PAGE
38

ON THE ROAD

YOUR COMPLETE DESTINATION GUIDE
In-depth reviews, detailed listings
and insider tips

TOP EXPERIENCES MAP | NEXT PAGE

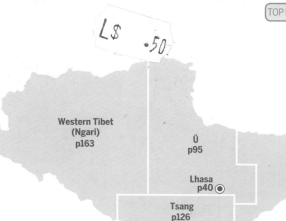

L$ .50

Western Tibet
(Ngari)
p163

Ü
p95

Lhasa
p40 ⊙

Tsang
p126

Eastern Tibet
(Kham)
p189

D1009889

PAGE
333

SURVIVAL GUIDE

YOUR AT-A-GLANCE REFERENCE
How to get around, get a room,
stay safe, say hello

Directory A-Z 334
Transport 349
Health 361
Language 368
Index 387
Map Legend 394

IN TIBET

**Availability &
Cost of Health
Care**

Self-diagnosis and treatment
can be risky, so you should
always seek medical help
where possible. Although
we do give drug dosages
in this section they are for
emergency use only. Correct
diagnosis is vital, and hotels

THIS EDITION WRITTEN AND RESEARCHED BY
Bradley Mayhew
Michael Kohn, Daniel McCrohan
John Vincent Bellezza

❯ Tibet

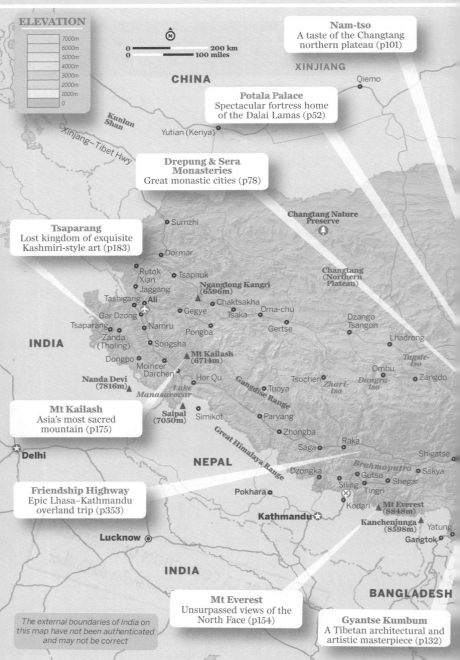

ELEVATION

	7000m
	6000m
	5000m
	4000m
	3000m
	2000m
	1000m
	0

0   200 km
0   100 miles

Ⓝ

CHINA

XINJIANG

Qiemo

Nam-tso
A taste of the Changtang
northern plateau (p101)

Potala Palace
Spectacular fortress home
of the Dalai Lamas (p52)

Yutian (Keriya)

Kunlun
Shan

Xinjang–Tibet Hwy

Drepung & Sera
Monasteries
Great monastic cities (p78)

Tsaparang
Lost kingdom of exquisite
Kashmiri-style art (p183)

Sumzhi

Changtang Nature
Preserve

Dormar

Rutok
Xian
Jaggang
Tashigang Ali

Nganglong Kangri
(6596m)
Tsaphuk
Chaktsakha

Gegye
Tsaka
Oma-chu

Changtang
(Northern
Plateau)

Gar Dzong

Dzango
Tsangon

Tsaparang
Namru
Pongba
Gertse

Lhadrong

INDIA

Zanda
(Tholing)
Songsha

Dongpo

Mt Kailash
(6714m)

Tugste-
tso

Ombu

Zangdo

Nanda Devi
(7816m)

Moincer
Darchen

Hor Qu

Lake
Manasarovar

Gangdise Range
Tuoya

Tsochen

Zhari-
tso

Dangra-
tso

Mt Kailash
Asia's most sacred
mountain (p175)

Saipal
(7050m)
Simikot

Paryang

Zhongba

Great Himalaya Range

Saga

Raka

Shigatse

Delhi

NEPAL

Dzongka

Brahmaputra
Gutso
Sakya

Siling
Shegar

Tingri

Friendship Highway
Epic Lhasa–Kathmandu
overland trip (p353)

Pokhara

Kathmandu ✪

Kodari

Mt Everest
(8848m)

Kanchenjunga
(8598m)
Yatung

Lucknow

Gangtok

INDIA

BANGLADESH

The external boundaries of India on
this map have not been authenticated
and may not be correct

Mt Everest
Unsurpassed views of the
North Face (p154)

Gyantse Kumbum
A Tibetan architectural and
artistic masterpiece (p132)

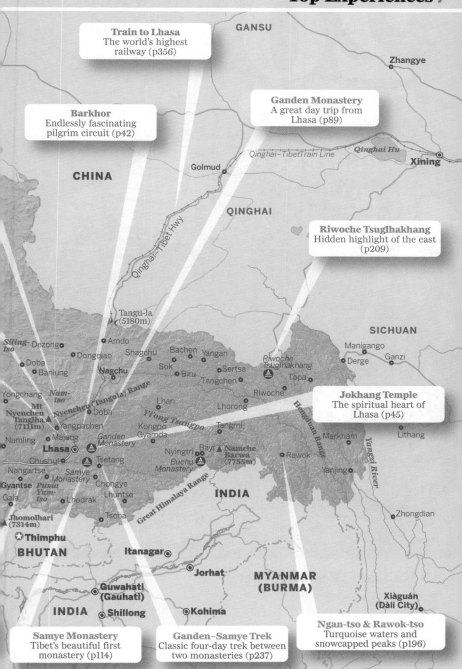

Train to Lhasa
The world's highest
railway (p356)

GANSU

Zhangye

Ganden Monastery
A great day trip from
Lhasa (p89)

Barkhor
Endlessly fascinating
pilgrim circuit (p42)

Qinghai–TibetTrain Line

Qinghai Hu

CHINA

Xining

Golmud

QINGHAI

Riwoche Tsuglhakhang
Hidden highlight of the east
(p209)

Qinghai–Tibet Hwy

Tangu-la
(5180m)

SICHUAN

*Siling-
tso* Dezong· Amdo·

Manigango·
Derge· Ganzi·

·Doba Dongqiao· Shagchu· Bachen· Yangan·
·Banlung **Nagchu** Sok· Biru· Sertsa· *Riwoche
Tsuglhakhang* Topa·

Yongchang· *Nam-
tso* **Nyenchen (Tangula) Range** Lhari· Lhorong· Riwoche·

**Mt
Nyenchen
Tangha**
(7111m) ·Nyenchen ·Doba *Yi'ong Tsangpo* Tangmi·

Jokhang Temple
The spiritual heart of
Lhasa (p45)

·Yangpachen

Markham· Lithang·

·Namling ·Majang *Ganden
Monastery* Kongpo
Gyamda·

Lhasa ◎ Nyingtri· Bayi· ▲ *Namche
Barwa*
(7755m) ·Rawok

·Chushul Tsetang· *Buchu
Monastery* Yanjing·

Nangartse· *Samye
Monastery* Chongye·

Gyantse *Puma
Yum-
tso* Lhuntse·

Gala· ·Lhodrak Tsona·

INDIA

Zhongdian·

Jhomolhari
(7314m)

✪Thimphu

BHUTAN Itanagar◎

INDIA ◎Jorhat

**MYANMAR
(BURMA)**

Xiàguán
(Dàli City)·

◎Guwahati
(Gauhati)

◎Shillong ◎Kohima

Ngan-tso & Rawok-tso
Turquoise waters and
snowcapped peaks (p196)

Samye Monastery
Tibet's beautiful first
monastery (p114)

Ganden–Samye Trek
Classic four-day trek between
two monasteries (p237)

20 TOP
EXPERIENCES

Mt Kailash, Western Tibet

1 Worshipped by more than a billion Buddhists and Hindus, Asia's most sacred mountain (p175) rises from the Barkha plain like a giant four-sided 6714m chörten. Throw in the stunning nearby Lake Manasarovar and a basin that forms the source of four of Asia's greatest rivers, and who's to say this place really isn't the centre of the world? Travel here to one of the world's most beautiful and remote corners brings an added bonus: the three-day pilgrim path around the mountain erases the sins of a lifetime.

Potala Palace, Lhasa

2 There are moments in travel that will long stay with you – and your first view of the iconic Potala Palace (p52) is one such moment. Even surrounded by a sea of Chinese development, the towering, mysterious building dominates Lhasa; it's simply hard to take your eyes off the thing. A visit to the former home of the Dalai Lamas is a spiralling descent past gold-tombed chapels, reception rooms and prayer halls into the bowels of a medieval castle. It's nothing less than the concentrated spiritual and material wealth of a nation.

Jokhang Temple, Lhasa

3 The atmosphere of hushed awe is what hits you first as you inch through the dark, medieval passageways of the Jokhang (p45). Queues of wide-eyed pilgrims shuffle up and down the stairways, past medieval doorways and millennium-old murals, pausing briefly to top up the hundreds of butter lamps that flicker in the gloom. It's the beating spiritual heart of Tibet. Welcome to the 14th century.

DENNIS WALTON

Views of Mt Everest

4 Don't tell the Nepal Tourism Board, but Tibet has easily the best views of the world's most famous mountain (p154). While two-week-long trekking routes on the Nepal side offer up only occasional fleeting glimpses of the peak, the view of Mt Everest's unobstructed north face framed in the prayer flags of Rongphu Monastery or from a tent at the Base Camp will stop you in your tracks.

TIM HUGHES

Samye Monastery

5 Tibet's first monastery (p114) is a heavily symbolic collection of chapels, chörtens and shrines arranged around a medieval Tibetan-, Chinese- and Indian-style temple called the Ütse. The 1200-year-old site is where Guru Rinpoche battled demons to introduce Buddhism to Tibet and where the future course of Tibetan Buddhism was sealed in a great debate. The location on the desert-like banks of the Yarlung Tsangpo is also superb.

Riding the Rails to Lhasa

6 For all its faults, China's railway to Tibet (the world's highest) is an engineering wonder and a delightful way to reach the holy city. Pull up a window seat to view huge salt lakes, plains dotted with yaks and herders' tents, and hundreds of miles of desolate nothing, as you inch slowly up onto the high plateau. Peaking at 5072m may send you diving for the piped oxygen, but it's still a classic rail trip (p356).

MERTEN SNIJDERS

Yak-Butter Tea

7 Some people prefer to call it 'soup', others liken it to brewed socks and sump oil. However you describe it, your first mouthful of yak-butter tea (p339) is the signal that you have finally reached Tibet. Our favourite thing about the Tibetan national drink is the view from the rim: a monk's quarters, a herder's yak-hair tent or a teahouse full of card-playing Tibetan cowboys. Definitely our cup of tea...

JULIET COOMBE

Sera & Drepung Monasteries, Lhasa

8 Lhasa's great religious institutions of Sera (p83) and Drepung (p78) are more than just monasteries – they are self-contained towns. A web of whitewashed alleyways climbs past medieval kitchens, printing presses and colleges to reach giant prayer halls full of chanting, tea-sipping red-robed monks. Don't miss the afternoon debating, an extravagant spectator sport of Buddhist dialectics and hand slapping.

Saga Dawa Festival

9 The line between tourist and pilgrim can be a fine one in Tibet, none more so than during the Saga Dawa Festival (p22), when thousands of pilgrims pour into Lhasa to visit the city and make a ritual procession around the 8km Lingkhor path. Load up on small bills and juniper incense before joining the pilgrims past chapels and prostration points, or travel west to Mt Kailash for the mountain's biggest annual party.

KEREN SU

BILL WASSMAN

IMAGEBROKER/OLAF SCHUBERT

Guge Kingdom, Western Tibet

10 The spectacular lost kingdom of Guge (p180) at Tsaparang is quite unlike anything you'll see in central Tibet; it feels more like Ladakh than Lhasa. There comes a point when you are lowering yourself down a hidden sandstone staircase or crawling through an inter-connected cave complex that you stop and think: 'This is incredible!' What's really amazing is that you'll likely have the half-forgotten ruins to yourself. Rank this as one of Asia's great travel secrets.

Ganden Monastery

11 A two hour-drive from Lhasa takes you to the stunning location of Ganden (p89), set in a natural bowl high above the braided Kyi-chu Valley. Brought back to life after nearly total destruction in the Cultural Revolution, the collection of restored chapels centres on Tsongkhapa's tomb, and offers a delightful kora path that will soon have you breathing hard from the altitude.

KRZYSZTOF DYDYNSKI

Ganden–Samye Trek

12 Tibet is one of those places you really should experience at the pace of one foot in front of the other. This classic four-day trek (p237) between two of Tibet's best monasteries takes you past herders' camps, high alpine lakes and a Guru Rinpoche hermitage, as well as over three 5000m-plus passes. Hire a horse for a wonderful wilderness trek, with just the marmots for company.

MERTEN SNIJDERS

Nam-tso

13 Just a few hours north of Lhasa, spectacular Nam-tso (p101) epitomises the dramatic but harsh scenery of northern Tibet. This deep blue lake is fringed by prayer flag–draped hills, craggy cliffs and nesting migratory birds, all framed by a horizon of 7000m peaks. It's cold, increasingly developed and devastatingly beautiful.

NICHOLAS REUSS

Gyantse Kumbum

14 The giant chörten at Gyantse (p132) is unique in the Himalayas. As you spiral around and up the snail shell–shaped building, you pass dozens of alcoves full of serene painted buddhas, bloodthirsty demons and unrivalled Tibetan art. Finally you pop out onto the golden eaves, underneath all-seeing eyes, for fabulous views of Gyantse fort and old town.

BRADLEY MAYHEW

Riwoche Tsuglhakhang, Eastern Tibet

15 Tibet is large enough to hold some hidden wonders. You'll have to overland for days to reach it and then haggle with the caretakers to let you in, but this dramatic, towering and remote temple (p209) in eastern Tibet feels like it's marooned in an earlier age. Enjoy the fact that you're among only a handful of foreigners to see it.

Adding Your Prayer Flags to a High Pass

16 Crossing a spectacular high pass, fluttering with prayer flags, to view an awesome line of Himalayan peaks is an almost daily experience in Tibet. Join your driver in crying a breathless 'so, so, so' and throwing colourful squares of paper into the air like good-luck confetti, as the surrounding multicoloured flags flap and crackle in the wind. Better still, bring your own string to the pass and add them to the collection for some super-good karma.

MERTEN SNIJDERS

Barkhor Circuit, Lhasa

NICHOLAS REUSS

17 You never quite know what you're going to find when you join the centrifugal tide of Tibetans circling the Jokhang Temple on the Barkhor Circuit (p45). Pilgrims and prostrators from across Tibet, stalls selling prayer wheels and turquoise, Muslim traders, Khampa nomads in shaggy cloaks, women from Amdo sporting 108 braids, thangka artists and Chinese military patrols are all par for the course. It's a fascinating microcosm of Tibet and an awesome backdrop for some souvenir shopping.

Koras & Pilgrims

18 All over Tibet you'll see wizened old pilgrims twirling prayer wheels, rubbing sacred rocks and walking around temples, monasteries and sometimes even entire mountains. It's a fantastic fusion of the spiritual and physical, and there are few better ways of spending an hour than joining a merry band of pilgrims on a monastery kora. En route you'll pass rock paintings, sacred spots and probably be invited to an impromptu picnic. See p19 for some of our favourites.

BRADLEY MAYHEW

IMAGEBROKER/STEFAN AUTH

Lhasa to Kathmandu by 4WD

19 Organising a 4WD trip across Tibet is the quintessential traveller experience (p32). It's hard to know what's toughest to overcome: the labyrinthine permit system, the terrible toilets or the rigours of bouncing around on a Tibet road for two weeks. Your reward is some wild and wholly Tibetan countryside, a satisfying sense of journey and a giant slice of adventure, until you finally drop off the plateau into the moist, green oxygen-rich jungles bordering Nepal.

Ngan-tso & Rawok-tso

20 Tibet is not short on spectacular, remote, turquoise-blue lakes. Of these, none surpasses the crystal-clear waters, sandy beaches and snowcapped peaks of these twin lakes (p196), more reminiscent of the Canadian Rockies than anything on the high plateau. Stay overnight at a hotel on stilts above the lake and explore nearby glaciers during the day.

DANIEL MCCROHAN

Preface

THE DALAI LAMA

The issue of Tibet is not nearly as simple and clear cut as the Chinese government often tries to make out. I believe that there are still widespread misunderstandings about Tibetan culture and misapprehensions about what is happening inside Tibet. Therefore, I welcome every opportunity for open-minded people to discover the reality of Tibet for themselves.

In the context of the growing tourist industry in Tibet, the Lonely Planet travel guide makes an invaluable contribution by providing reliable and authoritative information about places to visit, how to get there, where to stay, where to eat and so forth. Presenting basic facts and observations allows visitors to prepare themselves for what they will encounter and exercise their own choice.

There is a Tibetan saying: 'The more you travel, the more you see and hear.' At a time when many people are not clear about what is actually happening in Tibet, I am very keen to encourage whoever has the interest to go there and see for themselves. Their presence will not only instil a sense of reassurance in the Tibetan people, but will also exercise a restraining influence on the Chinese authorities. What's more, I am confident that once they return home they will be able to report openly on what they have seen and heard.

Great changes have lately taken place in this part of the world. Recent events have made it very clear that all Tibetans harbour the same aspirations and hopes. I remain confident that eventually a mutually agreeable solution will be found to the Tibetan problem. I believe that our strictly non-violent approach, entailing constructive dialogue and negotiation, will ultimately attract effective support and sympathy from within the Chinese community. In the meantime, I am also convinced that as more people visit Tibet, the numbers of those who support the justice of a peaceful solution will grow.

I am grateful to everyone involved in the preparation of this 8th edition of the Lonely Planet guide to Tibet for the care and concern they have put into it. I trust that those who rely on it as a companion to their travels in Tibet will enjoy themselves in what, despite all that has happened, remains for me one of the most beautiful places on earth.

2 April 2010

welcome to Tibet

Tibet is simply one of the most remarkable places in Asia. It offers fabulous monasteries, breathtaking high-altitude treks, stunning views of the world's highest mountains and one of the most likeable peoples you will ever meet.

A Higher Plain

For many people, the highlights of Tibet will be of a spiritual nature – magnificent monasteries, prayer halls of chanting monks and remote cliffside retreats. Tibet's pilgrims are an essential part of this appeal, from the local grannies mumbling mantras and swinging their prayer wheels in temples heavy with the intoxicating aroma of juniper incense and yak butter, to the hard-core walking or even prostrating around Mt Kailash. Tibet has a level of devotion and faith that seems to belong to an earlier age.

For travellers too, Tibet can be a uniquely spiritual place. Those moments of peace, fleeting and precious, when everything seems to be in its proper place, seem to come more frequently here, whether inspired by the devotion apparent in the face of a pilgrim or the dwarfing scale of a beautiful silent landscape.

After the dark days of the 1950s, '60s and '70s, when Tibetan monasteries and traditional culture were systematically dismantled, monasteries have been restored across the country, along with limited religious freedoms. A walk around Lhasa's lively Barkhor pilgrimage circuit is proof enough that the efforts of the communist government to build a brave new world in Tibet have foundered on the remarkable and inspiring faith of the Tibetan people.

The Roof of the World

For travellers nonplussed by Tibet's religious significance, the big draw is likely to be the elemental beauty of the highest plateau on earth. Geography here is on a humbling scale, from the world's highest peaks to lakes that look like inland seas and every view is lit with spectacular mountain light. Your trip will take you past glittering turquoise lakes, across huge plains dotted with grazing yaks and nomad's tents and over high passes draped with colourful prayer flags. Hike past the ruins of remote hermitages, stare up at the north face of the world's highest peak or make an epic overland trip along some of the world's wildest roads. The scope for adventure is limitless.

Even if your interest lies in adventure, your lasting memories of Tibet are likely to be of the bottle of Lhasa Beer you shared in a Lhasa teahouse, the yak-butter tea offered by a monk in a remote monastery or the picnic shared with a herders' family on the shores of a remote lake. Always ready with a smile and with a great openness of heart, it is the Tibetan people that truly make travelling in Tibet such a joy.

Tours & Permits

There's no getting away from politics in modern Tibet. Whether you see Tibet as an oppressed, occupied nation or simply an underdeveloped province of China, the normal rules for travel in China don't apply here. Non-Chinese travellers face ever-changing restrictions on getting into and around Tibet and finding your way around the latest restrictions is the major challenge to arranging travel here. Currently foreign travellers need to pre-arrange a tour with a guide for their time in Tibet and hire transportation for trips outside Lhasa. Truly independent travel may return during the lifetime of this book but at the time of writing it was almost impossible. See the Tours & Permits chapter (p29) for more.

Tourism in Tibet is changing fast. New airports, boutique hotels and paved roads are making travel ever more comfortable in many parts of the plateau. Once the remote preserve of hardy backpackers, it is now local Chinese tourists who dominate the queues for the Potala and Jokhang. For groups of three or four a 4WD trip across Tibet offers a grand adventure. If you are looking to explore Tibetan culture by yourself on foot or by public transport, you may be better off heading to the permit-free Tibetan areas of western Sìchuān or Qīnghǎi.

However you travel, a visit to Tibet will be memorable, fascinating and sometimes sobering experience. It's also a place that's likely to change the way you see the world and that will remain with you for years to come. And that's surely the definition of the very best kind of travel.

need to know

When to Go

Mt Kailash
GO May–Sep

Nagchu
GO Jun–Aug

Lhasa
GO Apr–Oct

Bayi
GO Feb–Nov

Everest Base Camp
GO May–Sep

Desert, dry climate
Warm to hot summers, mild winters
Mild to hot summers, cold winters
Cold climate

High Season
(May–Sep)

» The warmest weather makes travel, trekking and transport easiest

» Prices are at their highest

» The 1 May and 1 October national holidays bring the biggest crowds

Shoulder
(Mar–Apr, Oct–Nov)

» The slightly colder weather means fewer travellers and a better range of 4WDs

» Prices are slightly cheaper than during the high season

Low Season
(Dec–Feb)

» Very few people visit Tibet in winter, so you'll have the place largely to yourself

» Hotel prices are discounted by up to 50%, but some restaurants close

Your Daily Budget

Budget less than
US$50

» One-way hard sleeper Xīníng–Lhasa train and permits: $170

» Rooms without bathroom: $5–12

» Meal in local restaurant: $3

» Join a small group to share obligatory guide fees

Midrange
US $50–150

» One-way flight to Lhasa from Kathmandu/Chéngdū: $400/$200

» Daily 4WD rental per person: $40–60

» Double room with bathroom $20–50

Top end over
US $150

» Boutique or four-star hotel in Lhasa: $90–150

» Main meal in a top restaurant in Lhasa: $7.50–10

Money

» ATMs and travellers cheques only OK in Lhasa, Shigatse and a couple of other towns. Otherwise bring cash.

Visas

» Valid Chinese visa required.

Mobile Phones

» Buy a local SIM card for cheap local calls.

Transport

» 4WD rental is the most common form of transport, since most local public transport is officially off limits.

Websites

» **Australia Tibet Council** (www.atc. org.au) Useful travel information.

» **Central Tibetan Administration** (www. tibet.net) The view from Dharamsala.

» **China Tibet Information Center** (http://eng.tibet. cn/) News from the Chinese perspective.

» **Life on the Tibetan Plateau** (www.kekexili. typepad.com) Great blog for independent travellers.

» **Tibet Sun** (www. tibetsun.com) Good for Tibet-related news.

Exchange Rates

Australia	A$1	Y5.8
Canada	C$1	Y6.4
Europe	E	Y8.7
Japan	Y100	Y7.8
Nepal	Rs100	Y9.1
New Zealand	NZ$1	Y5.0
UK	UK£1	Y10.3
US	US$1	Y6.7

For current exchange rates see www.xe.com.

Important Numbers

Country code	☑86
International access code	☑00
Ambulance	☑120
Fire	☑119
Police	☑110

Arriving in Tibet

» **Gongkar Airport**
4WD – Your tour guide will most likely meet you in your rented vehicle.
Taxis – Y150 to Y200 to Lhasa's old town.

» **Train Station**
4WD – Your tour guide will most likely meet you in your rented vehicle.
Taxis – Around Y30 to Lhasa's old town.

Tours & Permits

» To board a plane or train to Tibet you need a Tibet Tourism Bureau permit, and to get this you must book a guide for your entire trip and pre-arrange transport for trips outside of Lhasa.

» Travel outside Lhasa requires additional permits, arranged in advance by your tour company so you need to decide your itinerary beforehand.

» Tour companies need 10 to 14 days to arrange permits and post you the TTB permit (the original permit is required if flying).

» Entering Tibet from Nepal you have to travel on a short-term group visa, which can make it tricky to continue into the rest of China.

» For details see p29.

if you like...

Off-the-Beaten-Track Monasteries

Beyond Lhasa's famous monastic cities there are hundreds of smaller lesser-visited places, each holding their own treasures and the chance to share some time (and a bowl of yak-butter tea) with some local monks. The following are a few of our favourites.

Sakya Monastery Towering golden buddhas reveal an important past tied to the Mongols (p147)

Phuntsoling Monastery Remote, little-visited and with a spectacular location (p146)

Dorje Drak Monastery A dramatic location surrounded by sand dunes and the flowing Yarlung Tsangpo river (p111)

Drak Yerpa A collection of hillside cave chapels that has housed hermits for generations (p92)

Korjak Monastery Delightful and quirky monastery at the far end of Tibet (p187)

Trekking & Hiking

Trekking 'the roof of the world' isn't easy. The altitude, weather and rugged terrain all present significant challenges. If you're up to it, hiking past nomad tents to remote settlements will take you out of reach of China's manic modernisation and into an older Tibet.

Ganden to Samye A classic route between two of Tibet's most important monasteries (p237)

Dode Valley, Lhasa It's hard to imagine a better way to spend half a day in Lhasa, with the best views in the city (p86)

Everest Base Camp There's something infinitely satisfying arriving on foot at the base of the world's highest mountain (p155)

Tsurphu to Yangpachen Get a taste of the wild northern plateau on this high trek past herding camps and black-haired nomads' tents (p240)

Palaces, Forts & Temples

There's more to Tibet than just monasteries. This mix of spectacular buildings represents a millennium of Tibetan history.

Potala Palace Towering home to the Dalai Lamas, full of priceless Tibetan art and jewel-studded tombs (p52)

Gyantse Dzong Pack your pith helmet and grow your best Younghusband moustache for this ruined fort with views over Gyantse's old town (p133)

Riwoche Tsuglhakhang Towering and totally unexpected temple about 30km from the middle of nowhere (p209)

Tsaparang Your inner Indiana Jones will love the caves, tunnels and hidden stairways of this ruined cliff-side fort (p183)

Gyantse Kumbum One of the great repositories of Tibetan art and a masterpiece of Himalayan architecture (p132)

TIM HUGHES

» Yak racing at the Gyantse Horse-Racing Festival (p22)

Incredible Scenery

You just have to turn your head to get another outstanding view in Tibet. Whether the rolling grasslands of the north, Mars-like deserts of the west, snowcapped Himalayan views to the south or the huge valleys and gigantic lakes of the centre, everywhere you turn are amazing high-altitude colours.

Everest Base Camp Jaw-dropping views of the north face that are *so* much better than from the Nepal side (p155)

Northern Route, Western Tibet Herds of antelope and wild ass graze by huge salt-water lakes in this empty end of the world (p170)

Tashigang area Sublime Swiss-style pine forests, green valleys and jagged peaks (p198)

Sutlej Valley Look out over weird eroded bluffs and former seabeds towards epic views of the Indian Himalaya (p181)

Cultural Encounters

Simple daily pleasures abound in Tibet. Whether it's spinning prayer wheels with a Tibetan granny, breathing in the heady fragrance of juniper incense in a medieval monastery or wondering at the devotion in a pilgrim's prostrations, the following encounters help you see Tibet through Tibetan eyes.

Tibetan Teahouses Kick back with a thermos of sweet milk tea (p339) and the world is instantly a better place

Koras Join a happy band of pilgrims for some prostrations and a sin test (see the box, p303)

Nangma A Tibetan nightclub is a mix of karaoke, line dancing and *American Idol*, but it's also very Tibetan (see the box, p74)

Chang & butter tea Join the locals for a jerry can of home-brewed barley beer or a never-ending cup of butter tea (p339)

Festivals Tibetan cultural life finds its best expression through festivals, opera, horse racing and some epic picnics (p21)

Pilgrim Paths

Tibet's koras (pilgrim routes) are the key to its soul. From 30m-long paths around a holy inner sanctum to month-long treks around a holy peak, koras are the ultimate fusion of the mind and the body, and the easiest way to meet Tibetans on their own terms.

Kailash Kora One of the world's great pilgrimages – a three-day walk around Asia's holiest mountain (p250)

Ganden Monastery Choose between the high kora with awesome views, or the lower route lined with sacred rocks and shrines (p89)

Sera Monastery A delightful walk past painted rock carvings with great views over monastery roofs (p83)

Barkhor Lhasa's most interesting corner, endlessly fascinating every time (p45)

Tashilhunpo Kora A fine hike that connects Shigatse's main monastery, old town and the restored fort, revealing the town's best views (p141)

If you like... lost art treasures, the frescoes at Thöling Monastery (p182) offer a splendid fusion of Kashmiri and Tibetan styles found almost nowhere else.

Overland Trips

Getting to Tibet is half the fun! From all four directions the overland routes to Lhasa deliver some of the world's most spectacular scenery. Organising a 4WD trip across Tibet is perhaps the plateau's quintessential travel experience.

Lhasa to Kathmandu Classic week-long 4WD or mountain-bike trip that delivers the highlights of the plateau (p25)

Chéngdū to Lhasa A wild roller-coaster route through the remote forested gorges and un-explored ranges of Kham (p28)

The Tibet Express Ride the world's highest railroad past huge grasslands dotted with yaks (p356)

Western Tibet The Northern Route to Kailash offers scenery, wildlife and isolation unparal-leled even in Tibet (p170)

Lakes

There's nothing quite like the deep turquoise blue of a high-altitude Tibetan lake. Whether sacred or just plain scenic, the following beauties beg you to pitch a tent or unwrap a picnic.

Manasarovar Yin to nearby Kailash's yang, sacred Mapham Yum-tso is utterly surreal in its beauty (p178)

Nam-tso Huge tidal salt lake lined with caves and a kora route and a traveller favourite (p101)

Rawok-tso A strong contender for Tibet's prettiest lake, fringed by sandy beaches and snowy peaks, with glaciers around the corner (p196)

Tagyel-tso Dramatic detour from the road to Kailash and a great place to spot wildlife (p170)

Yamdrok-tso Central Tibet's dramatic snaking scorpion lake (p127)

Outdoor Activities

Current travel restrictions make it difficult to arrange a DIY adventure but if you arrange things beforehand or join a specialised group there are plenty of adventures to be had in Tibet.

Mountain biking Certainly a challenge but ever-improving roads make the trips from Kathmandu or Chéngdū a once-in-a-lifetime adventure (p357)

Horse riding Add on an organ-ised trip from Lhasa or hire a horse at Kailash or Manasarovar for a multiday adventure (p335)

Rafting Day trip on the Kyi-chu or join a river expedition on the Reting Tsangpo (p336)

Watching wildlife Pack the binoculars and you'll likely spot black necked cranes, wild asses, antelope and a rich selection of summer birdlife (p295)

month by month

1 **Saga Dawa,** May

2 **Losar,** February

3 **Shötun Festival,** August

4 **Nagchu Horse Festival,** August

5 **Tashilhunpo Festival,** June

February

The depths of winter are very cold but still sunny, and are not a bad time to visit Lhasa and central Tibet. Lhasa sees few tourists but lots of visiting nomads. Ensure your hotel has heating!

✸ Year End Festival

On the 29th day of the 12th lunar month monks perform spectacular *cham* dances at Tsurphu, Mindroling and Tashilhunpo monasteries to dispel the evil of the old year and auspiciously usher in the new one. A huge thangka is unveiled the following day at Tsurphu Monastery.

✸ Losar (New Year Festival)

The first week of the first lunar month is a particularly colourful time to be in Lhasa. Tibetan opera is performed and streets are thronged with Tibetans in their finest cloaks. Prayer ceremonies take place at the Jokhang and Nechung Monastery and new prayer flags are hung.

March

Spring (March and April) brings pleasant temperatures but more than normal wind. Easier permits, few crowds and discounted hotel and 4WD rates make April a better month to visit.

✸ Tense Times

The anniversary of the 1959 Tibetan uprising on 10 March is just one of several politically sensitive dates in March. Permits are often suspended during the entire month, so travel agencies often suggest travellers avoid arriving in March.

✸ Chotrül Düchen (Butter Sculpture Festival)

Huge yak-butter sculptures have traditionally been placed around Lhasa's Barkhor circuit on the 15th day of the first lunar month. The festival is not currently celebrated in Lhasa, though it is in Labrang Monastery in Gansu province.

✸ Mönlam Chenmo (Great Prayer Festival)

Since 1409 monks from Lhasa's three main monasteries have assembled in the Jokhang to carry an image of Jampa (Maitreya) around the Barkhor circuit. The festival should culminate on the 25th of the first lunar month but was outlawed after political demonstrations ended in violence in 1988.

May

The warmer weather of late April and early May ushers in the start of the trekking season. Views are clear across the Himalaya, especially over Everest. Both April and May are good times to visit eastern Tibet.

✸ May Day

The major three-day national holiday on 1 May is a very popular time for Chinese travellers to come to Tibet, so expect flights and hotels to be booked solid and rates to be higher than usual, especially in Lhasa.

 Sakyamuni's Birthday

The seventh day of the fourth lunar month sees large numbers of pilgrims visiting Lhasa and other sacred areas in Tibet. Festivals are held around this time at Tsurphu, Ganden, Reting and Samye Monasteries.

⭐ Tsurphu Festival

Cham dancing (ritual dances performed by costumed monks), colourful processions and the unfurling of a great thangka are the highlights of this festival, held from the 9th to 11th days of the fourth lunar month.

⭐ Saga Dawa (Sakyamuni's Enlightenment)

The full moon (15th day) of the fourth lunar month marks the date of Sakyamuni's conception, enlightenment and entry into nirvana. Huge numbers of pilgrims walk Lhasa's Lingkhor circuit and visit Mt Kailash, where the Tarboche prayer pole is raised each year.

June

Tibet's high season starts in earnest in June. Lots of Indian pilgrims head to Kailash at this time and trekking is good. Even summer days can be chilly at higher elevations (above 4000m).

⭐ Gyantse Horse-Racing Festival

June or July brings this largely secular festival to Gyantse, featuring such fun and games as line dances,

yak races, archery and equestrian events. A large 480-year old thangka is unfurled at sunrise.

🏃 Worship of the Buddha

During the second week of the fifth lunar month, the parks of Lhasa, in particular the Norbulingka, are crowded with picnickers.

⭐ Tashilhunpo Festival

From the 14th to 16th days of the fifth lunar month, Shigatse's Tashilhunpo Monastery becomes the scene of three days of festivities. A huge thangka is unveiled at dawn and cham dances are performed.

⭐ Samye Festival

Held over two or three days from the full moon (15th day) of the fifth lunar month, the main events here are elaborate ritual ceremonies and cham dancing in front of the Ütse. The monastery guesthouse is normally booked out, so bring a tent.

July

Monsoon-influenced rain and glacial melting from mid-July to September can bring flooding and temporary road blockages to eastern and western Tibet, as well as the road to Nepal. Lowland Kathmandu and Chéngdū can be very hot.

⭐ Chökor Düchen (Drukwa Tsezhi) Festival

The fourth day of the sixth lunar month celebrates Buddha's first sermon at

Sarnath near Varanasi in India. Many pilgrims climb Gephel Ri (Gambo Ütse), the peak behind Drepung Monastery, and also the ridge from Pabonka to the Dode Valley, to burn juniper incense.

⭐ Guru Rinpoche's Birthday

Held on the 10th day of the sixth lunar month, this festival is particularly popular in Nyingmapa monasteries.

⭐ Ganden Festival

On the 15th day of the sixth lunar month, Ganden Monastery displays its 25 holiest relics, which are normally locked away. A large offering ceremony accompanies the unveiling.

⭐ Drepung Festival

The 30th day of the sixth lunar month is celebrated with the hanging at dawn of a huge thangka at Drepung Monastery. Lamas and monks perform opera in the main courtyard.

August

The warm weather combined with some major festivals and horse racing on the northern plateau makes this one of the most popular times to visit. Tibet sees half of its (minimal) rainfall in July and August.

⭐ Shötun (Yogurt Festival)

This major festival in the first week of the seventh lunar month starts with the dramatic unveiling of a giant thangka at Drepung

Monastery and then moves to Sera and then down to the Norbulingka for performances of *lhamo* (Tibetan opera) and some epic picnics.

Bathing Festival

The end of the seventh and beginning of the eighth lunar months sees locals washing away the grime of the previous year in an act of purification that coincides with the week-long appearance of the constellation Pleiades in the night sky.

 Horse-Racing Festival

During the first week of the eighth lunar month thousands of nomads head to Damxung and Nam-tso for a week of horse racing, archery and other traditional nomad sports. A similar and even larger event is held in Nagchu a few weeks earlier.

Onkor

In the first week of the eighth lunar month Tibetans in central Tibet get together and party in celebration of the upcoming harvest.

Tashilhunpo

More *cham* dances, from the ninth to 11th days of the eighth month, at Shigatse's Tashilhunpo Monastery.

October

Clear Himalayan skies and good driving conditions in eastern and western Tibet make this a good off-peak time to visit before the winter cold arrives, as the trekking season comes to a close.

October 1

Many people take a week off for National Day so expect flights and hotels to be full and rates higher than normal.

November

Temperatures are still pleasant during the day in Lhasa and Shigatse, but cold in the higher elevations of the north and west.

Lhabab Düchen

Commemorating Buddha's descent from heaven, the 22nd day of the ninth lunar month sees large numbers of pilgrims in Lhasa. Ladders are painted afresh on rocks around many monasteries to symbolise the event.

Palden Lhamo

The 15th day of the 10th lunar month sees a procession in Lhasa around the Barkhor bearing Palden Lhamo (Shri Devi), the protective deity of the Jokhang.

December

By December temperatures are starting to get seriously cold everywhere and some high passes start to close, but there's still surprisingly little snow in the Land of Snows.

Tsongkhapa Festival

Much respect is shown to Tsongkhapa, the founder of Gelugpa order, on the anniversary of his death on the 25th of the 10th lunar month. Monasteries light fires and carry images of Tsongkhapa in procession. Check for *cham* dances at the monasteries at Ganden, Sera and Drepung.

itineraries

Whether you have seven days or 40, these itineraries provide a starting point for the trip of a lifetime. Want more inspiration? Head online to lonelyplanet. com/thorntree to chat with other travellers.

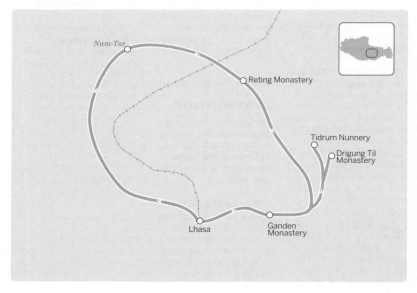

10 Days to Two Weeks
Lhasa & Around

❯ The chief goal of travellers is Lhasa itself, the spiritual heart of Tibet. The **train ride** from Xīníng or Běijīng is a great way to get to Lhasa, but ticket demand in high season means it's easier to leave Tibet by train rather than arrive.

There's enough to see in and around Lhasa to occupy at least a week. Highlights include the **Potala Palace** (a Unesco World Heritage Site), the **Jokhang Temple** and the **Barkhor** pilgrimage circuit. The huge monastic institutions of **Drepung** and **Sera** lie on the edge of town, and **Ganden Monastery** is a fantastic day trip away.

There are plenty of excursions to be made from Lhasa. An overnight return trip to stunning **Nam-tso** offers a break from peering at Buddhist deities, though you should allow at least a few days in Lhasa to acclimatise before heading out to the lake. Add a day or two and return via the timeless and little-visited **Reting Monastery** to avoid backtracking.

With another couple of days, visit atmospheric **Drigung Til Monastery** and **Tidrum Nunnery**, both east of Lhasa. You can visit these directly from Reting or on a two- or three-day excursion from Lhasa.

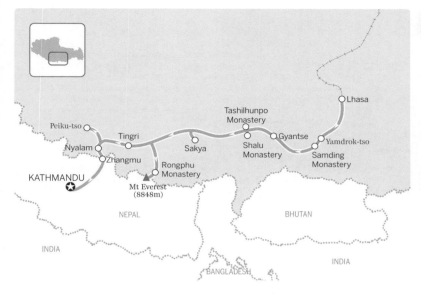

Seven Days
Lhasa to Kathmandu

❯ The 1300km Friendship Hwy between Lhasa and Kathmandu in Nepal is a classic overland journey and easily the most popular travellers' route through Tibet. It allows excellent detours to central Tibet's most important monasteries, plus views of the world's highest peak, and it's paved all the way! Combine it with the train route into Tibet for an epic overland tour.

From Lhasa you can head straight to the coiling scorpion-lake of **Yamdrok-tso** and take in the views from **Samding Monastery** before heading over the glacier-draped Karo-la pass to **Gyantse**. This town is well worth a full day: the *kumbum* (literally '100,000 images') chörten is a must-see and the fort is a fun scramble. A 90-minute drive away is Shigatse, with its impressive **Tashilhunpo Monastery**. **Shalu Monastery** is a worthwhile half-day trip from Shigatse, especially if you have an interest in Tibetan art.

A popular side trip en route to Kathmandu is to brooding **Sakya**, a small monastery town located just 25km off the Friendship Hwy. Overnight here and investigate the northern ruins.

The most popular excursion from the road is to **Rongphu Monastery** and **Everest Base Camp**, just a few hours from the main highway. An overnight here at 5000m guarantees both clear views and a pounding headache. It's not a good idea to stay here if you've come straight from Nepal, as the altitude gain is simply too rapid to be considered safe.

After Everest most people take the opportunity to stay the night in old **Tingri**, with its wonderful views of Mt Cho Oyu, before the scenic roller-coaster ride to **Nyalam** and nearby Milarepa's Cave. One interesting detour is to head east to overnight at **Peiku-tso**, a stunning turquoise lake nestled at the base of hulking Shishapangma. The highway drops like a stone off the dusty plateau, past misty waterfalls and lush green gorges to **Zhāngmù** and the gates of the Indian subcontinent at the Nepali border.

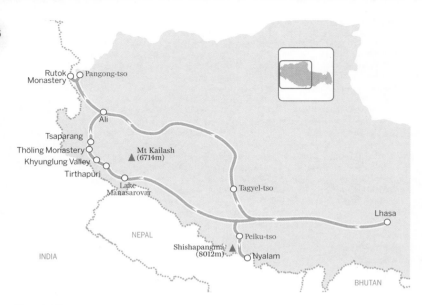

15 to 21 Days
Mt Kailash Pilgrimage

Much talked about but little visited, **Mt Kailash** occupies one of the most remote and sacred corners of Asia. Until very recently this trip entailed a rugged 4WD expedition, but the increasing number of paved roads under construction on the southern route is gradually making this a much more comfortable ride.

If you just want to visit Mt Kailash and Lake Manasarovar, the most direct route is the southern road (870km), a four-day drive from Lhasa along the spine of the Himalayas. Most people stop en route at Shigatse, Saga and Paryang, though Zhongba and Lhatse are also possibilities. Figure on a minimum of two weeks. See the first half of the Lhasa to Kathmandu itinerary for worthwhile extra stops in Gyantse and Sakya.

A *kora* (pilgrimage circuit) of the mountain will take three days and you should allow at least half a day afterwards to relax at **Lake Manasarovar**, probably at Chiu Monastery. You could easily spend a half-day at Darchen visiting Gyangdrak and Seylung monasteries. After the kora pilgrims traditionally then visit the sacred hot springs at **Tirthapuri**.

An ambitious but rewarding alternative is to travel one way to/from Lhasa along the longer (1700km) northern route to **Ali**, making a loop that will take three weeks. The six-day drive is astonishingly scenic but the towns en route are mostly charmless, so consider camping somewhere such as **Tagyel-tso**. From Ali you can make a good day trip to **Pangong-tso** and **Rutok Monastery**.

You'll need at least three extra days if you want to visit the Guge kingdom sites around Zanda: one day from Ali, one day to Mt Kailash (or vice versa) and at least one day to visit the sites. You need most of a day to explore the otherworldly ruins at **Tsaparang**, plus a few hours in Zanda at **Thöling Monastery**. En route to Kailash, adventurers could add on an extra day to explore the Bön school Gurugyam Monastery and the amazing ruins of the ancient Shangshung kingdom in the **Khyunglung Valley**.

Finally, if you are heading to Nepal from Mt Kailash, it's well worth taking the short cut south via stunning **Peiku-tso** and its views of Shishapangma to join the Friendship Hwy near Nyalam.

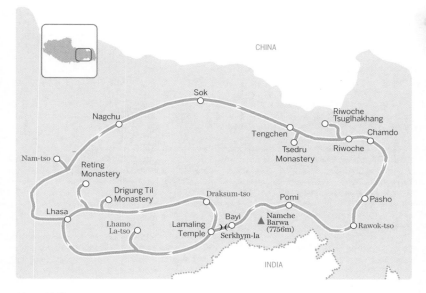

18 to 21 Days
Eastern Tibet Loop

Equally remote, but completely different scenically, are the wild valleys and gorges of eastern Tibet. Road conditions are best from late March to late April, and late September to early November. It's possible to enter or leave Tibet on a one-way trip but you can't beat the comprehensiveness of a loop route. The only snag is that permits can be hard to get even on a group tour. This is probably a trip for people who have already visited the major sights of central Tibet.

From Lhasa the southern route heads eastwards over a high pass to the beautiful but touristed lake of **Draksum-tso** and the fascinating Kongpo region, with its lovingly restored **Lamaling Temple**. From here the road climbs to the **Serkhym-la**, for excellent views in good weather of Namche Barwa, before dropping down into the dramatic gorges north of the Yarlung Tsangpo. There's some great accommodation on lake Ngan-tso, or camp by the shores of turquoise **Rawok-tso**, from where you can visit nearby glaciers; otherwise Pomi and Pasho are the logical overnight stops. Swing north over the high passes into the deep red-hued gorges of the Salween and Mekong Rivers. Reach the modern town of **Chamdo** after five or six days and rest for a day, visiting the large Galden Jampaling Monastery.

From Chamdo the northern route continues three or four days westwards to **Nagchu**, likely overnighting at **Riwoche**, Tengchen and Sok, all the time gradually climbing to the high-altitude pasturelands of Amdo. This road less taken passes the impressive temple of the **Riwoche Tsuglhakhang** and the incredibly sited **Tsedru Monastery**, the largest Bön monastery in Tibet.

From Nagchu visit **Nam-tso** and **Reting Monastery** en route to Lhasa (allow three to four days), though the direct road can be completed in a day's drive if you are short on time.

A shorter and cheaper five- to seven-day loop itinerary from Lhasa to Kongpo could take in **Drigung Til Monastery**, Draksum-tso and Lamaling Temple, overnighting in Bayi before swinging back via Tsetang and Samye. Adventurous add-ons include a visit to sacred Bönri mountain, the remote oracle lake of **Lhamo La-tso**.

Two to Three Weeks
Overland Routes to Lhasa

There are three main overland routes from the east: the northern route and southern route through Sìchuān and the shorter Yúnnán route. The Tibetan areas of western Sìchuān and northwestern Yúnnán do not require travel permits; the eastern Tibetan Autonomous Region does and these are sometimes tricky to get, even on an organised tour. If your 4WD has to come from Lhasa to pick you up, you can save some money by meeting your guide close to the TAR border at Bātáng, Derge or Déqīn.

The northern route through Sìchuān starts from Kāngdìng and passes the grasslands and monastery of **Tagong** and several large monasteries around **Gānzī**. The timeless printing press of **Derge** is a day's ride further but there are plenty of exciting excursions en route, including to the remote **Dzogchen Monastery** and the pretty **Yihun La-tso**. From Derge you cross into Tibet proper over some wild passes to **Chamdo**, the biggest town in eastern Tibet. For the route west of Chamdo, see the second half of the eastern Tibet loop; alternatively travel south to join the southern route.

The southern route through Sìchuān runs west from Kāngdìng past the important Khampa town and monastery of **Lithang**, home to an epic horse festival in August, and then low-lying **Bathang**. The road up into Tibet via Markham and over concertina passes to Pomda ranks as one of the wildest and remotest in Asia. For the route west, reverse the first half of the eastern Tibet loop itinerary, overnighting in Markham/Dzogang, Pasho and Pomi.

A popular alternative option is to start in Yúnnán at the Tibetan town of Zhōngdiàn (Gyeltang), from where it's a day's ride to Deqin. From here you cross into the Tibet Autonomous Region (TAR) near the salt pans of Yánjǐng; then it's 111km to Markham on the Sìchuān southern route.

From Zhōngdiàn to Lhasa, allow a week in a 4WD. From Chengdu it takes 10 days to two weeks along either the northern or southern route. You'll pass a number of hardcore Chinese cyclists en route.

Tours & Permits

Getting into Tibet

You need a Tibet Tourism Bureau (TTB) permit to be able to board a train or plane to Lhasa. For this you need to pre-arrange an itinerary through a travel agent before arriving in Tibet.

You need travel permits to travel outside Lhasa Prefecture and you can currently only get these by hiring transportation and a guide as part of your itinerary.

If you plan to enter Tibet from Nepal, you will have to travel on a short-term group visa, which is hard to extend (see p346).

All of these rules have exceptions and by the time you have finished reading this list, all of these rules will probably have changed.

Planning Your Trip

The million-dollar question everyone wants to know is: how do I get into Tibet? Tibet has never been the easiest place to visit, but these days the permit situation can be a harder obstacle than the mountain roads or lack of oxygen in the air.

The bottom line is that travel to the Tibet Autonomous Region (TAR) is radically different from the rest of China and a valid Chinese visa is not enough to visit Tibet. You'll also need several permits, foremost of which is a Tibet Tourism Bureau (TTB) permit, and to get these you have to book some kind of tour. Requirements change frequently. In the past they've been limited to a short three-day package (that then allowed you stay independently in Tibet), but currently at a minimum you need to arrange a guide for your entire stay and hired transportation for any travel outside Lhasa.

Tibet Tourism Bureau (TTB) Permit

A TTB permit is currently required to get into the TAR. Without one you will not be able to board a flight or train to Tibet and will not be able to secure the other permits you need to continue travelling throughout Tibet.

How these rules are interpreted depends on the political climate in Tibet. In the past travellers have been able to sign up for a nominal two- or three-day tour from one of the many budget travel agencies in China (especially Chéngdū) and get a permit that way. These days you can only get a TTB permit through a tour agency in Tibet (agencies outside Tibet can arrange trips, but ultimately they book through a Tibetan-based agency). You can no longer travel to Lhasa, meet up with some travellers and organise a tour there. Everything must now be arranged beforehand, including any trekking itinerary you have planned.

To get a permit you need to:

» work out an itinerary detailing exactly where you want to go in Tibet

» pay for a guide for every day of your tour, including arrival and departure, at a rate of Y200 to Y250 per day

» hire a vehicle (normally a 4WD) for all transportation outside Lhasa

» agree a price and send a deposit, normally through PayPal or a bank transfer (check transfer charges)

» send a scan of your passport information pages and China visa

» arrange an address in China (hotel, guesthouse or local agency) to receive your posted TTB permit, if flying to Lhasa

What your tour actually involves depends on the agency. Some offer all-inclusive tours, while others will arrange transport, a guide and permits but leave accommodation, food and entry fee costs up to you. You can book your own train or air ticket to Lhasa or have the agency arrange this. Some airline offices and online booking agencies will sell flights to Lhasa to foreigners, but others won't unless you can show you have a TTB permit. (See p352 for more information on buying air and train tickets into Tibet from Kathmandu, Chéngdū or elsewhere.) Some agencies require you to have a pre-booked ticket out of Tibet, but most are happy for you to arrange this in Lhasa.

Treks fall under the same permit requirements as normal tours. Some agencies offer pricey, fully organised treks, whereas others will let you arrange your own equipment, food, pack animals and local guides, as long as you take a guide and have transport arranged to and from the trailheads. It's unusual to be asked for any documentation while on a trek, though you might well at the trailheads.

You need to have the original permit in your hands in order to board a flight to Lhasa, so most agencies arrange to post the permit through an agency or hostel. This can cost anything from Y25 for normal post (four working days) to Y180/280/380 for 36-/24-/18-hour express post. A photocopy or scan of an original TTB permit is currently all that is required to board a train to Tibet, which saves on postage fees. The permit is actually free, though most agencies charge around Y600 per person for the bureaucratic run to secure this and other permits.

The fine print:

» Chinese residents of Hong Kong, Macau and Taiwan do not require a TTB permit to enter Tibet, though foreigners resident in China do.

» Journalists and embassy staff will find it impossible to get a TTB permit as a tourist. Visitors on a business or resident visa don't seem to have a problem.

» A few travellers have managed to sneak into Lhasa without a TTB permit and stay there without problems, but you still need to arrange one there in order to travel throughout the rest of Tibet.

» TTB permits generally take three days to process and are not available during weekends. The actual permit is a sheet of paper listing the names and passport numbers of all group members.

» If you are planning to arrive in Lhasa on a flight or dates that differ from those of your travel companions, your agency may have to issue a separate TTB permit for the time you are by

TRAVEL OUTSIDE TIBET

Note that TTB and Alien Travel Permits are only required for travel in the TAR. You can normally travel through the culturally Tibetan areas of Yúnnán, Sìchuān, Gānsù and Qīnghǎi (the former Tibetan provinces of Kham and Amdo) without the need for pesky permits. This includes the places in our Overland Routes from Sìchuān chapter. For details of Tibetan areas in Gānsù and Qīnghǎi, see Lonely Planet's *China* guide.

THE IMPERMANENCE OF TRAVEL

Travel regulations to Tibet are constantly in flux, dependent largely on political events in Lhasa and Běijīng. Don't be surprised if the permit system is radically different from that described in this guide. In fact, expect it. We've written the guide based on current travel restrictions, but have included some information on things like public transport and DIY trips to off-the-beaten-track monasteries, in the hope that regulations ease. One of the best places for updated information is the dedicated Tibet page of Lonely Planet's Thorn Tree at lonelyplanet.com/thorntree.

yourself. When you meet your friends you'll then join the main permit. There doesn't seem to be a problem getting on a flight with one or two group members not present.

» You will likely have to wire or transfer a deposit to your travel agency's Bank of China account in Lhasa, though some agencies accept PayPal. You will pay the balance in cash in Lhasa. Check with the agency.

Alien Travel Permits, Military Permits & Other Such Fun

Once you have a visa and have managed to wangle a TTB permit, you'd think you were home and dry. Think again. Your agency will need to arrange an alien travel permit for most of your travels outside Lhasa.

Travel permits are *not* needed for Lhasa or places just outside the city such as Ganden Monastery but most other areas do technically require permits. Permits are most easily arranged in the regional capital, so for Western Tibet you'll have to budget a couple of hours in Shigatse, and possibly also Ali, for your guide to process the permit. Lhasa PSB will not issue travel permits to individuals, and agencies can only arrange a travel permit to those on a tour with them. Permits cost Y50 and can list any number of destinations.

Sensitive border areas – such as Mt Kailash, the road to Kashgar and the Nyingtri region of eastern Tibet – also require a military permit and a foreign-affairs permit. For remote places such as the Yarlung Tsangpo gorges in southeastern Tibet, the roads south of Gyantse or for any border area, you may not be able to get permits even if you book a tour. Regions can close at short notice. In 2010 the entire region around Chamdo was closed, effectively blocking overland trips from Chéngdū. You'll have to check to see if this has changed.

You should give your agency a week to 10 days to arrange your permits, and two weeks if military or other permits are required. The authorities generally won't issue permits more than 15 days in advance and certain areas can close without warning, so you'll need a certain flexibility if headed off the beaten track.

Organising a Tour

Given the nature of the current restrictions, almost all travellers arrange a tour for their travels in Tibet. To arrange a tour you first need to pin down your itinerary. Some agencies offer fixed itineraries, but you can also customise your own. See our Itineraries chapter (p24) for some ideas. Your itinerary enables your agency to quote a firm price. Prices depend largely on the kilometres driven (roughly Y3.5 per km) not the time taken. It's a good idea to mention every place you intend to visit at this stage. Once on the road your driver will probably have been pre-paid for all the kilometres, so he'll be very reluctant to detour even a few kilometres off route.

Many agencies give a price breakdown for the vehicle, guide, permits, postage fees and transfers, which is very useful. Clarify whether the trip fee includes accommodation and/or entry tickets. It should include food and accommodation for your guide and driver. Transfers might be included or you might have to pay an additional Y300 for airport pick-up. Some agencies allow you to take the airport bus (Y25), but you'll still have to pay for your guide's ticket (both ways). Depending on your agency you may be able to take a modicum of public transport, such as the pilgrim bus to Ganden.

If you arrange your own tour you can expect to pay around US$50 to US$100 per person per day, depending on your itinerary, the amount of time in Lhasa (where

THE NITTY GRITTIES OF ORGANISING A 4WD TRIP

When finalising details with a tour agency it's a good idea to look through their contract (if they have one) and see where you stand in the event that things don't go according to plan. Bear the following in mind:

» You should agree on the rate for any extra days that may need to be tacked onto an itinerary. For delays caused by bad weather, blocked passes, swollen river crossings and so on, there should be no extra charge for jeep hire. At the very least, the cost for extra days should be split 50% between your group and the agency.

» For delays caused by vehicle breakdowns, driver illness etc the agency should cover 100% of the costs and provide a back-up vehicle if necessary.

» Ask the agency about its policy on refunds for an uncompleted trip. Some agencies refuse any kind of refund, while others are more open to negotiation. If you decide to cut a trip short for personal reasons it's unlikely you'll get a refund.

» Establish which vehicle costs are not covered in the price (eg the Y405 vehicle fee to drive to Everest Base Camp and Y40 vehicle fee at Peiku-tso), as well as entry fees for your guides (such as the entry ticket and 'environmental bus fee' for Everest).

Once you are sorted with the agency, it's a good idea to organise a meeting between your group and the driver(s) and guide a day or two before departure. Make sure the drivers are aware of your itinerary (it may be the first time they have seen it!). Ensure that the guide speaks fluent Tibetan, good Chinese and useable English. Strong personality clashes would suggest a change of personnel. It's not a bad idea to test the driver and car on a day trip to somewhere like Ganden Monastery before you head off on the big trip.

Unless you are a qualified mechanic, inspecting the soundness of the vehicle may prove to be difficult, but you should at least check that the windows open and close and that the handbrake works (ours didn't!). Make sure also that the 4WD can at least be engaged (not just that the stick moves) and that the 'diff lock' can be locked and unlocked (this is usually done via tabs on the front wheel hubs). Tyres and spares should be in reasonable condition. A long steel tow cable is advisable, since ropes are useless.

4WD rental is not required) and the number of people in the group.

On top of the costs of this kind of tour, you'll have to figure in the normal travel costs of accommodation, food and entry tickets etc, but these costs you can at least control. Some agencies want to book your hotels and indeed can often get cheaper rates for midrange or top-end hotels; others will let you arrange your own accommodation, which gives you greater flexibility in changing hotels.

In Lhasa you currently need to visit the major monasteries (the Jokhang, Drepung, Sera and Ganden) with your guide, but beyond that you can generally explore the city yourself, if you don't mind paying for a guide you don't use! The quality of guides in Tibet varies considerably. Some are great, many are next to useless and a few actually cause

more headaches than they solve. Asking for a Tibetan guide ensures you'll get a Tibetan perspective on monasteries and is highly recommended.

Solo travellers shouldn't be too put off by the official insistence on 'group travel'. For the purposes of getting permits and visas, a 'group' can be as small as one person. If you want to find people to share travel costs, the Lonely Planet Thorn Tree (lonelyplanet. com/thorntree) is full of travellers looking for travel partners. Some agencies (particularly the hostels) offer fixed departures and will help you find other travellers to form a small group. A 4WD can fit four people comfortably (including the guide). Some larger models also have a small jump seat in the rear, which makes it possible to squeeze in five. For a long overland trip to Kailash or

Eastern Tibet it's well worth paying a little extra to have a more space.

Note that the agency that arranges your TTB permit is legally responsible for you in Tibet. Should you get caught talking politics with the wrong person, or staying in Tibet after the date on your TTB permit, the agency will likely be questioned by the authorities and perhaps fined. This is one reason why some guides can appear over-protective.

Tibetan Tour Agencies

In general Tibetan tour agencies are not as professional as agencies in neighbouring Nepal. The following companies in Lhasa (☑0891) are used to arranging customised trips:

FIT Banak Shol Hotel (☑655 9938; fit0891@hotmail.com; 8 Beijing Donglu) Contact Xiaojin.

FIT Snowlands Hotel (☑634 9239; lhakpa88@yahoo.com; www.tibetfit.com; 2nd fl, Snowlands Hotel, 4 Zangyiyuan Lu/Mentsikhang Lam) Contact Lhakpa Tsering.

Namchen Tours (www.shangrilatours.com) At Barkhor Namchen Guest House; see p69.

Shigatse CITS (☑691 2080; tibetanintibet@yahoo.cn; Zangyiyuan Lu/Mentsikhang Lam) Contact Tenzin.

Shigatse Travels (☑633 0489; www.shigatse travels.com; Yak Hotel, 100 Beijing Donglu) Top-end tours.

Snow Lion Tours (☑134 3932 9243; www.snowliontours.com; 1 Danjielin Lu) Contact Wangden Tsering. Also a branch in Běijīng.

Spinn Café (☑136 5952 3997; www.cafespinn.com; 135 Beijing Donglu) Contact Kong or Pazu.

Tibet Wind Horse Adventure (☑683 3009; www.windhorsetibet.com; B32 Shenzheng Huayuan, Sera Beilu) Top-end trips.

Tibet Tourism Bureau FIT Travel Service Centre (☑632 0200; ttbfitsonam@hotmail.com; Zangyiyuan Lu) Contact Sonam.

Visit Tibet Travel and Tours (☑692 2114; www.visittibet.com; Niangre Lu) Can arrange Nepal add-ons.

Travellers have also recommended **Tibet Kyunglung Travel Service** (☑631 6298; www.tibetkyunglungtravel.com; 29 Sera Beilu) and **Great Tibet Tour/Tibet Niwei International Travel Service** (☑667 2062; www.greattibettour.com; 2 Linkuo Beilu).

There are also several good companies based outside the TAR. Many are based in the Tibetan areas of China and operate through local contacts in Lhasa. Depending on your itinerary it can be useful to arrange your tour through one of these. If catching the train from Xīníng, for example it's handy to use an agency there to help arrange hard-to-find train tickets and permit pickup. If overlanding from Zhōngdiàn, it's useful to book through a company based there to avoid having to send a vehicle all the way from Lhasa. The following companies all organise Tibet trips:

Access Tibet (☑028-8618 3658; www.access tibetour.com; Room 178-188, 4 F, Yuanheng Trade Bldg, 235 Shuhan Lu, Chéngdū) With an office in Lhasa.

China Yak (☑028-8663 0114; www.chinayak.com; Chéngdū) Part of CITS.

Dreams Travel (☑028-8557 0315; www.dreams-travel.com; 242 Wuhouci Dajie, Chéngdū)

Leo Hostel (☑10-8660 8923; www.leohostel.com; Guangjuyuan Binguan, 52 Dazhalan Xijie, Qianmen, Běijīng)

Mix Hostel (☑028-8322 2271; www.mixhostel.com/tibet.htm; 23 Renjiawan, Xinghui Xilu, Chéngdū)

Sim's Cozy Travel (☑028-8335 5322, 133 9819 5552; www.gogosc.com; Sim's Cozy Guest House, Chéngdū) Popular agency and hostel in Chéngdū.

Tibetan Connections (☑0971-820 3271; www.tibetanconnections.com; International Village/Guoji Cun Gongyu Bldg 5, 15th fl, Lete Youth Hostel, Xīníng) Recommended.

Windhorse Tour (☑028-8559 3923; www.windhorsetour.com; Ste 904, Wanheyuan, Bldg C, 1 Babao Lu, Chéngdū) Chinese agency, not connected to Tibet Wind Horse Adventure in Lhasa. Contact Helen.

See p263 for agencies in Kathmandu that arrange tours from Nepal.

Overland Tour Agencies in China

The following adventure travel agencies specialise in organised overland trips from or through the Tibetan areas of western Sìchuān and northwest Yúnnán, including organised trips to Lhasa.

China Minority Travel (☑0872-267 7824; www.china-travel.nl) Dutch-Chinese operation based at Jim's Tibetan Guesthouse in Dàlǐ, Yúnnán; contact Henriette.

Haiwei Trails (☏0887-828 9245; www.haiwei trails.com; 19 Beimen Jie, Zhōngdiàn) US-British company that runs 4WD trips and charters into central and eastern Tibet.

Khampa Caravan (☏0887-828 8648; www. khampacaravan.com; 117 Beimen Jie, Zhōngdiàn) Overland trips from Yúnnán to Lhasa, with an emphasis on sustainable tourism and local communities. Contact Dakpa.

Tibetan Connections (☏0971-820 3271; www.tibetanconnections.com; Guoji Cun Gongyu Bldg 5, 15th fl, Lete Youth Hostel, Xīníng) Excellent

for tours to Amdo and Kham, specialising in Qīnghǎi province.

Tibetan Trekking (☏028-8675 1783; www. tibetantrekking.com; Room 1614, Zhufeng Hotel, 288 Shuncheng Lu, Chéngdū) Contact Gao Liqiang for treks and 4WD trips, especially in Tibetan areas of western Sìchuān.

Wild China (☏010-6465 6602; www.wildchina. com; Room 801, Oriental Place, 9 Dongfang Donglu, North Dongsanhuan Rd, Chaoyang District, Běijīng) Professionally run trips.

Wind Horse Adventure Tours (☏971-613 1358; www.windhorseadventuretours.com; 19 Nan Dajie, Xīníng) Contact Tashi Phuntsok.

regions at a glance

Tibet is a huge land and you can't see all of it in a single trip. Almost everyone visits Lhasa, Tibet's holy city, which still has a lovely old town despite being at the forefront of Chinese-led modernisation. The valleys around Lhasa in Ü offer great scope for short excursions from Lhasa, as well as great trekking. Focus your efforts here if you're short on time.

For most travellers the central region of Tsang means the excellent overland route to Kathmandu and the trip to Everest Base Camp. More remote are the outlying regions of Western Tibet (Ngari) and Eastern Tibet (Kham), which require 4WD trips of two to three weeks through amazing scenery: one desert and steppe, the other forested valleys and alpine pastures.

Lhasa

Monasteries ✓
History ✓✓
Old Town ✓✓✓

Monasteries
The traditional seat of Tibetan power, the great Gelugpa monasteries of Drepung, Sera and Ganden still buzz with monks and pilgrims. Smaller but equally charming monasteries are in the old town.

History
Visit the Potala, the fortress-like home for nine Dalai Lamas; Norbulingka, from where the Dalai Lama made his escape in 1959; and Jokhang Temple, which dates from the arrival of Buddhism in Tibet.

Old Town
Lhasa's old town is the one corner of the city that feels truly Tibetan. The backstreets hide teahouses, guesthouses, chapels and craft shops, while the Barkhor Circuit is the spiritual heart of the city.

p40

Ü

Monasteries ✓✓
Activities ✓✓✓
Scenery ✓✓

Monasteries
Samye is perhaps the loveliest monastery in Ü, while the sky burial centre of Drigung Til is a travellers' favourite. Also charming are smaller monasteries of Mindroling, Dorje Drak and Reting, rarely visited by tour groups.

Activities
Trekking is superb in Ü. Ganden–Samye is the classic Tibetan trek but the Tsurphu–Yangpachen walk has equally superb scenery. Ü also offers rafting and horse riding.

Scenery
The grandest views are at Nam-tso, a giant salt lake fringed with the snowcapped Tanglha range. The sand dunes lining the braided Yarlung Tsangpo valley have a surreal beauty.

p95

Tsang

Monasteries ✓✓✓
Mountains ✓✓
Lakes ✓

Monasteries

Pelhor Chöde Monastery has the fabulous Kumbum chörten, but historic Sakya Monastery is an equally worthy destination. Off the beaten track explore the art of Shalu or a Bön monastery at Yungdrungling.

Mountains

Tsang is all about Mt Everest and the awesome views of its north face from Rongbuk Monastery. Himalayan views are superb all across southern Tsang en route from Lhasa to Kathmandu.

Lakes

Yamdrok-tso is a gorgeous coiling lake and there are great views from just below the Kamba-La. For epic scenery detour to Peiku-tso, just an hour or two off the Friendship Hwy towards Nepal.

p126

Western Tibet

Lakes ✓✓✓
Wildlife ✓✓
Adventure ✓✓✓

Lakes

The sight of Mt Kailash rising from the turquoise waters of Manasarovar is beyond words. The huge salt lakes of the northern route cry out for a picnic or overnight camp, especially at Dawatso and Tsogyel-tso.

Wildlife

Small herds of wild asses and antelope grazing the yellow steppe are a regular sight. Funnier are the marmots sitting up on their hind legs to watch you set up camp or the grunting yaks that haul trekkers' gear around Mt Kailash.

Adventure

Explore the tunnels, caves and mud walls of the ruined cities of Shangshung and Guge. Then shed your sins on a Mt Kailash pilgrimage or set up camp at the base of 8012m Shishapangma.

p163

Eastern Tibet

Monasteries ✓
Scenery ✓✓✓
Adventure ✓✓✓

Monasteries

The east has some real gems: Galden Jampaling Monastery is one of Tibet's largest, Riwoche is one of its great hidden sights and Tsedru Monastery has perhaps the region's most remote mountain crag location.

Scenery

Pine forests, lush jungle, alpine valleys, and the deep gorges of the upper Mekong and Salween Rivers make travel in the east a roller-coaster ride through a dozen climactic zones.

Adventure

Few people really explore Eastern Tibet and only the lucky few get a peek at Namche Barwa or the awesome gorges of the Yarlung Tsangpo. There's also one of the world's great road trips, if the permit situation allows.

p189

Look out for this icon:

TOP CHOICE Our author's recommendation

LHASA 40
AROUND LHASA 78
Drepung Monastery 78
Nechung Monastery 83
Sera Monastery 83
Pabonka Monastery 87
Ganden Monastery 89
Drak Yerpa 92
Drölma Lhakhang 93
Shugsheb Nunnery 94

Ü 95
NORTHERN Ü 98
Tsurphu Monastery 98
Nam-tso 101
Lhundrub County 103
Talung Monastery 104
Reting Monastery 105
Road to Drigung Til
Monastery 106
Drigung Til Monastery 108
Tidrum Nunnery 109
YARLUNG TSANGPO
VALLEY 109
Gongkar 109
Dorje Drak Monastery 111
Drak Yangdzong 112
Dratang Monastery 113
Mindroling Monastery 113
Samye Monastery 114
Around Samye 118
Namseling Manor 119
Tsetang 119
Yarlung Valley 121

Chongye Valley 124
Lhamo La-tso 125

TSANG 126
Yamdrok-tso 127
Nangartse 130
Gyantse 131
Around Gyantse 135
Gyantse to Shigatse 135
Shigatse 137
Around Shigatse 144
Phuntsoling Monastery &
Jonang Kumbum 146
Sakya 147
Lhatse 151
Around Lhatse 152
Baber & Shegar 152
Everest Region 154
Tingri 156
Around Tingri 157
Nyalam 157
Nyalam to Zhāngmù 160
Zhāngmù (Dram) 160

**WESTERN TIBET
(NGARI) 163**
Southern Route 167
Northern Route 170
Ali .173
Mt Kailash 175
Lake Manasarovar 178
Tirthapuri Hot Springs &
Kora 179
Guge Kingdom 180
Dungkar & Piyang 185
Rutok 186

On the Road

Western Nepal to
Mt Kailash 187

**EASTERN TIBET
(KHAM) 189**
THE SOUTHERN ROUTE
(HWY 318) 193
Markham 194
Pasho 194
Pasho to Rawok 195
Rawok 196
Pomi 196
Baha Gompa 197
Tangmi 198
Tashigang 198
Tashigang to Bāyī 198
Bāyī 199
Around Bāyī 200
Draksum-tso 201
Kongpo Gyamda 203
THE NORTHERN ROUTE
(HWY 317) 204
Chamdo 205
Riwoche 209
Riwoche Tsuglhakhang . . 209
Tengchen 210
Sok 212
Nagchu 213

**OVERLAND ROUTES
FROM SÌCHUĀN 216**
Kāngdìng (Dardo) 217
NORTHERN
ROUTE 222
Tǎgōng (Lhagong) 222
Gānzī (Garzê) 223

Around Gānzī 224
Manigango 224
Around Manigango 225
Derge 226
SOUTHERN ROUTE 227
Lithang 227
Bathang 229

TIBETAN TREKS . . . 230
PLANNING YOUR TREK . . 230
What to Bring 231
Maps 232
Trekking Agencies 232
Permits 234
ON THE TREK 234
Guides & Pack Animals . . 234
Food 235
Drink 236
TREKKING ROUTES 236
Ganden to Samye 237
Tsurphu to Yangpachen . . 240
Shalu to Nartang 244
Everest Base Camp to
Tingri 247
Mt Kailash Kora 250
Nyenchen Tanglha
Traverse 256
MORE TREKS 259
Lake Manasarovar Kora . 259
Everest East Face 260

GATEWAY CITIES . . . 261
KATHMANDU 262
CHÉNGDŪ 265

Lhasa ལྷ་ས

📞 0891 / POP 500,000 / ELEV 3650M

Includes »

Drepung Monastery . .78
Nechung Monastery . .83
Sera Monastery 83
Pabonka Monastery . .87
Ganden Monastery . . .89
Drak Yerpa. 92
Drölma Lhakhang 93
Shugsheb Nunnery . . .94

Best Places to Eat

» Snowland Restaurant (p71)

» Woeser Zedroe Tibetan Restaurant (p72)

» New Mandala Restaurant (p71)

Best Places to Stay

» Yabshi Phunkhang (p64)

» Kyichu Hotel (p64)

» Rama Kharpo (p65)

Why Go?

Despite rampant modernisation and expansion, Lhasa (the Place of the Gods) is still a city of wonders. Your first view of the red and white Potala Palace soaring above the holy city will raise the goosebumps, while the whitewashed old Tibetan quarter to the east continues to preserve the flavour of traditional Tibetan life. It is here in the Jokhang, an otherworldly mix of flickering butter lamps, wafting incense and prostrating pilgrims, and the encircling Barkhor pilgrim circuit that most visitors first fall in love with Tibet.

These days the booming boulevards of the modern Chinese city dwarf the winding alleyways of the whitewashed Tibetan quarter but it is in the latter that you should focus your time. Hired transport is not required in Lhasa and most guides will let you explore the city by yourself. If possible, budget a week to acclimatise, see the sights and explore the backstreets before heading off on an overland adventure.

When to Go

Temperatures are comfortable during April to September, with days surprisingly warm and nights pleasantly cool. Sunlight is strong at this altitude so always wear sunscreen.

The major festivals of Saga Dawa (spring) and Losar (winter) bring huge numbers of pilgrims to the city, and the August Shötun festival is also a major draw.

Accommodation can be tight during the first weeks of May and October and the months of July and August, when Chinese tourists flock to the city.

Lhasa Highlights

1 Follow monks, mendicants and fellow pilgrims around the fascinating medieval pilgrim circuit, the **Barkhor** (p43)

2 Join the lines of awed pilgrims around the glowing shrines of the **Jokhang** (p45), Tibet's holiest sanctum

3 Ogle the murals and stupas of the **Potala** (p52), the impressive but spiritless citadel of the Dalai Lamas

4 Take in a prayer meeting or some monk-debating at **Sera** (p83) or **Drepung** (p78), Tibet's great monastic cities

5 Take a day trip out to **Ganden Monastery** (p89) and test your sin on its fascinating kora (pilgrim path)

6 Explore the architecture, teashops and craft workshops of Lhasa's backstreets on our **old town walking tour** (p66)

7 Track down one of Lhasa's delightful off-the-beaten-track temples, such as the **Meru Nyingba Monastery** (p45) or **Tengye Ling** (p61)

History

Lhasa rose to prominence as an important administrative centre in the 7th century AD, when Songtsen Gampo (c 618–49), a local ruler in the Yarlung Valley, continued the task initiated by his father of unifying Tibet. Songtsen Gampo moved his capital to Lhasa and built a palace on the site now occupied by the Potala. It was at this time that the temples of Ramoche and the Jokhang were founded to house the priceless Buddha statues brought to Tibet as the dowries of Songtsen Gampo's Chinese and Nepali wives.

With the break-up of the Yarlung empire 250 years later, Buddhism enjoyed a gradual resurgence at monastic centres outside Lhasa and the centre of power shifted to Sakya, Nedong (Ü) and then Shigatse (Tsang). No longer the capital, Lhasa languished in the backwaters of Tibetan history until the fifth Dalai Lama (1617–82) defeated the Shigatse kings with Mongol support.

The fifth Dalai Lama moved his capital to Lhasa and started construction on his palace, the Potala, on the site of the ruins of Songtsen Gampo's 7th-century palace. Lhasa has remained Tibet's capital since 1642, and most of the city's historical sights date from this second stage of the city's development.

Modern Lhasa in many ways provides the visitor with both the best and the worst of contemporary Tibet. Photographs of the city taken before October 1950 reveal a small town nestled at the foot of the Potala, with a second cluster of residences surrounding the Jokhang, housing a population of between 20,000 and 30,000. Today the city has a population of around 500,000, and Chinese residents outnumber Tibetans.

Shöl, the village at the foot of the Potala, has long since disappeared, and the area in front of the Potala has been made into a Tiānānmén-style public square, complete with a 35m-tall monument to the 'liberation' of Tibet (under constant guard to prevent vandalism).

Physically the city has at least doubled in size in the last 20 years and it now takes at least 20 minutes to drive through the sprawling Chinese-style western suburbs. The Tibetan quarter is now an isolated enclave at the eastern end of town, comprising only around 4% of the city, and even these lingering enclaves of tradition are under threat from the bulldozers, despite official protection. Lhasa has probably changed more in the last 20 years than in the thousand years before.

Permits

Lhasa is currently the only part of Tibet that doesn't require you to hire pricey transportation. The only time you will be asked for your Tibet Tourism Bureau (TTB) permit is when you check in to a hotel. No other permits are required for the city or surroundings. At the time of research you had to visit the main monasteries of Drepung, Sera, Ganden and the Jokhang (but not the Potala) in the company of your guide, but other parts of the city were fine to explore by yourself.

◉ Sights

THE BARKHOR བར་འཁོར་ 八廓

The first stop for most newcomers to Lhasa is the Jokhang in the heart of the Tibetan old town. But before you even venture into the Jokhang it's worth taking a stroll around the **Barkhor** (Map p48), a quadrangle of streets that surrounds the Jokhang complex. It is an area unrivalled in Tibet for its fascinating combination of sacred significance and push-and-shove market economics. This is both the spiritual heart of the Holy City and the main shopping district for Tibetans.

The Barkhor is the one part of Lhasa that has most resisted the invasions of the modern world. Pilgrims from Kham, Amdo and further afield step blithely around a prostrating monk and stop briefly to finger a jewel-encrusted dagger at a street stall; monks sit cross-legged on the paving stones before their alms bowls muttering mantras, as armed police march by provocatively anti-clockwise in strict formation. It's an utterly fascinating place you'll want to come back to time after time.

PUBLIC TRANSPORT

At the time of research, foreigners were not allowed to travel on public transport out of Lhasa, with the possible exception of buses to the airport and the pilgrim bus to Ganden. Basic information is included here in case the situation changes.

Barkhor Square MONUMENT

For your first visit to the Barkhor, enter from Barkhor Sq (八角广场; Bājiǎo Guǎngchǎng; Map p48), a large plaza that was cleared in 1985. The square has become a focus for political protest and pitched battles between Chinese and Tibetans on several occasions, notably in 1998 (when a Dutch tourist was shot in the shoulder) and most recently in 2008. Look for the surveillance cameras recording everything from the rooftops above the square. The recent addition of a tacky Dico's fast-food joint at the west end of the square is a shame. At least the Chinese resisted the temptation to plunk a Mao statue in the middle of it all, like in almost every other provincial capital.

Close to the entrance to the Jokhang a constant stream of Tibetans follows the Barkhor circumambulation route in a clockwise direction. Look for the two pot-bellied, stone *sangkang* (incense burners) in front of the Jokhang. There are four altogether, marking the four extremities of the Barkhor circuit; the other two are at the rear of the Jokhang. Behind the first two *sangkang* are two joined enclosures. The northern **stele** is inscribed with the terms of the Sino-Tibetan treaty of 822. The inscription guarantees mutual respect of the borders of the two nations – an irony seemingly lost on the Chinese authorities. The southern one harbours the stump of an ancient willow tree, known as the hair

LHASA SIGHTS

DANGERS & ANNOYANCES

If you fly straight into Lhasa, remember to take things easy for your first day or two: it's not uncommon to feel breathless, suffer from headaches and sleep poorly because of the altitude. Don't attempt the steps up to the Potala for the first few days, drink lots of fluids and read p364 for details on acute mountain sickness (AMS).

Take care also when re-opening things such as tubes of sunscreen after a flight in to Lhasa or even jars of Coffee-mate from a local shop, as the change in pressure can cause messy explosions of volcanic proportions.

On a more serious note, Chinese armed police posts and riot squad teams currently occupy every street corner in the old town. Most Tibetans ignore them but you should take care not to photograph any military posts or armed patrols.

of the Jowo, allegedly planted by Songtsen Gampo's Chinese wife, Princess Wencheng (Wencheng Konjo), and a stele erected in 1793 commemorating smallpox victims.

For your first few visits to the Barkhor circuit, it's best to let yourself be dragged along

LHASA IN...

Two Days

On arrival in Lhasa you need at least two days to adjust to the altitude and you can expect to be tired and headachey most of the time. We recommend adding an extra day and taking the first day very easy.

The first item of business is for you or your guide to book a time to visit the Potala the next day. Then start off at **Barkhor Sq**, finding your legs on a relaxed stroll around the **Barkhor circuit** before visiting the **Jokhang** and afterwards grabbing lunch at nearby **New Mandala Restaurant**, **Snowland Restaurant** or **Lhasa Kitchen**. In the afternoon head to **Sera Monastery** to catch the monks debating. If your headache's gone, round off the day with a cold Lhasa Beer at **Dunya** or the roof of **Shambhala Palace**.

On day two visit the **Potala** at your allotted time and then spend the afternoon losing yourself in the fascinating old town on our **walking tour**.

Four Days

With four days you could leave the Potala until day three, and add on a stroll around the **Potala kora**, popping into the charming **Lukhang Temple** en route. On day four leave the city on a day trip out to **Ganden Monastery**, visiting the hermitage caves of **Drak Yerpa** on the way back.

Lhasa

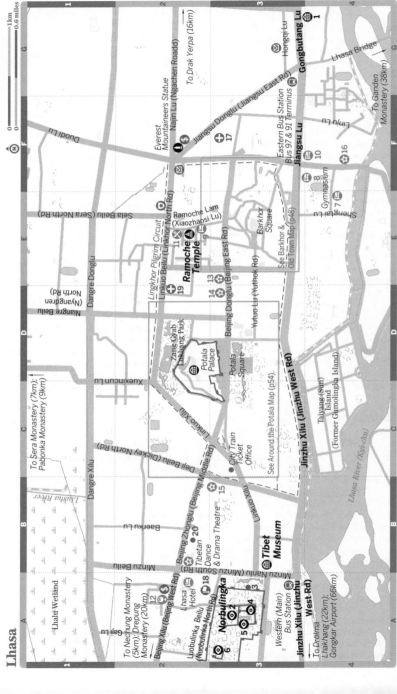

1 km
0.6 miles

Lhalu Wetland

To Nechung Monastery (5km); Drepung Monastery (20km)

Lhukha River

To Sera Monastery (7km); Pabonka Monastery (9km)

Duodi Lu

Everest Mountaineers Statue

Najin Lu (Ngachen Roadd)

To Drak Yerpa (16km)

Gongbutang Lu

1

Hongqi Lu

Lhasa Bridge

Jiangsu Donglu (Jiangsu East Rd)

Eastern Bus Station
Bus 97 & 91 Terminus

Jiangsu Lu

To Ganden Monastery (38km)

Linjiu Lu

Sela Beilu (Sera North Rd)

17

10

16

Niangre Beilu (Nyangdren North Rd)

Dangre Donglu

Lingkhor Pilgrim Circuit
Linkuo Beilu (Linkhor North Rd)

Ramoche Lam (Xiaozhaosi Lu)

Ramoche Temple

11

19

13

Barkhor Square

See Barkhor & Old Town Map (p48)

Gymnasium

8

7

Shengtai Lu

Dangre Xilu

Xuexincun Lu

Zang Gyab Lukhang Park

Potala Palace

Beijing Donglu (Beijing East Rd)

14

Yutuo Lu (Yuthok Rd)

Potala Square

See Around the Potala Map (p54)

Jinzhu Xilu (Jinzhu West Rd)

Linkuo Xilu

Taiyang (Sun) Island

Tuiyang (Sun) Island (Former Gtumolingka Island)

Lhasa River (Kyi-chu)

Deji Beilu (Dickey North Rd)

City Train Ticket Office

Baerku Lu

15

Beijing Zhonglu (Beijing Middle Rd)

Beijing Xilu (Beijing West Rd)

Tibetan Dance & Drama Theatre

20

Minzu Beilu

Minzu Nanlu (Minzu South Rd)

Tibet Museum

Liuobulinka Beilu (Nuobulinka North Rd)

Lhasa Hotel

12

18

Norbulingka

2

3

4

5

6

Western (Main) Bus Station

Jinzhu Xilu (Jinzhu West Rd)

To Drolma Lhakhang (22km); Gongkar Airport (66km)

Gala Lu

Lhasa

◎ Top Sights

Norbulingka	A3
Ramoche Temple	E2
Tibet Museum	B3

◎ Sights

1	Brahmaputra Grand Hotel	G4
2	New Summer Palace	A3
3	Norbulingka Ticket Office	A3
4	Palace of the Eighth Dalai Lama	A3
5	Retreat of the 13th Dalai Lama	A3
6	Summer Palace of the 13th Dalai Lama	A3

◎ Sleeping

7	Four Points	E4
8	Mandala Hotel	F4
9	Oh Dan Guest House	E2
10	St Regis	F4

◎ Eating

11	Norzing Selchung Tashi Yarphel Restaurant	E2

◎ Drinking

12	Qīpíngmǐ Bar	A2

◎ Entertainment

13	Gyelpo's Nangma	E3
14	JJ Nangma	D3
15	Queen	B3
16	Shöl Opera Troupe	F4

Information

17	City People's Hospital	F3
18	Nepali Consulate-General	A2
19	Tibetan Autonomous Region People's Hospital	D2

Transport

20	Air China	B2

by the centrifugal tide of pilgrims, but there are also several small, fascinating temples to pop into en route.

Barkhor Circuit PILGRIM CIRCUIT
As you follow the flow of pilgrims past sellers of religious photos, felt cowboy hats and electric blenders (for yak-butter tea!), you'll soon see a small building on the right, set off from the main path. This is the **Mani Lhakhang**, a small chapel that houses a huge prayer wheel set almost continuously in motion. To the right of the building is the grandiose entrance of the former city jail and dungeons, known as the Nangtse Shar.

If you head south from here, after about 10m you will see the entrance to the **Jampa Lhakhang** (also known as Jamkhang or Water Blessing Temple) on the right. The ground floor of this small temple has a huge two-storey statue of Miwang Jampa, the Future Buddha, flanked by rows of various protector gods and the meditation cave of the chapel's founder. Pilgrims ascend to the upper floor to be blessed with a sprinkling of holy water and the touch of a holy *dorje* (thunderbolt).

Continue down the alley following the prayer wheels, then pass through a doorway into the old **Meru Nyingba Monastery**. This small but active monastery is a real delight and is invariably crowded with Tibetans thumbing prayer beads or lazily swinging prayer wheels and chanting under their breath. The chapel itself is administered by Nechung Monastery, which accounts for the many images of the Nechung oracle inside. The building, like the adjoining Jokhang, dates back to the 7th century, though most of what you see today is recently constructed.

On the west side of the courtyard up some narrow stairs is the small Sakyapaschool **Gongkar Chöde** chapel. Below is the **Zhambhala Lhakhang**, with a central image of Marmedze (Dipamkara), the Past Buddha, and a small inner kora path. From here you can return north or head east to join up with the Barkhor circuit.

The eastern side of the circuit has more shops and even a couple of small department stores that specialise in turquoise. In the southeast corner is a wall shrine and a **darchen** (prayer pole), which mark the spot where Tsongkhapa planted his walking stick in 1409. The empty southern square of the Jokhang used to host annual teachings by the Dalai Lama during the Mönlam festival. The circuit finally swings north by a police station back to Barkhor Sq.

THE JOKHANG ཇོ་ཁང་ 大昭寺
Also known in Tibetan as the Tsuglhakhang, the **Jokhang** (Dàzhāo Sì; Map p48; admission Y85; ◎inner chapels 8am-12.30pm) is the most revered religious structure in Tibet. Thick with the smell of yak butter, the murmur of mantras and the shuffling of wide-eyed pilgrims, the Jokhang is an unrivalled Tibetan experience. Don't miss it.

The chapels can be very busy, with long lines of pilgrims, so try to view the most popular ones just after the temple opens or

STREET NAMES

In this edition we use Chinese street names, as that is what most locals (including many Tibetans) and almost all taxi drivers use. The traditional Tibetan names are included in brackets.

» Beijing Donglu (Beijing Shar Lam)
» Beijing Zhonglu (Beijing Kyil Lam)
» Danjielin Lu (Tengyeling Lam)
» Deji Lu (Dekyi Lam)
» Jiangsu Lu (Chingdröl Shar Lam)
» Linkuo Lu (Linkhor Lam)
» Minzu Lu (Mirig Lam)
» Niangre Lu (Nyangdren Lam)
» Xiaozhaosi Lu (Ramoche Lam)
» Yutuo Lu (Yuthok Lam)
» Zangyiyuan Lu (Mentsikhang Lam)
» Zhisenge/Qingnian Lu (Dosenge Lam)

just before it closes around noon. The complex is open in the afternoon via the side entrance but most chapels are closed then and there are no pilgrims. Once you've left the complex you can't re-enter without buying another ticket. Photos are not allowed inside the chapels.

History

Estimated dates for the Jokhang's founding range from 639 to 647 AD. Construction was initiated by King Songtsen Gampo to house an image of Mikyöba (Akshobhya) brought to Tibet as part of the dowry of his Nepali wife Princess Bhrikuti. The Ramoche Temple was constructed at the same time to house another Buddha image, Jowo Sakyamuni (Sakya Thukpa), brought to Tibet by his Chinese wife Princess Wencheng. It is thought that after the death of Songtsen Gampo, Jowo Sakyamuni was moved from Ramoche for its protection and hidden in the Jokhang by Princess Wencheng. The image has remained in the Jokhang ever since (Jokhang, or Jowokhang, means 'chapel of the Jowo'), and it is the most revered Buddha image in all of Tibet.

Over the centuries, the Jokhang has undergone many renovations, but the basic layout is ancient and differs from that of many other Tibetan religious structures. One crucial difference is the building's east–west ori-

entation, said to face towards Nepal to honour Princess Bhrikuti. A few interior carved pillars and entrance arches remain from the original 7th-century work of Newari artisans brought from the Kathmandu Valley in Nepal to work on the construction.

In the early days of the Cultural Revolution, Red Guards desecrated much of the interior of the Jokhang and it is claimed that a section was utilised as a pigsty. Since 1980 the Jokhang has been restored, and without the aid of an expert eye you will see few signs of the misfortunes that have befallen the temple in recent years.

GROUND FLOOR

In front of the entrance to the Jokhang is a forecourt that is perpetually crowded with pilgrims polishing the flagstones with their prostrations. For information on the monuments in front of the Jokhang see p43.

Just inside the entrance to the Jokhang are statues of the **Four Guardian Kings** (Chökyong), two on either side. Beyond this is the main assembly hall, or *dukhang,* a paved courtyard that is open to the elements. During festivals the hall is often the focus of ceremonies. The throne on the left wall was formerly used by the Dalai Lamas. You'll see a line of pilgrims filing past the main Jokhang entrance as they walk the pilgrim circuit around the temple.

The inner prayer hall of the Jokhang houses the most important images and chapels. Most prominent are six larger-than-life statues that dominate the central prayer hall. In the foreground and to the left is a 6m statue of Guru Rinpoche. The statue opposite it, to the right, is of Jampa (Maitreya), the Future Buddha. At the centre of the hall, between and to the rear of these two statues, is a thousand-armed Chenresig (Avalokiteshvara). At the far right are two more Jampa statues, one behind the other, and to the far rear, behind Chenresig and facing the main Jowo statue, is another statue of Guru Rinpoche, encased in a cabinet.

Encircling this enclosed area of statues is a collection of chapels, which Tibetan pilgrims visit in a clockwise direction. There are generally long queues for the holiest chapels, particularly the Chapel of Jowo Sakyamuni. Pilgrims rub the doorways and chain-mail curtains, touch their heads to revered statues, throw seeds as offerings and pour molten yak butter into the heat of a thousand prayer lamps. The hushed atmosphere of respect is broken only by groups of tourists chattering into their mobile phones.

The chapels, following a clockwise route, are as follows. The numbers marked here refer to those marked on the Jokhang map.

Tsongkhapa was the founder of the Gelugpa order, and you can see him seated in the centre of the **Chapel of Tsongkhapa & His Disciples (14)**, flanked by his eight disciples. The **Chapel of the Buddha of Infinite Light (15)** is usually closed. Just outside is the large Tagba chörten (stupa). The eight medicine buddhas in the **Chapel of the Eight Medicine Buddhas (17)** are recent and not of special interest.

The **Chapel of Chenresig (18)** contains the Jokhang's most important image after the Jowo Sakyamuni. Legend has it that the statue of Chenresig here sprang spontaneously into being and combines aspects of King Songtsen Gampo, his wives and two wrathful protective deities. The doors of the chapel are among the few remnants still visible of the Jokhang's 7th-century origins and were fashioned by Nepali artisans. This and the next four chapels are the most popular with pilgrims and lines can be long.

In the **Chapel of Jampa (19)** are statues of Jampa as well as four smaller bodhisattvas: Jampelyang (Manjushri), Chenresig (to the left), Chana Dorje (Vajrapani) and Drölma (Tara). Öpagme (Amitabha) and Tsongkhapa are also present here, as are two chörtens, one of which holds the remains of the original sculptor.

The image of Tsongkhapa in the **Chapel of Tsongkhapa (20)** was commissioned by the subject himself and is said to be a precise resemblance. It is the central image on top of the steps.

The **Chapel of the Buddha of Infinite Light (21)** is the second of the chapels consecrated to Öpagme (Amitabha), the Buddha of Infinite Light. The outer entrance, with its wonderful carved doors, is protected by two fierce deities, red Tamdrin (Hayagriva; right) and blue Chana Dorje (Vajrapani; left). There are also statues of the eight bodhisattvas. Pilgrims generally pray here for the elimination of impediments to viewing the most sacred image of the Jokhang, that of Jowo Sakyamuni, which awaits in the next chapel.

Outside the chapel to the right are statues of King Songtsen Gampo with his two wives, and of Guru Rinpoche (at the back).

The most important shrine in Tibet, the **Chapel of Jowo Sakyamuni (22)** houses the image of Sakyamuni Buddha at the age of 12 years, brought to Tibet by Princess Wencheng. You enter via an anteroom containing the Four Guardian Kings, smiling on the left and frowning on the right. Inside are statues of the protectors Miyowa (Achala) and Chana Dorje (Vajrapani, blue). Several large bells hang from the anteroom's Newari-style roof. The carved doorway has been rubbed smooth by generations of pilgrims.

The 1.5m statue of Sakyamuni is embedded with precious stones, covered in silks and jewellery, and surrounded by silver pillars with dragon motifs. The silver canopy above was financed by a Mongolian khan. Pilgrims touch their forehead to the statue's left leg before being tapped on the back by a monk 'bouncer' when it's time to move on.

To the rear of Sakyamuni are statues of the seventh and 13th Dalai Lamas (with a moustache), Tsongkhapa and 12 standing bodhisattvas. Look for the 7th-century pillars on the way out.

The Jampa (Maitreya, or Future Buddha) enshrined in the **Chapel of Jampa (23)** is a replica of a statue that came to Tibet as a part of the dowry of Princess Bhrikuti, King Songtsen Gampo's Nepali wife. Around the statue are eight images of Drölma, a goddess seen as an embodiment of the enlightened mind of Buddhahood and who protects against the eight fears – hence the eight statues. There are some fine door carvings here. As you exit the chapel look for the unexpected statues of the Hindu gods Indra and Brahma.

In the **Chapel of Chenresig Riding a Lion (24)**, the statue of Chenresig on the back of a *sengye* (snow lion) is first on the

Barkhor & Old Town

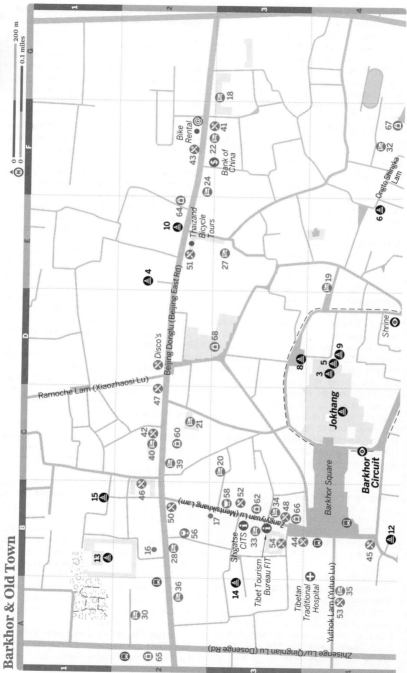

0 0
0.1 miles
200 m

13

15

16

30

36

28

56

50

46

42
40

39

21

60

47

Ramoche Lam (Xiaozhaosi Lu)

Disco's

4

10

64

51

Thaland Bicycle Tours

Beijing Donglu (Beijing East Rd)

68

Bike Rental
@
43
22
41
18

24

Bank of China
$

27

19

6

Ongto Shingka Lam

32
67

8
3 5
9

Shrine

Jokhang

Barkhor Square

Barkhor Circuit

14

Tibet Tourism Bureau FIT

Shigatse CITS

33
54
44
66
34
48
62

52
58

17

Zangyyuan Lu (Mentsikhang Lam)

20

Tibetan Traditional Hospital

Yuthok Lam (Yutuo Lu)

53
35

45

12

65

Zhisenge Lu/Qingnian Lu (Dosenge Rd)

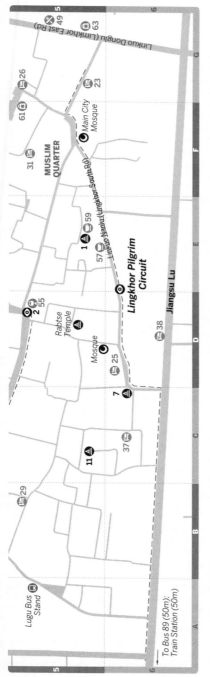

left (it's not the largest of the icons within). The other eight statues of the chapel are all aspects of Chenresig.

Some pilgrims exit this chapel and then follow a flight of stairs up to the next floor, while others complete the circuit on the ground floor. Unless you're chapelled out (you've seen the important ones already), continue on upstairs, but look out first for a small hole in the wall on the left as you exit the chapel, against which pilgrims place their ear to hear the beating wings of a mythical bird that lives under the Jokhang.

The **Guru Rinpoche Shrine (25)** contains two statues of Guru Rinpoche and one of King Trisong Detsen next to the stairs. Beside the shrine is a rock painting of the medicine buddha protected by a glass plate. Inside the **Chapel of Tsepame (26)** are nine statues of Tsepame (Amitayus), the red Buddha of Longevity, in *yabyum* (sexual and spiritual union) pose.

The **Chapel of Jampa (27)** holds the Jampa statue that was traditionally borne around the Barkhor on the 25th day of the first lunar month for the Mönlam festival. This yearly excursion was designed to hasten the arrival of the Future Buddha. Jampelyang and Chenresig flank the Buddha.

The chapel is also named Ramo Gyalmo (Chapel of the Sacred Goat), after the rough 'self-arisen' (ie not man-made) image of the goat emerging from the wall in the first corner, beside the god of wealth Zhambhala.

The **Chapel of the Hidden Jowo (28)** is where Princess Wencheng is said to have hidden Jowo Sakyamuni for safekeeping after the death of her husband. You can see the cavity on the eastern wall. Inside is a statue of Öpagme (Amitabha) and the eight medicine buddhas with characteristic blue hair.

From here there are several other chapels of limited interest to non-Tibetologists. The **Chapel of the Seven Buddhas (29)** is followed by the corner **Chapel of the Nine Buddhas of Longevity (30)**, whose deities hold vases of immortality. The last of the ground-floor chapels is the **Chapel of the Kings (31)**, with some original statues of Tibet's earliest kings. The central figure is Songtsen Gampo, flanked by images of King Trisong Detsen (left) and King Ralpachen (right). Pilgrims touch their head to the central pillar. On the wall outside the chapel is a fine mural depicting the original

Barkhor & Old Town

⊚ **Top Sights**

Barkhor Circuit C4
Jokhang C4
Lingkhor Pilgrim Circuit E6

⊚ **Sights**

1 Ani Sangkhung Nunnery E5
2 Darchen D5
3 Gongkar Chöde Chapel D4
4 Gyüme Tratsang E2
5 Jampa Lhakhang D4
6 Karmashar Temple E4
7 Lho Rigsum Lhakhang C6
8 Mani Lhakhang D3
9 Meru Nyingba Monastery D4
10 Meru Sarpa Monastery E2
11 Pode Kangtsang C5
12 Rigsum Lhakhang B4
13 Shide Tratsang B1
14 Tengye Ling A3
15 Tsome Ling B1
Zhambhala Lhakhang .... (see 3)

Activities, Courses & Tours

16 Braille Without Borders Blind
Medical Massage Clinic..................... B2
17 Tenzin Blind Massage Centre.............. B3

⊜ **Sleeping**

18 Banak Shol G3
19 Barkhor Namchen House E4
20 Cool Yak Hotel C3
21 Dhood Gu Hotel C2
22 Dongcuo International Youth
Hostel F2
23 Flora Hotel G5
24 Gang Gyen Hotel F2
25 Gorkha Hotel D6
26 Heritage Hotel.. G5
27 House of Shambhala E3
28 Kyichu Hotel B2
29 Lingtsang Boutique Hotel B5
30 Phuntsok Khasang International
Youth Hostel A2
31 Rama Kharpo F5
32 Shambhala Palace................................. F4
33 Shangbala Hotel B3
34 Snowlands Hotel B3
35 Thangka Hotel.. A4

36 Tibet Kailash Hotel A2
37 Trichang Labrang Hotel C6
38 Xiongbala Hotel D6
39 Yabshi Phunkhang C2
40 Yak Hotel C2

⊗ **Eating**

41 Alilang Korean Barbeque....................... F2
42 Dunya Restaurant C2
43 Lánqíng Qīngzhēn Fànguǎn.................. F2
44 Lhasa Kitchen B3
Nam-tso Restaurant .... (see 18)
45 New Mandala Restaurant B4
46 Pentoc Tibetan Restaurant B2
47 Shānchéng Chuāncàiguǎn C2
48 Snowland Restaurant B3
49 Sun Tribe Restaurant G5
50 Tashi I B2
51 Tashi II E2
52 Tengyelink Café...................................... B3
53 Tibet Kun Phan Vegetarian
Restaurant... A4
54 Woeser Zedroe Tibetan
Restaurant... B3

⊝ ⊝ **Drinking**

Dunya .... (see 42)
55 Makye Amye D5
56 Spinn Café B2
Summit Café .... (see 33)
57 Teahouse E5
58 Tengyeling Teahouse.............................. B3
59 Teahouse E5

Entertainment

Shangrila Restaurant..................... (see 51)

⊝ **Shopping**

60 Dorje Antique Shop................................ C2
61 Lhasa Village Handicrafts..................... F5
Kyichu Art Gallery .... (see 28)
62 Mani Thangka Arts................................. B3
63 Norling Supermarket.............................. G5
64 Outlook Outdoor Equipment................. E2
65 Sifang Supermarket............................... A2
66 Snow Leopard Carpet
Industries... B3
67 Tanva F4
68 Tromsikhang Market D3

construction of the Jokhang (right) and the Potala, alongside performances of Tibetan opera, yak dances, wrestling, stone weight-lifting and horse racing.

FIRST FLOOR

At this point you should return clockwise to the rear of the ground floor (if you did not do so earlier) and climb the stairs to the upper floor of the Jokhang. The upper floor of the Jokhang's inner sanctum is also ringed with chapels, though some of them are closed.

As you begin the circuit, you will pass by several newly restored rooms that feature **Sakyamuni (35, 37)** accompanied by his two main disciples, and one featuring the **eight medicine buddhas (36)**. The **Chapel of Lhobdrak Namka Gyaltsen (34)**, or Lamrin Chapel, near the southeast corner features Pabonka Rinpoche, Sakyamuni, Tsongkhapa and Atisha (Jowo-je). The chapel in the southwest corner is the **Chapel of Five Protectors (38)** and has some fearsome statues of Tamdrin (Hayagriva) and other protector deities, attended by Tantric drumming in the anteroom. Next is the **Chapel of the Three Kings (40)**, dedicated to Songtsen Gampo, Trisong Detsen and Ralpachen. Also featured in the room are the statues of Songtsen Gampo's two wives, various ministers, and such symbols of royalty as the elephant and horse on either side.

Also worth a look is the **Chapel of Songtsen Gampo (41)**, the principal Songtsen Gampo chapel in the Jokhang. It is positioned in the centre of the west wall (directly above the entry to the ground-floor inner sanctum). The bejewelled king, with a tiny buddha protruding from his turban, is accompanied by his two consorts, his Nepali wife to the left and his Chinese wife to the

right. During Losar Tibetan families queue up in front of the royal silver-embossed animal-headed *chang* (barley beer) container outside the chapel to make an offering of their first batch of home-brew.

Most of the other rooms are hidden behind grills, the main exception being the meditation cell of the **Chapel of Songtsen Gampo (46)** near the floor's northeastern corner, which has an incredible carved doorway smeared with decades' worth of yak butter. Murals to the right of the doorway depict the Jokhang. As you walk back to the stairs look at the unusual row of carved beams that look like half-lion, half-monkey creatures.

Back by the stairs, notice the round door frames of the **Chapel of Guru Rinpoche (48)** and the **Chapel of Samvara (49)**, showing Samvara with consort, which date back to the 7th century.

Before you leave the 1st floor by the stairs in the southeast corner, ascend half a floor up to two statues of the protectress **Palden Lhamo (50)**, one wrathful, the other benign. There's also a photo of the Nechung oracle here. You can sometimes gain access to a Tantric chapel up on the 2nd floor.

After you've explored the interior of the Jokhang, it's definitely worth spending some time on the **roof**, with its stunning views and small teahouse. The orange

---

DON'T MISS

WALK LIKE A TIBETAN: LHASA'S PILGRIM CIRCUITS

For Tibetan pilgrims the principal points of orientation in Lhasa are the city's three koras (pilgrimage circuits): the Nangkhor, Barkhor and Lingkhor. For the visitor, all the koras are well worth following, especially during festivals like Saga Dawa (p22), when the distinction between tourist and pilgrim can become very fine indeed. The following routes hold the keys to the soul of the city. Remember always to proceed clockwise.

» **Nangkhor** – this kora encircles the inner precincts of the Jokhang (Map p52).

» **Barkhor** – the most famous of Lhasa's pilgrimage circuits traces the outskirts of the Jokhang and is probably the best introduction to the old town for newcomers (Map p48).

» **Lingkhor** – this devotional route (Map p48) traditionally encompassed the entirety of the old city. Nowadays the Lingkhor includes a great deal of the modern city but it is still used by pilgrims. You can join the 8km-long circuit anywhere, but the most interesting section is covered in our Lingkhor walking tour (p68).

» **Potala Kora (Tsekhor)** – another popular kora encircles the Potala, passing by an almost continuous circuit of prayer wheels, chörtens (stupas), rock paintings and the Lukhang Temple (Map p54).

» **Other koras** – there are also excellent koras at Drepung, Ganden and Sera Monasteries.

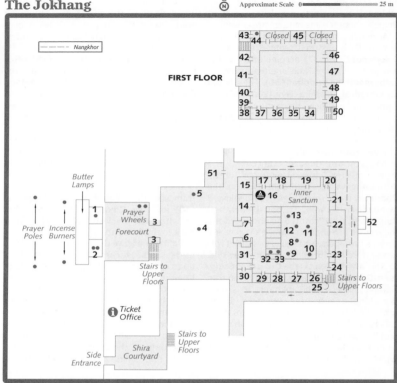

building on the north side holds the private quarters of the Dalai Lama.

Finish off the visit with a walk around the **Nangkhor** pilgrim path, which encircles the Jokhang's inner sanctum. If you're not exhausted, you can have a brief look at the **Drölma Chapel (51)**, featuring Drölma flanked by her green and white manifestations and others of her 21 manifestations. Pilgrims sometimes pop into the **Guru Rinpoche Chapel (52)**, a series of three interconnected shrines stuffed with images of Guru Rinpoche, at the back of the kora.

THE POTALA ཕོ་བྲང་ 布达拉宫

Lhasa's cardinal landmark, the **Potala** (Bùdálā Gōng; Map p54; admission Y100; ⊗9.30am-3pm before 1 May, 9am-3.30pm after 1 May, interior chapels close 4.30pm) is one of the great wonders of world architecture. As has been the case with centuries of pilgrims before you, the first sight of the

fortress-like structure will be a magical moment that you will remember for a long time. It's hard to peel your eyes away from the place.

The Potala is a structure of massive proportions, an awe-inspiring place to visit, but still many visitors come away slightly disappointed. Unlike the Jokhang, which hums with vibrant activity, the Potala lies dormant like a huge museum, and the lifelessness of the highly symbolic building constantly reminds visitors that the Dalai Lama has been forced to take his government into exile. It's a modern irony that the Potala now hums with large numbers of domestic tourists staring with wonder at the building that the generation before them tried to destroy.

History

Marpo Ri, the 130m-high 'Red Hill', which commands a view of all of Lhasa, was the site of King Songtsen Gampo's palace dur-

The Jokhang

Entrance
1 Sino-Tibetan Treaty Stele
2 Smallpox Stele and Ancient Willow Tree

Ground Floor
3 Guardian Kings
4 Courtyard
5 Throne of the Dalai Lamas
6 Naga Chapel (Lukhang)
7 Nojin Chapel
8 Jampa Statue
9 Jampa Statue
10 Jampa Statue
11 Guru Rinpoche Statue
12 Chenresig Statue
13 Guru Rinpoche Statue
14 Chapel of Tsongkhapa & His Disciples
15 Chapel of the Buddha of Infinite Light (Öpagme)
16 Chörten
17 Chapel of the Eight Medicine Buddhas
18 Chapel of Chenresig (Avalokiteshvara)
19 Chapel of Jampa
20 Chapel of Tsongkhapa
21 Chapel of the Buddha of Infinite Light
22 Chapel of Jowo Sakyamuni
23 Chapel of Jampa
24 Chapel of Chenresig Riding a Lion
25 Guru Rinpoche Shrine and Rock Painting
26 Chapel of Tsepame
27 Chapel of Jampa

28 Chapel of the Hidden Jowo
29 Chapel of the Seven Buddhas
30 Chapel of the Nine Buddhas of Longevity (Tsepame)
31 Chapel of the Kings
32 Songtsen Gampo Statue
33 Jowo Jampa Statue

First Floor
34 Chapel of Lhobdak Namka Gyaltsen (Lamrin Chapel)
35 Chapel of Sakyamuni
36 Chapel of Eight Medicine Buddhas
37 Chapel of Sakyamuni (Tupwang Lhakhang)
38 Chapel of Five Protectors
39 Anteroom
40 Chapel of the Three Kings (Dachok Lhakhang)
41 Chapel of Songtsen Gampo (Chögyel Lhakhang)
42 Chapel of Chenresig
43 Chapel of Sakyamuni (Tairab Lhakhang)
44 Prayer Wheel
45 Chapel of Guru Rinpoche & Sakyamuni
46 Chapel of Songtsen Gampo
47 Zhelre Lakhang (Inaccessible)
48 Chapel of Guru Rinpoche
49 Chapel of Samvara
50 Palden Lhamo Statues

Other Chapels
51 Drölma Chapel
52 Guru Rinpoche Chapel

ing the mid-7th century, long before the construction of the present-day Potala. There is little to indicate what this palace looked like, but it is clear that royal precedent was a major factor in the fifth Dalai Lama's choice of this site when he decided to move the seat of his Gelugpa government here from Drepung Monastery.

Work began first on the White Palace, or Kharpo Podrang, in 1645. The nine-storey structure was completed three years later, and in 1649 the fifth Dalai Lama moved from Drepung Monastery to his new residence. However, the circumstances surrounding the construction of the larger Red Palace, or Marpo Podrang, are subject to some dispute. It is agreed that the fifth Dalai Lama died in 1682 and that his death was concealed until the completion of the Red Palace 12 years later. In some accounts, the work was initiated by the regent who governed Tibet from 1679 to 1703, and foundations were laid in 1690 (after the fifth Dalai Lama's death). In other accounts, the Red Palace was conceived by the fifth Dalai Lama as a funerary chörten and work was well under way at the time of his death. In any event, the death of the fifth Dalai Lama was not announced until he was put to rest in the newly completed Red Palace.

There is also some scholarly debate concerning the Potala's name. The most probable explanation is that it derives from the Tibetan name for Chenresig's 'pure land', or paradise, also known as Potala. Given that Songtsen Gampo and the Dalai Lamas are believed to be reincarnations of Chenresig, this connection is compelling.

Since its construction, the Potala has been the home of each of the successive Dalai Lamas, although since construction of the Norbulingka summer palace in the late 18th century, it served as a winter residence only. It was also the seat of the Tibetan government, and with chapels, schools, jails and even tombs for the Dalai Lamas, it was virtually a self-contained world.

The Potala was shelled briefly during the 1959 popular uprising against the Chinese but the damage was not extensive. The Potala was spared again during the Cultural Revolution, reportedly at the insistence of Zhou Enlai, the Chinese premier, who is said to have deployed his own troops to protect it. The Potala was reopened to the public in 1980 and final touches to the US$4 million renovations were completed in 1995.

Entry Procedures

A quota system is now in place to cope with the huge numbers of domestic tourists trying to visit the Potala during the summer months. From mid-April to November you need to go to an **office** (⊙9am-6pm) at the southwestern gate the day before your intended visit. Present your passport and get a reservation slip detailing a time for your visit the next day. It can help to have your guide with you. One person can get slips for four people, so earn some good karma and take your friends' passports. After 2800 slips have been allotted (only 700 of which go to independent tourists) you'll be turned away, so start queuing early in peak seasons.

During the winter months (December to mid-April) you can just buy a ticket on the spot. Larger groups are officially limited to just one hour inside the Potala, which really isn't enough time. Individuals who book their own time slot at the western office face no such time restrictions.

The next day head to the main southern entrance 30 minutes before your allotted time (groups enter via the eastern gate) and then proceed through the rebuilt village of Shöl up into the palace. Halfway up is the office where you actually buy your ticket. From the roof you wind down into the laby-

Around the Potala

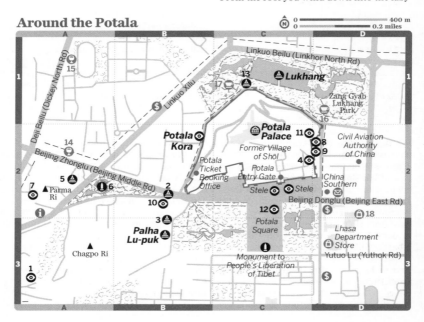

rinthine bowels of the Potala, before exiting at the rear of the palace and descending to either the Lukhang or the western entrance. Much of your visit will be in one huge shuffling queue.

Photography of the interior of the Potala is forbidden and all rooms are wired with motion sensors and video cameras.

SHÖL

Nestled at the southern foot of Marpo Ri, the former village of **Shöl** (admission Y30) was once Lhasa's red-light district, as well as the location of a prison, a printing press and some ancillary government buildings. Reconstructed buildings include an inn supposedly favoured by the licentious sixth Dalai Lama (see the box, p281), the residence of the monk police chief and an exhibition hall. Most people give the buildings a miss.

Entry to the Potala is up two steep access ramps that will soon leave you wheezing in the oxygen-depleted air (Shöl literally means 'at the base'). The stairs lead past the ticket office to the large **Deyang Shar**, the

When Princess Wencheng chose the site of the Jokhang, she chose Lake Wothang (perhaps because she was still upset at having to live in barbarian Tibet). The lake was eventually filled in, but it is said that a well in the precincts of the Jokhang still draws its waters from those of the old lake. Over the years, many legends have emerged around the task of filling in Lake Wothang. The most prominent of these is the story of how the lake was filled by a sacred white goat (the Tibetan word for goat, *ra*, is etymologically connected with the original name for Lhasa – Rasa). Look for a small image of the goat peeking out from the Chapel of Jampa on the south wall of the Jokhang's ground-floor inner sanctum.

Around the Potala

◎ Top Sights
Lukhang	C1
Palha Lu-puk	B3
Potala Kora	B2
Potala Palace	C2

◎ Sights
1	Chagpo Ri Rock Carvings	A3
2	Chörten (Former West Gate)	B2
3	Drubthub Nunnery	B3
4	Eastern (Group) Potala Entrance	C2
5	Gesar Ling	A2
6	Golden Yaks Statue	A2
7	Kunde Ling	A2
8	Nun's Chapel	D2
9	Phurbu Chok Hermitage Mani Lhakhang	D2
10	Potala Viewpoint	B2
11	Rock Paintings	C2
12	Stele	C2
13	Three Chörtens	C1

◎◎ Drinking
14	Bangda	A2
15	Easy Day	A1
16	Teahouse	D1
17	Teahouse	C1

◎ Shopping
18	Baiyi Supermarket	D2

external courtyard of the White Palace. At the top of the triple stairs leading up to the White Palace look out for the golden handprints of the fifth Dalai Lama on the wall to the left, and murals to the north depicting Songtsen Gampo's original Potala and the construction of the Jokhang.

ROOF OF THE WHITE PALACE

As you arrive on the roof, head right for the private quarters of the 13th and 14th Dalai Lamas. The first room you come to is the **throne room** (Simchung Nyiwoi Shar), where the Dalai Lamas would receive official guests. The large picture on the left of the throne is of the 13th Dalai Lama; the matching photo of the present Dalai Lama has been removed. There are some fine murals here, including a depiction of Bodhgaya (where the Buddha achieved enlightenment), the Chinese Buddhist mountain Wǔtái Shān and the mythical paradise of Shambhala (north of the entry).

The trail continues clockwise into the **reception hall** (Dhaklen Paldseg) from whose hidden balcony the Dalai Lama would have watched festival dances performed in the courtyard below. Next comes the **meditation room**, which still displays the ritual implements of the present Dalai Lama on a small table to the side of the room. Protector gods here include Nagpo Chenpo (Mahakala), the Nechung oracle and Palden Lhamo. The final room, the **bedroom of**

DEMONESS-SUBDUING TEMPLES

Buddhism's interaction with the pre-existing Bön – a shamanistic folk religion of spirits, ghosts and demons – combined with the wild and inhospitable nature of the Tibetan terrain has led to many metaphoric fables about Buddhism's taming of Tibet. The story of the early introduction of Buddhism to Tibet is represented by the story of a vast, supine demoness whose body straddled the entire plateau.

It was Princess Wencheng, the Chinese wife of King Songtsen Gampo, who divined the presence of this demoness. Through Chinese geomantic calculations she established that the heart of the demoness lay beneath a lake in the centre of Lhasa, while her torso and limbs lay far away in the outer dominions of the high plateau. As in all such fables, the demoness can be seen as a symbol, of both the physical hardships of Tibet and the existing Bön clergy's hostility towards Buddhism; both had to be tamed before Buddhism could take root here. It was decided that the demoness would have to be pinned down.

The first task was to drain the lake in Lhasa of its water (read life-blood of the demoness) and build a central temple that would replace the heart of the demoness with a Buddhist heart. The temple built there was the Jokhang. A stake through the heart was not enough to put a demoness of this size out of action, however, and a series of lesser temples, in three concentric rings, were conceived to pin the extremities of the demoness.

There were four temples in each of these rings. The first are known as the *runo* temples and form a protective circle around Lhasa, pinning down the demoness' hips and shoulders. Two of these are Trandruk Monastery in the Yarlung Valley (p122) and Katsel Monastery (p106) on the way to Drigung. The second group, known as the *tandrul* temples, pin the knees and elbows of the demoness. Buchu Monastery (p201) near Bayi in eastern Tibet is one of these. And the final group, known as *yandrul* temples, pin the hands and feet. These last temples are found as far away as Bhutan (Paro and Bumthang) and Sìchuān, though the location of two of them is unknown. You can see a representative image of the demoness and the temples that pin her down in the Tibet Museum (p63).

the **Dalai Lama** (Chimey Namgyal), has some personal effects of the Dalai Lama on show, such as his bedside clock. The mural above the bed is of Tsongkhapa, the founder of the Gelugpa order of which the Dalai Lama is the head. The locked door leads into the Dalai Lama's private bathroom.

RED PALACE

You can start the tour of the main palace building from the top. On the **third floor**, the first room is the Chapel of Jampa (Jamkhang), which contains an exquisite image of Jampa commissioned by the eighth Dalai Lama; it stands opposite the Dalai Lama's throne. To the right of the throne is a wooden Kalachakra mandala. The walls are stacked with the collected works of the fifth Dalai Lama. The chapel was unfortunately damaged in a fire in 1984 (caused by an electrical fault) and many valuable thangkas (religious paintings) were lost.

Next, the Chapel of Three-Dimensional Mandalas (Loilang Khang) houses spectacular jewel-encrusted mandalas of the three principal Tantric deities of the Gelugpa order. These are essentially three-dimensional versions of the mandalas you see painted on thangkas everywhere and act as meditation maps for the mind. Unfortunately you can no longer walk around to see the fine blackened murals near the throne of the seventh Dalai Lama.

The Chapel of the Victory over the Three Worlds (Sasum Namgyal) houses a library and displays examples of Manchu texts. The main statue is a golden thousand-armed Chenresig, while the main thangka is of the Manchu Chinese emperor Qianlong dressed in monk's robes, with accompanying inscriptions in Tibetan, Chinese, Mongolian and Manchurian.

Next, the Chapel of Immortal Happiness (Chimey Dedan Kyil) was once the residence of the sixth Dalai Lama, Tsangyang Gyatso, whose throne remains; it is now dedicated to Tsepame, the Buddha of Longevity, who sits by the window. Next to him in the corner is the Dzogchen deity Ekajati (Tsechigma), with an ostrich-feather hat and a single fang.

From here a locked corridor leads off the main circuit to a gallery that overlooks the **tomb of the 13th Dalai Lama**. You could at one time look down on the chörten from above and then descend to look at it at ground level, but the room has been closed for years.

Also in the northwest corner is the **Lhama Lhakhang** and the golden **tomb of the Seventh Dalai Lama** (Serdung Tashi Obar Khang), constructed in 1757 and encased in half a tonne of gold. To the right stands a statue of Kalsang Gyatso, the seventh Dalai Lama.

In the northwest corner, steps lead up into the small but important **Chapel of Arya Lokeshvara** (Phagpa Lhakhang). Allegedly this is one of the few corners of the Potala that dates from the time of Songtsen Gampo's 7th-century palace. It is the most sacred of the Potala's chapels, and the sandalwood image of Arya Lokeshvara inside is the most revered image housed in the Potala. The statue is accompanied on the left by the seventh Dalai Lama and Tsongkhapa, and on the right by the fifth, eighth and ninth Dalai Lamas and the protector Chana Dorje (Vajrapani). Relics include stone footprints of Guru Rinpoche and Tsongkhapa.

The last two rooms on this floor are the towering, jewel-encrusted **tombs of the Eighth and Ninth Dalai Lamas**, the former over 9m tall.

If you're exhausted already (not even halfway!), you can rest your legs at a reception area/teahouse in the middle of the **second floor**.

The first of the chapels you come to on the 2nd floor is the **Chapel of Kalachakra** (Dukhor Lhakhang), also known as the Wheel of Time. It is noted for its stunning three-dimensional mandala, which is over 6m in diameter and finely detailed with over 170 statues. Access to the room is limited.

The **Chapel of Sakyamuni** (Thubwang Lhakhang) houses a library, the throne of the seventh Dalai Lama, eight bodhisattvas and some fine examples of gold painted calligraphy.

In the **Chapel of the Nine Buddhas of Longevity** (Tsepak Lhakhang), look for the murals by the left window – the left side depicts Tangtong Gyelpo (see p279) and his celebrated bridge (now destroyed) over the Yarlung Tsangpo near Chushul. The images

of coracle rafts halfway up the wall add an intimate touch. Below is a mural of the Potala itself. There are also nine statues of Tsepame here, as well as green and white Drölma.

Passing the closed **Chapel of Sakyamuni** (Zegya Lhakhang), continue to the northwestern corner where you'll find a small corridor that leads to **King Songtsen Gampo's meditation chamber** (Chogyal Drupuk), which, along with the Chapel of Arya Lokeshvara on the 3rd floor, is one of the oldest rooms in the Potala. The most important statue is of Songtsen Gampo himself, to the left of the pillar. To the left is his minister Tonmi Sambhota (said to have invented the Tibetan script) and to the right are his Chinese and Nepali wives. A statue of the king's Tibetan wife (the only one to bear a son) is in a cabinet by the door. The fifth Dalai Lama lurks behind (and also on) the central pillar. Also here is Gar Tsongtsen, the Tibetan minister who travelled to the Tang court to escort Princess Wencheng back to Lhasa. Queues for this chapel can be long.

The last three rooms are all linked and are chock-a-block full of 3000 pieces of Chinese statuary, many donated by a Khampa businessman in 1995.

You can skip the **first floor**, which has been closed to visitors for years and is unlikely to reopen soon.

As you round the steps on the **ground floor**, enter the beautiful **assembly hall**, which is the largest hall in the Potala and is its physical centre. Note the fine carved pillar heads. The large throne that dominates one end of the hall was the throne of the sixth Dalai Lama. Four important chapels frame the hall.

The first chapel on this floor is the **Chapel of Lamrim**. *Lamrim* means literally 'the graduated path', and refers to the graduated stages that mark the path to enlightenment. The central figure in the chapel is Tsongkhapa, with whom *lamrim* texts are usually associated. Outside the chapel to the left a fine mural depicts the Forbidden City, commemorating the fifth Dalai Lama's visit to the court of Emperor Shunzhi in 1652.

The next chapel, the long **Rigzin Lhakhang**, is dedicated to eight Indian teachers who brought various Tantric practices and rituals to Tibet. The central figure is a silver statue of Guru Rinpoche (one of the eight), who is flanked by his consorts Mandarava

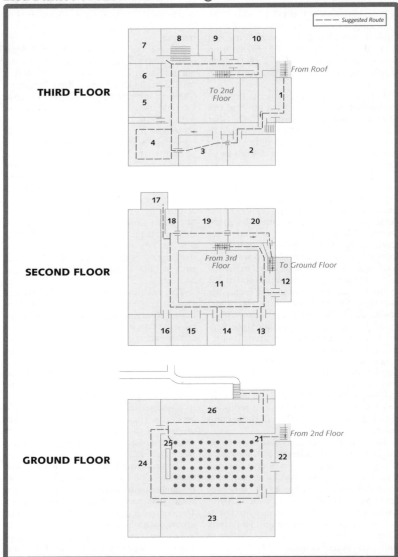
and Yeshe Tsogyel (with a turquoise headdress), as well as statues of the eight teachers on his left and a further eight statues of him in different manifestations on the right. As you exit the chapel, take an up-close look at the fine wall murals.

In the west wing of the assembly hall is one of the highlights of the Potala, the awe-inspiring **Chapel of the Dalai Lamas' Tombs** (Serdung Zamling Gyenjikhang). The hall is dominated by the huge 12.6m-high chörten of the great fifth Dalai Lama,

Third Floor

1 Chapel of Jampa (Jamkhang)
2 Chapel of Three-Dimensional Mandalas (Loilang Khang)
3 Chapel of the Victory over the Three Worlds (Sasum Namgyal)
4 Chapel of Immortal Happiness (Chimey Dedan Kyil)
5 Tomb of the 13th Dalai Lama
6 Lhama Lhakhang
7 Tomb of the Seventh Dalai Lama (Serdung Tashi Obar Khang)
8 Chapel of Arya Lokeshvara (Phagpa Lhakhang)
9 Tomb of the Eighth Dalai Lama (Serdung Gelek Siber Khang)
10 Tomb of the Ninth Dalai Lama (Serdung Sasum Ngongka Khang)

Second Floor

11 Rest Area
12 Chapel of Kalachakra (Dukhor Lhakhang)

13 Chapel of Sakyamuni (Thubwang Lhakhang)
14 Chapel of the Nine Buddhas of Longevity (Tsepak Lhakhang)
15 Treasures of the Potala Exhibition
16 Chapel of Sakyamuni (Zegya Lhakhang)
17 King Songtsen Gampo's Meditation Chamber (Chogyal Drupuk)
18 Kunsang Jedrokhang
19 Lima Lhakhang
20 Lima Lhakhang

Ground Floor

21 Assembly Hall
22 Chapel of Lamrim
23 Rigzin Lhakhang
24 Chapel of the Dalai Lamas' Tombs (Serdung Zamling Gyenjikhang)
25 Throne
26 Chapel of the Holy Born (Trungrab Lhakhang)

gilded with some 3700kg of gold. Flanking it are two smaller chörtens containing the 10th (right) and 12th (left) Dalai Lamas, who both died as children. Richly embossed, the chörtens represent the concentrated wealth of an entire nation. One of the precious stones is a pearl said to have been discovered in an elephant's brains and thus, in a wonderful piece of understatement, 'considered a rarity'. Eight other chörtens represent the eight major events in the life of the Buddha.

The last chapel is the **Chapel of the Holy Born** (Trungrab Lhakhang). Firstly, in the corner, is the statue and chörten of the 11th Dalai Lama, who died at the age of 17. There are also statues of the eight medicine buddhas, a central golden Sakyamuni and the fifth Dalai Lama (silver), and then Chenresig, Songtsen Gampo, Dromtönpa (founder of the Kadampa order) and the first four Dalai Lamas.

AROUND THE POTALA

A morning visit to the Potala can easily be combined with a circuit of the Potala kora

and an afternoon excursion to some of the temples nearby. One of the best ways to visit the following sights is on our Lingkhor walking tour – see p68.

Potala Kora   WALK

The pilgrim path that encircles the foot of the Potala (Map p54) makes for a nice walk before or after the main event. From the western chörten (formerly the west gate to the city), follow the prayer wheels to the northwest corner, marked by three large chörtens. There's a particularly nice teahouse here.

The northeast corner is home to several rock paintings and a delightful prayer hall alive with the murmurs of chanting nuns. Just past here, spin the large prayer wheel of the recently rebuilt Phurbu Chok Hermitage Mani Lhakhang and then swing past the Chinese-style square, where pilgrims often prostrate in front of the Potala. Look out for the three 18th-century *doring* (stele); the two to the north side of the road commemorate victories over the Central Asian Dzungars (left) and Nepali Gorkhas (right). King Trisong Detsen is said to have erected the single southern obelisk in the eighth century.

Drubthub Nunnery & Palha Lu-puk
NUNNERY & TEMPLE

Southwest of the Potala an unmarked road leads around the eastern side of Chagpo Ri, the hill that faces Marpo Ri, site of the Potala. Take this road past stone carvers and rock paintings to **Drubthub Nunnery** (Map p54). The nunnery is dedicated to Tangtong Gyelpo, the 15th-century bridge-maker, medic and inventor of Tibetan opera, who established the original nunnery on the top of Chagpo Ri. Gyelpo's white-haired statue graces the nunnery's main hall.

After the nunnery, head next door to the **Palha Lu-puk** (Map p54; admission Y20; ☺8am-8pm), where stairs lead up to an atmospheric cave temple said to have been the 7th-century meditational retreat of King Songtsen Gampo.

The main attraction of the cave is its relief rock carvings, some of which are over a thousand years old, making them the oldest religious images in Lhasa. Altogether there are over 70 carvings of bodhisattvas in the cave and on the cave's central column; the oldest carvings are generally the ones lowest on the cave walls. Songtsen Gampo is depicted on the west side.

The yellow building above the Palha Lu-puk is a chapel that gives access to the less interesting meditation cave *(drub-puk)* of King Songtsen Gampo's Chinese wife, Princess Wencheng.

Lukhang
TEMPLE

(Map p54; admission Y10, photos Y50; ☺9am-5pm) The Lukhang is a little-visited temple on a small island in a lake, behind the Potala. The lake is in the recently remodelled and very pleasant Zang Gyab Lukhang Park (Map p54).

The lake was created during the construction of the Potala. Earth used for mortar was excavated from here, leaving a depression that was later filled with water. *Lu* (also known as *naga*) are subterranean dragon-like spirits that were thought to inhabit the area, and the Lukhang, or Chapel of the Dragon King, was built by the sixth Dalai Lama to appease them (and also to use as a retreat). You can see Luyi Gyalpo, the *naga* king, at the rear of the ground floor of the Lukhang. He is riding an elephant, and protective snakes rise from behind his head. The *naga* spirits were finally interred in the nearby Palha Lu-puk.

The Lukhang is celebrated for its 2nd- and 3rd-floor murals, which date from the 18th century. Bring a torch (flashlight). The 2nd-floor murals tell a story made famous by a Tibetan opera, while the murals on the 3rd floor depict different themes on each of the walls – Indian yogis demonstrating yogic positions (west), 84 *mahisaddhas* or masters of Buddhism (east), and the life cycle as perceived by Tibetan Buddhists (north), with the gods of Bardo, the Tibetan underworld, occupying its centre. Look for the wonderful attention to detail, down to the hairy legs of the sadhus and the patterns on the clothes.

The 3rd floor contains a statue of an 11-headed Chenresig and a meditation room used by the Dalai Lamas. To reach the 3rd floor, walk clockwise around the outside of the building and enter from the back via a flight of stairs (access was closed during our last visit). Finish off a visit with a kora of the island.

For a detailed commentary on the murals check out Ian Baker and Thomas Laird's coffee-table book *The Dalai Lama's Secret Temple: Tantric Wall Paintings from Tibet.*

Parma Ri
TEMPLES

Several hundred metres west of Chagpo Ri, **Parma Ri** (Map p54) is a much smaller hill with a couple of interesting sights. At the foot of the hill, close to Beijing Zhonglu, is one of Lhasa's four former royal temples, **Kunde Ling** (Map p54; admission Y10; ☺9am-7pm). The *ling* (royal) temples were appointed by the fifth Dalai Lama, and it was from one of them that regents of Tibet were generally appointed. There are only a couple of restored chapels open, but it's a friendly place and worth a visit. Look for the upstairs mural of the original Kunde Ling, 80% of which has been destroyed.

On the north side of Parma Ri is the **Gesar Ling** (Map p54; ☺9.30am-7pm), a Chinese construction that dates back to 1793 and was recently renovated. It is the only Chinese-style temple in Lhasa. The main red-walled temple has a Chinese-style statue of Guandi, the Chinese God of War, while a separate yellow chapel holds the Tibetan equivalent, the mythical warrior Gesar, along with statues of Jampelyang, Chana Dorje (Vajrapani) and Chenresig.

Chagpo Ri Rock Carvings
ROCK CARVINGS

(Map p54; admission Y10; ☺dawn-dusk) This hidden corner of old Lhasa features over 5000 painted rock carvings that were created on the back side of Chagpo Ri over the course of 1000 years. Pilgrims perform full body prostrations in front of the images, beside several rooms full of glowing butter lamps, while nearby stalls sell pilgrim accessories like butter lamps and *tsa-tsas* (stamped clay icons). At the far end of the courtyard the trail is a collection of stone carvers and a large chörten, built entirely of the carvers' mani stones.

RAMOCHE TEMPLE ར་མོ་ཆེ་ 小昭寺

The sister temple to the Jokhang, the **Ramoche** (Xiǎozhāo Sì; Map p44; admission Y20; ☺8am-4.30pm) was constructed around the same time. It was originally built to house the Jowo Sakyamuni image brought to Tibet by Princess Wencheng but sometime in the eighth century the image was swapped for an image of Jowo Mikyöba (Akshobhya), brought to Tibet in the 7th century as part of the dowry of King Songtsen Gampo's Nepali wife, Princess Bhrikuti. By the mid-15th century the temple had become Lhasa's Upper Tantric College. It was badly damaged by Red Guards during the Cultural Revolution, but the complex has since been restored with Swiss assistance.

As you enter the temple, past pilgrims doing full-body prostrations and the first of two inner koras, you'll see a **protector chapel** to the left, featuring masks and puppets on the ancient pillars and an encased image of the divination deity Dorje Yudronma covered in beads on a horse. The main chapel is full of fearsome protector deities in *yabyum* pose, as befitting a Tantric temple.

The fabulously ornate Mikyöba (Akshobhya) image can be seen in the inner **Tsangkhang**, protected by the four guardian kings and a curtain of chain mail, which pilgrims rub for good luck. The image represents Sakyamuni at the age of eight. The lower half of the statue was discovered in 1983 in a Lhasa rubbish tip and the head was discovered in Beijing's Forbidden City and brought back to Lhasa by the 10th Panchen Lama.

As you exit the Ramoche, look for a doorway just to the right by a collection of yak-butter and incense stalls, leading to a delightful chapel, the **Tsepak Lhakhang**. The central image is Tsepame, flanked by Jampa and Sakyamuni. There are smaller statues of Dorje Chang (Vajradhara) and Marmedze (Dipamkara), and a protector chapel next door. This hidden corner is very popular with pilgrims.

OTHER TEMPLES

Down the alleys off Beijing Donglu are five obscure temples, which can be visited if you've seen everything else:

Tsome Ling   TEMPLE

One of the four *ling* temples of Lhasa (along with Kunde Ling and Tengye Ling), this small site (Map p48) is the most interesting of the three. To the east of the residential courtyard is the Kharpo Podrang (White Palace), built in 1777, and to the west is the Marpo Podrang (Red Palace), built at the beginning of the 19th century. Both buildings have fine murals and are well frequented by pilgrims who haul away day and night on the rope-pulled prayer wheels. Of equal interest is the small embroidery and Tibetan mattress workshop on site.

Tengye Ling   TEMPLE

This obscure and rarely visited Nyingmapasect temple (Map p48) is dedicated to the central red-faced deity Tseumar, as well as Pehar (a protector linked to Samye, right of the central statue) and Tamdrin (Hayagriva). The crates of *báijiǔ* (rice wine) stacked in the corner are there to refill the silver cup in Tseumar's hand; apparently he's in a better mood if constantly plastered. The entire chapel smells like a distillery. Look for the wonderful old photo of the Dalai Lama's pet elephant, stabled in the Lukhang behind the Potala. The chapel is hidden in the backstreets west of the Snowlands Hotel and is hard to find; enter through the gateway marked by juniper and *báijiǔ*-sellers, just south of the Tsen Bar.

Shide Tratsang   TEMPLE

Once one of the six principal temples encircling the Jokhang, this badly ruined temple (Map p48) is connected to Reting Monastery.

RAMOCHE LAM

Pedestrian-only **Ramoche Lam** (aka Xiaozhaosi Lu) is probably the most interesting street in Lhasa, jam-packed with teahouses, restaurants and stalls selling everything from saddles, traditional clothes and Tibetan-style tents to handmade potato chips, top-grade tsampa (roasted-barley flour) and Tibetan scriptures. It's well worth a stroll.

It's in a housing courtyard, down a back alley near Tashi I restaurant, and remains a rare example of what Lhasa looked like before the renovation teams moved in. Look for the brown walls.

Rigsum Lhakhang
TEMPLE

A small chapel (Map p48) hidden in a housing courtyard southwest of Barkhor Sq, this is dedicated to the Rigsum Gonpo trinity of Jampelyang, Chenresig and Chana Dorje (Vajrapani). Look for the line of prayer wheels disappearing down the alley.

Pode Kangtsang
TEMPLE

Die-hards can track down this hard-to-find chapel (Map p48) in the south of the old town, with its old upper-floor murals and large thangkas. It's accessed from the south.

THE NORBULINGKA

ནོར་བུ་གླིང་ཁ་ 罗布林卡

The summer palace of the Dalai Lamas, the **Norbulingka** (Luóbùlínkǎ; Map p44; Minzu Lu; admission Y60, Tibetans Y3; ⊙9am-6.30pm) is in the western part of town. It ranks well behind the other points of interest in and around Lhasa. The gardens are poorly tended and the lifeless palaces themselves are something of an anticlimax, since most rooms are closed to the public. Avoid the thoroughly depressing **zoo** (admission Y10).

This said, the Norbulingka is worth a visit if you don't mind the entry fee, and the park is a great place to be during festival times and public holidays. In the seventh lunar month of every year, the Norbulingka is crowded with picnickers for the Shötun festival, when traditional Tibetan opera performances are held here.

History

The seventh Dalai Lama founded the first summer palace in the Norbulingka (whose name literally means 'jewel park') in 1755. Rather than use the palace simply as a retreat, he decided to use the wooded environs as a summer base from which to administer the country, a practice that was repeated by each of the succeeding Dalai Lamas. The grand procession of the Dalai Lama's entourage relocating from the Potala to the Norbulingka became one of the highlights of the Lhasa year.

The eighth Dalai Lama (1758–1804) initiated more work on the Norbulingka, expanding the gardens and digging the lake, which can be found south of the New Summer Palace. The 13th Dalai Lama (1876–1933) was responsible for the three palaces in the northwest corner of the park, and the 14th (present) Dalai Lama built the New Summer Palace.

In 1959, the 14th Dalai Lama made his escape from the Norbulingka disguised as a Tibetan soldier (see p287). All the palaces of the Norbulingka were damaged by Chinese artillery fire in the popular uprising that followed. At the time, the compound was surrounded by some 30,000 Tibetans determined to defend the life of their spiritual leader. Repairs have been undertaken but have failed to restore the palaces to their full former glory.

PALACE OF THE EIGHTH DALAI LAMA

This palace (also known as Kelsang Podrang) is the first you come to. Every Dalai Lama from the eighth to the 13th has used it as a summer palace. Only the main audience hall is open; it features 65 hanging thangkas and some lovely painted wood.

NEW SUMMER PALACE

The New Summer Palace (Takten Migyü Podrang) in the centre of the park was built by the present Dalai Lama between 1954 and 1956 and is the most interesting of the Norbulingka palaces. You can only enter the walled complex from its east side.

The first of the rooms is the **Dalai Lama's audience chamber**. Note the wall murals, which depict the history of Tibet in 301 scenes that flow in rows from left to right. As you stand with your back to the window, the murals start on the left wall with Sakyamuni and show the mythical beginnings of the Tibetan people (from the union of a bodhisattva and a monkey in the Sheldrak Cave), as well as the first field in Tibet (representing the introduction of agriculture). The wall in front of you depicts the building of the circular monastery of Samye, as well as Ganden, Drepung and other monasteries to the right. The right wall depicts the construction of the Potala and Norbulingka.

Next come the **Dalai Lama's private quarters**, which consist of a meditation chamber and a bedroom. The rooms have been maintained almost exactly the same as the Dalai Lama left them, and apart from the usual Buddhist images they contain the occasional surprise (a Soviet radio, among other things).

The **assembly hall**, where the Dalai Lama would address heads of state, is home to a gold throne backed by wonderful cartoon-style murals of the Dalai Lama's court (left, at the back). Look out for British representative Hugh Richardson in a trilby hat, and several Mongolian ambassadors. The right wall depicts the Dalai Lamas. The first five lack the Wheel of Law, symbolising their lack of governmental authority. Last are the suites of the Dalai Lama's mother, whose bathroom sink overflows with offerings of one-mao notes.

South of the New Summer Palace is the artificial lake commissioned by the eighth Dalai Lama. The only pavilion open here at the time of research was the personal **retreat of the 13th Dalai Lama** in the southwestern corner, featuring a library, a thousand-armed Chenresig statue, and a stuffed tiger in the corner! The seats overlooking the duck pond offer a wonderful spot for a picnic.

SUMMER PALACE OF THE 13TH DALAI LAMA

The summer palace of the 13th Dalai Lama (Chensek Podrang) is in the western section of the Norbulingka, northwest of the awful zoo.

The ground-floor assembly hall is stuffed full of various buggies, palanquins and bicycles. The fine murals depicting the life of Sakyamuni are hard to see without a torch.

Nearby, the smaller **Kelsang Dekyi Palace** was also built by the 13th Dalai Lama but is closed.

TIBET MUSEUM

འགྲེམས་སྟོན་ཁང་ 藏博物馆

This grand-looking **museum** (Xīzàng Bówùguǎn; Map p44; Minzu Nanlu; ☎681 2210; admission free; ⏲9am-6.30pm May-Oct, 10.30am-5pm Nov-Apr), in the west of town just opposite the Norbulingka, isn't too bad as long as you can filter out the blatant propaganda. A useful audio tour (Y20) is available if you don't mind the odd pronunciation (Da-*lai* La-*maaarr!*).

The halls start logically with prehistory, highlighting the Neolithic sites around Chamdo and rock paintings at Rutok and Nam-tso, mixed in with a few oddities (5000-year-old grain; 4000-year-old musk deer teeth...). The 'Tibet is Inalienable in History' hall is full of boring seals and misleading Chinese political spin, but it's worth seeking out the Guge kingdom shields and the 18th-century gold urn and ivory slips (exhibit No 310) that were used by the Chinese to recognise their version of the Panchen Lama (see the box, p144). The more interesting third hall covers Tibetan script (with some fine 11th-century birch-paper scriptures), opera masks, musical instruments, divination guides, medical thangkas and statuary. The next hall concentrates on thangkas. The final hall has a good display of folk handicrafts, ranging from coracle boats to nomad tents, with some fine traditional Tibetan locks and leather bags used for carrying salt or tsampa.

The top floor has an inappropriate collection of Chinese jade and a hall of stuffed Tibetan wildlife, with a collection of python and leopard skins that were confiscated from local poachers. Photos are not allowed but everyone takes them anyway.

Activities

Braille Without Borders Blind Medical Massage Clinic MASSAGE
(Map p48; ☎632 0870; 3rd fl, Room 59, Door 42, Beijing Donglu; ⏲10am-10pm) This worthy enterprise, set up by the Braille Without Borders organisation (p345), offers hour-long traditional massages (Y80 to Y100) by blind therapists; it's perfect if you're recovering from a trek or a long overland trip stuffed in the back of a 4WD. The centre is in a courtyard, down an alley across from the Tashi I Restaurant. Call in advance. Ask at the Kyichu Hotel if you can't find it.

Tenzin Blind Massage Centre MASSAGE
(Map p48; ☎634 7591; Zangyiyuan Lu/Mentsikhang Lam; ⏲10am-11pm) A good private enterprise set up by a graduate of the Braille Without Borders clinic. Choose between Chinese (Y80 per hour) or Tibetan oil massage (Y100), the former clothed, the latter naked (don't be self-conscious, they're blind).

Festivals & Events

If at all possible, try to time your visit to Lhasa with one of the city's main festivals (p21). The **Saga Dawa** festival in particular sees huge numbers of pilgrims making circuits around the Barkhor late into the night. Follow the locals' cue and change Y10 into a fat wad of one-mao notes to hand out as alms during the walk.

A couple of months later, during the **Chökor Düchen** festival, Lhasa residents trek up to the summit of Gambo Ütse Ri, the high peak behind Drepung Monastery. In the olden days even the Dalai Lama would ascend the peak, riding atop a white yak.

🛏 Sleeping

The Tibetan eastern end of town is easily the most interesting place to be based, with accommodation options in all budgets. Apart from the hotels listed here there are dozens of shiny, characterless Chinese-style hotels scattered around town. You might find yourself in one of these if you arrive on a tour or book a hotel online.

Prices given here (and throughout this book) apply to the high season from May to October. We have listed the full rack rate, followed by the discount we were offered during high season. Between mid-October and April you can expect still deeper discounts.

Several new Chinese hostels and family-run guesthouses, popular with the ever-increasing number of Chinese backpackers, are giving the long-established Tibetan places a run for their money. Note that most of the budget places don't accept reservations. Several more top-end hotels are planned in Lhasa over the coming years, with a Radisson and Hyatt mentioned.

TOP CHOICE Kyichu Hotel HOTEL $$
(吉曲饭店; Jíqǔ Fàndiàn; Map p48; ☑633 1541; www.kyichuhotel.com; 149/18 Beijing Donglu; r standard/deluxe Y280/320; ❄@🛜) The recently (2010) renovated Kyichu is a friendly and well-run choice that's very popular with repeat travellers to Tibet. Rooms are simple but pleasant, with Tibetan carpets and private bathrooms, but the real selling points are the location and excellent service. There's also a good restaurant, a small library of English books and – that rarest of Lhasa commodities – a peaceful garden courtyard (with wi-fi and espresso coffee). Ask for a garden-view room at the back, as these are the quietest. Reservations are strongly recommended. Credit cards accepted.

Yak Hotel HOTEL $$
(亚宾馆; Yà Bīnguǎn; Map p48; ☑630 0008; fax 630 0191; 100 Beijing Donglu; dm Y30-40, d Y450-650, VIP Y880, discounts of 30%-50%; ❄@) The ever-popular Yak has matured in recent years from backpacker hang-out

---

LHASA'S BOUTIQUE HOTELS

A welcome recent trend in the Lhasa hotel scene is the collection of new hotels that has restored and converted several of Lhasa's crumbling historic courtyards into stylish atmospheric luxury lodgings. The following places ooze historic charm and traditional Tibetan decor.

TOP CHOICE Yabshi Phunkhang BOUTIQUE HOTEL $$$

(尧西平康; Yáoxī Píngkāng; Map p48; ☑632 8885; www.yabshiphunkhang.com; Beijing Donglu; deluxe/ste Y1000/1800, discounts of up to 60%; ❄@) Architectural integrity is rare in Lhasa these days, which makes the four-year restoration of this mid-19th-century mansion all the more special. The complex was built for the parents of the 11th Dalai Lama (yabshi is the title given to the parents of a Dalai Lama) and the collection of 21 large, well-equipped rooms linked by lovely courtyards and sitting areas is both stylish and very Tibetan. There's also a good restaurant, cafe and cosy winter bar.

House of Shambhala BOUTIQUE HOTEL $$$

(香巴拉府; Xiāngbālā Fǔ; Map p48; ☑632 6533; www.shambhalaserai.com; 7 Jiri Erxiang; d incl breakfast Y675-1015; @) Hidden in the old town in a historic Tibetan building, the romantic, boutique-style Shambhala mixes the earthy charm of the old town with good food and spa treatments, making it perfect for couples who prefer atmosphere over mod-cons. The nine rooms, decorated in natural wood and stone with antique Tibetan furniture, vary only in size. The spa even offers a herbal bath in holy water blessed by a local lama, and the hotel's soft furnishings are made in an on-site workshop by disadvantaged Tibetans. The fabulous rooftop terrace is a great to place relax over a Baileys and masala chai cocktail and pet the resident huskies. Just don't take it as seriously as the owners seem to.

Shambhala Palace BOUTIQUE HOTEL $$$

(香巴拉宫; Xiāngbālā Gōng; Map p48; ☑630 7779; www.shambhalaserai.com; 16 Taibeng Gang; r incl breakfast Y765-1200, discounts of 10%-20%; @🛜) The House of Shambhala's quiet

to tour-group favourite, eschewing the cramped dorm rooms (there are two left) for a range of comfortable en-suite rooms. Best bets are the colourful Tibetan-style decor of the quiet back block (Y600); the larger but noisier deluxe rooms overlooking the main street, which have better bathrooms (Y650); or the plush VIP rooms (*guìbīnlóu*) – all are currently discounted to Y380 to Y450. Reservations are recommended. The 5th-floor breakfast bar offers some great views of the Potala but foolishly closes at 6pm.

Snowlands Hotel
HOTEL $

(雪域宾馆; Xuěyù Bīnguǎn; Map p48; 632 3687; snowlandhotel@gmail.com; 4 Zangyiyuan Lu/Mentsikhang Lam; d/deluxe Y100/150, dm/d without bathroom Y20/60; @) Snowlands is another of Lhasa's popular old-timers, largely because of the almost perfect location beside Barkhor Sq. It's now best viewed as a lower midrange option, with some of the best-value en suite rooms in town. Check the water pressure in the

beaten-up cheaper rooms and the beds in the otherwise good-value newer block. You can expect something in the room to be non-functional but the cheery Tibetan floor ladies do their best to help and offer cheap laundry. The simplest rooms without bathroom suffer from paper-thin walls and are poorer value.

Rama Kharpo
HOTEL $

(热玛嘎布宾馆; Rèmǎ Gābù Bīnguǎn; Map p48; 634 6963; www.lhasabarkhor.com; 5 Ongto Shingka Lam; dm/r Y25/150;) Named the 'White Goat' after the legendary founder of the city (see the box, p55), this easily missed place is hidden deep in the old town near the Muslim quarter. Both dorm and en-suite rooms are comfortable (check for barking dogs) and the dark but pleasant cafe is a great meeting place, serving beer, breakfasts and simple food. The knowledgeable owner holds occasional lectures when in town. Vehicles can't reach here so you will have to carry your own luggage.

17-room annex is hidden deeper in the old town, offering identical styling but no spa. Avoid the smallest rooms here.

Gorkha Hotel
HOTEL $$

(郭尔喀饭店; Guō'ěrkā Fàndiàn; Map p48; 627 2222; tibetgorkha7@hotmail.com; 45 Linkuo Nanlu; r/ste Y280/300, tr per bed without bathroom Y50-80; @) This atmospheric Nepali-Tibetan venture is a nice blend of cultures, from the Tibetan-style entry murals and traditional architecture to the photographs of Nepali royalty and Nepali-style restaurant on the roof. The creaking back block housed the Nepali consulate in the 1950s. Other rooms are set around a pleasant courtyard but vary considerably, so take a look at a few. Still, it's a good choice and the suites are perfect for families. The hotel is in the south of the old town, near several lovely old temples and attached to a good Tibetan snack bar.

Trichang Labrang Hotel
BOUTIQUE HOTEL $$

(Map p48; 630 9555; www.trichanglabrang.com; 11 Luguwu Xinang; d & tr Y280-555, deluxe Y880) This new hotel occupies the former residence of Trijang Rinpoche, former tutor to the current Dalai Lama. Rooms are set around a charming courtyard garden and shrine and there is pleasant veranda seating. The building and rooftop are certainly charming, and a great place for dinner or a beer, but the rooms aren't all that well finished, with crummy carpets, blasé staff and modern but small bathrooms.

Lingtsang Boutique Hotel
BOUTIQUE HOTEL $$$

(林仓精品酒店; Líncāng Jīngpǐn Jiǔdiàn; Map p48; 689 9991; s/d/ste Y1000/2000/3000) There are just nine rooms in this traditional and intimate courtyard, the former residence of Nyi Rinpoche, a tutor of the Dalai Lama. The decor is a mixture of authentic architecture and modern stylish elements, with an open-plan wooden bathroom and dressed stone floors that add to the monastic feel. The suite occupies the former throne room. There's a rooftop restaurant/bar with views of the Jokhang and a jarringly modern ground floor restaurant and lounge.

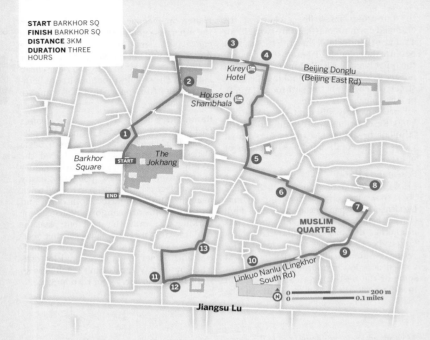

START BARKHOR SQ
FINISH BARKHOR SQ
DISTANCE 3KM
DURATION THREE HOURS

Kirey Hotel

Beijing Donglu (Beijing East Rd)

House of Shambhala

Barkhor Square

START

The Jokhang

END

MUSLIM QUARTER

Linkuo Nanlu (Lingkhor South Rd)

Jiangsu Lu

0   200 m
0   0.1 miles

Walking Tour
Old Town

❯ The fragile Tibetan old town shelters the soul of Lhasa, far from Chinese influence. This walk takes in craft workshops, backstreet chapels and pilgrim paths, passing en route some of Lhasa's last remaining traditional architecture.

At the first turn of the ❶ **Barkhor circuit** take a left and then quick right, past strips of dried yak meat and yellow bags of yak butter to the bustling ❷ **Tromsikhang Market**. After a quick look around the modern market (the original Tibetan-style building was demolished in 1997), head north to the main road, Beijing Donglu, and then right to visit the ❸ **Gyüme Tratsang**, Lhasa's Lower Tantric College. It's easy to miss this working temple; look for an imposing entrance set back from the road. It's a surprisingly impressive place and little visited by foreigners.

Gyüme was founded in the mid-15th century as one of Tibet's foremost Tantric training colleges. In Lhasa, its importance was second only to the monasteries of

Sera and Drepung. More than 500 monks were once in residence, and students of the college underwent a physically and intellectually gruelling course of study. The college was thoroughly desecrated during the Cultural Revolution, but a growing number of monks are now in residence. The main *dukhang* (assembly hall) has statues of Tsongkhapa, Chenresig and Sakyamuni. Look for the monks' alms bowls encased in crafted leather, hanging from the pillars. Behind are huge statues of Tsongkhapa and his two main disciples, and next door is a fearsome statue of Dorje Jigje (Yamantaka). The 2nd- and 3rd-floor chapels are sometimes open.

About 50m further down the road, opposite the Kirey Hotel, are the deceptively long white walls of the small but active ❹ **Meru Sarpa Monastery**. The building in the middle of the traditional housing compound has a traditional wood-block printing press but doesn't really welcome visitors. In the northwest corner is an atmospheric chapel with a statue of thousand-armed Chenresig, an unusual frog-faced Palden Lhamo and the preserved jaws of a crocodile-like gharial.

Cross Beijing Donglu, take the alley down the east side of the Kirey Hotel into the old town and follow the winding branch to the right, past the yellow walls of the House of Shambhala, which has a nice rooftop restaurant if you need a break. As you continue south you'll pass Tibetan craftspeople making statues, embroidery, cabinets, prayer wheels and Tibetan banners. At the junction there's the ❺ **Eizhi Thangka Shop** to the left; you want to take a left at this junction but first look down the alleyway to the right to see the brassware shop and monk's clothing store.

As you head southeast from the thangka shop, past statue makers and a small market, curve right to the quiet but interesting ❻ **Karmashar Temple**, once the home of the Karmashar, Lhasa's main oracle. Look for the Karmashar statue in the far right corner of the back chapel and for the spooky faded icon painted on a pigskin bag in the main hall, pacified with offerings of tsampa and barley beer. Enter from the southwest side.

Continue east to a T-junction past outdoor pool tables, furniture shops and blaring video teahouses. At the T-junction take a left to visit stylish ❼ **Lhasa Village Crafts**, where you can watch local craftsmen from the ❽ **Ancient Art Restoration Centre** (☺9am-1pm & 2-7pm Mon-Fri) across the courtyard, as they grind up mineral paints for thangka-painting and hammer away at metal sculptures in a corner workshop. Ask to see the centre's museum, which details the monasteries they have restored (everything from Samye to Ganden).

After loading up with souvenirs, head south towards the ❾ **Muslim quarter**, the focus of Lhasa's 2000-strong Muslim population. During Friday lunchtime weekly prayers and at dusk the quarter is full of men with wispy beards and skullcaps (non-Muslims are denied entry to the mosque itself). At other times the square bustles with wheeling-and-dealing *yartsa gunbu* traders (see the box, p294). Many women here wear black-velvet headscarfs, characteristic of the Línxià region of China's Gānsù province.

As you face the mosque, turn right and head southwest past Muslim tea stalls and butcher shops, branching along part of the Lingkhor pilgrim circuit to the yellow walls of the ❿ **Ani Sangkhung Nunnery** (29 Linkuo Nanlu; admission Y30; ☺8am-5pm).

This small, friendly and politically active nunnery is the only one within the precincts of the old Tibetan quarter. The site of the nunnery probably dates back to the 7th century, but it housed a monastery until at least the 15th century. The principal image, upstairs on the 2nd floor, is a thousand-armed Chenresig. A small alley to the side of the main chapel leads down to the former meditation chamber of Songtsen Gampo, the 7th-century king of Tibet. The busy nuns run a great teahouse in the courtyard, as well as a popular shop.

Continue past a second mosque to the ⓫ **Lho Rigsum Lhakhang**, one of four chapels surrounding the Jokhang at cardinal points. The lovely chapel, almost completely ignored by tourists, has a central statue of Tsepame (Amitayus) flanked by the four main bodhisattvas and its own inner kora. Monks from Ganden Monastery look after the site. A ⓬ **prayer-wheel shop** across the road offers the ultimate selection of prayer-wheel accessories; perfect for the pilgrim who has everything. Next door is a prayer-flag shop, should you want to pick up a string to leave at an upcoming pass crossing. If you are in need of refreshment, the pleasant garden and rooftop restaurant of the Trichang Labrang Hotel is just 100m to the west.

Take a right here headed north and then a right, then a left. At the junction you can see the ⓭ **Rabsel Tsenkhang**, a small temple affiliated to Sera Monastery.

The alley north takes you to the southeast corner of the Barkhor circuit, where you can continue clockwise to Barkhor Sq.

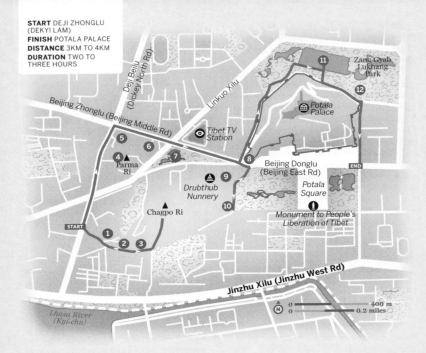

START DEJI ZHONGLU
(DEKYI LAM)
FINISH POTALA PALACE
DISTANCE 3KM TO 4KM
DURATION TWO TO
THREE HOURS

Deji Beilu
(Dickey North Rd)

Linkuo Xilu

11

Zang Gyab
Lukhang
Park

12

Beijing Zhonglu (Beijing Middle Rd)

Potala
Palace

Tibet TV
Station

5

6

7

4 Parma
Ri

8

Beijing Donglu
(Beijing East Rd)

END

9

Drubthub
Nunnery

Potala
Square

Chagpo Ri

10

Monument to People's
Liberation of Tibet

START

1

2 3

Jinzhu Xilu (Jinzhu West Rd)

Lhasa River
(Kyi-chu)

N

0   400 m
0   0.2 miles

Walking Tour
Lingkhor

> This walk follows the most interesting
section of the city's main pilgrimage
circuit, the Lingkhor. It's best walked in the
morning, when you'll be joined by hundreds
of Tibetan pilgrims.

To start the walk, take a taxi to Deji
Zhonglu (德吉中路; Dickey Lam in Tibetan).
An alley branches east of here to reach one
of the city's real gems: a lovely collection
of painted **1 rock carvings** centred on a
huge image of Tsepame. At the far end of
the courtyard the trail is a collection of
2 stone carvers and a large **3 chörten**,
built entirely of the carvers' mani stones.

From here, return along the alley back to
Deji Zhonglu and head north. Just before
you hit Beijing Zhonglu (the second crossroads) follow the alleyway to the right to
visit the friendly **4 Kunde Ling**. Back at
the intersection with Beijing Zhonglu, watch
the pilgrims as they rub their backs, shoulders and hips against a series of polished
5 holy stones. Head east along Beijing
Zhonglu to the yellow walls of the Chinese-
style **6 Gesar Ling**.

Continue east to the **7 Golden Yaks
statue**, erected for the 40th anniversary
of the 'liberation' of Tibet, before reaching
the former western **8 city gate** (Daggo
Kani). Black-and-white photos displayed in
the Brahmaputra Grand Hotel show British Army troops entering the city through
the original gate during the invasion of
1903–04.

Climb up to the **9 viewpoint** (admission
Y2; ⊙7am-7pm) just above the white chörten
for one of Lhasa's classic photo opportunities. The hilltop behind you is Chagpo Ri
(Iron Mountain) the site of Lhasa's principal
Tibetan medical college from 1413 until its
destruction in the 1959 popular uprising.

Head down the nearby alley, past
Drubthub Nunnery, to visit **10 Palha Lu-
puk**, the site of Lhasa's earliest religious
icons. If you have the energy, finish with a
quick circuit of the Potala kora, stopping in
at the **11 Lukhang**. Finish up with a well-
deserved thermos of sweet tea at either of
two nearby **12 teahouses** in the pleasant
park.

Even if you're not in the market for showy five-star digs, it's worth investing Y10 in a cab ride out to the opulent **Brahmaputra Grand Hotel** (雅鲁藏布大酒店; Yǎlǔzàngbù Dàjiǔdiàn; Map p44; www.tibethotel.cn; Section B, Yangcheng Plaza, Gongbutang Lu) in the east of town. Occupying a space somewhere between Vegas theme hotel and ethnographic museum, you could easily spend an hour wandering the hundreds of exhibits in the free 2nd-floor museum, from antique opera masks to armour and historic B&W photographs. Amazingly, it's all for sale. Pick up a floor plan from the lobby.

Dhood Gu Hotel
HOTEL $$

(敦固宾馆; Dūngù Bīnguǎn; Map p48; ☑632 2555; www.dhodguhotel.com; 19 Shasarsu Lu; s/d/ste Y280/300/520; @) If you're looking for a dash of style, this comfortable Nepali-run three-star place near the Tromsikhang market is a good choice, with ornate Tibetan-style decor, a decent restaurant and a superb location in the old town. Breakfast is included and rooms come with modern bathrooms, though the singles are cramped and some rooms lack views. The rooftop bar has fine Potala views. Credit cards are accepted.

Barkhor Namchen House
GUESTHOUSE $

(八廊龙乾家庭旅馆; Bākuò Lóngqián Jiātíng Lǚguǎn; Map p48; ☑679 0125; www.tibetnamchen.com; dm Y25, s Y60-70, d Y70; @) This small backstreet Tibetan-style guesthouse is a good budget choice. The old-town location just off the Barkhor is near perfect, the staff are friendly and the Asian-style bathrooms and hot showers are super-clean. Rooms are fairly small and some have limited natural light (ask for an upper-floor room) but the lounge area catches the winter sun, or you can head to the good rooftop restaurant for fine views. All rooms share the communal bathroom block.

Dōngcuò International Youth Hostel
YOUTH HOSTEL $

(东措国际青年旅馆; Dōngcuò Guójì Qīngnián Lǚshè; Map p48; ☑627 3388; www.yhalasa.com, in Chinese; tibetyouthhostel@163.com; 10 Beijing Donglu; dm Y15-40, s/d/tr Y100/120/180, s/d/

tr/q without bathroom Y80/90/105/120; @🛜) This modern, Chinese-run hostel attracts mainly Chinese backpackers, though a few foreign travellers make it here. Rooms are smallish but well maintained, with wooden floors and crisp white sheets, though a few don't have any exterior windows. The bunk-bed style dorms vary in size – the best deal is a bed in a triple for Y35. Solar-heated hot water is available in the evenings in the rooms with bathrooms, or 24 hours in the common showers. Prices rise in July and August. Bike rental (Y25 to Y30) and free laundry are bonuses, as are the three (!) bars.

Phuntsok Khasang International Youth Hostel
YOUTH HOSTEL $

(平措康桑青年旅舍; Píngcuò Kāngsāng Guójì Qīngnián Lǚshè; Map p48; ☑691 5222; www.tibetinn.cn, www.lhasahostel.com; 48 Duosenge Lu; dm Y25-40, d Y110-170) Lhasa's second Chinese-run youth hostel feels a bit too much like *Cell Block H* for us, with grafittied hallways and rooms set around an echoey courtyard. Try instead for a room in the huge annex (known as Lhasa International Youth Hostel) across the road, which has the advantage of two nice cafes with wi-fi, a foosball table and free breakfast (eight types of omelettes!). Useful perks include a laundry service and baggage storage. A YHA card (Y50) gets you a small discount.

Banak Shol
HOTEL $

(八郎学旅馆; Bālángxué Bīnguǎn; Map p48; ☑632 3829; 8 Beijing Donglu; d Y100-120, dm/s/d without bathroom Y20/40/70) Once *the* place to stay back in the early days of independent travel, the budget Banak Shol is looking pretty tired these days. It's still got several things going for it, including the good Nam-tso Restaurant (p71), free laundry and pleasant wooden verandas, but the staff are jaded, the walls of the cheaper rooms are paper thin, and most rooms look onto either the noisy main road or a courtyard full of reversing 4WDs. The doubles with a hot-water bathroom are among the cheapest of such rooms in Lhasa, though they have seen better days. The majority of the guests nowadays are Chinese backpackers.

Oh Dan Guest House
HOTEL $

(欧丹旅馆; Ōudān Bīnguǎn; Map p44; ☑634 4999; www.shangrilatours.com/ohdan.htm; oh dan_guesthouse@yahoo.com; 15 Xiaozhaosi Lu/ Ramoche Lam; d with/without bathroom Y130/60;

✳ @) One of several hotels owned by the Oh Dan group, this is a good lower-midrange, Tibetan-run choice with an interesting location on the pedestrian street leading to the Ramoche Temple (taxis can't go up this street during the day). The rooms are spacious and clean, though only the top-floor rooms get much natural light. The English-speaking staff are helpful; for Y30 they'll even teach you how to make *momos* (dumplings)! The cosy Nepali restaurant is a nice refuge and serves good breakfasts (try the breakfast burrito). The cheaper rooms share common hot showers and clean squat toilets.

Four Points
HOTEL $$$

(福朋酒店; Fúpéng Jiǔdiàn; Map p44; ✆634 8888; www.fourpoints.com/lhasa; no 5, 1 Xiang, Shengtai Lu; r Y1780-2580, ste from Y2880, discounts of 40%; ✳@☎) A solid four-star Sheraton property, this polished place is cool and understated, with pleasant courtyard seating serving everything from Lhasa Beer to Brazilian barbecue. Extra touches in the spacious rooms include a humidifier against Lhasa's dry climate and an emergency torch and panic button perfect for travelling paranoids. Prices include a breakfast buffet.

St Regis
HOTEL $$$

(Map p44; ✆630 5845; www.stregis.com/lhasa resort; Jiangsu Donglu; ✳@) Six-star travellers accustomed to uber-luxury, 24-hour butler service and, yes, a gold-plated pool, can finally consider a trip to the plateau. The new hotel promises a fortress-like lobby, three restaurants, a spa, tearoom and the largest selection of wines in Tibet (although any collection of more than 10 bottles qualifies as this). Proximity to the old town is an unexpected bonus. If you have to ask the price, you can't afford it. At least Richard Gere has a place to stay if he's ever allowed back into Tibet.

Cool Yak Hotel
HOTEL $$

(酷牦牛酒店; Kùmáoniú Jiǔdiàn; Map p48; ✆685 6777; coolyak@gmail.com; s/d/tr Y360/580/480, discounts of Y30%-50%; ✳) The great location and the giant Tibetan thangka in the central courtyard are the most eye-catching things about this modern place. The rooms are fresh and comfortable, though there's a definite lack of natural light. It's hidden down an alley off Zangyiyuan Lu (Mentsikhang Lam).

Heritage Hotel
HOTEL $$

(古艺酒店; Gǔyì Jiǔdiàn; Map p48; 11 Chaktsalgang Lam; s/d/ste Y380/480/680, discounts of 30%-40%; ✳☎) Hidden in the old town and part of the artsy courtyard holding Lhasa Village Handicrafts (see p75), the Heritage offers 21 stylish rooms, with stone-walled showers, wooden floors and Tibetan wall hangings. The good on-site Third Eye Nepali restaurant solves the dinner dilemma.

Flora Hotel
HOTEL $$

(哈达花神旅馆; Hǎdáhuāshén Lǚguǎn; Map p48; ✆632 4491; www.florahtl.piczo.com; Hebalin Lu; dm Y35, d/tr incl breakfast Y180/210) The Flora is a well-run and reliable hotel in the interesting Muslim quarter (it's run by a Nepali Muslim). Nice touches include a minibar at local-shop prices and a laundry service. There are three decent but slightly cramped three-bed dorms out the back (with attached toilet and shared hot shower). Credit cards and bookings are accepted.

Shangbala Hotel
HOTEL $$

(香巴拉酒店; Xiāngbālā Jiǔdiàn; Map p48; ✆632 3888; www.tibetshangbalahotel.com; 1 Danjielin Lu; r with breakfast Y680, discounts of 50%; ✳☎) Yes it's bland and boring, but this marbly tour-group blockhouse is also reassuringly familiar and ridiculously close to the Jokhang and local restaurants. The carpeted rooms are clean and have decent bathrooms, and there are good views from the 4th floor. It's not interesting but you could do a lot worse.

Lhasa has lots of other decent modern Chinese-style midrange choices with central locations. Consider the following if you score a bargain on an accommodation-booking website:

Gang Gyen Hotel
HOTEL $$$

(刚坚饭店; Gāngjiān Fàndiàn; Map p48; ✆630 5555; 83 Beijing Donglu; d with breakfast Y1280-1380, discounts of 50%; ✳☎) Modern and quiet four-star place.

Mandala Hotel
HOTEL $$

(满斋饭店; Mǎnzhāi Fàndiàn; Map p44; ✆636 7666; Jiangsu Lu; s Y250, deluxe Y350-400, ste Y650-700; ✳@) New Nepali-run three-star place.

Tibet Kailash Hotel
HOTEL $$

(凯拉斯酒店; Kǎilāsī Jiǔdiàn; Map p48; ✆675 9999; www.kailash.com.cn; 143 Beijing Donglu; r Y680, discounts of 50%-60%; @) Good location and lively bar.

Xióngbālā Hotel
HOTEL $$

(雄巴拉大酒店; Xióngbālā Dàjiǔdiàn; Map p48; ☎633 8888; xiongbl@public.ls.xz.cn; 28 Jiangsu Lu; r Y518, discounts of 50%; ☒) West-facing rooms offer views of the Potala from the 5th floor.

Thangka Hotel
HOTEL $$$

(康卡酒店; Kāngkǎ Jiǔdiàn; Map p48; ☎630 8866; 38 Yuthok Lam/Yutuo Lu; r Y880-1280, ste Y1880, discounts of 50%; ☎) A modern and friendly three-star place with some Tibetan touches and a super-convenient location near the Jokhang. Standard rooms are best value, as 'palace view' rooms don't offer much extra.

✗ Eating

As with accommodation, the best Tibetan, Nepali and Western restaurants are in the Tibetan quarter around the Barkhor Sq area. Almost all places offer decent breakfasts, perhaps the best being at the Lhasa Kitchen, Snowland and Nam-tso restaurants. All the eateries listed serve lunch and dinner, but you will struggle to find a meal after about 10pm. For the flashiest Chinese restaurants you'll have to head to the western districts.

With the arrival of half-a-dozen Nepali restaurants, Lhasa now rivals Kathmandu in its range of foreign foods (though prices are a bit higher). All offer a mix of Indian, pseudo-Chinese and Western dishes for about Y25, with Indian veggie dishes cheaper. If you're hankering for a *dal bhat* (lentils and rice), masala chai or banana lassi, make a beeline for these places.

TOP CHOICE Snowland Restaurant
WESTERN $$

(雪域餐厅; Xuěyù Cāntīng; Map p48; ☎632 0821; 4 Zangyiyuan Lu/Mentsikhang Lam; mains Y15-40; ☒) Attached to the Snowlands Hotel, this is a more upmarket and extremely popular place that serves a mix of excellent Continental and Nepali food in very civilised surroundings. The Indian dishes are particularly good, especially the tasty chicken butter masala and giant naan breads. The cakes are easily the best in town and discounted after 9pm; give the lemon pie our fond regards.

Nam-tso Restaurant
WESTERN $

(纳木措餐馆; Nàmùcuò Cānguǎn; Map p48; Banak Shol, 8 Beijing Donglu; mains Y20-30, set breakfast Y27; ☒) This old-timer is still one of the top hotel-restaurants, helped by jolly staff. Dishes stretch to vegetarian lasagne,

cream-cheese *momos* and yak burgers, and the sunny roof seating is one of the few places in town to sit outdoors. The chicken sizzler is a classic Lhasa meal. The restaurant's breakfasts (muesli brought in from Kathmandu, among other things) have also achieved a devoted following.

New Mandala Restaurant
NEPALI $$

(新满здай餐厅; Xīnmǎnzhāi Cāntīng; Map p48; ☎634 2235; west of Barkhor Sq; dishes Y20-35; ☒) This Nepali-run restaurant is definitely a winner for its fine views over the Barkhor, either from the mural-filled 2nd floor or the sunny rooftop. Try the excellent Nepali set meal. It also sells packaged Nepali foods such as muesli and soup mixes. The owner runs the Tashi restaurants in Shigatse and Tsetang.

Lhasa Kitchen
WESTERN $

(拉萨厨房; Lāsà Chúfáng; Map p48; 3 Zangyiyuan Lu/Mentsikhang Lam; mains Y15-30, Nepali sets Y20-30; ☒) With a wide-ranging menu of Nepali, Indian and Tibetan dishes, good breakfast options, decent prices, pleasant seating and a great location, it's no surprise that this is a popular place with travellers and locals alike. The menu covers everything from vegetable *dopiaza* (onion-based curry) to cheese and tomato toast.

Tashi I
WESTERN $

(Map p48; cnr Zangyiyuan Lu/Mentsikhang Lam & Beijing Donglu; mains Y10-25; ☺8am-10pm; ☒) Old Lhasa hands still like this unpretentious slice of old Lhasa, though other travellers may wonder what all the fuss is about, especially with the increased competition from slicker Nepali and foreign-run restaurants. Still, we like it for the cheerful service, cheap prices and great location, even if the food itself can be hit and miss. Try the *bobis* (chapati-like unleavened bread), which come with seasoned cream cheese and fried vegetables or meat, or some fried apple *momos* washed down with a mug of sweet milky tea. Tashi II in the Kirey Hotel on Beijing Donglu offers an identical menu.

Tengyelink Café
NEPALI $

(Map p48; ☎632 3866; Zangyiyuan Lu/Mentsikhang Lam; dishes Y15-25; ☒) This warm and cosy restaurant is popular with both foreigners and Tibetans, so get here early for a good table. The Western dishes are joined by a few Tibetan, Indian and even Korean options. Service is good and it's a well-run place. Time your meal to finish just after

8pm and you can snag half-price baked goods.

Dunya Restaurant
WESTERN $$

(Map p48; ☎633 3374; www.dunyarestaurant.com; 100 Beijing Donglu; dishes Y30-65; ☺8.30am-10pm; 🖬) With sophisticated decor, excellent and wide-ranging food (from yak enchiladas to Indonesian noodles), this cosy Dutch-run place best captures Lhasa's new tour-group zeitgeist, and is often packed with Dutch tourists and American school groups. It's pricier than most other places in town but the food is authentic, from the oregano-flavoured pizza crust to the imported Italian pasta. The homemade sandwiches and soups are good for a light lunch and it's one of the few places on the plateau to get a decent glass of wine or pina colada with dinner.

Pentoc Tibetan Restaurant
TIBETAN $

(Map p48; dishes Y10-15; 🖬) For something more authentically Tibetan, charming English-speaking Pentoc runs this local teahouse restaurant after working in Tashi I for many years. The menu includes breakfast (eggs, Tibetan bread, pancakes, yoghurt) and it's a good place to try homemade Tibetan standards, such as *momos, thugpa* (noodles), *shemdre* (rice, potato and yak meat), plus butter tea, *chang* and even *dal bhat*. It's 20m down an alleyway off Beijing Donglu, on the left.

Woeser Zedroe Tibetan Restaurant
TIBETAN $

(光明泽缀藏餐馆; Guāngmíng Zézhuì Zàngcānguǎn; Map p48; Danjielin Lu; mains Y6-28; 🖬) This is where visiting and local Tibetans come to fill up after a visit to the Jokhang. Add some pleasant traditional seating and a perfect location to the Tibetan vibe and it's a logical lunch stop. The *momos* are recommended, especially the fried yak meat or cheese varieties. Skip the boiled yak hooves and the phenomenally expensive dishes made with cordyceps.

Tibet Kun Phan Vegetarian Restaurant
TIBETAN $

(Bozhang Guenpan Gartse Sutsikhang in Tibetan; Map p48; Yuthok Lam/Yutuo Lu; mains Y10-18, buffet Y25; 🖬) Just to prove that vegetarian Tibetan food isn't a contradiction in terms, this Buddhist place serves excellent, healthy allveg dishes, including a nightly buffet (5pm to 8pm). It's a central place with a pleasant environment but no alcohol is served.

Sun Tribe
TIBETAN $$

(Nyima Ro Soltsek in Tibetan; 太阳部落藏餐; Map p44; Tàiyáng Bùluò Zàngcān; Linkuo Xilu; mains Y25-50; 🖬) This oddly named restaurant is a definite notch above the other old-town Tibetan restaurants and is a good place to splash out on top-end Tibetan cuisine. The decor is well done and the window seats are particularly pleasant. Alongside the predictable spinal marrow and fried lungs are such interesting dishes as mushroom pie and that rarest of things, a Tibetan salad. One nice touch is that the picture menu is divided into the regional cuisines of Tibet, so you can order Amdo-style yoghurt and mutton or sausage from Kham. The set meals (Y26) are good value.

Lánqīng Qīngzhēn Fànguǎn
MUSLIM $

(蓝青清真饭馆; Map p48; Beijing Donglu; dishes Y6-45) There are several Muslim restaurants in the old town but this one is unique in having cosy Tibetan-style seating in the side room. The Xīnjiāng specialty *xiǎopánjī* (小盘鸡; Y25) – chicken in a sauce with potatoes and carrots on a bed of noodles – is bony but very tasty. The photo menu on the wall is helpful, even if the images bear only a passing resemblance to the real thing. For lunch try one of the noodle dishes, such as *chǎomiànpiàn* (fried noodle squares) or *gānbànmiàn* (a kind of stir-fried spaghetti bolognaise).

Shānchéng Chuāncàiguǎn
SICHUANESE $

(山城川菜馆; Map p48; Beijing Donglu; mains Y10-25; 🖬) You won't have any problem finding Chinese food in Lhasa. This is one of several simple hole-in-the-wall Chinese places on Beijing Donglu, but one we kept coming back to for its tasty and cheap Sichuanese dishes like *gōngbào jīdīng* (diced chicken with peanuts) and *yúxiāng ròusī* ('fish-resembling' pork).

Ālǐláng Korean Barbeque
KOREAN $

(阿里郎烧烤; Ālǐláng Shāokǎo; Map p48; Beijing Donglu; mains Y13-25, barbecue meat/vegetables from Y20/5) For something a little different, this Korean Chinese place is popular for its barbecue, which you grill up on hot plates at the table and then eat wrapped in lettuce leaves. If that sounds like too much hard work, try the *bibambap* (rice, vegetables and fried egg in a stone pot), potato pancakes, kimchi soup or sushi-like rice rolls. The photo menu simplifies having to order Korean food in Chinese.

Norzing Selchung Tashi Yarphel Restaurant
TIBETAN **$**

(Map p44; Xiaozhaosi Lu/Ramoche Lam; dishes Y10-25) Super-convenient if you're visiting the next-door Ramoche Temple, this pleasant upstairs Amdo Tibetan restaurant offers great views over the street below from the low Tibetan-style tables. Try the set meal of *shemdre* for Y15 or choose something more adventurous from the photo menu, such as the tiger-skin chillies (虎皮青椒; *hǔpíqīngjiāo*; Y12).

Drinking
There's not a great deal when it comes to entertainment options in Lhasa. In the evening most travellers head to one of the restaurants in the Tibetan quarter and then retire to the roof of the Barkhor Namchen House or Banak Shol hotels for a cold Lhasa Beer.

Dunya
BAR

(Map p48; 100 Beijing Donglu; beer Y12) The breezy upstairs bar at this popular restaurant is a firm favourite of both local expats and tour groups. There's a nice terrace and a big-screen TV for major sports events.

Makye Amye
RESTAURANT/BAR

(玛吉阿米餐吧; Mǎjí'ǎmǐ Cānbā; Map p48; Barkhor; drinks from Y15, mains Y25-60) The past is tastier than the present at this watering hole overlooking the Barkhor. If the stories are to be believed, this was once a drinking haunt of the licentious sixth Dalai Lama, who met the famed Tibetan beauty Makye Amye here and composed a famous poem about her. Chinese tourists are drawn to the absorbing views of the Barkhor from the corner tables and fine rooftop terrace, but the food is just so-so.

Summit Café
CAFE

(顶峰咖啡店; Dǐngfēng Kāfēidiàn; Map p48; www.thetibetsummitcafe.com; 1 Danjielin Lu; coffee Y14-25, desserts Y10-24; ⊙7.30am-11pm; @⊚) With authentic espresso coffee and smoothies, sofas that swallow you up, free wi-fi and melt-in-your-mouth cheesecakes, this American-style coffeehouse is a mocha-flavoured nirvana for Starbucks addicts. It's in the courtyard of the Shangbala Hotel, a stone's throw from the Jokhang, with a couple of less useful branches around town. Other places for a real coffee include the courtyards of Yabshi Phunkhang (Illy coffee) or the Kyichu Hotel.

Spinn Café
BAR

(Map p48; www.cafespinn.com; ⊙2pm-midnight) This funky, tiny backstreet cafe/bar is a hang-out for cold beer, filter coffee, teas and snacks and is a good resource for travel information (especially biking). It's down a back alley off Beijing Donglu. Contact Kong or Oat.

There are several Tibetan teahouses around town where you can grab a cheap thermos of *cha ngamo* (sweet tea). Most of them are grungy Tibetan-only places, blasted by high-decibel kung fu videos, but there are a few exceptions. The bustling local **Tengyeling Teahouse** (Map p48; Zangyiyuan Lu/Mentsikhang Lam) beside the Tashi Takgay Hotel is very central, though the teahouse in the **Ani Sangkhung Nunnery** (Map p48; 29 Linkuo Nanlu) is probably the nicest for a quiet cup of tea. The two excellent **teahouses** (Map p54) in Zang Gyab Lukhang Park behind the Potala are also well worth the detour.

Entertainment
Unfortunately there is little in the way of cultural entertainment in Lhasa. Restaurants like the Shangrila in the courtyard of the Kirey Hotel have free song-and-dance performances for diners (buffet Y50). For authentic performances of Tibetan opera and dancing you'll probably have to wait for one of Lhasa's festivals (see p21).

For something a bit earthier there are several Tibetan *nangma* dance halls around town, which offer a mildly nationalistic mix of disco, traditional Tibetan line dancing, lots of beer and a bit of Chinese karaoke thrown in for good measure. See the box, p74, for some suggestions or ask a Tibetan friend for the latest places.

Shöl Opera Troupe
OPERA

(雪巴拉姆; Xuěbā Lāmǔ; Map p44; ☎632 1111; 6 Linkuo Donglu) Performs a selection of Tibetan operas nightly at 6.30pm at the Himalaya Hotel. Tickets for the 90-minute show cost Y180 with dinner and drinks, and there's a small museum on site.

Shopping
You can get most things in Lhasa these days, though water-purifying tablets, deodorant and English-language books and magazines are still not easy to find.

For souvenirs, the Barkhor circuit is lined with stalls selling everything a visiting Tibetan or tourist might possibly need.

LOCAL KNOWLEDGE

MILA-RAPPER: MC TENZIN'S NIGHTLIFE GUIDE

We asked MC Tenzin, the creator of Tibet's first hip hop album, to give us the lowdown on Lhasa nightlife.

Best Nangma?

For *nangma* my favourite place is **Gyelpo's Nangma** (雪域杰布; Xuěyù Jiébù; Map p44; Beijing Donglu; ☺7pm-2am). The seating is good, the floorshow and singers are the best in town and there's never any fighting here. Gyelpo was a famous dancer on Tibet TV. It's a great place to meet friends and it's cheaper than the discos, but get a seat before 9pm. Nearby **JJ Nangma** (Map p44; Beijing Donglu) is flashier and has a younger crowd.

Best Bars?

Bars change really frequently in Lhasa. **Easy Day** (简单日子; Jiǎndān Rìzi; Map p54; Lawei Yangguang Cheng A-47, Deji Beilu; beer Y10-15; ☺5pm-6am) has a lounge feel with dim lights and some live jazz and blues, and there are half a dozen other bars nearby. **Qīpíngmǐ Bar** (7平米; Map p44; beer Y8-10; Beijing Xilu; ☺4pm-4am) is a small, busy bar that has great music, from Chinese pop to the Eagles. **Bangda** (半打; Bàndá; Map p54; Beijing Donglu; ☺6pm-5am) is bigger and busier, with outdoor courtyard seating during the day.

Best Club?

Queen (皇后; Huánghòu; Map p44; Deji Beilu; ☺10pm-5am) is the biggest and best disco and the bouncers keep things in check. It's still known by its old name **Bābǐlā** (芭比拉俱乐部; Bābǐlā Jùlèbù). It's popular with young people and students and people here love to dance with foreigners! The music is mostly techno, Lady Gaga, Korean pop; you know, good beats. The people are very fresh.

MC Tenzin is a former tour guide who raps about morality, regret and impermanence and gets his guidance from both Buddhism and Eminem (favourite track: 'Lose Yourself'). 'Tibetan culture is changing,' says Tenzin, 'we can't live in the past; we should follow the world, not hide from it'. Check out www.myspace.com/tibetanhiphopmctenzin and the album 'One Day', available in Lhasa.

Expect to be asked an outrageous initial price and then settle down for some serious and persistent haggling. Popular purchases include prayer wheels, rings, prayer scarves and prayer flags, all of which are fairly portable. Most of the stuff on offer is actually made in Nepal and sold by Chinese or Hui Muslim traders.

Items of Tibetan clothing, such as *chubas* (long-sleeved sheepskin cloaks), cowboy hats, Tibetan brocade and fur hats, are good buys. There are several Tibetan dress shops on Beijing Donglu where you can get a formal Tibetan dress made or buy off the rack. One good place is opposite the Kyichu Hotel.

The majority of shops in the Barkhor sell jewellery, most of it turquoise and coral (Tibetans believe that turquoise is good for the liver and coral for the heart), but almost all of it is fake. The fake stuff is bluer and is

flawless; beware of a string of identically shaped and rounded beads – nature did not intend them to be this way. The final test is to scratch the surface with a sharp metal object; the fake turquoise will leave a white line, the real stuff won't show a thing. Take a close look at the stone to make sure it's all in one piece. Unscrupulous traders glue together tiny bits of turquoise to make larger pieces of stone.

You'll also see 'Buddha eye' beads, known as *dzi* – black or brown oblong beads with white eye symbols. These are replicas of natural fossils found in rocks in the mountains containing auspicious eye symbols thought to represent the eyes of the Buddha. The real things pass hands for tens of thousands of dollars.

Lhasa's glittering new supermarkets now offer a staggering range of imported goods, from frozen squid to ripe pineapples, alongside a bewildering array of dried yak meat. Cheese-heads desperate for a lactose fix can try the Dunya (p72) and Nam-tso (p71) restaurants for locally made 'yak' (actually *dri*, or female yak) cheese by the half-kilo.

To find basic items, such as thermoses and water canisters, the best places are the lanes that run from the Tromsikhang Market down to the Barkhor circuit. Cheap pots and pans (ideal for instant noodles) are available at the stalls on the east side of the Potala. For hard-to-find items such as sunscreen and deodorant, dig around in the Nepali-stocked shops dotted around the Barkhor circuit.

There are now dozens of trekking shops on Beijing Donglu and Zangyiyuan Lu/ Mentsikhang Lam, though most offer low-quality Nepali- or Chinese-made knock-offs.

Lhasa Village Handicrafts
HANDICRAFTS

(Map p48; ☏636 0558; www.tibetcraft.com; 11 Chaktsalgang Lam; ☻10am-8pm) This impressive nonprofit enterprise (formerly known as Dropenling) aims to bolster traditional Tibetan handicrafts in the face of rising Chinese and Nepali imports. Products are of high quality and employ traditional techniques (natural dyes, wool not acrylic etc) updated with contemporary designs. Prices are fixed, with proceeds going back to artisans in the form of wages and social funds. Artefacts for sale include woolly carpets from the Wangden region of southern Tsang, UNDP-supported weavings and silverware, Tibetan aprons, leather appliqué bags, table runners and horse blankets. Ask about its two-hour artisan walking tour of Lhasa's old town. Foreign currency and credit cards are accepted (the latter with a 4.2% fee), as are US dollars, and it can arrange international shipping. See also the walking tour on p66.

Tanva
CARPETS

(毯华编织; Tǎnhuá Biānzhī; Map p48; www.tora nahouse.com; ☻9.30am-1pm, 3-7.30pm Mon-Sat) After visiting Lhasa Village Handicrafts head to this upstairs showroom in the corner of the courtyard for a selection of Tibetan wool carpets given a modern designer twist. All carpets are handmade locally from 100% Tibetan handspun wool. To see the weaving process, pop into the workshop in Nam village, between Lhasa and the airport (kilometre marker 4671); the show-

room can arrange free transport. Expect to pay around Y4000 to Y5000 for a carpet, plus Y600 shipping. Credit cards accepted.

Snow Leopard Carpet Industries
CARPETS

(雪豹毯业有限公司; Xuěbào Tǎnyè Yǒuxiàn-gōngsī; Map p48; snowleopardcarpet@yahoo.com; 2 Zangyiyuan Lu/Mentsikhang Lam) Next to the Snowland Restaurant, this place sells a collection of high-quality carpets and yak-wool blankets at fixed prices. At around Y160 per sq ft, a 4ft by 6ft carpet costs around US$400. Credit cards are accepted and staff can arrange delivery abroad. Ask for friendly English-speaking Phurbu. The company uses some profits to fund a local orphanage.

Mani Thangka Arts
THANGKAS

(嘛呢唐卡艺术; Mání Tángkǎ Yìshù; Map p48; Zangyiyuan Lu/Mentsikhang Lam) Opposite the Shangbala Hotel, Mani Thangka Arts features thangkas made with mineral paints by local artist Phurbu Tsering. Most of the other thangka shops on this street are owned by Chinese traders who sell Nepali imports. The small thangka workshops on the south side of the Barkhor circuit and in the surrounding backstreets are also worth checking out.

For higher-quality items at higher prices, try shops like the **Dorje Antique Shop** (Map p48; Beijing Donglu), opposite the Yak Hotel, and the **Kyichu Art Gallery** (Map p48; 149 Beijing Donglu) in the Kyichu Hotel.

Bǎiyì Supermarket
SUPERMARKET

(百益超市; Bǎiyì Chāoshì; Map p54; Beijing Donglu; ☻10am-9pm) Next to Lhasa Department Store and boasting Lhasa's best range of foodstuffs.

Sìfāng Supermarket
SUPERMARKET

(四方超市; Sìfāng Chāoshì; Map p48; Beijing Donglu; ☻9am-10pm) This is the closest supermarket to the old town.

Tromsikhang Market
MARKET

(冲赛康市场; Chōngsàikāng Shìchǎng; Map p48) This bazaar-style area in the old town has the widest selection of dried fruits and nuts and is the place to buy such Tibetan specialities as tsampa and yak butter.

Norling Supermarket
SUPERMARKET

(罗林超市; Luólín Chāoshì; Map p44; 20 Linkuo Donglu) Located near the Muslim quarter, this Tibetan-run Nepali import shop sells everything from muesli and chocolate spread to Indian spices, olive oil and rolling tobacco, though at prices higher than in Nepal.

Outlook Outdoor Equipment OUTDOOR GEAR
(Map p48; 11 Beijing Donglu; ☺9.30am-9pm)
This reliable trekking shop across from the
Kirey Hotel has Western-quality sleeping
bags, Gore-Tex jackets and tents, plus hard-
to-find imported knick-knacks like altim-
eters, trekking socks and Primus cook sets.
Gear is also available for rent (Y10 to Y20
for a stove, Y25 to Y30 for a tent, per day).

ℹ Information

Internet Access

The most popular internet cafes are those at
the Snowlands and Yak Hotels, where you can
surf the internet (Y5) and burn CDs (Y15 to
Y20), from 9am to 11pm. If you have a laptop,
the Summit Café and Rama Kharpo and Yabshi
Phunkhang hotels offer free wi-fi. Local internet
cafes are cheaper, smokier and noisier.

Red Forest Net Café (红树村网城;
Hóngshùcūn Wǎngchéng; Map p48; Beijing
Donglu; per hr Y3; ☺24hr) One of several
places opposite the Banak Shol hotel.

Medical Services

Several hotels and pharmacies around town
sell Tibetan herbal medicine recommended by
locals for easing symptoms of altitude sickness. The most common medicine is known
as *solomano* in Tibetan and *hóngjīngtiān* (红景
天) in Chinese, though locals also recommend
gāoyuánníng (高原宁) and *gāoyuánkāng* (高原
康). A box of vials will cost you Y20 to Y35; take
three vials a day.

Military Hospital (西藏军区总医院; Xīzàng
Jūnqū Zǒngyīyuàn; Map p79; ☏628 0557;
Niangre Beilu) Travellers who have received
medical attention confirm that this place is the
best option (if you have an option).

Money

Bank of China branch (中国银行; Zhōngguó
Yínháng; Map p48; Beijing Donglu; ☺10am-
4.30pm Mon-Fri, 11am-3.30pm Sat & Sun) The
most conveniently located bank changes cash
and travellers cheques without fuss. It can't
give a cash advance on a credit card but the
ATMs normally work. It's between the Banak
Shol and Kirey Hotels.

Bank of China main office (中国银行;
Zhōngguó Yínháng; Map p54; Linkuo Xilu;
☺9am-1pm, 3.30-6.30pm Mon-Fri, 10.30am-
4pm Sat & Sun) West of the Potala. This is the
place to arrange a credit-card advance (3%
commission) or a bank transfer (p342). Take
a number as you walk in the door. The ATMs
outside the building are open 24 hours.

China Construction Bank ATM (中国建设
银行; Zhōngguó Jiànshè Yínháng; Map p48;
Zangyiyuan Lu/Mentsikhang Lam; ☺24hr) The

most centrally located ATM, outside Snowlands
Hotel.

Post

Main post office (中国邮政; Zhōngguó Yóuzhèng; Map p54; Beijing Donglu; ☺9am-8pm)
The counter in the far left corner sells stamps
and packaging for parcels. Leave parcels
unsealed until you get here, as staff will want
to check the contents for customs clearance.
Express Mail Service (EMS) is here. Postcards
are sold in the shop to the east.

DHL (中外运敦豪; Zhōngwàiyùn Dūnháo; Map
p44; ☏635 6995, 800 8108000; www.cn.dhl.
com; Room 4, 2nd fl, Back Block, Norpel Ling
Hotel/Baofa Jiudian, 6 Hongqi Lu) Free pick-up
and delivery service.

Public Security Bureau (PSB)

Lhasa City PSB (拉萨市公安局; Lāsà Shì
Gōng'ānjú; Map p44; ☏624 8154; 17 Linkuo
Beilu; ☺9am-12.30pm & 3.30-6pm Mon-Fri)
Visa extensions of up to a week are given, but
only a day or two before your visa expires and
only if you are on a tour.

Telephone

The cheapest way to make an international
call is through the various **private telephone
booths** (☺8.30am-11pm), often advertised as
'Telecom Supermarkets' (国际公话超市; Guójì
Gōnghuà Chāoshì). Useful outlets are on Zangyiyuan Lu (Mentsikhang Lam) and in front of the
Kirey Hotel. Rates are Y2.4 per minute to the US,
Y3.6 to Europe and Australia, or Y4.8 to other
countries.

Travel Agencies

FIT Banak Shol Hotel (散客旅游管理接待中
心; Sǎnkè Lǚyóu Guǎnlǐjiēdài Zhōngxīng; Map
p48; ☏655 9938; fit0891@hotmail.com; Banak
Shol, 8 Beijing Donglu) Contact Xiaojin. Good
prices, reliable and fairly transparent.

FIT Snowlands Hotel (高原散客旅游管理接
待中心; Gāoyuán Sǎnkè Lǚyóu Guǎnlǐjiēdài
Zhōngxīng; Map p48; ☏634 9239; www.tibet-
fit.com; lhakpa88@yahoo.com; 2nd fl, Snowlands Hotel, 4 Zangyiyuan Lu/Mentsikhang
Lam) Contact Lhakpa Tsering. Also goes under
the name Changtang.

Shigatse CITS (Map p48; ☏691 2080; www.
shambhalatour.com; tibetanintibet@yahoo.
cn; Zangyiyuan Lu/Mentsikhang Lam) Contact
Tenzin or Xiaojin.

**Tibet Tourism Bureau FIT Travel Service
Centre** (西藏旅游局; Xīzàng Lǚyóujú; Map p48;
☏632 0200; ttbfitsonam@hotmail.com; Zangyiyuan Lu/Mentsikhang Lam) Contact Sonam.
There are plenty of other travel agencies, though
most cater to Chinese tourists, who don't require travel permits.

❶ Getting There & Away

While there are a number of ways to get to Lhasa, the most popular routes are by air from Chéngdū (in Sichuān), by train from Xīníng, and overland or by air from Kathmandu. For details of getting *into* Tibet, see p352.

Air

Flying *out* of Lhasa is considerably easier than flying in. No permits are necessary – just turn up to the **Civil Aviation Authority of China office** (CAAC; 中国民航; Zhōngguó Mínháng; Map p44; ☑683 3446; 1 Niangre Lu; ☺9am-6.30pm) and buy a ticket. In August and around national holidays (p343), you'd be wise to book your ticket at least a week in advance. Ask about a free airport transfer if you buy your ticket here.

To book a ticket you need to complete a form, get a reservation and then pay the cashier (cash only). You can buy separate onward tickets from Chéngdū here, but not at discounted prices.

Air China (中国国际民航; Zhōngguó Guójì Mínháng; Map p48; ☑681 9777; www.airchina. com.cn; 48 Beijing Zhonglu; ☺9am-7.30pm) No credit cards.

China Southern (中国南方航空; Zhōngguó Nánfāng Hángkōng; Map p48; ☑683 1868; www.csair.com; 33 Beijing Zhonglu)

Bus & Minibus

TO/FROM CHINA

The arrival of the train has pushed the sleeper buses into irrelevancy. There are still daily sleeper services to Golmud (20 hours), Xīníng (2½ days) and even Chéngdū (three days and four nights, via Golmud) but you're better off taking the train.

AROUND TIBET

At the time of research foreigners were not allowed to take bus services around Tibet and had to arrange their own transport (see p29). In case this changes, the following public transport operates.

Buses to popular pilgrim destinations leave early in the morning from the west side of Barkhor Sq. Buses leave between 6.30am and 7.30am for Ganden Monastery, Tsurphu Monastery, Drak Yerpa, Tsetang (Shannan), Samye and Dranang. Samye tickets are sold from a tin shack just north of the square on Zangyiyuan Lu (Mentsikhang Lam). Buses depart when full, so expect lots of hanging around.

At the time of research the main **Western Bus Station** (西郊客运站; Xījiāo Kèyùnzhàn; Map p44; Jinzhu Xilu) wasn't selling bus tickets to foreigners. In case this changes there are hourly services to Shigatse (Y54 to Y84), Tsetang (Y33 to Y43) and Nagchu (Nàqū; Y57 to Y84), plus a daily service to Gyantse (Y74) and long-distance services to Chamdo, Markham,

Zhōngdiān, Golmud and Xīníng. Private cars also run from here and are more likely to take foreigners but cost about double the cheapest bus fare per seat.

Private buses to Shigatse, Nagchu and Damxung (Dāngxióng) also run from between the Yak and Kirey Hotels on Beijing Donglu between 7.30am and 8.30am.

The **Eastern Bus Station** (东郊客运站; Dōngjiāo Kèyùnzhàn; Map p44; Jiangsu Donglu) has frequent minibuses to Lhundrub (Línzhōu) and Medro Gongkar (Mòzhú Gōngkǎ), from outside the main station, plus daily buses to Drigung Til and Reting Monastery.

Lhasa's chaotic **Lugu Bus Stand** (Map p48) is southwest of Barkhor Sq and has several departures daily to Chushul, Yangpachen and Nyemo, but timings are awkward and information hard to find.

Lhasa's **Northern Bus Station** (北郊客运站; Běijiāo Qìchē Kèyùnzhàn; Map p79; Zaji Lu) has sleeper buses to Ali (Y650 to Y750, 60 hours) in western Tibet, as well as buses to Zhangmu, Yadong, Markham, Zhōngdiān and Shigatse.

Rental Vehicles

Rental vehicles are currently the only way to get around Tibet.

Train

It's possible to ride the rails up onto the Tibetan plateau all the way to Lhasa. There are daily trains to/from Běijīng, Xī'níng/Lánzhōu and Chéngdū/Chóngqìng, and services either daily or every other day to Xī'ān, Shànghǎi and Guǎngzhōu. See p356 for fares and other details. All trains from Lhasa depart between 7.30am and 1pm, while all trains to Lhasa arrive in the evening. The train station is 4km southwest of town. A service to Shigatse is due to begin in the next few years.

You can buy train tickets up to 10 days in advance at the Lhasa **train station ticket office** (☺7am-10pm) or the more centrally located **city ticket office** (火车票代售处; Huǒchēpiào Dàishòuchù; Map p44; Deji Beilu; ☺9-11.30am & 1-5pm). Note that it's generally much easier to get tickets from Lhasa than *to* Lhasa.

To get from the train station into town take bus 89 to the centre or take bus 91 over the Lhasa Bridge to the terminus near the Eastern Bus Station and then hop on bus 97 to Beijing Donglu. To get *to* the station catch bus 89 just south of the Barkhor on Jiangsu Lu or take bus 91/97 in the opposite direction. Buses run every 20 minutes from 6.30am to 10.30pm. A taxi costs around Y30.

❶ Getting Around

For those travellers based in the Tibetan quarter of Lhasa, most of the major inner-Lhasa sights are within fairly easy walking distance. For sights such as the Norbulingka over in the west of town, it's better to jump in a taxi or rent a bicycle.

To/From the Airport

Modern Gongkar airport is 66km from Lhasa, via the Gálá Shān tunnel and bridge. A new highway along the eastern side of the Kyi-chu river will further shave off some distance when it opens in 2011.

Airport buses (☑682 7727) leave up to 10 times a day (Y25, 1¼ hours) between 7.30am and 1pm from beside the CAAC building and are timed to meet flights. From the airport, buses wait for flights outside the terminal building. Buy tickets on the bus.

A taxi to the airport costs Y150 to Y200.

Bicycle

Bicycles are a good way to get around Lhasa once you have acclimatised to the altitude.

Thaizand Bicycle Tours (泰山单车; Tàishān Dānchē; Map p48; ☑691 0898; thaizand@ hotmail.com; Kirey Hotel, 105 Beijing Donglu) rents quality mountain bikes for Y40 to Y80 per day, with a helmet and pads, and can advise on routes and tours.

A couple of **bike rental places** (捷安特自行车专卖店; Jiéāntè Zìxíngchē Zhuānmàidiàn; Map p48; ☒10am-9pm) opposite the Banak Shol Hotel rent decent Giant-brand mountain bikes for Y30 per day. Bicycle theft is a problem in Lhasa, so be sure to park your bike in designated areas (Y1). A lock and chain is a good idea.

Minibuses & City Buses

Buses (Y1) and private minibuses (Y2) are frequent on Beijing Donglu, and if you need to get up to western Lhasa this is the cheapest way to do it.

Useful bus routes:

Bus 89 From the train station to the Eastern Bus Station, via the Western Bus Station, TTB office, Potala Palace, Lhasa Department Store and Jiangsu Lu.

Bus 106 From Beijing Donglu to the Potala, TTB office and Norbulingka.

Bus 109 From Beijing Donglu to the Western Bus Station, via the CAAC office, Linkuo Xilu, Bank of China, Beijing Zhonglu and Norbulingka; returning to Beijing Donglu via Luobulinka Lu.

Minibus 205 From Beijing Donglu to the Eastern Bus Station.

Minibus 301 From the Eastern Bus Station to Beijing Donglu, CAAC, Zang Gyab Lukhang Park, Bank of China, Lhasa Hotel and the turnoff to Drepung Monastery.

Pedicab

There is no shortage of pedicabs plying the streets of Lhasa, but they require endless haggling and are only really useful for short trips (around Y5). At least most are Tibetan owned. *Always* fix the price before getting in.

Taxi

Taxis charge a standard fare of Y10 for the first 5km (then Y2 per subsequent kilometre), resulting in a Y10 ride almost anywhere within the city.

AROUND LHASA

Within a short bus or taxi ride or easy cycling distance of central Lhasa are the impressive Gelugpa monasteries of Sera and Drepung. Both are must-sees, even if you have only a brief stay in Lhasa. Current regulations require foreign tourists to visit Drepung, Sera and Ganden Monasteries in the company of a registered guide.

See the Ü map (Map p96) for the location of Drak Yerpa, Drölma Lhakhang and Shugsheb Nunnery.

Drepung Monastery

འབྲས་སྤུངས་ 哲蚌寺

About 8km west of central Lhasa, **Drepung** (Zhébàng Sì; admission Y50, ☒9.30am-5.30pm) was once one of the world's largest monasteries. The word Drepung literally translates as 'rice heap', a reference to the huge numbers of white monastic buildings that once piled up on the hillside. It suffered through the ages with assaults by the kings of Tsang and the Mongols, but was left relatively unscathed during the Cultural Revolution and there is still much of interest intact. Rebuilding and resettlement continue at a pace unmatched elsewhere in Tibet and the site once again resembles a small village, with around 600 monks resident out of a pre-Liberation total of around 7000.

The best way to visit the chapels is to follow the pilgrims or, failing that, the yellow signs. Interior photography costs Y10 to Y20 per chapel. A restaurant near the bus stop serves reviving tea by the glass, as well as bowls of *shemdre* (Y6) and *momos*.

HISTORY

Drepung was founded in 1416 by a charismatic monk and disciple of Tsongkhapa

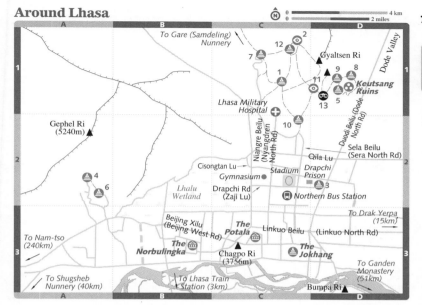

Around Lhasa

◎ Sights

1 Chupsang Nunnery	C1
2 Dadren Ritrö Hermitage	C1
3 Drapchi Monastery	D2
4 Drepung Monastery	A2
5 Keutsang Ritrö	D1
6 Nechung Monastery	A2
7 Pabonka Monastery	C1
8 Phurbu Chok Monastery	D1
9 Rakadrak Hermitage	D1
10 Sera Monastery	C2
11 Sera Ütse	D1
12 Tashi Chöling Hermitage	C1
13 Viewpoint	D1

called Jamyang Chöje. Within just a year of completion the monastery had attracted a population of some 2000 monks.

In 1530 the second Dalai Lama established the Ganden Palace, the palace that was home to the Dalai Lamas until the fifth built the Potala. It was from here that the early Dalai Lamas exercised their political as well as religious control over central Tibet, and the second, third and fourth Dalai Lamas are all entombed here.

GANDEN PALACE
From the car park, pass the woodblock and juniper stalls and follow the kora clockwise around the outside of the monastery until you reach the steps up to the Ganden Palace.

The first hall on the left is the **Sanga Tratsang**, a recently renovated chapel housing statues of the protectors Namtöse (Vairocana), Nagpo Chenpo (Mahakala), Dorje Jigje (Yamantaka), Chögyel (Dharmaraja), Palden Lhamo (Shri Devi; on a horse) and Dorje Drakden (the Nechung oracle; see the box, p83), all arranged around a central statue of the fifth Dalai Lama.

Head up the stairs and then across the main courtyard, where performances of *cham* (a ritual dance) are still performed

during the Shötun festival. The upper floor of the main building has three chapels that make up the apartments of the early Dalai Lamas. The second of the three chapels, to the right, is an audience room with wonderfully detailed **murals** and the throne of the fifth Dalai Lama, next to a thousand-armed statue of Chenresig. The third is a simple living room.

From here descend and cross over to a final chapel whose entrance is defaced by a Cultural Revolution–era political slogan

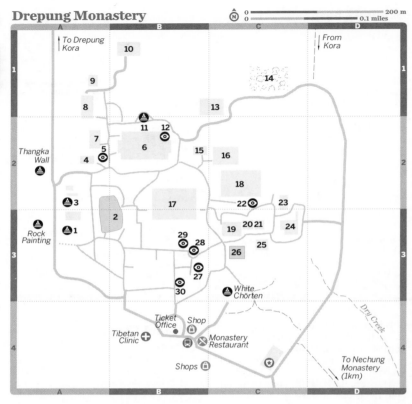

(Mao's image was only recently removed). Signs lead past a refreshment stand and a corner shrine to Drölma to the exit to the north.

MAIN ASSEMBLY HALL

The main assembly hall, or *tsogchen,* is the principal structure in the Drepung complex. The hall is reached through an entrance on the west side, just past a kitchen, whose medieval-looking giant cauldrons and ladles look like a set from the film *The Name of the Rose.*

The huge interior is very atmospheric, draped with thangkas and supported by over 180 columns, of which the ones near the western protector chapel are decorated with ancient chainmail and bows.

The back-room chapel features the protector deities Chana Dorje (Vajrapani, blue) and Tamdrin (Hayagriva, red), and contains statues of Sakyamuni with his two disciples, the Buddhas of the Three Ages, and nine chörtens above. The walls and pillars are lined with statues of the eight bodhisattvas. To the front centre there is also a youthful-looking statue of Lamdrin Rinpoche (a former abbot of Drepung recognisable by his black-rimmed glasses); next to it is his chörten. To the east is Tsongkhapa, the founder of the Gelugpa sect.

Sculptures of interest in the main hall include a two-storey Jampelyang (Manjushri), accompanied by the 13th Dalai Lama; Sakyamuni; Tsongkhapa; Jamyang Chöje, in a cabinet to the right; the seventh Dalai Lama; and to the right Sakyamuni, flanked by five of the Dalai Lamas. At either end of the altar you will find a group of eight *arhats* (literally 'worthy ones'). Pilgrims walk under the long cabinet on the eastern wall, which holds a huge building-sized thangka which is unveiled during the Shötun festival.

⊙ **Sights**

1	Sanga Tratsang	A3
2	Debating Courtyard	B3
3	Ganden Palace	A2
4	Nyango Kangtsang	A2
5	Kitchen	A2
6	Main Assembly Hall	B2
7	Chapel	A2
8	Ngagpa College	A1
9	Pindu Mitze	A1
10	Samlo Kangtsang	B1
11	Jampelyang Temple	B2
12	Jamyang Chöje Meditation Cave	B2
13	Residence	C1
14	Main Debating Courtyard	C1
15	Udu Kangtsang	B2
16	Tsor Kangtsang	C2
17	Loseling College	B2
18	Gomang College	C2
19	Deyang College	C3
20	Lamba Mitze	C3
21	Jurche Mitze	C3
22	Lumbum Kangtsang	C2
23	Hua Mitze	C2
24	Khamdung Kangtsang	C3
25	Tsokha Mitze	C3
26	Small Debating Courtyard	C3
27	College	B3
28	College	B3
29	Minyang Kangstang	B3
30	College	B3

Back by the main entrance, steps lead up to the 1st and 2nd floors. At the top of the stairs is the **Hall of the Kings of Tibet**, featuring statues of Tibet's early kings, as well as Lobsang Gyatso (the fifth Dalai Lama), and then a chapel containing the head of a two-storey **Jampa** statue. Pilgrims prostrate themselves here and drink from a sacred conch shell.

Continue moving clockwise through the **Sakyamuni Chapel**, stuffed with chörtens, and then descend to the **Miwang Lhakhang**. This chapel contains the assembly hall's most revered image, a massive **statue of Jampa**, the Future Buddha, at the age of 12. The statue rises through three floors of the building from a ground-floor chapel that is usually closed, and it is flanked by Tsongkhapa to the left and Jamyang Chöje to the right. The chörtens behind the statue contain the remains of the second Dalai Lama and Jamyang Chöje. At the front right are statues representing seven of the Dalai Lamas.

Descend to the **Drölma chapel**. Drölma is a protective deity, and in this case the three Drölma images in the chapel (to the immediate right) are responsible for protecting Drepung's drinking water, wealth and authority respectively. There are also some fine examples of gold-inked Tibetan Kangyur **scriptures** here. The central statue is a form of Sakyamuni, whose amulet contains one of Tsongkhapa's teeth.

Exit the building from the western side of the 2nd floor.

NGAGPA COLLEGE

Ngagpa is one of Drepung's four colleges, and was devoted to Tantric study. The chapel is dedicated to bull-headed Dorje Jigje (Yamantaka), a Tantric meditational deity who serves as an opponent to the forces of impermanence. The cartoon-style Dorje Jigje image in the inner sanctum is said to have been fashioned by Tsongkhapa himself. Walking clockwise, other statues include Palden Lhamo (first clockwise, riding a horse), Nagpo Chenpo (third), Drölma (fourth), Tsongkhapa (fifth), the fifth Dalai Lama (seventh) and, by the door, the Nechung oracle. Look for bull-headed Chögyel to the side, his hand almost thrusting out of the expanded glass cabinet.

To get a feel for what Drepung was like before the renovation teams arrived, detour briefly up to the **Samlo Kangtsang**, unrestored and surrounded by melancholic ruins.

As you follow the pilgrim path (clockwise) around the back of the assembly hall you will pass the small **Jampelyang Temple**, where pilgrims pour yak butter on the wall and then peer in to see a holy rock painting and get hit on the back with a holy iron rod. Just a little further, tucked in on the right, is the tiny **meditation cave** of Jamyang Chöje, with some fine rock paintings.

LOSELING COLLEGE

Loseling is the largest of Drepung's colleges, and studies here were devoted to logic. The **main hall** houses a throne used by the Dalai Lamas, an extensive library,

THE BUMPA RI TREK

The demanding but excellent five-hour return trek up imposing Bumpa Ri, the holy peak to the southeast of Lhasa, is worth attempting if you're fit and acclimatised. It's straight up and then straight down, but offers unparalleled views over the Holy City, either from the top or just part of the way.

From the Eastern Bus Station it's a 10-minute walk south over the Lhasa Bridge to the base of the hill, where a path ascends to a chörten and incense-burning site. From here faint trails head straight up the hillside to the third small ridge, where a faint trail branches to the right. In general, aim for the pylon, to meet up with the main trail. After an hour you reach a ridge with views of the summit spires ahead. It's another hour's climb from here to the summit, following the trail to the right of the spires, over a spur and then up a gully to the two main summits, festooned in prayer flags. From the top it's a two-hour descent back down the way you came.

and a long altar decorated with statues of the fifth, seventh and eighth Dalai Lamas, Tsongkhapa and former Drepung abbots. The two chörtens of Loseling's earlier abbots are covered with offerings. There are three chapels to the rear of the hall. The one to the left houses 16 *arhats,* which pilgrims walk under in a circuit. The central chapel has a large statue of Jampa and a self-arisen stone painting of the Nechung oracle; the chapel to the right has a small but beautiful statue of Sakyamuni.

On the 2nd floor you'll pass a small printing press to enter a small chapel full of angry deities, and then you pass under the body of a stuffed goat draped with one-mao notes before entering the spooky *gönkhang* (protector chapel). There are more protective deities here, including the main Dorje Jigje (Yamantaka), plus Nagpo Chenpo (six-armed Mahakala), Dorje Drakden and Dorje Lekpa.

If you have time, pop into the small **debating courtyard** west of Loseling College. Monks sometimes do their music practise in the garden here, blowing huge horns and crashing cymbals.

GOMANG COLLEGE

Gomang is the second largest of Drepung's colleges and follows the same layout as Loseling. The **main hall** has a whole row of images, including Jampa, Tsepame and the seventh Dalai Lama. Again, there are three chapels to the rear: the one to the left houses three deities of longevity, but more important is the **central chapel**, chock-a-block with images. As at Loseling, there is a single protector chapel on the upper floor. Women are not allowed into this chapel.

DEYANG COLLEGE & OTHER COLLEGES

The smallest of Drepung's colleges, this one can safely be missed if you've had enough. The principal image in the main hall is Jampa, flanked by Jampelyang, Drölma, the fifth Dalai Lama and others.

East of here is a cluster of friendly colleges that the tour groups never reach, including the Lamba Mitze, Lumbum Kangtsang, **Jurche Mitze**, once home to students from Inner Mongolia, and then round to the **Khamdung Kangtsang**, the upstairs back hallway of which is defaced with faded Mao slogans and images. More buildings sport English signs saying that visitors are welcome.

If you're here in the afternoon, save some time to watch the monk-debating (lots of shouting, hand slapping and gesticulation) between 2.30pm and 4.30pm in the **main debating courtyard** in the northeast corner of the monastery (photos Y15).

DREPUNG KORA

This lovely kora climbs up to around 3900m and probably should not be attempted until you've had four or five days to acclimatise in Lhasa. The walk takes about an hour at a leisurely pace (it is possible to do it more quickly at hiking speed). Look for the path that continues uphill from the turn-off to the Ganden Palace. The path passes several rock paintings, climbs up past a high wall used to hang a giant thangka during the Shötun festival (p22), peaks at a valley of prayer flags, then descends to the east via an encased Drölma (Tara) statue and several more rock carvings. There are excellent views along the way.

Getting There & Away

The easy way to get out to Drepung is by minibus 301, 302 and 303, which run from Beijing Donglu to the foot of the Drepung hill. From here a coach runs up to the monastery (Y1). A taxi from the Barkhor is Y30.

Nechung Monastery

གནས་ཆུང་གྲུ་ཚོང་ 乃琼寺

Only 10 minutes' walk downhill from Drepung Monastery, **Nechung** (Nǎiqióng Sì; admission Y10; ⊙8.30am-5pm) is worth a visit for its historical role as the seat of the Tibetan State Oracle until 1959. The oracle was the medium of Dorje Drakden, an aspect of Pehar, the Gelugpa protector of the Buddhist state, and the Dalai Lamas would make no important decision without first consulting him. The oracle was not infallible, however; in 1904 the oracle resigned in disgrace after failing to predict the invasion of the British under Younghusband. In 1959 the State Oracle fled to India with the Dalai Lama.

Nechung is an eerie place associated with possession, exorcism and other pre-Buddhist rites. The blood-red **doors** at the entrance are painted with flayed human skins and scenes of torture line the top of the outer courtyard. Tantric drumming booms from the depths of the building like a demonic heartbeat. For images of Dorje Drakden, the protective spirit manifested in the State Oracle, see the back-room chapel to the left of the main hall. The statue in the left corner shows Dorje Drakden in his wrathful aspect, so terrible that his face must be covered; the version on the right has him in a slightly more conciliatory frame of mind. The *la-shing* (sacred tree) in between the two is the home of Pehar.

The far right chapel has an amazing **spirit trap** and a statue of the Dzogchen deity Ekajati, recognisable by her single fang and eye and representing the power of concentration. On the 1st floor is an audience chamber, whose throne was used by the Dalai Lamas when they consulted with the State Oracle. The 2nd floor features a huge new statue of a wrathful Guru Rinpoche. Don't miss the fine murals in the exterior courtyard.

Nechung is easily reached on foot after visiting Drepung, en route to the main road. A path leads past stone-carvers to the monastery (10 minutes).

Sera Monastery

སེ་ར་དགོན་པ 色拉寺

Approximately 5km north of central Lhasa, **Sera Monastery** (Sèlà Sì; adult/under 8yr Y55/free; ⊙9am-5pm) was one of Lhasa's two great Gelugpa monasteries, second only to Drepung. Its once-huge monastic population of around 5000 monks has now been reduced by 90% and building repairs are still continuing. Nevertheless the monastery is worth a visit, particularly in the morning when the monastery is at its most active, but also between 3pm and 5pm (not weekends), when debating is usually held in the monastery's debating courtyard. Chapels start to close at 3pm, so it makes sense to see the monastery chapels before heading to the debating.

Interior photography costs Y15 to Y30 per chapel; video fees are an outrageous Y850. Near the monastery entrance there is a simple but pleasant restaurant-teahouse.

HISTORY

Sera was founded in 1419 by Sakya Yeshe, a disciple of Tsongkhapa also known by the honorific title Jamchen Chöje. In its heyday, Sera hosted five colleges of instruction, but

---

THE NECHUNG ORACLE

Every New Year in Lhasa until 1959, the Dalai Lama consulted the Nechung oracle on important matters of state. In preparation for the ordeal, the oracle would strap on eye-shaped bracelets and an elaborate headdress of feathers, so heavy that it had to be lifted onto his head by two men.

The oracle would then whip himself into a trance in an attempt to dislodge his spirit from his body. Eyewitness accounts describe how his eyeballs swelled and rolled up into his sockets, and how his mouth opened wide, his tongue curling upward as his face reddened. As he began to discern the future in a steel mirror, the oracle would answer questions in an anguished, tortured, hissing voice, and the answers would be interpreted and written on a small blackboard. After the trance the oracle would faint from the ordeal and have to be carried away.

at the time of the Chinese invasion in 1959 there were just three: Sera Me specialised in the fundamental precepts of Buddhism; Sera Je in the instruction of itinerant monks from outside central Tibet; and Sera Ngagpa in Tantric studies.

Sera survived the ravages of the Cultural Revolution with light damage, although many of the lesser colleges were destroyed.

SERA ME COLLEGE

Follow the pilgrims clockwise, past the Shompa Kangtsang and Tsa Kangtsang residential halls and several minor buildings, to the Sera Me College. This college dates back to the original founding of the monastery.

The central image of the impressive **main hall** is a copper Sakyamuni, flanked by Jampa (left) and Jampelyang. To the rear of the hall are four chapels. To the left is a dark chapel dedicated to the dharma protector of the east, Ta-og (in an ornate brass case and wearing a hat), alongside Dorje Jigje. Don't miss the **masks**, iron thunderbolts and antique bows hanging from the ceiling. Women cannot enter this chapel. To the left of the entrance is a three-dimensional wooden mandala.

Continue to the central chapel, which contains statues of the Past, Present and Future Buddhas, as well as 16 *arhats* depicted in their mountain grottos.

The next chapel is home to Miwang Jowo, a central Sakyamuni statue that dates from the 15th century and is the most sacred of the college's statues. At the back are Tsepame and eight bodhisattvas. The entrance to the chapel is guarded by the protectors Tamdrin (Hayagriva; red) and Miyowa (Achala; blue). The last chapel is dedicated to Tsongkhapa and there are also images of several Dalai Lamas, as well as of Sakya Yeshe, Sera's founder and first abbot.

There are two chapels on the upper floor. The first, after you mount the stairs,

Sera Monastery

is dedicated to Sakyamuni, depicted in an unusual standing form. The second is a Drölma chapel with 1000 statues of this protective deity. The third has 1000 statues of Chenresig, as well as a huge brass pot in the corner.

SERA NGAGPA COLLEGE

A Tantric college, Ngagpa is also the oldest structure at Sera. The **main hall** is dominated by a statue of Sakya Yeshe (wearing a black hat), behind the throne, surrounded by other famous Sera lamas. There are three chapels to the rear of the hall, the first featuring Jampa and thousand-armed Chenresig, the second with 16 *arhats* and a large Sakyamuni statue, and the third with a statue of the protective deity Dorje Jigje, as well as Namtöse (Vaishravana), the guardian of the north, to the right, who rides a snow lion and holds a mongoose that vomits jewels. There are also a couple of rooms upstairs featuring Tsepame and the eight medicine buddhas (Menlha).

After exiting, most pilgrims pay a visit to the **Jarung Kangtsang** residential college.

SERA JE COLLEGE

This is the largest of Sera's colleges, generally accessed from a western side entrance. It has a breathtaking **main hall**, hung with thangkas and lit by shafts of light from high windows. Several chörtens hold the remains of Sera's most famous lamas.

To the left of the hall is a passage leading, via a chapel dedicated to the Past, Present and Future Buddhas, to the most sacred of Sera Monastery's chapels, the **Chapel of Tamdrin**. Tamdrin (Hayagriva) is a wrathful meditational deity whose name means 'horse headed'. He is the chief protective deity of Sera, and there is often a long line of shuffling pilgrims waiting to touch their – and especially their children's – foreheads to his feet in respect. Monks sell holy threads, protective amulets and sacred pills here, as well as red slips of inscribed paper, which pilgrims buy to burn for the recently deceased. The ornate brass shrine recalls the temples of the Kathmandu Valley. Take a look at the weapons, hats and masks hanging from the ceiling. There is a second chapel for him on the upper floor, but there he is in another aspect with nine heads.

The first chapel to the rear of the hall is devoted to a lovely statue of Sakyamuni, seated below a fine canopy and ceiling mandala. Pilgrims climb steps to the right to touch his left leg. The next two chapels are dedicated to Tsongkhapa, with Sakyamuni and Öpagme (Amitabha); and to Jampelyang, flanked by Jampa and another Jampelyang. From here head to the upstairs chapels.

To the northeast of Sera Je is Sera's **debating courtyard**. There is usually debating practise here on weekday afternoons from around 3pm to 5pm, which provides a welcome relief from peering at Buddhist iconography. You will hear it (with much clapping of hands to emphasise points) as you approach Sera Je. Foreign photographers circle the site like vultures at a sky burial.

HAMDONG KANGTSANG

Hamdong served as a residence for monks studying at Sera Je College. The back left chapel contains a bearded image of a Sera lama who died in 1962; in a case to the right is an image of Drölma, who is said to protect Sera's water supply. Look for three

Sera Monastery

⊙ **Sights**

1	Mani Lhakhang	B3
2	Shompa Kangtsang	B3
3	Tsomoling	B3
4	Chetsa Kangtsang	B3
5	Sera Me College	B3
6	Minor Debating Courtyard	B2
7	Sera Ngagpa College	B2
8	Jarung Kangtsang	B2
9	Sera Je College	B2
10	Shedra	B1
11	Debating Courtyard	B2
12	Hamdong Kangtsang	B1
13	Dema Kangtsang	C2
14	Drölma Rock Shrine	C2
15	Main Assembly Hall	C2
16	Kitchen	C2
17	Gyansok Khang	C3
18	Sand Mandala	B2
19	Printing Press	B2
20	Gongbo Kangtsang	C3
21	Thangka Wall	C2
22	Chöding Hermitage	D2
23	Mani Lhakhang	C2
24	Hermit Caves	D3

DIY: TREKKING THE DODE VALLEY

From the Sera Monastery kora you can make a great half-day trek up to the Sera Ütse retreat above the monastery and then around the ridge to the little-visited retreats of the Dode Valley (Map p79). You shouldn't attempt the trek until you are well acclimatised to the altitude.

From Sera the steep relentless climb up to the yellow-walled **Sera Ütse** retreat takes at least an hour (look up and see it high on the cliff above Sera; if that doesn't put you off, you'll be fine!). Take the path towards the Chöding hermitage (see p87) and branch off to the left before you get there, climbing the ridge via a switchback path until you reach the yellow building perched high above the valley. Sera Ütse was a retreat used by Tsongkhapa (his *drub-puk*, or meditation cave, can be visited) and is currently home to two monks. You can also reach the retreat directly from Pabonka's Tashi Chöling hermitage (p88), but trailfinding is harder.

From the Ütse continue east along a level trail for 10 minutes to a superb **viewpoint**, probably Lhasa's most scenic picnic spot. From here the main trail continues east down into the Dode Valley, though it's possible for fit climbers to detour straight up the hillside to the summit, a knob of rock covered in prayer flags.

The main trail descends to the small **Rakadrak** hermitage, where you can visit three simple caves associated with Tsongkhapa. Five minutes' walk below Rakadrak is the larger **Keutsang Ritrö**, a retreat complex home to 23 monks. The original hermitage lies in ruins in an incredible location on the side of the sheer cliff-face to the east. A painting inside the main chapel (to the right) depicts the original. As you leave the complex a path to the left leads to the dramatic ruins but the trail is dangerous and ends in a sheer drop. The far section of the ruins can only be reached from the other side of the cliff.

From the Keutsang Ritrö follow the dirt road downhill and after 10 minutes branch left for the short uphill hike to the **Phurbu Chok Monastery** and its hilltop Rigsum Gonpo Lhakhang (an hour detour in total from the road). You can spot two nunneries from here; Negodong to the east and Mechungri to the southeast. Back at the junction, descend to the main road to flag down bus 601 or 603, which terminates at Linkuo Beilu, just north of the Ramoche Temple.

On the ride back it's worth getting off at Zaji (Drapchi) Lu to visit **Drapchi Monastery** (扎基寺; Zājī Sì), an active and unusual monastery that is located near Lhasa's most notorious political prison. Huge amounts of rice wine and *chang* (barley beer) are offered continuously to the local protectress Drapchi Lhamo and the site has an almost animist feel to it.

photos of **Ekai Kawaguchi**, the Japanese monk who studied here in disguise in 1901.

As you walk downhill, note the wonderful **rock paintings** depicting Jampelyang, Chenresig, Chana Dorje (Vajrapani) and Green Tara.

MAIN ASSEMBLY HALL (TSOGCHEN)

The main assembly hall is the largest of Sera's buildings and dates back to 1710. The central hall is particularly impressive and is noted for its wall-length thangkas and two-storey statue of Jampa. He is surrounded by other figures, including Dalai Lamas on the right, while to the left is the large throne of the 13th Dalai Lama. Left of the throne is a figure of Sakya Yeshe, recognisable by his black hat.

Of the three chapels to the rear of the hall, the central is the most important, with its 6m-high Jampa statue. The statue rises up to the upper floor, where it can also be viewed from a central chapel. Also on the upper floor (to the far left of the central chapel) is a highly revered statue of a thousand-armed Chenresig. Pilgrims put their forehead to a pole that connects them directly and literally to the heart of compassion. The pilgrim path enters the building from the back so this may be the first chapel you come across, before descending to the prayer hall.

PRINTING PRESS

Before leaving the monastery it's worth having a look at the printing blocks in this new hall. Photos are Y5. Prints made on site are for sale. A small building to the side holds a sand mandala.

SERA KORA

The Sera kora takes less than an hour and is well worth the time. It starts outside the entrance and heads west, following an arc around the monastery walls. On the eastern descent, look out for several brightly coloured **rock paintings**. The largest ones on the eastern side of the monastery are of Dorje Jigje, Tsongkhapa and others. Next to the rock paintings is a support wall used to hang a giant thangka during festivals.

A path leads up the side steps of this wall to the **Chöding hermitage**. The hermitage was a retreat of Tsongkhapa, and predates Sera. There is not a great deal to see, but it is a short walk and the views from the hermitage are worthwhile. A path continues south around the hillside past a holy spring to a point that has fine views of Sera and Lhasa beyond.

ⓘ Getting There & Away

Sera is only a half-hour bicycle ride from the Barkhor area of Lhasa. Alternatively, head down to the intersection of Beijing Donglu and Zhisenge/Qingnian Lu and catch minibus 503 (Y2, every 10 minutes) from just north of the intersection. Minibuses 501 and 502 also run to Sera. A taxi costs around Y10.

Pabonka Monastery
ཕ་བོང་ཁ་དགོན་པ་

One of the most ancient Buddhist sites in the Lhasa region, **Pabonka Monastery** (admission free; ☉dawn-dusk) is infrequently visited, but is only a one-hour walk (or short taxi ride) from the Sera Monastery turn-off and is worth the effort.

Built on a flat-topped granite boulder said to resemble a tortoise, Pabonka may even predate the Jokhang and Ramoche. King Songtsen Gampo built the monastery in the 7th century and he, his Chinese wife Princess Wencheng, Tibetan king Trisong Detsen, Guru Rinpoche and Tibet's first seven monks all meditated here at various times. The nine-storey tower was destroyed in 841 by the anti-Buddhist King Langdharma and rebuilt in the 11th century. The fifth Dalai Lama added an extra floor to the two-storey building. It suffered damage in the Cultural Revolution and has undergone repairs in recent years.

The first building you come across is the **Rigsum Gonpo Temple**, jam-packed with shrines, whose most famous relic is the blue and gold carved mantra *'om mani padme hum'* ('hail to the jewel in the lotus') that faces the entrance on the far side of the hall. The central shrine contains a 1300-year-old 'self-arising' (not man-made) carving depicting Chenresig, Jampelyang and Chana Dorje (Vajrapani) – the Rigsum Gonpo trinity after which the chapel is named. The stone carvings were buried during the Cultural Revolution and only dug up in 1985.

Continue uphill, turn left at the row of chörtens, and follow the road clockwise around the Pabonka rock (said to represent a female tortoise) to the **Palden Lhamo Cave** on the west side, where King Songtsen Gampo once meditated. Images inside are of Songtsen Gampo (with a turban), his two wives, Guru Rinpoche, Trisong Detsen (in the corner) and a rock carving of the protectress Palden Lhamo.

Pabonka Podrang sits atop the ancient rock. There is nothing to see on the ground floor, but the upper floor has an intimate assembly hall with a picture of the current Pabonka Lama and a 'self-arising' Chenresig statue hidden behind a pillar to the right. The inner protector chapel has a statue of red-faced local protector Gonpo Dashey Marpa (second from the right). The four-pillared Kashima Lhakhang next door is lined with various lamas, three kings and their wives. The cosy rooftop quarters of the Dalai Lama have a statue of the meditational deity Demchok (Chakrasamvara), and an ancient *dungkhar* (conch shell) wrapped in a *kathak* (prayer scarf), along with fine views back towards Lhasa.

Further above the Pabonka Podrang are the remains of 108 chörtens and the yellow **Gyasa Podrang**, or temple of Princess Wencheng. The two ground-floor rooms are dedicated to five manifestations of Tsongkhapa and the medicine buddhas, and an upper-floor chapel has a small statue of Wencheng herself in the far right, near an image of Thonmi Sambhota (who reputedly invented the Tibetan alphabet here). Songtsen Gampo's Nepali wife Bhrikuti is also present, as are images on the other side of the room of Green and White Drölma, of whom the two wives are thought to be emanations. Also present is Gar Tsongtsen, the Tibetan minister who travelled to the Tang

MONASTERIES IN TIBET

The great Gelugpa monasteries of Drepung, Sera and Ganden, collectively known as the *densa chenmo sum,* once operated like self-contained worlds. Drepung alone, the largest of these monasteries, was home to around 10,000 monks at the time of the Chinese takeover in 1951. Like the other major Gelugpa institutions, Drepung operated less as a single unit than as an assembly of colleges, each with its own interests, resources and administration.

The colleges, known as *tratsang* or *dratsang,* were (and still are) in turn made up of residences, or *kangtsang.* A monk joining a monastic college was assigned to a *kangtsang* according to the region in which he was born. For example, it is thought that 60% of monks at Drepung's Loseling College were from Kham, while Gomang college was dominated by monks from Amdo and Mongolia. This gave the monastic colleges a distinctive regional flavour and meant that loyalties were generally grounded much deeper in the colleges than in the monastery itself.

At the head of a college was the *khenpo* (abbot), a position that was filled by contenders who had completed the highest degrees of monastic studies. The successful applicant was chosen by the Dalai Lama. Beneath the abbot was a group of religious leaders who supervised prayer meetings and festivals, and a group of economic managers who controlled the various *kangtsang* estates and funds. There was also a squad of huge monks known as *dob-dobs,* who were in charge of discipline and administering punishments.

In the case of the larger colleges, estates and funds were often extensive. Loseling College had over 180 estates and 20,000 serfs who worked the land and paid taxes to the monastery. Monasteries were involved in many forms of trade. For the most part, these holdings were not used to support monks – who were often forced to do private business to sustain themselves – but to maintain an endless cycle of prayer meetings and festivals that were deemed necessary for the spiritual good of the nation.

Chinese court to escort Princess Wencheng back to Tibet.

WALKS AROUND THE MONASTERY

A few intrepid (and fit) travellers use Pabonka as a base for walks further afield. The half-day kora around Pabonka, Tashi Chöling hermitage and Chupsang Nunnery makes a nice addition to a visit to Sera Monastery. Midday can be hot here, so bring enough water.

For those who aren't so fit, an easier 20-minute walk from Pabonka leads up to **Tashi Chöling hermitage**. There's not a lot left to see at the hermitage, but it offers good views. Pilgrims drink holy spring water from the upper chapel before making a kora of the hermitage. To get here from the back of the Pabonka kora, follow the path diagonally up the hillside, following the electricity poles.

From Tashi Chöling, the trail drops into a ravine and follows this down for 30 minutes to **Chupsang Nunnery**. There are some 80 nuns resident at Chupsang and it's a very friendly place. It's about 40 minutes' walk from the nunnery to the main road into Lhasa.

An alternative route from Tashi Chöling is to hike for 40 minutes northeast up the ravine to the cliffside hermitage of **Dadren Ritrö**. You can see the hermitage from the trail. From here, trekkers can follow trails across the ridge for an hour or two to Sera Monastery or Sera Ütse (see the box, p86).

Gare (Samdeling) Nunnery is a tough four-hour trek from Tashi Chöling or Pabonka (allow around two hours for the descent). This is a serious day trek and should not be attempted until you are well adjusted to the altitude. The faint trail heads northwest from Tashi Chöling and follows a steep ridge. The nunnery, home to more than 80 nuns, is at an altitude of over 4200m.

ⓘ Getting There & Away

To get to Pabonka, take minibus 502 or 503 to the Sera Monastery turn-off on Nangre Beilu. A paved road branches left before the military hospital and leads all the way to the monastery, eventually branching right. You'll soon see Pabonka up ahead to the left, perched on its granite boulder. The 'monastery' to the right is actually Chupsang Nunnery. A ride from the junction in a rickshaw costs Y5 per person, or Y20/30 for a van/taxi.

Ganden Monastery
དགའ་ལྡན་ 甘丹寺

ELEV 4300M

Just 50km northeast of Lhasa, **Ganden** (Gāndān Sì; admission Y45; ☺dawn-dusk) was the first Gelugpa monastery and has been the main seat of this major Buddhist order ever since. If you only have time for one monastery excursion outside Lhasa, Ganden would probably be the best choice. With its stupendous views of the surrounding Kyi-chu Valley and fascinating kora, Ganden is an experience unlike the other major Gelugpa monasteries in the Lhasa area.

The monastery was founded in 1409 by Tsongkhapa, the revered reformer of the Gelugpa order, after the first Mönlam festival was performed here. Images of Tsongkhapa flanked by his first two disciples, Kedrub Je and Gyatsab Je, are found throughout the monastery. When Tsongkhapa died in 1411, the abbotship of the monastery passed to these disciples. The post came to be known as the Ganden Tripa and was earned through scholarly merit, not reincarnation. It is the Ganden Tripa, not, as one might expect, the Dalai Lama, who is the head of the Gelugpa order.

Ganden means 'joyous' in Tibetan and is the name of the Western Paradise (also known as Tushita) that is home to Jampa, the Future Buddha. There is a certain irony in this because, of all the great monasteries of Tibet, Ganden suffered most at the hands of the Red Guards, possibly because of its political influence.

Today it is the scene of extensive rebuilding, but this does not disguise the ruin that surrounds the new structures. In 1959 there were 2000 monks at Ganden; today there are just 360. The destruction was caused by artillery fire and bombing in 1959 and 1966. New chapels and residences are being opened all the time, so even pilgrims are sometimes unsure in which order to visit the chapels.

Ganden was temporarily closed to tourists in 1996 after violent demonstrations against the government's banning of Dalai Lama photos. There were further scuffles in 2006 when monks smashed a statue of the controversial deity Dorje Shugden. A new

police station and military barracks were built at the monastery following the riots of 2008.

Interior photography fees are Y20 per chapel; video fees are an amazing Y1500. For details of the trek from Ganden to Samye, see p237.

NGAM CHÖ KHANG
The first chapel you reach from the parking area is Ngam Chö Khang. It is built on the site of Tsongkhapa's original *dukhang*, and has a small shrine with images of Tsongkhapa. On the left is a *gönkhang* that houses four protective deities. The largest image is of Dorje Jigje.

DEBATING COURTYARD
Southeast of the Gomde Khang residence is the debating courtyard. You should be able to hear the clapping of hands as you pass if there is a debate in progress.

TOMB OF TSONGKHAPA
The red fortress-like structure of Tsongkhapa's mausoleum, also known as the Serkhang, is probably the most impressive of the reconstructed buildings at Ganden. It's above the prominent white chörten.

The main entrance leads to a new prayer hall with a small sand mandala and an inner Sakyamuni chapel. The protector chapel to the right is the domain of the three main Gelugpa protectors: Chögyel (far right), Dorje Jigje and Palden Lhamo. Women are not allowed into this chapel.

Exit this building, turn to the left and take the stairs leading to the upper floors. The holiest shrine here is the Yangpachen Khang (or Serdung) chapel, which houses Tsongkhapa's funeral chörten. The chapel is named after the stone in the back left, covered in offerings of yak butter, which is said to have flown from India. Red Guards destroyed both the original tomb and the preserved body of Tsongkhapa inside it. The new silver-and-gold chörten was built to house salvaged fragments of Tsongkhapa's skull. The images seated in front of the chörten are of Tsongkhapa flanked by his two principal disciples. The room also holds several holy relics attributed to Tsongkhapa. Pilgrims line up to buy votive inscriptions written in gold ink by the monks. Protective amulets and incense are sold outside the chapel and one-mao notes are stuffed in the grill outside as offerings.

Ganden Monastery

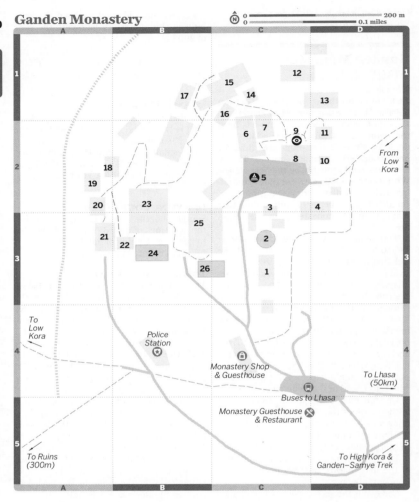

You can sometimes climb up to the roof for good views.

CHAPEL OF JAMPA

This small chapel (Jampa Lhakhang), just across from the exit of the Tomb of Tsongkhapa, holds two large images of the Future Buddha, plus the eight bodhisattvas.

ASSEMBLY HALL

The recently renovated assembly hall has statues of the 16 *arhats* and two huge statues of Tsongkhapa. Stairs lead up to the inner sanctum, the **Golden Throne Room**

(Ser Trikhang), which houses the throne of Tsongkhapa, where pilgrims get thumped on the head with the yellow hat of Tsongkhapa and the shoes of the 13th Dalai Lama.

There are two entrances on the north side of the building. The west one gives access to a 2nd-floor view of two Tsongkhapa statues, and the east one houses a library (Tengyur Lhakhang).

RESIDENCE OF THE GANDEN TRIPA

To the east of the Golden Throne Room and slightly uphill, this residence (also known as Zimchung Tridok Khang) contains the

Ganden Monastery

◎ **Sights**
1	Ngam Chö Khang	C3
2	Debating Courtyard	C3
3	Gomde Khang	C3
4	Nyare Kangtsang	D2
5	White Chörten	C2
6	Tomb of Tsongkhapa	C2
7	Chapel of Jampa	C2
8	Assembly Hall	C2
9	Golden Throne Room	C2
10	Kitchen	D2
11	Residence of the Ganden Tripa	D2
12	Samlo Kangtsang	C1
13	Shartse Kangtsang	D1
14	Lhowa Jikhang	C1
15	Lumbung Kangtsang	C1
16	Zingjung Kangtsang	C1
17	Serkong Kangtsang	B1
18	Tsar Kangtsang	A2
19	Dora Kangtsang	A2
20	Hamdong Kangtsang	A2
21	Dehor Kangtsang	A3
22	Barkhang (Printing Press)	B3
23	Jangtse Tratsang	B2
24	Debating Courtyard	B3
25	Shartse Tratsang	B3
26	Debating Courtyard	B3

living quarters and throne of the Ganden Tripa. Other rooms include a protector chapel, with statues of Demchok, Gonpo Gur (Mahakala) and Dorje Naljorma (Vajrayogini); a Tsongkhapa chapel; and a room with the living quarters of the Dalai Lama (note the photo of the 13th Dalai Lama). To the right is the 'Nirvana Room', which has a large shrine to Kurt Cobain (only kidding, it's Tsongkhapa again, who is said to have died in this room). The upper-floor library has a round platform used for creating sand mandalas.

OTHER BUILDINGS

From here, the pilgrim trail winds through various renovated *kangtsang*s (residences), which offer some good opportunities to meet the local monks away from the tourist trail.

Lumbung Kangtsang is also known as the Amdo Kangtsang. Tsongkhapa himself was from Amdo (modern-day Qīnghǎi), and many monks came from the province to study here. Look for the *rangjung* (self-arisen) and *sumjung* (with the power of speech) stone representation of Drölma.

The other two main buildings are the **Jangtse Tratsang**, an active college with an impressive main prayer hall, and the **Shartse Tratsang**, both large, recently reconstructed colleges. In the early afternoon (1.30pm to 3pm) listen out for debating in the enclosed courtyard south of the Shartse Tratsang. Nearby is the interesting Barkhang printing press.

Below the main assembly hall, the rather innocuous-looking **Nyare Kangtsang** houses a controversial statue of the deity Dorje Shugden. Worship of the deity has been outlawed by the Dalai Lama (for its alleged dangerous Tantric practices) and in 2006 monks stormed the building and smashed the statue, leading to the arrest of two monks. The statue was replaced in 2007 with the support of a Chinese government, seemingly more than happy to fan the flames of a sectarian split between local monks and the Dalai Lama. The standoff remains tense and on our last visit we found 30 Chinese soldiers barracked in the main chapel here. The statue is in the third chapel, in the far right corner, with a red face and third eye, wearing a bronze hat and riding a snow lion.

GANDEN KORA

The Ganden kora is a simply stunning walk and should not be missed. There are superb views over the braided Kyi-chu Valley along the way and there are usually large numbers of pilgrims and monks offering prayers, rubbing holy rocks and prostrating themselves along the way.

There are actually two parts to the walk: the high kora and the low kora. The high kora climbs Angkor Ri south of Ganden and then drops down the ridge to join up with the lower kora.

To walk the **high kora**, follow the path southeast of the car park, away from the monastery. After a while the track splits – the left path leads to Hepu village on the Ganden–Samye trek; the right path zigzags up the ridge to a collection of prayer flags. Try to follow other pilgrims up. It's a tough 40-minute climb to the top of the ridge, so don't try this one unless you're well acclimatised. Here, at two peaks, pilgrims burn juniper incense and give offerings of tsampa before heading west down the ridge in the direction of the monastery, stopping at several other shrines en route.

The **low kora** is an easier walk of around 45 minutes. From the car park the trail heads west up past the new police station and then around the back of the ridge behind the monastery. The trail winds past several isolated shrines and rocks that are rubbed for their healing properties or squeezed through as a karmic test. At one point, pilgrims all peer at a rock through a clenched fist in order to see visions.

A **sky-burial site** (*dürtro*) is reached shortly before the high point of the trail. Some pilgrims undertake a ritual simulated death and rebirth at this point, rolling around on the ground.

Towards the end of the kora, on the eastern side of the ridge, is **Tsongkhapa's hermitage**, a small building with relief images of Atisha, Sakyamuni, Tsepame and Palden Lhamo. These images are believed to have the power of speech. Above the hermitage is a coloured rock painting that is reached by a narrow, precipitous path. From the hermitage, the kora drops down to rejoin the monastery.

🛏 Sleeping & Eating

The simple **Monastery Guesthouse** (dm/d Y20/200) is occasionally used by trekkers headed to Samye. The better quality double rooms are above the well-stocked monastery shop just down from the car park. The **monastery restaurant** has low-grade *thugpa* (Tibetan noodles) and some fried dishes.

ℹ Getting There & Away

Ganden (Y25 return, 1¼ hours) is one of the few sights in Ü that is connected to Lhasa by public transport. At least one bus leaves from in front of the Barkhor Sq sometime between 6am and 7am, returning between 12.30pm and 1.30pm. A new paved road switchbacks the steep final 12km to the monastery.

Foreign tourists are currently required to visit the monastery with a guide but you should be able to take the pilgrim bus as long as your guide comes with you.

On the way back to Lhasa, the pilgrim bus normally stops at Sanga Monastery, set at the foot of the ruined Dagtse Dzong (or Dechen Dzong; *dzong* means 'fort').

A 4WD for a day trip to Ganden costs around Y400; a taxi might be cheaper.

Drak Yerpa ཟག་ལ་ར་པ་ 叶巴寺
ELEV 4885M

For those with an interest in Tibetan Buddhism, **Drak Yerpa** (Yèbā Sì; admission Y20) hermitage, about 16km northeast of Lhasa, is one of the holiest cave retreats in Ü. Among the many ascetics who have sojourned here are Guru Rinpoche and Atisha (Jowo-je), the Bengali Buddhist who spent 12 years proselytising in Tibet. King Songtsen Gampo also meditated in a cave, after his Tibetan wife established the first of Yerpa's chapels. The peaceful site offers lovely views and is a great day trip from Lhasa.

VISITING MONASTERIES & TEMPLES

Most monasteries and temples extend a warm welcome to foreign guests and in remote areas will often offer a place to stay for the night. Maintain this good faith by observing the following courtesies:

» Always circumambulate Buddhist monasteries and other religious objects clockwise, thus keeping shrines and chörtens (stupas) to your right.

» Don't take prayer flags or mani (prayer) stones.

» Refrain from taking photos during a prayer meeting. At other times always ask permission to take photos, especially when using a flash. The larger monasteries charge photography fees, though some monks will allow you to take a quick picture for free. If they won't, there's no point getting angry; you don't know what pressures they may be under.

» Don't wear shorts or short skirts in a monastery.

» Take your hat off when you go into a chapel (though there's generally no need to remove your shoes).

» Don't smoke in a monastery.

» Be aware that women are generally not allowed in *gönkhang* (protector chapels); always ask before entering.

At one time the hill at the base of the cave-dotted cliffs was home to Yerpa Drubde Monastery, the summer residence of Lhasa's Gyütö College at the Ramoche Temple. The monastery was destroyed in 1959. Monks have begun to return to Yerpa but numbers are strictly controlled by the government, which carries out regular patriotic study sessions.

THE CAVES
From the car park, take the left branch of the stairway to visit the caves in clockwise fashion. The first caves are the **Rigsum Gompo Cave** and the **Temjl Drubpuk**, the cave where Atisha (shown in a red hat) meditated. Look for the stone footprints of Yeshe Tsogyel in the former and the fifth Dalai Lama in the latter. At one nearby cave pilgrims squeeze through a hole in the rock wall; at another they take a sip of holy water.

The yellow **Jamkhang** has an impressive two-storey statue of Jampa flanked by Chana Dorje (Vajrapani) to the left and Namse (Vairocana) and Tamdrin (Hayagriva) to the right. Other statues are of Atisha (Jowo-je) flanked by the fifth Dalai Lama and Tsongkhapa. The upper cave is the **Drubthub-puk**, recognisable by its black yak-hair curtain. Continuing east along the ridge a detour leads up to a chörten that offers fine views of the valley.

Climb to the **Chögyal-puk**, the Cave of Songtsen Gampo. The interior chapel has a central thousand-armed Chenresig (Avalokiteshvara) statue known as Chaktong Chentong. Pilgrims circle the central rock pillar continually. A small cave and statue of Songtsen Gampo are in the right-hand corner.

The next chapel surrounds the **Lhalung-puk**, the cave where the monk Lhalung Pelde meditated after assassinating the anti-Buddhist king Langdharma in 842. A statue of the monk wearing his black hat occupies the back room.

The most atmospheric chapel is the **Dawa-puk** (Moon Cave), where Guru Rinpoche (the main statue) is said to have meditated for seven years. Look for the painting of Ekajati (Tsechigma) and other rock carvings in the left corner of the anteroom and the stone footprint of Guru Rinpoche in the inner room, to the right.

Below the main caves and to the east is the **Neten Lhakhang**, where the practice of worshipping the 16 *arhats* was first introduced. Below here is where Atisha is said to have taught. Further east is the holy mountain of Yerpa Lhari, topped by prayer flags and encircled by a kora.

There are several caves and retreats higher up the cliff-face and some fine hiking possibilities in the hills if you have time. A guesthouse is currently under construction and simple food is available.

ⓘ Getting There & Away
A daily pilgrim bus leaves from Barkhor Sq at around 7.30am for the caves, returning around 1pm. Bus drivers often call the site 'Drayab'. The paved road crosses the prayer-flag-draped 3980m Ngachen-la before turning into the side valley at Yerpa village and passing two ruined *dzongs* and a large disused dam en route to the caves. The bus does a final circuit of a large ruined chörten before screeching to a halt in a great cloud of dust.

Drölma Lhakhang
སྒྲོལ་མ་ལྷ་ཁང་ 卓玛拉康

This significant although small **monastery** (Zhuómǎlākāng; admission Y30; ⊙dawn-dusk) is jam-packed with ancient relics and hidden treasures. It's only 30 minutes drive southwest of Lhasa and is worth a stop for those interested in Tibetan Buddhism.

As you take the Lhasa–Tsetang road out of Lhasa, you'll pass a blue **rock carving** of Sakyamuni Buddha at the base of a cliff about 11km southwest of town (it's easily missed coming from the south). Nyetang village and the monastery are about 6km further on, between kilometre markers 4662 and 4663 (see the box, p149).

Drölma Lhakhang is associated with the Bengali scholar Atisha (982–1054). Atisha came to Tibet at the age of 53 at the invitation of the king of the Guge kingdom in western Tibet and his teachings were instrumental in the so-called second diffusion of Buddhism in the 11th century. Drölma Lhakhang was established at this time by one of Atisha's foremost disciples, Drömtonpa, who also founded the Kadampa order, to which the monastery belongs. It was here at Netang that Atisha died aged 72.

The 11th-century monastery was spared desecration by the Red Guards during the Cultural Revolution after a direct request from Bangladesh (which now encompasses Atisha's homeland). Apparently, Chinese premier Zhou Enlai intervened on its behalf.

The first chapel to the left is a *gönkhang*, decorated with severed stags' heads and arrow holders. As you enter and exit the main monastery building look for the two ancient guardian deities, which may even date back to the 11th-century founding of the monastery. An inner kora surrounds the main chapels.

From the entry, pass into the first chapel, the **Namgyel Lhakhang**, which contains a number of chörtens. The black-metal Kadampa-style chörten to the right reputedly holds the staff of Atisha and the skull of Naropa, Atisha's teacher. Statuary includes Atisha and the eight medicine buddhas.

The eponymous middle **Drölma Lhakhang** houses a number of relics associated with Atisha. The statues at the top include an 11th-century statue of Jowo Sakyamuni and statues of the 13th Dalai Lama (left), Green Tara, and Serlingpa (right, with a red hat), another teacher of Atisha. The lower central statue behind the grill is an image of Jampa that was reputedly saved from Mongol destruction when it shouted 'Ouch!'. There are also 21 statues of Drölma, after whom the monastery and the chapel are named.

The final **Tsepame Lhakhang** has original statues of Tsepame, cast with the ashes of Atisha, flanked by Marmedze (Dipamkara), the Past Buddha, Jampa (the Future Buddha) and the eight bodhisattvas. The small central statue of Atisha in a glass case is backed by his original clay throne. As you leave the chapel, look out for two sunken white chörtens, which hold Atisha's robes.

Upstairs is the throne room and living room of the Dalai Lamas, and to the right a library.

ⓘ Getting There & Away

Any bus heading to/from destinations south of Lhasa (eg to Shigatse, Samye Monastery, Tsetang) will take you past the entrance to Drölma Lhakhang, if you can get on it. Otherwise the temple is easily visited on a 4WD trip to or from Lhasa.

Shugsheb Nunnery

ཤུག་གཤེབ་ཨ་ནེ་དགོན་པ་ 雄色尼姑寺

ELEV 4410M

Trekkers and anyone who likes to get well off the beaten track will enjoy this excursion to Tibet's largest **nunnery** (Xióngsè Nígū

Sì; admission free), set in a large natural bowl about 65km south of Lhasa and home to over 280 nuns. The region is a favourite of bird-watchers.

From the end of the drivable road it's a steep 45-minute hike up to the village-like **nunnery**. The central hall contains a three-dimensional mandala of Drölma and statues of Guru Rinpoche, Dorje Semba (Vajrasattva), White Tara and several old lamas. Both Nyingma and Dzogchen schools are represented here. Stairs to the right lead upstairs to a chapel with a statue of Machik Labdronma (holding a double drum), the famous 11th-century adept who opened up the valley. There is also a B&W photo of one of her reincarnations.

You can hike up the hill, following the electric poles, for about 45 minutes to the **Gangri Tokar shrine** (Drubkhang), where Longchenpa, an important 14th-century Dzogchen lama, once meditated. The chapel has a cave shrine and a sacred tree stump in front of a rock image of the Dzogchen deity Rahulla.

From here fit and acclimatised hikers can climb for a couple of hours up past meditation caves (marked by prayer flags) to the ridgeline behind. The views of the Kyi-chu Valley are fantastic from here and if the weather is clear you'll get views of snowcapped 7191m Nojin Kangtsang and other Himalayan peaks to the south. From the ridgeline you can continue northwest across a boulder field for 15 minutes to a small hill (5160m) topped by a chörten that offers epic views northwards as far as Lhasa. Alternatively you can continue east along the ridge to summit the bowl's main peak.

If regulations change it might again be possible to overnight at the nunnery guesthouse. The small teahouse below the main complex offers simple meals.

ⓘ Getting There & Away

Access to the site will change once the new east-bank airport road is finished in 2011. Until then a nunnery bus leaves at 7am from Lhasa's Barkhor Sq on Monday, Wednesday and Saturday, returning to Lhasa around 5pm. The bus passes the picturesque cliffside Samanga Monastery en route and stops briefly at the small Ōshang Lhakhang on the way back.

Ü དབུས་

Includes »

Tsurphu Monastery . . .98
Nam-tso 101
Talung Monastery . . .104
Reting Monastery . . .105
Drigung Til
Monastery. 108
Tidrum Nunnery 109
Gongkar. 109
Dorje Drak
Monastery. 111
Drak Yangdzong 112
Dratang Monastery . . 113
Mindroling
Monastery. 113
Samye Monastery . . . 114
Tsetang 119
Lhamo La-tso 125

Best Places to Eat

» Friendship Snowland
Restaurant (p118)

» Yarlung Kitchen (p121)

» Tashi Restaurant (p121)

Best Places to Stay

» Drigung Til Monastery
(p108)

» Tidrum Nunnery (p109)

» Samye Monastery (p118)

Why Go?

Ü is Tibet's heartland and has almost all the landscapes you'll find across the plateau, from sand dunes and wide rivers to soaring peaks and alpine forests. Due to its proximity to Lhasa, Ü is the first taste of rural Tibet that most visitors experience, and exploring the region on foot is the best way to appreciate its scenery – fine walking opportunities abound, from day hikes to overnight treks. Ü is also the traditional power centre of Tibet, and home to its oldest buildings and most historic monasteries. A thousand-year-old temple or hilltop fort seems to lie around every bend in the road. Some of its best-known destinations are crowded in high season, so consider getting off the beaten path – there are endless valleys along the Yarlung Tsangpo river to explore. Head up one and you'll feel like you have Tibet all to yourself.

When to Go

Pilgrims converge on Tsurphu in May/June to take part in a festival of *cham* dancing, religious devotion and bouts of Tibetan-style drinking games. Festival season at Samye Monastery comes in June/July. Take part in the party then trek over the mountains to Ganden Monastery. Serene Lake Nam-tso comes alive in September for an annual horse festival. It's a good time to see horse racing and horse games before the cold sets in.

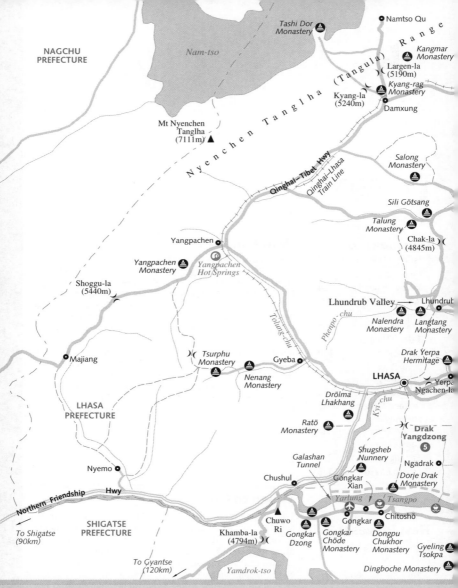

Ü Highlights

1 Divine your future by peering into the mystical waters of **Lhamo La-tso** (p125)

2 Take a scenic river journey across the Yarlung Tsangpo to the spectacular circular complex of **Samye** (p114), Tibet's first monastery

3 Hike the Yarlung Valley, including the iconic **Yumbulagang** (p123) – the first building in Tibet – and the ruins of **Rechung-puk** (p123)

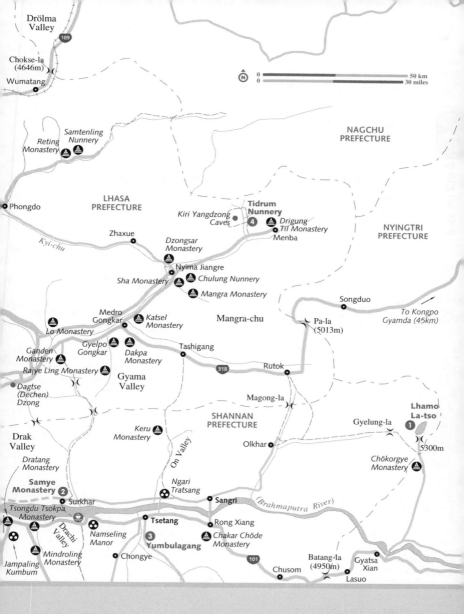

Soak your worries away in the picture-perfect hot springs of **Tidrum Nunnery** (p109)

Squeeze, drag and push yourself through the sacred cave complexes of **Drak Yangdzong** (p112), an adventurous overnight pilgrim destination

Permits

Travel in Lhasa prefecture (central and northern Ü) only requires the standard Tibet Tourism Bureau (TTB) permit. This includes such places as Tsurphu, Nam-tso, Reting, Drigung Til, Lhundrub and Nyemo. Most of the Yarlung Tsangpo Valley (formally Shannan prefecture) requires an additional permit (see p29), and you can expect your papers to be scrutinised particularly in Tsetang and possibly Samye. Lhamo La-tso requires five permits which need to be organized at least 15 days in advance of your trip.

Itineraries

Ü is a relatively small region compared to other areas of Tibet, resulting in shorter drives and fewer days on the road. The one exception is Lhamo La-tso – well off the beaten track. Some sights, including Tsurphu Monastery and even Nam-tso, can be visited as day trips from Lhasa, although spending your nights out of the city provides a slower pace and reduces backtracking.

Ü is tackled in three stages, usually broken up with stops in Lhasa (through which all roads run). If time is short your priority should be the Yarlung Valley (four to eight days), which houses the highest concentration of historic and religious sites. The road along the southern bank of the river to Tsetang is paved all the way and can be navigated in one or two days. The northern bank is rougher, more remote and requires more time. The sheer number of monasteries here can be overwhelming so it's best to just visit a few while allowing yourself more time for day hikes and treks.

With two or three more days at your disposal, head north of Lhasa to Drigung Til Monastery and Tidrum Nunnery. Some roads around here are unpaved but travel times are generally short. From Tidrum you can either go back to Lhasa or take the back roads to Reting (via Lhundrub). From Reting there is Nam-tso and Tsurphu Monastery (two to three days) to visit before heading back to Lhasa.

PUBLIC TRANSPORT

At the time of research, foreigners were not allowed to travel on public transport in Tibet. Basic information is included here in case the situation changes.

Keep in mind that at no part of this journey do you actually have to go back to Lhasa – roads from Ü connect with Tsang and eastern Tibet. From Nam-tso you can go to Yangpachen and then Majiang, eventually reaching the Friendship Hwy. From Medro Gongkar, there is the road heading east to Draksum-tso and Kham. From Gongkar (the airport), you can get onto the Southern Friendship Hwy and head west to Gyantse.

NORTHERN Ü དབུས་བྱང་

The featured sights in this section are best visited as part of a loop; first north to Tsurphu and the Nam-tso, then east to Talung and Reting and then further east to Drigung Til and Reting. The latter two places can be broken off to make a separate trip. If you are not acclimatised consider first exploring the Yarlung Valley, which is at a lower elevation.

Tsurphu Monastery
མཚུར་ཕུ་དགོན་པ་ 楚布寺

ELEV 4480M

Around 65km west of Lhasa, **Tsurphu Monastery** (Chǔbù Sì; admission Y40) is the seat of the Karmapa branch of the Kagyupa order of Tibetan Buddhism. The Karmapa are also known as the Black Hats, a title referring to a crown – a copy of which was given to the fifth Karmapa by the Chinese emperor Yong Lo in 1407. Said to be made from the hair of *dakinis* (celestial beings, known as *khandroma* in Tibetan), the black hat, embellished with gold, is now kept at Rumtek Monastery in Sikkim, India. You'll see images of the 16th Karmapa wearing the hat, holding it with his hand to stop it flying away (that's how powerful it is).

It was the first Karmapa, Dusum Khyenpa (1110–93), who instigated the concept of reincarnation and the Karmapa lineage has been maintained this way ever since.

The respected 16th Karmapa fled to Sikkim in 1959 after the popular uprising in Lhasa and founded a new centre at Rumtek. He died in 1981 and his reincarnation, Ogyen Trinley Dorje, an eight-year-old Tibetan boy from Kham, was announced amid great controversy by the Dalai Lama and other religious leaders in 1992 (see the box, p100). Over 20,000 Tibetans came to

Tsurphu to watch the Karmapa's coronation that year. In December 1999, the 17th Karmapa undertook a dramatic escape from Tibet into India via Mustang and the Annapurna region.

Tsurphu has an annual **festival** around the time of the Saga Dawa festival, on the ninth, 10th and 11th days of the fourth Tibetan month (around May). There is plenty of free-flowing *chang* (Tibetan barley beer), as well as ritual *cham* dancing and the unfurling of a great thangka on the platform across the river from the monastery.

History

Tsurphu was founded in 1187 by Dusum Khyenpa, some 40 years after he established the Karmapa order in Kham, his birthplace. It was the third Karmapa monastery to be built and, after the death of the first Karmapa, it became the head monastery for the order.

The Karmapa order traditionally enjoyed strong ties with the kings and monasteries of Tsang, a legacy that proved a liability when conflict broke out between the kings of Tsang and the Gelugpa order. When the fifth Dalai Lama invited the Mongolian army of Gushri Khan to do away with his opponents in Tsang, Tsurphu was sacked (in 1642) and the Karmapa's political clout effectively came to an end. Shorn of its political influence, Tsurphu nevertheless bounced back as an important spiritual centre and is one of the few Kagyud institutions still functioning in the Ü region. When Chinese forces invaded in 1950, around 1000 monks were in residence. Now there are about 300 monks.

VIEWING THE MONASTERY

The large **assembly hall** in the main courtyard houses a chörten (stupa) containing relics of the 16th Karmapa, as well as statues of Öpagme (Amitabha), Sakyamuni (Sakya Thukpa), and the eighth and 16th Karmapas. Look out for the mural depicting the original Tsurphu Monastery.

Scamper up the ladder to the right of the main entrance to visit the private quarters of the Karmapa; don't forget to slip the blue shower caps over your shoes before entering. An attendant monk inside will pat you with a shoe once worn by the Karmapa (bow slightly so he can tap the back of your neck). The monk will show off some of the 17th Karmapa's boyhood possessions, including a globe and toy car. His collection of books includes *Peter Pan, Fastest Cars from Around the World* and *Star Wars: The Empire Strikes Back*. He also had a good many books on bird watching and astronomy.

On the opposite side of the upper courtyard is the Karmapa's **classroom** (complete with chalkboard) and his **Audience Hall**. The Audience Hall contains the footprint of the 14th Karmapa as well as a picture of the 16th Karmapa wearing his holy headgear.

Walking west (clockwise) around the monastery complex you pass a large *darchen* (prayer pole) covered in yak hide and prayer flags to come to the main **protector chapel** *(gönkhang)*. There are five rooms, all stuffed to the brim with wrathful deities. A row of severed animal heads lines the entry portico.

The first room is dedicated to Tsurphu's protector deity, an aspect of blue Nagpo Chenpo (Mahakala) called Bernakchen. There are also statues of Palden Lhamo (Shri Devi) and Tamdrin (Hayagriva), as well as a spirit trap and several dead birds.

The third room features Dorje Drolo, a wrathful form of Guru Rinpoche astride a tiger, and the fourth room features the Kagyud protector Dorje Phurba holding a ritual dagger. The fifth room contains a statue of Tseringma, a protectress associated with Mt Everest, riding a snow lion.

The large building behind the *gönkhang* is the **Serdung Chanpo**, which once served as the residence of the Karmapa. The side chapel features new statues of all 16 previous Karmapas.

The **Lhakhang Chenmo**, which is to the right of the Serdung Chanpo, houses a new 20m-high statue of Sakyamuni that rises through three storeys; this replaced a celebrated 13th-century image destroyed during the Cultural Revolution.

Behind the Serdung Chanpo and Lhakhang Chenmo is the sprawling **Chökang Gang Monastery**, the residence of the exiled regent of Tsurphu.

The outer walls of the monastery are marked at four corners by four coloured chörtens.

TSURPHU KORA

The Tsurphu kora, a walk of around 4km (two hours), is quite taxing if you are not acclimatised to the altitude. It ascends 150m, past springs, shrines and meditation retreats, providing splendid views of Tsurphu below.

THE KARMAPA CONUNDRUM

Reincarnation is an integral part of Buddhist doctrine and culture but it is by no means an exact science. The controversy over the selection of the 17th Karmapa is a fine example of how things can go horribly wrong when opinions differ on the legitimacy of a newly chosen *trulku* (incarnate lama).

In 1981 the 16th Karmapa died in Chicago. Administration of the Karmapa sect in Sikkim was passed down to four regents, two of whom, Situ Rinpoche and Shamar Rinpoche, have become embroiled in a dispute that has caused a painful rift in the exiled Tibetan community.

In early 1992 the four regents announced the discovery of a letter written by the 16th Karmapa that provided critical clues as to the whereabouts of his reincarnation, eight-year-old Ogyen Trinley Dorje.

Two weeks after one of the regents was killed in a road accident, Shamar Rinpoche announced that the mystery letter was a fraud, but it was too late. By early June clues from the letter had been deciphered, Ogyen Trinley Dorje had been found in eastern Tibet and the Dalai Lama had made a formal announcement supporting the boy's candidature.

Shamar Rinpoche opposed the Dalai Lama's decision and began a letter-writing campaign. Meanwhile, the Chinese authorities formally enthroned the 17th Karmapa at Tsurphu, using the occasion to announce that they had a 'historical and legal right to appoint religious leaders in Tibet'. In March 1994, Shamar Rinpoche announced that he had discovered the rightful reincarnation, a boy named Tenzin Chentse (also known as Thaye Dorje), who had been spirited out of China to Delhi.

In December 1999, the then 14-year-old 17th Karmapa dramatically fled Tibet into India. In a letter left behind at Tsurphu he told the Chinese he was going to collect the black hat of the Karmapa (taken to India by the 16th Karmapa when he fled Tibet in 1959), as well as several relics, including a human skull encased in silver.

The flight of the Karmapa was a particular blow for the Chinese. The Karmapa ranks as the third-most important lama in Tibet after the Panchen Lama and the Dalai Lama and is the only high-level reincarnation recognised by both the Chinese and Tibetan authorities. China's fury over the escape was levelled at the Karmapa's tutor Yongzin Nyima who spent 15 months in jail for his alleged involvement.

For now the rivalry between the Karmapas is at a stalemate. Ogyen Trinley Dorje has been granted refugee status and residence at the Gyuto Monastery in Dharamsala, but the Indian authorities, in an attempt to avoid a political dispute with China, have not allowed him to travel to Rumtek (until recently China did not recognise India's claim to Sikkim). The other Karmapa, Tenzin Chentse, has established his base at Kalimpong, West Bengal. The rival Karmapas have never met, although both have indicated they are open to the idea.

For more on the starkly differing viewpoints, see the pro-Karmapa website at www.rumtek.org and the pro–Shamar Rinpoche sites at www.karmapa.org and www.karmapa-issue.org. Mick Brown's book *The Dance of 17 Lives* is a good investigation into the controversy.

To follow the kora take the track west of Tsurphu that leads up past walls of mani (prayer) stones to a walled garden (see p240). Bear right here up to a *dürtro* (sky burial site) and follow the cairns that snake up the hill to a small pass marked by prayer flags. The kora then winds in and out of the ridges above the monastery and detours up to the Samtenling retreat, before descending eastward into a gully to the chörten at the northeastern corner of the monastery.

💤 Sleeping

The small **Monastery Guesthouse** (dm Y25), opposite the main assembly hall, has damp and dark dorm rooms with four or six beds on concrete floors.

ℹ Getting There & Away

About 40km west of Lhasa, the road to Tsurphu crosses the Tolung-chu near the railroad bridge. From here it's another 25km up a rough dirt track to the monastery.

Most travellers come here as part of a 4WD tour, visiting Tsurphu as a side trip on the way to Nam-tso. The road to Tsurphu passes Nenang Monastery, home to the young 11th Powa Rinpoche. It's worth a quick stop, although you will probably need to have this listed on your itinerary.

A minibus (two hours) goes to Tsurphu from Lhasa's Barkhor Sq around 7am, leaving when full. It heads back to Lhasa at around 2pm, but confirm this with the driver.

Nam-tso གནམ་མཚོ 纳木错

ELEV 4730M

Approximately 240km northwest of Lhasa, **Nam-tso** (Nàmùcuò; adult/student Y120/60) is the second-largest saltwater lake in China and one of the most beautiful natural sights in Tibet. It is over 70km long, reaches a width of 30km and is 35m at its deepest point. When the ice melts in late April, the lake is a miraculous shade of turquoise and there are magnificent views of the nearby mountains. The wide open spaces, dotted with the tents of local *drokpas* (nomads), are intoxicating.

The Nyenchen Tanglha (Tangula) range, with peaks of more than 7000m, towers over the lake to the south – it was these mountains that Heinrich Harrer and Peter Aufschnaiter crossed on their incredible journey to Lhasa (their expedition is documented in the book *Seven Years in Tibet*).

The lake is at 4730m so you'll need to acclimatise in and around Lhasa for a few days before heading this way. It is not unusual for visitors to get altitude sickness on an overnight stay out at the lake.

For more on the trek to Nam-tso over the Kyang-la, see p256. Those seeking detailed information on Nam-tso should refer to *Divine Dyads: Ancient Civilization in Tibet* by John Vincent Bellezza (though this book may be hard to find).

TASHI DOR MONASTERY
བཀྲ་ཤིས་མདོ་དགོན་པ 扎西岛寺

Most travellers head for Tashi Dor (Zhāxīdǎo Sì in Chinese), situated on a hammerhead of land that juts into the southeastern corner of the lake. Here at the foot of two wedge-shaped hills are a couple of small chapels with views back across the clear turquoise waters to the huge snowy Nyenchen Tanglha massif (7111m).

Your initial experience here is unlikely to inspire visions of Shangri-La. The scraggly tourist base near Tashi Dor is hard on the eyes and the touts here can be pretty aggressive in forcing you onto the back of a yak or horse. Try to ignore all this and push ahead to the monastery.

The first **chapel** is the smaller but more atmospheric of the two. The main statue is of Luwang Gyelpo, the king of the *nagas* (snake spirits). Pilgrims test their sin by lifting the heavy stone of Nyenchen Tanglha, the god who resides in the nearby mountain of the same name (and who is also the protector of Marpo Ri, on which the Potala is built).

The second, main **chapel** features a central Guru Rinpoche statue and the trinity of Öpagme, Chenresig and Pema Jigme, known collectively as the Cholong Dusom. Protectors include Nyenchen Tanglha on a horse and the blue-faced Nam-tso, the goddess of the lake, who rides a water serpent. Both gods are rooted deep in Bön belief. Several other chapels and retreats are honeycombed into the surrounding cliffs.

There are some fine walks in this area. The short **kora** takes less than an hour (roughly 4km). It leads off west from the accommodation area to a hermit's cave hidden behind a large splinter of rock. The trail continues round to a rocky promontory of cairns and prayer flags, where pilgrims undertake a ritual washing, and then continues past several caves and a *chaktsal gang* (prostration point). The twin rock towers here look like two hands in the *namaste* greeting and are connected to the male and female attributes of the meditational deity Demchok (Chakrasamvara). Pilgrims squeeze into the deep slices of the nearby cliff face as a means of sin detection. They also drink water dripping from cave roofs and some swallow 'holy dirt'.

From here the path curves around the shoreline and passes a group of ancient rock paintings, where pilgrims test their merit by attempting to place a finger in a small hole with their eyes closed. At the northeastern corner of the hill is the **Mani Ringmo**, a large mani wall at the end of which is a *chörten* with a *chakje* (handprint) of the third Karmapa. From here you can hike up to the top of the hill for good views.

If you have enough time, it's well worth walking to the top of the larger of the two hills (6km, two hours return). There are superb views to the northeast of the Tangl-ha range, which marks the modern border between Tibet and Qīnghǎi (Amdo).

On the eastern edge of the peninsula is a **bird sanctuary** populated with migratory birds between April and November. Species to look out for include bar-headed geese and black-necked cranes.

For the seriously devout there is a pil-grim route that circles the entire lake. It takes around 18 days to make a full lap, staying at small chapels and hermitages along the way.

NOMADS

One attraction of a trip to Nam-tso is the opportunity to get a peek at the otherwise inaccessible life of Tibet's *drokpas*, seminomadic herders who make their home in the Changtang, Tibet's vast and remote northern plateau. In the Changtang, the *drokpas* are known as Changpa. You may also get the chance to visit a *drokpa* camp along the road from Sok to Nagchu or on the trek from Ganden to Samye.

Nomad camps are centred on their spider-like brown or black yak-hair tents. These are usually shared by one family, though a smaller subsidiary tent may be used when a son marries and has children of his own. The interior of a nomad tent holds all the family's possessions. There will be a stove for cooking and boiling water and also a family altar dedicated to Buddhist deities and various local protectors, including those of the livestock, tent pole and hearth. The principal diet of nomads is tsampa (roasted-barley flour) and yak butter (mixed together with tea), dried yak cheese and sometimes yak meat.

Tending the herds of yaks and sheep is carried out by the men during the day. Women and children stay together in the camp, where they are guarded by one of the men and the ferocious Tibetan mastiffs that are the constant companions of Tibet's nomads. The women and children usually spend the day weaving blankets and tan-ning sheepskins.

With the onset of winter it is time to go to the markets of an urban centre. The farm-ers of Tibet do the same, and trade between nomads and farmers provides the former with tsampa and the latter with meat and butter. Most nomads these days have a winter home base and only make established moves to distant pastures during the rest of the year.

The nomads of Tibet have also traditionally traded in salt, which is collected from the Changtang and transported south in bricks, often to the border with Nepal, where it is traded for grain (as documented in the film *The Saltmen of Tibet*). These annual caravans are fast dying out. Traditional life suffered its greatest setback during the Cultural Revolution, when nomads were collectivised and forcibly settled by the gov-ernment. In 1981 the communes were dissolved and the collectivised livestock divided equally, with everyone getting five yaks, 25 sheep and seven goats.

Nomads' marriage customs differ from those of farming communities. When a child reaches a marriageable age, inquiries are made, and when a suitable match is found the two people meet and exchange gifts. If they like each other, these informal meet-ings may go on for some time. The date for a marriage is decided by an astrologer, and when the date arrives the family of the son rides to the camp of the prospective daughter-in-law to collect her. On arrival there is a custom of feigned mutual abuse that appears to verge on giving way to violence at any moment. This may continue for several days before the son's family finally carry off the daughter to their camp and she enters a new life.

Drokpas now number around 500,000 across the plateau. Government incentives are forcing the settlement of nomads, further reducing their numbers and grazing grounds. The introduction of the motorbike has further transformed nomad life. Pres-sure also comes in the form of enforced migration dates and winter housing, as well as attitude changes within the *drokpas* themselves, as young people are fleeing the grasslands in search of a 'better life' in urban centres. How far into the 21st century their way of life will persist is a matter for debate among Tibetologists.

🛏 Sleeping & Eating

There are now half a dozen places to stay at Tashi Dor, which these days resembles a sort of Wild West mining camp, with lots of ugly metal shacks that serve as hotels, restaurants and shops.

Bedding is provided at all places but nights can get very cold, so it's a good idea to bring a sleeping bag and warm clothes. Between the altitude, cold and the barking dogs, most people sleep fitfully at best. Accommodation is only available between April and October. There are plenty of decent camping spots far away from the hubbub if you are prepared for the cold.

Tent restaurants offer Sichuanese dishes at slightly inflated prices. Several places sell delicious locally made yoghurt.

TOP CHOICE Holy Lake Namtso Guesthouse

GUESTHOUSE $

(神湖纳木措客栈; Shénhú Nàmùcuò Kèzhàn; ☏0891-696 4312; dm/d Y50/120) While most places at Nam-tso look like glorified toolsheds, this one is an actual structure. The rooms surround a comfortable sitting area where you can get Chinese or Tibetan meals. It's on the right as you enter, near the police station.

Yáng's Bīnguǎn Sheep Guesthouse

GUESTHOUSE $

(羊宾馆; Yáng Bīnguǎn; ☏0891-651 1201; dm/r Y50/160) This is one of the better-run camps at Nam-tso. The metal cabins aren't pretty, but the rooms inside are OK and include proper beds and clean sheets. Rooms have electrical outlets so you can power your devices (after 8pm). The nicest part about the place is its cosy restaurant warmed by a dung-fuelled stove. Chinese and Tibetan dishes are available, plus all the *shagambo* (dried yak meat) you can stomach.

Tashi Island Hotel

GUESTHOUSE $

(扎西岛宾馆; ☏136 3898 9497; Zhāxīdǎo Bīnguǎn; dm Y30-40) This place feels like a neglected stepchild compared to the better Sheep Guesthouse right next door. But it's a friendly place and has clean dorm rooms at bargain-basement prices.

Damshung Pema Hotel

HOTEL $$

(当雄县白马宾馆; Dāngxióng Xiàn Báimǎ Bīnguǎn; ☏0891-611 2098; dm Y30-48, d Y318, discounts of 25%; ❊) Located in the middle of the gateway town of Damxung (Dāngxióng; 4220m), this is the best place to stay in town if it's late. The Tibetan atmosphere

makes a pleasant change, with rooms with bathrooms decorated with Tibetan carpets and traditional furniture. The dorm rooms share squat toilets but no showers.

Damxung is a popular lunch spot en route to Nam-tso. There are several good Muslim noodle joints as you enter the town from the south, including the **Línxià Shuāngchéng Qīngzhēn Fànguǎn** (临夏双城清真饭馆; dishes Y6-10).

❶ Getting There & Away

By road it's 9km to the checkpost where you pay the entry fee, a further 16km steep uphill journey to the 5190m Largen-la, 7km to a junction and then a circuitous 30km to Tashi Dor. Around 4km before the checkpost, a drivable dirt road offers a possible detour to Kyang-rag Monastery (see p257). Another road leads north from the ticket gate to Kangmar Monastery.

Lhasa travel agencies offer minibus tours for around Y250 per person, which often includes the Y120 entry ticket. However, as day trips go, this one is pretty long and exhausting. It's better to make this a two-day trip, stopping off at Tsurphu and Yangpachen (see p244) en route.

Lhundrub County

ལྷུན་གྲུབ་གཞུང་

☏0894 / ELEV 3800M

The peaceful Lhundrub County, around 70km from Lhasa, is dotted with small monasteries and temples that rarely get a foreign visitor. Most of the sites here are spread across the lush and fertile Phenyul Valley. If you are on a 4WD tour you'll most likely pass through Phenyul while travelling between Medro Gongkar and Talung Monastery.

LHUNDRUB ལྷུན་གྲུབ་ 林周

The main town in the valley is Lhundrub (Línzhōu), which serves as a useful base. The northwestern section of town has the main shops and restaurants, the centre has the interesting **Ganden Chökhorling Monastery**, and the southeast has the minibus stand.

If you need to stay the night, the **Government Guesthouse** (政府招待所; Zhèngfǔ Zhāodàisuǒ; ☏139 8909 7905; r without/with bathroom Y80/120) has the best rooms in town. But take caution here because the compound is home to a pack of vicious dogs (our guide was surrounded and had to frantically beat them off with his satchel!).

DON'T MISS

STRETCHING YOUR LEGS

Tightly planned 4WD tours sometimes have the effect of dampening your desire for the unpredictable. Sitting in the car too long can also get your legs itchin' for a walk. One sure way of shaking things up is to embed some day hikes and koras into your itinerary. The following are some trips by foot you could consider taking while in Ü.

» Tsurphu kora (p99)

» Drak Yangdzong (p112)

» Chim-puk (p118)

» Dorje Drak kora (p111)

» Tashi Dor kora (p101)

» Gangpo Ri (p120)

» Hike to Jampaling (near Dratang; p113)

» Yarlung Valley Trek (p122)

It's best to drive into the compound and straight to the hotel.

Minibuses to Lhundrub (one hour) run every 20 minutes from Lhasa's Eastern Bus Station, departing when full. The last bus back to Lhasa returns around 7pm.

NALENDRA MONASTERY
ན་ལེན་ད་དགོན་པ་ 那仁札寺

Ruins still dwarf the rebuilding work at Nalendra Monastery (Nàrénzhá Sì in Chinese), founded in 1435 by the lama Rongtonpa (1367–1449), a contemporary of Tsongkhapa. It was largely destroyed in 1959.

To get an idea of the original layout, look closely at the mural on the immediate left as you enter the **main assembly hall**. The impressive *gönkhang* (women cannot enter) has a central Gompo Gur, a form of Nagpo Chenpo and protector of the Sakyapa school, as well as statues of Pehar (on an elephant) and Namse (Vairocana, on a snow lion), both in the left corner. Look for the three huge wild yak heads and the stuffed goat, in varying states of decay.

The main hall has a statue of Rongtonpa in a glass case. The inner sanctum features Rongtonpa in the front centre, flanked by two Sakyapa lamas. The same room contains the silver funeral stupa of Khenpo Tsultrim Gyeltsen, who is credited with rebuilding Nalendra after its destruction during the Cultural Revolution.

The chapel to the left contains hundreds of statues of Buddha Sakyamuni which pilgrims crawl under. The main statue in this chapel is Sakya Pandita Kunga Gyaltsen. In the centre is an unusual statue of Vairocana, which has four faces.

Other chapels worth popping into include the Tsar Kangtsang, still under renovation, the *shedra* (monastic college), the Jampa Kangtsang (with its interesting statue of skeletons in a *yabyum* pose), and the ruins of the *dzong* outside the monastery gate to the west.

Talung Monastery
སྟག་ལུང་དགོན་པ་ 达龙寺

ELEV 4150M

Dynamited by Red Guards and now in ruins in the green fields of the Pak-chu Valley, the sprawling monastic complex of Talung (or Taglung; Dálóng Sì in Chinese) is around 120km north of Lhasa by road. Rebuilding is currently underway, but not on the scale of other, more important, monasteries in the area.

Talung was founded in 1180 by Tangpa Tashipel as the seat of the Talung school of the Kagyupa order. At one time it may have housed some 7000 monks (it currently has 160), but was eventually eclipsed in importance and grandeur by its former branch, the Riwoche Tsuglhakhang in eastern Tibet (p209).

The site's most important structure was its **Tsuglhakhang** (grand temple), also known as the Red Palace. The building was reduced to rubble but its impressively thick stone walls remain.

To the south is the main assembly hall, the Targyeling Lhakhang. Look out for the destroyed set of three chörtens, one of which contained the remains of the monastery's founder.

To the west in the main monastery building, the Choning (Tsenyi) Lhakhang is used as a debating hall and has a statue of the bearded Tashipel to the right. The fine *cham* masks are worn during a festival on the eighth day of the eighth month (the festival clothes are in a metal box in the corner). Snarling stuffed wolves hang from the ceiling of the protector chapel next door. The Jagji Lhakhang behind the Choning

Lhakhang has fine new murals around a central mandala.

Down in the centre of the village is the renovated Tashikang Tsar, the residence of the local reincarnation Tsedru Rinpoche, who died in 2007. The Rinpoche's body is currently housed in the Targyeling Lhakhang. It will remain here for three years, drying under a pile of salt, after which it will be placed inside a new building, the Kumbun Lhakhang.

An hour's walk north of the turn-off to Talung brings you to Sili Götsang, an amazing eagle's-nest hermitage perched high above the main road. The monks at Talung have recently renovated the hermitage and added a new protector shrine dedicated to Nagpo Chenpo.

The monastery is 2.5km west of the main road to Phongdo. For information on reaching the monastery, see p106.

Reting Monastery

རྭ་སྒྲེང་དགོན་པ།　热振寺

ELEV 4100M

Pre-1950 photographs show Reting Monastery (Rèzhèn Sì; admission Y30) sprawled gracefully across the flank of a juniper-clad hill in the Rong-chu Valley. Like Ganden Monastery, it was devastated by Red Guards and its remains hammer home the tragic waste caused by the ideological zeal of the Cultural Revolution. Still, the site is one of the most beautiful in the region. The Dalai Lama has stated that should he ever return to Tibet it is at Reting, not Lhasa, that he would like to reside.

The monastery dates back to 1056. It was initially associated with Atisha (Jowo-je) but in its later years it had an important connection with the Gelugpa order and the Dalai Lamas. Two regents – the de facto rulers of Tibet for the interregnum between the death of a Dalai Lama and the majority of his next reincarnation – were chosen from the Reting abbots. The fifth Reting Rinpoche was regent from 1933 to 1947. He played a key role in the search for the current Dalai Lama and served as his senior tutor. He was later accused of collusion with the Chinese and died in a Tibetan prison.

The sixth Reting Rinpoche (Tenzin Jigne) died in 1997. In January 2001 the Chinese announced that a boy named Sonam Phuntsog had been identified out of 700 candidates as the seventh Reting Rinpoche; the Dalai Lama opposes the choice.

Reting is 25km from the crossroads settlement of **Phongdo** (旁多乡, Pángduō Xiāng), which has a ruined *dzong* and is overlooked by a mountain of near-perfect conical proportions. There are a handful of shops and restaurants here.

VIEWING THE MONASTERY

The current main assembly hall, or Tsogchen, is half its original size. Enter the hall to the right to get to the main inner shrine, the Ütse (women not allowed). The central statue of Jampai Dorje is an unusual amalgam of the gods Jampelyang (Manjushri), Chana Dorje (Vajrapani) and Chenresig (Avalokiteshvara). To the left is an ancient thangka of Drölma that, according to the resident monks, was brought here by Atisha himself. A wooden box beside the altar holds the giant molar of Sangye Wösong, the Buddha before Sakyamuni.

To the left of the Ütse entrance (on the outside of the Ütse) is a rare mural of the 14th (current) Dalai Lama (though it doesn't really resemble him). Next to the painting are some interesting photos of the monastery that date to 1948. To the right of the entrance is a picture of the current Reting Rinpoche and a footprint and photo of the fifth Reting Rinpoche. In front of the entrance is a platform used for creating sand mandalas. Behind the Ütse is a storeroom stuffed with Tantric drums and Buddha statues.

As you leave the chapel look for a second hall to your right. The hall contains a gold chörten with the remains of the sixth Reting Rinpoche. Lining the back wall are statues of all six previous Reting Rinpoches. The metal box in the right corner holds a giant thangka (known as a *thongdrol*), unveiled once a year.

The monastery is still graced by surrounding juniper forest, said to have sprouted from the hairs of its founder Dromtompa. A 40-minute kora leads from the guesthouse around the monastery ruins, passing several stone carvings, a series of eight chörtens and an active sky burial site. Further up the hillside is the *drubkhang* (meditation retreat) where Tsongkhapa composed the Lamrim Chenmo (Graduated Path), a key Gelugpa text. The large escarpment draped with prayer flags to the right is the Sengye Drak (Lion's Rock), where there are several more retreats.

A pleasant hour-long (2.5km) walk northeast of Reting leads to the village-like **Samtenling Nunnery**, home to over 240 nuns. The main chapel houses the meditation cave of Tsongkhapa; to the right is a stone footprint of Tsongkhapa and a hoofprint belonging to the horse of the protectress Pelden Lhamo. The trail branches off to the nunnery from the sky burial site to the northeast of the monastery.

The **monastery guesthouse** (dm Y40) offers basic dormitory rooms and simple meals.

ⓘ Getting There & Away

A two-day 4WD tour from Lhasa, taking in Reting and Talung monasteries, costs around Y1000 to Y1300.

A public bus departs for Reting (four hours) daily at 8am from the Lhasa Eastern Bus Station, passing near Talung and returning the following day.

Road to Drigung Til Monastery

Drigung Til Monastery and Tidrum Nunnery, around 120km northeast of Lhasa, are popular destinations for travellers looking for a short trip near the Tibetan capital. The steep-sided valleys are only a few hours' drive from the capital but offer a glimpse into rural life in Tibet. But change is coming to the region: towns are being developed, rivers dammed and hillsides mined. Despite these intrusions many locals carry on as usual and there are plenty of opportunities to stop off at remote villages as you monastery-hop your way through the region.

GYAMA VALLEY རྒྱ་མ་སྲོང་ 甲玛

This valley (Jiǎmǎ in Chinese), 60km east of Lhasa, is famed as the birthplace of Tibet's greatest king, Songtsen Gampo, who lived here until he became king at the age of 15. It's an easy detour if you are headed for Drigung Til, or a pleasant place to explore on bike.

From the main highway it's 2km south to the **Gyelpo Gongkar**, a chapel just east of the tarmac road and dedicated to Songtsen Gampo and his two wives. On his left is Nepali wife Bhrikuti Didev and on his right is Chinese wife Princess Wencheng. The original building dates from the 7th century and resembles a small Yumbulagang.

From here it's 3km up the valley to the **Rajye Ling Monastery** and, in the compound behind, the huge Kadam-style funeral **chörten** of Sangye On (1251–96), a master of the Talung School and founder of the Riwoche Tsuglhakhang (see p209). At the time of research, bulldozers were moving huge mounds of earth around the site as part of a plan to beautify the monastery grounds.

The small monastery boasts some fine murals and a stone mantra that is said to have appeared naturally at the moment of Songtsen Gampo's birth. You may be slightly confused upon entry because although this is in fact a monastery it is cared for by two nuns. The main statue is a 1000-arm, 1000-eye Avalokiteshrava.

From the monastery, head back down the main road and turn left towards the new Tibetan-style building with the chimney-like tower. The building was under construction at the time of research but workers here told us it was destined to be a **Songtsen Gampo Museum**. Just beyond the new museum are three **Dumburi chörtens** and the nearby shrine and natural springs that mark the birthplace of Songtsen Gampo. Archaeologists have linked the nearby ruins of Jampa Mingyur Ling to the palace that Songtsen Gampo's father built after leaving the Chongye Valley.

To get to the valley by public transport, take a frequent Medro Gongkar–bound minibus from Lhasa's Eastern Bus Station (40 minutes) and get off at kilometre marker 4572, 8km before Medro Gongkar.

MEDRO GONGKAR
མལ་གྲོ་གུང་དཀར 墨竹工卡
☏0891 / POP 2000 / ELEV 3600M

On the wide banks of the Kyi-chu, 75km northeast of Lhasa, Medro Gongkar (Mòzhú Gōngkǎ) is just a pit stop en route to Drigung. If you have time it's worth stopping at **Katsel Monastery**, 3km from town on the road to Drigung. Legend has it that this Kagyupa-order monastery was founded by the 7th-century King Songtsen Gampo, who was led here by the Buddha disguised as a doe with antlers. The temple is also significant as one of the original demoness-subduing temples (see the box, p56) – it pinned the monster's right shoulder.

There are several places to stay in Medro Gongkar, as well as lots of Chinese restaurants. An **internet cafe** (网吧; wǎngbā; Nan-

KILOMETRE MARKERS ALONG THE KYI-CHU

MARKER	FEATURE
4632	Lhasa Bridge
4611	Dagtse/Dechen Dzong and Sanga Monastery
4610/09	Dagtse bridge, turn-off to Lhundrub
4592/1	turn-off to Ganden Monastery
4587	large chörten surrounded by three others
4584/3	Lhamo Monastery
4572	Gyama village and valley
4569	roadside chörten
4564	Medro Gongkar

jing Xilu; ☉24hr) is located in the town centre. Walking out of the Tsijin La-Tso Bīnguǎn turn right and make the first left on Nanjing Xilu – it's a couple of doors down on the right.

Tsijin La-Tso Hotel　　　　　　HOTEL $
(思金拉措宾馆; Sījīn Lǎcuò Bīnguǎn; ☎613 2888; d/tr Y120/140) The best place in town is a Tibetan-style edifice in the middle of the main drag. Showers tend to dribble water and the toilets don't flush right but the rooms are bright and generally clean. A highlight is the billiards hall on the 2nd floor.

Jama Trigang Tashi Guesthouse　　　　BUDGET HOTEL $
(甲玛志康扎西旅馆; Jiǎmǎ Zhìkāng Zhàxī Lǚguǎn; ☎613 2666; d per bed Y30) There are plenty of types of rooms here but the best bet are the triples. Note that your guide may not allow you to stay here, on account of it being only a one-star hotel. It's near the east end of town, where the minibuses depart for Nyima Jiangre.

Minibuses go between Lhasa's Eastern Bus Station and Medro Gongkar (one hour) every 20 minutes or so until around 8pm. Smaller minibuses continue, when full, up to Nyima Jiangre from the east end of town.

NYIMA JIANGRE (DRIGUNG QU)
འབྲི་གུང་ཆུ་ཤུལ་ 尼玛江热
☎0891 / POP 1900
The small town of Nyima Jiangre (Nímǎ Jiāngrè in Chinese), halfway between Me-

dro Gongkar and Drigung Til, has a Wild West feel to it, with dusty traders coming in to stock up on goods, and rocky escarpments forming the town's backdrop. It's set at the auspicious confluence of three rivers. Chinese engineers have not overlooked the strategic location; an ugly dam has been stretched across the valley floor, forming a shallow reservoir. Most travellers blow through the town in a rush to reach Drigung Til, but the intrepid may want to stop off and explore some little-visited monasteries near the town.

About 1km northwest of town is the Drigungpa-school **Dzongsar Monastery**. A short but steep climb brings you up to a monastery located on a jagged slope; the name of the place soon becomes clear – the monastery is a converted *dzong*. Apart from the usual statues of Guru Rinpoche and Sakyamuni inside the main assembly hall, there is a two-armed standing Chenresig, as well as the founder of the Drigung school, Jikten Gonpo (and his golden footprints). On the left side of the hall, look out for the picture of the 13th Dalai Lama with his dog resting by his feet. The main altar also contains a couple of photos of the 14th Dalai Lama; a sight you will not see at larger monasteries. Below the hall in a protector chapel is an icon of Abchi, the white female protector of the region. The monastery is home to 29 friendly monks; if it's not too busy they may invite you into their quarters for a spot of Tibetan tea.

Also nearby is **Sha Monastery**, 2km southeast of Nyima Jiangre, dedicated to the Dzogchen suborder. A highlight of the monastery is the pair of 9th century *dorings* (inscribed pillars) that flank the entrance gate. These have inscriptions that detail the estates given to Nyangben Tengzin Zangpo, a boyhood chum of King Tritsug Detsen, who ruled Tibet and much of Central Asia. It was Nyangben Tengzin Zangpo who founded the monastery. Only one of the pillars remains intact.

Once inside the temple, look out for the remains of a stuffed snow leopard. To the right is a side protector chapel with the Dzogchen trinity of Dorje Lekpa, Rahulla and Ekajati, and a mask depicting the mountain deity Tseringma. This chapel contains the hoofprints of the goat that allegedly carried both Dorje Lekpa and the inscribed pillars to the monastery. Continue through an unusual courtyard encircling a huge chörten, to an upstairs chapel above the entrance.

If you need a place to stay, try **Amdo Naibeykhang** (安多招待所; Āndzuǒ Zhāodàisuǒ; ✆158 8909 6198; dm Y30) at the east edge of town. It has four-bed dorms in clean rooms with concrete floors. It also has the town's only real toilet. It's located above a tyre repair shop and next to a bathhouse.

For food, the **Báizhēn Fànguǎn** (白珍饭馆; meals Y10-20) is a cosy teahouse that offers sweet tea and *shemdre* (yak, potatoes and rice).

It's approximately 35km to Drigung Til from Nyima Jiangre.

Drigung Til Monastery

འབྲི་གུང་མཐིལ་ 直贡梯寺

ELEV 4150M

Although it suffered some damage in the Cultural Revolution, **Drigung Til Monastery** (Zhígòngtǐ Sì; admission Y30) is in better shape than most of the other monastic centres in this part of Ü. First established in 1167, it is the head monastery of the Drigungpa school of the Kagyupa order and the most famous sky burial site in central Tibet. By 1250 it was already vying with Sakya for political power – as it happened, not a particularly good move as the Sakya forces joined with the Mongol army to sack Drigung Til in 1290. Thus chastened, the monastery subsequently devoted itself to the instruction of contemplative meditation. There are around 200 monks at Drigung Til these days.

Drigung Til sprouts from a high, steep ridge overlooking the Zhorong-chu Valley. A steep thread of a path makes its way up into the monastic complex, although there is also vehicle access from the eastern end of the valley. The 180-degree views from the main courtyard are impressive and a serene stillness pervades the site. It's a joy just to hang out in the courtyard by the monastery to take in the view with the monks after their morning prayer.

The **main assembly hall** is probably the most impressive of the buildings. The central figure inside is Jigten Sumgon, the founder of the monastery. Guru Rinpoche (in the corner) and Sakyamuni are to the left. Upstairs on the 1st-floor Serkhang (golden room or chapel) you can see statues of Jigten Sumgon and his two successors, all wearing red hats. Jigten's footprint is set in a slab of rock at the foot of the statue. From the 1st floor you can go upstairs to a balcony and a circuit of prayer wheels. Steps lead up from here to the chörtens of two previous abbots.

The monastery **kora** heads up the hill to the main *dürtro*. This is the holiest sky burial site in the Lhasa region – people travel hundreds of kilometres to bring their deceased relatives here. Tourists are no longer welcome to view the sky burials, though monks say that it's fine to hike up to the site when no sky burials are taking place. It's possible to see the circular platform of stones where the bodies are cut up and the adjacent buildings where the shaved hair of the dead is stored (the site is purified once a year in the sixth lunar month and the hair is disposed of). If the birds are circling, don't go up to the site.

Back in the courtyard, look right to the reconstructed protector chapel, the **Abchi Lhakhang**, which houses an impressive bronze statue of the protector Abchi Chudu. In the rear chapel of this building is a photo of Bachung (Agu) Rinpoche, a hermit who lived in the caves above Drigung Til for 65 years. The monks of Drigung Til still praise Bachung Rinpoche for his efforts in helping to rebuild the monastery. Also look out for the pair of yak horns on the left wall of the chapel, after which Drigung is said to be named (a *dri* is a female yak and *gung* means 'camp'). The name may also derive from the hillside, which is said to be in the shape of a yak.

It's possible to stay at the scruffy **Monastery Guesthouse** (dm/d Y15/30) in the main courtyard. You can get simple meals at the monastery kitchen and there's a small shop. A second **Monastery Guesthouse** (per bed Y20), just as bare-boned but a little cleaner, is located in Menba (the village below Drigung). It's a popular base for visiting herb collectors who come to the Drigung area to scour the surrounding mountains for rare caterpillar fungus, which is used in traditional Chinese medicine.

ⓘ Getting There & Away

Most travellers get to Drigung Til and Tidrum by rented vehicle. The trip takes around three hours from Lhasa. It's worth spending at least one night in Tidrum or Drigung, more if you want to do any hiking. A two- or three-day trip will cost around Y1500.

A public bus runs daily from the Lhasa Eastern Bus Station to Drigung Til, departing at 8am. It leaves the monastery the next day at 9am, picks up passengers at Menba and continues to Lhasa via Nyima Jiangre.

Tidrum Nunnery

གདར་སྒྲོམ་བཙུན་དགོན་ 德仲寺

ELEV 4325M

Around three hours' walk (or a half-hour drive) from the main valley, northwest of Drigung Til and 13km up a side valley, is **Tidrum Nunnery** (Dézhòng Sì; admission Y20). Tidrum, with its **medicinal hot springs**, has a great location in a narrow gorge at the confluence of two streams. The entire valley is festooned with prayer flags. The small nunnery has strong connections to Yeshe Tsogyal, the wife of King Trisong Detsen and consort of Guru Rinpoche. The Kandro-la, the resident spiritual leader of the nunnery, is considered a reincarnation of Yeshe Tsogyal.

The delightful hot springs (free with admission to the nunnery) are surrounded by wooden canopies and there are separate men's and women's pools. The pools are surrounded concrete-free and the water is crystal clear. It is said to be rich in minerals, including sulphur, coal and limestone; a mixture of properties that locals say can cure everything from rheumatism to paralysis. The manager of the springs is adamant that you enter the pools buck naked, so there is no need for swimming trunks, though a towel and flip-flops would not go amiss. Photography is forbidden, even if no one is in the pool.

If you have a day to spare, you could do a tough day hike up to the **Kiri Yangdzong caves**, associated with Yeshe Tsogyal. The trail ascends to 5180m to visit the caves and then descends steeply down a scree slope to Dranang Monastery. Take a guide from the nunnery as the trail can be hard to find.

For a short walk, head north up the gorge behind the nunnery for about 1½ hours until you get to Dranang Monastery, where the valley divides.

🛏 Sleeping & Eating

There are two simple guesthouses near the springs – neither are worth writing home about. The one that overlooks the springs is a **private guesthouse** (dm Y20-40, d Y100). It's marginally better than the shabby **Nunnery Guesthouse** (dm Y25), which is closer to the main temple of the nunnery. A promising new option is **Shambhala Serai** (☎0891-632 6695; www.shambhalaserai.com), a Tibetan-style hotel located 5km before you reach Tidrum. The hotel has hot springs and a riverside location but was still under construction at the time of research.

At the nunnery, a shop sells biscuits and beer, and the restaurant above the government guesthouse serves hearty bowls of *thugpa* (noodle soup; Y6).

ℹ Getting There & Away

For information on reaching Tidrum Nunnery, see the directions for Drigung Til (p108).

YARLUNG TSANGPO VALLEY

ཡར་ཀླུང་གཙང་པོའི་གཞུང་ 雅鲁流域

The serene waters of the braided Yarlung Tsangpo meander through a swathe of land flanked by dramatic sand dunes and rich in Tibetan history. It's only a couple of hours from Lhasa and the numerous sights are relatively near one another, allowing you to see the main sights in two or three days. With more time you could spend days exploring the various side valleys on foot or by mountain bike.

Gongkar གོང་དཀར་ 贡嘎

☑0891 / ELEV 3600M

Gongkar (Gònggā) County's main claim to fame is its airport, but there are also a couple of interesting monasteries west of the airport, along the 'old' road to Lhasa. Note that there are three places called Gongkar: the airport, the monastery 10km to the west and the county town, about 10km to the east.

GONGKAR CHÖDE MONASTERY
གོང་དཀར་ཆོས་སྡེ་དགོན་ 曲德寺

Surprisingly large, the Sakyapa-school **Gongkar Chöde Monastery** (Qūdé Sì; admission Y20, photos Y15), founded in 1464, is famous for its 16th-century Kyenri-style murals. It lies 400m south of the highway, around 10km from the airport, back along the old road to Lhasa. The monastery has been renovated with the help of the Shalu Foundation (www.asianart.com/shalu).

The **assembly hall** has statues of Sakya Pandita, Drölma, Guru Rinpoche and the monastery founder Dorje Denpa (1432–96). To the left of the hall is the *gönkhang*, whose outer rooms have black murals depicting a sky burial. The inner hall has a statue of the Sakyapa protector Gonpo Gur and some amazing spirit traps (in a case to the right). The inner sanctum has fine Kyenri-style murals of the Sakyapa founders by the entrance, and an inner kora *(nangkhor)*. Art specialists say the murals show a marked Chinese influence. The chapel to the right of the assembly hall has particularly fine images of the Past, Present and Future Buddhas.

The upper floor has more lovely old murals, including some showing the original monastery layout. On either side of the roof is the Kyedhor Lhakhang, which has fine protector murals in *yabyum* (Tantric sexual union) pose, and the Kangyur Lhakhang.

As you walk clockwise around the main monastery building, look for the *shedra* on the northern side. The monks attend thangka-painting classes in the morning here and practice debating in the afternoon.

Die-hards can hike a further 5km up the side valley to visit the 13th-century **Dechen Chokhor Monastery** on the hillside. Most of the monastery lies in ruins, apart from a new chapel.

A further 13km along the road to Chushul are the impressive ruins of the Potala-like **Gongkar Dzong** and neighbouring **Sundruling Monastery**.

GONGKAR XIAN ས྄་གདོང་ཚེར་ 贡嘎县

This country town (Gònggā Xiàn; *xian*), 9km east of the airport, is of note for hosting Tibet's only public **Chairman Mao statue**, located next to a school west of the town centre. The 12m-tall icon, erected in 2006, has more to do with the town's economic connections to Mao's home province of Húnán than with a major ideological statement.

🛏 Sleeping & Eating

There are a couple of decent places to stay near the airport if you want to use Gongkar as a base from which to explore the valley.

Húnán Bīnguǎn HOTEL **$**
(湖南宾馆; ☑739 3282; Zangxing Lu, Gongkar Xian; ordinary/standard d Y80/150, discounts of 30%) Rooms at this clean modern hotel, 9km east of the airport, come with a Western bathroom, though only the pricier standard rooms have a shower.

Lántiān Bīnguǎn HOTEL **$$**
(蓝天宾馆; ☑139 0890 3354; 2nd fl, cnr Main & Airport Rds; r Y150) The 'Blue Sky' hotel won't win any awards for cleanliness but it does have a handy location above the main road junction. There's an internet cafe on the ground floor across the street.

Airport Hotel HOTEL **$$**
(机场宾馆; Jīchǎng Bīnguǎn; ☑621 6608; Gongkar airport; standard/deluxe d incl breakfast Y200/280; ❄) All rooms come with cleanish carpet, dim bathroom and a hot-water boiler. The cheaper standard rooms in the south block are a little darker but better value. The hotel is right by the terminal building.

KILOMETRE MARKERS ALONG THE YARLUNG TSANGPO

MARKER	FEATURE
72	Chuwo Ri, one of Ü's four holy mountains
73	monastery on side of Chuwo Ri
80-81	ruins of Gongkar Dzong and Shedruling Monastery
84	Gongkar Chöde Monastery
90	bridge and tunnel to/from Lhasa
93-94	Gongkar airport
100	Dakpo Tratsang Monastery
102-103	Gongkar Xian town, Mao statue and Rame Monastery
112	ferry to Dorje Drak Monastery
117-18	Chitoshö village, ruined *dzong* and Dongphu Chukhor Monastery
138	ferry to Drak Valley, for Drak Yangdzong Caves
142	Dratang Xian and turn-off to Dratang Monastery (2km)
147	road to Mindroling Monastery (8km)
148-149	Tsongdu Tsokpa Monastery
155	Samye ferry
161	Namseling Manor turn-off
170	sand dunes
190	Tsetang town

Chinese hydro-engineers, ever on the lookout for bigger and better rivers to dam, may have found their holy grail; the 2840km-long Yarlung Tsangpo (Brahmaputra). Damming the Yarlung Tsangpo is potentially the world's largest hydropower project, so says a research team that has studied the idea. The team has suggested building a 38-gigawatt power station on the upper reaches of the river. By comparison, the Three Gorges Dam can *only* create 22.5 gigawatts at full capacity.

According to the engineers, the best spot to build such a dam is on the 'Great Bend', an incredibly scenic curve in the river set at a strategic spot before it descends to the plains of India. One scientist on the team has equated the energy potential of the dam to 'all the oil and gas in the Yellow Sea'. Unsurprisingly, the Indian media has slammed the idea, stating that any attempt to harness or divert the waters of the Brahmaputra would have massive ecological implications for the sub-continent.

Politics may be the ultimate thorn in the side of the Chinese engineers, as the damming of this section of the river would surely strain relations with both India and Bangladesh. Thus far, even the Chinese government has been cool to the ideas put forward by the engineers. Even if the Great Bend is allowed to survive in its natural state, other dams are in the works further upstream. The first to get started is the 1.1-billion yuan Zangmu Dam, a 450-megawatt project being constructed in Gyantsa County. Zangmu is the first of five dams planned for this stretch of the Yarlung Tsangpo.

Gongkar has dozens of cheap Chinese restaurants, all overpriced but with decent food.

ℹ Information

Bank of China (中国银行; Zhōngguó Yínháng; ☯9.30am-5.30pm Mon-Fri, 11am-4pm Sat & Sun) is five minutes' walk south of the airport; it changes cash and travellers cheques and has a 24-hour ATM. It cannot change RMB back into foreign currency (see p342).

ℹ Getting There & Away

Airport buses run from the office of the Civil Aviation Authority of China (CAAC) in Lhasa to Gongkar seven times a day (75 minutes). Return buses to Lhasa are timed to coincide with the arrival of flights. Taxis to Lhasa cost around Y200.

Plenty of buses stop at Gongkar en route to Tsetang or Lhasa. Minibuses run when full from Gongkar Xian to Chitoshö village.

A chartered minibus from the airport to Gongkar Chöde Monastery costs around Y50 return, or Y15 one way to Gongkar Xian.

Dorje Drak Monastery

 རྡོ་རྗེ་བྲག་དགོན་པ་ 多吉扎寺

ELEV 3550M

Along with Mindroling Monastery, Dorje Drak (Duōjízhá Sì) is one of the two most important Nyingmapa monasteries in Ü. With a remote and romantic location, it is less accessible than Mindroling and consequently gets few Western visitors.

Dorje Drak was forcibly relocated to its present site in 1632 by the kings in Tsang. A line of hereditary lamas known as the Rigdzin leads the monastery. The title is named after the first Rigdzin Godemachen, thought to be a reincarnation of Guru Rinpoche. The fourth Rigdzin, Pema Trinley, was responsible for expanding the monastery in the early 17th century, though his efforts were for naught as the Dzungar Mongols sacked the place in 1717; Pema Trinley did not survive the onslaught. The 10th Rigdzin Lama currently resides in Lhasa.

The main assembly hall has statues of Guru Rinpoche and Pema Trinley, the fourth Rigdzin. The Samsum Namgyel Gönkhang to the right has five butter sculptures representing the chapel's five protectors. A cabinet holds the monastery's treasures, including a fragment of a staff belonging to Milarepa that was smashed in the Cultural Revolution. The upstairs chapel sells lovely ground juniper incense.

A demanding 1½ hour **kora** leads around the back of the *dorje* (thunderbolt symbol) shaped rock behind the monastery, up to a ruined retreat atop the rock. The path overlooks some dramatic sand dunes and the views from the retreat are simply stunning.

Tibetan-style beds are available at the **Monastery Guesthouse** (dm Y25). There are lots of duvets but it's a good idea to bring a sleeping bag and some food. A small shop sells soft drinks and instant noodles.

The monastery, on the northern bank of the Yarlung Tsangpo, can be reached via a ferry from kilometre marker 112 on the Lhasa–Tsetang road. Boats run in the morning and late afternoon (Y10, 30 minutes) or you can charter a boat for Y100. Hard-core trekkers can approach Dorje Drak from Lhasa, a trek of around four days. Four-wheel-drives can also get here on the road that runs along the northern bank of the Yarlung Tsangpo.

Drak Yangdzong

 སྒྲགས་ཡང་རྫོང་། 扎央宗

For an adventurous off-the-beaten-track trip, pack your sleeping bag and a torch (flashlight) and take the ferry across the Yarlung Tsangpo to explore the cave complexes of the Drak Valley (Drakyul). The best advice is to try and visit the sites with a band of Tibetan pilgrims. Note that the Drak Valley is not the same as the valley behind Dorje Drak Monastery.

There are several sacred spots in the valley and all are visited by pilgrims en route to the caves. The first stop is 4km past the ferry terminal at the **Dromochen Lhakhang**, which commemorates the birthplace of Nubchen Sangye Yeshe, a 9th-century Tantric master who was one of the 25 disciples of Guru Rinpoche.

Another 6km up the road comes **Tsogyel La-tso**, the spirit lake of Guru Rinpoche's consort Yeshe Tsogyal. Today the lake is more of a pond and covered by a protective fence. The golden-roofed chapel at the north end of the lake has a statue of Tsogyel, as well as a photo of her current reincarnation, who lives in Amdo.

Passenger trucks continue another 6km to Ngadrak village (pronounced Na-dra). There are several shops here and **Ngadrak Monastery** of the large Karma Kagyupa order. Look for the stone footprint of Yeshe Tsogyal by one of the assembly hall pillars.

The dirt road continues up the valley, past Gyarong village at the base of the ruined fortress Pema Dzong, and turns west up the valley at Ngalu village for the final climb to **Chusi Nunnery**. The 17th-century nunnery was largely left in ruins after the Cultural Revolution but has since been rebuilt and is now home to about 30 nuns.

From the nunnery it's a tough 1½-hour climb up to the **Drak Yangdzong caves** (Zhāyāngzōng). The large first cave has a chapel, an interesting side mural of Mindroling Monastery and a couple of resident nuns, who will act as your guide through the caves (Y5). Access to the upper caves is via a 10m ladder secured with strips of yak hide. Note that the caves are very narrow at times and are absolutely no place for those with claustrophobia, vertigo or a tendency to eat too many doughnuts. The spiritual and physical heart of the complex is a tiny Guru Rinpoche cave.

Back into the daylight (and after a quick round of butter tea) pilgrims continue to a side cave, which is smaller but with more limestone rock formations.

To visit the separate **Dzong Kumbum** cave complex you need to make your way back to Ngadrak village, 1½ hours' walk (roughly 5km) down the main valley. Pilgrims generally start the trek early the following morning at around 3am and return in the afternoon after visiting the four main caves. You can shave off some of the trek by hiring a tractor for the first section. The next day pilgrims take the bus down to the ferry.

🛏 Sleeping

Chusi Nunnery Guesthouse   GUESTHOUSE $
(dm Y10) Cosy, clean rooms and a small teahouse-restaurant make this a wonderful place to stay for a night or two.

There are several pilgrim guesthouses run by the families in Ngadrak village; none have signs so you just need to ask around. One such place is the family-run **Chimei Guesthouse** (☏152 8903 1312; dm Y10-50) located between the bridge and the monastery. Meals are available.

There are plenty of places to camp within the valley, if you are suitably equipped with a tent and sleeping bag.

ℹ Getting There & Away

Take the 7am bus from Lhasa's Barkhor Sq to Dratang and get off at the ferry, a couple of kilometres before Dratang (note: this is not the same dock as the ferry for Dorje Drak). Boats make the hour-long crossing (Y10) when there are enough passengers. At the far side, everyone piles into a converted truck for the ride up the Drak Valley to Ngadrak village. If you're lucky, you can share transport with pilgrims going all the way to the caves (Y20). Otherwise you may have to hike the final couple of hours.

When heading back, it's best to spend the night at Ngadrak and take the morning bus down to the ferry, otherwise you'll likely have to wait hours for a ferry or be forced to charter one (Y200).

Most 4WD tours come here by road; a sturdy jeep can now reach the valley from the south end of the Galáshān Tunnel.

Trekkers can access the Drak Yangdzong cave complex on foot from the Dorje Drak Valley over the Gur-la.

Dratang Monastery

ग्र་དང་གऋང་ 扎塘寺

About 48km east of Gongkar airport is the turn-off to the 11th-century **Dratang Monastery** (Zhātáng Sì; admission Y25), located 2km off the main road in the Dranang Valley. This small Sakyapa monastery of only eight monks is of interest mainly to art specialists for its rare murals, which combine Indian (Pala) and inner Asian (Western Xia) styles. Bring a torch to see the murals.

The assembly hall has central statues of Dorje Chang (Vajradhara; with crossed arms) and the monastery's founder, Drapa Ngonshe. Look for the interesting oracle costume and mirror (to the left of Dorje Chang) in which the oracle would discern his visions. The inner sanctum holds all that remains of the murals, the best of which are on the back (western) wall.

A side protector chapel is accessed by steps outside and to the left of the main entrance. The chapel (whose central image is that of a yak's head) has a passage at the back that leads to a rooftop chapel and kora.

If you need to spend the night, try the **Zhūzhōu Bīnguǎn** (株洲宾馆; ☎736 3333; dm Y30, d Y120-180), a clean modern place with a grassy garden area and dorms in spacious triples. It's at the junction with the main highway.

Also worth visiting if you have a particular interest are the ruins of the **Jampaling Kumbum**, on the hillside a half-hour walk (roughly 1km) southeast of Dratang. The 13-storey chörten, built in 1472, was one of the largest in Tibet with an attendant monastery of 200 monks before it was dynamited by the Chinese in 1963. Rebuilding efforts are limited to a two-storey Jampa chapel. Check out the little brass toe on the throne – all that remains of the original Jampa statue after which the complex was named.

To get to Jampaling, walk south out of Dratang Monastery and after a couple of minutes turn left, following a path to the base of the ruins visible on the hillside above.

A direct minibus (Y25) runs to Dratang from Barkhor Sq in Lhasa every day at 8am. Otherwise, take any Tsetang-bound bus to the Dratang junction, from where it's a short three-wheel motor rickshaw ride or 20-minute walk to the monastery. The pilgrim bus from Samye to Lhasa also stops here briefly (see p118).

Mindroling Monastery

སྨིན་གྲོལ་གླིང་དགོན་པ་ 敏珠林寺

A worthwhile detour from the Lhasa–Tsetang road, between the Dratang turn-off and the Samye ferry crossing, is **Mindroling Monastery** (Mǐnzhūlín Sì; admission Y25). It is the largest and most important Nyingmapa monastery in Ü.

Although a small monastery was founded at the present site of Mindroling as early as the 10th century, the date usually given for the founding of Mindroling is the mid-1670s. The founding lama, Terdak Lingpa (1646–1714), was highly esteemed as a *terton* (treasure finder) and scholar, and counted among his students the fifth Dalai Lama. Subsequent heads of the monastery were given the title Minling Trichen; the current titleholder lives in exile in Dehra Dun, India. The monastery was razed in the Mongol invasion of 1718 and later restored.

Mindroling has *cham* dancing on the 10th day of the fifth Tibetan lunar month and the fourth day of the fourth lunar month. The latter festival features the creation of a sand mandala nine days later.

The central **Tsuglhakhang** is an elegant brown stone structure on the west side of the courtyard. As you walk clockwise, the first chapel is the **Zhelre Lhakhang**, with statues of Guru Rinpoche and Terdak Lingpa (with a white beard and excellent hat). The bare main hall itself has another statue of Terdak Lingpa, along with Dorje Chang and a row of Kadam-style chörtens – the monastery originally belonged to the Kadampa school. The inner chapel has a large Sakyamuni statue. Only the statue's head is original; the body was ripped apart by Chinese troops for its relics.

Upstairs, the **Tresor Lhakhang** houses several treasures, including a stone hoofprint and a famed old thangka with the gold footprints and handprints of Terdak Lingpa, which was given to the fifth Dalai Lama.

The top floor holds the Lama Lhakhang, with some fine ancient murals of the Nyingma lineages, plus a central statue of Kuntu Zangpo (Samantabhadri). The Dalai Lama's quarters remain empty.

The other main building, to the right, is the **Sangok Podrang**, used for Tantric practices. To the left of the main entrance is a famous 'speaking' mural of Guru Rinpoche. Flanking the left wall is a huge thangka that is unfurled once a year on the 18th day of the fourth lunar month.

The new white chörten just outside the monastery, the **Kumbum Tongdrol Chenmo**, was constructed in 2000 with Taiwanese funds. It replaces an original 13-storey chörten destroyed in the Cultural Revolution. It's possible to climb past the ground-floor statue of Jampa to its upper floors.

Nice walks lead off from the **kora** around the Tsuglhakhang, west up the valley through the village to the ruins of what used to be a nunnery.

On the main road, 1.5km towards Tsetang, is the small **Tsongdu Tsokpa Monastery**. The original monastery across the road has been converted into a housing block.

🛏 Sleeping & Eating

It's possible to stay the night at the **Monastery Guesthouse** (r Y100), though you'd do well to bring a sleeping bag. Beware of dogs if you leave your room at night. A small shop sells noodles, Pepsi and the like.

ⓘ Getting There & Away

There is little direct transport to Mindroling. One possibility is to take the Lhasa–Tsetang bus and get off at kilometre marker 147 by the English sign to the monastery. The monastery is around 8km south of the road, up the Drachi Valley, and the last section involves a climb (it's not too punishing). You won't see the monastery until you round a ridge and are below it.

One daily bus leaves the monastery around 8.30am for Tsetang, returning in the afternoon.

Mindroling is easily slotted into a Yarlung Valley excursion if you have a rented vehicle.

Samye Monastery
བསམ་ཡས་དགོན་པ 桑耶寺

☏ 0893 / ELEV 3630M

Samye Monastery (Sāngyē Sì) is deservedly the most popular destination for travellers in the Ü region. Surrounded by barren mountains and dramatic sand dunes and approached via a beautiful river crossing, the monastery has a magic about it that causes many travellers to stay longer than they had intended.

As Tibet's first monastery and the place where Buddhism was established, the monastery is also of major historical and religious importance. No journey in Ü is complete without a visit to Samye.

For details of the popular trek between here and Ganden, see p237.

Permits

A travel permit is theoretically needed to visit Samye and you can only get one by organising a tour and guide (see p29). If you are on a 4WD tour your guide will probably pick up the permit in Tsetang; the process only takes a few minutes.

History

Samye was Tibet's very first monastery and has a history that spans more than 1200 years. It was founded in the reign of King Trisong Detsen, who was born close by, though the exact date is subject to some debate – probably between 765 and 780. Whatever the case, Samye represents the Tibetan state's first efforts to allow the Buddhist faith to set down roots in the country. The Bön majority at court, whose religion prevailed in Tibet prior to Buddhism, were not at all pleased with this development.

The victory of Buddhism over the Bön-dominated establishment was symbolised by Guru Rinpoche's triumph over the massed demons of Tibet at Hepo Ri, just to the east of Samye. It was this act that paved the way for the introduction of Buddhism to Tibet.

Shortly after the founding of the monastery, Tibet's first seven monks (the 'seven examined men') were ordained here by the monastery's Indian abbot, Shantarakshita (Kende Shewa), and Indian and Chinese scholars were invited to assist in the translation of Buddhist texts into Tibetan.

Before long, disputes broke out between followers of Indian and Chinese scholarship. The disputes culminated in the Great

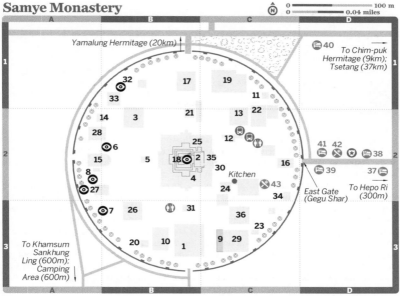

Samye Monastery

◉ Sights

1	Aryapalo Ling	B3
2	Assembly Hall	B2
3	Black Chörten	B2
4	Chenresig Chapel	B2
5	Chörten	B2
6	Chörten	B2
7	Chörten	B3
8	Chörten	A2
9	Debating Courtyard	C3
10	Drayur Gyagar Ling	B3
11	Dzogchen Lhakhang	C1
12	Gheku	C2
13	Green Chörten	C2
14	Jampa Lhakhang	A2
15	Jampa Ling	A2
16	Jampel Ling	C2
17	Jangchub Semkye Ling	B1
18	Jowo Khang	B2
19	Kordzo Pehar Ling	C1
20	Mani Lhakhang	B3
21	Moon Temple	B2
22	Namdok Trinang Ling	C2
23	Ngamba Ling	C3
24	Old Guesthouse	C2
25	Protector Chapel	B2
26	Red Chörten	B3
27	Sacred Tree	A2
28	Samtenling (Closed)	A2
29	Shetekhang	C3
30	Stele	C2
31	Sun Temple (Destroyed)	B3
32	Tree Shrine	B1
33	Triple Mani Lhakhang	B1
34	Tsengmang Ling	C2
35	Ütse	C2
36	White Chörten	C3

🛏 Sleeping

37	Agubaima Hotel	D2
38	Dawa Guesthouse	D2
	Friendship Snowland Hotel	(see 42)
39	Samye Monastery Guesthouse	D1
40	Samye Monastery Guesthouse Annex	D2
41	Tashi Guesthouse	D2

🍴 Eating

42	Friendship Snowland Restaurant	D2
43	Monastery Restaurant	C2

THE SAMYE MANDALA

Samye's overall design was based on that of the Odantapuri Temple of Bihar in India, and is a highly symbolic mandalic representation of the universe. The central temple represents Mt Meru (Sumeru), and the temples around it in two concentric circles represent the oceans, the continents and the subcontinents that ring the mountain in Buddhist cosmology. The complex originally had 108 buildings (an auspicious number to Tibetans). The 1008 chörtens on the circular wall that rings the monastery represent Chakravala, the ring of mountains that surrounds the universe.

Debate of Samye, an event that is regarded by Tibetan historians as a crucial juncture in the course of Tibetan Buddhism. The debate, which probably took place in the early 790s, was essentially an argument between the Indian approach to bodhisattvahood via textual study and scholarship, and the more immediate Chan (Zen) influenced approach of the Chinese masters, who decried scholarly study in favour of contemplation on the absolute nature of buddhahood. The debates came out on the side of the Indian scholars.

Samye has never been truly the preserve of any one of Tibetan Buddhism's different orders. However, the influence of Guru Rinpoche in establishing the monastery has meant that the Nyingmapa order has been most closely associated with Samye. When the Sakyapa order came to power in the 15th century it took control of Samye, and the Nyingmapa influence declined, though not completely.

Samye's most common icons are of the Khenlop Chösum – the trinity of Guru Rinpoche, King Trisong Detsen and Shantarakshita, the first abbot of Samye.

Samye has been damaged and restored many times throughout its long history. The most recent assault on its antiquity was by the Chinese during the Cultural Revolution. Extensive renovation work has been going on since the mid-1980s and there are now 190 monks at Samye.

Ütse   TEMPLE

The central building of Samye, the **Ütse** (admission Y40; ☺8am-5.30pm), comprises a unique synthesis of architectural styles. The ground and 1st floors were originally Tibetan in style, the 2nd floor was Chinese and the 3rd floor Indian. The corner parapets with green and gold *dorje* designs are also unique.

Just to the left of the main entrance is a **stele** dating from 779. The elegant Tibetan script carved on its surface proclaims Bud-

dhism as the state religion of Tibet by order of King Trisong Detsen. The doorway is flanked by two ancient stone lions and two stone elephants.

From here the entrance leads into the first of the ground-floor chambers: the **assembly hall**. As you enter the hall you pass a statue of Tangtong Gyelpo to the left and a row of figures greet you straight ahead: the translator Vairocana, Shantarakshita, Guru Rinpoche, Trisong Detsen and Songtsen Gampo (with an extra head in his turban). The photo to the right of the Guru Rinpoche statue is of the famous original statue (now destroyed), which physically resembled the guru and allegedly had the power of speech.

On the right are two groups of three statues: the first group is associated with the Kadampa order (Dromtompa and Atisha); the second group is multidenominational and includes lamas from the Nyingmapa, Sakyapa and Gelugpa orders.

To the rear of the assembly hall are steps leading into Samye's most revered chapel, the **Jowo Khang**. You enter the inner chapel via three painted doors – an unusual feature. They symbolise the Three Doors of Liberation: those of emptiness, signlessness and wishlessness. A circumambulation of the inner chapel follows at this point (take a torch).

The centrepiece of the inner chapel is a 4m statue of Sakyamuni. Ten bodhisattvas and two protective deities line the heavy side walls of the chapel, which are decorated with ancient murals. Look also for the blackened Tantric mandalas on the ceiling.

To the right of the hall is a *gönkhang*, reeking of *chang*, with statues of deities so terrible that they must be masked. There's a stuffed snake over the blocked exit.

Before ascending to the 1st floor, take a look at the **Chenresig Chapel**, outside and to the left of the main assembly hall, which features a dramatic 1000-armed statue of Chenresig.

The structure of the 2nd floor echoes the inner chapel and houses an image of Guru Rinpoche in a semiwrathful aspect, flanked by Tsepame and Sakyamuni, with Shantarakshita and Trisong Detsen flanking them. Look up to see the Chinese-influenced bracketing on the beams. There is an inner kora around the hall.

Some of the murals outside this hall are very impressive (photos Y10); those on the southern wall depict Guru Rinpoche, while those to the left of the main door show the fifth Dalai Lama with the Mongol Gushri Khan and various ambassadors offering their respects. The Dalai Lama's quarters are at the southeast corner of this floor. A relic chamber also exists on this floor, always under lock and key; among the objects here are the staff of Vairocana and a turquoise amulet that contains the hairs of Guru Rinpoche.

The 3rd floor is a recent addition to the Ütse. It holds statues of four of the five Dhyani Buddhas, with a mandala of the fifth (Namse) on the ceiling.

Walk around the back to a ladder leading up to the 4th floor. This chapel holds the sacred core of the temple, as well as an image of Dukhor (Kalachakra), a Tantric deity, but it is generally locked. As you descend from the 3rd floor look for a rare mural of the 14th (current) Dalai Lama beside the stairwell.

Back on the ground floor you can follow the prayer-wheel circuit of the Ütse, and look at the interesting murals showing the founding of the monastery. You can also ascend to the outer roof for views over the complex.

Ling Chapels & Chörtens   CHAPEL & CHORTENS

As renovation work continues at Samye, the original *ling* (royal) chapels (འགོན་ལང་དང་ཆོ་ རེན་; the lesser, outlying chapels) are slowly being restored. Wander around and see which are open. Following is a clockwise tour of those open at the time of research.

The square in front of the Monastery Guesthouse has some interesting elements. The stubby isolated building to the north constitutes the remains of a nine-storey tower used to display festival thangkas.

From the east gate *(gegyu shar)* follow the prayer wheels south to the **Tsengmang Ling**, once the monastery printing press, and look for the sacred stone in the centre of the chapel. If you pass the residential college of the **Shetekhang** around 9.30am or 6pm, listen out for the sounds of debating in the attached courtyard. The restored **Aryapalo Ling** was Samye's first building and has a lovely ancient feel. The statue of Arya Lokeshvara is similar to one seen in the Potala Palace (see p52). The **Drayur Gyagar Ling** was originally the centre for the translation of texts, as depicted on the wall murals. The main statue on the upper floor is of Sakyamuni, flanked by his Indian and Chinese translators.

The **Jampa Ling** on the west side is where Samye's Great Debate was held. On the right as you go in, look out for the mural depicting the original design of Samye with zigzagging walls. There is an unusual semicircular inner kora here that is decorated with images of Jampa. Just north of here is a chörten that pilgrims circumambulate; south is a **sacred tree** to which pilgrims tie stones. The **triple Mani Lhakhang** to the north has lovely murals.

The green-roofed, Chinese-style **Jangchub Semkye Ling** to the east houses a host of bodhisattvas around a statue of Marmedze, with a 3-D wooden mandala to the side. Take a torch to see the central Asian-style murals.

East of here is the **Kordzo Pehar Ling**, the home of the oracle Pehar until he moved to Nechung Monastery outside Lhasa. Pilgrims stick passport photos of themselves onto the locked entrance of the ground-floor chapel, which is flanked by two ancient-looking leather bags. The upstairs portico has some old cane helmets. The inner chapel reeks of alcohol, hooks hang from the ceiling and demons' hands reach out from their cases, as if trying to grab you.

It is also possible to enter the four reconstructed concrete chörtens (white, red, green and black), though there is little of interest inside.

Hepo Ri   SACRED HILL

Hepo Ri (ཧེ་པོ་རི; 哈不日神山; Hābùrì Shénshān in Chinese) is the hill some 400m east of Samye, where Guru Rinpoche vanquished the demons of Tibet. King Trisong Detsen later established a palace here. Pilgrims honour it as one of the four sacred hills of Tibet (the others being Gangpo Ri at Tsetang, Chagpo Ri in Lhasa and Chuwo Ri at Chushul). Even for the non-religious, it's worth coming up here for the views of Samye. Paths wind up the side of the hill from the road leading from Samye's east gate. A 30-minute climb up the side ridge takes you to an incense burner, festooned with prayer flags and with great views of Samye below. Head south along the ridge and descend from here. Early morning is the best time for photography.

🛌 Sleeping

Dawa Guesthouse   GUESTHOUSE $
(Dáwā Jiātíng Lǘguǎn; ☑799 5171; dm Y30) This place has a couple of dorm rooms in the back, behind a small courtyard garden. You can take tea in the sunny atrium. The staff is friendly and the bedding appears to be washed regularly.

Friendship Snowland Hotel   GUESTHOUSE $
(Xuěyù Tóngbāo Lǘguǎn, Gangjong Pönda Sarkhang; ☑136 1893 2819; dm Y30) Proper mattresses (not just foam) are on offer here, in concrete rooms above the cosy restaurant of the same name.

Samye Monastery Guesthouse   HOTEL $$
(Sāngyē Sì Lǘguǎn; ☑783 6666; dm/d Y50/150) This new slab of concrete is located outside the monastery walls in a fenced-in compound. Although devoid of charm, the double rooms are reasonably comfortable and probably the best in town. Doubles are en suite while the dorms utilize a bathroom down the hall. The Samye Monastery Guesthouse annex, even more bland and depressing, is run by the same people but it's at a completely different location, just outside the monastery's eastern gate.

There is fine camping in an orchard 10 minutes' walk south of the Ütse, near the Tibetan-style Khamsum Sankhung Ling. Take your own water.

Tashi Guesthouse   GUESTHOUSE $
(Zhāxī Zhāodàisuǒ; ☑783 6510; dm/r Y30/60) Pleasant five-bed dorms with clean foam beds, above a shop by the east gate. The best room, complete with a yak skull, overlooks the street.

Agubaima Hotel   GUESTHOUSE $
(Āgùbáimǎ Jiātíng Lǘguǎn; ☑139 0893 7199; dm Y25) This guesthouse is located over a small cafe and consists of three rooms with four or five rock-hard beds. It's probably the only place in town where you can get a view of the valley.

🍴 Eating

Friendship Snowland Restaurant
                                RESTAURANT $
(☑136 1893 2819; meals Y14-40; ⊗8am-midnight; 🏵) The backpacker-inspired menu at this pleasant Tibetan-style restaurant includes banana pancakes, hash browns and omelettes, as well as the normal menu gibberish ('Highland potato mud'?). Decent Chinese and Tibetan dishes are available (yak steak, fried mushrooms). It's outside the east gate of the monastery complex. Menu in English.

Monastery Restaurant   RESTAURANT $
(dishes Y7-15; ⊗8am-9pm) Loads of atmosphere, monks galore and decidedly average food at this place within the monastery compound.

There are also plenty of shops around town where you can load up on snacks and beer.

ℹ Getting There & Away
While it appears that Samye is easily reached by road from Lhasa, keep in mind that the main highway is south of the river, so if you come from Lhasa you need to cross over to the north bank, either by ferry (to the west) or bridge (to the east).

The only regular direct bus service from Lhasa to Samye, via the bridge at Tsetang, is a daily pilgrim bus (3½ hours), which departs from Barkhor Sq at around 6.30am. Buy your ticket the day before from the tin shack just north of the square opposite Snowlands Restaurant. The return bus leaves around 3.30pm and stops at Tsetang, Dratang Monastery and Rame Monastery en route, making a total trip of around five hours. Buy your ticket well in advance at the Samye Monastery Guesthouse.

Many travellers still opt for the ferry across the Yarlung Tsangpo, at least one way. River crossings (per person Y15, one hour) operate whenever there are enough people or a bunch of foreigners charter the boat for Y100. It is 9km from the ferry drop-off point to Samye, and everyone – Tibetans included – jumps on a truck or tractor for the ride (Y10, 20 minutes).

Trucks leave Samye for the ferry terminal whenever there are enough passengers, often around 8am and 2pm. Buses to Tsetang and Lhasa wait for their passengers on the other side of the river, as does the Public Security Bureau (PSB). This generally works out quicker than taking the pilgrim bus back to Lhasa.

Around Samye

Chim-puk Hermitage   HERMITAGE
Chim-puk Hermitage (མཆིམས་ཕུ་གུག་འཁང་; 青朴寺; Qīngpò Sì in Chinese) is a warren of caves northeast of Samye that was once a meditation retreat for Guru Rinpoche. It is a popular day hike for travellers spending

a few days at Samye. If you are lucky, you might find a pilgrim truck heading up there in the early morning, or you could hire a tractor in Samye (Y50). Ask at the reception of the Monastery Guesthouse. Otherwise, the walk takes around four or five hours up and three hours down (roughly 7km each way). Take plenty of water.

There is a small monastery built around Guru Rinpoche's original **meditation cave** halfway up the hill. Follow the pilgrims around the various other shrines. It's possible to stay the night here if you have a sleeping bag and food.

If you are feeling fit and acclimatised, it is possible to climb to the top of the peak above Chim-puk. You'll probably only have enough time to do this if you get a lift to Chim-puk or stay the night there. To make this climb from the Guru Rinpoche cave follow the left-hand valley behind the caves and slog it uphill for 1½ hours to the top of the ridge, where there are several clumps of prayer flags. From here you can drag yourself up along a path for another 1½ hours to the top of the conical peak, where there are a couple of meditation retreats and fine views of the Yarlung Tsangpo Valley. On clear days you can see several massive Himalayan peaks to the southeast.

Yamalung Hermitage — HERMITAGE

It is possible to head up the valley directly behind Samye to the Yamalung Hermitage (གཡའ་མ་ལུང་; 聂玛隆圣洞; Nièmǎlóng Shèngdòng in Chinese), around 20km from Samye. See p239 for details. It's really too far to hike there and back in a day, so it's best to build this into your itinerary so your driver can take you there. The recent upgrading of the road to Yamalung might bring regular transportation along this road.

Namseling Manor
 རྣམ་སྲས་གླིང་ 朗色林庄园

Perhaps the only building of its type still standing in Tibet, Namseling Manor (Lǎngsèlín Zhuāngyuán in Chinese) is a ruined multistorey family mansion. It's a minor site with just a few murals left, and the ruins are unstable in places so you should take care when exploring. At the time of research it was surrounded by a fence and off-limits. By the time you read this it may (or may not) be renovated and open as a tourist attraction.

The building is 3km south of the main highway near kilometre marker 161.

Tsetang ཙེ་ཐང་ 泽当
☑0893 / POP 52,000 / ELEV 3515M

An important Chinese administrative centre and army base, Tsetang (Zédāng) is the fourth-largest city in Tibet and the capital of huge Shannan (Lhoka) prefecture. The centre of town is a modern, thoroughly Chinese city where you'll find decent restaurants, overpriced accommodation and a couple of internet cafes. The more interesting area is the small traditional Tibetan town, clustered to the east around Gangpo Ri, one of Ü's four sacred mountains.

Most travellers use Tsetang as a base to visit outlying sites of the Yarlung Valley, including Samye Monastery, Yumbulagang and Chongye Valley. The PSB has a strong presence here so your guide may disappear for a few minutes to register your passport and possibly pick up extra permits for outlying sights (including Samye Monastery).

⊙ Sights & Activities

MONASTERY KORA

There are a couple of small monasteries in the Tibetan quarter that are worth a brief visit. Pilgrims visit them in a clockwise circuit.

From the market on Bairi Jie head east to a small square and continue down the street to the right of the bank. After 200m you'll come to **Ganden Chökhorling Monastery**. This 14th-century monastery was originally a Kagyupa institution, but by the 18th century the Gelugpas had taken it over, which is why the central statue is of Tsongkhapa.

From here head north and then east to **Ngamchö Monastery**, a somewhat livelier place. On the top floor are the bed and throne of the Dalai Lama. A side chapel is devoted to medicine, with images of the eight medicine buddhas. The protector chapel displays fine festival masks, representing snow lions, stags and demons.

A kora leads from the monastery around the base of Gangpo Ri up to a bundle of prayer flags and round to a throne-shaped incense burner. From here a side trail ascends the hill to the Monkey Cave, while the main kora descends to **Sang-ngag Zimche Nunnery** (桑阿赛津尼姑寺; Sāng'āsàijīn Nígū Sì; admission Y10). The principal image here

Tsetang

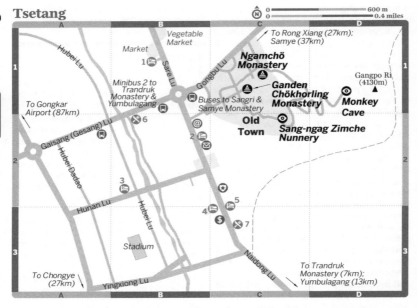

Tsetang

◉ Top Sights
Ganden Chökhorling Monastery C1
Monkey Cave D1
Ngamchö Monastery C1
Sang-ngag Zimche Nunnery C2

🛏 Sleeping
1 Dragon Horse Hotel B1
2 Shannan Post Hotel B2
3 Snow Pigeon Hotel B2
4 Tsetang Hotel C3
5 Yulong Holiday Hotel C2

✗ Eating
6 Tashi Restaurant B2
7 Yarlung Kitchen C3

is of a 1000-armed Chenresig, dating back to the time of King Songtsen Gampo. According to some accounts, the statue was fashioned by the king himself. There are around 70 resident nuns here.

GANGPO RI གངས་པོ་རི་ 贡不日神山

Gangpo Ri (4130m) is of special significance for Tibetans as the legendary birthplace of the Tibetan people, where Chenresig in the form of a monkey mated with the white demoness Sinmo to produce the beginnings of the Tibetan race. The **Monkey Cave**, where all this took place, can be visited near the summit of the mountain. Do it in the spirit of a demanding half-day walk in the hills, rather than as a trip specifically to see the Monkey Cave, as the cave itself is rather disappointing.

The most direct trail leads up from the Sang-ngag Zimche Nunnery, climbing about 550m to the cave. The walk up will take about two hours – bring plenty of water. If in doubt, follow the prayer flags. The walk up Gangpo Ri is a part of a long pilgrim route, which local Tibetans make each year on the 15th day of the 4th lunar month.

🛏 Sleeping

Finding good budget accommodation is a real problem in Tsetang. The town's cheaper hotels are prevented from accepting foreigners by a strong PSB presence, and those that will accept you will notify the PSB of your presence within minutes of you checking in.

TOP CHOICE **Snow Pigeon Hotel** HOTEL $$
(雪鸽宾馆; Xuěgē Bīnguǎn; ☏782 8888; cnr Xiangqu Nanlu & Hunan Lu; r incl breakfast Y480, discounts of 50%-60%; ❄) This place

has bright and tidy rooms at a competitive rate. You may need to leave the shower running for 10 minutes to get any hot water. The location off the main drag means that most of the rooms are reasonably quiet, however the common rooms above the bar are pretty noisy.

Dragon Horse Hotel
HOTEL $$

(龙马宾馆; Lóngmǎ Bīnguǎn; ☎783 5388; 28 Sare Lu; d Y288-388, tr Y388, discounts of 40%-60%; ❉@) Some of the cheaper ordinary rooms (pǔtōngfáng) here face out onto the noisy street so if you choose this block get a room that faces the courtyard. Standard rooms are much better looking and come with modern furnishings and air-con. Price includes breakfast and there is a business centre with internet.

Tsetang Hotel
HOTEL $$

(泽当饭店; Zédāng Fàndiàn; ☎782 5555; fax 782 1855; 21 Naidong Lu; d Y380-788; ❉@🛜) This is Tsetang's premier tour-group lodging, with money exchange (guests only), piped-in oxygen and comfortable four-star rooms. The souvenir shop sells slide film. Credit cards are accepted. The common room for Y380 is of similar size compared to standard rooms, but lacks the bells and whistles. It's the only hotel in town with wi-fi.

Yulong Holiday Hotel
HOTEL $$

(裕砻假日大酒店; Yùlóng Jiàrì Dàjiǔdiàn; ☎783 2888; 16 Naidong Lu; r incl breakfast Y580, discounts of 50%-60%; ❉) This new three-star place offers clean modern rooms, some containing computers with internet access. You can even listen to your favourite Chinese pop tunes in the power shower, if you can figure out how the damn thing works. On the downside, the mattresses here are springy and uncomfortable.

Shannan Post Hotel
HOTEL $$

(山南邮政大酒店; Shānnán Yóuzhèng Dàjiǔdiàn; ☎782 1888; 10 Naidong Lu; d incl breakfast Y240-340, discounts of 40%) Rooms in the main block are done up with Tibetan motifs while the older block in the back is dim and bland. It's reasonably priced but you might have to put up with charmless staff.

✖ Eating

Yarlung Kitchen
RESTAURANT $$

(雅砻厨房; Yǎlóng Chúfáng; ☎799 0800; Naidong Lu; mains Y20-40; ⊙8.30am-11.30pm) This very atmospheric restaurant is dressed up with colourful Tibetan decor. Despite the promise of Western food on the signboard,

the menu is primarily Tibetan and Chinese food. Some of the more intriguing options include 'lucky sheep's head' and 'snowland yak hoof'. At night it gets busy with local men swilling Budweiser beer from shot glasses.

Tashi Restaurant
RESTAURANT $

(扎西餐厅; Zhāxī Cāntīng; ☎783 1958; Gaisang Lu; mains Y20-30; ⊙7.30am-10.30pm; 🖻) Branch of the Tashi Restaurant in Shigatse (not Tashi's in Lhasa) that offers up Nepali-style Western goodies, such as pizza, curries and good breakfasts, in a nice Tibetan-style hall. Avoid the disappointing lassi. Menu in English.

❶ Information

Bank of China (中国银行; Zhōngguó Yínháng; Naidong Lu; ⊙9.30am-6pm Mon-Fri, 10.30am-4.30pm Sat & Sun) Changes cash and travellers cheques and has an ATM.

Chàngxiǎng Internet Cafe (畅想网吧; Naidong Lu; per hr Y4; ⊙24hr)

Post Office (邮局; Yóujú; 12 Naidong Lu; ⊙9.30am-7pm)

Public Security Bureau (公安局; Gōng'ānjú; Naidong Lu; ⊙9am-12.30pm & 3-6pm) Your guide will need to stop here to pick up permits if you are headed out of town.

❶ Getting There & Away

Buses run hourly between Tsetang and Lhasa's main Western Bus Station (2½ hours) until around 6pm, passing Dratang and Gongkar airport en route. Private cars also do the run at dangerous speeds for Y53 per seat.

Private buses to Samye (45 minutes) and Sangri (one hour) depart at 8am from near the main roundabout.

Yarlung Valley

ཡར་ཀླུང་ལུང་ 雅鲁流域

The Yarlung Valley (Yǎlǔ Liúyù) is considered the cradle of Tibetan civilisation. It was from Yarlung that the early Tibetan kings unified Tibet in the 7th century and their massive burial mounds still dominate the area around Chongye. Yumbulagang, perched on a crag like a medieval European castle, is another major attraction of the area and the site of Tibet's oldest building.

The major attractions of the Yarlung Valley can just about be seen in a day, but this is a beautiful part of Tibet for extended hiking

DIY: TREKKING THE YARLUNG VALLEY

Perhaps the best way to see the lesser sights of the Yarlung Valley is on foot, visiting a handful of pilgrimage sites, none of which are more than 40 minutes' walk apart. Bring water and a packed lunch for a fine day trip.

After visiting **Trandruk Monastery** and **Yumbulagang**, head north for 2km from Yumbulagang and get off at kilometre marker 373. Follow the side road westwards for 15 minutes, then curve to the left to visit the small **Tashi Chöden Monastery**, home to 20 monks.

From here, head north along the base of the hillside for 25 minutes and take a left where the canal branches left. A faint path climbs the ridge for 15 minutes up to **Rechung-puk**. Alternatively, carry on north to Khurmey village, from where it is an equally steep 20-minute walk up to the monastery, passing a white chörten.

After visiting the main **Heruka cave**, head over the back (west) side of the ridge, pick your way down through the ruins, past a looted chörten, to the minor road at the base of the ridge. Follow this southwest for 10 minutes to a small village. A path leads from here up to a cleft in the rock, decorated with prayer flags – this is the **Bhairo-puk**. The tiny cave is home to a couple of hermits and houses a stone handprint of the translator Vairocana.

From here descend back to the village and head west along a dirt track towards the large **Gongtang Bumpa chörten**, allegedly commissioned by Vairocana as a way to resolve a border dispute between rival kings. From here you can join the main road from Tsetang to Chongye.

and day walks. You'll need to specify on your permit exactly where you want to go.

When independent travel is possible, travellers usually band together in Lhasa for a three- or four-day trip out to the Yarlung Valley by way of Tsetang, taking in Samye and Mindroling en route. The total cost (including permits and guide) for a 4WD for such a trip is around Y2800.

Permits

Travel permits (see p29) are theoretically needed to visit anywhere outside Tsetang town, though there weren't any formal permit checks in the valley during our last few research visits. The only place you are likely to be checked is in Chongye, and then only if you stay the night.

TRANDRUK MONASTERY

ཁྲ་འབྲུག་དགོན་པ། 昌珠寺

Around 7km south of the Tsetang Hotel, **Trandruk** (Chāngzhū Sì; admission Y70, photos Y75; ☉dawn-dusk) is one of the earliest Buddhist monasteries in Tibet, having been founded at the same time as the Jokhang and Ramoche in Lhasa. Dating back to the 7th-century reign of Songtsen Gampo, it is also one of Tibet's demoness-subduing temples (see the box, p56; Trandruk pins down the demoness' left shoulder). In order to build the monastery here, Songtsen Gampo

had first to take the form of a hawk *(tra)* in order to overcome a local dragon *(druk)*, a miracle that is commemorated in the monastery's name.

Trandruk was significantly enlarged in the 14th century and again under the auspices of the fifth and seventh Dalai Lamas. The monastery was badly desecrated by Red Guards during the Cultural Revolution.

The entrance of the monastery opens into a courtyard area ringed by cloisters. The building to the rear of the courtyard has a ground plan similar to that of the Jokhang, and shares the same Tibetan name, Tsuglhakhang.

The principal chapel, to the rear centre, holds a statue of Tara known as Drölma Sheshema (under a parasol), next to the five Dhyani buddhas. The Tuje Lhakhang to the right has statues of Chenresig, Jampelyang and Chana Dorje, who form the Tibetan trinity known as the Rigsum Gonpo. The stove to the right is said to have belonged to Princess Wencheng (Wencheng Konjo), the Chinese consort of Songtsen Gampo.

Upstairs and to the rear is a central chapel containing a famous thangka of Chenresig made up of 29,000 pearls, as well as an ancient appliqué thangka showing Sakyamuni. Still, the admission price is very hefty compared with monasteries across Tibet.

Minibus 2 (Y1) runs here every 20 minutes from the main roundabout in Tsetang, picking up passengers along Naidong Lu.

YUMBULAGANG ཡུམ་བུ་བླ་སྒང་ 雍布拉康

A fine, tapering finger of a structure that sprouts from a craggy ridge overlooking the patchwork fields of the Yarlung Valley, **Yumbulagang** (Yōngbùlākāng; ⊙7am-7pm) is considered the oldest building in Tibet. At least that is the claim for the original structure – most of what can be seen today dates from 1982. It is still a remarkably impressive sight, with a lovely setting.

The founding of Yumbulagang stretches back into legend and myth. The standard line is that it was built for King Nyentri Tsenpo, a historic figure who has long since blurred into mythology. Legend has him descending from the heavens and being received as a king by the people of the Yarlung Valley. More than 400 Buddhist holy texts (known collectively as the 'Awesome Secret') are said to have fallen from the heavens at Yumbulagang in the 5th century. Murals at Yumbulagang depict the magical arrival of the texts.

There has been no conclusive dating of the original Yumbulagang, although some accounts indicate that the foundations may have been laid more than 2000 years ago. It is more likely that it dates from the 7th century, when Tibet first came under the rule of Songtsen Gampo.

The plan of Yumbulagang indicates that it was originally a fortress and much larger than the present structure. Today it serves as a chapel and is inhabited by around eight monks who double as guards – in 1999 some 30 statues were stolen from the main chapel. Its most impressive feature is its **tower**, and the prominence of Yumbulagang on the Yarlung skyline belies the fact that this tower is only 11m tall.

The ground-floor **chapel** (admission Y60) is consecrated to the ancient kings of Tibet. A central buddha image is flanked by Nyentri Tsenpo on the left and Songtsen Gampo on the right. Other kings and ministers line the side walls. There is another chapel on the upper floor with an image of Chenresig, similar to the one found in the Potala. There are some excellent murals by the door that depict, among other things, Nyentri Tsenpo descending from heaven, Trandruk Monastery, and Guru Rinpoche arriving at the Sheldrak meditation cave (in the mountains west of Tsetang).

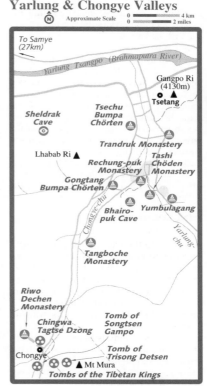

Perhaps the best part is a walk up along the ridge above the building, if only to get some peace from the syrupy Chinese pop music blasting up from the car park below. There are fabulous views from a promontory topped with prayer flags. It's an easy five-minute climb and no entry fee is needed.

Across the valley from Yumbulagang is an incredibly fertile and verdant crop field known as **zortang**, said to be the first cultivated field in Tibet. Farmers who visit the valley will often scoop up a handful of earth to sprinkle on their own fields when they return home, thereby ensuring a good crop.

Yumbulagang is 6km from Trandruk Monastery. Minibus 2 (Y5), originating from the Tsetang roundabout and passing Trandruk Monastery, terminates here.

RECHUNG-PUK MONASTERY རས་ཆུང་ཕུག 日琼布寺

A popular pilgrimage site associated with the illustrious Milarepa (1040–1123), the remains of Rechung-puk Monastery (Rìqióngbù Sì in Chinese) are set high on a dramatic escarpment that divides the two branches of the Yarlung Valley.

Milarepa, founder of the Kagyupa order, is revered by many as Tibet's greatest songwriter and poet. It was his foremost disciple, Rechungpa (1083–1161), who founded Rechung-puk as a *puk* (cave) retreat. Later a monastery was established at the site, eventually housing up to 1000 monks. This now lies in ruins. For pilgrims, the draw of the monastery is the atmospheric **cave of Black Heruka**, where they are thumped on the back with the stone footprint of Rechungpa.

See the box, p122, for how to visit the ruins as part of a day-long hike around the valley.

TANGBOCHE MONASTERY

ဘང်ဆိ်မ် 唐布齐寺

A minor site thought to date back to 1017, **Tangboche Monastery** (Tángbùqí Sì; admission Y10) is about 15km southwest of Tsetang on the way to Chongye. Atisha, the renowned Bengali scholar, stayed here in a meditation retreat. The monastery's **murals**, which for most visitors with an interest in things Tibetan are the main attraction, were commissioned by the 13th Dalai Lama in 1913. They can be seen in the monastery's main hall – one of the few monastic structures in this region that was not destroyed by Red Guards.

Heading towards Chongye, you should be able to see the building on the left once you're about 15km out of Tsetang. From the highway, look for the rusting metal sign that directs you down a dirt road to the monastery.

Chongye Valley

འཕྱོང་རྒྱས་གཤོངས་ 琼结山谷

Chongye (Qióngjié Shāngǔ in Chinese) holds a special place in the heart of every Tibetan, for it was here that the first great Tibetan monarchs forged an empire on the world's highest plateau. The capital eventually moved to Lhasa but the valley remained hallowed ground and the favoured place of burial for Tibetan kings. Rugged cliffs surround the scenic burial ground on all sides. It is also well worth climbing up to Riwo Dechen Monastery and the ruins of the old *dzong* behind it for more views of the

mounds. Most visitors to the Chongye Valley go as a day trip from Tsetang and combine it with attractions in the Yarlung Valley.

CHONGYE TOWN

འཕྱོང་རྒྱས་གྲོང་རྡལ་ 琼结镇

🗐 0893 / POP 3000

Chongye is a small, unassuming town where the pace of life is at a near standstill; you'll see just as many yaks saunter down the main road as people. There is little reason to stop, unless you need to fill up on water and snacks before setting out on a hike. Facilities are generally poor so most travellers will head back to Tsetang for the night. Buses run almost hourly between Tsetang and Chongye town (Y5), from where most of the important sights are easily accessible on foot.

CHONGYE BURIAL MOUNDS

འཕྱོང་རྒྱས་སྲོང་བཙན་བང་བས་ 藏王墓群

The **Tombs of the Kings at Chongye** (admission Y30) represent one of the few historical sites in the country that gives any evidence of a pre-Buddhist culture in Tibet. Most of the kings interred here are now firmly associated with the rise of Buddhism on the high plateau, but the methods of their interment point to the Bön faith. It is thought that the burials were probably officiated by Bön priests and were accompanied by sacrificial offerings. Archaeological evidence suggests that earth burial, not sky burial, might have been widespread in the time of the Yarlung kings, and may not have been limited to royalty.

Accounts of the location and number of the mounds differ. Erosion of the mounds has also made some of them difficult to accurately identify. It is agreed, however, that there is a group of 10 burial mounds just south of the Chongye-chu.

The most revered of the mounds, and the closest to the main road, is the **Tomb of Songtsen Gampo**. It has a small **Nyingmapa temple** atop its 13m-high summit. The furthest of the group of mounds, high on the slopes of Mt Mura, is the **Tomb of Trisong Detsen**. It is about a one-hour climb, but there are superb views of the Chongye Valley.

CHINGWA TAGTSE DZONG

འཕྱིང་བ་སྟག་རྩེ་རྫོང་ 青瓦达孜宫

This *dzong* (Qīngwǎ Dázī Gōng in Chinese) can be seen clearly from Chongye town and from the burial mounds, its crumbling ramparts straddling a ridge of Mt Chingwa. Once one of the most powerful forts in central Tibet, it dates back to the time of the early Yarlung kings. The *dzong* is also celebrated as the birthplace of the great fifth Dalai Lama. There is nothing to see in the fort itself, but again you are rewarded with some great views if you take the 40-minute or so walk (roughly 1km) up from Chongye. Paths lead up from the centre of town, from the nearby ruins of the red chapel and from the gully behind Riwo Dechen Monastery.

RIWO DECHEN MONASTERY
འབྲོང་རྒྱས་རི་བོ་བདེ་ཆེན་ 日乌德庆寺

The large, active, Gelugpa-sect **Riwo Dechen Monastery** (Rìwū Déqìng Sì; admission Y20) sprawls across the lower slopes of Mt Chingwa below the fort. There are some nice walks up to the ridge north of the monastery and then down to the fort.

Riwo Dechen Monastery can be reached by a half-hour walk (roughly 1km) from Chongye's atmospheric old Tibetan quarter. Turn west at the town's T-junction and ask for the 'gompa'. Halfway up is a grand, new chörten. It is sometimes possible to stay the night at the monastery – a magical experience.

Lhamo La-tso
ལྷ་མོ་བླ་མཚོ་ 拉姆拉措

One of Ü's most important pilgrimage destinations, Lhamo La-tso (Lāmǔ Lācuò) has been revered for centuries as an oracle lake.

The Dalai Lamas have traditionally made pilgrimages to Lhamo La-tso to seek visions that appear on its surface. The Tibetan regent journeyed to the lake in 1933 after the death of the 13th Dalai Lama and had a vision of a monastery in Amdo that led to the discovery of the present Dalai Lama. The lake is considered the home of the protectress Palden Lhamo.

The gateway to Lhamo La-tso is the dramatic, but mostly ruined, **Chökorgye Monastery** (琼果杰寺; Qióngguǒjié Sì; 4500m). Founded in 1509 by the second Dalai Lama, Gendun Gyatso (1476–1542), the monastery

served later Dalai Lamas and regents as a staging post for visits to the lake. On the nearby slope is a mani wall that consecrates a footprint stone of the second Dalai Lama.

Just short of the mountain pass that overlooks Lhamo La-tso is a ritual *shökde* (throne) built for the Dalai Lamas. It is now buried under a mound of *kathak* (silk scarves). It's a 15-minute walk from the *shökde* to the pass and another 1½ hours to get down to the lake (roughly 3.5km in total), which is encircled by a kora. The lake is a perfect place to camp and spending a night here allows you to watch the dramatic weather patterns change overhead; the micro-climate here ensures that the weather is in constant flux.

A visit to Lhamo La-tso requires five permits (seven to 15 days to process), which are only available with the help of a tourist company in Lhasa. The village has a checkpoint where you'll need to buy a ticket (Y100) for the area.

🛏 Sleeping & Eating

Chökorgye Monastery GUESTHOUSE **$**
(dm Y50) The nearest accommodation to Lhamo La-tso has a few basic dorm rooms. You are technically not allowed to stay here so check with your guide. There are good camping spots behind the temple walls if you have a tent (and if they let you stay).

Gyatsa Holy Lake Hotel HOTEL **$$**
(加查神湖宾馆; Jiāchá Shénhú Bīnguǎn; d Y160) Of the several hotels in Gyatsa Xian, this one, on the eastern edge of town, is the best.

ℹ Getting There & Away

The drive from Tsetang to Chökorgye Monastery can take four to six hours.

From the monastery, 4WD vehicles can drive 12km (about 40 minutes) up a twisting mountain road to the *shökde*. The most interesting way to reach the lake is to trek from Rutok (six days, via Dzingchi and Magong-la) or from Sangri, both routes via Gyelung-la. Coming from Sangri it's 42km along a driveable road to Olkhar, where you can break the journey at a hot-spring pool. A four- or five-day trip from Lhasa to Lhamo La-tso in a hired vehicle, including permits and guide, will cost around Y5000.

Tsang གཙང་

Includes »

Yamdrok-tso	127
Nangartse	130
Gyantse	131
Shigatse	137
Phuntsoling Monastery & Jonang Kumbum	146
Sakya	147
Lhatse	151
Baber & Shegar	152
Everest Region	154
Tingri	156
Nyalam	157
Zhāngmù (Dram)	160

Best Places to Eat

» Yak Head Restaurant 1st Branch (p142)

» Third Eye Restaurant (p142)

» Yak Restaurant (p134)

Best Places to Stay

» Everest Base Camp (p155)

» A campsite of your choice while trekking between Everest Base Camp and Tingri (p247)

» Shigatse, with its range of decent hotels (p141)

Why Go?

The great overland trip across Tibet – from Lhasa to the Nepali border via Gyantse, Shigatse and Mt Everest Base Camp – passes straight through Tsang. Most of the highlights of the region lie right along (or close to) the Friendship Hwy, making cross-country travel a relatively straightforward process. A great variety of sights and activities are experienced along the way, from hardcore treks in the Everest region to a smorgasbord of ancient Tibetan monasteries and historic towns. For many travellers, Tsang is either the first or last place they experience in Tibet, and the ride either up or down from Nepal is a border crossing for the ages.

When to Go

The best time of the year to visit Tsang is from May to June, when views of Mt Everest are usually clear before the monsoon brings cloud cover. This is also an excellent time for trekking in the Himalayas.

The colourful three-day festival at Tashilhunpo takes place in June or July (dates change each year) and culminates in the unrolling of a massive thangkas.

Visit Gyantse for the horse racing and archery festival in June (dates change each year), which includes traditional games, folk singing, picnics and much swilling of barley beer.

History

Tsang lies to the west of Ü and has shared political dominance and cultural influence over the Tibetan plateau with its neighbour. With the decline of the Lhasa kings in the 10th century, the epicentre of Tibetan power moved to Sakya, under Mongol patronage from the mid-13th to the mid-14th centuries.

After the fall of the Sakya government, the power shifted back to Ü and then again back to Tsang. But, until the rise of the Gelugpa order and the Dalai Lamas in the 17th century, neither Tsang nor Ü effectively governed all of central Tibet, and the two provinces were rivals for power. Some commentators see the rivalry between the Panchen Lama and Dalai Lama as a latter-day extension of this provincial wrestling for political dominance.

Permits

Most of Tsang's sights involve detours from the Friendship Hwy and you need permits to visit these areas. At the time of writing the only way to get permits was by travelling with an organised 4WD tour. Special trekking permits are needed if you plan to trek in the Everest region beyond the base camp. Trekking permits for Camp III (also known as Advanced Base Camp or ABC) are issued by the China Tibet Mountain Association. Trekkers will need help from an agency to get the permits. A number of trekking companies organise treks to ABC, including Great Adventure Treks (www.greatadventuretreks.com).

Itineraries

For most travellers, visiting Tsang means a straight shot from Lhasa to the Nepali border, with stops at Gyantse, Shigatse and Mt Everest. This journey takes about eight days if done at a reasonable pace.

From Lhasa, head out on the Southern Friendship Hwy, which takes you over the Kamba-la pass to the shores of Yamdrok-tso, then on to Nangartse and Gyantse. You'll need a full day in Gyantse before you can

PUBLIC TRANSPORT

At the time of research, foreigners were not allowed to travel on public transport in Tibet. Basic information is included here in case the situation changes.

move on to Shigatse. West of Shigatse the next obvious stop is Lhatse, but there are two worthy side trips on the way – Sakya Monastery and Phuntsoling Monastery. From Lhatse it's on to Baber and Shegar, a key stop before heading on to Everest Base Camp (EBC). Back on the main highway there is old Tingri and Nyalam before you finally reach the border town of Zhāngmù. The best hike in the region is from old Tingri to EBC (or vice versa), which will add another four days to your journey.

If you are in a hurry, it's quicker to take the Northern Friendship Road when travelling between Lhasa and Shigatse but going this way you'll miss Gyantse, one of the highlights of Tsang. Any way you go you'll find good facilities along the way and relatively easy drives as the Friendship Hwy is entirely paved. The exception is the Everest region, which has dirt roads and basic accommodation.

❶ Getting Around

The main road through Tsang, the Friendship Hwy, is paved almost all the way to the Nepali border (the final two kilometres before Zhāngmù were being sealed at the time of research, but should be done by the time you get there). The southern route via Yamdrok-tso has a brand-spankin' new paved highway that winds its way over Kamba-la to Yamdrok-tso and onto Shigatse. 4WD trips (the usual way to travel through the region) take this more scenic route.

Public transport runs along the Northern Friendship Hwy as far as Shegar. The Qīnghǎi–Tibet train from Lhasa to Shigatse is not due for completion until 2014.

The entries in this chapter follow a south-westerly route through Tsang from Lhasa to the border with Nepal, taking in the main attractions of the area on the way.

Yamdrok-tso

ཡར་འབྲོག་མཚོ 羊卓雍措

ELEV 4441M

Dazzling Yamdrok-tso (Yángzhuō Yōngcuò) is normally first seen from the summit of the Kamba-la (4700m). The lake lies several hundred metres below the road, and in clear weather is a fabulous shade of deep turquoise. Far in the distance is the huge massif of Mt Nojin Kangtsang (7191m).

Yamdrok-tso is shaped like a coiling scorpion. It doubles back on itself on the western side, effectively creating a large island within its reaches. For Tibetans, it

Tsang Highlights

① Scale the ruins and mighty cliffs of **Shegar Dzong** (p152), a fort and monastery in the Himalayan shadows

② Climb the dazzling **Gyantse Kumbum** (p132), a monumental chörten with mural-filled chapels

③ Absorb the holy atmosphere inside ancient **Sakya Monastery** (p147)

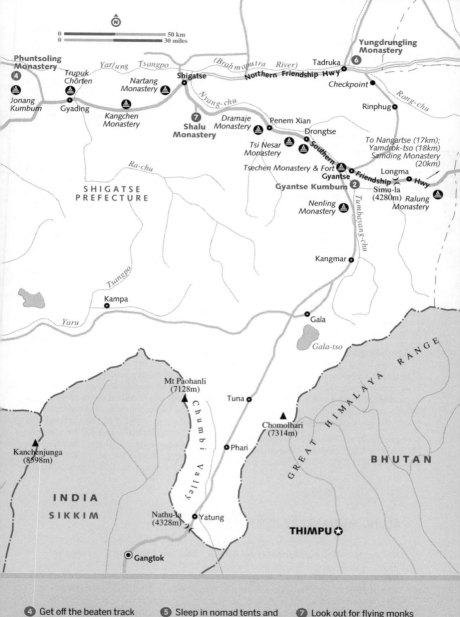

4 Get off the beaten track at photogenic **Phuntsoling Monastery** (p146), set at the base of a monstrous sand dune

5 Sleep in nomad tents and gaze upon the north face of **Mt Everest** (p155)

6 Get your Bön on at the Bönpo monastery **Yungdrungling** (p137)

7 Look out for flying monks at the mysterious **Shalu Monastery** (p144)

is one of the four holy lakes (the others are Lhamo La-tso, Nam-tso and Manasarovar) and home to wrathful deities. Devout Tibetan pilgrims circumambulate the lake in around seven days.

Most Western travellers are content with a glimpse of the lake from the Kamba-la and views from the town of Nangartse, where you can stay the night.

Nangartse ষ্ণ'ন্যাম'ৰ্ছ 浪卡子

☑0893 / ELEV 4400M

Nangartse (Làngkäzi) is the largest town on the lake and a popular stop for the night. It's not particularly attractive but there's a small monastery in the south of town, an old Tibetan quarter and a small *dzong* (fort) to the north (famed as the birthplace of the mother of the fifth Dalai Lama). There are also opportunities for walks, such as to Samding Monastery. You can't actually walk to the lakeshore as you'll soon find yourself up to your knees in bog, but the views are still good and bird-watchers will have a field day during the summer months.

There are several hotels and restaurants in Nangartse, including the following.

Yánghú Bīnguǎn   HOTEL $$
(羊湖宾馆; ☑738 2225; r Y200, discounts up to 25%) This Chinese-run pile of concrete is the best place in town. Hot showers are available to go along with relatively clean and comfortable rooms. It's located on the main highway, just at the end of the Yangzhuo Lu.

Nangartse Grain Hotel   BUDGET HOTEL $
(浪卡子粮食宾馆; Làngkäzi Liángshi Bīnguǎn; ☑136 5958 0813; r Y100) The Tibetan-owned Grain Hotel offers scruffy rooms that overlook the main intersection of this two-street town. There is no running water but each room comes with a big bucket of cold water for washing (and flushing).

Lhasa Restaurant   TIBETAN $$
(拉萨餐厅; Lāsā Cānting; ☑136 5893 6288; Yangzhuo Lu; dishes Y15-40; ☺8am-10pm) This well-established restaurant has a colourful dining hall with old photos of Lhasa and a range of Tibetan and Chinese dishes. The chicken chowmein is recommended.

Yamdrok Yak Restaurant   INTERNATIONAL $$
(羊卓亚餐厅; Yángzhuō Yà Cānting; ☑817 4971; dishes Y15-40; ☺7am-11pm) A branch of the Yak Restaurant in Gyantse, this place serves some tasty Western meals, as well as Indian and Chinese dishes. Amazingly, they specialise in French cuisine! A lunch buffet is spread out between 11am and 4pm. The restaurant is located on the road into town, just after you turn off the highway when coming from Lhasa.

SAMDING MONASTERY
བསམ་སྡིང་དགོན་པ་

Near the shores of Yamdrok-tso, about 10km east of Nangartse, **Samding Monastery** (admission Y20) is situated on a ridge that separates the northern arm of the lake from Dumo-tso (a smaller lake between the northern and southern arms of Yamdroktso). It provides excellent views of the Dumo plain and the mountains to the south.

Samding is noted for the unusual fact that it is traditionally headed by a female incarnate lama named Dorje Phagmo (Diamond Sow). When the Mongolian armies invaded Samding in 1716, Dorje Phagmo

---

WORTH A TRIP

RALUNG MONASTERY ར་ལུང་དགོན་པ་ 热龙寺

If you have your own transport and you want to get off the beaten track, make a 7km detour south to **Ralung Monastery** (Rèlóng Sì; admission Y15) from the road between Nangartse and Gyantse. Ralung was founded in 1180 and gets its name from the monastery's 'self-arising' image of a *ra* (goat).

The original *tsuglhakhang* (great temple) stands in ruins, as does a chörten (stupa) visible from the roof. As you wander around, look for images of the founder, Tsanpa Gyare, and the Drukpa Rinpoche (the monastery belongs to the Drukpa Kagyud school), who resides in India. The monastery is home to 15 monks. Ask one of them to point out the meaning of the mountains behind the monastery; each one stands for one of the eight auspicious symbols: right coiled conch, precious umbrella, victory banner, golden fish, the Wheel of Dharma, knot of eternity, lotus flower and vase of treasure. The highest peak in the range is 7191m high Nojin Gangtsang.

changed her nuns into pigs to help them escape. Her current incarnation works for the government in Lhasa.

It's possible to visit the main *dukhang* (assembly hall), to the right of the courtyard, which is dominated by a statue of Sakyamuni (Sakya Thukpa). There's also a footprint of the ninth Dorje Phagmo here, plus an eerie protector chapel and several chapels upstairs. There are 30 monks in residence.

❶ Getting There & Away

The main road from Lhasa climbs past the Yarlung Valley, over the 4794m Khamba-la, and drops to Yamdrok-tso. The distance is 140km. Departing Nangartse, buses usually congregate in the morning outside the Grain Hotel. Destinations are limited to Lhasa and Tsetang.

Gyantse རྒྱལ་རྩེ 江孜

☎0892 / POP 15,000 / ELEV 3980M

Lying on a historic trade route between India and Tibet, Gyantse (Jiāngzī) has long been a crucial link for traders journeying to the Himalayan plateau. It was once considered Tibet's third city, behind Lhasa and Shigatse, but in recent decades has been eclipsed in size and importance by up-and-coming towns like Bayi and Tsetang. Perhaps that's a good thing as Gyantse has managed to hang onto its small-town charm and laid-back atmosphere.

Gyantse's greatest sight is the Gyantse Kumbum, the largest chörten in Tibet and one of its architectural wonders. The white chörten contains a seemingly endless series of mural-filled chapels and offers outstanding views from its upper levels. For those with more time, there are some pleasant day trips that involve hikes to little-visited monasteries in the vicinity. And no matter what your schedule is, try to find a little time to wander the back streets of town: the mix of pilgrims, children, pop music, cows, motorcycles and mud is as true a picture of contemporary Tibetan life as you'll find.

If you happen to be in Tibet in early June, note that Gyantse has a horse-racing and archery festival during this time, though the date could change again (see p22).

History

Between the 14th and 15th centuries, Gyantse emerged as the centre of a fiefdom, with powerful connections to the Sakyapa order.

By 1440 Gyantse's most impressive architectural achievements – the *kumbum* and the *dzong* – had been completed. The Pelkor Chöde Monastery also dates from this period.

Gyantse's historical importance declined from the end of the 15th century, although the town continued to be a major centre for the trade of wood and wool between India and Tibet. Gyantse carpets, considered the finest in Tibet, were exported by yak cart to Gangtok and beyond. In 1904 it became the site of a major battle during Younghusband's advance on Lhasa.

◉ Sights

Pelkor Chöde Monastery MONASTERY
(དཔལ་འཁོར་མཆོད་རྟེན་དགོན; 白居寺; Pelkor Chötengön; ☎817 2680; admission Y40; ◉9am-6pm, some chapels closed 1-3pm) The sprawling compound in the far north of town houses Pelkor Chöde Monastery and the monumental Gyantse Kumbum, a chörten filled with fine paintings and statues. Both are deservedly top of the list on most travellers' must-sees.

Founded in 1418, the red-walled Pelkor Chöde was once a compound of 15 monasteries that brought together three different orders of Tibetan Buddhism – a rare instance of multidenominational tolerance. Nine of the monasteries were Gelugpa, three were Sakyapa and three belonged to the obscure Büton suborder whose head monastery was Shalu near Shigatse.

A climb up the nearby Gyantse Dzong will give you a clear birds-eye view of the original extent of the monastery and a sense of what a bustling place it must have been. Today, however, much of the courtyard, enclosed by high walls that cling to the hills backing onto the monastery, is bare and many buildings are empty. But the monastery has not yet become a mere museum. There's a small but visible population of monks and a steady stream of prostrating, praying, donation-offering pilgrims doing the rounds almost any time of the day.

The **assembly hall** is straight ahead as you walk into the compound, and most people begin their explorations here. The entrance is decorated with statues of the Four Guardian Kings, instead of the usual paintings, and a large Wheel of Life mural. Just by the entrance on the left is a particularly spooky protector chapel, with murals depicting sky burial in fairly graphic details. Look for the huge *tormas* (sculptures

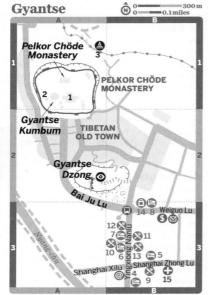

Gyantse

◉ Top Sights
Gyantse Dzong...A2
Gyantse Kumbum..A1
Pelkor Chöde Monastery.............................A1

◉ Sights
1 Assembly Hall..A1
2 Ganden Lhakhang.....................................A1
3 Rabse Nunnery..A1

🛏 Sleeping
4 Gyantse County Chǔgǔ Hotel..............B3
5 Gyantse Hotel..B3
6 Jiànzàng Hotel..B3
7 Wutse Hotel...B3
8 Zōngshān Hotel..B3

🍽 Eating
9 Gyantse Kitchen.......................................B3
10 Market...B3
11 Restaurant of Zhuāng Yuán.................B3
12 Tashi Restaurant.....................................B3
13 Yak Restaurant..B3

🛍 Shopping
14 Supermarket..B3

Information
15 Gyantse Hospital....................................B3

made out of tsampa) in a case outside the entrance.

The hall is quite dark inside and if you want a good look at the various murals and thangkas, it is a good idea to bring a torch (flashlight). The main chapel is located to the rear. There is an inner route around the chapel, which is lined with fine murals. The central image is of Sakyamuni (Sakya Thukpa), who is flanked by the Past and Future Buddhas.

To the left of the main chapel is the **Dorjeling Lhakhang**, with a four-headed Nampa Namse (Vairocana) and the other four Dhyani (or Wisdom) Buddhas.

Moving to the upper floor, the first chapel to the left is noted for a three-dimensional mandala, wall paintings of the Indian-looking *mahasiddhas* (highly accomplished Tantric practitioners) and lacquered images of key figures in the Sakyapa lineage. Each of the 84 *mahasiddhas* is unique and shown contorted in a yogic posture. Unfortunately, the room is seldom opened. Other chapels, which are open in the mornings, are dedicated to Jampa (Maitreya), Tsongkhapa and the 16 *arhats* (literally 'worthy ones'). Some chapels have fairly kitschy modern displays. Photos cost Y10 per chapel.

A new and easily overlooked **Ganden Lhakhang** chapel to the left of the *kumbum* is worth a quick peek for the largest Tsongkhapa statue in Tibet.

Gyantse Kumbum CHORTEN
(ཅན་ཐྲ་འབུམ; 江孜千佛塔; Jiāngzī Qiānfótǎ; admission incl in entry to Pelkor Chöde) Commissioned by a Gyantse prince in 1427, the Gyantse Kumbum is the town's foremost attraction. The 35m-high chörten, with its white layers trimmed with decorative stripes and its crown-like golden dome, is awe-inspiring. But the inside is no less impressive, and in what seems an endless series of tiny chapels you'll find painting after exquisite painting (*kumbum* means '100,000 images').

The Gyantse Kumbum has been described as the most important of its kind in Tibet. There are only two contemporaries, ruined and remote, in the Buddhist world: Jonang Kumbum, 60km northeast of Lhatse, and the even more remote Chung Riwoche in the west of Tsang. However, it is commonly held that neither could ever compare with the style and grandeur of the Gyantse Kumbum.

You can enter the *kumbum* and follow a clockwise route that leads murmuring pilgrims up through the six floors, taking in the dozens of rather tiny chapels that recede into the walls along the way. Much of the statuary in the chapels was damaged during the Cultural Revolution but the murals have weathered well. They date back to the 14th century, and if they were not created by Newari (Nepali) artisans then they were obviously influenced by Newari forms. Experts also see evidence of Chinese influence and, in the fusion of these Newari and Chinese forms with Tibetan sensibilities, the emergence of a syncretic but distinctly Tibetan style of painting.

There is a photography charge of Y10 for interior photography.

First Floor

This floor has four main chapels, two storeys high, and oriented according to the cardinal points. The four chapels are dedicated to: Sakyamuni (Sakya Thukpa; along with two disciples, medicine buddhas and Guru Rinpoche) in the south; Sukhavati, the 'pure land of the west' and home of red Öpagme (Amitabha) in the west; Marmedze (Dipamkara, the Past Buddha) in the north; and Tushita, another 'pure land' and home of Jampa (Maitreya), in the east. In between are some excellent murals depicting minor Tantric and protector deities. Statues of the Four Guardian Kings in the east mark the way to the upper floors.

Second Floor

The first four chapels in clockwise order from the stairs are dedicated to Jampelyang (known in Sanskrit as Manjushri), Chenresig (Avalokiteshvara), Tsepame (Amitayus) and Drölma (Tara). Most of the other chapels are devoted to wrathful protector deities, including Drölkar (White Tara; 12th chapel from the stairs), Chana Dorje (Vajrapani; 14th chapel) and Mikyöba (Akshobhya; 15th chapel), a blue buddha who holds a *dorje* (thunderbolt).

Third Floor

This floor is also dominated by a series of two-storey chapels at the cardinal points portraying the four Dhyani Buddhas: red Öpagme (Amitabha) in the south; yellow Rinchen Jungne (Ratnasambhava) in the west; green Donyo Drupa (Amoghasiddhi) in the north; and blue Mikyöba (Akshob-

hya) in the east. There are several other chapels devoted to the fifth Dhyani Buddha, white Namse (Vairocana). Again, most of the other chapels are filled with wrathful deities.

Fourth Floor

The 11 chapels on this floor are dedicated to teachers, interpreters and translators of obscure orders of Tibetan Buddhism. Exceptions are the Three Kings of Tibet on the north side (eighth chapel clockwise from the steps) and Guru Rinpoche (10th chapel).

Upper Floors

The 5th floor, which is also known as the Bumpa, has four chapels and gives access to the roof of the *kumbum*. Hidden steps behind a statue on the western side lead up to the 6th floor and take you onto the veranda at the level of the eyes painted on the wall. There is also a series of murals painted around a central cube, but most people are taken in by the outstanding views, especially looking south over the old town where, in the background, the white-walled Gyantse Dzong is perched atop a colossal outcrop.

The top floor of the *kumbum* portrays a Tantric manifestation of Sakyamuni (Sakya Thukpa), but you will likely find the way up locked.

Gyantse Dzong   FORT

(རྒྱལ་རྩེ་རྫོང་; ☎817 2116; admission Y40) Like most Tibetan towns, Gyantse radiates old-world charm when its whitewashed buildings are viewed from on high. So the stiff 20-minute climb to the top of the Gyantse Dzong is worth the effort for the great lookouts. In addition to Gyantse, clear views are afforded of the entire fertile Nyang-chu Valley and down into the compound of the Pelkor Chöde Monastery.

Many of the 14th-century fort's buildings and rooms are open for exploration, and a few have interesting murals and friezes, though most are bare. There's a kitschy attempt to re-create the old **tax office** behind the ticket booth, and a little further on to the left you'll find a dungeon, chapel and torture room with dioramas that leave nothing to the imagination. Bring a torch to explore the spooky lower chambers beneath the chapel.

Entry to the *dzong* is via a gate, just north of the main roundabout. 4WDs can drive up about halfway to the top.

Rabse Nunnery

NUNNERY

Hidden behind the hill that runs between the monastery and the *dzong* this nunnery (热赛尼姑庙; Rèsaìnígū Miào in Chinese) is a delightful place decorated with prayer flags, chörtens and *mani lhakhangs* (small chapels). The 'correct' way to visit is along the clockwise pilgrim trail that goes around the back of the Pelkor Chöde Monastery. To start, follow the road up beside the monastery and then swing right onto the dirt kora path. Bring a compass as the way back takes you through a maze of streets in the old town (but what views of the fort in the distance!). Bring water and lunch, too, as once you get out to this splendid open area you're going to want to continue to Retok Ganden Retreat. A round trip from central Gyantse to Rabse and back takes about two hours.

🛏 Sleeping

All of the following places have English signage out the front.

Zōngshān Hotel

HOTEL $$

(宗山饭店; Zōngshān Fàndiàn; ☑817 5555; 1 Weiguo Lu; d incl breakfast Y520, discounts of 50-70%; @) With 24-hour hot water, clean Western-style rooms and usual discounted rates of Y140 to Y160 a room, this is a solid-value midrange option. A top-floor restaurant (dishes Y15 to Y40) offers almost 360 degree views of Gyantse. Step outside onto the rooftop (access via the back of the restaurant) for the perfect shot of the Gyantse Dzong. Laundry service is available.

Jiànzàng Hotel

HOTEL $$

(建藏饭店; Jiànzàng Fàndiàn; ☑ 817 3720; Yingxiong Nanlu; tr per bed Y50, d Y180-200; @) Popular with overlanders, the English-speaking staff at the Jiànzàng offer rooms in a newer block that has en suite rooms and 24-hour hot water. If pressed, they will also show you the older block, which has triple rooms without shower. Prices start high but they are open to negotiation.

Gyantse Hotel

HOTEL $$

(江孜宾馆; Jiāngzī Bīnguǎn; ☑817 2222; 2 Shanghai Lu; d Y460; discounts up to 40%) This is the largest hotel in town and a popular place for groups. Heaters are in each room and there is 24-hour hot water. It has a cafe, a bright atrium and lots of Tibetan kitsch. Bike rental is available for Y5 per hour. Breakfast is an additional Y60.

Gyantse County Chǔgǔ Hotel

HOTEL $$

(江孜县楚古宾馆; Jiāngzīxiàn Chǔgǔ Bīnguǎn; ☑817 3165; Yingxiong Nanlu; r incl breakfast Y150) This courtyard hotel has 24-hour hot water, wood-floor rooms and friendly staff. It's a bit bland but still relatively new and seems well maintained.

Wutse Hotel

HOTEL

(乌孜饭店; Wūzī Fàndiàn; ☑ 817 2909; Yingxiong Nanlu) This popular place was undergoing renovations at the time of research. It may be worth checking out.

🍴 Eating

For a small town, Gyantse has a good range of decent restaurants. Most will cook at any time.

Yak Restaurant

WESTERN, TIBETAN $

(亚美食餐厅; Yàměishí Cāntīng; ☑817 4971; Yingxiong Nanlu; mains Y15-35; ⊙7am-11pm; @) The Yak offers backpacker treats like French toast (Y15), pizza, yak burgers, sizzlers (dishes served on a hot, sizzling plate) and Western breakfasts. The owner prides herself on her French cuisine so have a go at the yak liver paté or yak bourguignon.

Tashi Restaurant

INDIAN, WESTERN $

(扎西餐厅; Zhāxī Cāntīng; ☑817 2793; Yingxiong Nanlu; mains Y15-40; ⊙7.30am-11pm; @) This Nepali-run place (a branch of Tashi in Shigatse) whips up tasty and filling Indian fare. It also has the usual range of Western breakfasts, Italian and Chinese food. The decor is Tibetan but the Indian movies and Nepali music give it a sub-continent vibe.

Gyantse Kitchen

TIBETAN & INTERNATIONAL $$

(江孜厨房; Jiāngzī Chúfáng; ☑817 6777; Shanghai Zhonglu; dishes Y15-40; ⊙7am-midnight; @) This local favourite serves Western, Tibetan and Indian favourites, plus unique fusion dishes like yak pizza. The friendly owner, who may join you for a drink, donates a portion of his income to support poor families in Gyantse.

Restaurant of Zhuāng Yuán

CHINESE $$

(庄园餐厅; Zhuāngyuán Cāntīng; ☑139-8059 6328; Yingxiong Nanlu; dishes Y15-50; ⊙10am-10pm; @) The owners of the Zhuāng Yuán know how to promote themselves; the front window is covered with English signs and the chef is often standing on the steps, beckoning patrons. The Chinese dishes are tasty and while the prices are not cheap, portions are large. Poke your head in the kitchen and watch the chef throw flames from his frying pan.

Self-Catering

Yingxiong Nanlu has small shops selling drinks, fresh fruit and snack foods. There are a couple of **supermarkets** (超市; chāoshì; cnr Weiguo Lu & Yingxiong Nanlu), and a **market** (市场; shìchǎng; Yingxiong Nanlu) directly opposite the Restaurant of Zhuāng Yuán selling veggies and meat, including roasted chicken (great to take for lunch on a long hike).

ℹ Information

There is an **internet bar** (网吧; wǎngbā; cnr Shanghai Xilu & Yingxiong Nanlu; per hr Y4) in the south of town with decent connection speeds. For cash withdrawals the **Agricultural Bank of China** (中国农业银行; Zhōngguó Nóngyè Yínháng; Weiguo Lu) has an ATM that accepts foreign cards on the Plus, Visa or MasterCard networks. There are private telecom booths around town for cheap phone calls.

ℹ Getting There & Away

Minibuses to Gyantse depart from in front of Shigatse's main bus station between 10am and 8pm (1½ hours). Alternatively you can get a seat in a taxi (one hour). Minibuses from Gyantse back to Shigatse leave from the main intersection in Gyantse. Gyantse is 90km from Shigatse.

ℹ Getting Around

All of Gyantse's sights can be reached comfortably on foot, but there are rickshaws and even taxis if you need them. Negotiate all prices before you head out.

Around Gyantse

There are several excellent adventurous half-day trips to sights around Gyantse that could warrant an extra day or two in town.

TSECHEN MONASTERY & FORT

རྩེ་ཆེན་དགོན་པ། 慈青寺

The traditional village of Tsechen is located about 5km northwest of Gyantse and is a nice half-day trip from town. There is a small monastery (Cíqīng Sì in Chinese) above the village, but the main reason to hike out here is to climb the ruined fortress, wander along the defensive walls and enjoy great views of the (often flooded) river valley below. It's a good idea to bring a picnic.

The fortress is believed to have been built as early as the 14th century and was used by the British during their 1904 invasion,

although it was already partly ruined by then. Hike up to the right side of the fortress and then cross over to the highest ramparts on the left. Across the highway and behind a hill are more monastic ruins.

To get to Tsechen you can either walk, hitch (see p359) or take a taxi along the Southern Friendship Hwy toward Shigatse. The village is just past the turn-off south to Yatung. On the way back it's possible to cut through fields to the river and follow the dirt roads back to the Gyantse bridge.

RETOK GANDEN RETREAT

རེ་ཐོ་དགའ་ལྡན་དགོན་པ། 热托甘丹寺

Hidden in a fold of a valley north of town, this ruined and little-visited monastery (Rètuō Gāndān Sì in Chinese) is a fine 7km (two-hour) hike from Gyantse. It's uphill all the way but the last section is the only steep part, as you climb from a ruined manor house and herders' camp.

There are ruins all around the site, including what was once the main Drölma Lhakhang; compare it with the black-and-white photos taken of the monastery before it was destroyed. Today there are six Gelugpa monks here. Some guides may be wary of entering the monastery because of its association with the controversial deity Dorje Shugden. The central Tsongkhapa statue has a glass plate in his chest, which holds an older image of Tsongkhapa.

To get to Retok walk up the road beside the Pelkor Chöde Monastery and turn right onto the dirt track (a kora route) heading towards the Rabse Nunnery. Shortly you'll see a misspelled sign for Retok Ganden directing you north. The way is obvious; just follow the powerlines up the dirt road. From the sign it's 3.5km to the monastery.

Gyantse to Shigatse

Travelling by 4WD from Gyantse to Shigatse will lead you through the fertile Nyangchu Valley, a wide agricultural plain where colourfully decorated yaks and horses are used by Tibetan farmers to till the land. The red tassels are placed on the horns of yaks as a sort of lucky talisman before the serious spring ploughing begins. Besides the yaks and yak tenders there are a few sights of note along the way.

Drongtse Monastery and chörten, founded in 1442 and later adopted as a branch of Tashilhunpo, is located 19km past

Gyantse. A further 6km is **Tsi Nesar Monastery**, thought to be built by King Songsten Gampo. About 41km from Gyantse comes the county capital of Penem Xian. It's here that you'll spot the 15th century **Dramaje Monastery**. Levelled in the Cultural Revolution, the monastery was rebuilt in 2006 and is home to 20 monks. In the inner chapel

BAYONETS TO GYANTSE

The early-20th-century British invasion of Tibet, also known as the Younghusband expedition, began, as wars sometimes do, with unreliable intelligence. Newspapers were spreading the claim that Russia had designs on Tibet, and many were lapping it up. The British Raj feared losing a buffer state and so sent Major Francis Younghusband, an army officer with rich experience of Central Asia, on a diplomatic mission to Tibet. After six months of waiting, no Chinese or Tibetans had showed up for the meetings. A stronger message had to be sent. Younghusband was instructed to advance on Lhasa with 3000 troops (plus 7000 servants and 4000 yaks) to force a treaty on the recalcitrant Tibetans.

Despite previous brushes with British firepower, the Tibetans seem to have had little idea what they were up against. About halfway between Yatung and Gyantse, a small Tibetan army bearing a motley assortment of arms confronted a British force carrying light artillery, Maxim machine guns and modern rifles. The Tibetans' trump card was a charm marked with the seal of the Dalai Lama, which they were told would protect them from British bullets. It didn't. Firing began after a false alarm and the British slaughtered 700 Tibetans in four minutes.

The British buried the Tibetan dead (the Tibetans dug them up at night and carried them off for sky burial) and set up a field hospital, dumbfounding the wounded Tibetans, who could not understand why the British would try to kill them one day and save them the next. The British then continued their advance to Gyantse, but found the town's defensive fort (the Gyantse Dzong) deserted. Curiously, rather than occupy the *dzong*, the British camped on the outskirts of Gyantse and waited for officials from Lhasa to arrive. While they waited, Younghusband sped off up to the Karo-la with a small contingent of troops to take on 3000 Tibetans who had dug themselves in at over 5000m. The result was the highest land-based battle in British military history and a fine example of frozen stiff upper lip.

After nearly two months of waiting for Lhasa officials, the British troops received orders to retake the Gyantse Dzong (it had been reoccupied by Tibetans) and march on Lhasa. Artillery fire breached the walls of the fort, and when one of the shells destroyed the Tibetan gunpowder supply the Tibetans were reduced to throwing rocks at their attackers. The *dzong* fell in one day, with four British casualties and over 300 Tibetan dead.

With the fort under their command, the British now controlled the road to Lhasa. Younghusband lead 2000 troops to the capital with few incidents. In fact, the greatest challenge he faced was getting all the troops across the Yarlung Tsangpo (Brahmaputra River): it took five days of continual ferrying.

Once in Lhasa, Younghusband tried to ascertain where the Dalai Lama was (he had fled to Mongolia). After a month, Younghusband managed to get the Tibetan regent to sign an agreement allowing British trade missions at Gyantse and Gartok, near Mt Kailash. (Ironically, the troops discovered that British goods were already trickling into the bazaars – one British soldier wrote that he found a sausage machine made in Birmingham and two bottles of Bulldog stout in the Barkhor.) But the treaty and others that followed in 1906 were largely meaningless as Tibet simply had to no capacity to fulfil them.

As for Younghusband himself, the most significant event of the campaign was yet to come. On the evening before his departure, as he looked out over Lhasa, he felt a great wave of emotion, insight and spiritual peace. Younghusband had always been a religious man, but this moment changed him forever. 'That single hour on leaving Lhasa was worth all the rest of a lifetime,' he later quipped.

look for three life-like statues: King Trisong Detsen (wearing a white hat), Shantarakshita (wearing a red hat) and Padmasambhava. According to lore, it was Shantarakshita (at the behest of Trisong Detsen) who invited Padmasambhava to Tibet in order to subdue Tibetan devils and demons.

YUNGDRUNGLING MONASTERY

གཡུང་དྲུང་གླིང་ 雍竹林寺

Just visible across the river from the road between Lhasa and Shigatse is the Bönpo Yungdrungling Monastery (Yōngzhúlín Sì in Chinese). The monastery, founded in 1834, was once the second most influential Bön monastic institution in Tibet and home to 700 monks. The number is now limited to 35 by the Chinese government and consists largely of different factions of Bönpos from the Aba region of northern Sichuan.

To many, Yungdrungling looks much like a Buddhist monastery, but note the swastikas swirling anticlockwise and the reluctance of your guide and driver to enter the grounds (many Tibetan Buddhists have an aversion to Bön). The monks welcome visitors and one or two can even speak English. If someone is around who has a key, you can visit the large *dukhang* (assembly hall), with its impressive thrones of the monastery's two resident lamas. There are 1300 small iron statues of Shiromo (the equivalent of Sakyamuni) along the walls – look for the deity's characteristic swastika mace. You may also be able to visit a couple of chapels behind the main hall, including the Namjya Lhakhang. Just remember to make the rounds in an anticlockwise direction.

The monastery is 170km west of Lhasa on the north bank of the Yarlung Tsangpo (Brahmaputra River), just east of where the Nangung-chu meets it. Cross the bridge and follow the road 2km north along the Nangung-chu to a footbridge. From here it's about 1.5km up to the monastery (take the path diagonally up the hillside after crossing the stream). If the water level of the Nangung-chu is not too high, you can also take the dirt road 100m to the right after crossing the Yarlung Tsangpo.

Shigatse གཞིས་ཀ་རྩེ 日喀则

☑ 0892 / POP 80,000 / ELEV 3840M

About 250km southwest of Lhasa, or 90km northwest of Gyantse, lies Shigatse (Rìkāzé), Tibet's second-largest town and the traditional capital of Tsang province.

Shigatse is a sprawling place, with dusty, uneven streets humming with traffic (even the pedestrian-only lane). As you drive in across the plains, the site of the Potala-lookalike Shigatse Dzong, high on a hilltop overlooking the town, will probably fire up your imagination, but the fort is empty and most of what you see dates from a 2007 reconstruction. It is the Tashilhunpo Monastery, to the west of town, that is the real draw. Since the Mongol sponsorship of the Gelugpa order, Shigatse has been the seat of the Panchen Lama, and this seat was traditionally based in the monastery.

The town, formerly known as Samdruptse, has long been an important trading and administrative centre. The Tsang kings exercised their power from the *dzong* and the fort later became the residence of the governor of Tsang. The modern city is divided into a tiny old Tibetan town huddled at the foot of the fort, and a rapidly expanding modern Chinese town that has all the charm of, well, every other expanding modern Chinese town.

During the second week of the fifth lunar month (around June/July), Tashilhunpo Monastery becomes the scene of a three-day festival and a huge thangka is unveiled (p22).

⊙ Sights

Tashilhunpo Monastery MONASTERY

(བཀྲ་ཤིས་ལྷུན་པོ་དགོན་; 扎什伦布寺; Tashi Lhüngön; Zhāshílúnbù Sì; ☑ 882 2114; Qingdao Xilu; admission Y55; ⊗ 9am-7pm in summer, 10am-noon & 3-6pm in winter) One of the few monasteries in Tibet that weathered the stormy seas of the Cultural Revolution, Tashilhunpo remains relatively unscathed. It is a real pleasure to explore the busy cobbled lanes twisting around the aged buildings. Covering 70,000 sq metres, the monastery is essentially a walled town in its own right.

From the entrance to the monastery, visitors get a grand view. Above the white monastic quarters is a crowd of ochre buildings topped with gold – the tombs of the past Panchen Lamas. To the right, and higher still, is the **Festival Thangka Wall** that is hung with massive, colourful thangkas during festivals. Circumnavigating the compound is a one-hour kora that takes you into the hills behind the monastery.

As you start to explore the various buildings, you'll see a lot of photos of the ninth, 10th and 11th Panchen Lamas. The ninth

Panchen Lama is recognisable by his little moustache. The 11th Panchen Lama is the disputed Chinese-sponsored lama, now in his early 20s.

History

Tashilhunpo Monastery is one of the six great Gelugpa institutions, along with Drepung, Sera and Ganden Monasteries in Lhasa, and Kumbum (Tǎ'ěr Sì) and Labrang in Amdo (modern Gānsù and Qīnghǎi provinces). It was founded in 1447 by a disciple of Tsongkhapa, Genden Drup. Genden Drup was retroactively named the first Dalai Lama and he is enshrined within Tashilhunpo. Despite its association with the first Dalai Lama, Tashilhunpo Monastery was initially isolated from mainstream Gelugpa affairs, which were centred in the Lhasa region.

The monastery's standing rocketed, however, when the fifth Dalai Lama de-clared his teacher – then the abbot of Tashilhunpo – to be a manifestation of Öpagme (Amitabha). Thus Tashilhunpo became the seat of an important lineage: the Panchen ('great scholar') Lamas. Un-fortunately, with the establishment of this lineage of spiritual and temporal leaders – second only to the Dalai Lamas themselves – rivalry was introduced to the Gelugpa order.

The monastery has a very high profile as the largest functioning monastic institution in Tibet. The monks here can be somewhat cool: if you are seeking spiritual enlighten-ment, Tashilhunpo might not be the best place to begin your quest.

ⓘ Information

Morning is the best time to visit as more of the chapels are open. After 11am most tourists start to head out for lunch leaving many buildings practically empty.

◎ **Top Sights**
Shigatse Dzong..B1
Tashilhunpo Monastery.............................. A3

◎ **Sights**
1 Festival Thangka Wall A2

🛏 **Sleeping**
2 Gang Gyan Shigatse Hotel.................... B3
3 Qomolongma Friendship Hotel............ A4
4 Samdruptse Hotel................................. C2
5 Shigatse Hotel..D4
6 Tenzin Hotel C1

🍴 **Eating**
7 Fruit & Vegetable Market...................... C2
8 Gongkar Mountain Delicious
    Food Tibetan Restaurant.................. C2
9 Jin-Long Supermarket.......................... C2
10 Sifang Supermarket.............................. D3
11 Songtsen Tibetan Restaurant.............. B3

12 Tashi Restaurant...................................C2
    Tenzin Restaurant.........................(see 6)
13 Third Eye Restaurant...........................B3
14 Unequalled Coffee Bar.........................C3
15 Yak Head Restaurant 1st
    Branch D3

🛍 **Shopping**
16 Photo Shops...B3
17 Photo Shops...D2
18 Tibet Gang Gyen Carpet
    Factory...B3
19 Tibetan Market C1
20 Toread Outdoor Sports.......................D3

Information
FIT...(see 2)
21 Hospital..C3
22 Tibet-Shigatse Regional
    People's Hospital...............................D2
23 Ticket Booth...B3

Severe restrictions are in place on photography inside the monastic buildings. The going cost for a photograph varies, but be prepared for a pricey Y75 fee per chapel, and as high as Y150 in the assembly hall. Video camera fees are an absurd Y1000 to Y1500 in some chapels.

Chapel of Jampa (Jamkhang Chenmo)

Walk through the monastery and bear left for the first and probably most impressive of Tashilhunpo's sights: the Chapel of Jampa. An entire building houses the world's largest **gilded statue**, a 26m figure of Jampa (Maitreya), the Future Buddha. The statue was made in 1914 under the auspices of the ninth Panchen Lama and took some 900 artisans and labourers four years to complete.

The impressive, finely crafted and serene-looking statue looms high over the viewer. Each of Jampa's fingers is more than 1m long, and in excess of 300kg of gold went into his coating, much of which is also studded with precious stones. On the walls surrounding the image there are a thousand more gold paintings of Jampa set against a red background.

Victory Chapel (Namgyel Lhakhang)

This chapel is a centre for philosophy and houses a large statue of Tsongkhapa flanked by Jampa and Jampelyang (Manjushri). If it's not open, try to convince one of the monks to let you in.

Tomb of the 10th Panchen Lama (Sisum Namgyel)

This dazzling gold-plated funeral chörten holds the remains of the 10th Panchen Lama, who died in 1989. His image is displayed in front of the tomb. The ceiling of the chapel is painted with a Kalachakra (Dukhor in Tibetan) mandala and the walls are painted with gold buddhas.

Tomb of the Fourth Panchen Lama (Kundun Lhakhang)

The gold-roofed chapel holds the tomb of the Fourth Panchen Lama, Lobsang Choekyi Gyeltsen (1567–1662), teacher of the fifth Dalai Lama. This was the only mausoleum at Tashilhunpo to be spared during the Cultural Revolution. The 11m-high funerary chörten is inlaid with semiprecious stones and contains 85kg of gold. In front of the stupa are images of Amitayus, White Tara and Vijaya – deities of longevity.

From here you pass through a dark walkway that leads out to the Kelsang Temple Complex.

Kelsang Temple

The centrepiece of this remarkable collection of buildings is a large **courtyard**, which is the focus of festival and monastic activities. This is a fascinating place to sit and watch the pilgrims and monks go about their business. Monks congregate here before their lunch-time service in the

Tashilhunpo Monastery

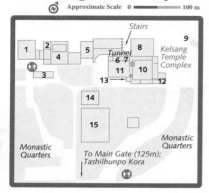

Tashilhunpo Monastery

Sights

1 Chapel of Jampa (Jamkhang Chenmo)
2 Victory Chapel (Namgyel Lhakhang)
3 Chörtens
4 Tomb of the 10th Panchen Lama (Sisum Namgyel)
5 Tomb of the 4th Panchen Lama (Kundun Lhakhang)
6 Jowo Sakyamuni Chapel
7 Drölma (Tara) Chapel
8 Tomb of the 5th to the 9th Panchen Lamas (Tashi Langyar)
9 Festival Thangka Wall
10 Courtyard
11 Assembly Hall
12 Printing Press (middle floor)
13 Kitchen
14 Tantric College
15 Philosophy College

main assembly hall. A huge prayer pole rears up from the centre of the flagged courtyard and the surrounding walls are painted with buddhas.

The **assembly hall** is one of the oldest buildings in Tashilhunpo, dating from the 15th-century founding of the monastery. The massive throne that dominates the centre of the hall is the throne of the Panchen Lamas. The hall is a dark, moody place, with rows of mounted cushions for monks, and long thangkas, depicting the various incarnations of the Panchen Lama, suspended from the ceiling. The central inner chapel holds a wonderful statue of Sakyamuni (Sakya Thukpa), while the chapel to the right holds several images of Drölma (Tara).

You can also visit the huge new **Tomb of the Fifth to the Ninth Panchen Lamas (Tashi Langyar)**, built by the 10th Panchen Lama to replace tombs destroyed in the Cultural Revolution. The central statue is of the ninth Panchen Lama. The 10th Panchen Lama returned to Shigatse from Běijīng to dedicate the tomb in 1989. He fulfilled his prediction that he would die on Tibetan soil just three days after the ceremony.

There are a dozen other chapels in the complex. Follow the pilgrims on a clockwise circuit, ending up in a tangle of chapels above the assembly hall. Here in the far left (upper) corner chapel you'll find views of the two-storey Jampa statue below and, to the right, the tombs of the first and third Panchen Lamas and first Dalai Lama. Then descend to the middle floor and do another clockwise circuit taking in the interesting **printing press** and monastic **kitchen**.

OTHER BUILDINGS

As you leave Tashilhunpo, it is also possible to visit the monastery's two remaining colleges. They are on the left-hand side as you walk down towards the main gate. The first is the **Tantric College** and the second is the brown **Philosophy College**. Neither is particularly interesting, but you might be lucky and find yourself in time for debating, which is held in the courtyard of the Philosophy College.

Shigatse Dzong   FORT

Once the residence of the kings of Tsang and later the governor of Tsang, very little remained of this *dzong* (གཞིས་ཀ་རྩེ་རྫོང་; 日喀则宗; Rìkāzé Zōng in Chinese) after it was destroyed in the popular uprising of 1959. Construction on a new building began several years ago and Shigatse is now once again graced with an impressive hilltop fort that bears a close resemblance to the Potala, albeit on a smaller scale.

The *dzong* was closed at the time of writing. A gallery is being built here and could be open by the time you read this.

Summer Palace of the Panchen Lamas

PALACE

(བདེ་ཆེན་སྐལ་བཟང་ཕོ་བྲང་; 德庆格桑颇彰; Déqìng Gésāng Pōzhāng; admission Y30; ☉9.30am-12pm & 3.30-6pm) Though it ranks far below Tashilhunpo, if you have extra time in Shigatse, pay a visit to this walled palace complex on the south end of town. Recent efforts at rehabilitating the gardens are taking fruit, as is the restoration or reworking of wall murals. While the new paintings cannot compare to the masterly works of the past, they are still quite lovely and, covering every surface of the rooms as they do with vibrant colours and fantastic images, form a rather awesome whole.

The palace was built in 1844 by the seventh Panchen Lama, Tenpei Nyima. It's a strange blend of Buddhist temple and Victorian-era mansion. Entrance is now though the backdoor. The bottom hallway has a pair of massive **murals**, one of which depicts the Buddhist version of Hell, complete with humans being boiled, dismembered, speared, hacked and disembowelled – enough to keep most believers on the straight and narrow. One image is so gruesome it's covered with a scarf.

To the left of the hallway (opposite the Panchen Lama's stuffed dog) are two rooms, which an attendant monk might open for you. The first room, the Gongkhang, is a small prayer chapel. The second room contains images of the 10th Panchen Lama's *yunze* (holy tutor).

Walk up the grand staircase to the 2nd floor where you will find the 10th Panchen Lama's **sitting rooms**, one of which contains his desk and telephones. The 2nd floor holds his **audience chamber**. Each room contains a throne *(shuegje)* to which pilgrims will bow. The attendant lama may even reveal one of the Panchen Lama's shoes, and proceed to bless you by rubbing the holy shoe on the back of your neck and head.

The palace is about 1km south of Tashilhunpo. Follow the road to the end and turn right into the gated compound.

Darawa Linka   PARK
(ཟླ་བ་གླིང་ཀ; 达热瓦林卡; Dárèwǎ Línkǎ; admission free; ☺9am-late, summer only) Locals make merry at this park on the eastern side of Shigatse. Grab a bottle of Lhasa beer and join them. There are a couple dozen tents where people kick back, drink beer and play *sho* (a Tibetan board game) and mahjong. This is also known as the local pick-up spot so you'll see lots of eligible youngsters prowling for potential mates. On weekends it's packed out with picnickers.

TASHILHUNPO KORA

The kora around Tashilhunpo Monastery takes about one hour to complete. From the main gate, follow the monastery walls in a clockwise direction and look out for an alley on the right. The alley curves around the western wall and climbs into the hills above the monastery where streams of prayers flags spread over the dry slopes like giant colourful spider limbs. The views of the compound below are wonderful from here. In about 20 minutes you pass the 13-storey white tower used to hang a giant thangka at festival time. The path then splits in two: down the hill to complete the circuit of the monastery, and along a ridge to the Shigatse Dzong, a walk of around 20 minutes. There is a small flat rock outcrop at this point for relaxing on and taking in the views.

🛏 Sleeping

Shigatse has a good range of decent hotels, most with flush toilets and 24-hour hot water. All the following have English signage out the front.

Gang Gyan Shigatse Hotel   HOTEL **$$**
(日喀则刚坚宾馆; Rìkāzé Gāngjiān Bīnguǎn; ☑882 0777; fax 883 0171; 77 Zhufeng Lu; tr without bathroom Y188, d with bathroom Y368, discounts up to 60%; ✲) Right next to the carpet factory is this well-managed hotel offering large Western-style rooms with comfortable beds and furnishings. The shared bathrooms are clean but the showers' water supply is iffy; rooms with bathrooms have a good supply of water. Breakfast is included, but best of all is the location of the hotel, less than 100m from the entrance of the Tashilhunpo Monastery.

Shigatse Hotel   HOTEL **$$$**
(日喀则饭店; Rìkāzé Fàndiàn; ☑ 882 2525; fax 882 1900; 12 Shanghai Zhonglu; d/tr Y560/660, discounts up to 20%; @) The biggest hotel in town has a grand Tibetan-style lobby and a number of facilities catering to the affluent tour groups that usually book the place out. There's in-house dry cleaning, laundry, an Internet centre, a games room and requisite dodgy massage parlour. The rooms are clean but characterless.

Tenzin Hotel HOTEL $$
(旦增宾馆; Dànzēng Bīnguǎn; ☎ 882 2018; fax 883 1565; 8 Bangjiakonglu; q per bed Y40, d/tr without bathroom Y180/120, d with bathroom Y220, discounts up to 30%) Popular with both backpackers and 4WD groups, though a little noisy for our tastes, especially on the lower floors. The shared bathrooms are excellent and have 24-hour hot water. The **restaurant** has a good range of Indian, Western and Nepalese dishes (Y15 to Y35).

Qomolangma Friendship Hotel HOTEL $
(珠峰友谊宾馆; Zhūfēng Yǒuyì Bīnguǎn; ☎882 1929; fax 882 2984; Puzhang Lu; d Y120) The reception desk is usually empty at this hotel because the staff always seems to be lounging around on the lobby sofas. Double rooms are cheap (and they are often willing to bargain) and reasonably clean and the price includes breakfast. It's not a bad choice if you don't mind the apathetic service.

Samdruptse Hotel HOTEL $$
(桑珠孜饭店; Sāngzhūzī Fàndiàn; ☎882 2280; 2 Qingdao Lu; dm Y40, d with bathroom Y260, discounts up to 30%) This hotel has a nice location near the pedestrian mall, a friendly staff and some OK rooms. Maintenance, however, is lacking a bit and parts of the place are starting to fall off. If you're on a shoestring budget they've got scruffy quad rooms for Y40 per bed and a separate bathroom one floor above.

Also recommended:

Young House Hotel HOTEL $$
(康勋宾馆; Kāngxūn Bīnguǎn; ☎ 882 7786; 262 Shanghai Nanlu; d Y288, discounts up to 40%) Solid midrange option with modern, comfortable rooms at reasonable rates. On the downside, it's a bit out of the city centre.

Yangtse Hotel HOTEL $$
(阳孜饭店; Yángzī Fàndiàn; ☎ 882 9899; Heilongjiang Beilu; d Y580, discounts up to 60%) Another midrange place that offers good discounts if it's not already full with prepaid package groups.

✗ Eating

Shigatse is swarming with good restaurants generally open for lunch and dinner.

Third Eye Restaurant INTERNATIONAL $
(☎698 9959; Zhufeng Lu; dishes Y10-30; ☉7.30am-10.30pm; 🅿) Nepali-run place that is popular with both locals and tourists; watch as monks sip tea under thangkas while travellers devour spicy Indian cui-sine. It's located in the same building as the Gang Gyen Shigatse Orchard Hotel.

Songtsen Tibetan Restaurant INTERNATIONAL $$
(松赞西藏餐厅; Sōngzàn Xīzàng Cāntīng; ☎883 2469; Buxing Jie; dishes Y20-40; ☉8am-10pm; 🅿) Popular Western-style place that does hearty breakfasts. It has a great location on the pedestrian-only street, offering good views of the pilgrims ambling past.

Unequalled Coffee Bar WESTERN $$
(哥比伦咖啡餐吧; Gēbǐlún Kāfēi Cānbā; ☎851 0666; Shandong Nanlu, Zanglong Guangchang; drinks Y28-50, meals Y30-70; ☉11am-1am; 🛜🅿) Elegant coffee shop and bistro with big couches and courteous service. The Western-style menu has tempting offerings like Brazilian steaks and pizza. Take the elevator to the 3rd floor.

Yak Head Restaurant 1st Branch TIBETAN $$
(牛头藏餐第一分店; Niútóu zàngcān Dìyī Fēndiàn; ☎884 1118; Yeshi Jie; meals Y15-40; ☉8am-11pm) This outrageous restaurant is so over-the-top kitsch you half expect Liberace to waltz out from behind a curtain to serenade you. Actually, it is the waitresses who do most of the serenading when their favourite Tibetan songs play on the TV on the screens. Dishes include boiled mutton platter, momos (dumplings) or kalifan (set plate lunch).

Tashi Restaurant INTERNATIONAL $$
(扎西餐厅; Zhāxī Cāntīng; ☎883 5969; Buxing Jie; dishes Y15-40; ☉9am-11pm; 🅿) This place makes nice tandoori-oven-baked naan and tasty Indian dishes but does a lousy job with pizzas. It's part of a chain of places run by brothers in Gyantse and Lhasa.

Gongkar Mountain Delicious Food Tibetan Restaurant TIBETAN $
(贡嘎山美味藏餐厅; Gònggā Shān Měiwèi Zàng Cāntīng; ☎882 1139; Xueqiang Lu; dishes Y10-20; ☉9am-11pm; 🅿) Hang out with the locals and enjoy good food. In addition to the standard momos and noodle dishes, you'll find some oddities such as yak-tongue soup. The signboard reads simply Gongar Tibetan Restaurant.

Self-Catering

Shigatse has a number of shops selling drinks and snacks along Zhufeng Lu and Shandong Lu. There's a traditional **market** (located behind a department store) selling fruit, vegetables, meats and breads.

Jin Long Supermarket (金龙; Jīnlóng), on the ground floor of the department store, has a small selection of goods. **Sifang Supermarket** (四方超市; Sìfāng; cnr Zhufeng Lu) has a wider selection.

🛍 Shopping

The **Tibetan market** (Bangjiakonglu) in front of the Tenzin Hotel is a good place to pick up souvenirs, such as prayer wheels, rosaries and thangkas. There are also dozens of souvenir and craft shops along the pedestrian-only street. Bargain hard.

Tibet Gang Gyen Carpet Factory   CARPETS (西藏刚坚地毯厂; Xīzàng Gāngjiān Dìtǎn Chǎng; ☏882 2733; www.tibetgang-gyencarpet.com; 9 Zhufeng Lu; ☺9am-1pm & 3-7pm) Beside the Gang Gyan Hotel, 100m down a dirt track (follow the huge signs), this workshop hires and trains impoverished women to weave some of the finest wool carpets available. Upon arrival you'll be directed to the workshop, where you can watch the women work on the carpets, singing as they weave, dye, trim and spin; you're free to take photos. A showroom contains carpets for sale, or you can have one made to order. They will even ship it to your home overseas. Expect to pay a few hundred US$, plus shipping, for a carpet measuring 185cm by 90cm. The factory is owned by Tashilhunpo Monastery, with some profits from carpet sales going back to supporting the monastery.

Toread Outdoor Sports   CAMPING (☏882 3195; Shanghai Zhonglu) If you are headed off on a trek but totally unprepared, you can pick up basic equipment such as tents, stoves and jackets here.

There are a couple of **photo shops** next to each other across from Monastery Square and also on Qingdao Lu where you can burn CDs.

ℹ Information

Internet Access

Internet bars (网吧; wǎngbā) go in and out of business quickly in Shigatse. Free wi-fi is available at Unequalled Coffee Bar.

Tiān Lè Internet Bar (天乐网吧; Shandong Lu; per hr Y5; ☺24hr) Has good connection speeds and window seats for those who need a little fresh air.

Spider Internet Bar (蜘蛛网吧; Zhīzhū Wǎngbā; Shandong Lu, Zanglong Guangchang Nei; per hr Y4; ☺24hr) To find this internet cafe, go through the archway on Shandong Lu and enter the night market area.

Money

Bank of China (中国银行; Zhōngguó Yínháng; Shanghai Zhonglu; ☺9am-6.30pm Mon-Fri in summer, 9.30am-6pm in winter, 10am-5pm Sat & Sun) Opposite the Shigatse Hotel, it changes travellers cheques and cash and gives credit-card advances. There's a 24-hour ATM outside.

Permits

At the time of writing, the **Public Service Bureau** (公安局; PSB, Gōng'ānjú; Qingdao Xilu) was not issuing permits for individual travel. Check with other travellers and on Lonely Planet's Thorn Tree forum for the latest information.

Post

Post Office (中国邮政; Zhōngguó Yóuzhèng; cnr Shandong Lu & Zhufeng Lu) It's possible to send international letters and postcards from here, but not international parcels.

Telephone

The cheapest places to make calls are the many private telecom booths around town.

Telephone Office (中国电信; Zhōngguó Diànxìn; Zhufeng Lu; ☺9am-6.30pm Mon-Fri, 9.30am-6.30pm Sat & Sun) You can send faxes and make international phone calls here, around the corner from the post office.

Travel Agencies

FIT (☏883 8068, 899 0505; Zhufeng Lu) Located in the lobby of the Gyang Gyan Shigatse Hotel. At the time of writing FIT could not arrange any travel for foreigners (due to restrictions on permits), except direct trips to the Tibet-Nepal border.

ℹ Getting There & Away

Minibuses to Lhasa leave from a stand on Qingdao Lu on the eastern side of Shigatse. You can also catch the similar public bus service, which runs from the main bus station on Shanghai Zonglu. Foreigners might be able to buy bus tickets to Lhasa on the minibuses, but not tickets on buses to Lhasa from the main bus station.

At the main bus station there are daily morning minibuses to Sakya (four hours), Lhatse (five hours) and Gyantse (1½ hours).

There are daily (sometimes twice daily) buses running to Saga (16 hours), and two or three buses daily to Shegar (seven hours).

Shigatse's Airport was completed in 2010. Commercial flights are expected to begin in 2011.

ℹ Getting Around

Shigatse is not that large and can be comfortably explored on foot. For trips out to the Shigatse Hotel or bank, you might want to use a pedicab (Y5). A ride anywhere in town in one of the many taxis will cost Y10.

Around Shigatse

There are many sights around Shigatse, but few are visited by Western travellers. En route to Lhatse stop at **Nartang Monastery**, a 12th-century Kadampa monastery famed for wood-block printing the Nartang canon in the 18th century, and **Kangchen Monastery**. Both are signposted in English just off the Friendship Hwy. There's a trek from Shalu to Nartang (p244). It is possible to visit Gyantse as a day trip from Shigatse. It's a very pleasant ride through a lightly wooded valley dotted with small villages.

SHALU MONASTERY

ཞ་ལུ་དགོན་པ་ 夏鲁寺

It's a treat for the traveller when a sight is both a pleasure to explore and of great importance in local history and culture. Such

is the **Shalu Monastery** (Xiàlǔ Sì; admission Y40), which dates back to the 11th century. The monastery rose to prominence in the 14th century when its abbot, Büton Rinchen Drup, emerged as the foremost interpreter and compiler of Sanskrit Buddhist texts of the day. (A suborder, the Büton, formed around him.) It also became a centre for training in skills such as trance walking and *thumo* (generating internal heat to survive in cold weather), feats made famous by the flying monks of Alexandra David-Neel's book *Magic and Mystery in Tibet*.

In the abstract, the design of the monastery represents the paradise of Chenresig (Avalokiteshvara), a haven from all worldly suffering. In the concrete, Shalu is the only monastery in Tibet that combines Tibetan and Chinese styles in its design. Much of the original structure was destroyed by

THE PANCHEN LAMAS

As the second-highest ranking lamas in the land, the Panchen Lamas' authority has often rivalled that of the Dalai Lamas. So great is their prestige, in fact, that the Panchen Lamas assist in the process of choosing new Dalai Lamas (and vice versa). And as with the latter, the Panchen lineage results from the rebirth of previous lamas, which in the 20th century has lead to a long series of unfortunate events.

The ninth Panchen Lama (1883–1937) spent his last days in the clutches of a Chinese nationalist warlord after attempting to use the Chinese as leverage in gaining greater influence in Tibet. His reincarnated self never knew anything but Chinese interference and control.

After the ninth's death, the usual search went on for his replacement. In 1951, the Chinese forced Tibetan delegates in Běijīng to endorse their choice. (They even claimed that in 1949, the 11-year-old future Panchen Lama had written to Mao Zedong asking him to 'liberate' Tibet.) Though little more than a tool of Běijīng when he arrived at Tashilhunpo Monastery in 1951, by the year of his death, 1989, he had become a hero to his people. What happened?

It seems that the Panchen Lama had a change of heart about his Chinese benefactors after the 1959 Lhasa uprising. In September 1961, the Panchen Lama presented Mao with a 70,000-character catalogue of the atrocities committed against Tibet, and a plea for increased freedoms. The answer was a demand that he denounce the Dalai Lama as a reactionary and take the latter's place as spiritual head of Tibet. Not only did the Panchen Lama refuse but, in 1964, with tens of thousands of Tibetans gathered in Lhasa for the Mönlam festival, he said to the crowds that he believed Tibet would one day regain its independence and the Dalai Lama would return as its leader.

It must have come as quite a shock to the Chinese to see their protégé turn on them. They responded in time-honoured fashion by throwing the Panchen Lama into jail, where he remained for 14 years, suffering abuse and torture. His crimes, according to the Chinese authorities, included participating in orgies, 'criticising China' and raising a private insurrectionary army. A 'smash the Panchen reactionary clique' campaign was mounted, and those close to the Panchen Lama were subject to 'struggle sessions' and in some cases were imprisoned.

After emerging from prison in early 1978, the Panchen Lama rarely spoke in outright defiance of the Chinese authorities, but continued to use what influence he had to press for the preservation of Tibetan cultural traditions. (He argued, for example, against

an earthquake in the 14th century and, as this was a time of Mongol patronage (see the box, p151), many Han artisans were employed in the reconstruction. The green-tiled Chinese style, clearly visible as you approach, is one of the monastery's most easily recognisable features.

What remained of the original 11th-century Tibetan-style monastery was largely destroyed in the Cultural Revolution, but the Chinese-influenced inner Serkhang has survived reasonably well. If you enjoy looking at murals, Shalu has some fine ones from the 14th century that fuse Chinese, Mongol and Newari styles. The best murals line the walls of a corridor that rings the central assembly hall; bring a powerful torch to really appreciate these.

The inner Serkhang contains a **kanjyur lhakhang** (scripture chapel), with lovely 14th-century mandala murals. The west chapel has a black stone statue of Chenresig Kasrapani, the monastery's holiest relic. The northern chapel has more fine murals, including one in the left corner depicting the monastery's founder. There are a couple of upper chapels, including the Mudu Lhakhang, which holds the **funeral chörten** of Büton.

From Shalu you can make the three-day trek to Nartang (p244) or take an hour's walk up to **Ri-puk Hermitage**, a former meditation centre built around a spring. There are lovely views of the Shalu Valley.

ⓘ Getting There & Away

Shalu Monastery is just a few kilometres off the Shigatse-Gyantse road and a side-trip here should not add much to the cost of a 4WD trip. If taking a Gyantse-bound minibus from Shigatse, get off at kilometre marker 19 or 21 and take a

the building of a hydroelectric power plant at Yamdrok-tso, one of Tibet's most sacred lakes.) It is believed that shortly before his death he again fell out with the Chinese, arguing at a high-level meeting in Běijīng that the Chinese occupation had brought nothing but misery and hardship to his people. Accordingly, many Tibetans believe that he died not of a heart attack, as was reported, but by poisoning. However, others maintain that, exhausted and perhaps despairing, the Panchen Lama came home in 1989 to die – as he always said he would – on Tibetan soil.

Of course, the story doesn't end here. In May 1995 the Dalai Lama identified Gedhun Choekyi Nyima, a six-year-old boy from Amdo, as the latest reincarnation of the Panchen Lama. Within a month the boy had been forcibly relocated to a government compound in Běijīng, causing him to be dubbed the 'world's youngest political prisoner', and an irate Chinese government had ordered the senior lamas of Tashilhunpo to come up with a second, Chinese-approved choice. Chadrel Rinpoche, the abbot who led the search that identified Gedhun, was later imprisoned for six years for 'splitting the country' and 'colluding with separatist forces abroad' (ie consulting the Dalai Lama), and Tashilhunpo was closed to tourists for a few months.

Tashilhunpo's lamas eventually settled on Gyancain Norbu, the son of Communist Party members, who was formally approved in a carefully orchestrated ceremony.

Běijīng's interest is not only in controlling the education of Tibet's number-two spiritual leader, but also influencing the boy who could later be influential in identifying the reincarnation of the Dalai Lama. Meanwhile, the Dalai Lama–appointed Panchen Lama, now in his early 20s, remains under house arrest at an undisclosed location. In 2010 Tibet's new governor stated publicly that he is alive and well and claimed that the boy and his family are living anonymously by their own volition. In the same year, the Chinese Panchen Lama made his political debut, being named a member of the CPPCC, China's top political advisory board.

There are a number of groups campaigning to free the Panchen Lama. Check out the websites of the **Tashilhunpo Monastery in exile** (www.tashilhunpo.org), which offers a reward for information on the whereabouts of Gedhun, the **Australia Tibet Council** (www.atc.org.au) and the **Canada Tibet Committee** (www.tibet.ca).

The Search for the Panchen Lama by Isabel Hilton is a look at the political intricacies of Tibet, with an emphasis on the controversial Panchen Lama and China's abduction of his current reincarnation.

dirt road heading south. Both approaches will lead you to Shalu village in an hour. As you walk through the small village look for the monastery (its green-tiled roof is a dead giveaway) on the right down an alley.

There are a number of shops outside Shalu Monastery gates selling soft drinks, water and noodles.

Phuntsoling Monastery & Jonang Kumbum

ཕུན་ཚོགས་གླིང་ངོ་ནང་སྐུ་འབུམ་

平措林寺觉囊千佛塔

If you're travelling down the paved Friendship Hwy and want to get a taste of what off-the-beaten track looks like, consider a few hours' diversion to **Phuntsoling Monastery** (Píngcuòlíng Sì; admission Y35). Not only is the drive here along the winding Yarlung Tsangpo highly scenic, but so is the monastery itself, situated at the edge of a gargantuan sand dune. A ruined red fort, seated high above the monastery on a rocky crag, just adds to the fantastic photogenic atmosphere.

Phuntsoling Monastery, now home to 50 monks, was once the central monastery of the Jonangpa. This Kagyu sect is especially known for the examination of the nature of emptiness undertaken at the monastery by its greatest scholar, Dolpopa Sherab Gyaltsen (1292–1361). He was one of the first proponents of the hard-to-grasp notion of *shentong*. Roughly, this is based on the idea that the Buddha-mind (which transcends all forms) is not ultimately empty, even though all forms are empty illusions.

Shentong has been debated among Buddhist philosophers for seven centuries. The Gelugpa school did not share Dolpopa's view, to the point where in the 17th century the fifth Dalai Lama suppressed the Jonangpa school and forcibly converted Phuntsoling into a Gelugpa institution.

The monastery was expanded by the writer and scholar Taranatha (1575–1634) whose next incarnation was the first Bogd Gegeen of Mongolia. Thereafter the monastery was closely associated with the Bogd Gegeens, which is why you will see pictures of the 8th and 9th incarnations in front of the main altar. The 9th Bogd fled to India as a young man but revisited Phuntsoling in 1986 and 1993, helping to reopen the monastery following its closure during the Cultural Revolution.

You can visit the monastery's large **assembly hall**, which is dominated by a statue of Chenresig (Avalokiteshvara). Other statues include those of the 10th Panchen Lama, Tsongkhapa and the fifth Dalai Lama. The inner sanctum of the hall contains a statue of Mikyöba (Akshobhya), while the murals on the roof tell the story of the life of Sakyamuni (Sakya Thukpa).

The highlight of the monastery is a walk up to the ruined **fortifications** behind the monastery, which offer stunning views of the valley. Look for the ruined *dzong* on a cliff across the Yarlung Tsangpo.

A festival is held at Phuntsoling around the middle of the fourth lunar month (or June/July) every year, and sees lamas and pilgrims from all over the county gathering in the courtyard for prayers and celebrations. Unfortunately the event is closed to foreigners and if you show up on this day, the PSB will quickly escort you off the premises.

From Phuntsoling you can head south up the valley for a two-hour (roughly 6km) walk to the ruins of the **Jonang Kumbum** (Juénáng Qiānfó Tǎ in Chinese). The former 20m-high chörten was built by Dolpopa in the 14th century and was the spiritual centre of the Jonangpas. It was said to be one of the best-preserved monuments in Tibet, resembling the Gyantse Kumbum, before it was wrecked during the Cultural Revolution.

LHATSE CHÖDE ལྷ་རྩེ་མཆོད་སྡེ་ 拉孜镇

If you continue on the road past Phuntsoling Monastery, in a couple of hours you'll reach Lhatse Chöde (Lāzī Zhèn in Chinese), with its small monastery and ruined *dzong*. (You can also reach the village by going 1km east of Lhatse on the Friendship Hwy to the 5052km mark and then heading north.) To the east of the village is **Drampa Gyang Temple**, one of Songtsen Gampo's demoness-subduing temples (see the box, p56). In this case it pins the troublesome demoness' left hip.

ⓘ Getting There & Away

Phuntsoling Monastery can be visited on the way from Shigatse to Lhatse. Take the dirt-road detour north of the Friendship Hwy at kilometre marker 4977/8. The monastery is 34km northwest from here (less than an hour's drive). It's a 61km journey from Phuntsoling to Lhatse on this road, but it's probably faster and more comfortable just to return to the Friendship Hwy, unless you plan to also visit Lhatse Chöde.

Sakya ས་སྐྱ 萨迦

☎ 0892 / ELEV 4316M

A detour to visit the small town of Sakya (Sàjiā Sì) is pretty much *de rigueur* for any trip down the Friendship Hwy. The town is southeast of Shigatse, about 25km off the Southern Friendship Hwy, accessed via a good dirt road through a pretty farming valley. The draw here is the **Sakya Monastery**, which, like Shalu, has great appeal to the eye (the high-walled monastery compound is dubbed the 'Great Wall of Tibet' by some) and the spirit (the dim, smoky assembly hall exudes sanctity like few others). Also like Shalu, Sakya occupies an important place in Tibetan history (see the box, p151).

Sakya actually has two monasteries, on either side of the Trum-chu. The heavy, brooding, fortress-like monastery south of the river is the more famous and if you only have time to visit one, make it this. The hillside northern monastery, mostly reduced to picturesque ruins, is undergoing restoration work.

One characteristic feature of the Sakya region is the colouring of its buildings. Unlike the standard whitewashing that you see elsewhere in Tibet, Sakya's buildings are ash grey with white and red vertical stripes. The colouring symbolises the Rigsum Gonpo (the trinity of bodhisattvas) and stands as a mark of Sakya authority. Sakya literally means 'pale earth'.

Sakya town has seen considerable change in recent years. The village has transformed into a small town but it's still a pretty laidback place. There are a handful of restaurants and hotels to choose from.

Permits

An Alien Travel Permit is required to visit Sakya Monastery. Your guide will probably arrange to pick this up en route, most likely in Shigatse.

◉ Sights

Sakya Monastery   MONASTERY
(☎ 824 2352; admission Y45; ⊗ 9am-6pm) The immense, grey, thick-walled southern monastery is one of Tibet's most impressive constructed sights, and one of the largest monasteries. The monastery was established in 1268 and is designed defensively, with watchtowers on each of the corners of its high walls. Before the Cultural Revolution, Sakya Monastery had one of the largest monastic communities in Tibet. At the time of writing there was much reconstruction work underway, and many areas were closed to visitors. As usual, morning is the best time to visit as more chapels are open.

Directly ahead from the east-wall main entrance is the entry to the inner courtyard. The dusty, somewhat pedestrian looking courtyard is a bit of a disappointment after the grandeur of the outside walls, but things pick up again as you enter the main **assembly hall (Lhakhang Chenmo)**, a huge structure with walls 16m high and 3.5m thick.

At first glance the assembly hall may strike you as being like most others in Tibet: a dark interior illuminated with shafts of sunlight and the warm glow of butter lamps; an omnipresent smell of burning butter from the lamps; slick stone floors (again from the butter); rows of red mounted cushions covered with old patterned rugs; tall columns decorated with colourful thangkas and photographs; and an array of gilded statues representing buddhas, bodhisattvas, Tibetan kings and holy men. But even weary tour groups seem to quickly recognise the age, beauty and sanctity of Sakya. Plan to spend time here just soaking up the atmosphere. You'll find few that are its equal.

A few things to look specifically for in the hall are the huge drum in the far left corner and the massive sacred pillars, some which are made of entire tree trunks and are famous throughout Tibet. One reputedly was a gift from Kublai Khan!

Another gift from Kublai to the monastery is Sakya's famous white **conch shell**, which can be blown only after the presentation of seven ounces of silver. The shell is supposedly all that remains of the Buddha when in a previous incarnation he lived his life as a modest shellfish.

The walls of the assembly hall are lined with towering **gilded buddhas**, which are unusual in that many also serve as reliquaries for former Sakya abbots. The buddha in the far left corner contains relics of Sakya Pandita; the one next to it houses those of the previous abbot of Sakya. The largest central buddha contains remains of the founder of the monastery. To the right of the central buddha are statues of Jampelyang (Manjushri), a seated Jampa (Maitreya) and a Dorje Chang (Vajradhara) that seemed to us to radiate holiness. Sakya's

KILOMETRE MARKERS ALONG THE FRIENDSHIP HIGHWAY

The following towns, geographical features and points of interest along with their appropriate kilometre markers (signifying distance from Shànghǎi) may be of help to travellers, hitchhikers and mountain bikers.

Lhasa to Shigatse

MARKER	FEATURE
4646	Lhasa's eastern crossroads to Golmud or Shigatse
4656	Blue Buddha rock painting
4661	sign to Nyetang Tashigang Monastery
4662/3	Netang village and Drölma Lhakhang
4683	new bridge and tunnel to Gongkar airport
4695-7	Chushul (Tibetan 'End of River')
4703	bridge over the Yarlung Tsangpo to Nangartse and Tsetang; shops and restaurants
4707	small monastery on right side of the road
4712	hydroelectric project on the far side of the river; the structure shaped like a golf ball atop the hill is a radar and meteorological centre
4717/8	ruined fortress on left and village
4724	village
4732	valley begins to narrow into rocky gorge
4757	road to Nyemo to north; restaurants; bridge
4768	suspension footbridge to left
4779	bridge over to south side of river
4794	bridge to Padang village
4800	checkpoint; turn-off to Rinbu (Rembu); old road to Shigatse; shops
4820	Traduka; bridge to Yungdrungling Monastery and Yangpachen; restaurants
4835	Drakchik Ferry
4840	Huda village
4855	Shigatse airport
4869	Ansa Monastery on hillside to south
4875	bridge north to Nanmulin (potato-growing region)
4900-5	Shigatse

Shigatse to Tingri

MARKER	FEATURE
4913	turn-off to Ngor Monastery
4917	Nartang Monastery
4928	Gyeli village
4932/3	very gentle mountain pass of Tra-la (3970m)
4936	Kangchen Monastery to right
4956/7	interesting ruined Trupuk Chörten 1km to the north
4960/1	Gyading; ruined fort; restaurants and shops
4972	Dilong village
4977/8	turn-off to Phuntsoling Monastery
4994	Daoban

MARKER	FEATURE
5000	marker showing 5000km from Shànghǎi; small monastery and ruined *dzong*
5009	village and start of climb to pass
5014	Tropu-la (Tsuo-la; 4500m)
5028	Sakya bridge; turn-off to Sakya; rebuilt hilltop monastery
5036	ruined *dzong*
5041	village and turn-off to Xiqian Hot Springs
5052	Lhatse
5058	checkpoint and turn-off to western Tibet
5063	start of climb to pass, with a height gain of around 1000m
5083	Gyatso-la (5100m)
5114	views of Everest and the Himalaya
5121	hermitage across river
5124	bridge; to nunnery and fortress
5128/29	Qiabu village, fort and caves
5133	Baber (Baipa) and turn-off to Shegar
5139	Shegar checkpoint
5145	turn-off to Everest Base Camp
5155	ruined *dzong* to left
5162	village
5170	village
5193-4	Tingri

Tingri to Nyalam

MARKER	FEATURE
5206	turn-off for Tsamda Hot Springs
5216	two small Tibetan guesthouses in village
5221-9	various ruins by side of road
5232-3	Gutso village; guesthouse and restaurant
5237	village on west side of the river
5254	village and small guesthouse and restaurant
5258	ruins by road
5263	start climb to La Lung-la
5265	turn-off to Saga and Mt Kailash via Peiku-tso
5276	La Lung-la (4845m)
5281	bridge, road workers' hostel
5289	Tong-la (Yarle Shung; 4950m) and view of Cho Oyu and Mt Everest
5303	roadworkers' hostel and village
5310	village, with ruins behind
5334	Gangka village and track to Milarepa's Cave
5345	Nyalam
5359	military checkpoint
5378	Zhāngmù
5386	Nepali border

famous library is accessible from this hall but hidden from sight and it is rarely opened up to tourists.

As you exit the assembly hall the chapel to the right (south) is the Purkhang Chapel. Central images are of Sakyamuni (Sakya Thukpa) and of Jampelyang (Manjushri), while wall paintings behind depict Tsepame (Amitayus) to the left, Drölma (Tara) and white Namgyelma (Vijaya) to the far left, as well as a medicine buddha, two Sakyamunis and Jampa (Maitreya). Murals on the left wall depict Tantric deities central to the Sakya school.

To the north of the inner courtyard is a chapel containing 11 gorgeous **silver chörtens**, which are also reliquaries for former Sakya abbots. Look to the left corner for the **sand mandala** inside a dirty glass case. A sometimes-locked door leads into another chapel with additional amazing chörtens and murals. Bring a torch as the room is even dimmer than others.

There are a couple of chapels open outside of this central complex (but still within the compound), the most interesting of which is the very spooky **protector chapel** of the Pakspa Lhakhang. If the thick incense doesn't get you, the terrifying monsters, the huge *cham* masks and the stuffed wolves that wait in the dark recesses just may. To the left is a **shrine** dedicated to Sakya Pandita.

It may be possible to climb up onto the wall-walk of the monastery for superb views of the surrounding valley, but ask first.

Northern Monastery Ruins RUINS

Very little is left of the original monastery complex that once sprawled across the hills north of the Trum-chu, but it is still worth climbing up through the Tibetan village and wandering around what does remain. The northern monastery predates the southern monastery (the oldest temple situated at the northern monastery was built in 1073), and it is alleged to have contained 108 buildings, like Ganden. It may once have housed some 3000 monks who concentrated on Tantric studies.

A new Tibetan village is hastily being constructed across the river at the base of the mountains and is adding to the charm of the area. Centred in the village is a large new **debating hall** with monks' quarters. Work was in progress at the time of writing but the wood and brick structure was looking like it was going to fit into its environment very nicely.

After passing through the new village, head for the white chörtens, or the ruins even further to the left. Near the chörtens are the three main complexes that are still open: the main **Labrang Shar**, the **Namja Choede** to the left and the **Rinche Gang** nunnery to the far right. Remember to walk in a clockwise fashion as this is a kora route.

🛏 Sleeping

Sakya Lowa Family Hotel GUESTHOUSE $
(萨迦镇鲁哇家庭旅馆; Sàjiā Zhèn Lǔwā Jiātíng Lǚguǎn; ☑824 2156; Baogang Beilu; per person Y50) The Lowa is a family-run guesthouse with basic but clean rooms. Walls are brightly painted and accented with traditional motifs. On the downside, there are no showers. It's down the street on the east side of the Manasarovar Sakya Hotel.

Manasarovar Sakya Hotel HOTEL $$
(神湖萨迦宾馆; Shénhú Sàjiā Bīnguǎn; ☑824 2222; Gesang Zhonglu; dm Y20-30, d/tr Y280/380, discounts of 20-30%) There is a mix of rooms in this rambling hotel; the ones that overlook the road are probably best. The thick walls keep the place cold and dark but rooms are comfortable enough and some have en suite hot showers. The eight-bed dorm rooms are OK; one includes a bathroom. There are superb views from the hotel's rooftop.

🍴 Eating

Sakya has a number of Chinese restaurants, all set up by Sichuanese immigrants. All restaurants serve lunch and dinner, and have no fixed opening hours.

Sakya Farmer Restaurant TIBETAN $
(萨迦农民餐厅; Sàjiā Nóngmín Cāntīng; ☑824 2221; dishes Y10-25) Looking over the main street, this Tibetan place has a cosy atmosphere amid Tibetan decor. The green-jacketed waitresses are friendly and will help explain the various Tibetan dishes available.

Manasarovar Sakya Hotel Restaurant
INTERNATIONAL $$
(神湖萨迦宾馆餐厅; Shénhú Sàjiā Bīnguǎn Cāntīng; ☑824 2222; dishes Y15-35; ⊙breakfast, lunch & dinner; 📶) For Western food, such as omelettes, burgers, sizzlers and pizza. There are also Tibetan, Nepalese and Indian dishes. The food is OK but the concrete dining

The 11th century was a dynamic period in the history of Tibetan Buddhism. Renewed contact with Indian Buddhists brought about a flowering of new orders and schools. During this time, the Kagyupa order was founded by Marpa and his disciple Milarepa, and in Sakya, the Kön family established a school that came to be called the Sakyapa. One interesting distinction between the latter school and others is that the abbotship was hereditary, restricted to the sons of the Kön family.

By the early 13th century, the Tsang town of Sakya had emerged as an important centre of scholastic study. The most famous local scholar was a Sakya abbot, Kunga Gyaltsen (1182-1251), who came to be known as Sakya Pandita, literally 'scholar from Sakya'.

Such was Sakya Pandita's scholastic and spiritual eminence that when the Mongols threatened to invade Tibet in the mid-13th century he represented the Tibetan people to the Mongol prince Godan (descendent of Genghis Khan). Sakya Pandita made a three-year journey to Prince Godan's camp (in modern-day Gansu), arriving in 1247. Sakya Pandita arrived to find the Mongols wantonly throwing Han prisoners in the river and set about instructing Godan in Buddhist philosophy and respect for human lives. Impressed by his wisdom, Godan made Sakya Pandita Viceroy of Tibet.

After Sakya Pandita's death in 1251, power was transferred to his nephew Phagpa, who went on to even greater fame than his uncle, being a close advisor to Kublai Khan. Phagpa's greatest legacy was a special script used by Kublai as the official alphabet of the Mongol court. Phagpa was named Imperial Preceptor (the highest religious title in the Mongol empire) and thus de facto leader of Tibet. The role of spiritual and temporal head of state became an important precedent for the Tibetan government. However, the association between Tibetan lamas and Mongol masters also set a precedent of outside rule over Tibet that the Chinese have used to justify current claims over the high plateau.

As it was, Mongol overlordship and Sakya supremacy were relatively short-lived. Mongol corruption and rivalry between the Sakyapa and Kagyupa orders led to the fall of Sakya in 1354, when power fell into the hands of the Kagyupa and the seat of government moved to Nedong in Ü.

Sakya was to remain a powerful municipality, however, and, like Shigatse, enjoyed a high degree of autonomy from successive central governments. Even today, you can see homes across the plateau painted with the red, white and blue-black stripes associated with Sakya Monastery.

hall is cold and lacks the charm of the other two places on this list.

Sakya Monastery Restaurant   TIBETAN **$**
(萨迦寺餐厅; Sàjiā Sì Cāntīng; ☎824 2988; dishes Y7-15) This Tibetan joint is owned by the monastery and serves fried rice, *thugpa* (noodles) and milk tea.

Self-Catering
For drinks and basic supplies there are several small supermarkets scattered about town.

❶ Getting There & Away

There's one daily minibus between Shigatse bus station and Sakya (four hours). The return bus departs from Sakya around 11.30am. Another option is to take a Lhatse-bound bus from Shigatse to the Sakya turn-off and then walk or hitch

the remaining 25km. See p359 for information regarding the risks associated with hitching.

Lhatse   ལྷ་རྩེ   拉孜

 0892 / ELEV 3950M

Approximately 150km southwest of Shigatse and some 30km west of the Sakya turn-off, the bleak town of Lhatse (Lāzī) is best considered a pit-stop for lunch or supplies or for staying overnight on the way to better destinations. Lhatse is more or less a one-street town with a small square near the town centre. The 3km-long main street runs east-west and used to be part of the Friendship Hwy, but this has now been diverted to the north. Passing 4WD traffic will mostly be heading to Everest Base Camp, the Tibet-Nepal border or the turn-off for Ali in western Tibet, about 6km out of town.

There's little to see in Lhatse save the small **Changmoche Monastery** at the western end of town. Nearby is the Xiqian Hot Springs, Lhatse Chöde and Drampa Gyang Temple.

🛏 Sleeping

Besides the following, there are also a few grubby, characterless hotels around the middle of town to consider if everything else is full. If you are coming from Lhasa or Shigatse, your stay here may be your first introduction to Tibet's infamous pit toilets.

Lhatse Tibetan Farmers Hotel
GUESTHOUSE **$**

(拉孜农民旅馆; Lāzī Nóngmín Lǚguǎn; ☎832 2333; d without/with bathroom Y35/130) Located on the east side of town, this courtyard guesthouse is popular with 4WD drivers and guides. The older block of basic rooms with hard mattresses still manages to survive but the owners have recently completed a new block in the back of the compound, complete with modern en suite rooms. The guesthouse's Tibetan-style **restaurant** is a very cosy place, with decent Tibetan and Western food (Y10 to Y25). Hot water showers are available.

Shànghǎi Hotel of Lāzī
HOTEL **$$**

(拉孜上海大酒店; Lāzī Shànghǎi Dàjiǔdiàn; ☎832 3678; fax 832 3786; d Y380, discounts up to 30%) This is the top hotel in Lhatse and, while overpriced, is the place to stay if you need Western comforts like good bed sheets, flush toilets and showers. Look carefully at your room before settling in; the one they showed us had a big hole in the bathtub. The hotel is obvious on the south side of the town square.

Dewang Hotel
GUESTHOUSE **$**

(☎832 2888; d Y120) The rooms at this family-run courtyard hotel are clean but they will have a hard time competing with the new rooms at the Farmer's Hotel. Still it makes a fine backup choice. The hotel is about 50m east of the Farmer's Hotel, on the other side of the road. The small sign above the door reads 'Plain Sailing'.

✕ Eating

Guesthouses all have their own inexpensive Tibetan-style restaurants (with English menus) and most travellers eat at these. You can also try the many Chinese and Muslim restaurants that line the south side of the main street.

Lhatse Kitchen
RESTAURANT **$**

(拉孜厨房; Lāzī Chúfáng; ☎832 2858; dishes Y10-35; ⊗7.30am-midnight; 🖥) Located in the same building as the Shànghǎi Hotel of Lāzī, the Kitchen serves a range of tasty Nepali, Indian and Western dishes in an upscale Tibetan-style setting.

ℹ Getting There & Away

Daily morning minibuses (five hours) run between Shigatse and Lhatse. Two or three buses a day from Shigatse pass through on the way to Shegar. There's no public transport all the way out to Mt Kailash, though daily (sometimes twice-daily) buses from Shigatse pass through on the way to Saga.

Around Lhatse

For the small traditional village of Lhatse Chöde, just north of Lhatse, see p146.

Xiqian Hot Springs
HOT SPRINGS

(ཚན་པ་ཚན; 温泉; Wēnquán; ☎0892-832 3999; baths per person Y60) Tibetans come from far and wide to bathe in the healing waters of these hot springs, which are said to cure a multitude of ills, especially skin irritations (so be careful who you share the pools with). The facilities have been upgraded in recent years and the odourless spring water is now piped into two large indoor pools, set under a canopy roof. It's a pleasant enough place for a dip, especially in the cooler months or in the evenings.

The hot springs are 10km east of Lhatse. Turn north off the Friendship Hwy at the town of Xiqian (or Xiqin; kilometre marker 5041) and continue 750m north. Hot spring fanatics can even stay here, in guestrooms just a few steps from the pools. The rooms contain small pools that you can fill up and soak in privacy. It's a good idea to agree beforehand about including the springs in your itinerary if you want to visit by hired 4WD.

Baber & Shegar

དབལ་འབར། 白坝协格尔

☎0892 / ELEV 4250M & 4150M

The last main stop on the way to Everest is a wind-raked truck stop called Baber (Báibà in Chinese), located at kilometre marker 5133, about 12km before the turn-off to

Everest. By the time most travellers arrive from Shigatse or Sakya it's already too late to visit Everest, so most spend the night in one of Baber's overpriced hotels. Baber is also the place to pick up entry tickets to Qomolangma Nature Reserve, which includes Everest Base Camp, Rongphu Monastery and Cho Oyu Base Camp. Purchase tickets at the **Qomolangma Service Centre** (☎135 1892 6785; ⏰9.30am-8.30pm) on the main road opposite the Kangjong Hotel.

Shegar (Xiégēr in Chinese; also known as New Tingri, but not to be confused with Tingri) is a small city located 7km northwest of Baber, easily reached from the crossroad in the middle of Baber. If you have time it's worth making a short trip to Shegar to check out the incredible ruins of **Shegar Dzong** (Crystal Fort), built into the side of an impossibly steep mountain. The remains of the *dzong's* defensive walls snake up the near vertical pinnacle that looms over the town. A 2km kora trail leads up from the western side of town to the top of the steep crag (think Mt Crumpit in *The Grinch Who Stole Christmas*). Along the way you can see Mt Everest in the distance. Morning light is best for taking photographs.

On the way up you'll pass the **Shegar Chöde Monastery** (admission Y10, photos Y10), a small Gelugpa institution built in 1269. The monastery originally followed Nyingma, Sakya, Gelug and Kargyu tradition until the period of the fifth Dalai Lama when the Gelugpa became the dominant order. A painting inside depicts the monastery at the height of its power, when it had around 800 monks. These days only 30 remain, but they are happy to have visitors sit and chat with them in the courtyard. Keep an eye out for the 'longevity sheep' (sheep that were saved from slaughter) that hang out in the courtyard.

🛏 Sleeping & Eating

Both Shegar and Baber offer accommodation. Most groups stay in Baber and head out early to catch the dawn over the Himalayas at Pang-la. Shegar is not a bad option as the town is a little more pleasant and has an interesting old Tibetan quarter that winds up toward the monastery.

Most guesthouses and hotels in Baber have attached restaurants. It seems like half the restaurants in town are either called 'Sìchuān' or 'Chéngdū'. You can pick up water and noodles and biscuits at any number of shops along the highway.

Kangjong Hotel HOTEL $$
(雪域宾馆; Xuěyù Bīnguǎn; ☎139 8992 3995; d without/with bathroom Y100/220) The Kangjong (Snowlands) has decent quality rooms in the new block with clean bathrooms and big duvets to keep the cold away. Rooms in the older block, with toilets down the hall, are dim and scruffy. The attached restaurant has wall-to-wall comfy sofas and is a great place to swap info with other travellers. Simple but good food is available (Y10 to Y15 per dish) and you can kick back with a thermos of sweet tea. The hotel is in the middle of town at the crossroads to Shegar.

Sunrise Hotel HOTEL $$
(阳光宾馆; Yángguāng Bīnguǎn; ☎139 8992 2770; d without/with bathroom Y50/220) Located at the beginning of town (coming from Lhatse) on the left. It has decent-looking doubles in a modern building and the price includes breakfast. Basic rooms without bath are located in a separate building. Note that the Hotel is called 'Sunshine' in Chinese but the English language sign outside says 'Sunrise'.

Qomolangma Hotel Tingri HOTEL $$$
(珠穆朗玛峰宾馆; Zhūmùlǎngmǎ Fēng Bīnguǎn; ☎826 2775; d/tr Y390/468, discounts up to 25%) The biggest place in town, this hotel is popular with tour groups. Rooms are modern and clean (though not better than the Kangjong). It's on the other side of the river on the way to Shegar.

Pentoc Guesthouse GUESTHOUSE $
(潘多旅馆; Pānduō Lǚguǎn; ☎139 0891 1167; per bed Y30) Manager Gele can set you up in a cabin with three beds. The open-air toilet is a tad basic, but affords great views. It's 100m south of the Kangjong (just past the T-junction).

The following two places are located in Shegar.

Shànghǎi Hotel HOTEL $$
(上海宾馆; Shànghǎi Bīnguǎn; ☎826 2858; Xuebao Nanlu; d/tr Y580/480, discounts up to 50%) The best place to stay in Shegar has a modern concrete block with en suite bathrooms and hot showers.

Tingri Guesthouse GUESTHOUSE $
(定日招待所; Dìngrì Zhāodàisuǒ; ☎152 8912 6282; Zhufen Nanlu; s/tr Y70/120) A small guesthouse with airless single rooms and better triples that look over the street. The

back of the guesthouse is an army barracks so be careful where you point your camera. The guesthouse is right above an **internet cafe**.

 Shopping

A gear shop at the Qomolangma Hotel sells jackets, sleeping bags, trekking boots and other camping gear. Prices are somewhat inflated compared to what you'd pay in Lhasa or Shigatse.

 Getting There & Away

Baber is around 81km from Lhatse. There are two or three buses (seven hours) a day between Shegar and Shigatse with a stop in Baber.

Everest Region

Everest's Tibetan name is generally rendered as Qomolangma, and some 27,000 sq km of territory around Everest's Tibetan face have been designated as the Qomolangma Nature Reserve (see the box, p296). For foreign travellers, Everest Base Camp has become one of the most popular trekking destinations in Tibet, offering the chance to gaze on the magnificent north face of the world's tallest peak, **Mt Everest** (珠穆朗玛峰, Zhūmùlǎngmǎ Fēng; 8848m). The Tibetan approach provides far better vistas than those on the Nepali side, and access is a lot easier as there is also a road all the way up.

The most satisfying way to get to Everest Base Camp is to make the popular three- or four-day trek from the Friendship Hwy at Tingri (p247). The road to Everest Base Camp from Chay was upgraded in 2007 to an elevated gravel road. Plans to pave the road with asphalt were met with international opposition (most strongly from India) and were abandoned. The road from Tingri to EBC has not been improved, so expect a rough and dusty trip if travelling this way by 4WD.

The Everest access road begins around 6km west of the Shegar/Baber checkpoint, shortly after kilometre marker 5145. The 91km drive takes around two to three hours. The locations this drive takes you through can be seen on Map p249.

About 3km from the Friendship Hwy you get to the village of Chay, where your entry permit is checked. From Chay, it's a winding drive up to Pang-la (5050m). The views here are stupendous on a clear day,

and feature a huge sweep of the Himalaya range, including Makalu, Lhotse, Everest, Gyachung and Cho Oyu.

The road then descends past a couple of photogenic villages and runs down into the fertile Dzaka Valley and the village of Tashi Dzom (also known as Peruche), where you can get lunch or a bed for the night at several places.

The dirt road then runs up the wide valley, to the village of Pagsum, which also offers accommodation. The next main village is Quzong (Chödzom) and from here the road turns south towards Rongphu (or Rong-puk or also Rongbuk). The first views of Everest appear half an hour before you arrive at Rongphu.

Permits

You need two permits to visit Everest Base Camp. The first is the usual Alien Travel Permit (only available if you were on a 4WD tour at the time of writing). The second, a park-entry permit for Qomolangma Nature Reserve, can be bought at the Qomolangma Nature Reserve in Baber or in the Snow Leopard Guest House in Tingri. The permit costs Y400 per vehicle, plus Y180 per passenger. Your guide will also need a ticket. Make sure you are clear with your agency if this cost is included in your trip (it usually isn't).

Your passport and PSB permit will be scrutinised at the checkpoint 6km west of Shegar. The park permit is checked at the Chay checkpoint, 3km after the turn-off from the Friendship Hwy. If you are hiking or driving in from Tingri, there is a checkpoint at Lungchang.

Dangers & Annoyances

Whatever you do, don't attempt to walk to Everest Base Camp directly after arriving in Tingri from the low altitudes of the Kathmandu Valley. The altitude gain of over 2600m leaves most people reeling from the effects of acute mountain sickness (AMS, also known as altitude sickness). Even those coming from Lhasa often have trouble.

It's also important to realise just how high and remote you are, and to carry warm clothing and some kind of rain gear no matter what time of year you visit and no matter how short your walk. Unlike on the Nepali side, there is no rescue service up here in the shadow of Everest. Get caught wearing shorts and a T-shirt when a sudden rain or snowfall hits and you could be in serious trouble.

The Chinese maintain a small military presence at Everest Base Camp to deal with any potential trouble, which include attempts to camp or trek past the base camp (you can only trek past the base camp if you have special trekking permits). Mostly, however, they are there to jump on any Tibetan-flag waving political activists.

◎ Sights

Rongphu Monastery
ELEV 4900M

Although there were probably some monastic settlements in the region for several hundred years previously, **Rongphu Monastery** (རོང་ཕོ་ཆེ་དགོན་པ་; admission Y25) is the main Buddhist centre in the valley and once coordinated the activities of around a dozen smaller religious institutions, all of which are now ruined. It was established in 1902 by a Nyingmapa lama. While not of great antiquity, Rongphu can at least lay claim to being the highest monastery in Tibet and thus the world.

Renovation work has been ongoing at the monastery since 1983, and some of the interior **murals** are superb. The monastery and its large **chörten** make a great photograph with Everest thrusting its head skyward in the background.

Tent Camp

New to the Everest scene is this group of yak fur tents lining the side of the dirt road between Rongphu and Base Camp. Don't come expecting an isolated camp of welcoming nomads – Tibetans from Tashi Dzom and other nearby villages run the tents like small hotels. So no one tent gets too much business, each tent is only allowed a maximum of five tourists. Large groups are divided into different tents, and some groups have reported that they were not even allowed to eat together in the same tent.

Be careful with your belongings as the tents are open all the time and offer no security. It's best to leave everything in your 4WD if possible. This may seem obvious, but also be careful not to touch the stovepipe, which can get scalding hot when the stove is burning. Some tents can get smoky inside; there is little you can do about this, apart from moving to a different tent.

This is the furthest point vehicles can drive to and is an incredibly scenic place to stay. You're hemmed in by high grey ridges to the east and west and as you look to the south, Everest's north face dominates the skyline. This is prime real estate and it's yours for a pittance.

Don't expect any privacy at the camp, though: tents sleep six people (your host and perhaps a relative or two will be sharing the space with you) in an open area around the central stove. Even with the fire going it's still bloody cold. Blankets are provided but you're better off with a sub-zero sleeping bag.

Everest Base Camp
ELEV 5150M

Endowed with springs, Everest Base Camp (རྫ་སྦོ་གྲུང་མའི་གཞས་ལོག་) was first used by the 1924 British Everest expedition. The site has a couple of permanent structures and a small army base. Clamber up the small hill festooned with prayer flags for great views of the star attraction, then have your photo taken at the base camp marker, which disappointingly does not even mention the word 'Everest'. It reads 'Mt Qomolangma Base Camp' and the Chinese below indicates that it is 5200m above sea level. (Other measurements have it at 5020m or 5150m.) The springs are just to the left of this marker.

If you drive up by 4WD, note that it's not possible to go all the way to Everest Base Camp anymore. All vehicles must stop at the tent camp a few kilometres past Rongphu Monastery. From here passengers must trek or take a bus (Y25) the last glorious 4km. The way up is gentle and the altitude gain is less than 200m: most people can cover the distance in less than an hour. Along the way you pass scree slopes, jagged ridges, and broad glacial valleys flowing with muddy water. About 1km uphill from the tent camp, on the left, is a Guru Rinpoche (Padmasambhava) meditation cave. The resident monk will allow you into the cave and tiny chapel.

If the altitude is bothering you, take the bus (Y25) from the tent camp. The ride includes an hour stay at Base Camp. Note that you can get mobile phone reception at Tent Camp and Base Camp. Call a friend. They'll be thrilled.

🛏️ Sleeping & Eating

Most travellers spend a night or two at the **tent camp**. Owners of tents all charge the same per-bed fee (Y40) and offer very simple

WHAT'S IN A NAME?

In 1856, Andrew Waugh, surveyor general of India, released the most important finding of the mapping of the 'Great Arc' of mountains from the south of India to the Himalayas: Peak XV was the highest mountain in the world and would henceforth be known as 'Mount Everest', in honour of Waugh's predecessor, Sir George Everest (actually pronounced 'eve-rest').

Waugh's proposal met with much initial opposition, including from Everest himself who thought a local name should be used. In response Waugh claimed that there was no 'local name that we can discover'. But this was almost certainly untrue, even if Waugh himself didn't know it. Very likely there were many scholars who knew the Tibetan name for the mountain: Qomolangma, which can be interpreted as 'Goddess Mother of the Universe' or (more literally, if less poetically) 'Princess Cow'. As early as 1733, the French produced a map on which Everest is indicated as Tschoumou Lancma. In addition, on the very day Waugh's paper on Everest was presented to the Royal Geographic Society, another was read that revealed the local Nepali name to be Deodhunga.

Still, the Everest contingent gained the upper hand (even the writer of the Nepali paper wanted the great man's name used) and in 1865 the Royal Geographic Society declared 'Mt Everest' would henceforth designate the world's highest mountain. Of course, this has had little effect on what the Tibetans and Chinese call the mountain.

meals and drinks. A few have beer for sale if you are in the mood to celebrate.

At Rongphu you can stay at the **Monastery Guesthouse**, located across the road from the monastery itself. The guesthouse was under renovation at the time of research but when completed it should offer some reasonably comfortable dorms and private rooms. The restaurant is also expected to reopen. Across from the Monastery Guesthouse, rooms are aging poorly at the **Government Hotel** (☎0892 858 4535; d per bed Y300). Despite the price, you won't get a private bathroom or a shower.

In the village of Tashi Dzom, try the **Chomolongma Benba Guesthouse** (☎139 0892 0952; per bed Y40), a family home with several dorm rooms and a cosy restaurant.

❶ Getting There & Away

There is no public transport to Everest Base Camp. It's either trek in or hire a 4WD.

Tingri དིང་རི་ 定日

ELEV 4250M

The village of Tingri (Dìngrì), 142km from Lhatse, comprises a half-kilometre of brick Tibetan homes, restaurants, guesthouses and shops lining the Friendship Hwy. Sometimes called Old Tingri, it overlooks a sweeping plain bordered by towering Himalayan peaks and is a usual overnight stop for 4WD

traffic heading to or from the Nepali border. On clear days there are stunning views of Cho Oyu from Tingri; if you can't make it to Everest Base Camp, at least pause here and take in the Himalayan eye-candy. Newcomers from Kathmandu will likely experience some mild altitude sickness if they have not acclimatised in Nyalam.

Ruins on the hill overlooking Tingri are all that remain of the Tingri Dzong. This fort was destroyed in a Nepali invasion in the late 18th century. On the plains between Shegar and Tingri, dozens more ruins that shared the same fate can be seen from the Friendship Hwy.

It is possible to trek between Everest Base Camp and Tingri (p247) or vice versa. If you are heading to EBC by vehicle there is a rough 4WD track from Tingri.

In Tingri, entry tickets to Qomolangma Nature Reserve are available at an office within the compound of the Snow Leopard Guesthouse.

🛏 Sleeping

Most places look like a trucker's hotel, which fits the mood as Tingri is little more than a truck stop en route to other places. Expect to see basic double rooms around a main courtyard with pit toilets, a hot shower block and a Tibetan restaurant or teahouse. All have English signage out the front.

Tingri Snowland Hotel
HOTEL **$**

(定日雪域饭店; Dìngrì Xuěyù Fàndiàn; ☎152 0802 7313; s/d Y60/70) About 800m west of the centre of town, Snowland has excellent views of the Himalayas when you step outside your room into the courtyard. Rooms have cloth-covered walls and are bright and clean. The restaurant has a large menu. Showers cost Y10/15 for guests/non-guests.

Himalaya Guest House
HOTEL **$**

(喜马拉雅旅馆; Xǐmǎlāyǎ Lǚguǎn; ☎826 2655; d per bed Y30) This is a new family-run place with cute cloth-covered walls that make the cheap doubles look rather cheery. The pit toilets are some of the cleanest in town. Showers cost an additional Y10. It's on the east side of town on the right as you drive in from the Baber.

Lhasa Guesthouse
HOTEL **$**

(拉萨饭店; Lāsà Fàndiàn; ☎136 1892 4906; s/d Y60/80) Prices rise with the quality of mattresses here. The restaurant (dishes Y5 to Y25) gets better reviews for the cleanliness of its kitchen. On the downside, there were no functioning showers when we visited. The hotel is east of Amdo Hotel.

Snow Leopard Guest House
HOTEL **$$**

(雪豹客栈; Xuěbào Kèzhàn; ☎826 2711; d without/with bath Y180/280) Some 4WD drivers and guides try to swing their customers here but look at a few other places in town first before deciding if this place is acceptable. It's a bit tatty and stained for the money.

✕ Eating

Third Eye Restaurant
NEPALI **$**

(☎826 2708; dishes Y14-30; ☺breakfast, lunch & dinner; 🖮) Like other Nepali-run places in this region, this one serves a range of Western, Tibetan, Nepali, Indian and Chinese dishes. Try whatever suits your mood – it's all good. The restaurant is located right in front of the Himalaya Guesthouse.

Around Tingri

Tsamda Hot Springs

(ཚ་མདའ་ཆུ་ཚན།; ☎139 0892 4147; dm Y35, d Y200-280) The odourless, iron-rich springs are about 12km west of Tingri, and are piped directly into the pools of the **Tsamda Snow Leopard Hot Spring Hotel.** Most travellers are not very impressed with the public pools (Y20), but you can rent a private room with bath for Y40 for a couple of hours if the place is not busy. The private bath is a bit rough,

too, and stained red in places from the iron in the water, but it's just the thing for cleaning yourself off after a day or two at Everest Base Camp.

The hotel makes for a better stop than Tingri. There's a common room on the 2nd floor with outstanding views, and some pleasant easy walks around the nearby hills. And the hot-spring water, despite the basic setup, is actually very good quality and the perfect temperature for soaking in.

The springs are 1km off the Friendship Hwy and are signposted in English near kilometre marker 5206.

Nyalam གཉའ་ལམ་ 聶拉木

☎0892 / ELEV 3750M

Nyalam (Nièlāmù) is a humid one-street town with a Chinese facade. It's about 30km from the Nepali border, 152km from Tingri, and is a usual overnight spot for 4WD trips to or from Nepal. It's also a base for trekking in the southern Shishapangma region.

The town has a couple of billiards halls, which can pass the time, but unless you are sleeping here your driver will probably bomb through the town, honking and scattering locals in his wake.

There is a good (read: clean) **Internet Bar** (网吧; wǎngbā; per hr Y8) across from the Nyilam Nga Dhom Hotel. There are numerous private telecom booths around town for cheap calls.

One possible day hike from here takes you up the valley behind Nyalam to Daratso, a holy lake from which glaciers of the Langtang and Jungal Himal, and maybe even Shishapangma (the only mountain over 8000m planted squarely in Tibet), are visible on a clear day.

Snowland Hotel can help organise porters and sells basic Chinese-made trekking gear from its shop across the road.

◉ Sights

The only cultural sight close to Nyalam is **Milarepa's Cave.** Milarepa was a famous Buddhist mystic and composer of songs (Tibet's St Francis of Assisi) who lived in the late 11th and early 12th centuries. During his time spent in long meditation in this cave he renounced all luxuries and survived on a diet of local weeds (famously turning green as a result).

A lot of construction has gone on around the cave in recent years. A brand new temple

THE ASSAULT ON EVEREST

There had been 13 attempts to climb Everest before Edmund Hillary and Sherpa Tenzing Norgay finally reached the summit as part of John Hunt's major British expedition of 1953. Some of these attempts verged on insanity.

In 1934 Edmund Wilson, an eccentric ex-British army captain, hatched a plan to fly himself from Hendon direct to the Himalaya, crash land his Gypsy Moth halfway up Everest and then climb solo to the summit, despite having no previous mountaineering experience (and marginal flying expertise). Needless to say he failed spectacularly. When his plane was impounded by the British in India he trekked to Rongphu in disguise and made a solo bid for the summit. He disappeared somewhere above Camp III, and his body and diaries were later discovered by the mountaineer Eric Shipton at 6400m. A second solo effort was later attempted by a disguised Canadian from the Tibet side. It was abandoned at 7150m.

From 1921 to 1938, all expeditions to Everest were British and were attempted from the north (Tibetan) side, along a route reconnoitred by John Noel – disguised as a Tibetan – in 1913. In all, the mountain claimed 14 lives. Perhaps the most famous early summit bid was by George Mallory and Andrew Irvine (just 22), who were last seen going strong above 7800m before clouds obscured visibility. Their deaths remained a mystery until May 1999 when an American team found Mallory's body, reigniting theories that the pair may have reached the top two decades before Norgay and Hillary. In 2005 teams were sent up to gather evidence, and the results prompted the writers at www.everestnews. com to publish an intriguing theory in support of a Mallory summit. It was Mallory, who when asked why he wanted to climb Everest famously quipped 'because it is there'.

With the conclusion of WWII and the collapse of the British Raj, the Himalayas became inaccessible. Tibet closed its doors to outsiders and, in 1951, the Chinese invasion clamped the doors shut even more tightly. In mountaineering terms, however, the Chinese takeover had the positive effect of shocking the hermit kingdom of Nepal into looking for powerful friends. The great peaks of the Himalaya suddenly became accessible from Nepal.

In 1951, Eric Shipton led a British reconnaissance expedition that explored the Nepali approaches to Everest and came to the conclusion that an assault via Nepal might indeed be met with success. Much to their dismay, the British found that the mountain was no longer theirs alone. In 1952 Nepal issued only one permit to climb Everest – to the Swiss. The Swiss, who together with the British had virtually invented mountaineering as a sport, were extremely able climbers. British climbers secretly feared that the Swiss might mount a successful ascent on their first attempt, something that eight

sits in front of the cave and at the time of research some guesthouses were being constructed. Most people can safely miss the cave without disappointment, though if the guesthouses are built they could make for a more interesting overnight location than bland Nyalam.

The cave is signposted 'Milaraba Buddist Practice Cave' and is 11km north of Nyalam, at Gangka village.

🛏 Sleeping

None of the guesthouses have showers (浴室; *yùshì*), but you can have one at Chéngdū Restaurant, opposite the Internet Bar, for Y20 between 8am and 11pm. All hotels have English signage out the front.

Shishapangma Guesthouse　　HOTEL $
(希夏邦马旅馆; Xīxiàbāngmǎ Lǚguǎn; ☎8277 2191; dm/tr Y40/200) This new hotel is located at the very edge of town, at the top of the hill on the Zhāngmù side (just past the petrol station). It has a choice of dorm rooms and a clean, shared bathroom. It has a cosy cafe and some rooms have valley views.

Nyalam Hotel　　HOTEL $
(聂拉木宾馆; Nièlāmù Bīnguǎn; ☎136 5956 8353; per bed Y40) The Nyalam has a few small bright rooms that overlook a parking yard. They are in contrast to the long, dark and cold hallway that leads to the loo. It's long been a favourite with overlanders but new rivals are starting to pick up some of their business. It's located a little way up the hill, just past the school.

major British expeditions had failed to achieve. As it happened, the Swiss climbed to 8595m on the southeast ridge – higher than any previous expedition – but failed to reach the summit.

The next British attempt was assigned for 1953. Preparations were particularly tense. It was generally felt that if this attempt were unsuccessful, any British hopes to be the first to reach the summit would be dashed. There was considerable backroom manoeuvring before the expedition set off. As a result, Eric Shipton, who had led three previous expeditions (including one in 1935), was dropped as team leader in favour of John Hunt, an army officer and keen Alpine mountaineer, though relatively unknown among British climbers.

Shipton's 1951 expedition had at the last minute accepted two New Zealand climbers. One of them was Edmund Hillary, a professional bee-keeper and a man of enormous determination. He was invited again to join Hunt's 1953 expedition. Also joining the expedition was Tenzing Norgay, a Sherpa who had set out on his first Everest expedition at the age of 19 in 1935.

On 28 May 1953, Hillary and Norgay made a precarious camp at 8370m on a tiny platform on the southeast approach to the summit, while the other anxious members of the expedition waited below at various camps. That night the two men feasted on chicken noodle soup and dates. The pair set off early the next day (29 May) and after a five hour final push they reached the top at 11.30am, planting the flag for Britain on the highest point on Earth.

By 2008, about 2700 people had reached the peak of Everest (including George Mallory II, Mallory's grandson), while 216 climbers had died in the attempt. The first woman to reach the summit was Junko Tabei from Japan on 16 May 1975. The youngest person was 13-year-old Jordan Romero from California, who reached the top in May 2010. The oldest person to make the climb was Min Bahadur Sherchan of Nepal, who scaled the peak in 2008 at the age of 76. The Nepali side is the easier and more frequently used.

Of all the controversies that Everest generates in the world of mountaineering, its height is not one that should still be an issue. But in May 1999 an American expedition planted a global positioning system (GPS) at the top of Everest and pegged the height at a controversial 8850m – 2m higher than the 8848m accepted since 1954. The Chinese dispute this claim (and indeed recently lowered the height by 1.5m due to melting of the summit ice cap.) Of course, plate tectonics are also at play. It is believed that the summit rises 4mm per year and is shifting 3 to 6mm per year in a northeasterly direction.

For the latest news on Everest, check out www.everestnews.com.

Snowland Hotel Nyalam HOTEL $
(雪域饭店聂拉木; Xuěyù Fàndiàn Nièlāmù; ☑827 2111; d per bed Y30) The Snowland is a quirky building. The floors are wobbly and ceilings a bit too low and the staircase/ladder thing can be a struggle to climb. But it also has loads of character, with a cheery staff, cosy cafe and the stickers of past overland groups plastered to the walls.

✗ Eating

Finding a place to eat in Nyalam is simple: just look around. All of the following serve breakfast, lunch and dinner but have no fixed opening hours.

Base Camp Restaurant INTERNATIONAL $$
(大本营; Dàbĕnyíng; ☑827 2992; dishes Y15-48; ⓜ) This is a branch of the Base Camp restaurant in Zhāngmù, with a similar menu and atmosphere. The food runs the gamut from Western to Chinese, Indian and Nepali. It's located in front of the Nyalam Hotel.

Snowland Restaurant INTERNATIONAL $$
(雪域餐厅; Xuěyù Cāntīng; ☑827 2111; dishes Y20-35; ⓜ) Popular with alpinists (every one of whom seems to leave a memento on the wall), the Snowland doles out Western dishes, including some filling pancakes, but is strongest on Tibetan and Chinese dishes. Locals like it too. It's located opposite the Snowland Hotel, above the Kailash Restaurant.

Nyalam Tongla Restaurant INTERNATIONAL $$
(☑827 2699; dishes Y20-48; ⓜ) This place has a lot of promise. There is an ambitious

Western-style menu, plus a slew of Indian and Chinese dishes. It's at the top of the hill, opposite the petrol station. Look for the big red sign saying 'Welcome to Pizza Center'.

ⓘ Getting There & Away

The only way here is by 4WD, hitching (see p359) or cycling.

Nyalam to Zhāngmù

The landscape along the 30km route from Nyalam to Zhāngmù should be touted as one of Tibet's great natural wonders. From Nyalam, the road drops like a stone off the Tibetan plateau into a deep gorge of evergreen forests, waterfalls and thundering rivers. Such noise and colour and drama after the dry, stark landscape of Tibet is a joy to the senses. Perhaps most amazing are the dozen or more falls, many well over 200m long, any one of which would be considered a great attraction anywhere else. Unfortunately, the road lacks turn-outs, making photo stops a little tricky. Ask your guide anyway and he may be able to convince the driver to pull over at a safe spot. During the summer monsoons, the road is submerged in a sea of cloud – no doubt one of the reasons why Nyalam means 'gateway to hell' in Tibetan.

After years of work a sealed road is nearly complete. At the time of writing the only unfinished section was the last 3km before Zhāngmù. By the time you read this it will most likely be finished.

Zhāngmù (Dram)

འགྲམ་ 樟木

☎ 0892 / ELEV 2250M

Zhāngmù, also known as Dram in Tibetan and Khasa in Nepali, hugs the rim of what seems a never-ending succession of hairpin bends down to the customs area at the border of China and Nepal. After Tibet, it all seems incredibly green and wet.

Zhāngmù is a typical border town, much larger than Nyalam, and has a restless, reckless feel to it. There is one far-too-narrow main road through town and it gets backed up frequently. During these times the squealing of Tata truck brakes as the vehicles inch their way down will drive you insane.

Evening reveals the town's seedy side as its numerous downmarket discos, bars and brothels open for business; a sort of Tijua-

Zhāngmù (Dram)

Zhāngmù (Dram)

◎ Top Sights

| Mani Lhakhang | A2 |
| Temple | A2 |

Activities, Courses & Tours

| 1 Bath House | A1 |

Sleeping

2 Gang Gyen Hotel	B2
3 Ji Ji Hotel	B2
4 Sherpa Hotel	A2
5 Zhāngmù Hotel	B2

Eating

Base Camp Restaurant	(see 2)
6 Chinese Restaurants	B2
7 Himalaya Restaurant	B2

Shopping

| 8 Supermarket | A2 |

Information

9 China Mobile	B2
10 Customs & Immigration	B2
11 PSB	B2

na-in-miniature. All in all, the town feels more like a part of Nepal than anywhere else, with only a few indications that you're still in Tibet (or China).

If you find yourself stuck here for a night and want a little peace and quiet, most of the traveller-oriented restaurants stay open late so it's easy to enjoy a late dinner or beer.

Orientation

All those hairpin bends can leave you spinning and upon first arrival it can be difficult to figure out where you are, relative to everything else on your map. The best way to orient yourself is to walk all the way downhill until you reach Chinese Customs Post; within a few minutes' walk back uphill you'll pass most of the hotels and restaurants listed in this guide.

Permits

Located above China Mobile, the **Zhāngmù PSB** (公安局; Gōng'ānjú; ☏874 2264) won't give you an Alien Travel Permit to head north into Tibet unless you have a guide, a driver and the mysterious Tibetan Tourism Bureau (TTB) permit – effectively making it impossible for independent travellers to come up from Nepal without having booked a tour in Kathmandu. The PSB cannot extend your visa.

🛏 Sleeping

Try to get a room off the road, preferably facing the mountains, as the noise from traffic can be awful.

Sherpa Hotel HOTEL **$$**
(夏尔巴酒店; Xià'ěrbā Jiǔdiàn; ☏874 2098; d/tr without bathroom Y80/120, d with bathroom Y200) The pink-painted rooms are clean (if a little small) at this friendly hotel and hot water is available most of the time. The two bars at street level can be noisy but the back rooms remain fairly quiet. In addition, the rooms that face the valley afford spectacular views.

Gang Gyen Hotel HOTEL **$$**
(刚坚宾馆; Gāngjiān Bīnguǎn; ☏874 2188; d without/with bathroom Y200/300) The double rooms are a little shabby and overpriced. Carpets are worn out, furnishings are old and the staircase is dirty. On a positive note, it has a nice location near Chinese Customs. Consider this place a backup option if others are full.

Zhāngmù Hotel HOTEL **$$$**
(樟木宾馆; Zhāngmù Bīnguǎn; ☏874 2221; fax 874 2220; d/tr Y480/580, deluxe Y680, discounts up to 15%) The modern rooms in this government-run hotel are luxurious by Tibetan standards, and back rooms have great mountain views, but it's overpriced and the management is a bit snooty. The hotel runs a legitimate massage centre (foot massage US$6) two doors up the road.

Ji Ji Hotel HOTEL **$**
(吉吉宾馆; Jíjí Bīnguǎn; ☏874 5688; tr per bed Y50, d without/with bathroom Y100/160) Rooms

are clean and basic. There are no showers for the dorms but you can grab one just up the road at Bath House. There are a couple of signs outside, one says Ji Ji Hotel, the other says JJ Hotel. Try not to get too confused.

🍴 Eating

Zhāngmù feels like a mini-Kathmandu, at least in its restaurant options. Wander up the hill for an excellent selection of Western, Chinese, Tibetan and Nepali cuisine. Opening hours appear to be very flexible. Many restaurants fix lunch boxes, which come in handy on the long ride to Kathmandu.

Base Camp Restaurant INTERNATIONAL **$$**
(大本营餐厅; Dàběnyíng Cāntīng; Ground fl, Gang Gyen Hotel; dishes Y20-45; ⏰9am-midnight; 📶) Looking a little like a Western sports bar (except with oxygen tanks and climbing gear instead of footballs and jerseys), this popular establishment serves a full range of Nepali, Chinese, Tibetan and Western mains, including steaks and breakfast foods. The curries are thick and delicious.

Sherpa Restaurant WESTERN, TIBETAN **$**
(夏尔巴餐厅; Xià'ěrbā Cāntīng; ☏874 2098; dishes Y15-40; ⏰breakfast, lunch & dinner; 📶) Located in the Sherpa Hotel, this place does everything from Tibetan momos and Chinese chow mien to pasta and burgers. It doesn't have much atmosphere but food quality is some of the best in town.

Himalaya Restaurant TIBETAN, NEPALI **$**
(喜马拉雅餐厅; Xīmǎlāyǎ Cāntīng; ☏874 3068; opposite Gang Gyen Hotel; dishes Y15-30; ⏰breakfast, lunch & dinner; 📶) A cheery place for decent Tibetan, Nepali or Chinese food.

🔒 Shopping

There are countless small shops on the main road selling drinks and snacks, and equally important in Zhāngmù, umbrellas. There's a small basic **supermarket** five minutes' walk up the hill from customs.

ℹ Information

If there was a contest to find the filthiest internet cafe in China the **Jídī Internet Cafe** (基地网吧; per hr Y10; ⏰10.30pm-2am) in Zhāngmù would be a strong contender.

For showers head to **Bath House** (Y10; ⏰9am-11.30pm).

Moneychangers deal openly in front of the Zhāngmù Hotel and change any combination of Chinese yuan, US dollars or Nepali rupees at better rates than on the Nepali side. **Bank of China** (中国银行; Zhōngguó Yínháng; ⊘9.30am-1.30pm & 3.30-6.30pm Mon-Fri, 11am-2pm Sat & Sun), way up the hill, will change cash and travellers cheques into yuan and also yuan into dollars, euros or pounds if you have an exchange receipt, but doesn't deal in Nepali rupees.

The **post office** near the bank has an ATM outside accepting foreign cards on the Visa and Plus networks. For telephone calls try the many private telecom booths around town.

ⓘ Getting There & Away

At **Chinese immigration** (⊘9.30am-6.30pm, sometimes closed 1.30-3.30pm) you will need to fill in an exit form and health declaration and you may be asked for your travel permit.

From customs, go on to Kodari in Nepal, around 8km below Zhāngmù. Cars and pickups offer lifts across this no-man's land (Y10). Tour groups often get taken across by their 4WD. The last stretch over the Friendship Bridge has to be walked.

At **Nepali immigration** (⊘8.30am-4pm) in Kodari it's possible to get a Nepali visa for the same price as in Lhasa (US$25/40/100 for up to 15/30/90 days, or the equivalent in rupees, plus one passport photo), although it is sensible to get one in Lhasa just in case.

If you are coming from Nepal into Zhāngmù, you won't find Chinese immigration open if you leave the Nepali side after 3.30pm. Note that Nepal is an odd 2¼ hours behind Chinese time.

There are four daily buses between Kodari and Kathmandu (Rs 240 to Rs 280, 4½ hours), with the 1.30pm an express service. Otherwise jump a local bus to Barabise (Rs 65, three hours) and change there. After 2pm your only option is to take a taxi for Rs3000, or Rs 800 per seat if shared.

Western Tibet (Ngari)
མངའ་རིས་

Includes »

Ali 173
Mt Kailash 175
Lake Manasarovar . . .178
Tirthapuri Hot Springs
& Kora 179
Guge Kingdom 180
Dungkar & Piyang . . .185
Rutok 186

Best Views

» Humla Karnali Valley from Shepeling (Simbaling) Monastery (p188)

» Tagyel-tso, or anywhere along the northern route (p170)

» Mt Kailash floating over the waters of Rakshas Tal (p178)

Best Places off the Beaten Track

» Gossul Monastery (p179)

» Ruins of Shangshung in the Khyunglung Valley (p181)

» Old Rutok (p186)

Why Go?

Vast, thinly populated and with an average altitude of over 4500m, Ngari is Tibet's wild west, a rough and ready frontier occupying one of the remotest corners of Asia. For most travellers the main attractions of what is likely to be a three-week overland trip are the almost legendary destinations of Mt Kailash and Lake Manasarovar. Indeed, many of the pilgrims on this road have been planning a visit all their lives. For those less fussed by the spiritual significance of Mt Kailash, getting to one of the most isolated and beautiful corners of high Asia is likely to be an attraction in itself.

Until recently only the hardiest of travellers made it to western Tibet, but freshly paved roads and a new airport means that the region is on the verge of embracing mass Chinese tourism.

When to Go

May to June and mid-September to early October are the best times to head to Ngari, though June and July see huge convoys of Indian pilgrims booking out entire hotels on their way to Mt Kailash. April to October is best for the Drölma-la pass on the Kailash kora, as it's normally blocked with snow during other months.

The festival of Saga Dawa in May/June is a particularly popular time to visit Mt Kailash, and hundreds of pilgrims and tourists descend on the mountain. Some find the pilgrim atmosphere a highlight; others find the large numbers of trekking groups off-putting.

INDIA

Pangong-tso

Dormar

LADAKH

Rutok
Lurulangkar
Rutok Xian
Rumudong
Tsaphuk

ALI PREFECTURE

Jaggang

Nganglong Kangri (6596m)

Chaktsakha

Ali

Tsaka
Peri-tso
Wenbu Dangsang
Sherm

Tashigang

Sengge Tsangpo
Indus River
Gegye
Drungba

Gar
Kunsha Airport
Zouzou

Sher-tso

Lalung-la (5330m)
Namru
Zhungba
Daman
Zhigon

Piyang
Dungkar
4938m
Ba'er
Yagra
Gunmidengli

Tsaparang 4

Zanda

Manam

Dawa

Moincer
Checkpoint
Mt Kailash (6714m) 1

Dongpo
Khyunglung
Gurugyam Monastery
Darchen

KINNAUR
Kamet (7756m)

Sutlej River

Tirthapuri Hot Springs
Rakshas Tal
Barkha
Checkpoint

Chiu Monastery
Hor Qu
Mayum-la (5220m)

INDIA
Nanda Devi (7817m)
Gurla-la (4715m)
Toyo
Purang
Khojarnath
Sher
Gurla Mandata (7728m)

Lake Manasarovar 2

Gung Gyu-tso
Checkpoint

G R E A T

Saipal (7050m)
Simikot

UTTARANCHAL

Pithoragarh

H I M A L A Y A

NEPAL
Kanjiroba (6883m)

Ganges River

Mahendranagar

R A

Rampur

The external boundaries of India on this map have not been authenticated and may not be correct

Western Tibet Highlights

1 Join fellow pilgrims looking to erase the sins of a lifetime on the three-day trek around sacred **Mt Kailash** (p175)

2 Hike the sandy shores of holy **Lake Manasarovar** (p178), or just marvel at the intensely turquoise waters and snowcapped-mountain backdrop

3 Camp on the shores of the spectacular otherworldly lakes of **Tagyel-tso** (p170), **Dawa-tso** (p171) and **Peiku-tso** (p168), as long as you are acclimatised

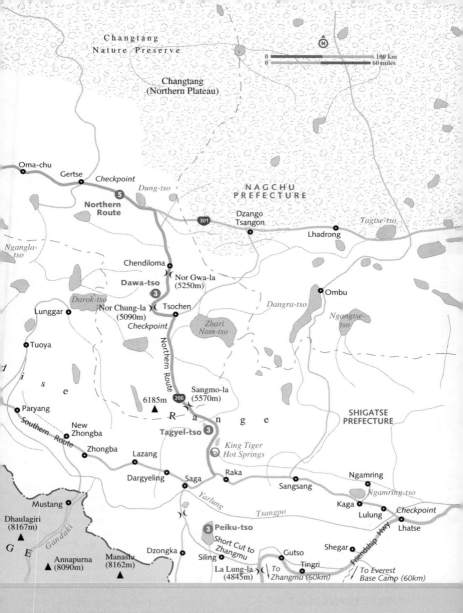

4 Scramble through tunnels, caves and secret passageways as you explore the ancient ruins and Kashmiri-influenced art of **Tsaparang** (p183), one of Asia's unknown wonders

5 Spot herds of wild asses, antelope and gazelle in the untrammelled wilderness of the Changtang, Tibet's Serengeti, along the **northern route** (p170) to Ali

History

Most histories of Tibet begin with the kings of the Yarlung Valley region and their unification of central Tibet in the 7th century. But it is thought that the Shangshung (or Zhangzhung) kingdom of western Tibet probably ruled the Tibetan plateau for several centuries before this. According to some scholars, the Bön religion made its way into the rest of Tibet from here. The Shangshung kingdom may also have served as a conduit for Tibet's earliest contacts with Buddhism. There is little material evidence of the Shangshung kingdom in modern Tibet, though the Khyunglung Valley, on the Sutlej River near Tirthapuri hot springs, marks the site of the old kingdom.

The next regional power to emerge in Ngari was the Guge kingdom in the 9th century. After the assassination of the anti-Buddhist Lhasa king Langdharma, one of the king's sons, Namde Wosung, fled to the west and established this kingdom at Tsaparang, west of Lake Manasarovar and Mt Kailash. The Guge kingdom, through its contacts with nearby Ladakh and Kashmir, spearheaded a Buddhist revival on the Tibetan plateau that at its peak fostered over 100 monasteries, most of them now in ruins.

In the late 16th century, Jesuit missionaries based in the enclave of Goa took an interest in the remote kingdom of Guge, mistaking it for the long-lost Christian civilisation of Prester John (a legendary Christian priest and king who was believed to have ruled over a kingdom in the Far East). The Jesuits finally reached Tsaparang over the Himalaya from India in 1624 after two failed attempts, but if their leader, Father Antonio de Andrede, had expected to find Christians waiting for him, he was disappointed. Nevertheless, he did meet with surprising tolerance and respect for the Christian faith. The Guge king agreed to allow de Andrede to return and set up a Jesuit mission the following year. The foundation stone of the first Christian church in Tibet was laid by the king himself.

Ironically, the evangelical zeal of the Jesuits led not only to their own demise but also to the demise of the kingdom they sought to convert. Lamas, outraged by their king's increasing enthusiasm for an alien creed, enlisted the support of Ladakhis in laying siege to Tsaparang. Within a month the city fell, the king was overthrown and the Jesuits imprisoned. The Guge kingdom never recovered.

At this point, Ngari became so marginalised as to almost disappear from the history books – with one notable exception. In the late Victorian era, a handful of Western explorers began to take an interest in the legend of a holy mountain and a lake from which four of Asia's mightiest rivers flowed. The legend, which had percolated as far afield as Japan and Indonesia, was largely ridiculed by Western cartographers. However, in 1908 the Swedish explorer Sven Hedin returned from a journey that proved there was indeed such a mountain and such a lake, and that the remote part of Tibet they occupied was in fact the source of the Karnali (the northernmost tributary of the Ganges), Brahmaputra (Yarlung Tsangpo), Indus (Sengge Tsangpo) and Sutlej (Langchen Tsangpo) Rivers. The mountain was Kailash and the lake, Manasarovar.

Permits

Foreigners require a fistful of permits: an Alien Travel Permit, military permit, Tibet Tourism Bureau (TTB) permit, foreign affairs permit... Your travel agency will organise all of these for you but it will take a week minimum. You may need to stop in Shigatse to process your Alien Travel Permit and may further need to get this endorsed in Darchen or Ali, depending on the direction of travel. This is particularly true if you wish to visit off-the-beaten-track places like Gurugyam Monastery. As you travel through the region your guide will need to register you with the Public Security Bureau (PSB) in some towns (such as Tsochen).

Western Tibet is a politically sensitive area and is periodically closed to foreigners, due either to political unrest on the Mt Kailash kora or military tension along the contested borders of China, India and Pakistan.

Itineraries

See p26 for an overview of itineraries from Lhasa to western Tibet. Most trips will

PUBLIC TRANSPORT

At the time of research, foreigners were not allowed to travel on public transport in Tibet. Basic information is included here in case the situation changes.

Warm clothes are essential, even in summer. The sun is strong and days can be hot, especially in a 4WD, so do bring something light to wear. A sleeping bag is recommended to avoid grubby truck-stop bedding. Many of the villages, towns and hotels in western Tibet are dusty, dirty, depressing places so a tent gives you the flexibility to camp out in some of the most glorious scenery on the planet. A tent is also useful (though not essential) if you are doing the Kailash kora. A face-mask can be useful to keep out the copious dust.

Supplies are now easy to get in all the settlements of the west but consider bringing luxuries like instant porridge, muesli (with powdered milk), chocolate, cheese and dehydrated foods from home. A snack supply gives you the flexibility to stop for a picnic lunch somewhere beautiful (or when the car breaks down).

The only places to change money in Ngari are banks in Ali and, less reliably, Purang – it's much easier to change cash US dollars than travellers cheques. It's best to bring as much cash as you expect to spend. There are ATMs in Ali and, less reliably, Zanda.

take between two and three weeks. Add in a spare day for delays or breakdowns and figure in some time to rest and wash up or you'll gradually get too tired to fully enjoy the trip.

From Lhasa there are two approaches to Ngari: a southern route and a northern. Both follow the same road west to Lhatse and beyond to Raka. About 6km past Raka the routes split, with the southern route continuing west and the northern route heading north. The southern route is the more popular one, largely because it is the fastest way to Mt Kailash. Although there are no stellar attractions on the longer northern route, the scenery is grander, traffic lighter and wildlife richer than the southern route.

The Xīnjiāng–Tibet Hwy is one of the highest, remotest and most spectacular roads in Asia. The route passes through the remote and disputed Aksai Chin region; with the unpredictability of breakdowns, it can take several days or more to travel the 1100km from Yecheng to Ali. The very few hardy adventurers who make this road do so mostly in a rented 4WD, and it's not cheap as you'll likely have to pay for the vehicle to travel all the way from Lhasa to Yecheng and back. Buses run every few days between Ali and Yecheng but foreigners are not officially allowed on them. For a rundown of the route, see p354.

If you're coming to/from Kathmandu via the Friendship Hwy, a shortcut to/from Saga (via beautiful Peiku-tso) will shave a full day's travel off your trip. It is also possible to enter Ngari on a four-day trek from Simikot in the Humla region of western Nepal to Purang on the Chinese border near Mt Kailash. This route is open only to tour groups that trek in from Humla, which is a restricted region.

Southern Route

The entire 500km section of road from Saga to Hor Qu was under reconstruction in 2010, qualifying the route as one of the world's largest construction sites. Once road upgrading has been completed, driving times will be slashed and you'll be able to drive from Lhatse to Kailash in two days. Until then, expect bone-crunching chaos as drivers divert off-road every few kilometres in a confused attempt to find the next road/detour/bridge. It's a serious grind. The good news is that bridges are now in place over all the major rivers, so getting stuck in a river is just a fond memory from the past.

LHATSE TO SAGA (306KM)
This is a full day's journey of about eight hours' driving. Just past the Lhatse checkpoint (6km after Lhatse itself), the road leaves the paved Friendship Hwy and bears northwest. The kilometre marker at the start of this route is 2141.

Just a couple of kilometres after leaving the Friendship Hwy the road crosses the Yarlung Tsangpo and then runs for an hour or so through alternating scenery: barren canyons (that swell in the summer rains) and green meadow land with scattered Tibetan villages on the edges. The photogenic **Lang-tso** (Ox Lake), which you pass in the first hour, has been stocked by the Chinese for sport fishing, a sore point with local

DANGERS & ANNOYANCES

If you've acclimatised for a few days in Lhasa, the gradual rate of gain along the southern route to Kailash shouldn't pose any serious problems, though the jump from Lhatse (3950m) to Raka (4925m) or Saga (4610m) involves a potentially dangerous jump in elevation. An overnight at Sakya (4280m) or Rongphu Monastery (4900m) en route will help your body adjust. If you're coming from Nepal you should be particularly careful as you won't be well acclimatised; an overnight in Nyalam (3750m) and either old Tingri (4250m) or Baber (4250m) or Lhatse is an excellent idea.

Tibetans. (Tibetans don't catch or eat fish because of the Buddhist prohibition on taking life.)

Past the lake the road climbs up to the Ngamring-la (4500m). At kilometre marker 2085, 60km from Lhatse, the road passes through the very small town of **Kaga** (Kajia), next to **Ngamring-tso**, which often appears brown because of the nearby mountains reflecting off its surface. A turn-off runs round the east side of the lake to the larger settlement and army base of **Ngamring** (Angren), visible on the northeast side of the lake and about 6km off the main route. Ngamring has food and accommodation if you need it.

Within 10km of passing Kaga, 70km west of Lhatse, you'll leave behind the last trees for many days, and soon after you'll also leave behind the last agricultural fields.

About 500m beyond kilometre marker 2060, prayer flags mark the start of a path to the **Drapsang Monastery**, which overlooks the road from a steep fairy-tale-like crag. The road then makes a zigzag ascent past photogenic nomads' camps and their flocks to the Bang-la (4720m), then down to a valley that time forgot, and up again to the 4800m Gor-la, before dropping down over one hour to Sangsang.

Sangsang (4590m), 113km and three hours west of Lhatse, is a small grubby town of a few hundred souls. The impressively named but overpriced **Symphonium Hotel** (桑福宾馆; Sāngfú Bīnguǎn; r Y80-150), and the simply unimpressive **Sāngsāng Bīnguǎn** (桑桑宾馆; per bed Y30-40) offer rooms, buckets of cold water and a few hours of electricity in the evenings. If you have time, you could visit the small Nyingma-school **Oserling nunnery**, which overlooks the town from the northern end and is home to 36 nuns.

The route passes through a succession of wide alleys before following a gorge into the ravine of the Raka Tsangpo with its dark, craggy peaks. Emerging from this ravine the road skirts a lake and then crosses a plain, which is prone to flood damage during July and August. The route then climbs to the 4925m Jye-la, before dropping down again and passing through the tiny settlement of **Raka** (4925m, kilometre marker 1912), about 6km before the junction of the northern and southern routes, and 115km from Sangsang.

The rooms in the misspelt **Lhato Hotal Teahoese** (拉妥旅馆; Lātuǒ Lǚguǎn; dm Y30) are rustic but clean and have their own yak-dung stoves for heat. The hotel is the first on the right as you drive through the one-horse village and is one of half a dozen identical guesthouses all in a line. For surprisingly good Sichuanese food, try the **Hóngchéng Fànguǎn** (洪城饭馆; mains Y20-25) across the road. Electricity is by generator only. If you're taking the northern route, this is pretty much the last accommodation for 240km, though you could camp at Tagyel-tso. Confusingly, many maps show Raka (or Raga) right at the crossroads; in fact the turn-off is 6km away.

If you are heading to Saga, it's another 60km.

ZHĀNGMÙ TO SAGA (280KM)

The scenic short cut from Zhāngmù on the Nepali border to Saga on the southern route to Ngari saves 250km (at least a day of travel) and is used mostly by 4WD groups visiting Ngari directly from Nepal.

See p157 and p160 for more details on the first part of this route. Past Nyalam the road climbs to the 4950m Tong-la and then the 4845m La Lung-la. Not long after, the short cut branches west off the Friendship Hwy (kilometre marker 5265-66; 113km from Zhāngmù), rounding some hills at the entrance of a vast stony plain. Keep your eyes peeled for ruins to the north. From here to Saga it's about 170km or four hours of driving.

The first village you see just north of the road, 24km from the junction, is Petse, huddled below a gompa and ruined hilltop *dzong* (fortress). Shortly afterwards at **Siling** (Seylong) village, travellers must pay Y65 per person and Y40 per car for entry to the western section of the Qomolangma Nature Reserve.

To the south come views of sand dunes and then massive **Shishapangma** (8012m), known to the Nepalese as Gosainthan, the world's 14th-tallest peak and the only 8000m-plus mountain planted completely inside Tibet. The road provides access to the mountain's north base camp before skirting the beautiful turquoise **Peiku-tso** (4590m), about an hour's drive from Siling. This is one of Tibet's magical spots, and there's fine camping by the lakeshore, with stunning views of snowcapped Shishapangma and the Langtang range bordering Nepal to the south. If you do plan to camp, bring your own drinking water and be well acclimatised. Also try to find a sheltered camp site as winds whip up in the afternoon.

The bumpy route then enters a side gorge before passing the turn-off to the scenic but off-limits Kyirong Valley and the border crossing with Nepal at Rasuwa (closed to foreigners). Some 14km after the junction look back for fine views over the plain. After passing small, salty Drolung-tso you climb to two passes at 4825m and 4760m and then drop steeply down to the bridge across the Yarlung Tsangpo. From here it's 3km to Saga, where you join the southern route.

SAGA ས་དགའ 萨嘎
📞 0892 / ELEV 4610M

The sprawling truck-stop town of Saga is the last of any size on the southern route and your last chance to eat a lavish meal and enjoy 24-hour electricity. Most facilities are found on the central street, Gesang Lu, at the intersection of the roads to Zhāngmù, Lhatse and Mt Kailash.

There's a fast and friendly **internet bar** (心语网吧; Xīnyǔ Wǎngbā; per hr Y10; ⏰24hr) at the square by the south end of Gesang Lu, and hot showers at a couple of **bathhouses** (淋浴; línyù; Y15-20; ⏰10am-midnight) on the main street. Cash-strapped optimists could try the ATM at the Agricultural Bank by the southern square. There are well-stocked supermarkets beside the Saga and Jiling hotels.

Saga Hotel (萨嘎宾馆; Sàgá Bīnguǎn; 📞820 2888; Gesang Lu; d/tr Y420/360, discounts of 10%;

❋ @) is the only decent hotel for hundreds of kilometres, with English-speaking reception staff and clean, carpeted rooms sporting modern bathrooms, though it's well overpriced. If it's full try the affiliated and similar Jiling Hotel at the other end of the street. The **Moon Star Restaurant** (dishes Y20-40; 🍴) attached to the Saga Hotel serves decent Chinese food, but the English menu is 60% pricier than the Chinese version.

Ālǐ Zhāodàisuǒ (阿里招待所; tr per bed Y40) is a modern concrete guesthouse at the eastern tip of Gesang Lu, opposite the Saga Hotel. The beds are comfortable and the location is central but the manager is cranky at best.

There are several Tibetan compound-style guesthouses on the road heading north from the T-junction, best of which is the cosy **Bo Tie The Clan Hotel** (Bodo Dronkhang; 博扎家族旅馆; Bózhá Jiāzú Lǚguǎn; dm Y30), with clean rooms, decent beds and clean squat toilets. It's a 10-minute walk from the centre.

Several buses a day run between Saga and Shigatse.

SAGA TO ZHONGBA (145KM)
There are several ruined monasteries along this stretch, including one just 1km out of Saga. **Dargyeling Monastery**, 42km from Saga (kilometre marker 1820) on the hillside and 1.5km off the main road, is the best preserved and worth a visit for its fine views and unusual chörtens.

From here, you cross a river and then pass the ruins of a large monastery, 12km from Dargyeling Monastery. The road then climbs to a pass marked by hundreds of miniature chörtens, before dropping 23km to Zhongba.

ZHONGBA འབྲོང་པ 仲巴
'Old Zhongba' (4570m) is a tiny, dusty town on the main road with a couple of basic guesthouses, restaurants and a small monastery. ('New Zhongba', 22km northwest, is a modern Chinese military town with good restaurants but little else to recommend it.) Given the choice between overnighting here and Paryang, take Old Zhongba.

The Sakayapa-school Dradun Gompa is worth the short stroll, especially for the remarkable Cultural Revolution–era newspapers still defacing religious murals in a side chapel of chörtens. The severed heads of goats and yaks dangle from a nearby roadside chörten.

The rustic but friendly **Yak Hotel** (☏0892-890 9863; dm Y35) has cosy yak-dung fireplaces and can provide basins of warm water for washing.

ZHONGBA TO PARYANG (101KM)

At New Zhongba you can enjoy a tantalising few kilometres of tarmac (and a petrol station) before the road deteriorates. A photogenic section of sand dunes, lake and mountains kicks in 60km from Zhongba. About 23km before Paryang you crest a 4780m pass and drop past more spectacular dunes to Paryang. Photos taken along this route can often get steppe, streams, desert dunes and snowcapped mountains in the same shot.

PARYANG པར་ཡངས་ 帕羊
ELEV 4750M

Guides have said that while many groups spend a night in Paryang (Pàyáng) on the way to Mt Kailash, none want to spend the night here on the return. The reason is obvious: it looks more like a refugee camp than a village, with foot-deep dust choking a central junction that consists largely of oil-soaked truck-repair shops.

If you must pass a night here, the **Shishapangma Hotel** (dm/d Y40/100) in the far west of town has modern rooms around a large courtyard and is popular with Indian pilgrims, though bed sheets can be grubby. The central **Tashi Hotel** (扎西旅馆; Zhāxī Lǚguǎn; dm Y30) is a smaller, simpler Tibetan-style place near a charming *mani lhakhang* (chapel with a large prayer wheel). There are several other hotels in town but no running water.

In the centre of the village, the yellow-signed **Meiyum Perse** (神湖藏餐; Shénhú Zàngcān; dishes Y10-20) is a cosy Tibetan-style teahouse and restaurant, and there are also several Sichuanese restaurants.

PARYANG TO HOR QU (223KM)

The route is a pleasant four-hour drive along the spine of the Himalaya, passing through yellow steppe, with craggy, snow-capped peaks looming to the south when the weather is clear.

There is a tricky section of sandy road 12km west of Paryang but all the major river crossings now have bridges. There's a checkpoint 103km from Paryang, where you must show your passport and permits.

At the Mayum-la (5220m), the road crosses from the drainage basin of the Yarlung Tsangpo to that of the Sutlej, as you cross from Shigatse to Ngari prefectures. A descent leads to the long Gung Gyu-tso, which nomads consider poisoned, even though it drains into Lake Manasarovar. Your first magical views of Mt Kailash come into view approximately 90km after the Mayum-la, just before the town of Hor Qu (4620m). A ticket office here collects a Y200 regional 'entry fee', when staffed.

Hor Qu (ཧོར་ཆུ; 霍尔; Huò'ěr) is another expanding village with little to recommend it but the views. Hulking 7728m Gurla Mandata is to the southwest, as is Lake Manasarovar, though the lake is a long hike away. Some trekkers walking the Lake Manasarovar kora (p259) spend the night here but most groups should give it a miss and continue to Darchen or Chiu Monastery at Lake Manasarovar, both less than an hour's drive away.

From Hor Qu, it's 22km to the crossroads settlement and checkpoint of Barkha (巴嘎; Bāgá), from where it's 15km south to Chiu Monastery, or 22km west to Darchen.

Northern Route

The northern route is the longer of the two routes from Lhasa to Ngari but it's arguably the more spectacular route, passing huge salt lakes and valleys of seminomadic herders, as well as marmots, blue sheep, wild asses and antelope. Although it's no freeway, the dirt road is well maintained and driving conditions are good.

The first part, like the southern route, follows the road from Lhatse to the turn-off near Raka (see p167). From Raka, there is almost no accommodation before Tsochen, 240km away. If you're travelling this route by 4WD, seriously consider camping at least once or twice, as the towns are uniformly dismal. You need to be well acclimatised if you intend to tackle this route before the rest of western Tibet as the road from Raka never really drops below 4500m and is often above 5000m.

KING TIGER HOT SPRINGS & TAGYEL-TSO ཐག་རྒྱལ་ཚ་ཚོ་
ELEV 5070M

Only 21km north of the Raka junction are the Tagyel Chutse, or **King Tiger Hot Springs**, a collection of gushing geysers, bubbling hot springs, puffing steam outlets and smoking holes that seem to lead straight down into the bowels of the earth. A grazing brontosaurus would not seem out of place in this smouldering, primeval landscape.

From the hot springs, the road skirts the western side of a beautiful lake, then through a wide valley, one of many stretches of open plateau in Ngari where you can see for tens of kilometres ahead of you. From a 5235m pass, the route descends to a much larger lake, **Tagyel-tso**, the waters of which are a miraculous shade of the deepest blue imaginable and ringed with snowy peaks. With luck you can spot gazelles, wild asses and even the occasional wolf, hungrily eyeing the valley's many fat marmots. This is a great place to camp but only if you're prepared for the cold and especially the altitude (around 5150m). If you've come from a night or two at Everest Base Camp you should be OK; from Lhatse this is too big a jump in altitude to be considered safe.

NORTH TO TSOCHEN

It's about 240km from Raka to Tsochen or six hours of driving on good but unpaved roads. For 25km the road runs along the eastern side of Tagyel-tso before climbing past herding camps to the 5570m Sangmola. The end-of-the-world Drolma Teahouse before the pass (5195m) offers instant noodles and a simple place to crash.

A further 45km after the pass the road crests a smaller pass and leads down to two conjoined lakes, past a small salt mine. Eventually you pop out into the wide sandy valley of the Yutra Tsangpo, where the road splits *Mad Max*–style into a dozen parallel tracks. About 230km from the turn-off, a small monastery and large collection of prayer flags and mani stones sit on a ledge above the road. Three kilometres later is a major checkpoint where your passport and permit will be checked. The town of Tsochen is just ahead, 5km across the plains.

TSOCHEN མཚོ་ཆེན་ 措勤
☑ 0897 / ELEV 4680M

Tsochen (Cuòqín), 235km from the northern turn-off and 173km south of the northern road proper, is probably the most interesting town on the northern route, full of wild-haired nomads in town on a shopping trip. At the east end of the 2km-long town, walk through the **Tibetan quarter** to reach a mass of mani stones, prayer poles and yak skulls that local pilgrims gravitate to daily at dusk.

From here you'll see a second larger collection of prayer flags and mani stones about 1km away on the plateau to the north; just below here is the **Mendong Monastery**, a small but friendly place with 36 monks. The atmospheric inner chapel of the main prayer hall holds the funeral chörten of local lama Sherab Rinpoche, plus his stone hand and footprints. The monastery belongs to the Kagyud school, so there are pictures of Milarepa, Marpa and the Karmapa here (as well as Chairman Mao!). The monastery is headed by an 88-year-old lama who fled to India in 1959 and returned in 1984 to rebuild the ruined monastery.

One potential excursion from Tsochen is to **Zhari (Tsari) Nam-tso**, a huge salt lake 50km east of town towards the town of Tseri (Tsitri). You will need to have this visit pre-arranged with your driver before leaving Lhasa or arrange extra payment for the half-day trip.

The PSB (公安局; Gōng'ānjú) maintains a strong presence in town and at the time of writing all foreign travellers had to go to the station to register. The station is about halfway up the road on the left from the start of town (coming from Lhasa). They'll be waiting for you.

The town has electricity between 7pm and 1am.

Friendship Feria Hotel (友谊宾馆; Yǒuyì Bīnguǎn; ☑ 261 2308; d/tr/q without bathroom Y120/150/200) is at the beginning of town on the left, before the petrol station. Rooms are clean and there's plenty of hot and cold water in drums, with outside pit toilets.

Lhatse Dronkhang (家庭旅馆; Jiātíng Lǚguǎn; ☑ 261 2561; s/d per bed Y80/50) Just 150m past the Feria, on the right, this friendly Tibetan-run place has decent, clean rooms on the 2nd floor. The walls are wooden and so potentially noisy but there's an inside toilet and showers are under construction.

The main street is lined with Chinese restaurants but don't expect to find an English menu. Opposite the Lhatse Dronkhang, the **Lhatse Tashi Restaurant** (mains Y10-30) is owned by the same people and offers cosy Tibetan seating and a good range of Chinese and Tibetan dishes. There are several supermarkets in town.

TSOCHEN TO GERTSE (257KM)

From Tsochen to the junction of the northern road (S301) is a journey of about 180km; Gertse is another 77km, making a total drive of around five hours. If you plan to stay in Gertse, take your time as the route is far more interesting and scenic than the town.

About 43km north of Tsochen, the road passes the 5090m **Nor Chung-la** (Small Wild Yak Pass) before descending to the dramatic turquoise waters of **Dawa-tso** (4680m), another superb camping spot. For the next 60km the route passes from one attractive valley to another, sometimes connected by the river and gorge, at other times by minor passes.

The road crosses the scenic **Nor Gwa-la** (Wild Yak Head Pass), another pass of 5250m, 94km (about two-and-a-half hours of driving) north of Tsochen. From the pass the route descends to a bridge, 109km from Tsochen, and for the next 50km the road runs alongside a dramatic range of 6000m-plus glaciated mountains. The valley narrows towards its northern end before the road suddenly pops out onto a wide plain to meet the northern road proper (linking Amdo with Ali).

It's a long 15km drive in an arrow-straight line towards **Dung-tso**, with its purple mountain backdrop and salt marsh foreground that looks like whitecaps on the water from a distance. Don't approach too close or you'll get stuck in the boggy shoreline.

From the junction it's 90km (two hours) west to Gertse through a wide valley dotted with sheep and prayer flags. There's a checkpoint 24km before Gertse.

GERTSE སྒེར་རྩེ 改则
☑ 0897 / ELEV 4445M

Gertse (Găizé) is the biggest town along the northern route before Ali. The main street (Luren Lu) begins from the yak statue roundabout and runs from east to west about 1.5km. Dazhong Lu is the most interesting street, lined with Tibetan teahouses and pool tables. Several shops sell colourful *chubas* (Tibetan cloaks) with fake sheepskin lining. Budget some time to visit the long wall of chörtens, mani stones, prayer flags and yak horns to the south of town.

The central **Hóngyùn Wăngbā** (鸿运网吧; Luren Lu; per hr Y5; ☺9am-2am) offers internet access. The **Yángguāng Línyù** (阳光淋浴; showers Y10; ☺10am-10.30pm), opposite the Grain Hotel, is one of a couple of places offering hot showers. Check the characters carefully on the doorway, as next door is a brothel.... None of the hotels in town have running water.

Xīnqìxiàng Zhāodàisuǒ (新气象招待所; r Y120) has spacious rooms for one to four people, all at the same price, with shared squatties down the hall. It's on the yak statue roundabout and gets quite a lot of 4WD traffic.

The **Gaize Hotel** (改则宾馆; Găizé Bīnguǎn; ☑265 2699; d Y120, d/tr per bed without bathroom Y50) is opposite the hospital west of the roundabout. The cheapest rooms are poorly maintained and favoured by truck drivers. The deluxe doubles have clean beds and bathrooms, though water comes in buckets only. The hotel is also known as the Zhèngfǔ Zhāodàisuǒ (Government Hotel) and Lǔrén Bīnguǎn.

Grain Hotel (粮食局招待所; Liángshíjú Zhāodàisuǒ; Wenhua Lu; s/d/tr Y80/100/120) is a decent place with clean rooms, a sunny greenhouse-style corridor and helpful floor ladies.

There are numerous Chinese and Tibetan restaurants (dishes Y10 to Y35) along the main road.

GERTSE TO GEGYE (368KM)

It's a seven- to eight-hour drive from Gertse to Gegye, the next town of any size. The initial landscape is a dreamy blur of lake and sky, cut by salt rings and brooding mountains of rust, mustard, turmeric and green barley. The isolated bunkers that look like tiny greenhouses are water wells. **Omachu** (kilometre marker 982), a small village huddled beneath a rocky splinter, is 50km west of Gertse. Keep your eyes open for the round, tomblike buildings that are actually tsampa (roasted barley) storage bins.

The road passes some impressive peaks to the south and then the village of Sherma, squeezed between the two lakes of Rali-tso and Loma Gyari-tso. After more peaks the road drops down to large and photogenic Peri-tso and the nearby village of Wenbu Dangsang, two hours from Gertse. It's another 50km past a stony plain and a huge salt lake that looks like it's full of icebergs to ramshackle **Tsaka** (擦咔; Cākā), a small salt- and sheepskin-processing community. The centre of town has Mínhé Fàngguăn, a good Muslim noodle place, and the decent **Fúpín Zhāodàisuǒ** (扶贫招待所; ☑263 5018; dm/r Y45/120), a two-storey Tibetan-style guesthouse, around the corner.

From Tsaka one route continues west to meet the Ali–Kashgar road just north of Pangong-tso. The road to Ali branches south and climbs a side valley to the 4895m

WESTERN TIBET (NGARI)

Gya-la, then descends past yak-hair nomads' tents to curve around salty Sher-tso (Bar-tso), before crawling to another pass (4855m) that has a large cave on one side. The road then descends to the pastures of **Zhungba** (Shungba; 雄巴; Xióngbā) via a Gobi-like stony desert. Zhungba is a dismal wool-trading centre for the nomads of the region, 96km from the turn-off and with a few simple teahouses.

At kilometre marker 1202, near Drungba, the road enters a gorge and follows the fledgling Indus River to Gegye, 105km (two hours) from Zhungba. The Indus has its source in the northern flanks of Kailash and is known here as the Sengge (or Sengye) Tsangpo, or Lion River. It's astonishing to think that this little stream continues through Ladakh and Pakistan, crossing the world's highest mountain ranges to become one of the great rivers of Asia.

GEGYE དགེ་རྒྱས་ 革吉

☎0897 / ELEV 4520M

The mildly interesting little town of Gegye (Géjí), nestled below a ridge, is a logical overnight point, though there's little to actually do except drink beer and play pool with the local nomads. The two main streets (Hebei Lu and Yanhu Lu) join at a T-junction by the Shuǐlì Bīnguǎn. Hebei Lu has several good supermarkets and internet access at the **Guāngxiān Wǎngsù** (光纤网速; 33 Hebei Lu; ⊙9am-midnight; per hr Y5). The Yángguāng Zhāodàisuǒ guesthouse across the road offers hot showers (Y15).

This 2nd-floor **Shuǐlì Bīnguǎn** (水利宾馆; ☎263 2146; cnr Yanhu Lu & Hebei Lu; r Y100) is easily the best choice in town. Rooms are clean and comfortable with TVs and DVD players, the shared indoor squat toilets are simple but clean and there's even some running water.

The government guesthouse **Géjí Bīnguǎn** (革吉宾馆; s/d Y100/120) is in a terminal state of decline. The carpeted rooms are OK but the bathrooms are locked, so you have to use the absolutely shocking outdoor latrines. The hotel is unsigned inside a compound with a white tiled arch.

Yanhu Lu boasts the excellent **Kange Nyima Tsangkhang** (mains Y14-30), a very pleasant Tibetan restaurant with a good range of Tibetan dishes and a recommended *shemdre* (meat and curried potatoes with rice). Next door is a glass-fronted Uighur restaurant that offers Xīnjiāng-style noodles and kebabs.

GEGYE TO ALI (112KM)

Ali is just three hours from Gegye. At first the road follows the infant Indus River, then at kilometre marker 1260 it crosses the river, swings southwest and enters a marshland rich in bird life, including golden ducks and large black-necked cranes. Many maps incorrectly show the main S301 road continuing northwest.

The road then passes through a canyon landscape painted in swirling desert hues of butterscotch, caramel and popcorn, then passes Zouzou village and a dramatic escarpment. At kilometre marker 1330 a lone concrete factory suddenly appears out of nowhere. Ali then gradually emerges like a desert mirage, gradually revealing paved grids of department stores, karaoke bars and taxis that come as quite a shock in such a remote location. It's a surreal experience to glide smoothly into town after five or six days bouncing around the northern plateau.

Ali ཨ་ལི་ 阿里/狮泉河

☎0897 / ELEV 4280M

Ali (Ālǐ), also known as Shīquánhé (Lion Spring River) in Chinese and Sengge Khabab (Town of the Lion) in Tibetan, is the capital of the Ngari (Ali) prefecture. There's nothing much to see, but it is a good place to clean up, have some decent food, top up supplies and check your email before heading off to the real attractions of western Tibet.

Ali is thoroughly Chinese. There are plenty of Tibetans wandering the streets but, like you, they are probably visitors from further afield. The town is expanding rapidly, especially to the south of the river, and there's a big army presence. The opening of the Kūnshā airport 50km from town in 2010 will only boost the city's growth.

For views of the town, climb up to the pagoda-topped hill to the north of town. Don't take pictures of the army compound to the west (recognisable by the huge '八一' army symbol painted on the hillside above).

🛏 Sleeping

Your sleeping options are limited in Ali as many hotels are off-limits to foreigners. The better hotels fill up quickly.

Shénhú Bīnguǎn　　　　HOTEL $
(神湖宾馆; ☎136 3897 7982; Shiquanhe Donglu; s/d Y140/150, s/d without bathroom Y50/80)

Ali

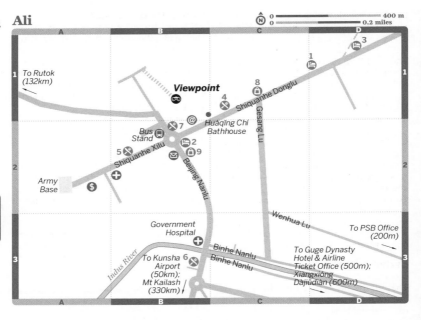

Ali

◎ Top Sights
Viewpoint B1

🛏 Sleeping
1 Ali Hotel D1
2 Heng Yuan Guesthouse B2
3 Shénhú Bīnguǎn D1

🍴 Eating
4 Baiyi Supermarket C1
5 Chinese Restaurants B2
6 Effendi Ashkhana B3
7 Uighur Ashkhana B2

🛍 Shopping
8 Fruit & Vegetable Market C1
9 Supermarket B2

Owned by the Yak Hotel in Lhasa, this place is a good first choice. The cheaper rooms have communal squat toilets but no showers. Rooms are arranged around an inner atrium.

Heng Yuan Guesthouse   HOTEL $$
(恒远宾馆; Héngyuǎn Bīnguǎn; ☎282 8288; cnr Beijing Nanlu & Shiquanhe Donglu; s/d Y120/140, tr without bathroom Y150) A popular place with 4WD tours, it has decent rooms in the main building (avoid the back courtyard rooms) but chaotic management when we visited. You access the rooms through a ground-floor department store.

Ali Hotel   HOTEL $$
(狮泉河饭店; Shīquánhé Fàndiàn; ☎280 0004; 17 Shiquanhe Donglu; d Y260, d/tr without bathroom Y120/130) This charmless two-star government hotel offers exhausted Western-style rooms with broken fixtures and small bathrooms, and very spartan rooms without. There's hot water in the evenings and mornings only.

Xiàngxióng Dàjiǔdiàn   HOTEL $$$
(象雄大酒店; ☎283 0888; www.xiangxiong hotel.com, in Chinese; Binhe Nanlu; d Y488; ❈) Currently the best hotel in town, in the southeast suburbs, shortly to be eclipsed by the next-door Guge Dynasty Hotel.

🍴 Eating

Ali has numerous Chinese restaurants south and west of the main junction and, given the town's remote location, they are surprisingly good value for money. There are also a few Tibetan places around (don't expect English menus). For supplies try the Baiyi Supermarket on Shiguanhe Donglu or the supermarket next to Hengyuan Guesthouse. For fresh produce try the fruit and vegetable market on Shiquanhe Donglu.

Uighur Ashkhana
UIGHUR $

(Beijing Beilu; noodles Y12) For a taste of Central Asia head to this popular Uighur restaurant (*ashkhana* in Turkic), 100m from the main roundabout. Fresh nan bread, a bowl of *suoman* (fried noodle squares) and a couple of kebabs makes for a great meal. The barbecue grill and smell of mutton is a sign that you're close.

Effendi Ashkhana
UIGHUR $$

(Beijing Nanlu; dishes Y15-100) For something a bit fancier, this great *1001 Nights*–style restaurant feels lifted from Istanbul. The *pilov* (pilau rice) and kebabs are great but the best dish is the *dàpánjī* (大盘鸡), a chicken, potato and noodles extravaganza big enough for three people.

ⓘ Information

Electricity is on and off in Ali, shifting every 12 hours between different districts like a nomad.

Agricultural Bank of China (中国农业银行; Zhōngguó Nóngyè Yínháng; Shiquanhe Xilu; ☻10am-7pm Mon-Fri) Near the army post, west of the roundabout. Will change cash US dollars, euros and UK pounds only (no travellers cheques). There's an ATM outside on the Visa, MasterCard and Cirrus networks.

Gésāng Wǎngchéng (格桑网城; Shiquanhe Donglu; per hr Y10; ☻24hr) Reliable internet access.

Huáqīng Chí Bathhouse (华清池; Shiquanhe Donglu; showers Y10; ☻10am-11pm) Hot-water showers.

PSB (行政公署公安处; Xíngzhèng Gōngshǔ Gōng'ānchù; ☏282 1545; 17 Wenhua Lu; ☻10am-1pm & 4-7pm Mon-Fri) Groups may need to get their travel permit endorsed here if they haven't done so in Darchen. The office is in the southeast of town.

ⓘ Getting There & Away

From Ali to Darchen, at the base of the Mt Kailash kora, it's a day's journey of around 330km.

AIR Tibet's fourth airport, at Kūnshā (昆莎; Gunsa in Tibetan; 4274m) opened in 2010, 50km south of Ali. There are currently twice-weekly flights to Lhasa (Y2500) and on to Chéngdū, with services planned to Kashgar. Buy tickets and enquire about airport buses at the airline ticket office in the new **Guge Dynasty Hotel** (古格王朝大酒店; Gǔgé Wángcháo Dàjiǔdiàn; Binhe Nanlu).

BUS Sleeper buses run every couple of days to Lhasa (50 hours) and Yèchéng (30 hours)

in Xīnjiāng and there are also daily services to Rutok Xian, Zanda, Darchen/Purang and Gertse. Passenger 4WDs also run to Lhasa for Y300/500/800 for a back/middle/front row seat.

ⓘ Getting Around

Fleets of taxis are part of the mirage-in-the-desert shock of arriving in Ali (*We wonder how they got there...?*). Within the city limits there's a standard taxi fare of Y5, but the centre of town is actually compact enough that you can walk anywhere.

Mt Kailash
ᠨᠠᠩᠰ ᠷᠢᠨ ᠫᠣ ᠼᠧ   冈仁波齐峰

Going to western Tibet and not completing a kora around Mt Kailash (Kang Rinpoche, or Precious Jewel of Snow, in Tibetan) would be like visiting a great capital and stopping short outside its most famous treasure. Mt Kailash dominates the region with the sheer awesomeness of its four-sided summit, just as it dominates the mythology of a billion people.

The mountain has been a lodestone to pilgrims and adventurous travellers for centuries but until recently very few had set their eyes on it. With road conditions improving every year, this is fast changing. Large numbers of Indian pilgrims visit the mountain between June and August and you can expect visitor numbers to increase dramatically now that flights are operating to Ali, just a few hours' drive away.

Any reasonably fit and acclimatised person should be able to complete the three-day walk, but come prepared with warm and waterproof clothing and equipment. For more information about the kora, including a map of the route, see p250.

HISTORY

Throughout Asia, stories exist of a great mountain, the navel of the world, from which flow four great rivers that give life to the areas they pass through. The myth originates in the Hindu epics, which speak of Mt Meru – home of the gods – as a vast column 84,000 leagues high, its summit kissing the heavens and its flanks composed of gold, crystal, ruby and lapis lazuli. These Hindu accounts placed Mt Meru somewhere in the towering Himalaya but, with time, Meru increasingly came to be associated specifically with Mt Kailash. The confluence of the myth and the mountain is no coincidence. No-one has been to the

WORTH A TRIP

WARM-UP HIKES AROUND MT KAILASH

If you've got extra time at Darchen, or you want to spend a day acclimatising before setting out on the Mt Kailash kora, you can find some interesting short walks in the area. The ridge to the north of the village obscures Mt Kailash, but an hour's walk to the top offers fine views of the mountain. To the south you will be able to see the twin lakes of Manasarovar and Rakshas Tal.

A switchbacking dirt road just to the east of Darchen branches right after 1km to the **Gyangdrak Monastery**, largest of the Mt Kailash monasteries and 6km from Darchen. Like other monasteries, it was rebuilt (in 1986) after the depredations of the Cultural Revolution. The left branch of the road follows a stream west to **Selung Monastery**, where a short walk leads to a viewpoint popular with Indian pilgrims for its views of Kailash and Nandi peaks. The secret 'inner kora' of Kailash starts from here but is only open to pilgrims who have completed 13 main koras of the mountain.

For an excellent warm-up and acclimatisation hike, get dropped off at Gyangdrak and then follow the obvious path over the ridge and down to Selung (45 minutes). At the pass on the ridge a side path leads up the hillside straight towards Kailash for epic views of the south face and back towards Manasarovar, Rakshas Tal and tent-shaped Gurla Mandata. From Selung you can drive back or continue over the ridges to the south to eventually drop down steeply to Darchen. Views of the Barkha plain from the ridge above Darchen are awesome but it gets very windy in the afternoons. For a map of the region see Map p252.

summit to confirm whether the gods reside there (although some have come close), but Mt Kailash does indeed lie at the centre of an area that is the key to the drainage system of the Tibetan plateau. Four of the great rivers of the Indian subcontinent originate here: the Karnali, which feeds into the Ganges (south); Indus (north); Sutlej (west); and Brahmaputra (Yarlung Tsangpo, east).

Mt Kailash, at 6714m, is not the mightiest of the mountains in the region, but with its distinctive shape – like the handle of a millstone, according to Tibetans – and its year-round snowcapped peak, it stands apart from the pack. Its four sheer walls match the cardinal points of the compass, and its southern face is famously marked by a long vertical cleft punctuated halfway down by a horizontal line of rock strata. This scarring resembles a swastika – a Buddhist symbol of spiritual strength – and is a feature that has contributed to Mt Kailash's mythical status. Kailash is actually not part of the Himalaya but rather the Kangri Tise (Gangdise) range.

Mt Kailash has long been an object of worship. For Hindus, it is the domain of Shiva, the Destroyer and Transformer, and his consort Parvati. To the Buddhist faithful, Mt Kailash is the abode of Demchok (Sanskrit: Samvara) and Dorje Phagmo. The Jains of India also revere the mountain as the site where the first of their *tirthankara* (saints)

entered Nirvana. And in the ancient Bön religion of Tibet, Mt Kailash was the sacred Yungdrung Gutseg (Nine-Stacked-Swastika Mountain) upon which the Bönpo founder Shenrab alighted from heaven.

In May 2001 Spanish climbers gained permission to climb the peak, only to abandon their attempt in the face of international protests. Reinhold Messner also gained permission to scale the peak in the 1980s, but abandoned his expedition in deference to the peak's sanctity when he got to the mountain.

DARCHEN དར་ཆེན། 塔钦
📞 0897 / ELEV 4670M

Nestled in the foothills of Mt Kailash, the small town of Darchen (Tǎqīn) is the starting point of the kora. It is a rapidly expanding settlement of hotel compounds, tourist restaurants and newly built blocks, much improved on the miserable hovel that greeted travellers to Kailash a few years ago. Most travellers make use of the town's hot showers, restaurants and supermarkets, either before or after their kora, though it's perfectly feasible to sleep instead at Lake Manasarovar just over an hour's drive away. If you need medical attention, there's a Swiss-funded traditional Tibetan clinic in the northwest of Darchen.

If you haven't already bought your 'ticket' for the Kailash–Manasarovar–Purang area (Y200) you will have to get one on the approach road to Darchen.

✦✦ Festivals & Events

The festival of **Saga Dawa** marks the enlightenment of Sakyamuni, and occurs on the full-moon day of the fourth Tibetan month (in May or June). Saga Dawa is a particularly popular time to visit Mt Kailash, though you will have to share the Tarboche camping area with several hundred other foreigners, most of them on group tours. You can also expect that all the hotels in Darchen will be booked solid throughout this time. The presence of so many tourists and their ever-present camera lenses can spoil the occasion. Other times offer a less colourful but more personally spiritual time to make your kora.

The highlight of the festival is the raising of the Tarboche prayer pole on the morning of Saga Dawa. Monks circumambulate the pole in elaborate costumes, with horns blowing. There are plenty of stalls, a fair-like atmosphere and a nonstop tidal flow of pilgrims around the pole. After the pole is raised at about 1pm everyone sets off on their kora.

How the flagpole stands when it is re-erected is of enormous importance. If the pole stands absolutely vertical all is well, but if it leans towards Mt Kailash things are not good; if it leans away towards Lhasa, things are even worse.

Particularly large numbers of pilgrims assemble at Mt Kailash every 12 years, in the Tibetan Year of the Horse. The next gathering is in 2014.

🛏 Sleeping & Eating

There's not a great deal to choose between Darchen's hotels. Almost all offer foam beds in clean rooms with an outdoor pit toilet in the corner of a large courtyard. Just pick one that doesn't have a large convoy of 4WDs parked outside.

Pilgrim Hotel GUESTHOUSE $
(朝圣宾馆; Cháoshèng Bīnguǎn; ☑298 0833; dm Y60; @) Turn right at the T-junction for this good place that has a cosy dining room, patchy internet access and donates part of its profits to local monasteries.

Lhasa Holyland Guesthouse GUESTHOUSE $
(拉萨圣地康桑旅馆; Lāsà Shèngdì Kāngsāng Lǚguǎn; ☑139 8907 0818; dm Y60-70) This friendly new place has modern rooms, a cosy Tibetan-style teahouse and, for better or worse, the local PSB office. It is currently adding 150 beds.

Sun & Moon Guesthouse GUESTHOUSE $
(Ninda Dronkhang; 日月宾馆; Rìyuè Bīnguǎn; ☑260 7102; q per bed Y60) This easily overlooked place in the far top (northwest) end of town offers the nicest accommodation, with cosy rooms and clean communal toilets, though it's a bit out of the way. It's part of the Tibet Medical and Astrological Institute (Menkhang).

Other good and almost identical places include the Fresh Peacock Hotel and the Darchen Local Aid the Poor Programme Hotel (Poverty Alleviation Hotel), both on the main street and with four-bed rooms for Y60 per bed. Bigger places like the Gandisi Hotel are often fully booked with huge groups of Indian pilgrims.

Darchen Local Aid the Poor Programme Hotel Restaurant TIBETAN $
(塔尔青利民扶贫宾馆; Tǎ'ěrqīng Lìmín Fúpín Bīnguǎn; mains Y10-25) Good breakfasts, the best-value *shemdre* and other dishes in town and a cosy Tibet-style decor make this our favourite restaurant in town, and the hotel is pretty good also.

❶ Information

A couple of places are trying to start internet service without much success, though it's surely only a question of time.

God Water Bathing (圣水淋浴; Shèngshuǐ Línyù; showers Y20; ⊗9.30am-midnight)

Lobsang Blind Massage House (☑136 3899 9712; Chinese/Japanese/Tibetan massage Y100/120/150) The perfect end to a kora is a relaxing massage from blind English-speaking Lobsang, a graduate of Braille Without Borders (see p345) who has set up shop in the Poverty Alleviation Hotel.

PSB (公安局; Gōng'ānjú) Travellers need to register and have their travel permit endorsed at the PSB office in the Lhasa Holyland Guesthouse.

❶ Getting There & Away

Darchen is 3km north of the main Ali–Saga road, about 12km from Barkha, 107km north of Purang, 330km southeast of Ali and a lonely 1200km from Lhasa.

Buses pass through town daily to Ali (Y150) and Purang (Y100) but currently not to Saga.

The following books about Mt Kailash, Lake Manasarovar and the surrounding area are guaranteed to whet your appetite for adventure. Charles Allen's *A Mountain in Tibet* chronicles the hunt for the sources of the region's four great rivers and is perhaps the best introduction to the region. Allen's follow up, *The Search for Shangri-La*, focuses on the region's pre-Buddhist heritage and is also a great read. *The Sacred Mountain* by John Snelling reports on early Western explorers, including those who turned up in the early 1980s when the door to China and Tibet first creaked narrowly open.

The Kailash chapters in German-born Lama Anagarika Govinda's *The Way of the White Clouds* (1966) includes a classic account of the pilgrimage during a trip to Tibet in 1948. Sven Hedin's three-volume *Transhimalaya: Discoveries & Adventures in Tibet* (1909–13) will keep you company for many a long night on the Changtang plateau. Hedin was the first Westerner to complete the Kailash kora.

Books such as *Kailas: On Pilgrimage to the Sacred Mountain of Tibet* by Kerry Moran (with photos by Russell Johnson) and *Walking to the Mountain* by Wendy Teasdill may make you jealous that you didn't get to the mountain just a decade or two earlier. Both highlight the much greater difficulties (and, in their eyes, rewards) that one would experience on a pilgrimage as recently as the late 1980s.

The more scientifically inclined can turn to Swami Pranavananda's *Kailas Manasarovar*, an account of the author's findings over numerous stays in the region between 1928 and 1947. The book was reprinted in India in 1983 and you should be able to find a copy in a Kathmandu bookshop or online.

Most recent is Manosi Lahiri's *Here be Yaks*, an unpretentious travelogue that details a more recent Indian pilgrimage to the region, with a special focus on defining the source of the Sutlej.

Lake Manasarovar

མཚོ་མ་ཕམ་   玛旁雄错

ELEV 4560M

Lake Manasarovar, or Mapham Yum-tso (Victorious Lake) in Tibetan, is the most venerated of Tibet's many lakes and one of its most beautiful. With its sapphire-blue waters, sandy shoreline and snowcapped-mountain backdrop, Manasarovar is immediately appealing, and a welcome change of venue from the often-forbidding terrain of Mt Kailash.

Manasarovar has been circumambulated by Indian pilgrims since at least 1700 years ago when it was extolled in the sacred Sanskrit literature the *Puranas*. A Hindu interpretation has it that *manas* refers to the mind of the supreme god Brahma, the lake being its outward manifestation. Accordingly, Indian pilgrims bathe in the waters of the lake and circumambulate its shoreline. Tibetans, who are not so keen on the bathing bit, generally just walk around it. Legend has it that the mother of the Buddha, Queen Maya, was bathed at Manasarovar by the gods before giving birth to her son. It is said that some of Mahatma Gandhi's ashes were sprinkled into the lake.

The Hindi poet Kalidasa once wrote that the waters of Lake Manasarovar are 'like pearls' and that to drink them erases the 'sins of a hundred lifetimes'. Be warned, however, that the sins of a hundred lifetimes tend to make their hasty exit by way of the nearest toilet. Make sure that you thoroughly purify Manasarovar's sacred waters before you drink them, however sacrilegious that may sound.

Manasarovar is linked to a smaller lake, Rakshas Tal (known to Tibetans as Lhanag-tso), by the channel called Ganga-chu. Most Tibetans consider Rakshas Tal to be evil, home in Hindu minds to the demon king Ravanna, though to the secular eye it's every bit as beautiful as Manasarovar. The two bodies of water are associated with the conjoined sun and moon, a powerful symbol of Tantric Buddhism. On rare occasions, water flows through this channel from Lake Manasarovar to Rakshas Tal; this is said to augur well for the Tibetan people and most are pleased that water has indeed been flowing between the two lakes in recent years.

Most groups and individuals base themselves at the picturesque Chiu village, site of the Chiu Monastery, on the northwestern shore of the lake. Dirt roads encircle most of the shoreline now and some tour groups have already started doing a circuit of the lake by 4WD. For an overview of the kora and a map of the lake, see p259.

◉ Sights & Activities

Chiu Monastery   MONASTERY
(admission free) Thirty-three kilometres south of Darchen, Chiu (Sparrow) Monastery enjoys a fabulous location atop a craggy hill overlooking Lake Manasarovar. The main chapel here contains the meditation cave of Guru Rinpoche, who is said to have passed away here, but most people focus on the lake views, the winding stone staircases and old wooden doorframes of this fairytale-like structure. A short kora path leads to a second chapel. On a clear day Mt Kailash looms dramatically to the north.

For a hike, walk along the ridge to the southeast of the monastery or make a half-day trek along part of the lake kora to the ruined chörten and prayer wall at Cherkip, returning via the shoreline cave retreats. There are fine views and lots of nesting birds along this route, but bring repellent against the annoying shoreline flies.

If you fancy a long post-hike soak, the small but overpriced **hot springs** (bath Y50; ☺10am-8pm) beside the village pipes water into private wooden tubs.

There are over a dozen simple, friendly guesthouses between the monastery and the lake, all charging an identical Y50 per bed in a four- or five-bed room, with an outdoor pit toilet. There's little to choose between them except perhaps the availability of food and where the big groups are staying.

Gossul Monastery   MONASTERY
Further south along the shore of Manasarovar, this charming monastery is part of the Manasarovar kora (see p259) but can now be reached by road. The three resident monks can show you the meditation cave of Götsangpa (the ascetic who opened up the Kailash kora in the 13th century) and a sacred stone conch shell, and you can buy amulets or packets of holy Manasarovar sand, incense and salt. The views of the lake are breathtaking.

The best way to reach the road is if you are driving from Purang; an unsigned dirt road branches off the main road 10km north of the Gurla-la (around kilometre marker 36), crosses a pass and then swings left to follow the lakeshore for 10km. From Gossul it's 7km north to the paved main road and then a further 6km to Chiu Monastery.

Tirthapuri Hot Springs & Kora ཏི་ར་ཕུ་རི་ཆུ་ཚན 芝达布日寺

On the banks of the Sutlej, only a few hours' drive northwest of Darchen, the hot springs at **Tirthapuri** (admission Y15) is the place where pilgrims traditionally bathe after completing their circuit of Mt Kailash. The one-hour kora route around the site is interesting, though most people can safely give this place a miss if time is tight. Thirteen Tirthapuri koras are considered to bring equal merit as one Kailash kora.

Starting from the hot springs the kora trail climbs to a cremation point, an oval of rocks covered in old clothes and rags. From this point, an alternative longer kora climbs to the very top of the ridge, rejoining the trail near the long mani wall (a wall made of mani stones). The regular kora trail continues past a hole where pilgrims dig 'sour' earth for medicinal purposes. Further along, there's a 'sweet' earth hole. The trail reaches a miniature version of Mt Kailash's Drölma-la, marked with mani stones and a large collection of yak horns and skulls.

Where the trail doubles back to enter the Guru Rinpoche (Tirthapuri) Monastery, there is a rock with a hole in it right below the solitary prayer wheel, which is a handy karma-testing station. Reach into the hole and pull out two stones. If both are white your karma is excellent; one white and one black means that it's OK; and if both are black you have serious karma problems. Perhaps another Mt Kailash kora would help?

The monastery *dukhang* (assembly hall) has stone footprints of Guru Rinpoche and his consort Yeshe Tsogyel to the right of the altar. Outside the monastery a large circle of mani stones marks the spot where the gods danced in joy when Guru Rinpoche was enshrined at Tirthapuri. Beside it is a 200m-long mani wall, the result of a demon firing an arrow at the guru. (The guru stopped the arrow's flight and transformed it into this wall.) Finally, the kora drops back down to the river, passing several small shrines and a series of rocky pinnacles revered as *rangjung*, or self-manifesting chörtens.

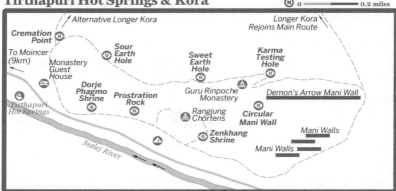

Accommodation is limited. The **monastery guesthouse** (d Y40) has a couple of very simple rooms, as does a crummy nearby 'resort' trying to attract people with water siphoned off from the springs. There's nice riverside camping (Y15) just below the kora.

Tirthapuri is 9km south of **Moincer** (Mensi), which in turn is 65km west of Darchen along the main paved road to Ali. There's better choice of food and accommodation at Moincer, including at the friendly **Dekyi Neylingkhang** (美满招待所; Měimǎn Zhāodàisuǒ; dm Y50), a simple but cosy guesthouse just by the Tirthapuri turn-off. The excellent **Chuānyuè Xiǎochǎo** (川粤小炒; dishes Y20-30) in the centre of town offers great food and is a favourite with the local People's Liberation Army (PLA) officers.

Guge Kingdom
གུ་གེ་རྒྱལ་རབ་ 古格王国

The barren, eroded landscape around modern Zanda is unlike any you will have encountered so far, and seems an improbable location for a major civilisation to have developed. Yet the ancient Guge kingdom (Gǔgé wángguó) thrived here as an important stop on the trade route between India and Tibet. Today, the remains of Thöling Monastery, once a major centre of Tibetan Buddhism, and neighbouring Tsaparang, a 9th-century fortress etched into the very stone of a towering ridge, are two of western Tibet's highlights, though few Western tourists manage to make it this far.

Tsaparang is 18km west of Zanda, while Thöling Monastery is now merely an adjunct to the town. To visit both you need to budget at least three days (two merely for getting there and back from Darchen). Both sites are in the valley of the Langchen Tsangpo (Sutlej River), the 'elephant river', which rises west of Manasarovar and continues over the border with India into Ladakh and finally Pakistan.

HISTORY
By the 10th century the Guge kingdom was already a wealthy trade centre supporting several thousand people when the great Guge king Yeshe Ö began to nurture an exchange of ideas between India and Tibet. The young monk Rinchen Zangpo (958–1055) was sent to study in India and returned 17 years later to become one of Tibet's greatest translators of Sanskrit texts and a key figure in the revival of Buddhism across the Tibetan plateau. Rinchen Zangpo built 108 monasteries throughout western Tibet, Ladakh and Spiti, including the great monasteries of Tabo (Spiti) and Alchi (Ladakh). Two of the most important were those at Tsaparang and Thöling. He also invited Kashmiri artists to paint the unique murals still visible today. It was partly at Rinchen Zangpo's behest that Atisha, a renowned Bengali scholar and another pivotal character in the revival of Tibetan Buddhism, was invited to Tibet. Atisha spent three years in Thöling before travelling on to central Tibet.

The kingdom fell into ruin just 50 years after the first Europeans arrived in Tibet in

EXPLORING THE GARUDA VALLEY

Adventurers with a day up their sleeve could explore the Khyunglung (Garuda) region of the upper Sutlej Valley, southwest from Moincer. Around 16km from Moincer (8km from Tirthapuri), the Bönpo-school **Gurugyam Monastery** (གུར་འབུམ་དགོན་པ།; 故如甲木寺; Gùrújiǎmù Sì) is worth a visit, primarily for the dramatic cliffside retreat of 10th-century Bön master Drenpa Namka.

A further 14km down the Sutlej Valley, 2km past Khyunglung (曲龙; Qūlóng) village, is the extensive ruined cave city that archaeologists believe belonged to the early kingdom of **Shangshung**. The 20-minute trail to the site leads from a roadside chörten and drops past hot-spring terraces to cross the Sutlej over a bridge hung with severed animal heads. Nearby is a riverside hot-springs pool. You could easily spend a fantastic couple of hours exploring the troglodyte caves and buildings but it's dangerous to continue to the upper citadel. On the way back stop off at **Khyunglung Monastery** just above the village, which also has a couple of simple teahouses.

There are no checkpoints on route to Khyunglung though it would be prudent to have the valley added to your travel permit, either in Ali or Darchen. From Khyunglung the dirt road continues southwest to seriously remote monasteries at Dongpo, Dawa (Danba) and Manam (Malang) en route to Zanda, but also passes near several military bases so you need to bring watertight permissions and to be prepared for some serious exploration.

1624, after a siege by the Ladakhi army (see p175). The centre of Tibet soon became the middle of nowhere.

ℹ️ Getting There & Away

From Ali there are buses (Y260) every couple of days to Zanda. There are two main roads to Zanda from the Darchen–Ali road. Both are rough and go over some very high passes. In a 4WD it's possible to make it to Zanda from either Ali or Mt Kailash in a single day.

To/From Darchen

It's about an eight-hour drive from Darchen to Zanda, though the distance is only about 243km. It's 65km along a paved road from Darchen to Moincer, which is the turn-off to Tirthapuri, and then another 50km from there to the army base at Ba'er, where the road branches south. The 122km from Ba'er to Zanda takes four hours of winding up and down fantastically eroded gorges and gullies. Road improvements should speed things up by 2012.

To/From Ali

Coming from Ali, the road is equally scenic and will take around five hours of driving to cover the 200km. The first hour on a paved road climbs to the 4720m Pe-la and then drops down past a great scenic viewpoint to the Gar Valley, home to Ali's new airport at Kūnshā at kilometre marker 1109. About 64km from Ali the route crosses a bridge to the western side of the valley. A further 10km and the road branches right off the main road towards Zanda. The recently upgraded

road climbs huge switchbacks up to the 5330m Lalung-la (Laling Gutsa), then the 5390m Laochi-la before descending into a valley. About 65km from the turn-off you have to buy a ticket to the area (Y200, including Thöling and Guge).

The road branches left onto a plateau from where there are stunning 180-degree views of the Indian Himalaya, stretching from Nanda Devi in the south to the Ladakh range in the north. Around 90km from the turn-off (36km from Zanda) look for a village surrounded by eroded cliffs with hundreds of tombs carved into the soft rock. The turn-off for Dungkar and Piyang (see p185) is just before the village.

The route then drops down into deep, fantastically eroded wadi-like gullies before finally reaching the Sutlej Valley. The layers of the former sea bed are clearly visible and the scenery is a wonderland of eroded cliff faces that have taken on the most astonishing shapes. You'll swear over and over again that you're seeing the melted ruins of an ancient monastery, or a castle, or the high pillars that once held the roof of a mighty palace.

Just before reaching Zanda, 130km from the turn-off, you cross the Sutlej River on a long bridge before pulling into town.

ZANDA རྩ་མདའ་ 札达
📞 0897 / ELEV 3760M

Zanda (Zhada), or Tsamda, is the bland, one-street town that has been built up alongside Thöling Monastery. The town consists of a few hotels, restaurants, supermarkets, two army bases and some brothels.

Budget a couple of hours to visit Thöling Monastery and an hour to wander the cliff-side chörtens at dusk. If you have more time the two sets of ruins south and particularly southwest of town offer amateur archaeologists plenty of scope to explore crumbling monastery walls, ruined chörtens and elaborate cave complexes.

🛏 Sleeping & Eating

Héběi Bīnguǎn
HOTEL $$
(河北宾馆; ☎262 2475; old block d Y180, new block from Y350, discounts 10%-20%) Conditions here appear grim at first – the rooms have bathrooms but no shower or sinks and the toilets don't flush – but friendly staff makes this quiet place surprisingly ok. There's lots of hot water in thermoses for washing and a bucket by the toilet for flushing. The brand-new next-door annex has luxury, carpeted rooms that boast the town's only en suite hot showers.

Chóngqìng Hotel
HOTEL $$
(重庆宾馆; Chóngqìng Bīnguǎn; ☎290 2650; d Y180, tr without bathroom Y210) This large, quiet compound is a favourite with overlanders but the rooms with TV and en suite squat toilet are well overpriced. Triples without bathroom are a decent deal if you bargain hard.

Transportation Hotel
HOTEL $$
(交通宾馆; Jiāotōng Bīnguǎn; ☎262 2686; s/d/tr Y130/140/180, 5-bed r without bathroom Y200) The spacious tiled rooms here come with attached squat toilet and sink. There's no hot water but guests can get a free hot shower next door in the attached public shower. The down side is that it always seems full.

Sìchuān Eats Mill
SICHUANESE $$
(四川食坊; Sìchuān Shífáng; dishes Y20-40) Gets the thumbs up from many travellers and has pleasant outdoor tables. It's opposite the Transportation Hotel.

The main street has at least half-a-dozen other places to eat, mostly generic Chinese restaurants, though also a couple of Tibetan options, one Muslim eatery, and an Uighur restaurant that does excellent *suoman* (Y10 to Y12) and kebabs (no nan bread).

ℹ Information

A couple of 'telephone supermarkets' offer standard international phone rates.

Agricultural Bank of China (中国农业银行; Zhōngguó Nóngyè Yínháng; ⊙10am-1pm, 4-7pm Mon-Fri) Has a 24-hour ATM.

Internet Bar (金鑫网吧; jīnxīn wǎngbā; per hr Y8; ⊙9am-midnight) Next door to the Masses Bath.

Jiāotōng Yùshì (交通浴室; showers Y10; ⊙10am-11pm) A second shower, attached to the Transportation Hotel.

Masses Bath (大众浴室; Dàzhòng Yùshì; showers Y15; ⊙9am-10pm) For a hot shower head to beside the Chóngqìng Hotel. On the 1st floor you can get your laundry done for Y6 per piece.

THÖLING MONASTERY མཐོ་གླིང་ 托林寺

Founded by Rinchen Zangpo in the 10th century, **Thöling Monastery** (Tuōlín Sì; joint admission ticket with Tsaparang Y200) was once Ngari's most important monastic complex. It was still functioning in 1966 when the Red Guards shut down operations and took a sledgehammer to the chapel's magnificent interiors. Three main buildings survive within the monastery walls. If you have little interest in Buddhist statues and murals, stick to the chörtens, mani walls and open views across the Sutlej Valley just north of the monastery.

Main Assembly Hall (Dukhang)

The dimly lit chamber of the *dukhang* has especially fine wall murals, showing strong Kashmiri and Nepali influences; bring a powerful torch (flashlight) to enjoy the rich detail. The Kashmiri influences are noticeable in the shading on the hands and feet, the ornate jewellery and dress, the tight stomach lines and non-Tibetan images of palm trees and *dhotis* (Indian-style loincloths). Scholarly opinion varies on whether the murals date from the 13th and 14th, or 15th and 16th centuries.

The main statues here are of the past, present and future buddhas (all of recent origin), and there's also a footprint of Rinchen

---

DON'T MISS

AN AFTERNOON STROLL

A few steps east of the monastery compound is the recently restored **Serkhang chörten**. A similar chörten stands in total isolation just to the west of the town. To the north, between the monastic compound and the cliff-face that falls away to the Sutlej River below are two long lines of miniature chörtens. The area is superbly photogenic at dusk, when locals do a kora of the complex.

Zangpo. The lower walls of the inner area have murals depicting the life of the Buddha and the founders of the monastery. Murals of the protectors Dorje Jigje (Yamantaka) and Namse (Vairocana) decorate the main entry.

White Chapel (Lhakhang Karpo)

The entry to this side chapel is marked by a finely carved deodar (cedar) doorframe that originated in India. Inside are detailed 15th- and 16th-century murals, somewhat affected by water damage and recently restored by Swiss assistance. The central statue is an old Sakyamuni Buddha; only his hands are of recent origin. Lining the sides are the eight medicine buddhas in various states of destruction. Male deities line the left wall; female bodhisattvas are on the right. The far-right-corner murals depict a gruesome sky burial.

Yeshe Ö's Mandala Chapel (Nampar Nang Lhakhang)

Once the main building in the Thöling complex, Yeshe Ö's Mandala Chapel was also known as the Golden Chapel. Before its destruction in the Cultural Revolution, the square main hall had four secondary chapels at the centre of each wall. Figures of the deities were arrayed around the wall facing towards a central image atop a lotus pedestal, in the form of a huge three-dimensional Tibetan mandala (a representation of the world of a meditational deity). All the images have been destroyed but the four chörtens remain along with a few remaining torsos, disembodied heads and limbs, scattered around the chapel like the leftovers from a sky burial. The mood created by the senseless loss of such magnificent art hangs heavy in the air.

You enter the Mandala Chapel through the Gyatsa Lhakhang and finish off a visit by walking around an interior kora of chapels. Most are closed and devoid of statues but a few open to reveal broken legs and empty plinths.

TSAPARANG རྩ་རེང་ 古格古城

The citadel of **Tsaparang** (Gŭgé Gŭchéng; joint admission ticket with Thöling Y200, optional guide per person Y10), 18km west of Zanda, has been gracefully falling into ruin ever since its slide from prominence in the 17th century. The ruins seem to grow organically out of the hills in tiers and are crowned by a red Summer Palace atop a yellow cocks-comb-like outcrop. It's a photogenically

To Zanda (18km)
Mummy Cave
Lotsang Lhakhang
Ticket Office
Entrance
Caves
P
Lhakhang Karpo
Chapel of the Prefect
Lhakhang Marpo
Dorje Jigje Lhakhang
Monastic Quarters
Tunnel
Summer Palace
Stairs Down to Winter Palace
Very Steep Cliff
Mandala (Demchok) Lhakhang
Very Steep Cliff

surreal landscape that resembles a giant termites' nest.

The site's early Tantric-inspired murals are of particular interest to experts on early Buddhist art. Even without the magnificent art, it's worth the trip for the views over the Sutlej Valley and to explore the twisting paths and secret tunnels that worm their way through the fortress.

The ruins climb up the ridge through three distinct areas. At the bottom of the hill is the monastic area with the four best-preserved buildings and their murals. From there the trail to the top climbs through former residential quarters, where monks' cells were tunnelled into the clay hillside. Finally, the route burrows straight into the hillside through a tunnel before emerging in the ruins of the palace citadel at the very top of the hill. The vast, rough-hewn landscape of the Sutlej Valley that spreads out before you is both terrifying and sublime: you can't take your eyes off its beauty, but you know you wouldn't last a day alone in it.

Early morning and evening (particularly around 8pm) offers the best light. No photography is allowed inside the chapels and guardians will watch you like a hawk. Bring a strong torch, snacks and water, and

WESTERN TIBET (NGARI) GUGE KINGDOM

expect to spend at least half a day exploring the ruins.

◎ Sights

Chapel of the Prefect   CHAPEL

Just inside the entrance to the complex is a small building that was a private shrine for Tsaparang's prefect or regent. The caretaker has named it the 'Drölma Lhakhang' after his own sculpture of Drölma (Tara) displayed here. The wall murals date from the 16th century, by which time the style evinced in other Tsaparang murals was in decline. The exuberant murals include fantastic multicoloured images of elephants, Garuda-people (beside the Buddha's arms), hermits and dog-like snow lions, among others. The main mural on the back wall shows Sakyamuni flanked by Tsongkhapa and Atisha (Jowe-je). Small figures of the Buddha's disciples stand beside his throne.

Lhakhang Karpo   CHAPEL

Slightly above the entrance, the large **Lhakhang Karpo**, or White Chapel, holds the oldest paintings at Tsaparang and is probably the most important chapel in Ngari. The murals of the chapel date back to the 15th or 16th century but their influences extend back to 10th-century Kashmiri Buddhist art, and for this reason are of particular interest to scholars of Buddhist art. Apart from Tsaparang, very little material evidence of early Kashmiri art remains (notably at Alchi Monastery in Ladakh). Laypeople can spot the Kashmiri influence in the slender torsos, thin waists and long fingers of the Hindu-inspired deities.

The ceiling is beautifully painted, as are the many thin supporting columns, made from composite pieces of wood (trees are scarcer than hen's teeth in Ngari). The carvings and paintings of Sakyamuni that top each column are particularly noteworthy. At one time, 22 life-size statues lined the walls; today only 10 remain and these are severely damaged. In the far left corner are the legs of Jampa; to the right is Yeshe Ö. Originally each statue would have been framed by a *torana* (halo-like garland) and a Kashmiri-style plinth. Only partial sections of these remain (look in the far left corner and back recess), but you can still see the holes where these structures were once anchored to the walls.

The doors are flanked by two damaged 5m-high guardian figures, red Tamdrin (Hayagriva) and blue Chana Dorje (Vajrapani). Even armless they hint at the lost marvels of the chapel.

The huge figure of Sakyamuni that once stood in the recess, the Jowo Khang, at the back of the hall has been replaced by one of the caretaker's statues. On the side walls at the back were once row after row of smaller deities, each perched on its own small shelf.

Lhakhang Marpo   CHAPEL

Above the Lhakhang Karpo is the equally large **Lhakhang Marpo**, or Red Chapel, which was built around 1470, perhaps 30 years earlier than the Lhakhang Karpo. The murals in this chapel were repainted around 1630, shortly before the fall of the Guge kingdom, so they are actually younger than those in the Lhakhang Karpo.

The beautiful original chapel door, with its concentric frames and carvings of bodhisattvas, elephants and the syllables of the *om mani padme hum* ('hail to the jewel in the lotus') mantra in six panels, has survived and is worth close inspection. Inside, many thin columns support the chapel roof, similar to those of the neighbouring Lhakhang Karpo. By the main door are images of Chenresig (Avalokiteshvara), Green Tara and an angry eight-armed White Tara, with Drölma and Jampelyang (Manjushri) to the right.

The statues that once stood in the chapel were placed towards the centre of the hall, not around the edges, and although only the bases and damaged fragments remain, the crowded feel to the space, the intense colours and the eerie silence combine to create a powerful atmosphere. You almost expect Indiana Jones to come striding out from behind the wreckage.

Although the wall murals have been damaged by vandalism and water leakage, they remain so remarkably brilliant that it's easy to forget they are actually over 350 years old. On the left wall are the famous murals chronicling the construction of the temple: animals haul the building's huge timber beams into place as musicians with long trumpets and dancing snow lions celebrate the completion of the temple. Officials stand in attendance (a Kashmir delegation wears turbans), followed by members of the royal family, the king and queen (under a parasol), Öpagme (Amitabha) and, finally, a line of chanting monks. The royal gifts frame the bottom of the scene.

Murals on the far right (northern) wall depict the life of the Buddha, showing him tempted by demons and protected by a naga serpent, among others. On the eastern wall are eight stylised chörtens, representing the eight events in Buddha's life.

The main deities in the chapel have very ornate *toranas,* decorated with birds and crocodiles, and topped with flying *apsaras* (angels). At the back of the hall, statues of the 35 confessional buddhas once sat on individual shelves; a handful of them still have bodies but all the heads have gone.

Dorje Jigje (Jikji) Lhakhang   CHAPEL
The murals in the smaller **chapel** a few steps above the Lhakhang Marpo are also painted red and gold, and are almost solely devoted to wrathful deities such as Demchok (Chakrasamvara), Hevajra and the buffalo-headed Dorje Jigje (Yamantaka), to whom the chapel is dedicated. On the left as you look back at the door is Namtöse (Vaishravana), the God of Wealth, who is depicted riding a snow lion and surrounded by square bands of Tibetan warriors. Beside him is a strange dog-faced protector riding a panther.

Like the Chapel of the Prefect, the paintings here are of later origin, central Tibetan in style (rather than Kashmiri-influenced) and of lower quality; the golden years had passed by this point. All the statues that once stood here were destroyed, including the central Dorje Jigje.

Summer Palace   CHAPEL
From the four chapels at the base of the hill, the path to the top climbs up through the monastic quarters and then ascends to the palace complex atop the hill via a tunnel. The **Summer Palace**, at the northern end of the hilltop, is empty, with a balcony offering wonderful views. The Sutlej Valley is just to the north. Across the smaller valley to the northeast is the ruined Lotsang Lhakhang.

The small but quite well-preserved, red-painted **Mandala (Demchok) Lhakhang** in the centre of the hilltop ridge once housed a wonderful three-dimensional mandala with Tantric murals, only the base of which survived the desecrations of the Cultural Revolution. It is often closed to visitors.

Winter Palace   RUINS
Accessed by a steep and treacherous eroded staircase (now with an iron railing in place), the **Winter Palace** is an amazing ants' nest of rooms tunnelled into the clay below the Summer Palace. The rooms were built 12m underground in order to conserve warmth, and the eastern rooms have windows that open out onto the cliff-face. There are seven dusty chambers, all empty, linked by a cramped corridor. Branching off from the stairs you will see a dim passage that provided vital access to water during sieges and served as an emergency escape route for the royal family.

The easily missed stairs to the Winter Palace lead down from between the Summer Palace and the Mandala (Demchok) Lhakhang. Don't go down if you're prone to vertigo or claustrophobia.

OTHER SIGHTS
North of the main entrance to Tsaparang a trail follows a green river valley down about 700m to a **cave** on the left that holds the mummified remains of several bodies. On the way back, visit the chörten and ruined chapel of the **Lotsang Lhakhang**. Only the feet of the main statue remain. Also worth a quick visit are the **caves** and **chörtens** to the west of the main site, near the public toilet behind the caretaker's compound.

Dungkar & Piyang ষ্ট্রন্শ্মীর

Caves with extensive wall paintings were discovered at remote **Dungkar** (4250m; N 31°40.638', E 079°49.471') approximately 40km northeast of Zanda, during the early 1990s. At around 1100 years old, the cave paintings are possibly the oldest in Ngari and have much in common stylistically with the Silk Road cave murals of Dunhuang in China (particularly in their almost cartoon style, and the flying *apsaras,* painted on a blue background). There are three main caves in a side valley before the main village, of which the best preserved is the mandala cave. You need to have an interest in early Tibetan and Silk Road art for the trip to be worthwhile. Lovely nearby Dungkar village also has a ruined **monastery** above the town.

A couple of kilometres west, the village of **Piyang** (4180m; N 31°40.962', E 079°47.784') is also worth the small detour. It lies at the foot of a large ridge honeycombed with thousands of caves and topped with a ruined monastery and two caves with fine murals.

Entry to both Dungkar and Piyang are technically included in the Y200 entry fee for Thöling and Tsaparang, though the Piyang caretaker charges an extra Y30 to enter the caves there since no money from the ticket makes it to the village.

Getting to Dungkar and Piyang is not easy. Most 4WD drivers don't know the area and the dirt roads are poorly signposted. If you come from the Ali–Zanda road, look for the turning east, just north of a village with caves behind it, 36km from Zanda. From here it's 9km past a stunning Himalayan viewpoint to Piyang and then another 5km to Dungkar. From Dungkar you can continue 8km to a junction, then turn right for 16km to join the main Zanda–Moincer road. From here it's 86km to the main Ali–Darchen road. This way you can get an early start and visit Piyang and Dungkar en route between Zanda and Darchen.

Rutok ᠌᠌ᡃ᠋ᢅᠯ᠌ 日土县

The new Chinese town of Rutok Xian (Rìtǔ Xiàn), 132km from Ali, is a modern army post, but there are a couple of great sights nearby that warrant a day trip, especially now that the upgraded road between Rutok and Ali has cut travel time down to just two hours.

Most people visit Rutok Xian as a day trip from Ali, though there are a couple of hotels in town and many restaurants. There's no accommodation or any other facilities at old Rutok.

About 8km north of Rutok Xian, the road hits the east end of lovely turquoise **Pangong-tso** (4241m). The long lake extends 110km into Ladakh in India. It's worth continuing here for views of the lake but beware the tour boats; several Chinese tourists died here in 2010 when theirs capsized.

⊙ Sights

Ancient Petroglyphs   ROCK CARVINGS
In 1985 prehistoric rock carvings, or petroglyphs, were found at several sites in Rutok County. This was the first time such finds had been made in Tibet, although similar finds have since been made at numerous other sites.

The extensive collection of rock carvings at **Rumudong** is right beside the road, about 36km south of the old Rutok turn-off, or about 96km north of Ali. There are kilometre markers every 5km along this road. Travelling north from Ali, start looking on the east side of the road at kilometre marker 970 (though the kilometre markers may change with the upgraded road); the petroglyphs are at around 967. There are two distinct groups on the rock face right beside the road, just before it crosses a bridge to travel along a causeway over the marshy valley floor of the Maga Zangbu-chu.

The first, and more extensive, group also features a number of more recent Buddhist carvings, some of them carved right over their ancient predecessors. The most impressive of the rock carvings features four extravagantly antlered deer racing across the rock and looking back at three leopards in hot pursuit. Also depicted are eagles, yaks, camels, goats, tigers, wild boars and human figures.

Less visited are the **Lurulangkar** paintings, about 12km southwest of Rutok. The relatively primitive carvings are right beside the road, up to a height of 4m above the ground, and show a variety of pre-Buddhist symbols and animals, including dogs, yaks, eagles, deer and goats. Human figures are shown standing in isolation or riding on horses. There are a number of hunting scenes showing dogs chasing deer and hunters shooting at them with bows and arrows.

Old Rutok   VILLAGE
The old Tibetan village of Rutok lies about 10km off the main road from a turn-off about 5km south of Rutok Xian. The drive passes the pretty chörtens of Bankor village en route. Lovely white-painted traditional Rutok huddles at the base of a splinter of rock, atop which is **Rutok Monastery**, flanked at both ends of the hill by the crumbling, but still impressive, ruins of **Rutok Dzong**. From here, you can see the reservoir below and Pangong-tso in the distance. The surrounding villages are largely deserted in summer, as herders move to higher pastures.

The intensely atmospheric main chapel of the monastery has a large statue of Jampa (Maitreya) and a bronze Garuda to the left. Clearly, at one time the whole eastern face of the hill was covered in monastic buildings. The monastery was destroyed during the Cultural Revolution and rebuilt in 1983–84; it now has just six monks.

🛈 Getting There & Away

From Ali there are daily buses (Y50) to Rutok Xian, but there's no public transport to old Rutok and very little traffic on the road.

Western Nepal to Mt Kailash

Fully organised trekking groups can trek to the Nepal–China border from Humla, a restricted region in the far west of Nepal. You will need a Nepali liaison officer, a specially endorsed Chinese visa and a full trek crew. See Lonely Planet's *Trekking in the Nepal Himalaya* for details of the five-day approach from Humla and the optional return via the Limi Valley.

From the Nepali border at Sher, the road makes a long descent to a stream and then follows the Humla Karnali to the village of Khojarnath, 10km north.

KHOJARNATH འཁོར་ཇ་ན
ELEV 3790M

For those travelling north from Nepal, Khojarnath, 21km south of Purang, is the first large village over the border in Tibet. It boasts the wonderful **Korjak Monastery** (admission Y30), an important monastery of the Sakya order. The blood-red compound, which dates back to 996, escaped the worst excesses of the Cultural Revolution and the damage sustained has been repaired with financial assistance from German and Italian sponsors.

The eight-pillared Rinchen Zangpo Lhakhang adjoining the main hall is dominated by the trinity of Chenresig (Avalokiteshvara), Jampelyang (Manjushri) and Chana Dorje (Vajrapani). To the right of these statues is a small *rangjung* speaking Tara. The revered 2ft-high statue once warned the monastery's abbot how to prevent flooding of the local area. During the Cultural Revolution the statue was buried for safekeeping.

The atmospheric main hall is entered via an ancient wooden door with particularly fine carvings. The hall itself is presided over by a figure of Jampa (Maitreya). To the far left is a small chamber with paintings from the earliest days of the monastery. Hanging from the ceiling to the right of the entrance are the stuffed carcasses of a yak, Indian tiger, snow leopard, bear, wolverine and a wolf. The inner kora gives access to a hidden protector chapel. When you finish inside do a final kora around the compound to see the unusual *om mani padme hum* mantra painted on the back wall.

Khojarnath is 130km from Darchen or about 107km from Chiu Village on Lake Manasarovar and is a worthy detour. The drive south from Lake Manasarovar is one of the most scenic in western Tibet and it's easy to visit as a day trip.

PURANG སྤུ་ཧྲེང་ 普兰
☑ 0897 / ELEV 3800M

Purang (Pǔlán to the Chinese; Taklakot to the Nepalis) is a large trading centre comprising a number of distinct settlements separated by the Humla Karnali River, known in Tibetan as Mabja Tsangpo (Peacock River). Nepali traders come up from the Humla and Darchula regions in the extreme west of Nepal to trade a variety of goods, including rice, carried up from Nepal in huge trains of goods-carrying goats. Indian consumer goods and Nepali rice are traded for Tibetan salt and wool in the **Darchula Bazaar**, a 15-minute walk south of Purang.

Purang is also the arrival point for the annual influx of Hindu pilgrims from India, intent on making a *parikrama* (the Hindu equivalent of a kora) of Mt Kailash,

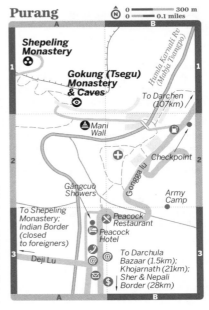

Purang

which devout Hindus consider the abode of Shiva.

The hill northwest of town is the site of a huge army base said to extend far into the mountain in a series of caves. It's even rumoured there are missiles here.

◉ Sights

In the hills above the Humla Bazaar are many retreat **caves** formed around the cliffside **Gokung (Tsegu) Monastery**. Here, a ladder leads up to a couple of upper-floor cave chapels decorated with prayer flags and impressive murals.

The ruined **Shepeling (Simbaling) Monastery** towers over the town from its dramatic hilltop position. In 1949 the Swami Pranavananda described this Kagyud monastery, which housed 170 monks, as the biggest in the region. The monastery's treasures allegedly included one testicle of Indian invader Zowar Singh, displayed every four years during a festival! The Chinese army shelled the monastery during the Cultural Revolution and today only the assembly hall is partially restored. The views south over the valley and north towards a cave complex are superb but be surreptitious in taking photos. Slogans marked in stones above the military base praise Chairman Mao and the Chinese Communist Party.

🛏 Sleeping & Eating

There are several hotels in town, but the PSB only allows foreigners to stay in the Peacock Hotel.

Peacock Hotel HOTEL **$**
(孔雀宾馆; Kǒngquè Bīnguǎn; ☏290 0139; Gongga Lu; old block s/d Y120/1600, new block d Y280) This government hotel is actually divided into two hotels: a rundown old block with back-breaking beds, no running water and disinterested staff, and a **new block** (Xī'ān Yíng Bīnguǎn; ☏260 3266) with clean bathrooms with hot water and good spacious triples without bathrooms (Y200).

Peacock Restaurant CHINESE **$$**
(孔雀饭庄; Kǒngquè Fànzhuāng; ☏290 0139; Gongga Lu; dishes Y20-50; 🖼) Despite the

DANGERS & ANNOYANCES

Be careful not to photograph – even inadvertently – the Chinese military base to the east or any of the small compounds in town. This is unlawful and you or your local guide could get in serious trouble for it.

proximity to Nepal, there's little flavour of the subcontinent in Purang's restaurants. This place has the normal range of good Chinese dishes in pleasant surroundings.

❶ Information

Agricultural Bank of China (中国农业银行; Zhōngguó Nóngyè Yínháng; Gongga Lu; ◷10am-1pm & 4-7pm Mon-Fri) Changes cash and has a 24-hour ATM.

Bǎixīng Wǎngba (百兴网吧; Gongga Lu; per hr Y6-8; ◷24hr) Internet cafe next to the Bǎixīng Supermarket, on the upper floor.

Gǎngcuò Showers (岗措淋浴; Gǎngcuò Línyù; Gongga Lu; showers Y10; ◷10am-11pm) Outside the gate of the Peacock Hotel.

Lóngténg Internet Bar (龙腾网吧; Lóngténg Wǎngba; Deji Lu; per hr Y6-8; ◷24hr)

❶ Getting There & Away

Western trekkers arriving from Nepal usually arrange to be met at the border town of Sher for the 28km drive via Khojarnath to Purang.

Daily buses (Y230) run every two days from Ali to Purang via Darchen. From Purang it's 74km north to Chiu Monastery on the shores of Lake Manasarovar and another 33km from there to Darchen, the starting point for the Mt Kailash kora.

The road north from Purang passes the picturesque villages of Toyo and Deraling, with its unusual red chörtens on a ledge above town, en route to the Gurla-la (4715m). Though still part of western Tibet, the lush terraced fields and distinct architecture feels connected to Himalayan communities of Nepal and India. Just beyond the pass, Rakshas Tal and (on a clear day) Mt Kailash come into view. Keep looking back south for dramatic views of the Himalayas.

Eastern Tibet (Kham)
ཁམས་

Includes »

Pasho 194
Pomi 196
Tashigang 198
Bāyī 199
Draksum-tso 201
Chamdo 205
Riwoche
Tsuglhakhang 209
Tengchen 210
Sok 212
Nagchu 213

Best Places to Eat

» Lo Les Traditional
Emotion Palace (p199)

» Guzel (p197)

» Lhasa Wealth God
Restaurant (p213)

» Qílín Cānguǎn (p209)

» Yīpīnxiāng Lǚròuguǎn
(p211)

Best Places to Stay

» Ránwūhú Fēngqíngyuán
(p196)

» Tashigang Village (p198)

» Rinchen Family
Guesthouse (p197)

» Bāngdá Qīngnián Lǚshè
(p194)

Why Go?

Kham is the face you never knew Tibet had: a land of raging rivers and deep gorges, alpine forests and rolling grasslands, outspoken monks and rebel cowboys. Compared with the rest of this largely barren land, it's a world apart.

It's still part of the Tibetan plateau, but Kham is where Tibet begins its descent towards the subtropical Sìchuān basin, and the landscapes here represent both extremes: one day you'll drive over a breathtakingly high mountain pass, the next you'll slide your way through rainforest on a mud-bath road. This is off-the-beaten-track adventure travel at its most exhilarating, and the chances are you'll be the only foreigner in sight.

Kham gains much of its charm from its people. Khampas dressed in sheepskin cloaks and with braided hair cruise the region on motorbikes. It can sometimes feel like America's Wild West, only with the cowboys and buffalos replaced by Khampas and yaks.

When to Go

May and June are the best months to travel in eastern Tibet. There's hardly any rain, temperatures are at their most comfortable and much of the landscape is covered in blankets of bright-yellow rapeseed flowers.

If you're here in early August, try to pop in on the Nagchu Horse Festival; well worth a look if you're on the Northern Route.

And don't discount coming in winter (November–February). Temperatures are warmer than you'd think (apart from in the Nagchu region, of course), there's hardly any rain and usually not another tourist in sight.

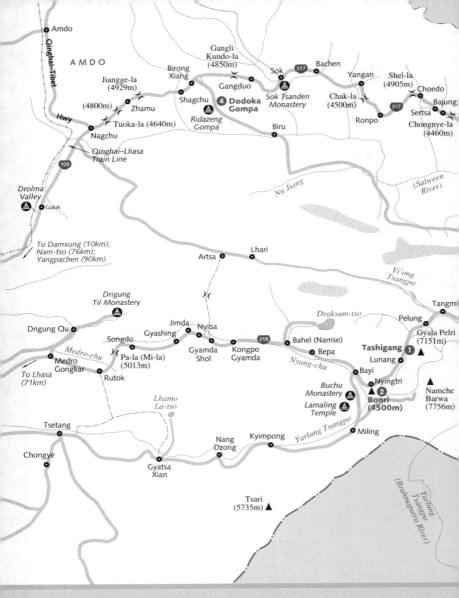

Eastern Tibet Highlights

❶ Stay with a Tibetan family in the charming village of **Tashigang** (p198)

❷ Join devout Bön pilgrims on an unforgettable seven-hour trek around holy mountain **Bönri** (p200)

❸ Sleep in Tibet's most romantic guesthouse,

suspended on stilts above the cool blue waters of **Ngan-tso** (p196)

❹ Detour to Dodoka Gompa to see its remarkable **skull wall** (p214), in one of Tibet's

least-visited and creepiest sights

5 Clamber up wooden ladders to cliff-top shrines at the spectacularly sited **Tsedru Monastery** (p211)

6 Hike towards the magnificent **Midui Glacier** (p197)

7 Hunt down the three closely guarded keys needed to unlock the treasures of **Riwoche Tsuglhakhang** (p209)

History

The area around Chamdo was one of the first settled in Tibet, as indicated by the 5000-year-old Neolithic remains at nearby Karo. Fossilised millet hints at a 5000-year tradition of agriculture in the region.

Kham was the home of many early lamas, including the founders of the Drigungpa and Karmapa schools. In 1070 many Buddhists fled persecution in central Tibet to Kham, where they set up influential monasteries, later returning to central Tibet to spearhead the so-called second diffusion of Buddhism in Tibet.

Lhasa's control over the region has waxed and waned over the centuries. Lhasa first gained control of Kham thanks to Mongol assistance, but the majority of the region has traditionally enjoyed de facto political independence. Until recently, much of Kham comprised many small fiefdoms ruled by kings (in Derge, for instance), lamas (Lithang) or hereditary chieftains (Bathang). Relations with China were mostly restricted to the trade caravans, which brought in bricks of Chinese tea and left with pastoral products.

Chinese warlords such as Zhao Erfeng and Liu Wenhui swept through the eastern part of Kham (modern-day western Sìchuān) in the late 19th and early 20th centuries, eventually setting up the Chinese province of Xīkāng (western Kham). Khampa rebellions occurred frequently, notably in 1918, 1928 and 1932, though not all were against the Chinese; in 1933 the Khampas tried to shake off Lhasa's nominal rule.

In 1950 Chamdo fell to the People's Liberation Army (PLA) and much of eastern Tibet came under Chinese control. In 1954 the part of Kham east of the upper Yangzi River was merged into Sìchuān province and a program of land reforms was introduced, including the collectivisation of monasteries. When in 1955 the Chinese tried to disarm the Khampas and settle the nomads, the Kāngdìng Rebellion erupted and fighting spread to Lithang, Zhōngdiàn and Dàochéng. When the PLA bombed monasteries in Dàochéng and Lithang, the rebels fled to Chamdo, and later to India and Nepal, to organise armed resistance from Mustang in Nepal with CIA assistance.

Today eastern Tibet remains quite heavily Sinicised along the southern Sìchuān–Tibet Hwy, where the controversial construction of new towns (with multicoloured corrugated-iron roofs) is fast altering the face of the region. Off the main highways, Khampa life remains culturally strong.

Permits

Military presence is strong in eastern Tibet, and this has for a long time been a heavily restricted area for general travel. Since 2008 the whole of the Chamdo and Nyingtri regions (an area which covers almost all of eastern Tibet, save the area closest to Lhasa) have been closed to foreigners for around three weeks every year during March. At other times travel is allowed, although foreigners cannot normally take public transport and must, of course, have all the necessary permits.

At the time of research, foreign visitors needed three permits to travel in eastern Tibet: an Alien Travel Permit, a military permit and a Tibet Tourism Bureau (TTB) permit. These permits were registered at the Public Security Bureau (PSB), Foreign Affairs Office and Military Office. They also needed to be shown at a number of checkpoints along the Sìchuān–Tibet Hwy. Your travel agency will organise all these permits for you (and the registration process), but it will take a minimum of 15 days.

Itineraries

There are three main routes for those wanting to see eastern Tibet: the southern route of the Sìchuān–Tibet Hwy, the northern route of that same highway, and a big loop, taking in parts of both the southern and the northern route.

Scenery in these parts is stunning wherever you travel, but the southern route probably just about edges the northern route when it comes to landscape diversity. It also has more in terms of sights. Bank on needing between one and two weeks to drive from Bathang, in Sìchuān province, to Lhasa.

You need about the same amount of time to drive the drier, more barren northern route from Derge, also in Sìchuān province, to Lhasa. For both routes it's worth factoring in one or two rest days to help you ac-

---

PUBLIC TRANSPORT

At the time of research, foreigners were not allowed to travel on public transport in Tibet. Basic information is included here in case the situation changes.

Following a failed rebellion against new Chinese rule in the late 1950s, a core of Khampa fighters managed to regroup in Lhoka, in southern Tibet, and in a rare moment of Khampa unity formed an organisation called Chizhi Gangdrung (Four Rivers, Six Ranges), the traditional local name for the Kham region. Soon 15,000 men were assembled.

The Khampa's cause attracted attention from abroad, and before long Tibetan leaders were liaising with CIA agents in Kolkata (Calcutta), arranging secret meetings through dead letter drops. The first batch of six Khampa agents trekked over the border to India, were driven to Bangladesh and then flown to the Pacific island of Saipan, where they were trained to organise guerrilla groups. Agents were later parachuted behind enemy lines into Samye and Lithang.

In 1957 guerrilla attacks were made on Chinese garrisons and road camps, and in 1958, 700 Chinese soldiers were killed by guerrillas near Nyemo. The movement met with the Dalai Lama in southern Tibet when he fled Lhasa in 1959 as the CIA readied three planeloads of arms – enough for 2000 people.

The flight of the Dalai Lama to India marked a setback for the resistance and the focus switched to a base in Mustang, an ethnically Tibetan area in Nepal, where initially at least the Nepalis turned a blind eye to the movement. Between 1960 and 1962 over 150 Tibetans were sent to Colorado for training.

Yet the resistance was living on borrowed time. By the mid-1960s CIA funding had dried up. By 1972 the international political climate had changed; US president Richard Nixon's visit to China and the coronation of Nepal's pro-Chinese king left the Khampas out on a limb. Moreover, the resistance was riddled with feuds – most of the Khampa rebels had always been fighting more for their local valley and monastery than for any national ideal. In 1973 the Nepalis demanded the closure of the Mustang base and the Dalai Lama asked the rebels to surrender. It was the end of the Khampa rebellion and the end of Tibetan armed resistance to the Chinese.

EASTERN TIBET (KHAM)

climatise to the altitude, if nothing else, but this is particularly the case for the northern route. An alternative route here starts in Derge but heads south from Chamdo before joining the southern route at Pomda junction. Allow the same amount of time.

Those with more time on their hands could try a big loop, starting and finishing in Lhasa, taking in both southern and northern routes as well as the short stretch between Chamdo and Pomda junction. You'll need between two and three weeks for this, whichever direction you go in.

At the time of research, foreigners weren't allowed into Chamdo prefecture, the region that stretches along the TAR border with Sìchuān province. This means it was impossible to complete any of the three itineraries mentioned above. If this is still the case when you're planning your trip, consider driving only the western stretch of the southern route, from Lhasa to Rawok, before coming back the same way. This stretch includes some of the best sights and most stunning scenery in the whole region,

so you won't feel like you're missing out. Allow between one and two weeks.

THE SOUTHERN ROUTE (HWY 318)

This chapter covers the two main overland routes from Sìchuān province to Lhasa. Both are part of the legendary Sìchuān–Tibet Hwy, which splits in two about 200km east of the Tibetan border to form the Northern Hwy (Hwy 317) and the Southern Hwy (Hwy 318), both of which eventually lead to Lhasa.

The slightly busier and strategically more important southern route takes in the best of the alpine scenery. Here you'll see (and hear) rivers powering their way through deep gorges and subtropical forests before opening out to form sublime mirror lakes overlooked by distant snowcapped peaks.

Most of the road is paved these days, the muddy single-lane track just west of Tangmi being a notable exception.

Markham ब्लूर:ावबाब्य 芒康

☑0895

It's possible to make it all the way to Pomda from Bathang in one long day's drive (about eight hours), but stopping in Markham (pronounced Mángkāng in Chinese) makes some sense. Markham has for centuries been a strategic crossroads town on the salt and tea trade routes between Tibet and China. The road leading south from here goes to the remote but fascinating riverside salt-mining town of **Tsakalho** (盐井; Yánjǐng), which still produces salt from its open salt pans beside the Mekong River, before continuing across the border into Yúnnán province. Foreigners haven't been allowed to use this border for some time now, although, as always, getting out of Tibet is considerably easier than getting in.

These days Markham has a largely Han Chinese feel to it, plus a strong police presence, so make sure you have your papers in order before showing up.

Xuěyù Bīnguǎn (雪域宾馆; ☑454 3399; tw Y110) is a reliable backpacker-friendly guesthouse with OK rooms. Private bathrooms have sit-down loos. It's on the southbound road, about 200m from the T-junction with Hwy 318.

Between Xuěyù Bīnguǎn and the Hwy 318 junction is a cluster of decent Sichuanese restaurants, some of which are open round the clock.

It takes about three hours to drive here from Bathang. Public buses passing through Markham tend to stop at the hotel Jiāotōng Bīnguǎn (交通宾馆) to fill up any spare seats they may have.

POMDA ब्लॅस्रॅट्न 邦达

☑0895 / ELEV 4390M

The roller-coaster road east from Markham crosses three high mountain passes and some stunning scenery before arriving at Pomda. Known as Bāngdá in Chinese, Pomda comes in two parts: the T-junction, where Hwy 318 meets Hwy 317; and the village, about 5km north of the junction, where you'll find Pomda Monastery.

The junction is full of restaurants, teahouses and guesthouses and makes an OK place to bunk up for the night before heading north to Chamdo, west towards Lhasa or east towards Sìchuān province.

Pomda Monastery (邦达寺; Bāngdá Sì), a colourfully decorated whitewashed building, lies in the lovely village of Pomda, set at

REMAINING KHAM

The traditional Tibetan province of Kham incorporates much of the eastern part of the Tibetan Autonomous Region (TAR), most of western Sìchuān and a small part of northwest Yúnnán. This chapter covers only the eastern TAR, where travel permits are required. For information on overland travel through western Sìchuān, see p216. For information on Yúnnán province, see Lonely Planet's *China* guide.

the edge of a wide valley. It dates back 360 years, but was destroyed in 1959 and rebuilt between 1984 and 1988. It is now home to 70 monks. The main entry hallway of the assembly hall has excellent murals depicting monastic dress codes and the *gelong* examination that all monks must pass. There is also a protector chapel and a debating courtyard, as well as a huge mani wall (a wall made of engraved prayer stones) and mani *lhakhang* (prayer-wheel chapel).

At Pomda junction, **Bāngdá Qīngnián Lǚshè** (邦达青年旅舍; ☑139 0895 0026, 189-0895 2463; dm/tw/tr Y20/50/60; @🛜) is a popular hostel. Simple rooms have clean and comfy beds. Shared toilets are with the bedrooms on the 1st floor, while a hot shower is available on the ground floor. There's free laundry and, if you're touring, management will wash your bicycle for free! It's right on the main junction. Look for 'youth hostel' in English on the sign. The Sichuanese restaurant (dishes Y15 to Y40) on the ground floor is decent.

Nearby **Gāoyuán Xuěniú Bīnguǎn** (高原雪牛宾馆; ☑133 9805 2677; tw Y60-80, tr Y45-60) is a cheaper, Tibetan-run option. Rooms aren't the cleanest and there's no shower, but it's fine for one night. There's a popular Tibetan restaurant on the ground floor.

Buses travelling in all three directions tend to stop in Pomda for lunch, but times vary. Buses heading towards Lhasa are most frequent.

Pasho ८ময়র্শ্র 八宿

☑0895 / ELEV 3270M

Heading west from Pomda the paved road only lasts for 13km, as far as the 4618m-high pass Zar Gama-la (业拉山; Yèlā Shān).

From here a 72-switchback dirt track descends into the Salween Valley, crossing the Ngul-chu (怒江; Nù Jiāng or Salween River) before hitting the pleasant one-street town of Pasho, known as Bāsù in Chinese.

Sights & Activities

On the northwestern outskirts of the town is **Neru Monastery**, a Gelugpa monastery that's home to 36 monks and is worth a visit if you have a couple of spare hours. The renovated central chapel holds the throne of the Pakhpala, a religious leader based in Chamdo, whose current incarnation is a government minister. It was the current Pakhpala who paid for the restoration of Neru Monastery. To the right of the main chapel is the funeral chörten of the monastery's last *trulku* (reincarnated lama) and the back room has a large seated Jampa (Maitreya) statue made by craftsmen from Chamdo. The top floor contains a *gönkhang* (protector chapel) loaded with old Khampa weaponry. The monastery is a 25-minute walk from the centre of town along a winding road leading north from town centre and across a river bridge. You can drive here via the sturdier bridge west of town.

About 4km east of town, beside the main highway, is **Dola Gompa Monastery** (多拉神山; Duōlā Shénshān), home to just 12 monks these days. The older lower chapel here is surrounded by chörtens and ancient yak-hide prayer wheels, and is a great place to meet local pilgrims. A popular kora leads up the mountainside to a plateau and then descends west to Pasho town, with fine views of the arid valley. The leisurely half-day kora is chock-a-block with jovial pilgrims during the Saga Dawa festival (p22).

Sleeping & Eating

Bāsù Bīnguǎn　　　　　　HOTEL $$
(八宿宾馆; ☎456 3333; d/tw Y200/300) This new place is the best hotel in town and worth considering for a splurge. Good-quality, clean rooms have sparkling bathrooms and there's a nice cafe and restaurant on the 1st floor plus a well-stocked supermarket (open from 7.40am to 11pm) below.

Jiāotōng Bīnguǎn　　　　　HOTEL $
(交通宾馆; ☎465 2235; dm/tr Y15/75; tw with bathroom Y140) There's a wide range of reasonably clean rooms on offer here at this unofficial bus station hotel in the western end of town (24-hour hot water too).

CHEAP HOTELS

Contrary to how things appear in this chapter, there are actually a lot of very cheap hotels in eastern Tibet – it's just that most don't accept foreign guests. We've tried to list hotels that traditionally have been foreigner friendly, and they tend to be the more expensive ones. Rules change, though, so don't be surprised if a hotel we recommend here turns you away. And before you get into an argument with reception, remember it's the PSB that decides which hotels can and can't register foreigners.

Piāoxiāng Fàndiàn　　　　SICHUAN $
(飘香饭店; dishes Y10-30; ◷9am-10pm) This 22-year-old establishment, opposite Jiāotōng Bīnguǎn, still knocks up excellent Sìchuān cuisine.

Information

Agricultural Bank of China ATM (农业银行; Nóngyè Yínháng) On main strip. Accepts foreign bank cards.

Wǎngyuán Wǎngbā (网缘网吧; per hr Y5; ◷7am-midnight) Internet cafe down a side street off main highway.

Getting There & Away

Buses to Chamdo leave from Jiāotōng Bīnguǎn every morning at around 8am. Buses to other destinations – Bāyī, Markham and Lhasa – are through buses, so are less predictable.

Pasho to Rawok

The landscape changes dramatically along this 90km stretch of road. Rocky purples and reds, reminiscent of Utah or Arizona in the United States, make way for arid khaki colours in an area sprinkled with traditional whitewashed villages. The road then climbs the 4462m-high pass, Ngajukla, which marks the end of the arid plateau and the start of the descent into the subtropical Parlung Tsangpo Valley.

Around 13km before the pass, it's worth detouring 2km west to the lovely village of **Dzongsar**, which has the small Sangha Lhakhang (recognisable by the stuffed sheep outside) and the fort-like ruins of Ramo Monastery. This is a very friendly village and you'll need to allocate extra time for yak-butter tea breaks with the locals. A 20-minute walk to the west leads to the active Lhorong Monastery. Be on the look out for dogs here. On the hillside further west is the ruined Yarlo Monastery.

Back on the main highway, you'll cross Ngajuk-la and descend into the valley past a small azure lake and some nomads' camps before reaching Rawok and its two stunning alpine lakes.

Rawok ར་འོག 然乌

☎0895 / ELEV 3880M

Rawok (Ránwū in Chinese) has the ramshackle and temporary feel of a frontier outpost, but without the charm. The short main drag is strewn with guesthouses and noodle joints, not to mention the occasional body part (we found a human skull lying ignored in the gutter a few years back). Fortunately, you can skip all this by staying a few hundred metres east of town in what is quite possibly the coolest guesthouse in all of Tibet, situated literally *on* the waters of **Ngan-tso**.

It is, after all, the stunning lakes of Ngan-tso and Rawok-tso that most travellers stop here for, and there are great opportunities for walking round them.

The old town is also worth a wander. A road leads into the warren from the north end of the Rawok strip. From here you can work your way through to the large chörten, mani wall and small temple overlooking the lake in the southeast of town. The surrounding fields are full of wooden platforms for drying barley.

It's worth heading north of town and taking the side road southeast for around 6km to the second lake, **Rawok-tso**. The views here are excellent and it's a great place for a picnic. It's a popular location for Chinese tourists, who come to watch the sunrise.

🛏 Sleeping & Eating

There are great camping spots around either of the two lakes, but it's worth checking first that you are allowed to camp; sometimes the authorities don't permit it.

TOP CHOICE **Ránwūhú Fēngqíngyuán**

GUESTHOUSE **$$**

(然乌湖风情园; ☎456 2606; dm/tw Y60/180; 🛜) This excellent place, a few hundred metres east of the main strip, is traveller central for Rawok. There's a lively restaurant-cafe at the front with decent twin rooms around the car park out the back. But it's what's behind the main building that makes this place eastern Tibet's stand-out guesthouse: a pinewood cabin with stilts hovering above the cool-blue waters of Ngan-tso. It's a dream location on a stunning lake surrounded by snowcapped mountains, and could hardly be more romantic. The long cabin with verandas on three sides is joined to the lakeside by a narrow wooden walkway, and has a handful of rooms: some dorms, some twins. All are neat and clean and come with wi-fi access. The only downside is that you have to walk back onto dry land if want to use the shared toilets. There is, of course, the peeing-in-the-lake option, but we didn't say that.

Ránwū Bīnguǎn

GUESTHOUSE **$$**

(然乌宾馆; ☎139 8905 8387; dm Y40; tw without/with bathroom Y80/180) Slightly further into town from Ránwūhú Fēngqíngyuán, this place has acceptable twins, some of which have bathrooms. The shared showers and toilets are suspended precariously above ground in a wooden shack at the end of the 1st-floor corridor. This place also has a restaurant.

ⓘ Getting There & Away

Although 'through buses' between Pomi and Pasho do stop here, times are unpredictable, so if you haven't organised a tour you may have to hitch.

Pomi སྤོ་མེས། 波密

☎0894 / ELEV 2740M

Known as Bōmì in Chinese, this bustling county capital has well-stocked shops and several hotels and restaurants, making it a logical place to spend the night. The town itself isn't pretty to look at (although the old town over the river is more interesting), but the surrounding scenery is lovely and there's scope for exploring nearby valleys.

◎ Sights

Around 6km west of Pomi is the tranquil, 600-year-old Nyingma-sect **Dodung Monastery**, set on a pine-clad hill overlooking the valley and home to 56 monks. The main prayer hall includes the footprint of the seventh Khamtrul Rinpoche, Sangye Tenzin (1909–29). Upstairs are murals depicting the life story of two forms of Gesar, as well as Guru Rinpoche and Tsepame (Amitayus). The monastery is a branch of Chayab Monastery (see the box, p211) and so there are some photos of the sixth Taksam Rinpoche. Several delightful mani *lhakhangs* (buildings holding prayer wheels) make up the rest of the lovely complex.

To reach the monastery from Pomi, cross the road bridge over the Parlung Tsangpo, opposite the Jiāotōng Lǚguǎn, and take the first right. The dirt track you're on continues all the way to Metok (this road when completed will make Metok the last county in China to be connected by road!), but after about three to four kilometres you need to turn sharp left uphill to the monastery.

🛏 Sleeping & Eating

Míngzhū Bīnguǎn   HOTEL $$
(明珠宾馆; ☎542 4688; Zhamuxi Lu; 扎木西路; tw/d Y288, discounted to Y140; @) Among the best-quality rooms in town, they come with clean bathrooms, 24-hour hot water, internet access for laptop users and, in some cases, river views. At the west end of the main road, next to the petrol station.

Jiāotōng Lǚguǎn   HOTEL $
(交通旅馆; ☎542 2798; dm Y20, tw without/with bathroom Y40/80) Pretty basic rooms here, but claims to have 24-hour hot water. If they let you pay per bed, this is a pretty good deal. Not to be confused with the larger hotel of the same name just opposite.

TOP CHOICE **Guzel**   TIBETAN TEAHOUSE $
(艺人; Yìrén; Píng'ān Jiē; 平安街; dishes Y4-10) Run by local artist Gyatso, who speaks a little English, this lovely pocket-sized teahouse has its walls adorned with Mr Jiang's unusual Tibetan calligraphy, which is for sale, although doesn't come cheap. The atmosphere is very welcoming and the food simple but decent with *shemdre* (Y10), *momos* (Y10), *thugpa* (Y5), *tsampa* (Y4) and butter tea (Y10) all on the menu. Ping'an Jie is a small tree-lined street that leads south off the main road towards the river.

ℹ Information

Agricultural Bank of China ATM (农业银行; Nóngyè Yínháng) On main road; accepts foreign cards.

Internet cafe (网吧; wǎngbā; per hr Y5; ⏰24hr) On Shangmao Jie, the road with the archway entrance, just east of Ping'an Jie.

ℹ Getting There & Away

The bus station, opposite Míngzhū Bīnguǎn, has one daily service to Chamdo, plus a bus to

WORTH A TRIP

MIDUI GLACIER

The most popular excursion from Rawok is to the **Lhegu Glacier** (来古冰川; Láigǔ Bīnchuān; admission/parking Y20/10), 31km south of Rawok, but this was off-limits to foreigners at the time of research. In any case, it's becoming so popular with Chinese tourists that it can be a bit of a zoo. Quieter, and actually more picturesque, is **Midui Glacier** (米堆冰川; Mǐduī Bīngchuān; admission Y50; ⏰8am-5pm) about 35km west of Rawok, on the road to Pomi. You can drive 7km from the entrance on the main highway to a car park from where it's a two-hour horse ride (Y100) or walk to **Midui Village** (Mǐduī Cūn; 米堆村). The glacier is a further 2km away, but tourists (of any nationality) aren't allowed beyond the village after two Korean travellers went missing hiking up to the glacier in 2009. The views from the village, though, are stunning.

Chéngdū every two days. Minibuses for Bāyī wait outside.

Baha Gompa བྷ་ཧ་

This 800-year-old Nyingma monastery – officially called Orgyen Sanga Chöling – is home to 12 monks and an enormous, tusked, 20-year-old pet pig, and is reputed to have been built on the site of the grave of the illegitimate child of Princess Wencheng. The monks here say the child was born in secrecy while the Chinese princess was on her way to Lhasa to marry Tibetan king Songtsen Gampo.

You'll get a friendly welcome here, but sadly travellers are no longer allowed to camp either in the grounds of the monastery or anywhere around the beautiful nearby lake. Luckily, a gorgeous two-storey pine guesthouse recently opened in a pretty rapeseed field next to the monastery. **Rinchen Family Guesthouse** (仁青家庭旅馆; Rénqīng Jiātíng Lǚguǎn; ☎139 0894 0848, 136 5959 0828; dm without bathroom Y40, tw with bathroom Y100), or Rinchen Khyimtshang Dönkhâng in Tibetan, has basic but spotless rooms, some of which have bathrooms, and fabulous views of the lake and surrounding countryside, which is perfect for walking. They serve simple but tasty home-cooked Tibetan food.

Keep walking past the monastery, which itself is accessed from the highway by crossing a suspension bridge over a fast-flowing river.

Tangmi 通麦

This tiny, one-street lunch-stop, known in Chinese as Tōngmài, has a handful of restaurants and guesthouses. The ugly blue-grey concrete block that is **Jiāotōng Bīnguǎn** (交通宾馆; ☏138 8904 8533; dm/tw Y20/140) has clean, comfortable twins with bathroom in the main building and a row of rustic, bathroomless wooden huts in the back garden, which go for Y20 per bed. There's an OK restaurant next door, with others to be found 200m further up the road in Tangmi proper.

A couple of kilometres beyond here, the southern highway crosses **Tangmi Suspension Bridge** at the confluence of three rushing rivers. Photography here is strictly forbidden.

Immediately after the bridge, a poor-quality side road heads 23km northwest up to **Yigong-tso** (elevation 2150m), a stunning but hard-to-reach lake that was created in this area.

The main highway, though, bears left and turns into a narrow and often treacherous, cliff-hugging dirt track. This is arguably the most stunning stretch of scenery on the southern route – subtropical, mist-shrouded forests line steep-sided gorges above raging rivers, framed most of the time by distant snowcapped mountains – but it's also the most dangerous with the road becoming particularly susceptible to landslides after rain.

Tashigang

བཀྲ་ཤིས་སྒང་དམར་གསོལ་གོང་ཚོ
扎西岗民俗村

☏0894 / ELEV 2530M

A stay in this gorgeous tiny rural village, a couple of kilometres east of the small town of **Lunang** (鲁朗; Lǔlǎng), is for many travellers a highlight of a trip to this part of eastern Tibet. Surrounded by fields of deep green barley and bright yellow rape-seed, and framed by forested mountains, Tashigang (or Zhāxīgǎng in Chinese), with its pigs and chickens roaming free, is made up of a handful of large stone Tibetan block homes, six of which have been converted into fabulous family guesthouses.

This is a wonderful chance to stay with a Tibetan family and eat genuine Tibetan home-cooked food, and the countryside offers an almost endless selection of **walks**. Locals are also on hand to rent **horses** (Y10 to Y100) for short treks into the hills.

Be aware that a couple of kilometres east of here is the **Lunang Scenic Area** (鲁朗风景区; Lǔlǎng Fēngjǐngqū; entrance Y170), where you have to pay an extortionate fee for the pleasure of walking around the countryside. Everywhere else, it's free.

Local villager Po Phuntsok turned his home into a **family guesthouse** (☏136 5894 6031; beds Y30-40; meals Y20-40) in 2004, the first Tashigang villager to do so. It's made up of two stone-walled, wood-beamed buildings that house clean, tidy bedrooms decked out in beautifully painted traditional wood furniture, a shared bathroom with a hot-water shower-pod and a large, fabulously atmospheric old kitchen that doubles as a communal dining area. Five other neighbours have since followed suit. All have almost identical facilities and prices, but we like Tangci Ren's the most – there's just something about it. Apart from the generic tourism-board plaque that all the guesthouses here have over their front gate, there's no sign or name, but as the village lane bends round to the left, it's the white stone house right in front of you. A wooden sign with the village name on it stands outside its end wall.

If you're pining for shops or a restaurant, walk 20 minutes east along the main highway to the one-street town of Lunang where you'll find a couple of Tibetan teahouses and a string of Chinese restaurants selling the expensive local speciality **shíguōjī** (石锅鸡; stone-pot chicken; Y100-280), as well as the usual Chinese fare.

Tashigang to Bāyī

The 70km-stretch from Tashigang to Bāyī passes over the 4582m **Serkhym-la** (色齐拉; Sèqí Lā). On a rare clear day there are dramatic views of shark-toothed Namche Barwa (7756m) and Gyala Pelri (7151m). The road then descends around the back of the forested holy mountain, Bönri (4500m), passing the point at which the Bönri kora meets the highway, marked by a flurry of prayer flags, before continuing on to the small, two-street county capital of Nyingtri, 18km east of Bāyī.

Just down from where the Bönri kora meets the main highway, a side road turns left into the village of Kāngzhā Cūn (康扎村) from where you can see **Takdrugtse Monastery** about 3km away, up in the hills to your left. This Bön pilgrimage site contains a large central stone with 'tiger paw prints' on it. Long ago, legend says, monks decided to build a temple here after seeing an auspicious *tak* (tiger) crouching on the rock.

Bāyī བརྒྱད་གཅིག་ 八一

☎0894 / POP 60,000 / ELEV 2990M

Bāyī, a recent Chinese creation close to the small county capital of Nyingtri, is the largest town along this stretch of the southern route so an obvious choice for an overnight stay, especially if you fancy hiking the nearby Bönri kora.

This is also where you or your guide will almost certainly need to register with the rather unwelcoming local PSB. Just keep smiling.

🛏 Sleeping

Azalea Hotel HOTEL $$
(杜鹃花酒店; Dùjuānhuā Jiǔdiàn; ☎582 3222; Guangdong Lu; tw/tr Y688/588, discounted to Y120/200; ✳@) The smartest affordable option in town, Azalea has clean, bright doubles with decent bathrooms and free internet for laptop users.

Post Hotel HOTEL $$
(邮政大酒店; Yóuzhèng Dàjiǔdiàn; ☎588 9666; cnr Xianggang Lu & Xiamen Lu; d without/with bathroom Y168/488, discounted to Y80/120; ✳) Twins here are modern and very comfortable with carpeted floors, TV and piping-hot showers in admittedly slightly grubby bathrooms. The bathroomless versions are basic but clean, but you might struggle to land one as they tend to be for drivers and guides only.

Bātáng Línqiáo Zhùsùbù GUESTHOUSE $
(巴塘林桥住宿部; ☎136 5894 8880; Xiamen Lu; dm/s/tw Y20/40/60) The cheapest place we could find that was allowing foreigners to stay, rooms here are pretty shabby but the

Bāyī

🛏 Sleeping

1 Azalea Hotel.................................A2
2 Bātáng Línqiáo Zhùsùbù..............A1
3 Post Hotel.....................................A1

🍴 Eating

4 Bātáng Zàngcān...........................A2
5 Héngyuán Xiǎochī........................A2
6 Lo Les Traditional Emotion
    Palace.......................................B1

common showers are hot (once you've waited 30 minutes for them to warm up).

🍴 Eating

TOP CHOICE **Lo Les Traditional Emotion Palace** TIBETAN $$$
(拉列思藏餐厅; Lālièsī Zàng Cāntīng; Zhuhai Lu; dishes Y10-68; ⊙9am-10pm) Fabulous food, regal Tibetan decor and fantastically dressed staff make this easily the best place in town to sample Tibetan food. English menu, too.

Bātáng Zàngcān TIBETAN $
(巴塘藏餐; Xiamen Lu; meals from Y7; ⊙8am-midnight]) Hang with the locals in this salt-of-the-earth, pocket-sized Tibetan teahouse serving tsampa (Y2), *thugpa* (Y7/8), *momo* (Y1 each) and butter tea (Y6).

Héngyuán Xiǎochī CHINESE $
(恒源小吃; Fujian Lu; dishes Y8-18; ⊙9am-6am) This almost 24-hour establishment, specialising in pigs trotters (猪蹄; zhūtí; half a trotter Y7), gets good reviews from Chinese travellers. Also serves decent noodles – try

the spicy dàndàn miàn (担担面; Y8/10 per small/large bowl).

Information

Agricultural Bank of China ATM (农业银行; Nóngyè Yínháng; Fujian Lu) Accepts foreign cards.

Eastern Express Internet Café (东方快车网吧; Dōngfāng Kuàichē Wǎngba; Aomen Lu; per hr Y4; ⊙24hr) Another 24-hour internet cafe sits above Kodak Express.

Kodak Express (柯达快速彩色; Kēdá Kuàisù Cǎisè; Xiamen Square; Xiamen Guangchang) CD burning from Y20.

Post Office (中国邮政; Zhōngguó Yóuzhèng; Zhuhai Lu; ⊙9.30am-7pm)

Telephone Office (中国电信; Zhōngguó Diànxìn; ☑582 1048; Zhuhai Lu; ⊙9.30am-7.30pm)

ℹ Getting There & Away

Several buses run daily to Lhasa from the **Bus Station** (客运站; Kèyùn Zhàn; Guangdong Lu). There are also buses every other day to Chamdo, Chéngdū and Markham.

Shared 4WDs and minivans leave for other destinations from outside the bus station, including Nyingtri, Miling (for the airport), Lunang and Pomi.

Línzhī Airport (林芝机场; Línzhī Jīchǎng), about 70km south of Bāyī near Miling (米林; Mǐlín), has daily flights to Chéngdū.

Around Bāyī

BÖNRI བོན་རི་ 苯日神山

Bönri, or Běnrì Shénshān in Chinese, is the Bön religion's most sacred mountain, a sprawling massif where Bön founder Tonpa Shenrab fought and defeated his arch-rival Khyabpa Lagring. Bönpo pilgrims come from all over Tibet to circumambulate the mountain in an anticlockwise direction.

The full 60km kora starts and finishes in Nyingtri, 18km west of Bāyī, and takes two or three days, climbing to the 4500m Bönri-la on the second day. It passes many sites connected to Tonpa Shenrab, as well as an ancient burial tumulus, a 9th-century stele and a cemetery for babies.

Thanks to a new road built around the back of the mountain, it's now possible to complete the main part of the kora in around seven hours. It's a tough trek because of the steepness of the climb, not to mention the altitude, but it's incredibly rewarding to follow pilgrims over such sacred

ground and among such fabulous scenery. The forested mountainside eventually opens up onto grasslands at the top where nomads graze their yaks. Rhododendron bushes also cover parts of the top of the mountain in blankets of colour. If it's raining be particularly careful on the descent as the path is unmade and can get very muddy.

This seven-hour section of the kora starts in the tiny but modern village of **Miru** (米瑞; Mǐruì). From Nyingtri's main street, turn south and continue past a military base to a T-junction. Turn left and follow the road a few kilometres to a road barrier where non-Tibetans have to pay Y50 entrance fee to enter the **Nyang River Tourism Area** (尼洋河风光带; Níyánghé Fēngguāngdài).

Immediately after the barrier is a 2km-long signposted track on your left that leads to **Taktse Yungdrungling Monastery**, which houses some interesting iconography (was it us or is one deity in the main chapel holding a Rubik's cube?) as well as some lovely ruined chörtens and water-driven prayer wheels.

From the road barrier it's a 20km drive past charming farming villages and a beautiful, wide river valley to Miru, where you can get a bite to eat and stock up on provisions. There are also cheap lodgings here if you want to get an early start up the mountain.

Locals in Miru can act as your hiking guide (Y80), but it's just as easy to follow the pilgrims. In any case, prayer flags line pretty much the whole route.

The path will take you up and over Bönri-la until you eventually meet the main Sìchuān–Tibet Hwy (Hwy 318) where your driver can pick you up or you can hitch back to Bāyī or the other way to Lunang.

Don't be persuaded by your guide or driver to either start from the highway, or to trek up and down the same side of the mountain. Doing this may be quicker, and more convenient for your driver of course, but will result in you walking part of the kora in a clockwise instead of anti-clockwise direction and will be considered highly disrespectful by the Bönpo pilgrims.

LAMALING TEMPLE
ཟླ་མ་གླིང་དགོན་པ། 喇嘛宁寺

About 30km south of Bāyī is the attractive Lamaling Temple (Lǎmaníng Sì). This monastery was the seat of the exiled Dudjom Rinpoche (1904–87), the former head of the

Nyingma order. It is now looked after by his son-in-law Chuni Rinpoche and is home to around 40 monks and 30 nuns.

The octagonal main Zangtok Pelri temple was wonderfully restored in the early '90s and rises through four storeys, bringing to mind the Ütse of Samye Monastery. The building is draped in long strands of cannonball-sized wooden prayer beads. The grassy courtyard in front is home to a few doleful mountain goats brought here from Tsodzong Monastery at Draksum-tso. Don't get too close: they buck.

Take your shoes off before entering the temple. The ground floor has a statue of Guru Rinpoche, with two stone footprints of the guru on the altar (curiously, both the right foot!) and puppet-like images of the protector Tseumar to the left. A passageway behind the altar leads up to a mezzanine level with four protector chapels in each corner. The chapel above this houses statues of Chenresig (Avalokiteshvara), flanked by Jampelyang (Manjushri) and Chana Dorje (Vajrapani), known collectively as the Rigsum Gonpo. The top-floor chapel contains a statue of Öpagme.

The other main building, to the right, is the assembly hall, where religious services are held on the 10th, 15th and 25th days of each lunar month. The hall is dominated by a huge statue of Sakyamuni and more images of Dudjom Rinpoche wearing his characteristic sunglasses. Pilgrims circumambulate both this building and the main temple.

If you want to stretch your legs, a trail leads off from the corner of the car park to an atmospheric prayer-flag-draped chörten and then winds up the hillside for about 40 minutes (follow the prayer flags) to Norbu Ri, where the original Lamaling Temple stood before it was destroyed in a 1930 earthquake. Look out for the Sakyamuni footprint on a cloth above the door.

WHICH WAY TO CIRCUMAMBULATE?

Even if you're not a pilgrim, you'll still be expected to walk in the correct direction around or inside monasteries and around kora trails. This means clockwise for Buddhist monasteries and koras, but anti-clockwise for the Bön-religion equivalents.

About one kilometre before the turning for Lamaling Temple you pass the small but ancient Gelugpa monastery of Buchu (Bùjiǔ Sì). The original dates from the 7th century, when it was built at the command of King Songtsen Gampo as one of the demoness-subduing temples (see the box, p56); it pins the demoness' right elbow. The monastery is recognisable by its striking golden roof.

The entrance to the main chapel is flanked by unusual murals of several protector gods, including the Kongpo deity Kongtsun Demo (in the far right on horseback, next to the wheel of life). The main hall has statues of the standing form of Guru Rinpoche and a large Jampa (Maitreya), and there are two small statues of the protectors Dorje Lekpa and Kongtsun Demo in the left corner.

The inner sanctum houses statues of Chenresig (Avalokiteshvara), with Songtsen Gampo in the left corner. Behind these is the trinity of Guru Rinpoche, the Indian translator Shantarakshita and King Trisong Detsen.

A lovely kora surrounds the timeless temple.

NECHE GOSHOG MONASTERY 尼池寺

This small, golden-roofed Bön monastery about 17km east of Bāyī, on your right just before you reach the town of Nyingtri, was rebuilt in 2008 after being gutted in a fire. It's home to around 25 monks and is famous for its 2000-year-old juniper tree that is sacred to Bönpos. The manicured courtyard includes a small side shrine dedicated to the Bön founder Tonpa Shenrab.

Draksum-tso
བྲག་གསུམ་མཚོ། 巴松措

☎ 0894 / ELEV 3470M

Eastern Tibet is blessed with many beautiful lakes but this is arguably the best of the lot. Known as Bāsōngcuò in Chinese, Draksum-tso (admission Y100), and particularly its monastery island, is a photographer's dream. It's also a great opportunity to dust off those hiking boots and that tent that you've been lugging around.

Apart from the sheer beauty of the lake and its surrounding 6000m peaks, the site has strong connections to Gesar of Ling, the semi-mythical ruler of eastern Tibet, and Guru Rinpoche, the Indian sage, both

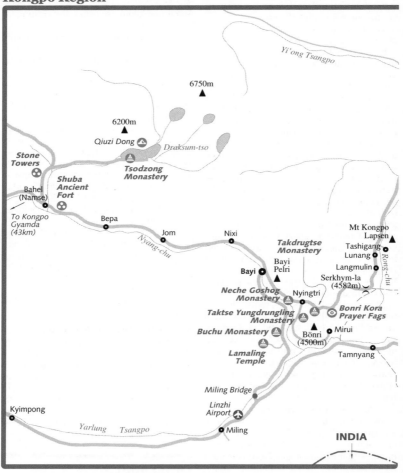

Yi'ong Tsangpo

6750m ▲

6200m ▲

Qiuzi Dong ⚠

Draksum-tso

Stone Towers ☢

Shuba Ancient Fort ☢

⚠ **Tsodzong Monastery**

Bahel (Namse) ●

To Kongpo Gyamda (43km)

Bepa ●

Jom ●

Nyang-chu

Nixi ●

Mt Kongpo Lapsen ▲

Takdrugtse Monastery

Tashigang ●
Lunang ●

Langmulin ●

Rong-chu

Bayi ● Bayi Pelri ▲

Serkhym-la (4582m)

Neche Goshog Monastery ⚠ Nyingtri ●

Bonri Kora Prayer Fags ⊙

Taktse Yungdrungling Monastery ⚠

Buchu Monastery ⚠ Bönri (4500m) ▲ ● Mirui

Lamaling Temple ⚠

Tamnyang ●

Miling Bridge ●

Linzhi Airport ⚠

Kyimpong ●

Yarlung   Tsangpo

● Miling

INDIA

of whom are said to have resided at the lake.

The entrance fee to the area is payable at a toll gate 33km past the Hwy 318 turn-off at **Bahel**, and 4km before the lake. PSB officers here and at the hotel by the lake will want to see your travel permits. A free shuttle bus takes visitors from the gate to the lake, although it's fine to walk.

The highlight of the lake is the charming **Tsodzong Monastery** (The Fortress on the Lake), a small Nyingmapa chapel sited on a photogenic island just off the southern shore. This is where the bus drops you off.

The monastery was founded by Sangye Lingpa in the 14th century. The main chapel has statues of a wrathful and peaceful Guru Rinpoche and smaller statues of Sakyamuni, Chenresig (Avalokiteshvara) and Kongtsun Demo, a local protector, on horseback. The statues were actually shot and then burned by Red Guards during the Cultural Revolution, before being restored by the famous local lama Dudjom Rinpoche and his son Chuni Rinpoche (now resident at Lamaling Monastery). In the corner of the monastery is what is said to be a stone hoofprint of Gesar's horse. You may see Tibetans rubbing

across from Tsodzong Monastery at a place known as **Qiúzǐ Dòng** (求子洞) or 'Searching for a Son Cave'. From the bus drop-off point, walk clockwise around the lake for about three hours until you reach the cave, leaving you with another four-hour hike to complete your circuit of the lake the next morning.

For something more comfortable, walk a few hundred metres beyond Tsodzong Monastery to **Basomtso Holiday Resort** (巴松措度假村; Bāsōng Cuò Dùjià Cūn; ☏541 3508; dm Y80-100, d/tw Y120/240, tw cabin Y380; dishes Y18-188), which has clean, well-kept rooms as well as private wood cabins. There's an upmarket restaurant in reception with (as you'd imagine) a lot of fish dishes. There are cheaper restaurants as well as small shops just outside the toll gate.

Draksum-tso is about a five-hour drive from Lhasa, or a couple of hours from Bāyī. The road to the lake branches off the Sìchuān–Tibet Hwy at Bahel (also known as Namse), where there's a cluster of teahouses, restaurants and lodgings. From there it's around 40km to the lake, turning right about halfway at a blue sign in Chinese for the lake (巴松措; Bāsōngcuò).

AROUND DRAKSUM-TSO

About 12km from the highway junction, the road up to the lake passes three tall 12-sided **stone towers**, on your left, which can be reached with a bit of scrambling. No one quite knows for what purpose the enigmatic towers were built – they stand empty and entryless. Locals refer to them as *dudkhang* (demons' houses) and recite legends connecting them to Gesar of Ling.

A more accessible group of half-ruined towers, known as the **Shuba Ancient Fort** (秀巴千年古堡; Xiùbā Qiānnián Gǔbǎo; admission Y20), stands on the main highway, 7km east of Bahel. These five magnificent towers are said to date from the reign of Songtsen Gampo (r 630–49).

Kongpo Gyamda

ཀོང་པོ་རྒྱ་མདའ་ 工布江达

☏0894 / ELEV 3400M

Unless it's getting late in the day, there's little reason to stop in this modern town. But there's a decent range of accommodation and restaurants if you do stop.

The **Kathok Nunnery**, located in the hills to the north of town, has eight nuns

---

this on their backs to take advantage of its healing powers. The steps to the monastery are flanked by ancient-looking male and female fertility symbols.

A small kora squeezes its way around the back of the monastery.

Six- to 10-person **motorboats** (per hour Y400-800) leave from beside Tsodzong Monastery for trips on the lake.

There's plenty of scope for **hiking** around the lake. One good spot for camping – if the authorities allow you to camp, that is (check with your guide or with people at the toll gate) – is near the far corner of the lake

HOT SPRINGS

There are a couple of places between Kongpo Gyamda and Lhasa where you can stop for a good long soak.

Less than an hour's drive from Kongpo Gyamda, the one-street town of **Songdo** (松多; Sōngduō) has hot springs (per person Y10) in a cute little wooden hut, accessed by crossing a small, rickety suspension bridge on the right-hand side of the highway about 1km before you reach Songdo. You could also stop for lunch here. Among the Chinese restaurants is the **Tashi Teahouse** (扎西茶馆; Zhāxī Cháguǎn), a simple Tibetan teahouse serving delicious *diru* (yak-meat noodle soup, Y12), *tsampa* (Y2), Tibetan bread (Y2) and butter tea (Y6).

About 50 mins further towards Lhasa, over the 5013m-high Pa-la pass, is **Rutok** (日多; Rìduō; elev 4300m), which has a monastery on the hillside north of town and several Tibetan teahouses. Rutok is named after the hot springs that are on the main road here, which take the form of a large **swimming pool** (per person Y60) in the main building, or smaller **private pools** (per pool Y150) down by the river behind it. Rutok is also the trailhead for the six-day trek to Lhamo La-tso (p125).

and a small chapel housing an image of Guru Rinpoche and King Trisong Detsen. A path (a 30-minute walk) leads up to the nunnery from the plaza on the main road, climbing some steps and weaving through the old quarter to offer fine views.

The nunnery is backed by a cleft in the forested Baripo Mountain, which has a small **hermitage** marked by fluttering prayer flags; it takes 45 minutes to walk here from the nunnery.

🛏 Sleeping & Eating

The main street is lined with Sichuanese restaurants and Tibetan teahouses. There's also a couple of popular Tibetan teahouses opposite the internet cafe.

Guolinka Hotel HOTEL **$**
(果林卡宾馆; Guǒlínkǎ Bīnguǎn; ☑541 2046; tw Y100-120, tr Y120) Housed in an unattractive white block set back from the main strip, this place, one of the few that were accepting foreigners at the time of research, has spacious, tidy rooms with TV, bathroom and hot water in the evenings.

Huátíng Kāngshà Dàjiǔdiàn HOTEL **$$$**
(华庭康厦大酒店; ☑541 3111; tw Y480; ❋) This plush place is probably the best in town, with soft carpets, Western-style bathrooms and hot water in the evenings. It's down a side street on the north side of the main strip, opposite the police station.

❶ Information

Internet cafe (网吧; wǎngba; per hr Y4; ⏲24hr) First side street on left off main road.

❶ Getting There & Away

Shared minibuses to Bāyī leave from the main strip, over the river from Hwy 318. Minibuses to Lhasa tend to leave from the highway.

It's about 4½ hours' drive from here to Lhasa.

THE NORTHERN ROUTE (HWY 317)

The less well-paved northern route is a higher roller-coaster ride past ancient temples, remote Bön monasteries and herding communities. Far fewer travellers take this route, and those that do tend to head south from Chamdo to join up with Hwy 318 before carrying on to Lhasa. Those that stay on the northern route will not only have most of it to themselves, they'll also have the opportunity to visit some of Tibet's most unusual and least-visited sights.

Roads here are mostly unpaved (although the relative lack of rain means they are normally passable). However, there was some serious road repairing going on at the time of research, especially south and west of Chamdo, meaning journeying along smooth tarmac should be just around the corner.

JOMDA  江达

☑0895 / ELEV 3665M

You can break the 347km-journey from Derge to Chamdo by stopping first in Jomda (Jiāngdá in Chinese) and then in Topa, both of which have lunch options as well as monasteries that are worth a peek. If you want to stay the night, Jomda is the more comfortable choice.

The 700-year-old **Wara Monastery** (瓦拉寺; Wǎlā Sì; www.warabuddhism.com), 30km east of Jomda, contains Tibet's largest Sakyapa monastic school with more than 200 monks studying here at any time. The monastery has two main sites: one, which contains the school, is beside the river and can be seen from the main highway; the other is home to just 30 monks and overlooks the school from a scenic hilltop perch a few hundred metres above the river. The recently renovated but undeniably attractive main hall of the hilltop monastery has an interesting mix of Tibetan, Mongolian and Chinese architectural styles. Both sites are monitored on a regular basis by plainclothes security guards who may ask to see, and then delete, the photographs you've just taken. Monks are arrested here as recently as July 2010 for their alleged role in riots that took place in Jomda county in 2008.

In Jomda itself, **Jiāotōng Fàndiàn** (交通饭店; ☑493 1188; tw Y120) is a decent hotel on the main strip. Twins come with 24-hour hot-water showers. A cheaper option is **Chéngdū Lǚguǎn** (成都旅馆; ☑451 2451; beds Y20), also on the main strip. Corridors are a bit grotty and there are no showers, but the beds are comfy and clean.

There are a number of Sichuanese and Muslim restaurants on the main road, where you'll also find a foreign-friendly ATM, an **internet cafe** (网吧; wǎngbā; per hour Y4; ☺9am-1am) and the bus station with daily buses to Chamdo.

There tends to be a strong police presence in Jomda.

TOPA 妥坝
☑0895 / ELEV 3981M

The small, one-street town of Topa (Tuǒbà in Chinese), 115km west of Jomda and about the same distance from Chamdo, makes a nice lunch stop, especially if you decide to picnic in the surrounding grasslands.

Five kilometres east of the main strip on the south side of Hwy 317 is the turn-off for two nearby monasteries. The first, and better known of the two, is the Kagyupa-sect **Chugu Gompa** (珠古寺; Zhūgǔ Sì), about 6km south of the turn-off. Home to more than 100 monks and nuns, it has an enormous courtyard and a lovely grassland setting. It dates back to 1670, although the main hall is a recent rebuild.

Overlooking it is the rarely visited Nyingmapa monastery, **Söda Gompa** (索德寺; Suǒdé Sì), which was built in 1872 and is home to 30 monks. The hilltop grassland setting here is stunning, with wonderful views of the surrounding mountains and Chugu Gompa below.

The first hall you reach on the approach to the monastery is original; the main hall to the left is a newer construction. Friendly monks set up Tibetan-style tents outside during summer, while the surrounding grasslands make for some wonderful picnic spots – if you bring along some food from Topa or Jomda. Take the same turn-off as Chugu Gompa, but turn right at the prayer flags after about 3km then head up the winding hillside track.

In Topa itself, the main strip is made up of newer Chinese-style buildings at its eastern end and older Tibetan-style ones at its western end. At the Tibetan end, on the south side of the road, is the cute **Tuǒchāng Fàndiàn** (妥昌饭店), which makes a nice lunch stop. It takes about two hours to carry on from here to Chamdo.

Chamdo ཁམས་མདོ། 昌都
☑0895 / POP 80,000 / ELEV 3300M

Chamdo (or Chāngdū in Chinese), at the strategic river junction of the Dza-chu and the Ngon-chu, is a surprisingly pleasant town. It is dominated by the hilltop Galden Jampaling Monastery, while below huddles the tiny Tibetan old town and a much larger, sprawling Chinese new town. Over 1000km from Lhasa and 1250km from Chéngdū, the town is the major transport, administrative and trade centre of the Kham region. Make sure you have your permits in order, otherwise the PSB here are likely track you down, fine you and kick you out.

Chamdo has had a troubled relationship with nearby China. The Chinese warlord Zhao Erfeng (the 'Butcher of Kham') captured Chamdo in 1909 and ruled the region until the Tibetans recaptured it in 1917. Chamdo fell to communist troops in 1950, marking the beginning of the end for independent Tibet.

◉ Sights

Galden Jampaling Monastery MONASTERY
This active hilltop monastery (དགའ་ལྡན་བྱམས་པ་གླིང་དགོན་; 强巴林寺; known in Chinese as Qiángbālín Sì) of around 1000 monks

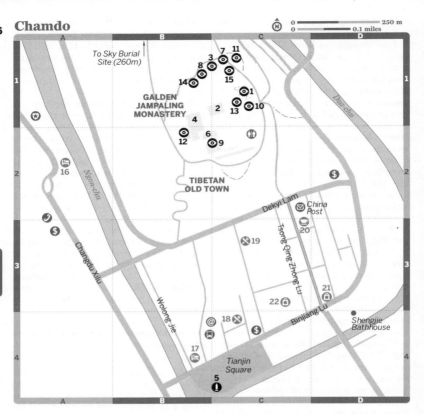

dominates Chamdo. The monastery was founded in 1444 by Jangsem Sherab Zangpo, a disciple of Tsongkhapa. It was destroyed in 1912 and then rebuilt in 1917, after the Tibetan army retook Chamdo.

Pilgrims circumambulate the exterior of the walled compound in the mornings and it's worth following them on at least one circuit. Behind the monastery, to the north of town, trails lead up to a sky-burial site and views over the city. The steep paved road up to the east gate is one of the town's most interesting, lined with Tibetan teahouses, tailors and prayer-wheel repair workshops.

The first building on the right is the impressive **Tsenyi Lhakhang** (Dialectic College), behind which is a debating courtyard. Just to the left of the college is a side entrance; go in here, take an immediate left up the stairs and then turn right at the top. This leads to a *gönkhang* (protector chapel) packed with guns, knives and pistols – echoes of the region's warrior past.

Back outside, the monastery's enormous **kitchen** is well worth a look, but only men can enter.

The main **dukhang** (assembly hall) is particularly impressive, especially when it is packed with hundreds of murmuring monks. This is probably the largest assembly of monks you will see in Tibet these days, outside festival times. The glorious inner sanctum is dominated by Sakyamuni, Tsongkhapa and Atisha. The statue second to the left is the Pakhpala, the line of religious leaders that head the monastery. The bearded statue in the far right is of the monastery's founder.

In the main monastery courtyard is the **gönkhang**, lined with fantastic murals and statues of protector gods, and lots of old armour. The **Jamkhang** to the south holds a large new statue of Jampa (Maitreya).

Chamdo

◎ **Top Sights**

Galden Jampaling Monastery....................B1

◎ **Sights**

1 Debating Courtyard.............................C1
2 Dukhang (Assembly Hall)...................C1
3 Dukhor (Kalachakra) Tratsang..........B1
4 Former Residence of the
   Phakhpala....................................B1
5 Golden Eagle Statue............................C4
6 Gönkhang (Protector Chapel)............B2
7 Guhyasamaja Tratsang........................C1
8 Hevajra Tratsang...............................B1
9 Jamkhang..C2
10 Kitchen..C1
11 Prayer Flags......................................C1
12 Tsenkhang (Earth Spirit
   House)..B2
13 Tsenyi Lhakhang................................C1
14 Vairocana (Namse) Tratsang.............B1
15 Yamantaka Tratsang..........................C1

◉ **Sleeping**

16 Chamdo Hotel...................................A2
17 Jīnchuān Bīnguǎn.............................B4

◈ **Eating**

18 Sichuanese Restaurants....................C4
19 Vegetable Market.............................C3

◌ **Drinking**

20 Zhèngzōng Lāsà Tiáncháguǎn............C3

◎ **Shopping**

21 Kodak Express..................................D3
   Supermarket..............................(see 17)
22 Toread..C3

Behind the *gönkhang* is the **former residence of the Pakhpala**, whose 11th reincarnation currently works for the Tibetan government in Lhasa. The exit in the southwest corner leads to the **Tsenkhang** (earth spirit house), hidden around the back of the interior courtyard, with a fantastic collection of protectors strung up on a series of pillars like a crack squad of gravity-defying martial arts warriors. Look also for the skeleton and monkey outfits worn during cham dances, as well as a stuffed bear. Around the back is a small tsampa mill.

🛏 Sleeping

Jīnchuān Bīnguǎn   HOTEL **$$**
(金川宾馆; ☑484 4998; Wolong Jie; tw Y320, discounted to Y192) Large rooms come with

bathrooms with 24-hour hot water. Rooms are arranged around a smoke-filled mahjong hall, but it closes at 9pm.

Chamdo Hotel   HOTEL **$$**
(昌都饭店; Chāngdū Fàndiàn; ☑482 5998; 22 Changdu Xilu; tw Y350, discounted to Y210; 🖥) A bit posher than Jīnchuān, rooms at the back look out over a pleasant garden. Internet access for laptop users is free. Service can be grumpy.

🍴 Eating & Drinking

The narrow streets one block east of Jīnchuān Bīnguǎn have loads of cheap Sichuanese restaurants where you'll get dishes for around Y20. There's a decent vegetable market in the lanes south of Dekyi Lam where you can pick up fruit and snacks.

Zhèngzōng Lāsà Tiáncháguǎn   TEAHOUSE **$**
(正宗拉萨甜茶馆; tea per pot Y10) Very popular with the locals, this no-nonsense teahouse is *the* place to come for your fix of Tibetan sweet tea. Sit on plastic stools or wooden benches either inside or under the tarpaulin on the pavement out front.

🛍 Shopping

The well-stocked supermarket on the ground floor of the Jīnchuān Bīnguǎn has items such as batteries as well as foodstuffs.

Toread (探路者; Tànlùzhě; Pedestrian Market) An outdoor shop that offers down vests, camping gas canisters, sleeping bags and the like.

Kodak Express (柯达快速彩色; Kēdá Kuàisù Cǎisè; Binjiang Lu; ◷10am-10pm) Burns CDs from around Y10.

❶ Information

A couple of ATMs around town now accept foreign bank cards. We've marked them on the map.

Jiāhuá Wǎngluò (嘉华网络; per hr Y4; ◷24hr) Internet cafe near the Jīnchuān Bīnguǎn.

Post Office (中国邮政; Zhōngguó Yóuzhèng; Zhong Lu; ◷9am-7.30pm)

PSB (公安局; Gōng'ānjú; ☑482 5085; Changdu Xilu; ◷9am-12pm & 3.30-5.30pm Mon-Fri) Visa extensions are possible if travel permits are in order. The phone is sometimes answered by English speakers.

Shèngjié Bathhouse (圣洁淋室; Shèngjié Línshì; Binjiang Lu; shower/bath Y8/Y25; ◷9am-midnight)

Telephone Office (中国电信; Zhōngguó Diànxìn; Changdu Xilu; ◷10am-9pm) Sells phonecards.

THE ROAD SOUTH FROM CHAMDO

Most public buses heading to Lhasa from Chamdo head south rather than west, mainly because the state of the road on the southern route is better, although major work to improve the northern route was being done at the time of research.

This southern splinter of Hwy 317 passes by or near a number of interesting monasteries and small villages as well as Chamdo-Pomda Airport before joining Hwy 318 at Pomda.

The road follows the Mekong River (Dza-chu; 澜沧江; Láncāng Jiāng) 65km to Kyitang, passing a Willy Wonka-esque landscape of spearmint green fields, raspberry purple hills and chocolate streams. A few kilometres before Kyitang, and just 7km before a 3465m-high pass (Nya-la) a turn-off to your left takes you along a 42km dirt track to **Drayab** (察雅; Cháyǎ) and the **Endun Monastery** (烟多寺; Yānduō Sì).

Back on the main highway, the road climbs the pass then descends into the village of **Kyitang** (吉塘; Jítáng). **Tra'e Monastery**, on the southeastern edge of the village, is worth a look. The kora around the ancient-feeling old chapel is lined with animal skulls. The turn-off for the 10-minute walk to the monastery is marked by a huge new white chörten. The barracks-style **Jíxiáng Bīnguǎn** (吉祥宾馆; dm Y15) at the north end of town offers basic rooms and pit toilets in an emergency. There's a Tibetan-style restaurant opposite.

Leaving Kyitang, the road climbs dramatically 29km to a 4572m-high pass, Lang-la (浪拉山; Lànglà Shān) before descending again, past the turn-off for the old caravan trail to Lhasa and on to the airport.

Around 10km past the old caravan-trail turn-off, and 6km before the airport, is a turn-off onto a dirt road that heads 7km to the remote and welcoming **Yushig Monastery**, home to 50 Kagyupa monks and three *trulkus* (reincarnated lamas), one of whom is considered a manifestation of Rechungpa, a disciple of Milarepa. The main hall contains images of Sakyamuni, Marpa and Milarepa. The spirited debating that takes place here in the afternoons sounds more like a pub brawl than a theological discussion! The turn-off for the monastery is to the right (west) about 100m after the bridge. The wide plain here supports large herds of grazing yaks.

If you're flying in or out of **Chamdo-Pomda Airport** (昌都邦达机场; Chāngdū Bāngdá Jīcháng), about 130km south of Chamdo, the previously shoddy airport hotel **Xīzàng Chāngdū Bāngdá Jīcháng Bīnguǎn** (西藏昌都邦达机场宾馆; ☑0895 462 3166, 136 5955 0479; tw Y228) has been spruced up and now has quite plush twin rooms with laminated wood flooring and bathrooms with squat loos. The canteen is open from 7am to 11pm. If that option is too expensive, you can stay in one of the guesthouses on the main highway right by the turn-off for the airport. **Rújiā Chuāncàiwáng** (如家川菜王; ☑152 8915 1243; per bed Y40) has a ground-floor Sichuanese restaurant and basic but clean rooms with metal-framed beds upstairs. From here it's about 200m to the airport turn-off and less than 1km to the airport itself.

About 20km beyond the airport a bridge gives access to the yellow-painted and rather derelict **Shongba Guen Tashi Chöling Monastery**. It is visible from the highway, across a glorious grassy plain; a pleasant walk here takes about 25 minutes.

Another 10km brings you to **Kyidrup Monastery**, which is home to a handful of monks and nuns and is about 15km from Pomda.

ℹ️ Getting There & Away

Air

There's a weekly flight to Lhasa (Y1170, 9am) on Monday and to Chéngdū (Y900, 9.15am) every day except Sunday. An extra midday flight to Chéngdū is laid on Monday and Wednesday.

The **ticket office** (中国民航售票处; Zhōngguó Mínháng Shòupiàochù; ☑482 1004; ☺9.30–11.30am) is 500m south of the Dza-chu River. Staff might sell you a ticket without checking for permits, but you'll probably still be asked for them at the airport when you check in.

Chamdo-Pomda Airport (昌都帮大机场; Chāngdū-Bāngdà Jīcháng) is 130km south of Chamdo. Airport buses (Y40) depart from opposite the ticket office before flights, but the unreliability of the roads here means it may be safer to leave the day before your morning flight, then overnight near the airport. A taxi from Chamdo costs around Y120 per person and takes about two hours.

Bus

Chamdo Bus Station (顺康客运站; Shùnkāng Kèyùn Zhàn; ☑482 7351) has daily services to Jomda and Markham, services every other day to Pomi, and two services a week to Nagchu and Yùshù.

CHAMDO TO RIWOCHE (110KM)

A couple of monasteries en route to Riwoche are worth a visit. Soon after the road leaves the Dza-chu (Mekong River; 澜沧江; Láncāng Jiāng) and swings south, it climbs past the stunningly located **Dragu (or Trugu) Monastery** (朱吉寺; Zhūjí Sì) perched on a grassy plateau at around 4200m and backed by granite bluffs and snowcapped peaks. The 50 or so monks are friendly and will point out the tiger and snow leopard pelts in the upper protector chapel. A huge thangka is unfurled on a platform outside the monastery gate during the Losar festival.

To drive here, take the steep 3km dirt road to the right just after some houses, before kilometre marker 1331 and about 38km past Chamdo. The best views of the monastery are actually from the main road.

The main road continues to climb for 17km through sections of 1500-year-old juniper forest to cross the 4612m Chabi-la before making a long descent past herders' huts into a lovely alpine valley. About 88km past Chamdo, next to the road, is the restored **Dzonglho Monastery** (宗洛兴旺林寺; Zōngluò Xīngwànglín Sì) If you fancy a walk, a suspension bridge leads across the river to the ruins of the original monastery, at the base of a bluff with the ruins of the old *dzong* atop it.

Riwoche རི་བོ་ཆེ། 类乌齐县

☑0895 / ELEV 3800M

The mid-sized town of Riwoche (known as Lèiwūqí Xiàn in Chinese) is of limited interest but makes a good base from which to explore the village of Riwoche, 26km to the north, which houses the fascinating monastery Riwoche Tsuglhakhang.

🛏 Sleeping & Eating

Zìgòng Bīnguǎn GUESTHOUSE $
(自贡宾馆; ☑4932 798; s/tw/tr Y30/40/60) This simple but clean Sichuanese-run place

on the corner of Hwy 317 and a side road in the centre of town is probably the best of several cheapies. Rooms are small but clean. Common bathrooms have squat toilets and no showers.

Dàshān Bīnguǎn HOTEL $$
(大山宾馆; ☑450 4433; d/tw Y160/200) Decent rooms with clean bedding and laminated wood flooring come with bathrooms with slightly tight shower cubicles but hot water. Like Zìgòng Bīnguǎn, it's also on the corner of Hwy 317 and a side road, but further east.

Qílín Cānguǎn CHINESE $
(麒麟餐馆; Yúzhōng Lù; dishes Y7-30; ☺8.30am-midnight) A couple of doors down a side road by Sunny Hotel (which is between the two hotels mentioned above), this place, run by a guy from Shaanxi province, does delicious clay-pot stews (砂锅; shāguō; Y15). Try the shāguō niúròu miàn (砂锅牛肉面), which is cooked with beef and noodles. The braised pork belly (红烧猪肉; hóngshāo zhūròu; Y35) is also delicious.

ℹ Information

Agricultural Bank of China ATM (农业银行; Nóngyè Yínháng) On main highway opposite Zìgòng Bīnguǎn; accepts Visa and Mastercard.

Fēixiáng Internet Bar (飞翔网吧; Fēixiáng Wǎngba; per hr Y4; ☺24hr) Far side of the square past Qílín Cānguǎn.

Meijie Yushi (美洁浴室; shower/bath Y10/25; ☺8am-10pm) Public bathhouse in same square as Fēixiáng Internet.

ℹ Getting There & Away

Buses from the station, Kèyùn Zhōngxīn (客运中心), which is down the same side road as Zìgòng Bīnguǎn, go to destinations including Chamdo, Nagchu and Yùshù.

Riwoche Tsuglhakhang
 རི་བོ་ཆེ་གཙུག་ལག་ཁང་ 类乌齐寺

From the western edge of Riwoche town, a road branches northwest off the main highway, crosses the river and follows a newly paved section of the road north to Yùshù in Qīnghǎi province. A couple of kilometres before **Riwoche village** (类乌齐镇; Lèiwūqí Zhèn) the road crests a ridge and you get the first view of the amazing golden-roofed Riwoche Tsuglhakhang (Lèiwūqí Sì).

Founded in 1276 by Sangye On, who relocated to Kham after the death of his master

UNDER LOCK & KEY, TIMES THREE

The ground-floor courtyard of the **Riwoche Tsuglhakhang** is always open, but access to the 1st and 2nd floors is through a triple-locked door at the side of the courtyard. You will need to find three separate monks who look after the three separate keys that each open one of the locks. The monks will then have to follow you up each floor because there are more doors to unlock along the way, not least the one to the highly revered treasures inside the monastery's rooftop hut.

Sangye Yarjon (1203–72), the third leader of the Talung order, Riwoche started as an off-shoot of Talung Monastery in Ü. Eventually it grew to eclipse its parent monastery and it now ranks as one of Tibet's most impressive monasteries. It is still the more vibrant of the two, retains the characteristic red, white and black vertical stripes of the Talung school, and is home to more than 500 monks.

The Monastery

The huge *tsuglhakhang* towers over Riwoche village, dwarfing the pilgrims who circumambulate the massive structure. You enter through 20m-tall doors into a breathtaking open inner courtyard covered with a plastic-glass roof. Photos are not allowed in the chapels.

The eye is immediately drawn to the huge statues that loom out of the half-light. The entry is flanked on the left by Jampa (Maitreya) and eight chörtens, and on the right by two dramatic protector masks that peer down at you from a high pillar. The left wall has statues of Tsepame (Amitayus), Guru Rinpoche (one peaceful and one smaller wrathful variety with a scorpion in his hand) and Sakyamuni. The west wall has the funerary chörten of a local rinpoche, three Sakyamunis, two abbots and the two early Talung lamas – Sangye Yarjon on the right and Sangye On to the left. The altars are fronted by elephant tusks and long banners made of petals. Along the right wall is a white statue of Namse (Vairocana) in front of a mandala, a gold chörten, a seated Jampa (Maitreya), Matrö Bodhisattva, Sakyamuni Buddha and finally two 1000-armed statues of Chenresig (Avalokiteshvara).

The middle floor is relatively bare but has some fine murals and statues of Guru Rinpoche, a 1000-armed Chenresig (Avalokiteshvara) and Sakyamuni.

A small hut on the roof is where the real gems are kept, though. Again you'll need to have the door here unlocked for you, and photography is strictly prohibited inside the hut. Items include some beautiful antique statues and ancient horse saddles that are said to belong to Gesar of Ling and his general. Look for the very old statue of Dorje Chang (Vajradhara), with the slender waist. There are fine views of the village, the valley and the surrounding mountains from the roof top here.

Monks' quarters lie to the north, and it's worth walking up the hillside a little to get overviews of the site.

🛈 Getting There & Away

You'll need to catch a shared minibus or a taxi to the monastery (about Y200 return including waiting time) from Riwoche.

Tengchen   སྟེང་ཆེན་   丁青

🖉 0895 / ELEV 3820M

The largely Tibetan town of Tengchen (Dīngqīng in Chinese) is a forlorn outpost of crumbling concrete blocks and half-broken facilities. Both Tengchen and the surrounding area of Khyungpo are strong centres of the Bön religion.

👁 Sights & Activities

The main reason to stop here is to visit the **Tengchen Monastery**, on a hillside about three kilometres west of town. This interesting Bön monastery, home to more than 200 monks, is made up of two separate institutions. The main building, founded in 1110, has an impressive assembly hall and upper-floor chapel. Bön deities include Tonpa Shenrab and an amazing Palpa Phurbu, whose lower half consists of a ritual dagger.

To the east is the Ritro Lhakhang, built in 1180. The main chapel, the Serdung, contains three funerary chörtens, another many-armed Palpa Phurbu and a statue of Monlam Tai, the founder of the monastery. Another chapel displays a row of six Bön gods on a variety of mounts. There are fine views from the roof.

To get here, take Hwy 317 west for about 3km out of town. The road crosses a bridge then climbs steeply. As you round a tight

The 148km stretch of Hwy 317 from Riwoche to Tengchen is littered with monasteries. Here are the standout ones:

» Chayab Monastery (大香寺; Dàxiāng Sì) Also known as Taksam or Dashang Gompa, this small but very charming Nyingma-school monastery, 17km from Riwoche, is surrounded by over 100 chörtens, thousands of mani stones and a short kora. The design of the main chapel is similar to that of Lamaling Temple, but on a much smaller scale. Look for a photo of the current Taksam Rinpoche, the reincarnation of Taksam Nuden Dorje, an 18th-century *terton* (treasure finder) who founded the monastery (and whose portrait is painted in the right-hand corner of the chapel). There are good camping possibilities nearby. Only three monks actually live here, although others visit regularly.

» Rìbā Sì (日巴寺) One or two kilometres north of the highway, and 57km west of Riwoche, is a turn-off marked by large collection of prayer flags and chörtens that leads to this 240-year-old Nyingma-school monastery, last renovated in 1984. It's set among grassland with an eye-catching backdrop of unusual jagged mountains. Just one monk lives here, although even he's not always in, so you might just have the whole area to yourself.

» Jinkar Monastery (金卡寺; Jīnkǎ Sì) This 500-year-old walled Gelugpa-school monastery, 95km from Riwoche, was rebuilt in 1984 and is now home to around 200 monks. The kitchen and metal workshop to the side of the main assembly hall are particularly worth visiting here. The monastery is on the south side of Hwy 317, after the highway descends through a series of red-rock gorges.

» Rotung Monastery (绒通寺; Róngtōng Sì) A few minutes' walk west of Jinkar, past a chörten and through some barley fields, brings you down to this remarkable small monastery that's home to around 40 monks. The monastery is surrounded by a large number of chörtens and tens of thousands of votive-carved mani stones, the first of which is said to have been laid by Princess Wencheng when she passed through here on her way to Lhasa. Pilgrims circle the monastery from dawn to dusk. A road leads south from here back to Hwy 317 so you don't need to go back via Jinkar Monastery.

» Tsedru Monastery (孜珠寺; Zīzhū Sì) At 4800m this is one of Tibet's highest monasteries, and its location, strung out along a ridgeline below a series of natural cliffs and caves, is one of the most fantastical you can imagine. This is considered Tibet's largest and oldest Bön monastery and is home to more than 200 monks. Once you've visited the main chapels (there's debating in the afternoon), walk up to the large natural arch to the left, where ancient wooden ladders lead up the cliff-face to a precarious ridge-top shrine that features a stone footprint of the monastery's founder inlaid in the floor. If you have time, it's well worth walking the kora around the base of Ngon Ri, the mountain to the east. When you reach a small chapel on the south side, climb the kora path to the peak for amazing views. The skies around the cliffs are sometimes full of soaring eagles and vultures, attracted by the sky-burial site in the valley below. The turn-off for Tsedru is 18km past Jinkar Monastery and marked by a blue sign. From here, follow the track over a bridge and, 2km from the highway, turn left up an 11km-long switchback dirt track that climbs 800m to the monastery. All told, it's a half-day detour.

right-hand bend, turn right up a small 500m-long track that takes you to the monastery.

🛏 Sleeping & Eating

There's a row of decent Sichuanese restaurants on the right side of the town square. On the left of the entrance to the square, is a very popular deli, **Yīpǐnxiāng Lǔròuguǎn**

(一品香卤肉馆), that's been around for years. It sells cold portions of pre-cooked pig meat including ears, trotters and tongues; takeaway nibbles for the brave.

Gōnglù Bīnguǎn   GUESTHOUSE **$**
(公路宾馆; ☑459 3389; dm Y20, tw from Y60) Cheap but a bit on the shabby side, with no

showers and pretty grim shared toilets, it's on the right of Hwy 317, just as you enter the town.

Yōuyǎ Bīnguǎn HOTEL $$
(优雅宾馆; ☑152 8905 0412, 136 1895 7963; 13-19 Dongqing Dadao; tw Y168) New and very clean rooms have bathrooms with sit-down loos and multijet shower pods, with round-the-clock hot water. It's on Hwy 317 on your left just before the town square.

ℹ️ Information

Agricultural Bank of China ATM (农业银行; Nóngyè Yínháng; 8 Jiāmùtáng Lù; 甲木塘路8号) Accepts Visa bank cards.

E'wǎng Qíngshēn Wǎngba (E网情深网吧; per hr Y4; ⊙10am-midnight) Internet cafe down an alley to the left side of the main square.

Qióngbù Línshi (琼布淋室; shower Y10) Public bathhouse on right-hand side of town square.

ℹ️ Getting There & Away

Buses go to Chamdo and Nagchu. Tickets are sold at Gōnglù Bīnguǎn.

TENGCHEN TO SOK (270KM)

The 33km stretch of Hwy 317 from Tengchen to the 4460m-high pass Chongnye-la (Chuni-la) launches you up into the highlands of northeastern Tibet, offering fabulous views across nomad camps and yak herds to the huge range of snowy peaks to the south. In June and July wild flowers cover the grasslands here in a blanket of colour.

The road then descends for 9km to the lovely village of **Bajung**, where you can explore the cliff-top Bön-sect Yongdzong Monastery and the Gelugpa-sect Tashiling Monastery.

Just below Bajung, and 44km from Tengchen, is the run-down modern town of **Sertsa** (色扎; Sèzhā, also known as Khardong), which offers restaurants, a couple of simple guesthouses and a large collection of mani stones in the southwest corner. About 14km from Sertsa keep an eye out for the Bön-sect **Targye Monastery** perched dramatically across the valley on the face of a high ridge. Some 66km past Tengchen, the unremarkable town of **Choedo** has some shops and another guesthouse.

Here the road swings north and starts to climb up to the stunning 4905m-high **Shel-la**, 102km past Tengchen and the highest and most dramatic pass along the northern route. Some 40km past the Shel-la brings you to **Ronpo** (荣布; Róngbù), a one-street

town that offers food and basic accommodation. For lunch, try **Chuānhóng Fàndiàn** (川洪饭店; dishes from Y20), a good Sichuanese restaurant set slightly below road level on the south side of the highway at the eastern end of the town. There is a large mani wall at the western end of town.

The road climbs yet again to the 4500m **Chak-la**, where you turn a corner for a dramatic view of one of the Salween's many tributaries. The road then makes a long descent past scattered nomad camps and a chörten to the village of **Yangan**, where there is a collection of basic teahouses.

From here it's another 48km to the dull county town of **Bachen** (巴青; Bāqīng), which has plenty of places to eat and sleep if you need to stop. Bus passengers overnight at the aircraft-hanger-like **Jiāotōng Bīnguǎn** (交通宾馆; ☑0896-390 1656, 0896-3612 755; tw & tr Y120), which has twins with bathrooms and triples without, as well as pool tables in the simply enormous lobby. There's an **internet cafe** (网吧; wǎngbā; per hr Y7; ⊙9am-3am) a few doors east.

From Bachen it's 33km to Sok.

Sok ষོག་ 索县

☑0896 / ELEV 4000M

This crossroad town's claim to fame is the impressive **Sok Tsanden Monastery** (索赞丹寺; Suǒzàndàn Sì) perched on an outcrop in the southern suburbs. Built in 1667 by the Mongol leader Gushri Khan, this Gelugpa monastery, home to 150 monks, looks like a miniature version of the Potala. The best views of the building are from the south as you leave town.

The monastery was made off limits to foreigners in 2001 after tourists smuggled out a letter from the monks to the Dalai Lama. Local authorities remain very suspicious of foreign visitors and threaten a Y20,000 fine for anyone trying to sneak into the monastery. If you want to try to get permission to visit the monastery, make sure that Sok Monastery (not just the town) is specifically written on your travel permits. Even this is no guarantee.

The **Repung Nunnery** to the northeast of town is also technically off limits.

🛏️ Sleeping & Eating

There are lots of Tibetan teahouses around the roundabout crossroads in the centre of town.

Yàlā Xìnyuàn Jiǔdiàn/Diànxìn Bīnguǎn
HOTEL **$$**

(亚拉信苑酒店/电信宾馆; ☑370 3000, 189 0896 1577; dm/tw/q Y30/150/150; ✱) With a decent range of rooms, this hotel with two names is probably the best choice overall, though like all Sok hotels there's no shower facilities. The four-bed economy rooms are perfect for accommodating 4WD groups, while the doubles with TV and air-con are a bit overpriced considering all rooms use the same shared squat toilets. Guests can use the washing machine in the shared bathroom.

Chéngdū Xiǎochī
GUESTHOUSE **$**

(成都小吃; r from Y80; dishes Y10-30) This good Sichuanese restaurant doubles as a guesthouse with OK 1st-floor rooms and clean shared toilets. Coming from the east, turn left at the roundabout crossroads and it's on your right almost immediately.

Dōngpō Jiǔlóu
CHINESE **$$**

(东坡酒楼; mains Y18-38) The best restaurant in town is this relatively pricey option by the main junction. Coming from the east, turn right at the roundabout crossroads and it's on your right.

ⓘ Information

Xīnshìjì Wǎngba (新世纪网吧; per hr Y5; ☺24hr) Internet cafe on main highway just west of the roundabout crossroads.

Yīhéyuán Línyù (伊河源淋浴; shower/bath Y10/40; ☺7am-midnight) A clean bathhouse on the right just before the roundabout crossroads if coming from the east.

ⓘ Getting There & Away

The bus station is south of the roundabout, just beyond Chéngdū Xiǎochī. It's 237km from here to Nagchu, which takes around nine hours in a 4WD. Once the new road surface is laid it shouldn't take more than five hours.

Nagchu ནག་ཆུ 那曲

☑0896 / POP 70,000 / ELEV 4500M

Nagchu (Nǎqū in Chinese) is one of the highest, coldest and most windswept towns in all of Tibet. Perched on the edge of the Changtang (northern plateau), it is an often-dismal town of mud and concrete, but is still an important stop on both the road and railway line between Qīnghǎi and Tibet. In fact, this is where Hwy 317 ends as it joins the Qīnghǎi–Tibet Hwy (Hwy 109) on its way to Lhasa.

Nagchu is a literally breathtaking place: oxygen levels here are only 60% of those at sea level, so be prepared for headaches and watch for the symptoms of altitude sickness (AMS). Bring warm clothes, even in summer.

The town holds a large **horse-racing festival**, which usually falls at the beginning of August, when Nagchu swells with up to 10,000 nomads and their tents from all over the Changtang. Accommodation can be very tight at this time, but it's a fascinating spectacle.

On the western outskirts of the town is the surprisingly large **Shabten Monastery** (founded 1814), a branch of Lhasa's Sera Monastery, with more than 90 monks. The main hall here is particularly atmospheric. Look in the back hall for the strings of dried tamarind pods, said to have been brought here from India as gifts for the Buddha.

Samtenling Nunnery, home to 47 nuns, is a 30-minute walk northwest of here above the Qīnghǎi–Tibet Hwy.

⎙ Sleeping & Eating

Nǎqū Fàndiàn
HOTEL **$$**

(那曲饭店; ☑382 2424; 23 Zhejiang Zhonglu; d Y268, discounted to Y180; ✱) The best-value of the three hotels that were accepting foreigners at the time of research, this place has smart clean rooms (spoiled only by the mosaics of cigarette burns on the carpets) and decent bathrooms with 24-hour hot water and squat toilets. Nice touches include mist-free bathroom mirrors and oxygen canisters and altitude sickness pills for sale in each room. Coming from Chamdo, Zhejiang Zhonglu is on your left off the main highway (called Lasa Donglu at this point) that bisects the town. The hotel is then on your left.

Post Hotel
HOTEL **$$**

(邮苑宾馆; Yóuyuàn Bīnguǎn; ☑382 0999; cnr Zhejiang Zhong Lu & Liaoning Zhonglu; tw without/with bathroom Y188/338, discounted to Y100/188; ✱) Next to the post office, this place is a bit on the grimy side, but tends to have the cheapest rooms available for foreigners. Common bathrooms have no shower, but if you want a private bathroom, you're much better off going to Nǎqū Fàndiàn. The Post Hotel is on the right before Nǎqū Fàndiàn.

⎰TOP CHOICE Lhasa Wealth God Restaurant
TIBETAN TEAHOUSE **$**

(拉萨财神藏餐; Lāsà Cáishén Zàngcān; Liaoning Zhonglu; dishes Y4-30) Beautifully decorated, and so popular you may have to share

BIRU'S SKULL WALL

About halfway between Sok and Nagchu is a turn off, south of Hwy 317, that brings you to **Dodoka Gompa** (达木寺; Dámù Sì), a remote monastery in Biru County containing one of Tibet's strangest, creepiest and least-visited sights: the mysterious **skull wall** (骷髅墙; kūlóu qiáng; entrance Y10).

Making up the southern part of a half-open courtyard in the monastery, the wall looks like any other Tibetan mani wall from a distance. But as you approach it you realise that instead of being made of engraved prayer stones, it's made of hundreds and hundreds of human skulls.

The skulls, which are still being added to from sky burials carried out within the courtyard, are placed in neat rows and set into wooden blocks, looking not unlike large bookshelves which are in turn set into the inside of the courtyard's 6ft clay walls.

At the northern end of the courtyard is a small building (usually locked) that is used by the monks who carry out the sky burials and that contains religious scriptures and icons.

It is thought that only three monasteries in Tibet – all in Biru County – have ever carried out the practice of displaying human skulls like this. **Ridazeng Gompa** (日丹寺; Rìdān Sì), just across the river from Dodoka, and **Quedai Gompa**, on a separate site some distance away, still contain a few human skulls, but nothing like the number on display at Dodoka. The practice was stopped for a number of years during the Cultural Revolution and the walls were destroyed with many of the skulls damaged or lost, but it has been revived by monks at Dodoka in the past 10 years, using old, recovered skulls then adding to them with the skulls of recently deceased locals. No one really knows when or why the ritual of displaying human skulls started here, but monks say that they display row upon row of identical-looking skulls to illustrate to people that no matter what we do in life, we are all equal after death.

Dodoka Monastery is about 50km from the highway turn-off on a well paved road leading to the town of **Biru** (比如; Bǐrú), which is about 75km further south. There's no sign for the monastery on the Biru road, but you can see the main hall on your left from the road. A track leads to the hall and nearby chörtens. To get to the skull wall, either walk south from the main hall, through monks living quarters, or take the right fork in the road to the main hall.

The skull wall's courtyard has two entrances: the west gate is for living people so can be opened (although you'll need to find a monk to unlock it for you). The south gate is for the dead, so is never unlocked.

Note there is an extortionate fee for foreigners wishing to take photos (Y200) or videos (Y2000).

If you don't have time to make it back to Sok or Nagchu, you can overnight in Biru. **Liángmào Bīnguǎn** (粮贸宾馆; ☎0896-362 2810; tw Y150-160) has decent rooms with bathrooms and hot showers.

a table, this place just up from Post Hotel has a pretty extensive menu of Chinese and Tibetan dishes, including Tibetan noodles (藏面; zàngmiàn; Y4 to Y6), yak-meat dumplings (牛肉包子; niúròu bāozi; Y1 each) and an excellent *shemdre* (咖喱饭; gālí fàn; Y10), although most locals just come here for a game of cards and some butter tea.

ℹ Information

Agricultural Bank of China ATM (农业银行; Nóngyè Yínháng; cnr Zhejiang Zhonglu & Liaoning Zhonglu) Opposite the post office, it accepts foreign cards.

Kāngdá Wǎngluò Shìjiè (康达网络世界; cnr Zhejiang Donglu & Chaodan Zhonglu; per hr Y3-4, ⊗24hr) Fast internet access, just past Nàqū Fàndiàn.

Post Office (中国邮局; Zhōngguó Yóujú; cnr Zhejiang Zhonglu & Liaoning Zhonglu; ⊗9.30am-7pm)

ℹ Getting There & Away

The main bus station (客运中占; Kèyùn Zhōngzhàn), round the corner from Nàqū Fàndiàn (turn right out of the hotel, then first right) on Liaoning Zhonglu, has regular buses to Lhasa and Sok. You can get cheaper, less comfortable Lhasa-bound buses or minibuses from Nǎqū Kèyùn Zhàn (那曲客运站), a smaller bus station on the main highway (called Lasa Nanlu here), on the way to the train station.

The train station (火车站; huǒchē zhàn) is 8km south of town. Hard-seat tickets to Lhasa (Y51, five hours, seven daily) or Golmud (格尔木; Gé'ěrmù; Y106, 10 hours, seven daily) in Qīnghǎi, are reasonably easy to obtain, depending on the permit situation.

DRÖLMA VALLEY

An interesting place to break the seven-hour journey from Nagchu to Lhasa is the rocky Drölma Valley, home to 80 monks, 49 nuns and a beautiful mountain lake.

The 800-year-old monastery **Bamrim Gompa** was undergoing extensive renovation when we visited, including construction work for a guesthouse just outside the main chapel.

A short walk further up the valley, the small nunnery known as **Drölma Lhakang Ani Gompa** (Tara Nunnery) already has a basic guesthouse with dorm rooms (Y20 per bed), but no showers or anywhere to eat, so bring instant noodles if you plan to stay over. Travellers are also welcome to set up their own tent on the nunnery's small lawn, home to five extremely cute half-tamed marmots. The main hall here contains 1000 silver statues of the female bodhisattva Drölma (Tara).

A two-hour walk up the valley brings you to a **mountain lake** and fine views of the surrounding snowcapped mountains.

The turn-off for Drölma Valley (not signposted) is between kilometre markers 3666 and 3667, 9km past the wind-swept one-street town of Gulok (古露; Gǔlù) if you're coming from Nagchu; or 61km past Damxung if you're coming from Lhasa. The valley is on the west side of the highway. **Damxung** (当雄; Dāngxióng) is the best place for a lunch stop on this stretch of the highway. Try Snowland Tangla Yak Tibetan Restaurant. From here it's about three hours' drive to Lhasa.

Overland Routes from Sìchuān

Includes

Kāngdìng (Dardo) . . . 217
Tǎgōng (Lhagong) . . 222
Gānzī (Garzê) 223
Manigango 224
Derge 226
Lithang 227
Bathang 229

Best Places to Eat

» Tibetan Restaurant (p224)

» Khampa Café & Arts Centre (p223)

» Tibetan Culture Dew (p221)

» Tiantian Restaurant (p228)

» Street barbecues in Bathang (p229)

Best Places to Stay

» Dala Gong (p225)

» Jya Drolma and Gayla's Guesthouse (p223)

» Camping at Yilhun Lha-tso (p225)

» Zhilam Hostel (p221)

» Potala Inn (p228)

Why Go?

Wild, mountainous and deliciously remote, the tradition-ally Tibetan areas of western Sìchuān are a cultural and geographical extension of the Tibetan plateau in all but name. This area was once part of the eastern Tibetan re-gion of Kham, and has long been the meeting point of the Chinese and Tibetan worlds.

In many ways Tibetan culture is better preserved here than in the Tibetan Autonomous Region (TAR). It's cer-tainly subject to fewer religious restrictions, and you'll see photos of the Dalai Lama displayed freely.

Unlike the TAR, western Sìchuān is also permit-free, meaning foreign travellers can explore to their heart's con-tent. If you do manage to get those pesky permits to contin-ue over the high passes and deep gorges into the even more remote eastern Tibet, you'll deserve to feel a little smug in the knowledge that you have completed one of the world's great road trips.

When to Go

May and June are the prime times for western Sìchuān. It's generally warm and sunny with occasional afternoon rains. If you're in the Kāngdìng area in May, it's worth try-ing to pay a visit to Pǎomǎ Shān for the Walking Around the Mountain Festival.

In July and August the grassland areas are green and full of flowers, and play host to horse festivals such as the one in Lithang. It's worth keeping an umbrella handy for this time of year, though!

Rains lessen in September and October, and days are sunny again, but it's starting to get pretty chilly by this time. Sightseeing can still be on the agenda but think twice before planning any hiking.

Permits

The good news is that no permits are required anywhere in western Sìchuān, although it's worth noting that from time to time certain areas are closed to foreigners temporarily. You will, though, need permits to continue into the Tibetan Autonomous Region (TAR) – if the border is open (see the box below). For more details, see the Tours & Permits chapter (p29).

Dangers & Annoyances

Western Sìchuān experiences up to 200 freezing days per year; summers are blistering by day and the high altitude invites particularly bad sunburn. Lightning storms are frequent from May to October, when cloud cover can shroud the scenic peaks.

If you're thinking of crossing into Tibet from Bathang or Derge without the necessary permits, you may want to reconsider. The PSB keeps a very close eye on foreigners straying west of these towns, and drivers can be severely punished for carrying foreigners across the border, so think twice before potentially putting locals at risk.

Kāngdìng (Dardo) 康定

♪ 0836 / POP 110,000 / ELEV 2616M

The 'do' of Kāngdìng's Tibetan name, Dardo, means 'river confluence', and this lively town is nestled in a deep river valley at the point where the fast-flowing Yǎlā (Tse in Tibetan) meets the raging Zhéduō (Dar) which roars its way right through the town centre. More poignantly, Kāngdìng has for centuries also been the point at which two very different cultures converge.

This is the gateway into Sìchuān's Tibetan world, and it's long been a trade centre between Tibetans and Han Chinese, with wool and yak hides travelling in one direction, and bricks of tea in the other. It also served as an important staging post on the road to Lhasa, as indeed it still does today.

Historically, Kāngdìng was the capital of the local Tibetan kingdom of Chakla (or Chala) before, briefly, being the capital of the now defunct Chinese province of Xīkāng. Today, although there is a large Tibetan population, the city feels more Chinese, but you can still find elements of Tibetan culture in the food, the dress and, to a lesser extent, in the architecture.

The steep river valley here is set amidst distant snowcapped mountains, includ-

ing the imperious Gònggā Shān (Minyak Gangkar in Tibetan; 7556m), and Kāngdìng is famed throughout China for Kāngdìng Qínggē, a popular love song inspired by the town's surrounding scenery.

⊙ Sights

There are several small monasteries in and around Kāngdìng. The central **Ānjué Temple** (安觉寺; Ānjué Sì; Ngachu Gompa in Tibetan) dates back to 1652 and was built under the direction of the fifth Dalai Lama.

Nánwú Temple (南无寺; Nánwú Sì) belongs to the Gelugpa (Yellow Hat) sect of Tibetan Buddhism and is the most active monastery in the area. It also affords good views of Kāngdìng and the valley. Walk south along the main road, cross the river and keep going for about 200m until you see a rusty old sign for the monastery (in traditional Chinese characters: 南無寺) on your right. Follow that track up hill, beside a stream, and the monastery will be on your right.

Nearby, about 100m further along the main road, is **Jīngāng Temple** (金刚寺; Jīngāng Sì), a 400-year-old Nyingma monastery set around a lawned courtyard. Turn right at the sign for Knapsack Inn.

You can head up 2900m **Pǎomǎ Shān** (admission Y50) for some excellent views of Kāngdìng and the surrounding mountains and valleys. The ascent takes you past oodles of prayer flags and several Buddhist temples up to a white chörten. Avoid hiking alone, as a British tourist was murdered here in 2000 and one or two muggings have been reported.

To reach the hill, bear left at the fork in the road south of the bus station and walk about 10 minutes until you reach a monastery on the left; a stairway leads up the

TIBET BORDER CLOSED

At the time of research foreigners were forbidden from travelling overland from Sìchuān into Tibet proper because Tibet's far eastern prefecture of Chamdo, which borders Sìchuān, was completely off limits. Check the Tibet branch of Lonely Planet's online forum, Thorn Tree (lonelyplanet.com/thorntree), for the latest information.

Overland Routes from Sìchuān Highlights

1 Stay with Tibetan nomads on the beautiful grasslands of **Tăgōng** (p222)

2 Watch traditional Tibetan block printing done by hand at Derge's fabulous **printing monastery** (p226)

3 Hang with the butter-tea-sipping locals in any one of western Sìchuān's fabulously down-to-earth **Tibetan teahouses**

4 Bunk with the monks in the dorms at **Dala Gong** (p225), a monastery guesthouse set among some of the most spectacular scenery imaginable

5 Hike around the turquoise-blue waters of the stunning holy **Yilhun Lha-tso** (p225)

6 Get swept up by religious fervour as you join pilgrims on a **kora circuit** of one of western Sìchuān's numerous Buddhist monasteries

7 Hike, horse ride or ride motorbikes over the mountain grasslands around popular **Lithang** (p227)

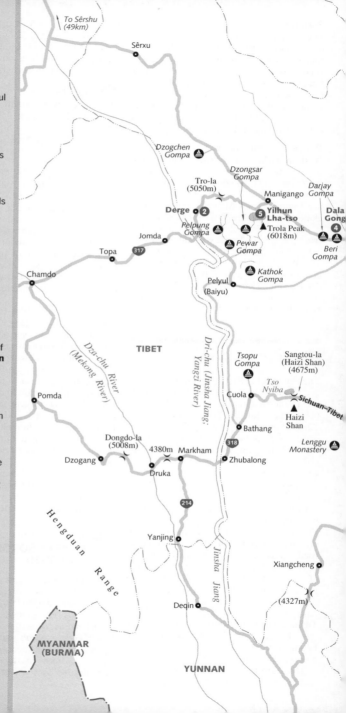

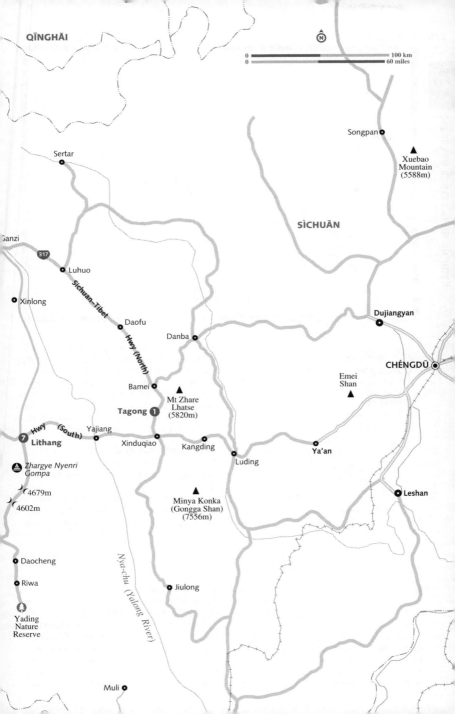

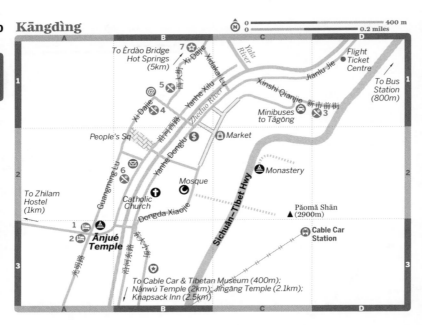

Kāngdìng

◎ Top Sights
Ānjué Temple A3

🛏 Sleeping
1 Kāngdìng Hotel A3
2 Yǒngzhū Hotel A3

🍴 Eating
3 A'Re Tibetan Restaurant...................D1
4 Barbecue Stalls..................................B1
5 Dàtóng Xiaochi..................................B1
6 Tibetan Culture Dew B2

⚙ Entertainment
7 Happiness in Heaven...........................B1

hill from here. A second, more direct route, heads up the hill further south, beginning above the staircase on Dongda Xiaojie. You could also ride up in the **cable car** (suǒdào; 索道; one way/return Y20/30). By the entrance to the cable car is a small **Tibetan museum** (admission Y30; ☺8am-6pm).

About 5km north of Kāngdìng are the **Èrdào Bridge Hot Springs** (二道桥温泉; Èrdàoqiáo Wēnquán; admission Y10-120; ☺7am-midnight) where you can have an hour-long soak in hot, sulphurous water. For Y10 to

Y20 you get your own private room with jacuzzi-sized sunken pool. For Y80 to Y120, the rooms and pools are larger, have bathrooms and towels are provided. There's also a communal hot-spring swimming pool (Y45). All prices are per person, not per room. It's a pleasant 45-minute walk here, along the Yǎlā River, or an Y8 taxi.

🎎 Festivals & Events

Kāngdìng's biggest annual festival, the **Walking Around the Mountain Festival** (Zhuànshānjié), takes place on Pǎomǎ Shān on the eighth day of the fourth lunar month (normally in May) to commemorate the birthday of the Historical Buddha, Sakya Thukpa (Sakyamuni). White-and-blue Tibetan tents cover the hillside and there's wrestling, horse racing and visitors from all over western Sìchuān.

🛏 Sleeping

Yǒngzhū Hotel　　　　　　GUESTHOUSE **$$**
(拥珠驿栈; Yǒngzhū Yìzhàn; ☎283 2381, 159 8373 8188; off Guangming Lu; dm Y30-40, d Y120-160) Hidden in a lane beside Kāngdìng Hotel, this small, friendly guesthouse has comfortable, well-kept rooms, including three- and four-bed dorms decorated with colourful Tibetan furnishings and built

around an inner atrium. There's 24-hour hot water in both the common and private bathrooms.

Kāngdìng Hotel HOTEL $$$
(康定宾馆; Kāngdìng Bīnguǎn; ☑283 2077; 25 Guangming Lu; r from Y360; ❉ @) For something more comfortable, this decent hotel, right beside Ānjué Temple, had standard twins going for Y240 when we were there.

Two hostels that were closed at the time of research, but which get good reviews from travellers, are **Zhilam Hostel** (汇道客栈; Huìdào Kèzhàn; ☑283 1100; www.zhilamhostel.com; Bái Tǔkǎn Cūn; dm Y35/60, ste Oct-Apr/May-Sep Y260/450; @ ☎), whose American owners had gone back home for a few months, and **Knapsack Inn** (背包客栈; Bèibāo Kèzhàn; ☑283 8377; dm Y25-35, d without bathroom Y80; @), which was being renovated. Both are walking distance from the Ānjué Temple area or a Y6 to Y8 taxi ride from the bus station. Knapsack is next door to Jīngāng Temple. Zhilam is a 10-minute walk up behind Yǒngzhū Hotel. Once the short lane ends, keep following the winding footpath.

✖ Eating

On mild evenings, Sìchuān **barbecue stalls** (烧烤; shāokǎo) set up around the northeast corner of People's Sq.

TOP CHOICE **Tibetan Culture Dew** TIBETAN $$
(西藏雨; Xīzàng Yǔ; ☑158 0836 6530; Yanhe Xilu; dishes Y15-38; ☺11am-11pm) Hang out with the yak-butter-tea-sipping locals at this lovely teahouse/restaurant with a rustic stone-and-wood interior decorated with colourful Tibetan prayer flags. There are all sorts of tea if you don't like the yak-butter variety, plus coffee and beer. The English menu is limited, but includes tsampa, Tibetan yoghurt, a few yak-meat dishes and some delicious dumplings.

BRING PLENTY OF CHINESE CASH

At the time of research it was impossible to change money or travellers cheques or get advances on credit cards or use ATMs with foreign bank cards anywhere in western Sìchuān, apart from Kāngdìng. So bring plenty of rénmínbì.

A'Re Tibetan Restaurant TIBETAN $$
(阿热藏餐; Ā'rè Zàngcān; ☑669 6777; Xinshi Qianjie; dishes Y12-78; ☺9am-10pm) More of a proper restaurant than Tibetan Culture Dew, and with a bigger menu, this place does tasty soups, tsampa and yak-meat dishes including a whole yak hoof, if that sort of thing takes your fancy? English menu too.

☆ Entertainment

Happiness in Heaven TIBETAN DANCE HALL
(天地吉祥; Tiāndì Jíxiáng; Xi Dajie; ☺7pm-midnight; drinks from Y20) Traditional Tibetan and Chinese songs, including the famous Kāngdìng Love Song, are performed to ear-splitting techno beats and appreciative audiences, and you can get up and dance once the performances are finished.

ℹ Information

ATM (自动柜员机; Zìdòng Guìyuán Jī; Yanhe Donglu) China Construction Bank ATM. One of a few around town that takes foreign cards.

Internet cafe (网吧; wǎngbā; per hr Y3; ☺24hr)

Public Security Bureau (公安局; PSB; Gōng'ānjú; ☑281 1415; Dongda Xiaojie; ☺8.30am-noon & 2.30-5.30pm) Next-day visa-extension service.

ℹ Getting There & Away

Air

Kāngdìng airport only serves Chéngdū (35 minutes), and only has one daily flight (8.13am). Tickets cost around Y1000 before discounts, but can often be had for Y500 or less. Either buy them online (www.elong.com is good) or from the **flight ticket centre** (机场售票中心; Jīchǎng Shòupiào Zhōngxīn; ☑287 1111; 28 Jianlu Jie; ☺8.30am-5.30pm) at the north end of town. An airport bus (Y22) leaves from outside the ticket centre at 6.30am.

Bus

The bus station is a 10-minute walk north of the centre and has services to Bathang (Y142.5, 12 hours, one daily, 6am), Chéngdū (Y121 to Y131, eight hours, hourly 6am to 4pm), Derge (Y176, 16 hours, 6am), Gānzī (Y113, 11 hours, 6am), Lithang (Y87.5, eight hours, 6.30am) and Tǎgōng (Y39, three hours, 6am).

Minibuses to all destinations on the following pages leave from outside the bus station. Ones to Tǎgōng are cheaper from Xinshi Qianjie. Remember, private hire: 'bāochē' (包车) and shared vehicle: 'pīnchē' (拼车).

DON'T DOUBLE UP ON TRAVEL INSURANCE

Save yourself a couple of yuán each time you buy a long-distance bus ticket by saying that you don't need road insurance: 'bùyòng bǎoxiǎn'. Most ticket sellers don't realise that foreign tourists usually have their own travel insurance, so they'll assume you want it.

NORTHERN ROUTE

It may have only been around since 1954, but the Sìchuān–Tibet Hwy has a well-deserved reputation for being one of the highest, roughest, most dangerous and most beautiful roads in the world. Around 70km west of Kāngdìng it splits in two to form the Northern Route (Hwy 317) and the Southern Route (Hwy 318).

The Northern Route is around 300km longer and is generally less travelled. This is 'big sky' country, with wide-open grasslands, beginning near Tǎgōng, leading to soaring snow-topped mountains, and it passes through traditional Tibetan communities with their remote monasteries and motorcycle-riding yak herders. It also crosses Tro-la (5050m), the highest pass this side of Lhasa, before descending towards the Tibet border.

You *must* come prepared with warm clothing; even in mid-summer, it can be very cold at higher elevations once the sun goes down. Remember that bus services can be erratic – this is no place to be in a hurry.

Tǎgōng (Lhagong) 塔公

☑ 0836 / ELEV 3750M

The small Tibetan village of Tǎgōng and its beautiful surrounding grasslands offer plenty of excuses to linger. As well as an important monastery and a fascinating nearby nunnery, there's also horse trekking and hiking, and travellers give rave reviews to the Tibetan homestays here. Some even have an opportunity to watch sky burials nearby.

Tǎgōng is well above 3000m, so take time to adjust to the altitude if you're coming from lower terrain to the east.

◉ Sights

Tǎgōng Monastery MONASTERY
(塔公寺; Tǎgōng Sì; admission Y20) The story goes that when Princess Wencheng, the Chinese bride-to-be of Tibetan king Songtsen Gampo, was on her way to Lhasa in the 7th century, a precious statue of Jowo Sakyamuni Buddha toppled off one the carts in her entourage. A replica of the statue was carved on the spot where it landed and a temple then built around it. You'll find the statue in the right-hand hall here. The original, which is the most revered Buddha image in all of Tibet, is housed in Lhasa's Jokhang Temple.

Also note the beautiful 1000-armed Chenresig (Avalokiteshvara) in the hall to the left. And don't miss the impressive collection of over 100 chörtens behind the monastery.

Hépíng Fǎhuì NUNNERY
Lama Tsemper was a revered local hermit who spent much of his life meditating in a cave about two hours' walk across the grasslands from Tǎgōng. Local nuns would bring him food and generally look after him. Just before his death in the 1980s, he requested a temple be built here, so it was decided to build a nunnery too. Hépíng Fǎhuì (和平法会), known locally as *ani gompa* ('nunnery' in Tibetan), is now home to around 500 nuns and more than 100 monks and is a fascinating place to visit.

Lama Tsemper's remains are in a chörten inside the original cave; you may have to ask a nun to unlock the door to look inside. Below the cave is the temple and a huge mani wall as big as the temple itself, which has its own kora that attracts many pilgrims.

From the mani wall, you can see a hill, covered in thousands of prayer flags, where **sky burials** take place. If you see some activity up there, feel free to take a look, but remember to act with the same respect you would any funeral ceremony. Some families donate the deceased's possessions to the nunnery, and these genuine Tibetan family heirlooms can actually be bought in the small convenience shop at the foot of the hill. Next to the shop is a **canteen** (noodles/tsampa/butter tea Y6/6/8) with a simple **guesthouse** (dm Y20) upstairs.

Getting to the nunnery is half the fun. Heading north out of town, turn right just after the Golden Temple, then, at some point soon after crossing the river bridge, roll up your trouser legs and bound your way over the grasslands on your left, towards the golden-roofed *shedra* (monastic college) that you'll see way off in the distance. The nunnery is just down the hill from the *shedra*.

🏃 Activities

Angela, at Khampa Café & Arts Centre (p223), can arrange **Tibetan homestays** (per person per night Y40), **horse trekking** (per person per day Y250) and guided **grassland hikes** (per day per person Y150). Prices are all inclusive. She will also point people in the right direction who want to hike out into the grasslands on their own. The homestays get particularly good reviews from travellers.

🎉 Festivals

Like many places in this part of Tibetan Sìchuān, Tǎgōng holds an annual **horse-racing festival** (*sàimǎhuì*), during the fifth lunar month (usually early July), which features thousands of Tibetan herdsmen and Tibetan opera.

🛏 Sleeping & Eating

Jya Drolma & Gayla's Guesthouse
GUESTHOUSE $
(☏266 6056; dm Y25, tw with shared bathroom Y50) Bedrooms here – even the dorms – are a riot of golds, reds and blues, with elaborately painted ceilings and walls. There are common toilets on each floor and one shower with 24-hour hot water. Look for the English sign on the opposite side of the square from the monastery. No English is spoken, but the welcome is very friendly.

Snowland Guesthouse
GUESTHOUSE $
(雪城旅社; Xuěchéng Lǚshè; ☏286 6098, 130 5645 7979; tagongsally@yahoo.com; dm from Y10, s without bathroom Y20, tw with bathroom Y80) This long-standing backpacker hangout, right beside Tǎgōng Temple, has less character than Gayla's but is still a fine choice. Sally, who also runs the adjacent cafe-restaurant, **Sally's Kham Restaurant** (☏139 0564 7979; tagongsally@yahoo.com; dishes Y3-35; ☺8am-10pm), speaks a bit of English.

TOP CHOICE **Khampa Café & Arts Centre**
TIBETAN-WESTERN $
(☏136 8449 3301; definitelynomadic.com; dishes Y9-28; ☺8am-11pm) Run by Angela, a super-helpful American woman, and her Tibetan husband Djarga, this fantastic new cafe serves authentic Tibetan cuisine as well as Westernised Tibetan dishes (think yak burger) and straightforward Western food, including good breakfasts. The fresh coffee is excellent, as is the yak-butter tea, and there should be wi-fi up and running by the time you read this. They also sell beautiful clothes, handicrafts and jewellery, handmade by locals from various parts of western Sìchuān and Tibet. Also next to Tǎgōng Temple.

ℹ Getting There & Away

A bus from Gānzī to Kāngdìng (Y40, two hours, 7.30am) passes Tǎgōng Temple, but you might not get a seat. Alternatively, take a shared minivan (Y50). Note, you might struggle to find fellow passengers after about 10am.

To get to Lithang, take the Kāngdìng bus or a shared minivan to Xīndūqiáo (新都桥; Y15, one hour) from where you can flag down the Kāngdìng–Lithang bus (Y64, seven hours), which passes by at around 9am, or a minibus (Y80).

For Gānzī, you can try to snag a seat on the bus from Kāngdìng which passes here between 9am and 10am. You may be able to arrange a shared minivan too.

Gānzī (Garzê) 甘孜

☏0836 / ELEV 3394M

This dusty but lively market town in a picturesque valley surrounded by snow-capped mountains is the capital of the Gānzī Autonomous Prefecture and is populated mostly by Tibetans. It's easy to spend a couple of days here exploring the beautiful countryside, which is scattered with Tibetan villages and monasteries. Photo opportunities abound.

👁 Sights

North of the town's Tibetan quarter, **Garzê Gompa** (甘孜寺; Gānzī Sì; admission Y15) is the region's largest monastery, dating back more than 500 years and glimmering with blinding quantities of gold. Encased on the walls of the main hall are hundreds of small golden Sakya Thukpas (Sakyamunis). In a smaller hall just west of the main hall is an awe-inspiring statue of Jampa (Maitreya or Future Buddha), dressed in a giant silk robe. The views into the mountains from here are fantastic.

The monastery is about a 25- to 30-minute walk from the bus station. Turn left out of the station and keep going until you reach the Tibetan neighbourhood. Then wind your way uphill around the clay and wooden houses.

🛏 Sleeping & Eating

Jīntàiyáng Bīnguǎn   HOTEL $
(金太阳宾馆; ☑752 5479; 53 Jiefang Jie; r without bathroom Y30-50, r with bathroom Y80; 🛜) Simple but clean rooms sit around a courtyard out back. Round-the-clock hot water, even in the common bathrooms and, believe or not, wi-fi! (Not the quickest, mind.) Turn left out of the station and it's on your left. Another building off Chuanzang Lu houses smarter twins with bathrooms that usually go for Y100, and also has wi-fi. Turn left out of the station, take the first right and it's on your left through an archway.

Golden Yak Hotel   HOTEL $$
(金牦牛酒店; Jīnmáoniú Jiǔdiàn; ☑752 2353; Dajin Tan; r without/with hot water Y60/150) This dependable chain has branches at a number of bus stations in western Sìchuān. This particular one has a main building at the back of the bus station forecourt with standard doubles discounted to Y120 and a separate building across the forecourt housing enormous, but slightly shabby, twin rooms with bathrooms but no hot water.

TOP CHOICE **Tibetan Restaurant**   TIBETAN $
(藏餐馆; Zàngcānguǎn; 47 Dajin Tan, 2nd fl; dishes Y10-35; ⏲7am-11pm) This wonderfully decorated teahouse/restaurant, just across from the bus station, is run by a local nun and is the main Tibetan hang-out in town. Sip butter tea, tuck into hearty plates of yak meat and get your hands covered in dough as you attempt to mix your own *tsampa*. English menu.

❶ Information

Internet cafe (网吧; wǎngbā; per hr Y4; ⏲24hr) Turn left out of the bus station and take the second road on your right. It's on the 2nd floor.

❶ Getting There & Away

Heading east, there's one daily bus to Kāngdìng (Y115, 11 hours, 6.30am) and one to Chéngdū (Y220, 18 hours, 6am). Heading west, a bus to Derge (Y66, eight to 10 hours), via Manigango (Y30, three hours), passes through here at 9am, but it's often full. Minibuses ply the same route for Y10 to Y20 more, but leave before the bus arrives (between 7.30am and 8.30am). After 9am it's hard to find fellow passengers so you'll either have to fork out for the whole vehicle or hitch.

Around Gānzī

There are a number of Tibetan villages and monasteries in the fabulous countryside west of Gānzī.

Perched attractively on a hill up a rutted dirt track, **Beri Gompa** (白利寺; Báilì Sì) is a mid-sized monastery about 15km west of town, on the road to Derge. On sunny days, its gold top sparkles against the deep blue sky. The scenery from Gānzī to here is lovely so you might consider hiking to the monastery, stopping for a picnic en route and hiking back to Gānzī. Turn left out of the bus station then take the first left and follow the road over the bridge then along the river all the way, passing plenty of Tibetan villages and temples en route. Otherwise, hitch a ride on any Derge-bound vehicle.

Further along the same road, about 30km from Gānzī, is **Darjay Gompa** (大金寺; Dàjīn Sì). This monastery was once home to more than 3000 monks. Many were killed during the Cultural Revolution; others escaped to India. Nowadays, around 300 monks reside here. They spend much of their time having animated, hand-slapping debates in the courtyard outside the main hall. Inside the hall, you'll find large photos of the 14th Dalai Lama and, right at the back, a row of impressive 3m-tall Buddha images. You may have to get one of the monks to unlock the door to the hall.

Travellers who wish to stay the night here and soak up the sumptuous scenery should consider the wonderfully located Dala Gong Guesthouse (see the box, p225), a 10-minute walk from the monastery and just a short stroll from some hot springs.

To get to Darjay Gompa from Gānzī, either grab a seat on the Derge-bound bus (Y10, 45 minutes, 8.30am) or take a minibus (Y30). Note, the bus is often full and the shared minibuses leave before it (around 7.30am). A private taxi will cost at least Y50 one way. Keen hikers could consider walking here but it will take a whole day. Walk to Beri Gompa and just keep going.

Manigango 马尼干戈
📞0836 / ELEV 3800M
Despite market stalls piled with yak innards and crimson-robed monks on motorbikes, there's not much going on in this dusty two-street town halfway between Gānzī and Derge. Nearby, though, is the stunning

DALA GONG GUESTHOUSE

Sick of staying in dusty market towns and seeing drop-dead-gorgeous scenery only through the window of a vehicle? Then you'll adore **Dala Gong Guesthouse** (dm Y30, r with bathroom Y100).

A 10-minute walk from Darjay Gompa, one of the area's most revered monasteries, the small temple of Dala Gong is home to three friendly monks who welcome guests to share their mud-brick, wood-beamed living quarters set among the prettiest scenery you can imagine – snowcapped mountains to one side; rolling grasslands and a river to the other. This place could well push your camera's memory card to the limit.

Climb up onto the roof for 360-degree views and to plot your next hike to one of the nearby villages, monasteries or mountains.

Accommodation was dormitory-only when we stayed, and as basic as it gets, but two small modern blocks were being built in the courtyard at the time of research, promising private rooms with bathrooms and, wait for it...hot water! We shall see.

If, as we suspect, the showers are cold, fear not – there are some free-to-use, open-air **hot springs** a five-minute walk away over the other side of the river. Locals use them to wash themselves, their children, their clothes and sometimes even their motorbikes, but there's plenty of room for everyone, so squeeze on in.

The only food options are eating with the monks (offer them whatever money you feel is right). If you tire of eating nothing but tsampa three times a day (we're not joking), there's a small **shop** (◷8am-9pm) on the main road outside the monastery, which sells drinks, snacks and instant noodles.

To get to the guesthouse from Darjay Gompa, walk for 10 minutes along the only track that leads away from the back entrance of the monastery.

turquoise Yilhun Lha-tso, which has great hiking and camping possibilities.

The town is known in Chinese as Yùlóng or Mǎnígāngē, but it's most commonly referred to by its Tibetan name, Manigango.

🛏 Sleeping & Eating

Mǎnígāngē Pàní Hotel　　　HOTEL **$$**
(马尼干戈怕尼酒店; Mǎnígāngē Pàní Jiǔdiàn; dm Y10-20, tw without/with bathroom Y80/160) This good hotel has become the town's centre of gravity with its car park used as the unofficial bus station and its buffet-style restaurant the most popular lunch stop for passing motorists. Sleeping-wise there are rooms for everyone, from dirt-cheap five-bed dorms to really quite decent twins with bathrooms and hot water (8pm to 11pm only) that go for Y130 when it's quiet. The **restaurant** (vegetable/meat dishes Y10/15; ◷7am-11pm) has an easy-to-order, point-and-choose buffet with surprisingly good results.

Qīngzhēn Gānsù Líntán Fàndiàn　MUSLIM **$**
(清真甘肃临潭饭店; noodles from Y8; ◷8am-11pm) This popular Muslim restaurant run by a friendly guy from Gānsù province makes a nice change from Sichuanese or Tibetan. There's no menu, but noodle dishes

on offer include beef noodle squares (牛肉面片; niúròu miànpiàn; Y8) and glass noodles with beef (牛肉粉条; niúròu fěntiáo; Y8). The shǒuzhuā yángròu (手抓羊肉; Y35 per *jīn*) is the restaurant's speciality lamb dish. One *jīn* (500g) is enough for one person. It's at the town crossroads.

❶ Information

Internet cafe (网吧; wǎngbā; per hr Y5; ◷noon-11pm) About 100m along the lane opposite Mǎnígāngē Pàní Hotel.

❶ Getting There & Away

A daily bus to Derge (Y40, three to four hours) passes through Manigango at about 11am, but is often full. Going the other way, there are usually some empty seats on the Gānzī-bound bus (Y30, three to four hours), which passes by at a similar time. Catch both from Mǎnígāngē Pàní Hotel.

Plenty of minibuses congregate outside Mǎnígāngē Pàní Hotel waiting to scoop up bus-less passengers.

Around Manigango

YILHUN LHA-TSO 新路海

The fabulous turquoise-blue waters of **Yilhun Lha-tso** (Xīnlù Hǎi; admission Y20), a holy alpine lake 13 kilometres southwest of

Manigango, are the main reason most travellers stop in this area. The stunning lake is bordered by chörten and dozens of rock carvings, and is framed by snowcapped mountains. You can walk an hour or two up the left (east) side of the lakeshore for views of the nearby glacier.

This is also a great place to camp – some travellers have even slept in caves here – although you'll need to bring your own equipment and guard against mosquitoes. You may be hit with a Y15 tent-pitching charge. Monks from Darjay Gompa sometimes camp here during the summer in colourful Tibetan nomad tents.

To get here, you can either nab a seat in a Derge-bound minibus (Y20), hitch a ride or hike. The lake is a five-minute walk from the main road, along a signposted track. Motorbikes (Y20) wait to take you back to Manigango.

Derge 德格

📞 0836 / ELEV 3270M

Your bumpy bus rides just got bumpier. Derge, or Dégé in Chinese, is cut off from the rest of western Sìchuān by the towering Chola Mountain, and to get here from the east you will probably have to endure a highly uncomfortable, slightly scary three-hour minibus ride along a dirt track that goes up and over the 5050m Tro-La pass. Here, Tibetans on board will throw coloured prayer paper out the window and chant something that you can only hope will carry you all to safety.

Unless you've managed to secure the correct permits to enter the rarely travelled Chamdo prefecture of Tibet proper, the only reason you'll have made the arduous trek out here is to see Derge's famous printing monastery. It may only be one reason, but it's reason enough: this is one of the region's stellar sights.

◎ Sights

TOP
CHOICE
Bakong Scripture Printing Press & Monastery
MONASTERY
(德格印经院; Dégé Yìnjīngyuàn; www.degepark hang.org; admission Y50; ⊙8.30am-noon & 2-6.30pm) This striking 18th-century monastery houses one of western Sìchuān's star attractions: a fascinating printing press that still uses traditional wood-block printing methods and that houses an astonishing 70% of Tibet's literary heritage.

There are more than 217,000 engraved blocks of Tibetan scriptures here from all the Tibetan Buddhist orders, including Bön. These texts include ancient works about astronomy, geography, music, medicine and Buddhist classics, including two of the most important Tibetan sutras. A history of Indian Buddhism, comprising 555 wood-block plates in Hindi, Sanskrit and Tibetan, is the only surviving copy in the world.

Within the monastery, dozens of workers hand-produce over 2500 prints to order each day, as ink, paper and blocks fly through the workers' hands at lightning speed. In one side room you'll find an older crowd of printers who produce larger and more complex prints of Tibetan gods on paper or coloured cloth.

You can also examine storage chambers, paper-cutting rooms and the main hall of the monastery itself, protected from fire and earthquakes by the guardian goddess Drölma (Tara). There are some nice murals in the two ground-floor chapels, so bring a torch.

You aren't allowed to take photos in the storerooms or the main hall, but the workers were happy for us to snap away while they worked frantically to meet their quota.

To get here, turn right out of the bus station then left over the bridge and keep walking up the hill.

Other Monasteries

If you continue following the road up the hill beyond the printing house, you'll reach **Gonchen Gompa**, which is over 1000 years old. At the time of research it was still closed for major renovations (which had been going on for more than two years!) so just how much of the original building will be left once the work's completed is anybody's guess.

High in the mountains to the south and east of Derge are several other monasteries, including **Pelpung Gompa**, **Dzongsar Gompa** and **Pewar Gompa**. To head out this way, try to get a seat in a minibus leaving from outside the bus station.

🛏 Sleeping & Eating

Héxié Hotel
HOTEL $$
(Héxié Lûguăn; 和谐旅馆; 📞822 6111; Chamashang Jie; tw Y200-250) A friendly Tibetan-run hotel with a homely feel to it, spacious carpeted rooms come with coat stand, hot-water flask and pinewood table and chairs,

while the comfy beds have clean sheets and warm puffy duvets. Bathrooms are shared but have 24-hour hot-water showers. Best of all are the discounts: rooms normally go for Y60, and sometimes for as little as Y40, making this the best-value stay in Derge. Turn left out of the bus station and it's on your left after five minutes.

Róngmài Ángzhā Bīnguǎn HOTEL $$
(绒麦昂扎宾馆; Chamashang Jie; dm Y30, tw from Y188) The private rooms with showers, some overlooking the river, are of decent quality and can be nabbed for Y120. The three-bed dorms are clean and reasonably spacious and come with a TV. The common bathrooms, though, don't have showers. On the right before Héxié Hotel.

Kāngbā Zàngcān TIBETAN $
(康巴藏餐; Chamashang Jie; dishes Y10-35; ☺midday-midnight) The decor is half-Tibetan and half-African safari, but the food and the clientele are as Tibetan as it gets. There's butter tea, Tibetan yoghurt, Tibetan dumplings and various yak-meat dishes including a hearty yak pie (牛肉饼; níuròu bìng; Y20). Tsampa (Y5) isn't on the menu, but is of course available. No English menu. No English sign. No English spoken. Turn left out of the bus station and it's on your right on the 2nd floor.

There are several small restaurants and noodle shops near the bus station.

❶ Information
Internet cafe (网吧; wǎngbā; per hr Y3; ☺8.30am-midnight) Turn right out of the bus station, left over the bridge and down steps to your right. Entrance is just past the pool hall.

❶ Getting There & Away
Just one daily eastbound bus leaves from here, at 7.30am, heading for Kāngdìng (Y179, next-day arrival) via Manigango (Y41, three hours), Gānzī (Y68, six hours) and Lúhuò, where it stops for the night. Otherwise, there are minibuses.

There's normally a daily bus to Jomda (江达; Jiāngdá) in Tibet proper, from where you can catch onward transport to Chamdo and Lhasa, but foreigners haven't been allowed to ride public transport in Chamdo prefecture for many years, so you will almost certainly have to had to pre-arrange a private vehicle in advance if you want to cross the border here. You will, of course, need a Tibet permit. There is a checkpost at this border crossing.

A shared minivan from Derge to Lhasa costs around Y600 per person and takes two days.

SOUTHERN ROUTE

The southern section of the Sìchuān–Tibet Hwy (Hwy 318) is shorter and less remote (relatively speaking, of course), so is more commonly used both by travellers (especially those who decide to cycle out this way) and pilgrims (who you'll pass from time to time as they prostrate their way slowly along the main road, often walking as far as Lhasa).

Travel here takes you through vast grasslands dotted with Tibetan block homes and contentedly grazing yaks, while majestic peaks tower beyond. While journeying along this route is slightly easier than taking the northern route, it's still not for the faint-hearted: road conditions vary from rough to rougher and, just like on the northern route, cold weather and altitude can be an issue.

Lithang 理塘
☑ 0836 / ELEV 4014M

Lithang, pronounced Lǐtáng in Chinese, claims to be the world's highest town. It isn't. That accolade is shared by Wēnquán in Qīnghǎi province and La Rinconada in Peru, both of which stand at a wheeze-inducing 5100m. Nevertheless, at a dizzying altitude of 4014m, Lithang is still exceptionally high, so be sure to look out for signs of altitude sickness.

The surrounding scenery will certainly leave you breathless, and there are great opportunities to get out and see it – whether by horse, motorbike or simply hiking – making this a decent place to spend a couple of days.

Lithang is famed as the birthplace of the seventh and 10th Dalai Lamas, but the town's large monastery, Chöde Gompa, is the most absorbing sight. In the hills behind the monastery is a sky burial site, which is often visited by travellers.

In the 1950s, Lithang was one of the main areas of Tibetan armed resistance to the Chinese occupation and, in 1956, the Chinese army bombed Chöde Gompa.

❻ Sights & Activities
At the northern end of town you will find the large **Chöde Gompa** (长青春科尔寺; Chángqīngchūn Kě'ěr Sì), a monastery built for the third Dalai Lama. Inside is a statue of Sakya Thukpa (Sakyamuni) that is

believed to have been carried from Lhasa by foot. Don't miss climbing onto the roof of the furthest right of the three main halls for great views of the Tibetan homes leading up to the monastery and the grasslands and mountains beyond. Monks climb up here every day to sound the temple's long horns. To get here, walk past the post office, turn left at the end of the road then take the first right.

Báitǎ (白塔) is a 33m-tall chörten that worshippers seem to be perpetually circling as they recite mantras and spin prayer wheels. You can join the locals hanging out in the surrounding park. Turn left out of the bus station and just keep walking.

There are **hot springs** (温泉; wēnquán; admission Y15) 4km west of the centre. Keep walking past Báitǎ.

Hiking opportunities abound outside of town. The hills behind the monastery are one fine option. For more ideas, talk to Mr Zheng at Tiantian Restaurant, or to the English-speaking managers at either Potala Inn or Peace Guesthouse.

Potala Inn can also help organise **horse trekking**, while Peace Guesthouse can arrange renting **motorbikes** for the day.

Lǐtáng has a **sky burial** site just behind the monastery. Sky burials are usually held on Wednesdays, Fridays and Sundays, and travellers have reported being made to feel very welcome. If you do attend a sky burial, though, be sure to remember exactly what you are watching and treat the ceremony and all those involved with the utmost respect. For more details, ask Longlife, the manager of Peace Guesthouse, or Mr Zheng at Tiantian Restaurant.

✳️ Festivals & Events

One of the biggest and most colourful Tibetan festivals, the annual **Lithang Horse Festival**, includes horse racing, stunt riding, dance competitions and an arts-and-crafts fair.

At the time of research, the festival was still being suspended following a protest at the 2007 event from a local activist calling for the release of Gedhun Choekyi Nyima, who went missing in 1995, at the age six, after the 14th Dalai Lama had named him as his choice for the next Panchen Lama.

The festival usually starts on 1 August and lasts several days, but check at the hostels in Kāngdìng or Chéngdū for the current situation.

🛏️ Sleeping & Eating

TOP CHOICE Potala Inn YOUTH HOSTEL $$
(布达拉大酒店; Bùdálā Dàjiǔdiàn; ☑532 2533; dm Y25-35, tw Y140-180; @🛜) Run by an English-speaking Tibetan woman called Metok, this large hostel has a mixed bag of rooms, ranging from basic bunk-bed dorms to Tibetan-style twins with bathrooms. Pretty much everything is on offer here – hiking, horse trekking, sky-burial visits, bike rental – but what makes this place stand out from the crowd is its excellent wi-fi-enabled 2nd-floor cafe, which wouldn't seem out of place in Běijīng. Those without laptops can get online on the ground floor (Y4 per hour). Turn left from the bus station and it's on the right, set back from the main street.

Peace Guesthouse YOUTH HOSTEL $
(和平酒店; Hépíng Jiǔdiàn; ☑532 1100, 152 8360 5821; dm/tw Y20/40; @🛜) A favourite with Israeli travellers, this friendly and no-nonsense hostel, run by helpful English-speaking manager Longlife, has large, clean, albeit basic rooms and a small cafe. Turn right out of the bus station and walk 50m up the hill.

Tiantian Restaurant FUSION $
(天天饭食; Tiāntiān Fànshí; ☑135 4146 7941; 108 Xingfu Donglu; dishes Y12-40; ⏱7.30am-11pm; 🛜) The ever-friendly, English-speaking ace chef Mr Zheng has moved his popular travellers' haven across the road to a larger location. Look for the Lonely Planet logo. The same good food – a mix of Chinese, Tibetan and Western – is still on offer, as is the excellent fresh coffee and reliable travel advice. Turn left out of the bus station and it's on your left after 10 minutes.

ℹ️ Information

Internet cafe (网吧; wǎngbā; Tuanjie Lu; per hr Y5; ⏱8.30am-midnight) Next to the post office.

Post office (邮局; yóujú; Tuanjie Lu; ⏱9-11.30am & 2-5.30pm) Turn left out of the bus station then right at main crossroads.

ℹ️ Getting There & Away

Lithang's bus station, at the town's east end, has buses to Kāngdìng (Y87, eight hours, 6.30am), Xīndūqiáo (Y63, six hours, 6.30am) and Bathang (Y63, 3½ hours, 3pm). Times are unpredictable so double check. It's normally easy to bag Kāngdìng or Xīndūqiáo tickets (same bus), but the others are through buses, so are often full by the time they get here. Minibuses hang around outside the bus station to save to the day. There's an OK road north to Gānzī, but no public buses ply the route so you'll have to try your luck with the minibuses.

Bathang 巴塘

📞0836 / ELEV 2589M

Just around 32km from the Tibetan border, Bathang (pronounced Bātáng in Chinese) is one of Sìchuān's main gateways into Tibet proper. Foreigners will need to have all their paperwork in order, of course, but it is easy to catch minibuses from here to Markham or even Lhasa. Bathang itself has a welcoming monastery, while outside the town are lovely suburbs of ochre-coloured Tibetan houses. Bathang is much lower than surrounding areas, so when it's late winter in Lǐtáng, it's already spring here.

The Gelugpa monastery **Chöde Gaden Pendeling Gompa** (康宁寺; Kāngníng Sì) was undergoing heavy renovations at the time of research, but is usually well worth a visit. There are three rooms behind the main hall: a protector chapel, giant statue of Jampa and a 10,000 Buddha room. Up some stairs via a separate entrance is a room for the Panchen Lama, lined with photos of exiled local lamas who now reside in India. Most images here are new, but one upstairs statue of Sakya Thukpa is claimed to be 2000 years old. To get here, continue down the hill from Jīnsuì Bīnguǎn.

There are some fine **walks** around town, including a lovely Tibetan hillside village, a riverside chörten and a hilltop covered in prayer flags offering views of the town.

Hotels and restaurants abound in Bathang. **Jīnsuì Bīnguǎn** (金穗宾馆; 📞562 2700; 1 Ba'an Lu; dm Y30, tw Y100-280) is an old standby with basic rooms. Ones at the back are quieter and face Tibetan homes. Twins are discounted to Y60 or Y100. Turn left out of the bus station and take the first right after the hard-to-miss golden eagle.

On mild evenings you can find excellent roadside Sìchuān **barbecues** (烧烤; shāokǎo; per skewer Y1). For something more Tibetan, try **Xuěyǔ Zàngcān** (雪雨藏餐; dishes from Y5; ⏰8.30am-11pm). Dishes include Tibetan noodles, yak dumplings, tsampa and yak-butter tea. Turn left out of the bus station and it's soon on your left.

ℹ️ Information

Internet cafe (网吧; wǎngbā; per hr Y3; ⏰9am-midnight) Turn left out of the bus station then right at the golden eagle statue and keep going to the end.

ℹ️ Getting There & Away

All public buses are eastbound and leave Bathang's bus station at 6am. You can go to Lǐtáng (Y58, 3½ hours), Xīndūqiáo (Y121, 10½ hours), Kāngdìng (Y140, 12 hours) and even Chéngdū (Y245, one day). The Chéngdū bus is not a sleeper bus, though.

Tibet proper is served by shared minibuses that congregate at the crossroads just down from Jīnsuì Bīnguǎn. Markham (芒康; Mángkāng; Y50, 2½ hours) and Lhasa (拉萨; Lāsà; Y500, two days) are popular destinations.

Tibetan Treks

Includes »

Ganden to Samye . . . 237

Tsurphu to
Yangpachen 240

Shalu to Nartang . . . 244

Everest Base Camp
to Tingri 247

Mt Kailash Kora 250

Nyenchen Tanglha
Traverse 256

Best Long Trek

» Ganden to Samye (p237)

Best Short Trek

» Shalu to Nartang (p244)

Best Cultural Trek

» Mt Kailash (p250)

Best Trek to Spot Wildlife

» Nyenchen Tanglha (p256)

Best Trek to Follow Great Explorers

» Mt Everest (p247)

Why Go?

Tibet, the highest land on earth, is a trekker's dream. Its towering mountains, deep valleys and verdant forests offer unbounded opportunities for walking. On foot the joys of the Tibetan landscape are heightened and immediate, and all other modes of transport pale in comparison. The wonders of Tibet's natural environment are enhanced by the people met along the trail, heirs to an ancient and fascinating way of life. By plying the highland paths one can enter into the same solemn relationship with nature that has sustained Tibetans through the ages.

When to Trek

The best time to trek in Tibet is during the warmer half of the year. May and June are excellent months without much rain or snowfall but some high alpine passes may still be closed. July and August are the hottest months of the year, but they tend to be rainy and this can make walking messy and trails harder to find. September and October are excellent months for trekking, but in high areas the nights are cold and early snow is always a possibility.

PLANNING YOUR TREK

For all its attractions, Tibet is a formidable place where even day walks involve survival skills and generous portions of determination. The remoteness of Tibet combined with its extreme climate poses special challenges for walkers – and unique rewards. As it's situated on the highest plateau on earth and crisscrossed by the world's loftiest mountains, nothing comes easily and careful preparation is all important. Even on the most popular treks, which can involve several days of travel without any outside help, high passes up to 5600m are crossed.

Cities such as Lhasa and Shigatse provide bases from which to equip and launch treks. Walking the classic treks presented here will serve you well. Should you decide to venture further afield, there are certainly many more frontiers beckoning the experienced, well-equipped trekker.

It's a good idea to budget in one or two extra days for your trek, especially if a lot of road travel is needed to get to the trailhead: roads can be blocked, especially in the wet summer months. If on your own, you might also need additional time hiring local guides and beasts of burden.

Trekkers must be prepared for extremes in climate, even in the middle of summer. A hot, sunny day can turn cold and miserable in a matter of minutes, especially at higher elevations. Night temperatures above 4700m routinely fall below freezing, even in July and August. At other times of the year it gets even colder. In midwinter in northwestern Tibet, minimum temperatures reach –40°C. Yet Tibet is a study in contrasts, and in summer a scorching sun and hot, blustery winds can make even the hardiest walker scurry for any available shade. Between the two extremes, the Tibetan climate – cool and dry – is ideal for walking, but always be prepared for the worst.

Before embarking on a trek, make sure you're up to the challenge of high-altitude walking through rugged country. Test your capabilities by going on day walks in the hills around Lhasa and Shigatse. Attempt a hike to the top of a small mountain such as Bumpa Ri, the prayer-flag–draped peak on the far side of the Kyi-chu from Lhasa.

What to Bring

There is a great deal to see while trekking and you will be revitalised by the natural surroundings, but you must be prepared for extremes in weather and terrain. The time of year and the places in which you choose to walk will dictate the equipment you need.

CLOTHING & FOOTWEAR

As a minimum, you will need basic warm clothing, including a hat, scarf, gloves, down jacket, long underwear, warm absorbent socks, all-weather shell and sun hat, as well as comfortable and well-made pants and shirts. Women may want to add a long skirt to their clothing list. Bring loose-fitting clothes that cover your arms, legs and neck, and a wide-brimmed hat like the ones Tibetans wear. For information on culturally appropriate dress, see the box, p300.

If you attempt winter trekking, you will certainly need more substantial mountaineering clothing. Many people opt for synthetic-pile clothing, but also consider wool or sheep fleece, which have proven themselves in the mountains of Tibet for centuries. One of your most important assets will be a pair of strong, well-fitting hiking boots. And remember to break them in before starting the trek!

TREKKING DISCLAIMER

Although the authors and publisher have done their utmost to ensure the accuracy of all information in this guide, they cannot accept any responsibility for any loss, injury or inconvenience sustained by people using this book. They cannot guarantee that the tracks and routes described here have not become impassable for any reason in the interval between research and publication.

The fact that a trip or area is described in this guidebook does not mean that it is safe for you and your trekking party. You are ultimately responsible for judging your own capabilities in the conditions you encounter.

EQUIPMENT

Three essential items are a tent, sleeping bag and portable stove. There are few restaurants in the remote areas of Tibet and provisions hard to come by, so you or your support staff will end up preparing most of your meals. Expect to camp most nights – except in certain villages on the main trekking routes, it can be difficult to find places to sleep. Invest in a good tent that can handle big storms and heavy winds. A warm sleeping bag is a must. Manufacturers tend to overrate the effectiveness of their bags, so always buy a warmer one than you think you'll need.

You will also need a strong, comfortable backpack large enough to carry all of your gear and supplies. To save a lot of misery, test the backpack on day hikes to be certain it fits and is properly adjusted.

Other basic items include water containers with at least 2L capacity, a system for water purification, a torch (flashlight), compass, pocketknife, first-aid kit (see p362), waterproof matches, sewing kit, shrill whistle and walking stick or ski pole. This last item not only acts as a walking aid, but also as a defence against dog attacks. Tibetan dogs can be particularly large and brutal, and they roam at will in nearly every village and herders' camp. Bring your walking stick or pole from home, or purchase Chinese-made trekking poles in Lhasa.

Petrol for camping stoves is widely available in towns and cities but is of fairly poor quality. To prevent your stove from getting gummed up you will have to clean it regularly. Kerosene (煤油, *méiyóu* in Chinese; *sanum* in Tibetan) can also be obtained in cities.

For details on buying and hiring trekking gear in Lhasa, see p73. Nowadays, there are scores of shops in Lhasa selling such equipment.

Maps

There are numerous commercially available maps covering Tibet, but very few of these maps are detailed enough to be more than a general guide for trekkers. For details of general overview maps of Tibet, see p341.

The Chinese government produces small-scale topographic and administrative maps, but these are not for sale to the general public. The US-based Defense Mapping Agency Aerospace Center produces a series of charts covering Tibet at scales of 1:1,000,000, 1:500,000 and 1:250,000. The most useful of the American 1:500,000 references for trekking in Tibet are H-10A (Lhasa region, Ganden to Samye, Tsurphu to Yangpachen), H-9A (Kailash and Manasarovar) and H-9B (Shigatse region, Shalu to Nartang, Everest region).

Soviet 1:200,000 topographic maps can now be consulted in many large university library map rooms. Buying them has become easier with commercial outlets in the West stocking them. Punch 'Tibet maps' into your computer search engine to see who carries them in your area.

Digital maps are freely available at www.earth.google.com. To access them you will have to download the Google Earth Installer. The images currently available vary widely in quality but are expected to soon reach a standard by which you can closely chart your trekking routes.

The Swiss company **Gecko Maps** (www.geckomaps.com) produces a 1:50,000-scale Mt Kailash trekking map.

Trekking Agencies

The kind of trek you take will depend on your experience and the amount of time you have. Unless you have already hiked extensively in the Andes or Himalayas and are willing to try and skirt travel regulations, it is far better to organise your walk through a travel agency.

The main advantage of going with an agency is that it takes care of all the red tape and dealings with officials. Most agencies offer a full-package trek, including transport to and from the trailhead, guide, cook, yaks, horses or burros to carry the equipment, mess tent and cooking gear. The package may even include sleeping bags and tents if these are required.

There is a plethora of private agencies that can arrange treks. Let the buyer beware though, for the standard of service fluctuates wildly and may bear little relation to what you pay. Shop around online or better yet on the ground. Competition between agencies is strong, impelling the smarter ones to up the quality of their trekking services. Be prepared to provide all your own personal equipment.

Make sure the agency spells out exactly what is included in the price it is quoting you, and insist on a written contract, detailing all services that are to be provided as well as a money-back guarantee should it fail to deliver what has been agreed. For the standard contents of tour contracts, have a look at the brochures of adventure-travel companies in your home country. It is prudent to pay one-half of the total cost of a trip up front and the balance after the trek is completed. This is now more or less standard operating procedure in Tibet.

All the Lhasa-based agencies listed here have run many successful treks. Trekkers are particularly at the mercy of those driving them to and from the trailheads. To avoid problems, it is prudent to test the driver and guide on a day trip before heading off into the wilds with them. Always have the phone number of your agency so that you can contact them should something go awry. Mobile (cell) phone coverage has now been extended to all the trailheads.

Prices vary according to group size, ranging from US$90 to US$200 per person per day. For treks in remote and border areas, your agency will need up to two weeks to sort out the permits. If you feel you have been cheated by your agent, you may find help with the department of marketing and promotion of the **Tibet Tourism Bureau** (☎0891-683 4315; fax 683 4632) in Lhasa. This government organisation is in charge of training tour guides and monitoring the performance of all trekking and tour companies.

The agencies listed below tend to be tucked away in hard-to-find spots. If you are in Lhasa call first and ask the staff to come and pick you up.

LHASA AGENCIES

Higher Ground Treks and Tours (☎0891-681 7072; higherground_treks_tours@yahoo.com; 75 Beijing Middle Rd) The head of this agency, Karma Khampa, was once a manager at Tibet International Sports Travel.

Tibet Highland Tours and Treks (☎0891-632 8808; tibethighland@tfol.com; www.tibethighland.com; 1 Nangtse Huayuan, Yixuwupaiqi Huo) Run by Dawa, the ex-sales manager of Tibet International Sports Travel, this outfit has oodles of trekking experience.

Tibet International Sports Travel (Xīzàng Shèngdì Guójì Lǚxíngshè; ☎0891-633 4082; pella_1@hotmail.com; www.sdtist.com; 6 Lingkhor Shar Lam) The oldest agency specialising in trekking. Located next to the Himalaya Hotel, it has been managed for some years by Peldon.

Tibet Wind Horse Adventure (☎0891-683 3009; jampa_w@hotmail.com; www.tibetwindhorse.com; B32 Shenzheng Huayuan, Sera Beilu) One of the best-managed agencies in town. The running of treks and white-water rafting trips is handled by Jampa, the general manager.

Tibet Yungdru Adventure (Xizang Yunzhu Tanxian; ☎0891-683 5813; info@tnya.com.cn; No 5 Bldg, 1st fl, New Shol Village) A main focus of the sales director Thupden is trekking in the more remote regions of Tibet.

KATHMANDU AGENCIES

If you want to organise your Tibet trek from Kathmandu, here are some of the most qualified agencies.

Dharma Adventures (☎01-443 0499; pawan@dharmaadventures.com; www.dharmaadventures.com; GPO Box 5385, 205 Tangal Marg, Tangal)

Sunny Treks and Expeditions (☎01-443 2190; sunny@mos.com.np; www.sunnytravel.com.np; PO 7823, Baluwatar)

Tibet International Travels and Tours (☎01-444 4339; tibetexport@gmail.com; www.tibetintl.com; 29 Tridevi Marg, Thamel)

Ying Yang Tibet Treks (☎01-442 3358; yinyang.travels@gmail.com; www.yinyangtibet.com; 208, 1st fl, A-one Business Center, Thamel)

RESPONSIBLE TREKKING

With average temperatures increasing rapidly, the environment of Tibet is under unprecedented pressure. It is imperative that trekkers make their way lightly and leave nothing behind but their proverbial footprints. Tibet's beautiful but vulnerable landscape deserves the utmost respect. A fire, for instance, can scar the landscape for centuries. Stay off fragile slopes and do not tread on delicate plants or sensitive breeding grounds. Follow the Tibetan ethos, killing not even the smallest of insects. This approach guarantees that later visitors get to enjoy the same pristine environment as you.

Rubbish

» Carry out every piece of your rubbish including toilet paper, sanitary napkins, tampons and condoms.

» Have a dedicated rubbish bag and minimise packaging materials.

» Do not burn plastic and other garbage as this is believed to irritate the Tibetan divinities.

Human Waste Disposal

» Where there is a toilet, use it.

» Where there is none, human waste should be left on the surface of the ground away from trails, water and habitations to decompose. If you are in a large trekking group, dig a privy pit. Be sure to build it far from any water source or marshy ground and carefully rehabilitate the area when you leave camp. Ensure it's not near shrines or any other sacred structures.

Washing

» Don't use detergents or toothpaste in or near watercourses, even if they are biodegradable.

» For all washing use biodegradable soap and a lightweight, portable basin at least 50m away from the water source.

» Try using a scourer, sand or snow instead of detergent. Widely disperse the waste water to allow the soil to filter it.

WESTERN AGENCIES

A few Western companies organise fixed-departure treks in Tibet. These tours can be joined in your home country or abroad, usually in Chéngdū or Kathmandu. Prices are higher than treks arranged directly in Tibet or Kathmandu, but they save you a lot of effort and are useful if you have the money but only a couple of weeks to spend.

A trek organised at home includes a Western leader, a local guide, porters, a cook and so on. All your practical needs will be taken care of freeing you up to enjoy the walking.

Permits

Officially, individuals are not permitted to trek independently in Tibet and must join an organised group. Trekking, as with all travel in Tibet apart from in Lhasa prefecture, requires travel permits (see p29).

ON THE TREK

Trekking trails in Tibet are not marked and in many places there are no people to ask for directions. Paths regularly merge, divide and peter out, making route-finding inherently difficult. Government regulations aside, if you're not good at trailblazing, your only alternatives are to employ a local guide or to go through a travel agency.

Guides & Pack Animals

The rugged terrain, long distances and high elevations of Tibet make most people think twice about carrying their own gear. In

Erosion

» Hillsides and mountain slopes are prone to erosion, so stick to existing tracks and avoid short cuts.

» Do not trench around tents.

» Never remove the plant life that keeps topsoil in place.

Fires & Low-Impact Cooking

» Building fires is not an option. Wood is nonexistent in much of Tibet and where there are trees and bushes they are desperately needed by locals.

» Cook on a lightweight kerosene, petrol, alcohol or multifuel stove and avoid those powered by disposable butane gas canisters.

» Make sure you supply your guide and porters with stoves.

» Ensure that all members are outfitted with adequate clothing so that fires are not needed for warmth.

Good Trekking Partnerships

» Monitor all your staff members closely and make it clear that any gratuities will hinge upon good stewardship of the environment.

» Stress to your agency that you will not tolerate rubbish being thrown along the trail or at the trailheads.

» Explain to your drivers that rubbish should not be thrown out the windows (a common practice in Tibet).

Wildlife Conservation

» Do not engage in or encourage illegal hunting.

» Don't buy items or medicines made from endangered wild species.

» Discourage the presence of wildlife by cleaning up your food scraps.

Camping

» Seek permission to camp from local villagers or shepherds. They will usually be happy to grant permission.

villages and nomad camps along the main trekking routes it's often possible to hire yaks or horses to do the heavy work for you.

It's helpful to know some Tibetan to negotiate what you want and how much you are willing to pay. Otherwise write out the figures involved and make sure the owners of the pack animals understand them. To avoid any misunderstandings, be sure to spell out the amount of time you expect from your helpers and the exact amount you intend to pay. Your mule skinner or yak driver will also serve as your guide, which is an important asset on the unmarked trails of Tibet. Consider just hiring a guide if you don't want or can't get pack animals – this could save you a lot of frustrating hours looking for the route. Guides can also share their knowledge of the natural history and culture of the place, greatly adding to your experience.

The rates for pack animals vary widely according to the time of the year and location. Horses and yaks are pricey at Mt Kailash, costing upwards of Y150 per animal. In most other places burros and horses can be had for Y60 to Y100 per head. Local guides and livestock handlers usually command Y60 to Y90 per day. Remember that your hired help will want to be paid for the time it takes them to return home. Sometimes a discount on the daily rate can be negotiated for their homeward travel.

Food

You should be self-sufficient in food since there isn't much to eat along the trail. Bring anything you cannot live without from home, such as high energy bars and your

SOCIAL TREKKING

In most out-of-the-way places trekkers can quickly become the centre of attention, and sometimes just a smile may lead to dinner invitations and offers of a place to stay. If you really detest being the star of the show, don't camp in villages. If you do, don't expect Western notions of privacy to prevail.

If you have any religious sentiments, your trek probably qualifies as a pilgrimage, in which case you will generally receive better treatment than if you are 'just going someplace'. Another helpful hint: if all else fails try a song and dance. Even the most amateur of efforts is met with great approval.

For other cultural considerations related to trekking, see the box, p300.

favourite chocolates. In Lhasa there are thousands of stalls and shops selling a huge variety of foodstuffs, making well-balanced, tasty meals possible on the trail. Even in Shigatse and the smaller cities there are many foods suitable for trekking.

Vacuum-packed red meat and poultry, as well as packaged dried meat, fish and tofu, are readily found in Lhasa. Varieties of packaged and bulk dried fruits are sold around the city. You can even find almonds and pistachios imported from the USA.

Dairy- and soybean-milk powders can be used with several kinds of prepackaged cereals. Oatmeal and instant barley porridge are widely available in the supermarkets. Pickled and dried vegetables are good for dressing up soups and stir-fries. On the Barkhor are stalls selling Indian pickles and curry powders for an added touch. Lightweight vegetables such as seaweed and dried mushrooms can do wonders for macaroni and instant noodles. Wholemeal Chinese noodles made of various grains are now on the supermarket shelves as well.

Cooking mediums include butter, margarine, vegetable oil and sesame oil. Butter can be preserved for long treks or old butter made more palatable by turning it into ghee (boil for about 20 minutes and then strain). All kinds of biscuits and sweets are sold in Lhasa and the larger regional towns, while decent-quality Chinese and Western chocolate is available in Lhasa. Check out p73 for details of good supermarkets in the capital.

Drink

As wonderfully cold and clear as much of the water in Tibet is, do not assume that it's safe to drink. Livestock contaminate many of the water sources and Tibetans do not always live up to their cultural ideals. Follow Tibetan tradition and eliminate the monotony of drinking plain water by downing as much tea as you can. You can buy Chinese green tea in all its varieties in every city and town in Tibet. If you're offered Tibetan yak-butter tea, have it served in your own cup as per tradition – this eliminates the risk associated with drinking from used cups. More like a soup than a tea, it helps fortify you against the cold and replenishes the body's salts. For information on water purification and traditional beverages, consult the Health chapter (p366).

TREKKING ROUTES

Detailed descriptions of several popular treks are given here. They offer fantastic walking, superb scenery and, with the exception of Lake Manasarovar and Mt Kailash, are close to Lhasa or the main highways. Walking times given are just that: they don't include breaks, nature stops or any other off-your-feet activities. On average, plan to walk five to seven hours per day, interspersed with frequent short rests.

PASS HEIGHTS

Elevations in Tibet, especially for passes, are notoriously inconsistent, with maps and road signs rarely agreeing over the correct elevation. In this book we have tried to use composite measurements, incorporating the most accurate maps, the most consistently agreed figures and on-the-spot GPS readings (which have their own inconsistencies and inaccuracies). Most figures should be accurate within 100m or so, but use the elevations in this book as a guide only.

You will also need time to set up camp, cook and just plain enjoy yourself.

The trek stages can be used as a daily itinerary, but plan ahead to avoid spending the night at the highest point reached in the day.

Ganden to Samye

This trek has much to offer: lakes, beautiful alpine landscapes, herders' camps and sacred sites, as well as two of Tibet's greatest centres of religious culture. With so much to offer, its popularity is understandable, but you should not underestimate this walk. Only those with experience hiking and camping in higher-elevation wildernesses should attempt this trek.

The best time for the trek is from mid-May to mid-October. Summer can be wet but the mountains are at their greenest and wildflowers spangle the alpine meadows. Barring heavy snow, it's also possible for those with a lot of trekking experience and the right gear to do this trek in the colder months. If you're coming straight from Lhasa, you should spend at least one night at Ganden Monastery (4190m) to acclimatise.

If you're fit, acclimatised and have a pack animal to carry your bags, it's not difficult to do the trek in 3½ days, overnighting in Hepu/Yama Do, Tsotup-chu and Yamalung, though some groups take the full five days. You'll experience at least three seasons on this trek, probably in the same day! From the wintry feel of the Chitu-la you rapidly descend to the spring-time rhododendron blooms of the middle valley until the summer heat hits you on the final approach to Samye. Pack accordingly.

Guides and pack animals can be procured in the villages of Trubshi and Hepu, situated in the Tashi-chu Valley near Ganden. An improved road now connects these villages to the Kyi-chu Valley.

STAGE 1: GANDEN TO YAMA DO
5-6 HOURS / 17KM / 300M ASCENT / 450M DESCENT

The trek begins from the car park at the base of Ganden Monastery. It may be possible to find a pack animal or porter here to help carry your bags to Hepu or beyond; ask among the incense and prayer-flag sellers near the car park.

Leave the car park and look for the well-trodden trail heading south along the side of Angkor Ri, the highest point on the

At the time of research, foreigners were not allowed to travel on public transport in Tibet. Basic information is included here in case the situation changes.

Ganden kora. After 20 minutes the Ganden kora branches off to the right (4360m; N 29°44.891', E 091°28.788'); keep ascending to the south for another 30 minutes. You quickly lose sight of Ganden but gain views of Samadro village below you, before reaching a **saddle**, marked by a *lapse* (cairn) 2m tall and 3m in diameter (4530m; N 29°44.130', E 091°29.729').

From the saddle, look south to see the approach to the Shuga-la in the distance. Traversing the west side of the ridge from the saddle, you briefly get views of Trubshi village below and the Kyi-chu Valley to the west. After 45 minutes the trail descends towards Hepu village. Twenty minutes from the spur is a spring. From here it's a further 30 minutes to the village, 2½ hours or so from Ganden.

There are around 30 houses in the village of **Hepu** (4240m; N 29°42.387', E 091°31.442') and it's possible for trekkers to camp or find accommodation among the friendly locals. There's good camping to the south and west of the village. Look for a red-and-yellow masonry structure and white incense hearths at the southeastern edge of the village. This is the **shrine** of Hepu's *yul lha* (local protecting deity), the Divine White Yak.

From Hepu, the trail climbs towards the Shuga-la, 3½ hours away. Walk west downhill from the village towards a bridge crossing the Tashi-chu, near the confluence with another stream. Round the inner side of the confluence and head south upstream along the east bank. You are now following the watercourse originating from the Shuga-la. Near the confluence are good camp sites.

One hour from Hepu you reach **Ani Pagong**, a narrow, craggy bottleneck in the valley. A small nunnery used to be above the trail. Across the valley is the seasonal herders' camp of Choden. From Ani Pagong, the trail steadily climbs for one hour through marshy meadows to **Yama Do** (4490m; N 29°40.511', E 091°30.918').

GANDEN TO SAMYE AT A GLANCE

Duration 4–5 days

Distance 80km

Difficulty medium to difficult

Start Ganden Monastery

Finish Samye Monastery

Highest Point Shuga-la (5250m)

Nearest Large Towns Lhasa and Tsetang

Accommodation camping

Best Time to Trek mid-May to mid-October

Summary This demanding trek crosses two passes over 5000m, connects two of Tibet's most important monasteries and begins less than 50km from Lhasa. It has emerged as the most popular trek in the Ü region.

Yama Do offers extensive camp sites suitable for larger groups. Consider spending the night here as it's still a long climb to the pass and there are few other camping places along the way.

STAGE 2: YAMA DO TO TSOTUP-CHU VALLEY

5-7 HOURS / 10KM / 1000M ASCENT / 450M DESCENT

Above Yama Do the valley's watercourse splits into three branches. Follow the central (southern) branch, not the southeast or southwest branches. The route leaves the flank of the valley and follows the valley bottom. The trail becomes indistinct but it's a straight shot up to the pass. Thirty minutes from Yama Do are two single-tent camp sites, the last good ones until the other side of the pass, at least five hours away. One hour past Yama Do leave the valley floor and ascend a shelf on the east side of the valley to avoid a steep gully that forms around the stream. In another 45 minutes you enter a wet alpine basin studded with tussock grass.

The Shuga-la is at least 1¼ hours from the basin. Remain on the east side of the valley as it bends to the left. You have to negotiate boulders and lumpy ground along the final steep climb to the pass. The **Shuga-la** (5250m; N 29°38.472', E 091°32.015') cannot be seen until you're virtually on top of it. It's marked by a large cairn covered in prayer flags and yak horns, and is the highest point of the trek.

The route continues over the Shuga-la and then descends sharply through a boulder field. Be on the lookout for a clear trail

Ganden to Samye

marked by cairns on the left side of the boulder field. This trail traverses the ridge in a southeasterly direction, paralleling the valley below. Do not head directly down to the valley floor from the pass unless you have good reason. It's a long, steep descent and once at the bottom you have to go back up the valley to complete the trek. In case of emergency, retreat down the valley for a bolt back to the Lhasa–Ganden Hwy, a long day of walking away.

The trail gradually descends to the valley floor, 1½ hours from the pass and 200m below it. The views of the valley and the lake at its head are one of the highlights of the trek. Cross the large **Tsotup-chu** (4980m; N 29°37.366', E 091°33.288'), which flows through the valley and keep an eye out for the herders' dogs. During heavy summer rains, take special care to find a safe ford. The pastures in the area support large herds of yaks, goats and sheep, and during the trekking season herders are normally camped here. Known as Tsogo Numa, this is an ideal place to camp and meet the *drokpas* (nomads).

An alternative route to Samye via the **Gampa-la** (5050m) follows the main branch of the Tsotup-chu past a couple of lakes to the pass. South of the Gampa-la the trail plunges into a gorge, crisscrossing the stream that flows down from it. These fords may pose problems during summer rains or when completely frozen. See Gary McCue's *Trekking in Tibet – A Traveler's Guide* for details of this route.

STAGE 3: TSOTUP-CHU VALLEY TO HERDERS' CAMPS
5 HOURS / 14KM / 300M ASCENT / 400M DESCENT

From the Tsotup-chu ford, the main watercourse flows from the southeast and a minor tributary enters from the southwest. Follow this tributary (which quickly disappears underground) steeply up for about 30 minutes until you reach a large basin and a cairn that offers fine views down onto Palang Tsodü lake. Stay on the west side of the basin and turn into the first side valley opening on the right. A couple of minutes into the valley you'll pass a large group **camp site** (5079m; N 29°36.604', E 091°33.544'). This is a good alternative camp site to the Tsotup-chu, but only if you're acclimatised as it's 100m higher.

Follow this broad valley, which soon arcs south to the Chitu-la. The pass can be seen in the distance, a rocky rampart at the head of the valley. At first, stay on the west side of the valley; there is a small trail. As you approach the pass, the trail switches to the east side of the valley. If you miss the trail just look for the easiest route up: the terrain is not particularly difficult.

The **Chitu-la** (5225m; N 29°34.810', E 091°33.160') is topped by several cairns and a small glacial tarn. Move to the west side of the pass to find the trail down and to circumvent a sheer rock wall on its south

flank. A short descent will bring you into a basin with three small lakes. The trail skirts the west side of the first lake and then crosses to the eastern shores of the second two. It takes 45 minutes to reach the south end of the basin. Drop down from the basin on the west side of the stream and in 30 minutes you'll pass a collection of **cairns** (5077m; N 29°33.924', E 091°32.790') to the right. A further 20 minutes brings you the stone walls of a camp where herders have carved out level places for their tents.

Below the herders' highest camp, the valley is squeezed in by vertical rock walls, forcing you to pick your way through the rock-strewn valley floor. Pass a side stream after 15 minutes and then cross over to the west side of the widening valley to recover the trail. In 20 more minutes you will come to a flat and a seasonal **herders' camp** on the east side of the valley, which is good for camping. At the lower end of the flat, return to the west side of the valley. The trail again disappears as it enters a scrub willow and rosebush forest, but there is only one way to go to get to Samye and that is downstream.

In 30 minutes, when a tributary valley enters from the right, cross to the east side of the valley. Ten minutes further, you will reach another seasonal **herders' camp**, inhabited for only a short time each year. Another 20 minutes beyond this camp, hop back to the west bank to avoid a cliff hugging the opposite side of the stream. Pass through a large meadow and ford the stream back to the east bank. From this point the trail remains on the east side of the valley for several hours.

Camp sites are numerous here. Soon you'll pass herders' tents camped near the spot where the side valley coming from the Gampa-la joins the main valley. Descend the finger of land formed by the river junction and then cross the **stream** (4460m; N 29°31.603', E 091°32.980'). Unless an impromptu wooden bridge has been erected by the herders, during heavy summer rain you might have to wait for the water to subside in order to cross safely.

STAGES 4 & 5: HERDERS' CAMPS TO SAMYE MONASTERY
10 HOURS / 39KM / 1200M DESCENT

The trail is now wide and easy to follow as it traces a course down the east side of the valley. Walk through the thickening scrub forest for one hour and you will come to another stream entering from the east side of the main valley. Look for the wood-and-stone **Diwaka Zampa bridge** (4335m; N 29°30.439′, E 091°33.165′) 50m above the confluence. The valley now bends to the right (west) and the trail enters the thickest and tallest part of the scrub forest. The right combination of elevation, moisture and aspect create a verdant environment, while just a few kilometres away desert conditions prevail.

The next two-hour stretch of the trail is among the most delightful of the entire trek. According to local woodcutters, more than 15 types of trees and shrubs are found here, some growing to as high as 6m. Fragrant junipers grow on exposed south-facing slopes, while rhododendrons prefer the shadier slopes. The rhododendrons start to bloom in early May and by the end of the month the forest is ablaze with pink and white blossoms.

The trail winds through a series of meadows. After 40 minutes the stony flood plain of a tributary joins the river from the north. In another 30 minutes look for a mass of prayer flags and an ancient juniper tree at a place known as Gen Do. This is a **shrine** (4165m; N 29°29.525′, E 091°31.805′) to the protector of the area, the goddess Dorje Yudronma. Just past the shrine, cross a small tributary stream. In one hour the forest rapidly thins and **Changtang**, the first permanent village since Hepu, pops up. There's good camping just before the village.

Look south to the distant mountains; this is the range on the far side of the Yarlung Tsangpo Valley. Forty-five minutes down the valley at a prominent bend in the valley is the turn-off for the **Yamalung Hermitage**, visible on the cliff face high above the valley. A small shop run by the nuns of Yamalung sells soft drinks, beer and instant noodles. There's fine camping across the bridge; the path to Yamalung also leads up from here. It's a 45-minute steep climb to the hermitage. Yamalung (also called Emalung) is where the Tibetan wonder-worker Guru Rinpoche is said to have meditated and received empowerment from the long-life deity Tsepame (Amitayus).

From the turn-off to Yamalung the walking trail is a full-fledged motorable road and the valley much wider. Nowadays many groups opt to end their trek at Yamalung, but if the weather is good and you want a taste of southern Tibetan cultural life, consider carrying on. In 15 minutes you will reach a bridge; the road now sticks to the west side of the valley all the way to Samye, a 3½-hour walk away. Twenty minutes from the bridge you will come to the village of **Nyango** with its substantially built stone houses. A big tributary stream, entering from the northwest, joins the Samye Valley here. The old trade route from Lhasa to Samye via the Gokar-la follows this valley.

Thirty minutes' walk past Nyango is the village of **Wango** and, an hour beyond it, the hamlet of **Pisha**. From the lower end of Pisha, a hill can be seen in the middle of the mouth of the Samye Valley. This is **Hepo Ri**, one of Tibet's most sacred mountains. The entire lower Samye Valley – a tapestry of fields, woods and villages – can be seen from Pisha. Pisha is the last place where water can be conveniently drawn from the river. From here on, the trail only intersects irrigation ditches.

Fifteen minutes past Pisha a ridge spur called **Dragmar** meets the trail. On the ridge is the partially rebuilt palace where King Trisong Detsen is said to have been born. Formerly a lavish temple, it now stands empty. Below, just off the road, is a small red-and-white **temple** (3687m; N 29°22.802′, E 091°30.399′), which is often locked and enshrines the stump of an ancient tree. Legend has it that a red-and-white sandalwood tree grew here, nourished by the buried placenta of Trisong Detsen. During the Cultural Revolution the tree was chopped down.

Twenty minutes further down the trail is **Sangbu** village, from where there are good views of the golden spires of Samye. The route follows the 4WD track direct to Samye along the margin of woods and desert; it takes about one hour. The closer you get to Samye the hotter the valley can become; in May and June it can be fiery hot. You finally enter the perimeter wall of **Samye** (3630m), about three hours from Nyango. See p114 for details of the stunning monastery complex.

Tsurphu to Yangpachen

Beginning at Tsurphu Monastery, this rugged walk crosses several high valleys before emerging into the broad and windswept Yangpachen Valley. Combining alpine tundra and sweeping mountain panoramas with visits to monasteries, this trek nicely balances cultural and wilderness activities.

TSURPHU TO YANGPACHEN AT A GLANCE

Duration 3–4 days

Distance 60km

Difficulty medium to difficult

Start Tsurphu Monastery

Finish Yangpachen Monastery

Highest Point Lasar-la (5400m)

Nearest Large Town Lhasa

Accommodation camping

Best Time to Trek mid-April to mid-October

Summary An excellent choice for those who want to get a close look at the lifestyle of the *drokpas* (herders; see the box, p102). You need to be well acclimatised for this high-elevation trek, which never dips below 4400m.

The best time for this walk is from mid-April to mid-October. Summer can be rainy but be prepared for snow at any time. As you will be in nomad country, beware of vicious dogs, some of which take a sadistic pride in chasing hapless foreigners. Fuel and food are not available, so come prepared. There are few permanent settlements along the way and the inhabitants are often away from home. Your only option on this trek is to be fully self-sufficient.

Tsurphu Monastery (4500m) is a good place to spend a night acclimatising. The area around the Karmapa's former *lingka* (garden), 10 minutes' walk upstream from the monastery, is ideal for camping. Some of the area's herders spend a lot of time at the monastery, so this is a good place to start looking for guides and yaks. Villagers in Tsurphu ask around Y400 for a guide and horse/yak for a five-day return trip to Yangpachen.

If you're well acclimatised, it's possible to do this trek in three days by continuing on to Tajung on day two and finishing at Yangpachen on day three.

Minibuses leave the Barkhor in Lhasa daily around 7am for Tsurphu (Y15, 2½ hours). Minibuses shuttle regularly from Yangpachen back to Lhasa (Y25, three hours). Taxis are also available en route.

STAGE 1: TSURPHU MONASTERY TO LETEN
3½-4 HOURS / 11KM / 500M ASCENT

The trek begins by heading west or up the valley. Follow the kora trail 10 minutes west to the **lingka** (4550m; N 29°43.436', E 090°34.128'), a walled copse of old trees

Tsurphu to Yangpachen

with a brook. This garden-like wood is used by the monks in the summer, so ask permission before you set up camp. The trees here are the last you will see until after finishing the trek. Just above the copse, the valley splits: follow the northwest branch and remain on the north side of the stream.

Forty-five minutes of walking through a rocky gorge along a well-graded trail brings you to **Shupshading** (4700m; N 29°43.574', E 090°32.876'), a seasonal herders' camp on an easily missed shelf above the trail. After 30 minutes look for a line of ruined chörtens to your right. After a further 10 minutes the valley looks like it splits; follow the main river valley (to the left) and descend to cross the stream on a stick-and-sod **bridge** (4890m; N 29°43.396', E 090°31.859'). The trail now continues on the south side of the valley. In another 20 minutes you'll pass a popular camping spot. Look out for small herds of *na* (blue sheep) on the slopes to the north.

Twenty-five minutes further on, by a **mani wall** (N 29°43.373', E 090°30.856'), the trail forks. Both branches lead to Leten, about an hour away, but it's easier to take the right fork that follows the valley floor. This trail passes to the right of a small cliff, past the remains of winter ice, before swinging to the left up into the natural bowl of Leten.

Several families live year-round in the *drokpa* settlement of **Leten** (5090m; N 29°43.557', E 090°30.094'), braving the severe climate with their livestock. Leten is the last chance to find yaks and a guide, both of which are highly recommended because the route to and from the Lasar-la is not easy to find. Camping spots are limited by the lumpy terrain and over-protective dogs. If you value your peace and quiet, consider camping in the valley below Leten.

Spend at least one night (and preferably two) in Leten acclimatising.

STAGE 2: LETEN TO BARTSO
5 HOURS / 15KM / 300M ASCENT / 600M DESCENT

It's about a three-hour walk from Leten to the Lasar-la. Head for the northern half of the settlement (assuming you aren't already there). The route climbs steeply up a short ridge, reaching the highest house. Bear northwest into a steep side valley. As you ascend, a reddish knob of rock looms up ahead. Angle to the north, or right, of this formation, past a mani wall in the centre of the bowl, and leave the valley by climbing to the top of a spur marked by three **cairns** (5270m; N 29°43.973', E 090°29.869'). It's a 45-minute walk to here from Leten. The peak attached to this spur is called **Damchen Nyingtri** and is holy to the god ruling the environs.

As per Buddhist tradition, stay to the left of the three cairns and descend sharply into a narrow valley. As you look into the curved valley ahead you'll notice a round, bald, red peak called Tamdrim Dora; the main trail

you'll be following for the next hour or so keeps to the right of that.

Once on the valley bottom, cross to the east side of the stream and strike out north (up the valley). In 15 minutes a side-stream enters from the west: keep following the main north branch. Cross back to the left side of the stream as the terrain here is easier to traipse over. In another 10 minutes you'll see O-Lha peak, the prominent jagged mountain to the northeast. Walk up the widening valley through arctic-like mounds of tundra for 40 minutes, following a minor trail. Then, as the valley floor veers west, look for a **cairn** (5310m; N 29°45.631', E 090°29.813') on the opposite bank of the stream.

Using this cairn as a marker, bear northwest over an inclined plain. This plain parallels the valley floor before the two merge. Continue ascending as the plain opens wider in the direction of the pass. The **Lasarla** (5400m; N 29°46.165', E 090°29.600') is a broad gap at the highest point in the plain, beside a small tarn, and is heralded by cairns and prayer flags. (A separate pass to the northwest, the Tigu-la, also descends towards Yangpachen, but this is not the route described here.)

From the Lasar-la descend steeply into the north-running valley. A faint trail can be found on the east side of this valley. Thirty minutes from the pass the trail passes a decent camp site, just before descending into a short gully. A side valley joins from the right, offering fine views of the back side of O-Lha. When this side stream joins the main stream, cross over to the west side of the valley. There are many possible camp sites along this next stretch, as well as views of the snowcapped Nyenchen Tanglha range to the north.

The valley is covered with hummocks, but a trail avoids the ups and downs of these mounds of turf and earth. About an hour from the pass, just past a large corral, you meet a large westward bend in the valley. If water levels are high, you should ford the river here and continue on the north side of the valley. In early summer when water levels are lower you can simply follow the valley as it bends to the west and ford the river further downstream.

As you now head westwards, along the north side of the river, there are superb views of the surrounding mountains. In the north is Brize, which is a heavily glaciated peak enclosing the south side of the Yangpachen Valley, and towards the west is a distinctive pinnacle named Tarze. Brize, the 'female-yak herder', and Tarze, the 'horse keeper', are just two of many topographical features in a mythical society ruled by the great mountain god Nyenchen Tanglha. These two mountains make convenient landmarks for trekkers as you go against the grain by heading north over a series of drainage systems that run from east to west.

Thirty minutes after the big bend the trail hits the settlement of **Bartso** (4950m; N 29°48.962', E 090°28.091'). This *drokpa* village of five homes with a permanent source of water is a decent place to camp. The hills around the village are still covered in juniper. In the 1960s and '70s huge amounts of this valuable bush were extracted from the region and trucked to Lhasa to feed the hearths of the new provincial city.

STAGE 3: BARTSO TO DORJE LING NUNNERY
3½-4 HOURS / 15KM / 150M ASCENT / 150M DESCENT

Look northwest from Bartso to the far end of the valley. A clearly visible trail winds up from the valley to the top of the ridge. Make for this trail, 25 minutes' walk over marshy ground from Bartso, following the fence line. It's another half-hour to the summit of the ridge. If you have a guide, a trail leads up to a saddle north of the valley for fine views of Nyenchen Tanglha. However, the more straightforward main path continues down into a gully in about 25 minutes to the village of **Tajung** (4660m; N 29°50.286', E 090°25.116'), a walk of around 90 minutes from Bartso. Tajung is a decent alternative spot to end the second stage, though the insatiably curious villagers can be demanding of your time and supplies.

Stay to the left of the 14 whitewashed houses and ford the stream below the village. Bear northeastwards into the parting in the ridge and, after a few minutes, cross a low saddle. Continue going northeast in the direction of Brize until a large dip appears in the ridgeline to the west, 40 minutes from Tajung. Leave the trail going towards Brize and head cross-country between the ridgeline and a large hill to the right, using a **cairn** (4630m; N 29°51.353', E 090°25.740') on the saddle as your marker. If you have gained enough height, you will be able to see a group of white houses at the base of a hill to the far northwest. The Dorje Ling Nunnery is just downstream of here.

One excellent possible side trip from here is the 20-minute climb to the top of the hill to the right (east), known as **Nyinga Ri** (4800m; N 29°51.688', E 090°25.990'). Views of the Nyenchen Tanglha Range, and the distinctive flat-topped 7111m massif that gives its name to the entire range, are fantastic from here. Nyenchen Tanglha is the holiest mountain in central Tibet, the haunt of a divine white warrior on a white horse. The range is part of the trans-Himalaya, which circumscribes the plateau, dividing southern Tibet from the Changtang.

A 25-minute traverse down the valley (or a short, steep descent north from Nyinga Ri) will bring you to a stream at the base of a ridge, aligned east to west. (If you decide to climb Nyinga Ri, you can send your guide ahead to meet you here.) Two trails climb the ridge: one to the right just past a corral; and a gentler path, favoured by herders, 10 minutes downstream. From the top of the ridge, you'll have good views of the village just upstream of Dorje Ling Nunnery. The nunnery, which is out of view, sits at the bottom of a rock outcrop visible from the ridge top.

SAFETY GUIDELINES FOR WALKING

Before embarking on a walking trip, consider the following points to ensure a safe and enjoyable experience:

» Be sure you are healthy and feel comfortable walking for a sustained period.

» Only undertake treks that are well within your physical capacity and level of experience.

» Obtain reliable information about the terrain and current conditions along your intended route from local inhabitants.

» Be aware of local laws, regulations and customs about wildlife and the environment.

Strike out directly across the plain for the village, taking in the awesome views of the glaciers tumbling off Brize and the fertile flood plain below. After dipping briefly into a dry gully you crest a small ridge and see **Dorje Ling** (4474m; N 29°53.600', E 090°24.782'); the nunnery is about one hour away (two to three hours from Tajung).

The centrepiece of this friendly nunnery is the red *dukhang* (assembly hall). Good camping is found in the meadow to the southwest of the nunnery, by a small chapel, or you can stay in a room at the nunnery.

STAGE 4: DORJE LING NUNNERY TO YANGPACHEN MONASTERY
3½-4½ HOURS / 14KM / MOSTLY LEVEL

From Dorje Ling follow the motorable road west, or downstream. After a couple of minutes fill up your water bottle at a spring, the waters of which power a prayer wheel. After 40 minutes or so, past a fenced area, take the right fork over a ruined concrete **bridge** (4426m; N 29°54.216', E 090°23.247') and continue down the east bank of the stream as the valley drains into the huge Yangpachen plain. Below you to the left is **Tsaburing** village. The track quickly turns into a motorable road and runs north, paralleling the course of the Nyango-chu, which drains the upper Yangpachen Valley. The road stays close to the east bank of the silty river, skirting meadows that afford some fine picnic spots, offering encompassing views of the trans-Himalaya.

Once you've entered the Nyango drainage area, it's a level but draining two-hour walk through the giant landscape to a steel **bridge** (4400m; N 29°59.072', E 090°24.451') spanning the river. Cross over the bridge to meet the northern road to Shigatse. Walk northwards on the road for about 10 minutes, suddenly coming to Yangpachen Monastery.

Perched on top of a ridge above the village, the 15th-century **Yangpachen Monastery** overlooks a broad sweep of trans-Himalaya peaks. The monastery was once home to 115 monks, but many of them have fled to Rumtek Monastery in Sikkim and less than half that number remain. Yangpachen is headed by Shamar Rinpoche (also known as the Sharmapa), a leading lama of the Kagyupa order, whose 14th incarnation is based in India. You'll see images here of the important fourth

Sharmapa (wearing a red hat), the 16th Karmapa (a black hat) and the 'alternative' rival Karmapa, who is supported by the Sharmapa in India.

From Yangpachen Monastery it's an 18km road journey to Yangpachen town. You might be able to hitch there, but there's not a lot of traffic along this road, so consider hiring a minibus or taxi in the village (around Y50). Look out for **Galo Nunnery**, nestled in the hills to the left after about 7km.

For a post-trek treat, the swimming-pool-sized **hot-springs complex** (Yangbajian Wenchuan; admission Y40-60; ☉7am-9pm), located 7km west of Yangpachen town, is great to ease your aching limbs, though it's undergone rapid development in recent years.

From Yangpachen town there are minibuses back to Lhasa (three hours), or continue 2km further to the main Qīnghǎi–Tibet Hwy and hitch from there.

Shalu to Nartang

This trek follows the old trade route between the great Buddhist centres of Shalu and Nartang, marking a glorious chapter in Tibetan history. Treading the ancient trail you can almost feel the caravans laden with scriptures and treasures that once passed this way.

The trek begins at the historic Shalu Monastery and traverses west over a couple of small ranges to Ngor Monastery. From Ngor it's a downhill roll to Nartang Monastery. The route passes through several villages as well as uninhabited dry canyons. It's about a 10-hour walk to Ngor from Shalu, which is best divided into two days, and another five hours from there to Nartang. Finding guides and burros to carry your gear in Shalu is easier than before. Expect to pay Y60 to Y80 for each. Having local support is a good thing because the route tends to vanish in the canyons.

The optimal walking season is from the beginning of April to the end of October. In summer the trail can be sizzling hot, and in other months cold and windy, so be prepared.

For information on getting to Shalu, see p145. Lhatse–Shigatse minibuses travel the Friendship Hwy and pass near Nartang.

SHALU TO NARTANG AT A GLANCE

Duration 2–3 days

Distance 45km

Difficulty medium

Start Shalu Monastery

Finish Nartang Monastery

Highest Point Char-la (4550m)

Nearest Large Town Shigatse

Accommodation camping

Best Time to Trek early April to late October

Summary This walk will give you a good feel for trekking in Tibet. The trail and passes are not particularly high or difficult and the trailheads are easily accessible from Shigatse.

Shalu to Nartang

STAGE 1: SHALU MONASTERY TO UPPER LUNGSANG
5½-6½ HOURS / 19KM / 420M ASCENT / 240M DESCENT

From **Shalu Monastery** (3980m; N 29°07.625′, E 088°59.590′) walk the motorable road south (up the valley). Thirty minutes from Shalu you will pass by the **Ri-puk Hermitage**, set on a hillside on the west side of the valley. If you wish to visit, cut across the fields and head directly up to the hermitage – the way is not difficult and there are several trails leading up to it.

Forty-five minutes from Shalu the road forks: take the south fork. In the south, a conical-shaped hill and a village at its base can be made out. If you struck out in Shalu, stay on the road to this village, called **Phunup**, about a one-hour walk away. You

may also find a guide and pack animals here. Otherwise, there is a short cut that saves 2km of walking. A few minutes from the fork in the road, look for the base of a long red ridge. Leave the road and skirt the base of this ridge, going in a southerly direction. First cross a flood plain to reach a rectangular red shrine and, beyond it, enter a plain bounded in the south by the red ridge.

Gradually the trail climbs to a small white ridge blocking the route to the south. As you approach you will see a line of white cairns marking its **summit** (4030m; N 29°06.011′, E 088°59.590′). Look for the trail that ascends to the cairns, a one-hour walk from the fork in the road. From the ridge's summit, Phunup village is to the south and the Showa-la is to the west. The pass is the obvious low point in the range at least one hour away. The trail descends gradually to enter the stream bed coming from the Showa-la, 30 minutes from the cairns. If you came via Phunup, your route will converge with the main trail here.

The climb up to the pass and the descent on the other side is through some heavily eroded, waterless ravines and slopes. Bring plenty of drinking water from the trailhead. From the stream bed the trail soon climbs back up the right side of the valley only to drop back in and out of the stream bed in quick succession. Don't make the mistake of walking up the stream bed as you will encounter ledges and other difficult terrain. After twice briefly dropping into the narrow stream bed, be alert for a trail carving a route up the right slope. It's situated just a few metres before a fork in the stream bed. The trail climbs steeply to a group of ruins and then winds around to the pass in 30 minutes. The top is marked by white cairns.

From the **Showa-la** (4170m; N 29°06.371', E 088°56.939'), the second pass, the Char-la, can be seen in the range of hills west of an intervening valley. The easy-to-follow trail descends from the pass along the south side of a ravine. In one hour you will reach the valley floor. Leave the trail just before it crosses a small rise marked with cairns and continue west towards a distant group of trees. Cross over the sandy north–south valley, intersecting a road. Shigatse is about three hours north along this road.

The valley watercourse is dry except during summer flash floods. West of it is a **poplar and willow copse** (3950m; N 29°06.572', E 088°54.093'), the only bit of shade in the area. Consider stopping here for lunch and a rest. From the copse, you enter a side valley, continuing in a westerly direction towards the Char-la. There are places suitable for camping along the length of this valley and water is available in the villages. In a few minutes you will reach the village of **Manitinge**, on the southern margin of the valley, and pick up the main cart track going up the valley. The track passes through the village of Siphu and, one hour from the copse, crosses to the south side of the valley. You can glimpse the Char-la from here, which for most of the trek is hidden behind folds in the mountains.

In 30 minutes you will reach **Lower Lungsang** (4060m; N 29°06.265', E 088°51.824'), a few minutes later **Upper Lungsang**. There is a fine old wood here ideal for camping and resting.

STAGE 2: UPPER LUNGSANG TO NGOR MONASTERY
3½-4 HOURS / 8KM / 550M ASCENT / 240M DESCENT

From Upper Lungsang the trail cuts across the valley floor, gradually making its way back to the northern side of the valley. The cart track does not extend past the village and the trail up to the pass may be difficult to find in places. If you are in doubt, try to hire a local person to show you the way. It is at least three hours from Upper Lungsang to the Char-la. At first, the trail skirts the edge of a gravel wash. However, in 15 minutes a series of livestock tracks climbs out of the stream bed and onto an eroded shelf that forms above it. Observe the old agricultural fields here, many of which have been long abandoned due to a lack of water.

The terrain becomes more rugged and a gorge forms below the trail. There is a sidestream and small **reservoir** (4190m; N 29°06.619', E 088°50.763') 45 minutes above Upper Lungsang. This is the last convenient place to collect water until over the pass. From the reservoir, the trail descends back to the stream bed but quickly exits the opposite side of the valley.

Look for a series of switchbacks on the southern side of the gorge and then follow them up. A further 15 minutes on, the trail crosses a gully and then another gully in 15 more minutes. The final leg to the pass is pretty much cross-country over a steep slope of raw expanses of rock. From the second gully, the Char-la can be reached in 45 minutes of steep uphill walking. At one time this trail was well maintained and formed a main trade link between Shalu and Sakya Monasteries, but it has fallen into disrepair.

Eventually, the white cairns along the summit ridge come into focus. The pass is the obvious notch in the ridge line. From the **Char-la** (4550m; N 29°07.000', E 088°49.850'), mountain ranges stretch to the west across the horizon and Ngor Monastery is visible directly below. Ngor is a 45-minute steep descent from the pass. The route from the Char-la descends the south side of a ravine that forms below it. Several trails cross the stream that flows from the pass and provide access to Ngor, but the first trail is the quickest route – it climbs the right side of the ravine and traverses directly to the monastery. Consider camping near Ngor or staying in the monastery's little guesthouse and save the last five hours of walking for the next day, when you're rested.

Sakya master Ngorchen Kunga Sangpo founded **Ngor Monastery** in 1429, giving rise to the Ngorpa suborder, a distinctive school of Buddhist thought. Once an important centre of learning, Ngor used to boast four monastic estates and 18 residential units inhabited by about 340 monks. Only a portion of the monastery has been rebuilt, but what is has is pleasing to behold. The largest structure is the assembly hall, called the Gonshung. The outer walls of its gallery are painted in vertical red, white and blue stripes, a characteristic decorative technique used by the Sakya order. The three colours represent the Rigsum Gonpo, the three most important bodhisattvas. The present head of Ngor, Luding Khenpo, resides in northern India.

STAGE 3: NGOR MONASTERY TO NARTANG MONASTERY
5-6 HOURS / 19KM / 410M DESCENT

From Ngor, a road runs down the valley that is now suitable for all types of vehicles. Fifteen minutes from the monastery is the sizable village of **Pero**. Ninety minutes from Ngor the valley and road bend to the north, while the old trade route to Sakya continues west over a saddle. Thirty minutes further, there is a copse at the edge of the flood plain that is good for fair-weather camping.

The road now swings to the west side of the wide alluvial valley and 30 minutes past the copse is the village of **Dzong Lugari** (3910m; N 29°08.171', E 088°45.741'). The road exits the north side of the village and extends northeast for 10km before joining the Lhatse–Shigatse Hwy 11km from Shigatse, just east of the 4914 road marker. The trail to Nartang Monastery, however, splits from the road on the northern outskirts of Dzong Lugari and heads north. From Dzong Lugari, it's at least a two-hour trek across a broad valley to **Nartang** (N 29°11.490', E 088°45.927').

The trail to Nartang crosses over a small stream and an electric utility line. The track tends to merge with a welter of agricultural trails and if you miss it, simply continue walking north. Soon the massive ramparts that surrounded the Nartang Monastery come into view. Just before arriving, cross the Lhatse–Shigatse Hwy, about 14km west of Shigatse. Donations are expected if you want to visit the chapels and famous printing presses at the **monastery**. There are several shops selling soft drinks and noodle soup on the roadside. It should be pretty easy to catch a ride from here to Shigatse.

Everest Base Camp to Tingri

Walking in the shadow of iconic Mt Everest provides a heady mix of solitude, wildlife sighting and physical challenge. Wild asses and gazelle thrive around the trail, and you might even get lucky and see a Tibetan brown bear rambling in the pastures.

If you are looking for an alternative exit route from Everest Base Camp, this trek to Tingri is an excellent choice. The route passes through an isolated valley on the way up to the Pang-la and then enters a region used by herders and their livestock. Following the Ra-chu Valley, the route swings northwards along a motorable track to the plains of Tingri. It's also possible to do this trek in the opposite direction. If you get tired of trekking along the road, you can always try to get a lift. Vehicles now regularly ply this route during summer.

If you do decide to trek into Everest from Tingri, it is possible to hire yaks, guides and even pony carts in Tingri. Animals and helpers can set you back as much as Y100 per head, but try your benevolent powers of persuasion to get the best deal possible.

The trekking season in the Everest region extends from April to late October. This is a difficult high-elevation region with altitudes ranging between 4400m and 5400m, and one high point is at the beginning of the trek! Careful preparation and the right gear are imperative. Subfreezing temperatures can occur even in summer at higher elevations and, conversely, hot gusty winds in May and June can make walking a sweaty experience. For well-equipped and seasoned walkers, winter treks to Everest Base Camp are often possible. Thanks to the rain shadow created by Mt Everest (Qomolangma) and its lofty neighbours, even the monsoon months are relatively dry in the region.

The trek via the Pang-la is the fastest route from Everest Base Camp to Tingri. Keep in mind, however, that once you leave

Rongphu Monastery there are no permanent settlements until well in reach of Tingri, three days away.

Be aware that expeditions beyond Base Camp are only for those very experienced in trekking and mountaineering. It's all too easy, once you have reached Base Camp, to succumb to the temptation to push further up the mountains. Do not do it without adequate preparation. At the very least, spend a couple of days acclimatising in the Rongphu area and doing day hikes to higher altitudes.

For highly fit and prepared groups, with the right permits from Lhasa, it's possible to trek beyond Base Camp as far as Camp III. Including time for acclimatising, you would need to allow at least one week for this trek. The route skirts the Rongphu Glacier until Camp I and then meets the East Rongphu Glacier at Camp II. This glacier must be crossed in order to reach Camp III (6340m). For detailed information on reaching the advanced camps, see Gary McCue's *Trekking in Tibet*.

Without the proper permits it is now virtually impossible to reach Everest. These days there are no fewer than six police and army checkpoints between Shekar and Base Camp.

For additional information relating to the Everest region, including the Everest Base Camp, see p155.

STAGE 1: EVEREST BASE CAMP TO BEYOND THE PANG-LA
9½ HOURS / 27KM / 550M ASCENT / 620M DESCENT

A walk between EBC and Rongphu takes about two hours, but it is hardly under-taken anymore as this stretch of the road has a steady stream of traffic. Setting out downstream from Rongphu along the road, the meadows soon recede as the valley narrows between boulder-strewn slopes. After 10km a trail angles down a steep embankment from the road to the bridge. Cross the bridge and look for the trail along the west bank of the river (4700 m; N 28°16.521', E 086°48.424'). Soon the trail starts to ascend the embankment and emerges onto a shelf above the Dza-chu. In a few minutes the trail climbs further and traverses around the base of a slope into the mouth of a side valley. It takes 30 minutes to reach the mouth of this valley from the bridge.

While the majority of the Dzaka Valley is dry and barren, this side valley is relatively luxuriant, hosting a variety of plants and shrubs, and plenty of fresh water. This is a nice place to camp or take a long lunch break. The valley bends to the west as the trail to Pang-la leaves the valley floor and climbs past a corral onto a plain abutting the north side of the valley. The route to the pass now bears west all the way to the summit, paralleling the valley floor. It's at least a 3½-hour hike to reach the pass.

As you begin your ascent towards the pass there is a saddle in the ridge bounding the northern side of the valley – this is the most direct route to the Zombuk Valley. Walk close to the ridge enclosing the northern side of the valley. Past the corral there is no trail. The route clambers over rock-strewn shrubby terrain and then over big plates of tundra that fit together like a giant jigsaw puzzle. About one hour from the corral, a steep slope blocks the view to the

---

EVEREST BASE CAMP TO TINGRI AT A GLANCE

Duration 3–4 days

Distance 70km

Difficulty medium to difficult

Start Everest Base Camp

Finish Tingri

Highest Point Pang-la (5350m)

Nearest Large Town Shigatse

Accommodation camping

Best Time to Trek early April to late October

Summary This is fine alpine trekking in the shadow of the legendary Mt Everest. See wild asses and other wildlife in the valleys and pastures along the way.

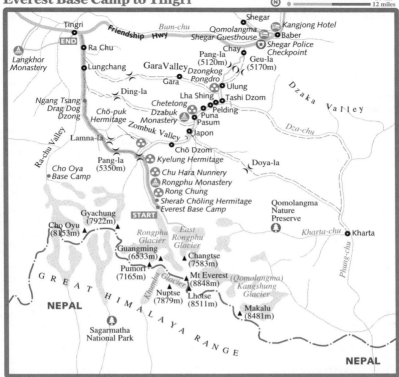

west. It takes 10 minutes to climb over this onto another broad tundra-covered pitch. In 10 more minutes you will be able to see the head of the valley; however, the Pang-la is out of sight, tucked behind the folds in the ridge.

The route gradually levels out and in 15 minutes descends into a marshy side valley. There is a small stream in this valley, the last place you can count on for water until well beyond the pass. Look for a small corral on the far side of the side valley and bear to the left of it. Continue walking upward for 10 minutes before gradually descending into the main valley floor in another 15 minutes.

Remain on the north side of the valley, taking the trail that steeply climbs towards the pass. The trail remains clear for 40 minutes until it's absorbed by the tussock grass of the valley floor. The pass is near where the ridge south of the valley bends around to the west. It is still 40 minutes from here

to the Pang-la over alpine meadows, but the terrain is now much more open and the gradient less steep.

Proceed west, looking out for the lowest point on the horizon. The **Pang-la** (5350m; N 28°18.194′, E 086°45.371′) is a very broad summit simply delineating the parting of drainage basins over a vast plain. There are a few small cairns on top of the pass, seen only when you are already upon them. Towards the west, and across a wide, wet, downhill slope, is a small valley and the Ra-chu Valley far beyond that. North of the Pang-la, with only a small summit in between, is the **Lamna-la** coming from the Zombuk Valley. This is the way that the road goes to reach the Ra-chu Valley.

Descend from the pass in a northwesterly direction over tussock grasses and tundra for one hour, and cross the road coming from the Lamna-la. If the time is right, you may see gazelles during your descent. From the road take a short cut along a precipitous slope to the valley floor. There are both springs and a stream in this swampy valley of grasses and wildflowers, a tributary of the Ra-chu. Great camp sites are found on the drier margins of the valley. It's at least a five-hour trek from here to the first village, Lungchang.

STAGE 2: BASE OF PANG-LA TO LUNGCHANG
5-6 HOURS / 21KM / 200M DESCENT

From the base of Pang-la the dirt road cutting across the ridge goes all the way to Tingri, making route-finding easy. In one hour the track passes through a narrow constriction in the valley formed by a series of **orange cliffs** (4830 m; N 28°21.243', E 086°40.318'). There are excellent camp sites here and plenty of fresh water. Beyond the cliffs the valley turns north and retains this bearing all the way to Tingri.

The view to the north is now dominated by the blue or purple Tsebu Mountains. Tingri is in front of these mountains, south of the Bum-chu. The road unfolds along the bank of the stream for 45 minutes. It then ascends above the bank and traverses the side of a ridge with the stream running through a narrow channel directly below. Look south to see the glittering white Cho Oyu massif. In 30 minutes descend into the widening valley floor. In 10 more minutes cross a small side valley.

The track unrolls over a level shelf above the stream for 30 minutes before climbing over a small ridge that circumvents the gorge below. Just upstream of the gorge, the stream you've been following from the base of the pass flows into the much higher-volume main branch of the Ra-chu. The summit of the ridge is marked with a cairn and prayer flags and takes 10 minutes to reach from the shelf.

From the summit, the track descends to cross a side valley before ranging across a long and barren stretch of valley. In the distance you can see two rocky knobs at the end of the long eastern ridge line. It takes about one hour to reach the knobs and the disintegrating walls of the long-abandoned fort known as **Ngang Tsang Drag Dog Dzong**. Thirty minutes after passing beneath the ramparts of the ancient fort you reach **Lungchang** (N 28°28.188', E 086°39.814'), which is the first permanent settlement since Rongphu. Simple meals and beds are usually available here with village families.

STAGE 3: LUNGCHANG TO TINGRI
3½ HOURS / 12KM / 150M DESCENT

From Lungchang, you can see several low-lying hills in the mouth of the Ra-chu Valley: Tingri is at the foot of the northernmost of these. It is easy to catch a ride in a horse cart or on a tractor from Lungchang to Tingri. From Lungchang, the road moves towards the middle of the valley, following a bluff along the edge of the Ra-chu. In 1½ hours it reaches the outskirts of the **Ra Chu** village. Before the village, at a white shrine, the track splits: the south (or main) branch goes to Tingri via Ra Chu village, while the other jogs west and then north over wide pastures to Tingri. The left fork is the shorter route and is a more pleasant walk. The lower part of the Ra-chu Valley is green during the warmer half of the year; extensive meadows support flocks of goats and sheep.

Fifteen minutes south of Ra Chu you will pass ruins on the slopes bounding the east side of the valley – look back to see Everest rise up from behind the anterior ranges. The two tracks that split near Ra Chu are reunited 45 minutes beyond the village.

Thirty minutes further on, you reach a bridge over the Ra-chu, which allows you to access the south side of Tingri. You can cross the Ra-chu here and pass through the village to the highway or remain on the east bank and cross the new highway bridge. It's only 15 minutes to the highway.

Mt Kailash Kora

The age-old pilgrims' path around Mt Kailash is one of the world's great pilgrimages, completely encircling Asia's holiest mountain. With a 5630m pass to conquer, this kora is a test of both the mind and the spirit.

There's some gorgeous mountain scenery along this trek, including close-ups of the majestic pyramidal Mt Kailash, but just as rewarding is the chance to see and meet your fellow pilgrims, many of whom have travelled hundreds of kilometres on foot to get here. Apart from local Tibetans, there are normally dozens of Hindus on the kora during the main pilgrim season (June to September), normally on horseback, with yak teams carrying their supplies.

MT KAILASH KORA AT A GLANCE

Duration 3 days

Distance 52km

Difficulty medium to difficult

Start/Finish Darchen

Highest Point Drölma-la (5630m)

Nearest Large Town Ali

Accommodation camping or monastery guesthouses

Best Time to Trek mid-May until mid-October

Summary The circuit, or kora, of Mt Kailash (6714m) is one of the most important pilgrimages in Asia. It's been a religious sanctuary since pre-Buddhist times, and a trek here wonderfully integrates the spiritual, cultural and physical dimensions of a trip to Tibet. Being able to meet pilgrims from across Tibet and other countries is another allure.

The route around Mt Kailash is a simple one: you start by crossing a plain, then head up a wide river valley, climb up and over the 5630m Drölma-la, head down another river valley, and finally cross the original plain to the starting point. It's so straightforward, and so perfect a natural circuit, it's easy to see how it has been a pilgrim's favourite for thousands of years.

The Mt Kailash trekking season runs from mid-May until mid-October but trekkers should always be prepared for changeable weather. Snow may be encountered on the Drölma-la at any time of year and the temperature will often drop well below freezing at night. The pass tends to be snowed in from early November to early April.

The kora is getting more and more popular (and there's litter everywhere to prove it). A tent and your own food is recommended, although there is now accommodation and simple food at Dira-puk and Zutul-puk. Bottled water, instant noodles and snacks are available every few hours at nomad tents. Natural water sources abound.

Horses, yaks and porters are all available for hire in Darchen, the gateway town to the kora. Big groups often hire yaks to carry their supplies but yaks will only travel in pairs or herds, so you have to hire at least two. Horses are an easier option but are surprisingly expensive because they are in great demand by Indian pilgrims. Most hikers carry their own gear or get by with the services of a local porter for Y100 to Y120 a day. Guesthouse owners can normally help

put you in touch with porters and guides. See p176 for details on Darchen and for suggestions of nearby warm-up hikes.

STAGE 1: DARCHEN TO DIRA-PUK MONASTERY
6 HOURS / 20KM / 200M ASCENT

The kora path begins rather obviously on the western edge of Darchen. Quickly leaving all traces of the village behind, you head westward across the Barkha plain, a sandy expanse speckled with greenery like a massive camouflage jacket. To the north, the east–west ridge blocks your view of Mt Kailash, but to the southeast are clear views of huge Gurla Mandata (7728m). Api and other peaks in Nepal are visible to the south, while look to the southwest for the twin, sharp humps of Kamet (7756m) in India.

Only 4km from Darchen the trail climbs up over the southwest end of the ridge to reach a **cairn** at 4790m. The cairn is bedecked with prayer flags and marks the first views of Mt Kailash's southern or lapis lazuli face and a *chaktsal gang,* the first of the kora's four prostration points.

Very quickly the trail bends round to the north and enters the barren Lha-chu Valley. From here on, the narrow Lha-chu River provides a steady supply of water all the way to Dira-puk Monastery. For the best water, however, look for the occasional side-stream flowing down from the cliffs.

The valley is so open at this point you can see ahead to the tall Tarboche flag-pole (4750m) in the distance. The Tarboche area is one of the most significant sites for Tibet's most important festival, Saga Dawa,

when hundreds of pilgrims clamour to watch the annual raising of the flagpole. The pole was first erected in 1681 during the reign of the fifth Dalai Lama to commemorate a military victory over Ladakh.

Just west of Tarboche is the 'two-legged' **Chörten Kangnyi**. It's an auspicious act for pilgrims to walk through the small chörten's archway. A short climb above Tarboche to the east is the sky-burial site of the 84 *mahasiddhas* (Tantric practitioners who reached a high level of awareness). The site is revered, as it was once reserved for monks and lamas, but is no longer used: too few birds these days and too many wild dogs (it's wise not to hike alone). The first of the kora's three Buddha footprints is here, but it's hard to find. The views of the valley are superb from here.

Beyond Tarboche the valley narrows dramatically at an area called Sershong. You can begin to get clear shots of Mt Kai-

lash now, standing to attention above the eastern ridge. After passing a series of ruined chörtens and a number of long mani (prayer) walls, the trail reaches a small bridge across the Lha-chu at 4710m. The bridge is less than an hour's walk from Tarboche, about 2½ hours from Darchen, and is directly below Chuku Monastery. Most Indian pilgrims begin their kora here, so there's lots of loading and unloading of 4WDs, horses and yaks.

Chuku Monastery (4820m), founded in the 13th century by Götsangpa Gompo Pel, a Kagyupa-order master, is perched high above the valley floor on the hillside to the west. It blends so secretively into its rocky background you may not even notice it's there. All Mt Kailash monasteries were wrecked during the Cultural Revolution and the Chuku (or Nyenri) Monastery was the first to be rebuilt. Inside look for a glass case over the altar: there's a highly revered marble statue called Chuku Opame (originally from India and reputed to talk) inside and a conch shell inlaid with silver. Beside the altar there's a copper pot and elephant tusks, the latter a leftover from when Bhutan exerted religious control over the monasteries around Kailash.

From the Chuku bridge there are alternative trails along the east and west banks of the river. Either way it's about three hours to Dira-puk Monastery. The trail along the eastern bank is the regular pilgrim route, but on the western trail there are some fine grassy camp sites at **Damding Donkhang** (4890m), about an hour before the monastery. The west or ruby face of Mt Kailash makes a dramatic backdrop to this camp site and in the early morning Tibetan pilgrims can be seen striding past on the other side of the river, already well into their one-day circuit.

Be aware, though, that walking on the western side may require crossing the side streams that flow into the Lha-chu. Even in early summer these can be waist high. Wear socks or rubber sandals when you cross; it helps on the slippery rocks.

Take your time between Chuku Monastery and Dira-puk Monastery as this stretch has some of the best scenery of the entire kora. High sedimentary faces, wonderfully puckered and dented, and chiselled into shapes that seem alive, hem you in on both sides. When the weather is warmer there's even the occasional ribbon of water tumbling down the slopes from hundreds of metres high.

Many of the formations along the way have mythical connections, with a number of them related to Tibet's legendary hero Gesar of Ling – but you're unlikely to find them without a guide. Along the eastern route, however, you will have no problem finding the **second prostration point** (N 31°04.430', E 081°16.942'), with its prayer flags and clear view of the east side of Mt Kailash. Thirty minutes later, just past a tea tent selling the usual drinks and snacks, look for the second Buddha footprint, and a **carving** (N 31°05.126', E 081°17.264') of the god Tamdrin, a wrathful horse-headed deity, on a black stone smeared with aeons of yak butter.

From the rock, the trail starts to climb and heads northeast toward Dira-puk Monastery. Cross the bridge to head directly to the monastery or continue straight ahead for the main trail. Eventually you'll spot a couple of buildings. To the right is the old **Indian guesthouse** (dm Y50), a series of simple stone dormitory rooms with a cosy tented teahouse and several shops. Below and to the left is the huge new **Shishapangma Guesthouse** (西夏邦马宾馆; Xīxiàbāngmǎ Bīnguǎn; r per bed Y80), a two-storey concrete guesthouse boasting real beds and real toilets. The third and quietest option is a bed in the **Monastery Guesthouse** (dm

ESSENTIAL CONSIDERATIONS FOR WALKING AROUND MT KAILASH

There are several important questions to consider when planning to walk the 52km Mt Kailash circuit. Firstly, will you be walking the mountain in a clockwise or anticlockwise direction? Hindus, Jains and Buddhists go clockwise, but followers of Bön (the native religion of Tibet) anticlockwise.

If you're a Tibetan, you'll probably plan to complete the circuit in one hard day's slog. Achieving this feat requires a predawn start and a late-afternoon return to Darchen. Otherwise plan on a comfortable three days around the holy mountain. Some very devout Tibetans make the round much more difficult by prostrating themselves the entire way. Count on around three weeks to complete a kora in this manner and be sure to wear knee padding and thick gloves.

It is said by Tibetans that circling the mountain once will wipe out the sins of a lifetime, while 108 circuits guarantees instant nirvana. Cost-cutters should note that koras completed during a full moon or in the Tibetan Year of the Horse are more beneficial than ordinary ones.

Assuming you're not a Buddhist, Bönpo or Hindu, the promise of liberation may not grab you no matter how caught up in the moment you are. And yet, many foreigners go truly expecting to experience something holy or profound. This is a little like wanting to fall in love. But why not?

THE FACES & RIVERS OF MT KAILASH

On a mystical level, Tibetans identify Mt Kailash with the mythical world mountain known as Meru, which reaches from the lowest hell to the highest heaven. According to ancient tradition, four rivers flow down the flanks of Kailash. While no major river really issues from this mountain, four do begin within just 100km of it.

DIRECTION	FACE	MYTHICAL RIVER	REAL RIVER
south	lapis lazuli	Mabja Kambab (Peacock Fountain)	Karnali
west	ruby	Langchen Kambab (Elephant Fountain)	Sutlej
north	gold	Sengge Kambab (Lion Fountain)	Indus
east	crystal	Tamchog Kambab (Horse Fountain)	Yarlung Tsangpo (Brahmaputra)

Y50), though food here is limited to instant noodles.

If you're camping, head for the grassy flats below the monastery or the northern valley (that leads to the source of the Indus River) east of the monastery.

Dira-puk (Lhalung Dira) Monastery (5080m) sits in a superb location on the hillside north of the Lha-chu across from the Shishapangma Guesthouse. It directly faces the astonishing north face of Mt Kailash, which from this angle appears as a massive, jet-black slab of granite ornamented with alabaster-white stripes of snow. Three lesser mountains are arrayed in front of Mt Kailash: Chana Dorje (Vajrapani) to the west, Jampelyang (Manjushri) to the east and Chenresig (Avalokiteshvara) in the centre, but there's no doubting who is the superstar in this band.

Dira-puk Monastery takes its name from the words *dira* (meaning 'female yak horn') and *puk* ('cave') – this is where the Bön warrior god king Gekho tossed boulders around with his horns. The great saint Götsangpa, who opened up the kora route around Mt Kailash, was led this far by a yak that turned out to be the lion-faced goddess Dakini (Khandroma), who guards the Khando Sanglam-la. Colourful murals mark the entry to Götsangpa's atmospheric meditation cave. The monastery was rebuilt in 1985.

To get to the monastery, cross the bridge just north of the Shishapangma Hotel and then cross the river on stones or head to the bridge further upstream – a trying ordeal at the end of a long day.

If you have the time, consider walking up to the **Kangkyam Glacier** that descends from the sheer north face of Mt Kailash. It takes about two hours there and back and you feel you're getting so close to the peak that you could touch it.

STAGE 2: DIRA-PUK MONASTERY TO ZUTUL-PUK MONASTERY
7-8 HOURS / 18KM / 550M ASCENT / 600M DESCENT

No doubt when you wake in the morning and step outside you'll want to revel in the glory of your surroundings. Mt Kailash's dramatic black face dominates the skyline, while the middle slopes echo with the moans of yak teams complaining as drivers load them with the day's supplies.

The main kora path heads off to the east, crossing the Lha-chu by bridge and then climbs on to a moraine to meet the trail on the east bank. The long ascent up the Drölma-chu Valley that will eventually lead to the Drölma-la has begun. Bring water to last a few hours.

Less than an hour along is the meadow at **Jarok Donkhang** (5210m), where some trekking groups set up camp. It's not wise to camp any higher up than here because of the risk of problems with altitude.

Near Jarok Donkhang a trail branches off to the southeast, leading over the snow-covered Khando Sanglam-la. This shortcut to the east side of Mt Kailash bypasses the normal route over the Drölma-la, but only those on their auspicious 13th kora may use it. That lion-faced goddess Dakini, who led Götsangpa to Dira-puk, makes sure of that.

Also nearby, another **glacier** descends from the east ridge off the north face of Mt Kailash, down through the Pölung Valley between Chenresig (Avalokiteshvara) and Jampelyang (Manjushri). This glacier can be reached in a return trip of a couple of hours from Jarok Donkhang. You can follow the glacial stream that runs down the middle of the valley to merge with the Drölma-chu, or you can avoid losing altitude from Jarok Donkhang by terracing around the side of Jampelyang.

Only a short distance above Jarok Donkhang, about two hours from the day's starting point, is the rocky expanse of **Shiva-tsal** (5330m; N 31°05.795', E 081°20.856'). Pilgrims are supposed to undergo a symbolic death at this point, entering in the realm of the Lord of the Dead, until they reach the top of the Drölma-la and are reborn again. It is customary to leave something behind at Shiva-tsal – an item of clothing, a drop of blood or a lock of hair – to represent the act of leaving this life behind.

After Shiva-tsal the trail mercifully flattens for a time and proceeds along a glacial ridge. There are a number of interesting sights ahead, such as the sin-testing stone of **Bardo Trang** (a flat boulder that pilgrims are supposed to squeeze under to measure their sinfulness), but even your guide may not know where they are.

About 30 minutes from Shiva-tsal the trail turns eastward for the final ascent. The saddle is fairly dull looking, just a long slope of boulders and scree, but there are some stark, jagged peaks to the right. Look south for your last glimpse of the north face of Mt Kailash, since there are no views of the mountain from the pass.

Allow around an hour for the 200m climb to the top of the **Drölma-la** (5640m; N 31°05.719', E 081°22.204'). The trail disappears at times, merging with glacial streams in summer, but the way up, up, up is obvious. Take your time. Let the children and old women pass you, and if you can't go more than a few metres at a time, then don't.

After a few false summits, the rocky pass is reached. The great cubic **Drölma Do** (Drölma's Rock) that marks the top is barely visible behind an enormous number of prayer flags. Pilgrims perform a circumambulation nonetheless, pasting money onto the rock with yak butter, and stooping to pass under the lines of prayer flags and add a new string or two to the collection. They also chant the Tibetan pass-crossing mantra, *'ki ki so so, lha gyalo'* (*'ki ki so so'* being the empowerment and happiness invocation, *'lha gyalo'* meaning 'the gods are victorious'). They have now been reborn, and, by the mercy and compassion of Drölma, their sins have been forgiven.

The tale associated with the revered Drölma Do is worth telling. When Götsangpa pioneered the kora and wandered into the valley of Dakini (Khandroma), he was led back to the correct route by 21 wolves that were, of course, merely 21 emanations of Drölma (Tara), the goddess of mercy and protector of the pass. Reaching the pass, the 21 wolves merged into one and then merged again into the great boulder. To this day Drölma helps worthy pilgrims on the difficult ascent.

Weather permitting, most pilgrims and trekkers pause at the pass for a rest and refreshments before starting the steep descent. Almost immediately, **Gauri Kund** (5608m; the Tibetan name Tukje Chenpo translates as 'Lake of Compassion') comes into view below. Hindu pilgrims are supposed to immerse themselves in the lake's green waters, breaking the ice if necessary, but few actually do.

It takes approximately an hour to make the long and steep 400m descent to the grassy banks of the Lham-chu Khir. You may have to cross snowfields at first, sometimes leaping across streams that have cut through the valley floor, but later the trail turns dry, and rocky. Walking sticks are useful here.

En route there is a much-revered footprint of Milarepa, though again, spotting it on your own is difficult. When the trail reaches the valley, you may find nomad tents and a teahouse selling drinks and noodles. A huge rock topped by the kora's third **Buddha footprint** stands nearby (5245m).

As with the Lha-chu Valley on the western side of Mt Kailash, there are routes that follow both sides of the river. The eastern bank trail presents better views and there's less marshy ground, but it requires crossing the river by boulder hopping, and later recrossing by wading into the river itself (which may be quite deep during the wetter months).

About 30 minutes south, a valley comes down from the Khando Sanglam-la to join the western trail. This valley provides the only glimpse of Mt Kailash's eastern or crystal face. The kora's third prostration point is at the valley mouth, but it's easy

All around Mount Kailash there are signs of a legendary contest for control that involved Milarepa, the Buddhist poet-saint, and Naro Bönchung, the Bön master. According to the Buddhists, Milarepa came out the victor in all the various challenges, but despite this Naro Bönchung still argued for a final, winner-takes-all duel: a straightforward race to the top of the mountain.

Mounting his magic drum, Naro Bönchung immediately set out to fly to the summit. Unperturbed by the progress made by his rival, Milarepa rose from his bed at dawn and was carried by a ray of light directly to the summit. Shocked by this feat, Naro Bönchung tumbled off his drum, which skittered down the south face of the mountain, gouging the long slash marking Mt Kailash to this day. Gracious in victory, Milarepa decreed that Bön followers could continue to make their customary anticlockwise circuits of Mt Kailash, and awarded them Bönri as their own holy mountain.

to miss this point if you're walking on the eastern bank.

Grassy fields start to appear alongside the river, affording those with tents endless spots to set up camp. A couple of hours from the third Buddha footprint a side valley enters from the left. From here on the river changes name to the Dzong-chu, translated as 'Fortress River'. Soon afterwards you'll likely see a neat line of tents set up for one of the Indian pilgrim groups. Trekkers can often stay here if there's space.

Ten minutes from the Indian camp is **Zutul-puk Monastery** (4820m). The *zutul phuk* (miracle cave) that gives the monastery its name is at the back of the main hall. As the story goes, Milarepa and Naro Bönchung were looking for shelter from the rain. They decided to build a cave together, but Milarepa put the roof in place without waiting for Naro Bönchung to make the walls (thus once again showing the supremacy of Buddhism). Milarepa then made a couple adjustments to the cave, which left a footprint and handprint that can still be seen today.

The monastery has a simple **guesthouse** (beds Y50), but the half-dozen rooms sometimes get booked out by Indian groups. The area around the monastery is also littered with rubbish mounting with every pilgrim season.

STAGE 3: ZUTUL-PUK MONASTERY TO DARCHEN
3-4 HOURS / 14KM / 150M DESCENT

From the monastery the trail follows the river closely for an hour or so then climbs above the river and enters the lovely Gold & Red Cliffs, a narrow canyon whose walls are stained purple, cobalt and rust.

When the canyon narrows look for holes gouged into the cliff walls. These are not natural but made by pilgrims looking for holy stones. Also look for prayer flags festooned across the river, and in the far distance the blue waters of the lake Raksas Tal.

Where the trail emerges onto the Barkha plain, close to the fourth prostration point (4700m), Gurla Mandata is again visible in the distance. It's now an easy one-hour walk back to Darchen along a dirt road. While not a very scenic stretch of the kora, the steady ground below does allow you to drift off and reflect on the past three days.

Nyenchen Tanglha Traverse

This is a fabulous trek for those who want to see the ecological mosaic of northern Tibet in all its splendour. Close encounters with the *drokpa,* the seminomadic shepherds of the region with their ancient customs and traditions, enliven the trail. Herds of blue sheep live in the crags and in the woodlands the endangered musk deer makes its home.

The trek begins on the main road to the Nam-tso, 5km beyond the Damxung–Lhasa Hwy turn-off. The trail cuts across the mighty Nyenchen Tanglha range and heads directly for Tashi Dor, the celebrated headland on the southeast shore of Nam-tso. From Tashi Dor there is an almost constant stream of Lhasa-bound vehicles, making prospects for a ride back easy. For further information on accessing Damxung and Tashi Dor, see p103.

The route leaves the Damxung valley and wends its way through a rocky defile, the gateway to a high-elevation forest in which dwarf willow and rhododendron are dominant species. A number of stream crossings await you. A tundra-filled upper valley gradually climbs to the Kyang-la (Onager pass), followed by a steep descent onto the Changtang plains. Fantastic views of sparkling Nam-tso and Tashi Dor are visible from many vantage points on the trail. And colourful *drokpa* camps dot the way.

The best time to make the Nyenchen Tanglha traverse is from May to October. A winter crossing is also sometimes possible but don't attempt one unless you have the green light from local residents. This is a very high elevation trek with a 5330m pass and minimum elevations of 4310m, so factor in plenty of time for acclimatising. It's prudent to spend two nights in Damxung before setting out. You will have to be fully equipped with a tent and stove and enough food to reach Tashi Dor, three days away. Temperatures even in the summer regularly dip below freezing and gale force winds are common.

Horses and guides should be available in the villages near the trailhead for Y60 to Y90 apiece per day. In June when locals are out collecting caterpillar fungus (see the box, p294), horses may be hard to get. If you're not successful in the nearby villages of Nakya or Baga Ara, try Nya Do, Largen Do or Tren Do, which are a little further afield but larger in size.

STAGE 1: NAKYA TO THE TREELINE
5 HOURS / 18KM / 480M ASCENT

This trail sets off from villages outside Damxung and makes a beeline directly into the Kyang Valley. From the turn-off for Nam-tso at Damxung proceed along the black-top road 4.5km to the village of Nakya or 6km to Baga Ara. In both villages there are motorable tracks that head northwest over a plain entering the narrow mouth of the Kyang Valley in just over 2km. Perched 50m above the northeast side of the valley is Kyang-rag Monastery (4370; N 30°31.694′, E 091°05.759′).

All the way to the Kyang-la the valley runs in a northwest direction. From Kyang-rag remain on the east side of the valley heading upstream. Along the narrow valley floor are plenty of small places to camp. About one hour from Kyang-rag Monastery ford the crystal waters of the Kyang-chu to the west side of the valley and enter a narrow rocky gorge. The gorge coincides with the high mountains that close in around the Kyang-chu. Five more fords await, so it's a good idea to bring canvas tennis shoes or rubber sandals especially dedicated to this purpose. A walking stick is also very helpful. The Kyang-chu is a fairly shallow stream but with a swift current, so make sure your legs are up to the task.

The trail is clear and easy to follow. In 10 minutes it crosses to the east side of the valley. There are rocks but these may be slippery and it's safer to get your feet wet. Within half an hour the trail crosses the river four more times, breaking out of the gorge at the last ford and landing on the east side of the valley.

The valley is now a little more open and the west slopes quite heavily forested. The trail remains in the valley bottom or along the east edge of the slope. There are a number of places to camp provided they are not already occupied by the *drokpa* shepherds. In two or 2½ hours, reaching the treeline,

KYANG-RAG

It is said that the 6th Panchen Lama, Palden Yeshe (1738–80), and his retinue once camped along the Kyang-chu. One day a *kyang* (wild ass) wandered into camp and entered the tent used by him in his religious practice. The Panchen Lama tossed a sack containing sacrificial cakes on the back of the wild ass. The *kyang* exited the tent, wandered to the other side of the river and disappeared into a cliff. Curious, Palden Yeshe went in pursuit of the *kyang* and reached the cliff where it was last seen. Here he found an old monk who had covered the very spot with his cloak. The Panchen Lama demanded to know what was going on and pulled off the cloak. Immediately his nose began to bleed. Taking this as a mystic sign, he used the blood to paint an image of Palden Lhamo on the rocks. This site became the inner sanctum of Kyang-rag Monastery. As it turned out the *kyang* was no ordinary animal but a local deity and the mount of the great goddess Palden Lhamo. For that reason the place became known as Kyang-rag (Wild Ass Beheld).

the trail skips over stones to the west side of the valley (4790m; N 30°34.662', E 91°02.350'). There are a number of excellent camp sites in the vicinity.

STAGE 2: TREELINE TO KYANG DO
8-9 HOURS / 25KM / 540M ASCENT / 490M DESCENT

Twenty minutes up the valley **springs** gush out of the base of a cliff. In about 200m the trail returns to the east side of the valley where it remains until the pass crossing. There are good camping sites on both sides of the stream ford. Now the valley becomes more sinuous and somewhat steeper. The trail enters the tundra zone and becomes faint in places. Stay in the valley floor and head upstream. In around 45 minutes enter a long, wide section of the valley gravitating towards its east flank. You will need at least 1½ hours to trek over this stretch of the valley. High peaks of the Nyenchen Tanglha range tower above your line of travel.

Above this point you're not likely to find any more *drokpa* camps until well after the Kyang-la, but there are quite a few places to set up your tent should you decide to tarry in the flower-spangled meadows. Further up the valley narrows a little and becomes steeper. The trail is still near the east edge of the valley but hardly visible in places. In 1½ hours ascend the broad shelf east of the valley. It's only about 10m higher than the valley floor. In the vicinity the Kyang-chu forks: the larger branch flows down from the southwest originating in a group of dark-coloured rocky peaks. The smaller branch cascades down from the pass in the northwest. This is the last place to collect

water until after the pass. Paralleling the smaller branch of the stream the trail heads in a northwest and then westerly direction to meet the base of the Kyang-la (5240m; N 30°37.522', E 090°58.080') in about 45 minutes.

Climb up to a higher and narrower bench continuing in a westerly direction. The way is moderately steep. Soon a line of brown cairns come into view. These mark the broad saddle rising to the Kyang-la. Continue up walking parallel to these cairns. The high point is **Kyang-la** (5330m; N 30°37.700', E 090°57.320'), about a 45-minute hike from the base of the pass.

It's only about a 30m descent to the head of the valley on the Changtang side of the pass. This valley is also known as Kyang. Good drinking water is had here – fill up because water can be scarce down valley. The valley now bends to the north, the direction it takes all the way down to the Nam-tso basin. Soon the great lake in all its glory comes into view. The eastern tip of Tashi Dor and a long headland jutting deep into the lake, bright gems on a scintillating cobalt-blue surface, are clearly visible.

Stay on the east side of the valley. In a few minutes the trail leaves the valley and steeply descends through rocky slopes, followed by grassy slopes. In about 45 minutes you reach the **valley floor** (5120m; N 30°38.505', E 090°56.954'). Note that the Kyang-chu on this side of the pass is much smaller and prone to disappear underground in places.

The trail soon crosses to the west side of the valley before returning to the east side

---

NYENCHEN TANGLHA TRAVERSE AT A GLANCE

Duration 3 days

Distance 60km

Difficulty moderate to demanding

Start Damxung

Finish Tashi Dor

Highest Point Kyang-la (5330m)

Nearest Large Town Damxung

Accommodation camping

Best Time to Trek May to October

Summary Passing through gorges, forested slopes, alpine meadows and the plains of the Changtang, this is a great walk for those interested in the ecological diversity of northern Tibet.

in only five minutes. The trail traces the east edge of the valley. In 45 minutes the magnificent Tashi Dor comes into full view. In 20 minutes recross to the west side of the stream and point your feet downstream. The terrain is quite gentle and Nam-tso is your constant companion, so going cross-country is easy and fun. The valley is wide open and in 30 minutes there are many excellent camps by the stream at **Kyang Do**.

STAGE 3: KYANG DO TO TASHI DOR
4-5 HOURS / 17KM / 80M DESCENT

A tawny-coloured hill appears in the distance. Leave the valley and skirt its west side by walking across the plain. The base of this hill is reached in approximately one hour. Do not make the mistake of staying in the valley floor, although this may seem the best route. Further down swampy ground would come between you and Tashi Dor. After walking around the base of the tawny hill look for a complex of mainly white buildings to the north. Hike directly to it in about one hour. This complex at the base of the Tashi Dor headland is part of its management apparatus.

The tourist centre of **Tashi Dor** (4730m; N 30°46.652', E 090°52.243') is still 8km away on a black-top road. It should be easy should you want to hitch a ride from there.

MORE TREKS

Lake Manasarovar Kora

Although there is now a road all the way around Lake Manasarovar (4575m), this is still a very lovely walk. Fortunately, the road can be avoided for much of the 110km mostly level route. Lake Manasarovar reflects the most lucid shades of blue imaginable. It represents the female or wisdom aspect of enlightenment and is a symbol of good

Lake Manasarovar Kora

fortune and fertility, explaining why Tibetans are always very eager to circumambulate it. There are five Buddhist monasteries along the way. Public buses now ply the north side of the lake. Horses and guides can be hired in Hor Qu and at Chiu Monastery, the town on the northeastern side of the lake. Expect to pay at least Y100 per day for each.

Due to the elevation (averaging 4600m) this is a moderately difficult trek. May, June and September are the best months for the four- or five-day trek; July and August are also good, save for the hordes of gnats that infest the shores. A tent and stove are required and you should be prepared for any kind of weather at any time.

The best place to start the walk is at **Chiu Monastery** on the northwest corner of the lake. Go in either a clockwise or counter-clockwise direction, depending on whether you more closely relate to the Buddhists and Hindus or the Bönpos. If walking in a clockwise direction you will reach **Langbona Monastery** in about

four hours. From Langbona, the pilgrims trail cuts inland to avoid lagoons that form along the north shore of Manasarovar. Look for cairns, prayer flags and other signs of pilgrim activity that herald the way. Do not make the mistake of hugging the lakeshore unless you are up for an icy-cold swim or have a raft in tow. It's about four hours from Langbona to Hor Qu.

Seralung Monastery, on the east side of Lake Manasarovar, is approximately three hours beyond Hor Qu and a good place to camp and experience Tibetan religious life. Four or five more hours brings you to **Trugo Monastery** on the southern flank of the lake. Camp well away from the monastery to avoid the hordes of Indian pilgrims that have become a regular feature of the pilgrim scene in recent years. You can make it back to Chiu Monastery via Gossul Monastery in nine to 10 hours of walking from Trugo Monastery. On either side of Gossul Monastery are caves where one can shelter and get a feel for the meditator's way of life that once ruled in Tibet.

Everest East Face

Follow a river conduit breaching the Himalaya to the spectacular forested east flank of Mt Everest. Small lakes and fantastic camping make this a most attractive trek, but route finding is demanding and the terrain difficult so consider a local guide. Drive to **Kharta**, with its alpine hamlets, some 90km from Shegar on the Friendship Hwy. Budget at least 10 days for the trek. There are two main passes accessing the east or Kangshung side of Everest: **Langma-la** (5330m) and **Shao-la** (5030m). The huge **Kangchung glacier** reposes on the west end of the Karma Valley. For detailed information, see *Tibet Handbook* by Victor Chan and *Trekking in Tibet* by Gary McCue.

Gateway Cities

Includes »

Kathmandu. 262
Chéngdū 265

Best Places to Stay Kathmandu

» Hotel Ganesh Himal (p264)

» Kantipur Temple House (p264)

» Kathmandu Guest House (p264)

Best Places to Stay Chéngdū

» Sim's Cozy Garden Hostel (p265)

» Traffic Inn (p265)

» Loft (p266)

Which City?

Given the complicated logistics of getting into Tibet, it's advisable to at least overnight in a gateway city en route to Lhasa, either to pick up your TTB permit, meet up with your fellow travellers or to buffer potential delays in your international flights. Most travellers reach Lhasa from Chéngdū or Kathmandu, though it's equally feasible to fly or train in from Běijīng, Xīníng, Guǎngzhōu or a half-dozen other Chinese cities.

Kathmandu

Crowded, colourful and chaotic Kathmandu has been a popular destination for travellers since the Hippy Trail in the '60s and '70s, but there are a couple of drawbacks to entering Tibet from here. Prime among these is the time needed to get a Chinese visa (group visas only; see p346) and the hassle that this group visa brings if you plan to travel onwards inside China. However, if you're looking for a cheap overland tour to Lhasa (or even Mt Kailash) and plan to return to Nepal, it's a fairly good choice. It's also a great way to end a trip to Tibet.

Chéngdū

Sìchuān's huge capital city has long been the main logistical gateway to Tibet. With ever-increasing international air connections and excellent hostels well used to helping travellers headed to Tibet, it's still a logical choice (unless you want to travel by train, then Xīníng is better). It's also a great starting point for overland trips to Lhasa or into the ethnically Tibetan areas of western Sìchuān.

KATHMANDU

♪ 01 / POP 822,000 / ELEV 1300M

Kathmandu is a fascinating, sometimes maddening city that seems to straddle both the 15th and 20th centuries. Most people head straight for the Thamel district, a travellers' mecca and the place to get a yak steak, buy a cut-priced down jacket, shop for Buddhas or hard-to-find books on Tibet. But it's also a bit of a zoo, with too many vehicles, Tiger-balm pedlars and trekking touts all sharing the same narrow, footpath-less roads. A few days here is plenty. For more info, see Lonely Planet's *Nepal* guide.

During the June to August monsoon season (when most visitors travel to or from Tibet) it is usually humid and rainy in Kathmandu.

Dangers & Annoyances

Public disturbances have been standard in Nepal for years now and can turn ugly. Check news reports and your own country's travel warnings for the current situation.

City-wide strikes *(bandh)* occasionally paralyse the city, shutting down businesses and making transport and getting to the airport difficult. The Nepal Tourism Board often runs tourist buses to the airport at this time, or ask your hotel whether taxis can run to the airport.

Kathmandu is currently plagued by power strikes lasting up to 16 hours a day – choose a hotel with a generator (and a room at the other end of the building). Congestion and pollution are crippling problems in Kathmandu and many people wear a face mask when moving around town.

◉ Sights

Durbar Square   SQUARE
(admission Rs 200) Kathmandu's royal collection of Newari-styled buildings has been designated a World Heritage Site. An early morning walk here through the maze-like

Central Kathmandu

alleys of the medieval old town is one of Kathmandu's highlights.

Durbar Square (Patan)
SQUARE

(admission Rs 200) The nearby city of Patan (really a suburb of Kathmandu) has its own Durbar Square, which has equally impressive architecture, as well as the wonderful **Patan Museum** (admission Rs 250; ⊙10.30am-4.30pm), with an outstanding collection of Hindu and Buddhist art. The detailed English text is a fantastic primer on the iconography of the two religions and especially useful for those planning to visit a lot of monasteries in Tibet. Patan is south of Thamel, about a 20-minute taxi ride (Rs 200).

Swayambhunath
STUPA

(admission Rs 75) To the west of central Kathmandu, a short taxi ride (Rs 150) or 30-

minute walk is the great Buddhist stupa also known as the Monkey Temple, whose iconic all-seeing eyes offer fine views over the city.

Bodhnath
STUPA

East of Kathmandu is the huge Tibetan chörten at Bodhnath (Boudha), which serves as a focus for the exiled Tibetan community. Here you'll find Tibetan hotels, restaurants and half a dozen monasteries, as well as places to learn Tibetan. Come at dusk to join the local Tibetans on a ritual kora or base yourself here as a quieter alternative to Thamel. Bodhnath is a 6km taxi ride (Rs 200) from Thamel.

Pashupatinath
HINDU TEMPLE

(admission Rs 250) Set along the *ghats* (steps) of the Bagmati River, Pashupatinath is a major cremation site, and the most sacred Hindu site in Kathmandu. Hindu cremations are visible here, but show sensitivity when observing and don't take photos. A taxi costs around Rs 150.

☞ Tours

Several agencies in Thamel offer seven-day budget tours to Tibet (US$350; most leave Tuesday, Thursday and Saturday) which are the cheapest way to see Tibet from Nepal. Regardless of who you book with, at the border everyone ends up on the same bus. See p353 for details of the seven-day trip. Other options include five-day, fly-in and fly-out tours to Lhasa. The following agencies offer tours to Tibet.

Eco Trek
TRAVEL AGENCY

(☏4423207; www.ecotrek.com.np, www.eco treknepal.com; Thamel) Seven-day overland trips, plus tours to Kailash, the latter in conjunction with Indian pilgrim groups.

Green Hill Tours
TRAVEL AGENCY

(☏4700803; www.greenhill-tours.com; Thamel)

Royal Mount Trekking
TRAVEL AGENCY

(☏4241452; www.royaltibet.com; Durbar Marg)

Tashi Delek Nepal Treks & Expeditions
TRAVEL AGENCY

(☏4410746; www.tashidelektreks.com.np; Thamel)

Other agencies include **Earthbound Expeditions** (www.trektibet.com) and **Adventure Silk Road** (www.silkroadgroup.com).

🛏 Sleeping

There are dozens of places to stay in the tourist ghetto of Thamel; here are just a few.

Central Kathmandu

◎ Top Sights
Durbar Square..................................A4

Activities, Courses & Tours
1 Eco Trek B2
2 Green Hill Tours..........................B2
3 Royal Mount Trekking..................C2
4 Tashi Delek Nepal Treks & Expeditions B2

🛏 Sleeping
5 Hotel Ganesh Himal......................A3
6 Hotel Potala B2
7 Kantipur Temple House................B3
8 Kathmandu Guest House..............B2
9 Tibet Peace Guest House A1

🍴 Eating
10 Fire & Ice B2
11 La Dolce Vita..............................B2
12 New Orleans Café B2
13 Or2K B2
    Third Eye Restaurant ....(see 17)
14 Utse Restaurant B2
15 Yak Restaurant B2
16 Yangling Tibetan Restaurant.......B1
17 Yin Yang.....................................B2

Transport
18 Air China....................................D1
19 Air India D3
20 Gulf Air D2
21 Qatar Airways D2
22 Nepal Airlines Corporation B4
23 Thai International Airways...........C3
24 Wayfarers..................................B2

KATHMANDU PRICES

For Kathmandu we have used the following price indicators:

Sleeping (double room)

$	less than US$15
$$	US$15–60
$$$	over US$60

Eating (per dish)

$	less than Rs 300
$$	Rs 300–600
$$$	over Rs 600

Discounts of 30% are commonplace, especially in the low season (May to September).

TOP CHOICE **Hotel Ganesh Himal** HOTEL $
(☑4263598; www.ganeshhimal.com; Chhetrapati; s US$11-16, d US$14-19; @🛜) This booming family-run hotel offers midrange comfort at budget prices. Perks include garden and balcony seating, free airport pickup and free internet access. It's a 10-minute walk southwest of Thamel, well out of range of the tiger-balm sellers. Deluxe rooms offer the best value.

Kathmandu Guest House HOTEL $$
(☑4413632; www.ktmgh.com; simple r US$2-22, standard r US$30-65, deluxe r US$70-130; ✳@🛜) The KGH is a Thamel institution. The cheapest rooms come without bathroom, while US$20 to US$30 will get you a bathroom and basic midrange comfort. Rooms over US$50 have air-con. The large quiet grounds, with a well-tended garden and a wi-fi-enabled courtyard restaurant, provide an oasis that many travellers appreciate in this hectic city. Reservations recommended.

Hotel Potala HOTEL $
(☑4419159; s/d/tr without bathroom US$5/8/12, with bathroom US$8/12/15; @) Right in the heart of Thamel is this backpacker place with small, darkish rooms but a good cafe and internet access.

Kantipur Temple House BOUTIQUE HOTEL $$
(☑4250131; www.kantipurtemplehouse.com; s US$55-85, d US$66-125; discounts of 25-40%) Along a short alley at the southern end of Jyatha is this gorgeous, well-run hotel built in the style of an old Newari temple. It's a tasteful, quiet retreat, and ecofriendly to boot.

Tibet Peace Guest House GUESTHOUSE $
(☑4381026; www.tibetpeace.com; r without bathroom Rs 200-400, r with bathroom Rs 400-800) This mellow family-run hang-out has a nice garden on the quieter fringes of Thamel. Rooms vary so look at a few. There are several good similar places nearby.

 Eating

Central Thamel offers an amazing range of food, with dozens of backpacker-friendly cafes, bakeries and restaurants. Most places add 13% tax and 10% service onto listed prices. Bakeries offer a useful 50% discount in the evenings. All places are open lunch and dinner and menus are in English.

New Orleans Cafe WESTERN $$
(mains Rs 270-425; 🛜) Hidden down an alley, cool New Orleans has a globe-trotting menu, live blues music and candlelit tables in a Newari courtyard.

Fire & Ice PIZZA $$
(Sanchaya Kosh Bhawan, Tridevi Marg; pizzas Rs 320-380) Nepal's best pizza was a favourite of Prince Dipendra before he massacred the royal family in 2002 (don't worry: no one's blaming the pizza).

Utse Restaurant TIBETAN $$
(dishes Rs 60-80) In the hotel of the same name in Jyatha, this long-running place has a lovely Tibetan teahouse style restaurant and better Tibetan dishes than you ever had in Tibet.

For quality Indian food we recommend **Third Eye Restaurant** (main Rs 250-400), or head next door to **Ying Yang** (main Rs 400) for the best Thai spices. **La Dolce Vita** (main Rs 250) offers fine pasta and espresso. Fresh and funky **Or2K** (mains Rs 130-200; 🛜) serves light vegetarian Middle Eastern food.

Our favourite cheapies are the Tibetan diner-style **Yak Restaurant** for Tibetan dishes and *tongba* (hot millet beer), and **Yangling Tibetan Restaurant** (momos Rs 75-130; ☉Sun-Fri), which has the best momos in town.

 Shopping

The Thamel area is crammed with shops selling camping gear and clothing. What you purchase probably won't be genuine, but it should last at least one trip through Tibet.

ℹ️ Information

Money

The many licensed moneychangers are the easiest places to change cash; all offer the same rate.

Himalayan Bank (Sanchaya Kosh basement, Tridevi Marg; ☺8am-8pm Sun-Fri) Close to Thamel, changes travellers cheques and gives cash advances on Visa cards.

Standard Chartered Bank Has two ATMs in Thamel, with one inside the grounds of the Kathmandu Guest House.

Travel Agencies

Wayfarers (☎4266010; www.wayfarers.com.np; Thamel) Straight-talking agency for air tickets, including domestic Indian routes.

ℹ️ Getting There & Away

For details about flights into Kathmandu, see p349. Visas are available on arrival at the airport for US$25/40/100 for up to 15/30/90 days. You'll need to fill out a visa form and arrival form and give one photo.

ℹ️ Getting Around

Taxis are reasonably priced and most of the drivers will use the meter for short trips around town, which rarely come to more than Rs 100. Note that in the evening you may have to negotiate a fare.

Cycle rickshaws cost Rs 40 to Rs 50 for short rides around town but require considerably more bargaining. Always agree on a price before you get in.

To/From the Airport

Kathmandu's **Tribhuvan International Airport** (☎4472265; www.tiairport.com.np) is about 2km east of town. International airport departure tax is included in the price of air tickets.

You'll find a **pre-paid taxi service** (☎4112521) in the ground-floor foyer area immediately after you leave the baggage collection area. The fixed fare to Thamel is currently Rs 500 (and rising), plus Rs 100 after 9pm.

Hotel touts outside the international terminal will offer you a free lift to their hotel, but you are less likely to get a discounted room rate after the tout gets his hefty commission.

CHÉNGDŪ 成都

🎵028 / POP 4.1 MILLION / ELEV 500M

The modern, surprisingly laid-back city of Chéngdū is the largest and most important in China's southwest. Temperatures can hit an uncomfortable 35°C during muggy July and August. For details on the city see

Lonely Planet's *China* or *China's Southwest* guides.

👁️ Sights

Giant Panda Breeding Research Base

RESEARCH BASE

(大熊猫繁殖研究中心; Dàxióngmāo Fánzhí Yánjiū Zhōngxīn; www.panda.org.cn; admission Y30; ☺8am-6pm) If you have a half day to fill, take a taxi or bus out to this research base, 18km north of the city. Feeding is around 9.30am, which is when the bears are most active. It's easiest to take one of the tours run by the budget guesthouses; they cost around Y50, which includes the entrance fee.

Wénshū Temple

MONASTERY

(文殊院; Wénshū Yuàn; Renmin Zhonglu; admission Y5; ☺6am-9pm) This Buddhist monastery (Chéngdū's largest) has an excellent vegetarian restaurant and the surrounding alleys are also worth a visit.

People's Park

PARK

(人民公园; Rénmín Gōngyuán; admission free; tea Y5-25; ☺6.30am-10pm) For a distinctly Sichuanese experience visit the teahouses here.

Wǔhóu Temple

TEMPLE

(武侯祠; Wǔhóu Cí; admission Y60; ☺8am-6pm) South of the river. Opposite is a small Tibetan neighbourhood that's worth a stroll.

🛏️ Sleeping

TOP CHOICE Sim's Cozy Garden Hostel

YOUTH HOSTEL $

(老沈青年旅舍; Lǎoshěn Qīngnián Lǚshè; ☎8196 7573; www.gogosc.com; 211 Yihuan Lu Bei Siduan; dm Y30-40, s without/with bathroom Y80/120, d Y160-240; ⊕❄️@🛜) Run by a Singaporean-Japanese backpacker couple, this exceptional hostel set around two garden courtyards gets all the details right, from lockable storage boxes in the dorms to DVD players in the doubles. There's a wide range of rooms, lots of places to hang out and Sim is a great resource on travel to Tibet. Staff are used to receiving posted TTB permits.

Traffic Inn

YOUTH HOSTEL $

(交通青年旅舍; Jiāotōng Qīngnián Lǚshè; ☎8545 0470; www.redcliffinn.cn; 6 Linjiang Zhonglu; dm Y20-30, s/d/tr without bathroom Y60/80/120, with bathroom Y140/160/210; ❄️@🛜) If Sim's wasn't so damn good, this place would be the best hostel in town. Rooms without bathrooms are the best, the mosaic-tiled shared showers are spotless, and the excellent Highfly Cafe is just round

GATEWAY CITIES

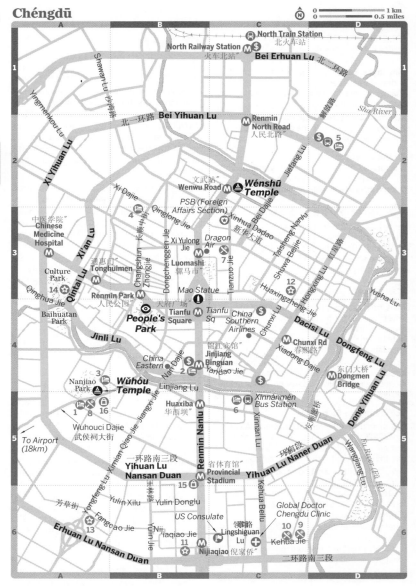

the back. Dorms and rooms with bathrooms are housed in the adjoining **Traffic Hotel** (交通酒店; Jiāotōng Jiǔdiàn; ☎8545 1017), where rates for rooms with bathrooms are cheaper than those at the youth hostel. The location, near Xīnnánmén bus station, is perfect if you are headed to Kāngdìng and beyond.

Loft YOUTH HOSTEL $
(四号工厂旅馆; Sìhào Gōngchǎng Lǘguǎn; ☎8626 5770; www.lofthostel.com; 4 Shangtongren Lu, Xiaotong Xiang; dm Y40, tw without bathroom Y100,

tw & d with bathroom Y180; ❄@☎) Exposed brick walls, minimalist furnishings and sexy black-tiled bathrooms make this converted printing factory the coolest place in town. Pluses include a cafe serving Western food and free internet access.

Holly's Hostel YOUTH HOSTEL $
(九龙鼎青年客栈; Jiǔlóngdǐng Qīngnián Kèzhàn; ☑8554 8131; hollyhostelcn@yahoo.com; 246 Wuhouci Dajie; dm Y25-35, d without bathroom Y80, d/tw/tr with bathroom Y120/140/180; @☎) Rooms at this lovely little hostel tucked down a lane near the Tibetan quarter are a bit bland, but staff are friendly and there's a great roof-terrace cafe, plus bikes for rent (Y20 per day).

Jǐnlǐ Hotel HOTEL $$
(锦里客栈; Jǐnlǐ Kèzhàn; ☑6631 1335; 231 Wuhouci Dajie; s/d Y480/560; discounts of 40%; ❄) If you don't mind the touristy surroundings on the Jǐnlǐ shopping street near Wǔhóu Temple, this upmarket inn set in two courtyard-style buildings is a fun place to stay. Rooms mix traditional Chinese

Chéngdū

⊙ Top Sights
People's Park..B4
Wénshū Temple.......................................C2
Wǔhóu Temple..A4

⊜ Sleeping
1 Holly's Hostel.....................................A5
2 Jǐnjiāng Hotel.....................................B4
3 Jǐnlǐ Hotel...A4
4 Loft..B3
5 Sim's Cozy Garden Hostel................D2
6 Traffic Inn..C5

⊗ Eating
7 Chén Mápó Dòufu...............................C3
8 Kampa Tibetan Restaurant...............A5
9 Xīnjiāng Hóng Mǔdàn Mùsīlín
   Kuàicān..C6
10 Yùlín Chuànchuàn Xiāng..................C6

⊙ Entertainment
11 Bookworm...B6
12 Jǐnjiāng Theatre...............................C3
13 New Little Bar...................................A6
14 Shǔfēng Yǎyùn Teahouse.................A3

⊜ Shopping
15 52 Camp..B5
16 Tibetan Shops...................................A5

For Chéngdū we have used the following price indicators:

Sleeping (double room)

$	less than Y160
$$	Y160–500
$$$	over Y500

Eating (per dish)

$	less than Y20
$$	Y20–50
$$$	over Y50

wooden furnishings with modern trappings like white duvets and TVs.

Jǐnjiāng Hotel HOTEL $$$
(锦江宾馆; Jǐnjiāng Bīnguǎn; ☑8550 6050; www.jjhotel.com; 80 Renmin Nanlu; 人民南路二段80号; r from Y1587; discounts around 50%; ❄@✉) Sìchuān's first five-star hotel retains a charm that the bigger international chains lack. Rooms are comfortable not luxurious, but were good enough for Spanish tenor Plácido Domingo when he stayed here in 2009.

✗ Eating

TOP CHOICE **Yùlín Chuànchuàn Xiāng** HOTPOT $
(玉林串串香; 2-3 Kehua Jie; per skewer Y1; ⊙11am-late) This popular open-fronted branch of the popular Yùlín chain specialises in hotpot. Choose your own skewers from a side room then cook them yourself in the boiling, spicy broth on your table for the quintessential Chéngdū eating experience. There's another, slightly smaller branch near the Traffic Inn.

Chén Mápó Dòufu SÌCHUĀN $$
(陈麻婆豆腐; Pockmarked Grandma Chen's Bean Curd; 197 Xi Yulong Jie, 2nd fl; dishes Y12-58; ⊙11.30am-9pm) This Chéngdū institution specialises in its signature mápó dòufu (small/large Y12/20) – soft, fresh bean curd in a fiery sauce of garlic, minced beef, salted soybean, chilli oil and Sichuanese pepper. Photo menu.

Kampa Tibetan Restaurant TIBETAN $
(康巴藏餐; Kāngbā Zàngcān; off 246 Wuhouci Dajie; dishes Y8-28; ⊙8am-11pm; ⓓ) This small, friendly Tibetan-run restaurant located next to Holly's Hostel serves tasty

Tibetan classics such as tsampa, yak meat and butter tea.

Xīnjiāng Hóng Mǔdān Mùsīlín Kuàicān
MUSLIM **$**

(新疆红牡丹穆斯林快餐; cnr Kehua Jie & Guojiaqiao Xijie; dishes Y6-50; ☺10am-11.30pm) This extremely popular Uighur restaurant beside Sìchuān University is a great place to sample *dàpánjī* – chicken, potatoes and peppers stewed in a savoury, spicy sauce. When you're part way through the meal, staff dump a pile of handmade noodles into your dish, perfect for sopping up the sauce. Kebabs and naan bread are also available.

☆ Entertainment

A night out at the Sichuanese opera is a must-do in Chéngdū. Most of the budget guesthouses run tours and some can even get you backstage.

Shǔfēng Yǎyùn Teahouse
SÌCHUĀN OPERA

(蜀风雅韵; Shǔfēng Yǎyùn; ☎8776 4530; www.shufengyayun.com; Culture Park; tickets Y150-260) Located in Culture Park, this large teahouse puts on excellent shows that include music, puppetry, comedy, Sìchuān opera and the province's famed face-changing performances. Shows run nightly from 8pm to 9.30pm. If you come at around 7.30pm you can watch performers putting on their make-up.

Jǐnjiāng Theatre
SÌCHUĀN OPERA

(锦江剧院; Jǐnjiāng Jùyuàn; ☎8662 0019; 54 Huaxingzheng Jie; tickets Y120-260; ☺8-9.30pm) Similar mixed-performance shows are held daily at this renowned opera theatre. The adjoining Yuèlái Teahouse (悦来茶楼; Yuèlái Chálóu; tea Y6-15; ☺8.30am-9.30pm) also has performances on its small stage every Saturday from 2pm to 5pm. Tickets for the teahouse shows cost Y20 to Y35.

Bookworm
CAFE

(老书虫; Lǎo Shūchóng; ☎8552 0177; www.chengdubookworm.com; 2-7 Yulin Donglu, 28 Renmin Nanlu; ☺9am-1am) This excellent bookshop-cafe is a peaceful spot for a drink or a coffee and often hosts author talks, concerts and other events. Check its website for a schedule.

New Little Bar
BAR

(小酒馆/芳沁店; Xiǎo Jiǔguǎn/Fāngqìn Diàn; ☎8515 8790; Fangqin Jie, behind 47 Yongfeng Lu; 永丰路47号芳沁街; beer from Y10; ☺6pm-2am) This small pub-like venue is *the* place

in Chéngdū to catch local bands performing live Friday and Saturday night (cover around Y30). Fangqin Jie is the small road on the east side of Yongfeng Jie.

Shopping

52 Camp
OUTDOOR GEAR

(户外用品商城; Hùwài Yòngpǐn Shàngchéng; Renmin Nanlu; ☺9am-9.30pm) For a last-minute Chinese-made tent or Gore-Tex jacket, try this place for good quality gear. More outdoor shops line Wuhouci Dajie, opposite Wǔhóu Temple. Quality varies and fakes abound.

❶ Information

Best sources for up-to-the-minute restaurant, bar and entertainment listings are free monthly magazines **More Chéngdū** (www.morechengdu.com) and **GoChengdoo** (www.gochengdoo.com/en). **Chéngdū Living** (www.chengduliving.com) is also good.

Bank of China (中国银行; Zhōngguó Yínháng; 35 Renmin Zhonglu, 2nd Section; ☺8.30am-5.30pm Mon-Fri, to 5pm Sat & Sun) Changes money and travellers cheques and offers cash advances on credit cards. Other branches also change money. Most ATMs in the city accept foreign cards.

Global Doctor Chéngdū Clinic (环球医生成都诊所; Huánqiú Yīshēng Chéngdū Zhěnsuǒ; ☎8528 3660, 24hr helpline 139 8225 6966; 2nd fl, 9-11 Lippo Tower Bldg, 62 Kehua Beilu; 科华北路62号力宝大厦2层9—11号; ☺8.30am-6pm Mon-Fri) English-speaking doctors and a 24-hour English-language helpline.

Public Security Bureau (公安局; PSB; Gōng'ānjú; ☎8640 7067; 391 Shuncheng Dajie; ☺9am-noon & 1-5pm Mon-Fri) Foreign affairs office on 2nd floor; extends visas in five working-days.

Tourist hotline (☎8292 8555) Free English-speaking hotline.

❶ Getting There & Away

For details about flights into Kathmandu, see p349.

Buses to destinations in western Sìchuān, such as Kāngdìng (Y119 to Y129, seven hours, hourly) depart from the Xīnnánmén (新南门) bus station.

❶ Getting Around

The most useful bus is route 16 (Y1 to Y2), which connects the north and south train stations along Renmin Nanlu. Taxis have a flag fall of Y5 or Y7 (Y1 extra at night), though this is set to rise. Most budget accommodation rent bikes for Y20 per day.

The new subway should be open by the time you read this. The useful Line 1 links the North Train Station with the length of Renmin Lu. The east–west Line 2 meets Line 1 at Tianfu Square before continuing west to Chádiànzì Bus Station.

To/From the Airport

Shuāngliú airport (双流飞机场; Shuāngliú Fēijīchǎng) is 18km west of the city. Airport bus 303 (Y10) runs frequently between the airport and Yandao Jie. A taxi costs around Y60 to Y70, depending on the traffic. Most of the hostels will pick you up from the train station for free or arrange an airport pickup for around Y70.

Understand
Tibet

TIBET TODAY **272**

Between the economic boom and the political unrest, what does China's 'great leap west' mean for Tibet?

HISTORY **274**

Follow the transformation of Tibet from a warring empire to a Buddhist nation, and its perennially complex relationship with China.

LANDSCAPES IN THE LAND OF THE SNOWS . . . 293

The Tibetan plateau is home to species on the brink of extinction as well as resources vital for the planet's future.

THE PEOPLE OF TIBET **299**

Nomadic lifestyle, exiled communities, pilgrimage tradition – learn about the various unique facets of Tibetan identity.

TIBETAN BUDDHISM **307**

Before immersing yourself in the monasteries and temples, get an understanding of the religion that permeates everything in Tibet.

TIBETAN ART **322**

Buddhism is the dominant inspiration in Tibetan art, from masked dances and poems of lamas, to chörtens, murals and mandalas.

THE FUTURE OF TIBET **330**

Does Tibet's best hope for the future lie in the international community, in reincarnation or in its traditional culture?

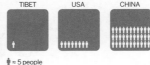

population per sq km

TIBET   USA   CHINA

👤 ≈ 5 people

Tibet Today

There is an increasing economic and social divide in Tibet. Per capita disposable income currently stands at over US$1800 in the towns, but only US$460 in the countryside.

Change is afoot in Tibet. The economy is booming; extended train links, airports and paved roads are revolutionising transport on the plateau; and Tibet's urban areas are expanding at an unprecedented rate. As part of its 'great leap west', the Chinese government has poured billions of US dollars into Tibet's infrastructure and resettled 1.3 million Tibetans in new housing, while a domestic tourist boom is fuelling hotel and restaurant construction across the plateau.

In most parts of the world this would all be good news, but herein lies Tibet and China's conundrum. Alongside the short-term tourists has come a flood of Chinese immigrants, whom Tibetans claim are the real beneficiaries of Tibet's economic boom. Although no figures are available, it is obvious that many Chinese people – attracted by preferential loans and tax rates, a less strictly enforced one-child policy, stipends for a hardship posting and easy business opportunities – are setting up shop in urban centres all over Tibet.

As the face of Tibet changes, many Tibetans feel they are becoming increasingly marginalised in their own land. China reminds them that it has brought in education, health and infrastructure, and spent millions renovating monasteries. Tibetan groups maintain that it is mostly Chinese immigrants who run Tibet's businesses, and that monasteries remain under tight political control and exist largely for tourism. The Chinese counter that they are just trying to bring economic prosperity to one of its most backward provinces, at a large financial loss. (Then everyone storms out of the room.)

Tibet's long-simmering tensions boiled over on 10 March 2008, the anniversary of the Dalai Lama's flight into exile, kicking off several days of protests by monks from Lhasa's big monasteries. As protest turned to violence, at least 19 people, mostly Han Chinese, were killed in rioting

Dos & Don'ts

» Don't wear brief skirts or shorts, especially at religious sites.

» Don't point at people or statues with your finger, use your full upturned hand.

» Don't pat children on the head, as the head is considered sacred.

» Always circle a Buddhist monastery building or chörten clockwise.

Top Books

The Open Road: The Global Journey of the Fourteenth Dalai Lama (Pico Iyer) An engaging look at the warmth and contradictions of the 14th Dalai Lama.

Fire Under the Snow (Palden Gyatso) A moving

where Tibetans live (%)

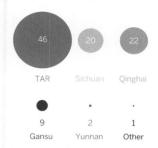

TAR	Sichuan	Qinghai
46	20	22

Gansu	Yunnan	Other
9	2	1

that left Beijing Donglu (east Lhasa's main road) smouldering and full of tear gas. The disturbances quickly spread to Tibetan towns outside the Tibetan Autonomous Region, from Labrang and Hézuò in southern Gānsù, to Aba, Gānzī and Lithang in western Sìchuān and Rebkong and Machu in Qīnghǎi, making this the worst political unrest in Tibet for 20 years.

In the wake of the riots Tibet remains a tightly controlled place, with armed riot police posted on every street corner in Lhasa's old town. Basic religious and political freedoms are lacking and political propaganda campaigns have been stepped up. Monasteries are repeatedly the focus of 'patriotic education' and 'civilising atheism' campaigns, with political management teams and police posted in every monastery. To show support for the Dalai Lama continues to result in long jail sentences. Even tourism regulations have been tightened, limiting the contact foreign tourists have with Tibetans.

Cosmetic changes and tightened political controls are unlikely to solve the frustration and resentment that runs deep in Tibet. As Tibetans struggle to adapt to the daily changes taking place in their land, the root causes remain unaddressed. The longest-lasting result of Tibet's economic boom is clear though: the ties that bind China and Tibet are stronger than ever.

The Qīnghǎi–Tibet railway line to Lhasa is the world's highest, reaching 5072m at the Tangula Pass, 200m higher than the summit of Mt Blanc.

Top Films

autobiography of a Buddhist monk imprisoned in Tibet for 33 years.
Tears of Blood (Mary Craig) A riveting and distressing account of the Tibetan experience since the Chinese takeover.

Kundun (1997) Martin Scorsese's beautifully shot depiction of the life of the Dalai Lama.
Vajra Sky Over Tibet (2006) John Powers' Buddhist-inspired cinematic pilgrimage to the principal sites of central Tibet.

When the Dragon Swallowed the Sun (2010) Explores the increasingly tense debate inside Tibet's exile community on how best to deal with China, featuring music by Damien Rice and Thom Yorke.

History

Tibet's history has been a curious mixture of invasion and intrigue, of soaring religious debate, reincarnation, miracles and murders, all taking place under the backdrop of one of the world's most extreme environments. If one event has defined Tibet, it has been the nation's remarkable transformation from warring expansionist empire to introspective non-violent Buddhist nation. Since Tibet took on the mantle of Buddhism from its neighbour India 1300 years ago, it has created one of the world's most spiritually advanced religious traditions, weaving it into a unique, precious and sophisticated culture.

Core to Tibet's history, of course, is its knotty, intertwined relationship with its giant neighbour China. At the heart of the matter is the ill-defined medieval relationship between priest and patron; between the Mongol khans and the Yuan Chinese empire they ruled; and between an ever-shifting Chinese empire and its remote Tibetan borderlands. Over the centuries the shifting balance of power has brought Tibet everything from de facto independence to full-scale Chinese invasion, all underpinned by contested concepts of sovereignty and suzerainty.

Tibetan history depends on whom you are talking to and these irreconcilable versions of history lie at the heart of the Tibetan problem. Was Tibet an independent nation invaded by an aggressive ideologically driven Chinese army keen to avenge the humiliations of its past, or has Tibet always been part of the loosely defined Chinese empire, tied by tribute to Běijīng just like the other nations of a multi-ethnic China?

For centuries Tibet resisted outside influence, a policy that contributed in large part to its downfall in 1950. Not only has Tibet been swamped by a resurgent China and ignored by a world unwilling to risk billion-dollar trade deals, it has also been victim of its own historic inability to engage with the world. For centuries the world has seen Tibet as a timeless, impossibly remote Himalayan fantasy, a forbidden Land of Snows, whose people are somehow detached from the suffering of

TIMELINE	28,000 BC	300 BC	c 600
	The Tibetan plateau is covered in ice. It's cold. Very cold. But there are people living there. Tools, stone blades and hunting instruments are in use in Chupsang, 85km from Lhasa.	Throughout the plateau people are building stone dwellings and producing fine pottery; petroglyphs indicate that Buddhism may have started to spread by this time.	Nyatri Tsenpo, the first king of Tibet, founds the Yarlung dynasty and unifies the people and the land; according to legend he is responsible for the first building in Tibet.

invasion and political oppression. In the words of Donald Lopez, Tibet has become a 'prisoner of Shangri-la'.

As modern Tibet teeters on the edge of losing its cultural identity, one faint hope lies in the cyclical nature of Chinese history. Over the centuries China has grown, cracked and collapsed. If that happens again, or if fundamental changes occur in Chinese domestic politics, Tibet may well once again have a say in its own affairs.

The definitive (but weighty) account of Tibetan history since 1947 is *The Dragon in the Land of Snows* by Tsering Shakya.

Murky Origins

The origins of the Tibetan people are not clearly known. Today Chinese historians claim the Tibetan people originally migrated from the present-day areas of the Qīnghǎi–Gānsù plains and were descended from people known as Qiang. Although there is evidence of westward migration, it is not possible to trace a single origin of the Tibetan people. Matthew Kapstein, one of the leading Western Tibetologists writes, 'the people of Tibetan plateau became Tibetan primarily owing to cultural developments during the past two millennia, rather than to common genetic origins'.

The Tibetan people have mythic stories of their origin. According to legend, the earth was covered in a vast sea; eventually the water receded and land appeared in the present-day Tsetang area in central Tibet. A monkey and an ogress first inhabited the land and were later identified as the emanations of Avalokiteshvara (the Buddha of Compassion)

SHANGRI-LA

The slippery notion of Shangri-la has been captivating foreigners for over 80 years now, but mention the phrase to a Tibetan and you'll likely get little more than a blank stare. The origins of Shangri-la lie in James Hilton's novel *Lost Horizon,* a post-WWI fable of a lost Himalayan utopia, where people live in harmony and never age. Hilton's inspiration may well have been National Geographic articles on the remote kingdom of Muli in Kham, and may have even adapted the idea from Tibetan tradition.

Tibetan texts talk of Shambhala, a hidden land to the north whose king will eventually intervene to stop the world destroying itself. The notion of Shangri-la also bears strong similarities to the Tibetan tradition of *baeyul,* hidden lands visible only to the pure of heart that act as refuges in times of great crisis. Tibetan Buddhism also refers directly to various heavenly lands, from the Western Paradise of Ganden to Guru Rinpoche's paradise of Zangtok Pelri.

Whatever the origins, Shangri-la is firmly lodged in the Western psyche. The name has been adopted as a hotel chain and even as a US presidential retreat. In 2001 the Chinese county of Zhōngdiàn upped the ante by renaming itself 'Shanggelila' in a blatant ploy to boost local tourism. Shangri-la is probably best filed under 'M' for the mythologising of Tibet, on the shelf in between levitating monks and yetis.

608	629	640s	7th century
The first mission is sent to the court of Chinese Emperor Yang-ti. This brings Tibet in direct contact with China and sees increasing Tibetan interest in the frontier of China.	Namri Songtsen is assassinated and his son, Songtsen Gampo, aged 13, inherits the throne. He will be regarded as the founder of the Tibetan empire and a cultural hero for the Tibetan people.	Songtsen Gampo marries Chinese Princess Wencheng and Nepalese Princess Bhrikuti. They are credited with bringing Buddhism, silk weaving and new methods of agriculture to Tibet.	The Tibetan empire stretches to include north Pakistan and the Silk Road cities of Khotan and Dūnhuáng.

and the goddess Tara. The first people were descendents of the union between the monkey and ogress. The children of the monkey and ogress gave rise to the Tibetan people and as the number of children increased, the people evolved into six families known as Se, Mu, Dong, Tong, Wra and Dru. They became the six clans of the Tibetan people.

Traces of the Yarlung Kings

» Yumbulagang (Yarlung Valley), the first building in Tibet

» Yarlung Tombs, Chongye

» Zortang (Yarlung Valley), the first field in Tibet

Kings, Warriors & the Tibetan Empire

As early myths of the origin of the Tibetan people suggest, the Yarlung Valley was the cradle of central Tibetan civilisation. The early Yarlung kings, although glorified in legend, were probably no more than chieftains whose domains extended not much further than the Yarlung Valley itself. A reconstruction of Tibet's first fortress, Yumbulagang, can still be seen in the Yarlung Valley, and it is here that the 28th king of Tibet is said to have received Tibet's first Buddhist scriptures in the 5th century AD, when they fell from heaven onto the roof of Yumbulagang.

By the 6th century the Yarlung kings, through conquest and alliances, had made significant headway in unifying much of central Tibet. Namri Songtsen (c 570–619), the 32nd Tibetan king, continued this trend and extended Tibetan influence into inner Asia, defeating the Qiang tribes on China's borders. But the true flowering of Tibet as an important regional power came about with the accession to rule of Namri Songtsen's son, Songtsen Gampo (r 629–49).

Under Songtsen Gampo the armies of Tibet ranged as far afield as northern India and threatened even the great Tang dynasty in China. Both Nepal and China reacted to the Tibetan incursions by reluctantly agreeing to alliances through marriage. Princess Wencheng, Songtsen Gampo's Chinese bride, and Princess Bhrikuti, his Nepali bride, became important historical figures, as it was through their influence that Buddhism first gained royal patronage and a foothold on the Tibetan plateau.

Songtsen Gampo went as far as passing a law making it illegal *not* to be a Buddhist.

Contact with the Chinese led to the introduction of astronomy and medicine, while a delegation sent to India brought back the basis for a Tibetan script. It was used in the first translations of Buddhist scriptures, in drafting a code of law and in writing the first histories of Tibet.

For two centuries after the reign of Songtsen Gampo, Tibet continued to grow in power and influence. By the time of King Trisong Detsen's reign (r 755–97), Tibetan influence extended over Turkestan, northern Pakistan, Nepal and India. In China, Tibetan armies conquered Gānsù and Sìchuān and gained brief control over the Silk Road, including the great Buddhist cave complex of Dūnhuáng.

Introduction of Buddhism

By the time Buddhism arrived in Tibet during the reign of Songtsen Gampo, it had already flourished for around 1100 years and had become

763

Trisong Detsen attacks the Chinese capital Chang'an (Xī'ān) after a Chinese tribute of 50,000 bolts of silk is late.

822

The Sino-Tibetan treaty is signed, confirming Tibet's right to rule all the conquered territories. The bilingual inscription of the treaty is erected outside the Jokhang.

» Samye, Tibet's first monastery, is built from 765 to 780

the principal faith of all Tibet's neighbouring countries. But it was slow to take hold in Tibet.

Early Indian missionaries, such as the famous Shantarakshita, faced great hostility from the Bön-dominated court. The influence of Songtsen Gampo's Buddhist Chinese and Nepali wives was almost certainly limited to the royal court, and priests of the time were probably Indian and Chinese, not Tibetan.

It was not until King Trisong Detsen's reign that Buddhism began to take root. Trisong Detsen was responsible for founding Samye Monastery, the first institution to carry out the systematic translation of Buddhist scriptures and the training of Tibetan monks.

Contention over the path that Buddhism was to take in Tibet culminated in the Great Debate of Samye, in which King Trisong Detsen is said to have adjudicated in favour of Indian teachers over the Chan (Zen) approach of Chinese advocates. There was, however, considerable opposition to this institutionalised, clerical form of Buddhism, largely from supporters of the Bön faith. The next Tibetan king, Tritsug Detsen Ralpachen, fell victim to this opposition and was assassinated by his brother, Langdharma, who launched an attack on Buddhism. In 842, Langdharma was himself assassinated – by a Buddhist monk – and the Tibetan state soon collapsed into a number of warring principalities. In the confusion that followed, support for Buddhism dwindled and clerical monastic Buddhism experienced a 150-year hiatus.

Marco Polo and Alexandra David-Neel both wrote about the magical powers of Tibetan monks, including the ability to move cups with their minds, travel cross-country while levitating or keep warm in subzero temperatures simply through the power of their minds.

Second Diffusion of Buddhism

Overwhelmed initially by local power struggles, Buddhism gradually began to exert its influence again, giving the Tibetan mind a spiritual bent and turning it inward on itself. As the tide of Buddhist faith receded in India, Nepal and China, Tibet slowly emerged as the most devoutly Buddhist nation in the world. Never again was Tibet to rise to arms.

WRITTEN IN STONE

A Sino-Tibetan treaty was signed in 822 during the reign of King Tritsug Detsen Ralpachen (r 817–35), heralding an era in which 'Tibetans shall be happy in Tibet and Chinese shall be happy in China'. It was immortalised in stone on three steles: one in Lhasa, outside the Jokhang; one in the Chinese capital of Chang'an; and one on the border of Tibet and China. Only the Lhasa stele still stands, in Barkhor Square.

Signatories to the treaty swore that '…the whole region to the east…being the country of Great China and the whole region to the west being assuredly that of the country of Great Tibet, from either side of that frontier there shall be no warfare, no hostile invasions, and no seizure of territory…'.

842	996	1042	1073
Monk Lhalung Palgye Dorje assassinates anti-Buddhist king Langdharma in disguise. The event is still commemorated by the Black Hat Dance performed during monastic festivals.	Thöling Monastery is founded in far western Tibet and becomes the main centre of Buddhist activities in Tibet, translating large numbers of Buddhist texts from Kashmir.	Atisha, the Bengali Buddhist scholar and abbot, arrives in Tibet. With his disciple Drömtonpa (1004–64) he is credited with founding the Kadampa, the first distinctive Tibetan Buddhist School.	The Khon family, which traces its lineage from the nobility of the Yarlung dynasty, founds the Sakya school of Tibetan Buddhism. The family remains the hereditary head of Sakya tradition to this day.

**Famous
Early
Monasteries**

» Trandruk
Monastery (7th
century)

» Samye (765)

» Tholing (996)

» Reting (1056)

The so-called second diffusion of Buddhism corresponded with two developments. First, Tibetan teachers who had taken refuge in Kham, to the east, returned to central Tibet in the late 10th century and established new monasteries. The second great catalyst was the arrival of two figures in far western Tibet: the Bengali Buddhist scholar Atisha (Jowo-je in Tibetan; 982–1054), whom the kings of Guge in far western Tibet invited to Tibet in the mid-11th century; and the great translator Rinchen Zangpo (958–1054), who after travelling to India brought back Buddhist texts and founded dozens of monasteries in the far West. Disciples of Atisha, chiefly Dromtönpa, were instrumental in establishing the Kadampa order and such early monasteries as Reting. For an overview of the spectacular Guge Kingdom, which reached its peak between the 10th and 16th centuries, see p180.

The Sakyas & the Mongols

With the collapse of a central Tibetan state, Tibet's contacts with China withered. By the time the Tang dynasty collapsed in 907, China had already recovered almost all the territory it had previously lost to the Tibetans. Throughout the Song dynasty (960–1276) the two nations had virtually no contact with each other, and Tibet's sole foreign contacts were with its southern Buddhist neighbours.

This was all to change when Genghis (Chinggis) Khan launched a series of conquests in 1206 that led to a vast Mongol empire that straddled Central Asia and China. By 1239 the Mongols started to send raiding parties into the country. Numerous monasteries were razed and the Mongols almost reached Lhasa before turning back.

Over the centuries Tibet has suffered from ill-defined borders and a lack of internal unity, with large parts of Amdo, Kham and Ngari and independent tribes like the Goloks only nominally ruled by Lhasa.

Tibetan accounts have it that returning Mongol troops related the spiritual eminence of the Tibetan lamas to Godan Khan, grandson of Genghis Khan and ruler of the Kokonor region (which means 'Blue Sea' in Mongolian) in modern-day Qīnghǎi. In response Godan summoned Sakya Pandita, the head of Sakya Monastery, to his court. The outcome of this meeting was the beginning of a priest-patron relationship that has come to dog the definition of Tibetan independence and its relationship to China. Tibetan Buddhism became the state religion of the Mongol empire in east Asia, and the head Sakya lama became its spiritual leader, a position that also entailed temporal authority over Tibet (see the box, p151). The Sakyapa ascendancy lasted less than 100 years but had profound effects on Tibet's future.

Tibetan Independence (Part I)

Certain Chinese claims on Tibet have looked to the Mongol Yuan dynasty overlordship of the high plateau, and the priest-patron relationship existing at the time, as setting a precedent for Chinese sovereignty over

1110–1193	1201	1240	1249
The first Karmapa introduces the concept of reincarnation, which eventually spreads to other schools of Tibetan Buddhism and to the institution of the Dalai Lamas.	Sakya Pandita (1182–1251) travels to India, studying under great Indian gurus. He becomes a great religious and cultural figure, creating a Tibetan literary tradition inspired by Sanskrit poetry.	The grandson of Genghis Khan, Godan, invades central Tibet with 30,000 troops, ransacking the monastery of Reting.	Sakya Pandita becomes the spiritual advisor to Godon Khan and converts the Mongols to Buddhism. Godon invests Sakya Pandita as the secular ruler of Tibet.

Tibet. The Yuan dynasty may have claimed sovereignty over Tibet, yet this 'Chinese' dynasty was itself governed by the invading Mongols and their ruler Kublai Khan. Pro-independence supporters state that this is like India claiming sovereignty over Myanmar (Burma) because both were ruled by the British.

In reality, Tibetan submission was offered to the Mongols before they conquered China and it ended when the Mongols fell from power in that country. When the Mongol empire disintegrated, both China and Tibet regained their independence. Due to the initial weakness of the Ming dynasty, Sino-Tibetan relations effectively took on the form of exchanges of diplomatic courtesies by two independent governments.

The Tibetans undertook to remove all traces of the Mongol administration, drawing on the traditions of the former Yarlung kings. Officials were required to dress in the manner of the former royal court, a revised version of King Songtsen Gampo's code of law was enacted, a new taxation system was enforced, and scrolls depicting the glories of the Yarlung dynasty were commissioned. The movement was a declaration of Tibet's independence from foreign interference and a search for national identity.

The Tibetan Lama Phagpa, nephew of Kunga Gyetsen, enjoyed a close relationship with the Mongol leader Kublai Khan, likely met Marco Polo in Běijīng and even helped create a new Mongol script.

Rise of the Gelugpa & the Dalai Lamas

In 1374, a young man named Lobsang, later known as Tsongkhapa, set out from his home near Kokonor in Amdo to central Tibet, where he undertook training with all the major schools of Tibetan Buddhism. By the time he was 25, he had already gained a reputation as a teacher and a writer.

Tsongkhapa established a monastery at Ganden, near Lhasa, where he refined his thinking, steering clear of political intrigue, and espousing doctrinal purity and monastic discipline. Although it seems unlikely that Tsongkhapa intended to found another school of Buddhism, his teachings attracted many disciples, who found his return to the original teachings of Atisha an exciting alternative to the politically tainted

TANGTONG GYELPO

Tangtong Gyelpo (1385–1464) was Tibet's Renaissance man *par excellence*. Nyingmapa yogi, treasure finder, engineer, medic and inventor of Tibetan opera, Tangtong formed a song-and-dance troupe of seven sisters to raise money for his other passion, bridge building. He eventually built 108 bridges in Tibet, the most famous of which was over the Yarlung Tsangpo near modern-day Chushul. Tangtong is often depicted in monastery murals with long white hair and a beard, and is usually holding a section of chain links from one of his bridges.

1260	1268	1290	1357–1419
Kublai Khan appoints Phagpa as an imperial preceptor. This ushers in what the Tibetans call the priest–patron relationship between Mongol Khans, later Chinese Emperors and Tibetan lamas.	The first census of central Tibet counts some 40,000 households. Basic taxation and a new administrative system is established in Tibet.	Kublai Khan's army supports the Sakya and destroys the main centres of the Kagyud school. With the death of Kublai Khan in 1294, the power of the Sakya school begins to wane.	Tsongkhapa establishes himself as a reformer, founds the reformist Gelugpa school, writes the influential Lamrin Chenpo and introduces the popular Mönlam Festival.

REINCARNATION

Sakyapa and Kagyupa orders. Tsongkhapa's movement became known as the Gelugpa (Virtuous) order, which remains today the dominant school in Tibet.

By the time of the third reincarnated head of the Gelugpa, Sonam Gyatso (1543–88), the Mongols began to take a renewed interest in Tibet's new and increasingly powerful order. In a move that mirrored the 13th-century Sakyapa entrance into the political arena, Sonam Gyatso accepted an invitation to meet with Altyn Khan near Kokonor in 1578. At the meeting, Sonam Gyatso received the title of *dalai,* meaning 'ocean', and implying 'ocean of wisdom'. The title was retrospectively bestowed on his previous two reincarnations, and so Sonam Gyatso became the third Dalai Lama.

Their relationship with the Mongols marked the Gelugpa's entry into the turbulent waters of worldly affairs. It is no surprise that the Tsang kings and the Karmapa of Tsurphu Monastery saw this Gelugpa-Mongol alliance as a direct threat to their power. Bickering ensued, and in 1611 the Tsang king attacked Drepung and Sera Monasteries. The fourth (Mongolian) Dalai Lama fled central Tibet and died at the age of 25 in 1616.

The Great Fifth Dalai Lama

A successor to the fourth Dalai Lama was soon discovered, and the boy was brought to Lhasa, again under Mongol escort. In the meantime, Mongol intervention in Tibetan affairs continued in the guise of support for the embattled Gelugpa order.

Unlike the Sakya-Mongol domination of Tibet, under which the head Sakya lama was required to reside in the Mongol court, the fifth Dalai Lama was able to rule from within Tibet. With the backing of the Mongol Gushri Khan, Tsang was brought back into the fold. All of Tibet was pacified by 1656, and the Dalai Lama's control ranged from Mt Kailash in the west to Kham in the east. Ngawang Lobsang Gyatso, the fifth Dalai Lama, had become both the spiritual and temporal sovereign of a unified Tibet.

The fifth Dalai Lama is remembered as having ushered in a great new age for Tibet. He made a tour of Tibet's monasteries, and although he stripped most Kadampa monasteries – his chief rivals for power – of their riches, he allowed them to re-establish. A new flurry of monastic construction began, the major achievement being Labrang Monastery (in what is now Gānsù province). In Lhasa, work began on a fitting residence for the head of the Tibetan state: the Potala.

The concept of reincarnation was first introduced by the Karmapa and adopted in the 15th century by the Gelugpa order and the Dalai Lamas.

Manchus, Mongols & Murder

Reincarnation lineages were probably first adopted as a means of maintaining spiritual authority within monastic orders, where there was no

1368

The Mongol Yuan dynasty in China ends, and the Ming dynasty begins. This coincides with the final demise of Sakya rule in Tibet.

1565

The kings of Tsang became secular rulers of Tibet from Shigatse. Spiritual authority at this time is vested in the Karmapa, head of a Kagyupa suborder at Tsurphu Monastery.

» Painting in the Tashilhunpo Monastery, founded in 1447

THE PLAYBOY LAMA

Tsangyang Gyatso (1683–1706), the young man chosen as the sixth Dalai Lama, was, shall we say, unconventional. A sensual youth with long hair and a penchant for erotic verse, he soon proved himself to be far more interested in wine and women than meditation and study. He refused to take his final vows as a monk and he would often sneak out of the Potala at night to raise hell in the inns and brothels of Lhasa, under the pseudonym Norsang Wangpo. A resident Jesuit monk described him as a 'dissolute youth' and 'quite depraved', noting that 'no good-looking person of either sex was safe from his unbridled licentiousness'.

hereditary line of succession. With the death of the fifth Dalai Lama in 1682, however, the weakness of such a system became apparent. The Tibetan government was confronted with the prospect of finding his reincarnation and then waiting 18 years until the boy came of age. The great personal prestige and authority of the fifth Dalai Lama had played no small part in holding together a newly unified Tibet. The Dalai Lama's regent decided to shroud the Dalai Lama's death in secrecy, announcing that the fifth lama had entered a long period of meditation (over 10 years!).

In 1695 the secret was leaked and the regent was forced to hastily enthrone the sixth Dalai Lama, a boy of his own choosing. The choice was an unfortunate one (see the box, p281) and could not have come at a worse time.

In China the Ming dynasty had been replaced by the Manchu Qing dynasty (1644–1912). The events that followed were complicated. Basically, Tibet's ineffectual head of state, the Qing perception of the threat of Tibetan relations with the Mongols, disunity within the ranks of Tibet's Mongol allies and Qing ambitions to extend its power into Tibet led to a Qing intervention that was to have lasting consequences for Tibet.

Tibet's dealings with the new Qing government went awry from the start. Kangxi, the second Qing emperor, took offence when the death of the fifth Dalai Lama was concealed from him. At the same time, an ambitious Mongol prince named Lhabzang Khan came to the conclusion that earlier Mongol leaders had taken too much of a back-seat position in their relations with the Tibetans and appealed to Emperor Kangxi for support. It was granted and, in 1705, Mongol forces descended on Lhasa, deposing the sixth Dalai Lama. Depending on your source, he either died at Lithang (where he was probably murdered), or he lived

The fifth Dalai Lama wrote a detailed history of Tibet and his autobiography is regarded as a literary treasure of Tibet.

The Dalai Lamas are depicted in wall paintings holding the Wheel of Law (Wheel of Dharma) as a symbol of the political power gained under the Great Fifth Dalai Lama.

1578	1588	1601	1624
Mongolian Altan Khan converts to Buddhism and bestows the title 'Dalai Lama' to Sonam Gyatso, who becomes the third Dalai Lama (the first two are honoured retroactively).	Ties with the Mongols deepen when, at the third Dalai Lama's death, his next reincarnation was conveniently found in a great-grandson of the Mongolian Altyn Khan.	The Mongolian grandson of Altyn Khan is recognised by the Panchen Lama as the fourth Dalai Lama. This establishes the tradition of the Dalai Lamas being recognised by the Panchen.	Jesuits open their first mission at Tsaparang in far western Tibet after an epic journey across the Himalaya from bases in Goad.

to a ripe old age in Amdo. The seventh Dalai Lama was subsequently found in Lithang, fulfilling a famous poem written by the sixth.

In 1717 the Dzungar Mongols from Central Asia attacked and occupied Lhasa for three years, killing Lhabzang Khan and deposing the seventh Dalai Lama. The resulting confusion in Tibet was the opportunity for which Emperor Kangxi had been waiting. He responded by sending a military expedition to Lhasa. The Chinese troops drove out the Dzungar Mongols and were received by the Tibetans as liberators. They were unlikely to have been received any other way: with them, they brought the seventh Dalai Lama, who had been languishing in Kumbum Monastery under Chinese 'protection'.

Emperor Kangxi wasted no time in declaring Tibet a protectorate of China. Two Chinese representatives, known as Ambans (a Manchurian word), were installed at Lhasa, along with a garrison of Chinese troops. It was just a beginning, leading to two centuries of Manchu overlordship and serving as a convenient historical precedent for the communist takeover nearly 250 years later.

Kate Teltscher's *The High Road to China* details the 1774–45 journey of 27-year-old George Bogle to Shigatse and his fascinating relationship with the Panchen Lama.

Manchu Overlordship

The seventh Dalai Lama ruled until his death in 1757. However, at this point it became clear that another ruler would have to be appointed until the next Dalai Lama reached adulthood. The post of regent (*gyeltshab*) was created.

It is perhaps a poor reflection on the spiritual attainment of the lamas appointed as regents that few were willing to relinquish the reins once they were in the saddle. In the 120 years between the death of the seventh Dalai Lama and the adulthood of the 13th, actual power was wielded by the Dalai Lamas for only seven years. Three of them died very young and under suspicious circumstances. Only the eighth Dalai Lama survived into his adulthood, living a quiet, contemplative life until the age of 45.

Barbarians at the Doorstep

Early contact between Britain and Tibet commenced with a mission to Shigatse headed by a Scotsman, George Bogle, in 1774. Bogle soon ingratiated himself with the Panchen Lama – to the extent of marrying one of his sisters. With the death of the third Panchen Lama in 1780 and the ban on foreign contact that came after the Gurkha invasion of Tibet in 1788, Britain lost all official contact with Tibet.

Meanwhile, Britain watched nervously as the Russian empire swallowed up Central Asia, pushing its borders 1000km further towards India. The reported arrival of Russian 'adviser' Agvan Dorjieff in Lhasa exacerbated fears that Russia had military designs on British India, the 'jewel in the crown' of the empire.

The process of reincarnation has been likened to a flame that passes from candle to candle, yet remains the same flame.

1640–42	1652	1706	1716–21
Mongolian Gushri Khan executes the King of Tsang and hands over religious and secular power to the fifth Dalai Lama. Lhasa becomes the capital and construction begins on the Potala.	The Manchu Emperor Shunzhi invites the fifth Dalai Lama to China; to mark the occasion the Yellow Temple is built on the outskirts of Běijīng.	Lhabzang Khan's army marches into Lhasa, deposes (then likely executes) the sixth Dalai Lama and installs Yeshi Gyatso, who is not accepted by Tibetans as a Dalai Lama.	Italian priest Ippolito Desideri travels to the Guge Kingdom and Lhasa, where he lives for five years, trying to convert Tibetans to Catholicism. He is the first Westerner to see Mt Kailash.

There are thought to be several thousand *trulku* (also spelt *tulku*; 'incarnate lamas') in contemporary Tibet. The abbots of many monasteries are *trulku,* and thus abbotship can be traced back through a lineage of rebirths to the original founder of a monastery. The honorific title *rinpoche,* meaning 'very precious', is a mark of respect and does not necessarily imply that the holder is a *trulku.*

A *trulku* can also be manifestation of a bodhisattva that repeatedly expresses itself through a series of rebirths. The most famous manifestation of a deity is, of course, the Dalai Lama lineage. The Dalai Lamas are manifestations of Chenresig (Avalokiteshvara), the Bodhisattva of Compassion. The Panchen Lama is a manifestation of Jampelyang (Manjushri), the Bodhisattva of Insight. There is no exclusivity in such a manifestation: Tsongkhapa, founder of the Gelugpa order, was also a manifestation of Jampelyang (Manjushri), as traditionally were the abbots of Sakya Monastery.

Lamas approaching death often leave behind clues pointing to the location of their reincarnation. Potential reincarnations are often further tested by being required to pick out the former lama's possessions from a collection of objects. Disputes over *trulku* status are not uncommon (see The Karmapa Conundrum, p100). A family's fortunes are likely to drastically improve if an incarnate lama is discovered among the children; this creates an incentive for fraud.

It is possible to see in the *trulku* system a substitute for the system of hereditary power (as in Western royal lineages) in a society where, historically, many of the major players were celibate and unable to produce their own heirs. Not that celibacy was overwhelmingly the case. The abbots of Sakya took wives to produce their own *trulku* reincarnations, and it is not uncommon for rural *trulkus* to do the same.

The major flaw in the system is the time needed for the reincarnation to reach adulthood. Regents have traditionally been appointed to run the country during the minority of a Dalai Lama but this tradition takes on an added dimension under modern political circumstances. The current Dalai Lama has made it clear that he will not be reincarnated in Chinese-occupied Tibet and may even be the last Dalai Lama.

When Dorjieff led an envoy from the Dalai Lama to Tsar Nicholas II in 1898, 1900 and 1901, and when British intelligence confirmed that Lhasa had received Russian missions (while similar British advances had been refused), the Raj broke into a cold sweat. There was even wild conjecture that the tsar was poised to convert to Buddhism.

It was against this background that Russophobe Lord Curzon, viceroy of India, decided to nip Russian designs in the bud. In late 1903, a British military expedition led by Colonel Francis Younghusband entered Tibet via Sikkim. After several months waiting for a Tibetan delegation, the British moved on to Lhasa, where it was discovered

1774	**1879**	**1893**	**1904**
Scotsman George Bogle, aged 27, travels to Tibet to investigate the opening of trade and spends the winter at Tashilhunpo Monastery in Shigatse.	The 13th Dalai Lama is enthroned. In 1895 he takes his final ordination and becomes the secular and spiritual ruler of Tibet.	Tibet cedes Sikkim and opens the Chumbi Valley to trade with British India.	The British mobilise over 8000 soldiers and launch an invasion of Tibet from the Sikkim frontier. The ill-equipped Tibetan army is no match. The 13th Dalai Lama escapes to Mongolia.

that the Dalai Lama had fled to Mongolia with Dorjieff. However, an Anglo-Tibetan convention was signed following negotiations with Tri Rinpoche, the abbot of Ganden whom the Dalai Lama had appointed as regent in his absence. British forces withdrew after spending just two months in Lhasa. For more on the story of the British invasion, see p136.

The missing link in the Anglo-Tibetan accord was a Manchu signature. In effect, the accord implied that Tibet was a sovereign power and therefore had the right to make treaties of its own. The Manchus objected and, in 1906, the British signed a second accord with the Manchus, one that recognised China's suzerainty over Tibet. In 1910, with the Manchu Qing dynasty teetering on collapse, the Manchus made good on the accord and invaded Tibet, forcing the Dalai Lama once again into flight – this time into the arms of the British in India.

Tibetan Independence Revisited

In 1911 a revolution finally toppled the decadent Qing dynasty in China, and by the end of 1912 the last of the occupying Manchu forces were escorted out of Tibet. In January 1913 the 13th Dalai Lama returned to Lhasa from Sikkim.

In reply to overtures from the government of the new Chinese republic, the Dalai Lama replied that he was uninterested in ranks bestowed by the Chinese and that he was assuming temporal and spiritual leadership of his country.

Tibetans have since read this reply as a formal declaration of independence. As for the Chinese, they chose to ignore it, reporting that the Dalai Lama had responded with a letter expressing his great love for the motherland. Whatever the case, Tibet was to enjoy 30 years free of interference from China. What is more, Tibet was suddenly presented with an opportunity to create a state that was ready to rise to the challenge of the modern world and, if need be, protect itself from the territorial ambitions of China. The opportunity foundered on Tibet's entrenched theocratic institutions, and Tibetan independence was a short-lived affair.

Attempts to Modernise

During the period of his flight to India, the 13th Dalai Lama had become friends with Sir Charles Bell, a Tibetan scholar and political officer in Sikkim. The relationship was to initiate a warming in Anglo-Tibetan affairs and to see the British playing an increasingly important role as mediators between Tibet and China.

In 1920 Bell was dispatched on a mission to Lhasa, where he renewed his friendship with the Dalai Lama. It was agreed that the British would supply the Tibetans with modern arms, providing they agreed

Scott Berry's *A Stranger in Tibet* tells the fascinating story of Ekai Kawaguchi, a young Japanese monk, who was one of the first foreigners to reach Lhasa in 1900 and who managed to stay over a year in the capital before his identity was discovered and he was forced to flee the country.

1907	1909	1910	1913
Britain and Russia acknowledge Chinese suzerainty over Tibet in a resolution of Great Game tensions.	The 13th Dalai Lama returns to Lhasa.	Chinese resident in Tibet, Zhao Erfeng, attempts to re-establish Qing authority and storms Lhasa. The Dalai Lama escapes again, this time to India. On his return he declares Tibet independent.	The Simla Convention between Britain, China and Tibet is held in India. The main agenda for the conference is to delimit and define the boundary between Tibet and China.

to use them only for self-defence. Tibetan military officers were trained in Gyantse and India, and a telegraph line was set up linking Lhasa and Shigatse. Other developments included the construction of a small hydroelectric station near Lhasa and the establishment of an English school at Gyantse. Four Tibetan boys were even sent to public school at Rugby in England. At the invitation of the Dalai Lama, British experts conducted geological surveys of parts of Tibet with a view to gauging mining potential.

It is highly likely that the 13th Dalai Lama's trips away from his country had made him realise that it was imperative that Tibet begin to modernise. At the same time he must also have been aware that the road to modernisation was fraught with obstacles, foremost of which was the entrenched Tibetan social order.

Since the rise of the Gelugpa order, Tibet had been ruled as a (some would say feudal) theocracy. Monks, particularly those in the huge monastic complexes of Drepung and Sera in Lhasa, were accustomed to a high degree of influence in the Tibetan government. And the attempts to modernise were met with intense opposition.

Before too long, the 13th Dalai Lama's innovations fell victim to a conservative backlash. Newly trained Tibetan officers were reassigned to nonmilitary jobs, causing a rapid deterioration of military discipline; a newly established police force was left to its own devices and soon became ineffective; the English school at Gyantse was closed down; and a mail service set up by the British was stopped.

However, Tibet's brief period of independence was troubled by more than just an inability to modernise. Conflict sprang up between the Panchen Lama and the Dalai Lama over the autonomy of Tashilhunpo Monastery and its estates. The Panchen Lama, after appealing to the British to mediate, fled to China, where he stayed for 14 years until his death.

In 1933 the 13th Dalai Lama died, leaving the running of the country to the regent of Reting. The present (14th) Dalai Lama was discovered in Amdo but was brought to Lhasa only after the local Chinese commander had been paid off with a huge 'fee' of 300,000 Chinese dollars. The boy was renamed Tenzin Gyatso and he was installed as the Dalai Lama on 22 February 1940, aged 4½.

In 1947 an attempted coup d'état, known as the Reting Conspiracy, rocked Lhasa. Lhasa came close to civil war, with 200 monks killed in gunfights at Sera Monastery. Reting Rinpoche was thrown into jail for his part in the rebellion and was later found dead in his cell, though it remains unclear whether he was set up or not.

It was not a good time for Tibet to be weakened by internal disputes. By 1949 the Chinese Nationalist government had fled to Taiwan and

The Younghusband invasion of Tibet included 10,091 porters, 7096 mules, 2668 ponies, 4466 yaks and six camels, in a train that stretched for 7km!

Charles Allen's *Duel in the Snows* brings to life the 1903–4 Younghusband expedition to Tibet, through the letters and accounts of its main protagonists.

1923	1933	1935	1950
A clash with Lhasa sends the Panchen Lama into exile in China. This is to have disastrous consequences for Tibet: he comes under Chinese influence and never returns.	The 13th Dalai Lama dies, and secular authority is passed to Reting Rinpoche, who rules as regent until 1947. He is an eminent Gelugpa Lama, but young and inexperienced in state affairs.	Birth of the present 14th Dalai Lama in Taktser village, Amdo, just outside Xīníng in present Qīnghǎi; his younger and older brothers are also *trulkus* (reincarnated lamas).	China attacks Chamdo; the Tibetan army is greatly outnumbered and defeat is swift. The Tibetan government in Lhasa reacts by enthroning the 15-year-old 14th Dalai Lama. There is jubilation in the streets.

Mao Zedong and his Red Army had taken control of China. Big changes were looming.

Liberation

Fans of Great Game history can visit Gyantse Dzong and nearby Tsechen Dzong, both of which were taken by Younghusband in 1904, as well as the Karo La, scene of the highest battle in British Imperial history.

Unknown to the Tibetans, the communist takeover of China was to open what is probably the saddest chapter in Tibetan history. The ensuing Chinese 'liberation' of Tibet eventually led to the deaths of hundreds of thousands of Tibetans, a full-on assault on the Tibetan traditional way of life, the flight of the Dalai Lama to India and the large-scale destruction of almost every historical structure on the plateau. The chief culprits were Chinese ethnic chauvinism and an epidemic of social madness known as the Cultural Revolution.

On 7 October 1950, just a year after the communist takeover of China, 40,000 battle-hardened Chinese troops attacked central Tibet from six different directions. The Tibetan army, a poorly equipped force of around 4000 men, stood little chance of resisting, and any attempt at defence soon collapsed before the onslaught. In Lhasa, the Tibetan government reacted by enthroning the 15-year-old 14th Dalai Lama, an action that brought jubilation and dancing on the streets but did little to protect Tibet from advancing Chinese troops.

Presented with a seemingly hopeless situation, the Dalai Lama dispatched a mission to Běijīng with orders that it refer all decisions to Lhasa. As it turned out, there were no decisions to be made. The Chinese had already drafted an agreement. The Tibetans had two choices: sign on the dotted line or face further military action.

The 17-point *Agreement on Measures for the Peaceful Liberation of Tibet* promised a one-country-two-systems structure much like that offered later to Hong Kong and Macau, but provided little in the way of guarantees. The Tibetan delegates protested that they were unauthorised to sign such an agreement but were strongarmed and the agreement was ratified.

The Snow Lion and the Dragon by Melvyn Goldstein is worth wading through if you want an unsentimental analysis of the historically complex issue of China's claims to Tibet, and the Dalai Lama's options in dealing with the current Chinese leadership.

Initially, the Chinese occupation of central Tibet was carried out in an orderly way, with few obvious changes or reforms, but tensions inevitably mounted. The presence of large numbers of Chinese troops in the Lhasa region soon affected food stores and gave rise to high inflation. Rumours of political indoctrination, massacres and attacks on monasteries in Kham (far eastern Tibet) slowly began to filter back to Lhasa.

In 1956 uprisings broke out in eastern Tibet (see the box, p193) in reaction to enforced land reform, and in 1957 and 1958 protests and armed guerrilla revolt spread to central Tibet (with covert CIA assistance). With a heavy heart, the Dalai Lama returned to Lhasa in March 1957 from a trip to India to celebrate the 2500th anniversary of the birth of the Buddha. It seemed inevitable that Tibet would explode in

1950	1951	1954	1955
El Salvador sponsors a UN motion to condemn Chinese aggression in Tibet. Britain and India, traditional friends of Tibet, convince the UN not to debate the issue.	The 17 Point Agreement is signed by the Governor of Kham, acknowledging Tibet as a part of the People's Republic of China (PRC). Chairman Mao's first remark is 'Welcome Back to the Motherland'.	In 1954 the Dalai Lama spends almost a year in Běijīng, where, amid cordial discussions with Mao Zedong, he is told that religion is 'poison'.	Xikang province is absorbed into Sichuān province, eating up a large chunk of the traditional Tibetan province of Kham.

revolt and equally inevitable that it would be ruthlessly suppressed by the Chinese.

Uprising & Bloodshed

The Tibetan New Year of 1959, like all the New Year celebrations before it, attracted huge crowds to Lhasa, doubling the city's population. In addition to the standard festival activities, the Chinese had added a highlight of their own – a performance by a Chinese dance group at the Lhasa military base. The invitation to the Dalai Lama came in the form of a thinly veiled command. The Dalai Lama, wishing to avoid offence, accepted.

As preparations for the performance drew near, however, the Dalai Lama's security chief was surprised to hear that the Dalai Lama was expected to attend in secrecy and without his customary contingent of 25 bodyguards. Despite the Dalai Lama's agreement to these conditions, news of them soon leaked, and in no time simmering frustration at Chinese rule came to the boil among the crowds on the streets. It seemed obvious to the Tibetans that the Chinese were about to kidnap the Dalai Lama. A huge crowd (witnesses claim 30,000 people) gathered around the Norbulingka (the Dalai Lama's summer palace) and swore to protect him with their lives.

The Dalai Lama had no choice but to cancel his appointment at the military base. In the meantime, the crowds on the streets were swollen by Tibetan soldiers, who changed out of their People's Liberation Army (PLA) uniforms and started to hand out weapons. A group of government ministers announced that the 17-point agreement was null and void, and that Tibet renounced the authority of China.

The Dalai Lama was powerless to intervene, managing only to pen some conciliatory letters to the Chinese as his people prepared for battle on Lhasa's streets. In a last-ditch effort to prevent bloodshed, the Dalai Lama even offered himself to the Chinese. The reply came in the sound of two mortar shells exploding in the gardens of the Norbulingka. The attack made it obvious that the only option remaining to the Dalai Lama was flight. On 17 March, he left the Norbulingka disguised as a soldier and surrounded by Khampa bodyguards. Fourteen days later he was in India. The Dalai Lama was 24 years old.

With both the Chinese and the Tibetans unaware of the Dalai Lama's departure, tensions continued to mount in Lhasa. On 20 March, Chinese troops began to shell the Norbulingka and the crowds surrounding it, killing hundreds of people. Artillery bombed the Potala, Sera Monastery and the medical college on Chagpo Ri. Tibetans armed with petrol bombs were picked off by Chinese snipers, and when a crowd of 10,000 Tibetans retreated into the sacred precincts of the Jokhang, that too was bombed. It is thought that after three days of violence,

While laying in state the head of the 13th Dalai Lama's corpse allegedly repeatedly turned towards the northeast, indicating that the 14th Dalai Lama would be born in Amdo.

A scholarly account of modern Tibet is Melvyn Goldstein's *A History of Modern Tibet 1913–1951: The Demise of the Lamaist State*, which pulls no punches in showing the intrigues, superstitions and ineptitude that led to the demise of the Lhasa government. A second volume covers the years 1951–55.

HISTORY UPRISING & BLOODSHED

1956	late 1950s
Rebellions break out in monasteries in Kham (modern-day western Sichuan). The siege of Lithang rebellion lasts 67 days and ends in aerial bombardment of the monastery.	The Khampas found the resistance group Four Rivers, Six Ranges. The Tibetan exile groups in India make contact with the CIA; Tibetans are sent for training to the Pacific island of Saipan.

ANTHONY PLUMMER

» Norbulingka palace, shelled by the Chinese in 1959

hundreds of Tibetans lay dead in Lhasa's streets. Some estimates put the numbers of those killed far higher.

Socialist Paradise on the Roof of the World

The Chinese quickly consolidated their quelling of the Lhasa uprising by taking control of all the high passes between Tibet and India and disarming the Khampa guerrillas. As the Chinese themselves put it, they were liberating Tibet from reactionary forces, freeing serfs from the yoke of monastic oppression and ushering in a new equitable social-ist society, whether the Tibetans liked it or not.

The Chinese abolished the Tibetan government and set about re-ordering Tibetan society in accordance with their Marxist principles. The monks and the aristocratic were put to work on menial jobs and subjected to violent ideological struggle sessions, known as *thamzing,* which sometimes resulted in death. A ferment of class struggle was

THE FALL OF CHAMDO

In spring 1950, Chamdo was in real trouble. Although there were still pockets of re-sistance at Derge and Markham, the communist Chinese had taken control of most of Kham without even a fight. Chinese armies were moving in on Tibet from Xīnjiāng and Xikang (now Sìchuān) provinces in a strategy masterminded by, among others, Deng Xiaoping.

The first skirmish between Chinese and Tibetan troops took place in May 1950 when the People's Liberation Army (PLA) attacked Dengo on the Dri-chu (Yangzi River). Then on 7 October 1950 the PLA moved in earnest, as 40,000 troops crossed the Dri-chu and attacked Chamdo from three directions: Jyekundo to the north, Derge to the east and Markham to the south.

As panic swept through Chamdo, the city responded to the military threat in char-acteristic Tibetan fashion – a frenzy of prayer and religious ritual. When the local Tibetan leader radioed the Tibetan government in Lhasa to warn of the Chinese inva-sion, he was coolly told that the government members couldn't be disturbed because they were 'on a picnic'. To this the Chamdo radio operator is said to have replied *'skyag pa'i gling kha!',* or 'shit the picnic!'. It was to be the last ever communication between the Chamdo and Lhasa branches of the Tibetan government.

The city was evacuated (with the Chamdo government commandeering most of the town's horses) but the PLA was one step ahead. Chinese leaders know that speed is of the essence (the Chinese described the military operation as 'like a tiger trying to catch a fly') and had already cut the Tibetans off by taking Riwoche. The Tibetans surrendered without a shot on 19 October. The Tibetan troops were disarmed, given lectures on the benefits of socialism, and then given money and sent home. It was the beginning of the end of an independent Tibet.

1962	1964	1 September 1965	1967–76
The Indo-Chinese war ends in defeat for India, but territorial disputes over Arunachel Pradesh and Aksai-Chin continue to this day between the two rising giants.	The Panchen Rinpoche writes the 70,000 Characters Petition, accusing China of committing genocide. Arrested, he is charged with instigating rebellion and planning to flee to India.	The Tibetan Autonomous Region (TAR) is formally brought into being with much fanfare and Chinese talk of happy Tibetans fighting back tears of gratitude at becoming one with the great motherland.	The Cultural Revolution sweeps China and Tibet. Ideological frenzy results in the destruction of monasteries, shrines and libraries and the imprisonment of thousands of Tibetans.

whipped up and former feudal exploiters – towards some of whom Tibet's poor may have harboured genuine resentment – were subjected to punishments of awful cruelty.

The Chinese also turned their attention to Tibet's several thousand 'feudal' monasteries. Tibetans were refused permission to donate food to the monasteries, and monks were compelled to join struggle sessions, discard their robes and marry. Monasteries were stripped of their riches, Buddhist scriptures were burnt and used as toilet paper. The wholesale destruction of Tibet's monastic heritage began in earnest.

Notable in this litany of disasters was the Chinese decision to alter Tibetan farming practices, as part of an economic 'Great Leap Forward'. Instead of barley, the Tibetan staple, farmers were instructed to grow wheat and rice. Tibetans protested that these crops were unsuited to Tibet's high altitude. They were right, and mass starvation resulted. It is estimated that by late 1961, 70,000 Tibetans had died or were dying of starvation.

By September 1961, even the Chinese-groomed Panchen Lama began to have a change of heart. He presented Mao Zedong with a 70,000-character report on the hardships his people were suffering and also requested, among other things, religious freedom and an end to the sacking of Tibetan monasteries. Four years later he was to disappear into a high-security prison for a 10-year stay. Many more would soon join him.

The Cultural Revolution

Among the writings of Mao Zedong is a piece entitled 'On Going Too Far'. It is a subject on which he was particularly well qualified to write. What started as a power struggle between Mao and Liu Shaoqi in 1965 had morphed by August 1966 into the Great Proletarian Cultural Revolution, an anarchic movement that was to shake China to its core, trample its traditions underfoot, cause countless deaths and give the running of the country over to mobs of Red Guards. All of China suffered in Mao's bold experiment in creating a new socialist paradise, but it Tibet suffered more than most.

The first Red Guards arrived in Lhasa in July 1966. Two months later, the first rally was organised and Chinese-educated Tibetan youths raided the Jokhang, smashing statues, burning thangkas and desecrating whatever religious objects they could get their hands on. It was the beginning of the large-scale destruction of virtually every religious monument in Tibet, and was carried out in the spirit of destroying the 'Four Olds': old thinking, old culture, old habits and old customs. Images of Chairman Mao were plastered over those of Buddha, as Buddhist man-

An illuminating glimpse of the Tibetan experience is provided by *Freedom in Exile: The Autobiography of the Dalai Lama*. With great humility the Dalai Lama outlines his personal philosophy, his hope to be reunited with his homeland and the story of his life. *Kundun* by Mary Craig is a biography of the Dalai Lama's family.

John Avedon's *In Exile from the Land of Snows* is largely an account of the Tibetan community in Dharamsala, but is an excellent and informative read.

1975	1979–85	1982	1987–89
The last CIA-funded Tibetan guerrilla bases in Mustang, northern Nepal, are closed down, bringing an end to armed rebellion and CIA involvement in the Tibetan resistance movement.	China enters a period of liberalisation and reform and limited religious freedoms are restored in Tibet. Out of a pre-1950 total of around 2000 monasteries, only 45 are reopened.	A three-person team sent to Běijīng from Dharamsala is told Tibet is part of China and that the Dalai Lama would be given a desk job in Běijīng on his return. By 1983 talks had broken down.	Pro-independence demonstrations take place in Lhasa; the response is violent, several tourists are injured and martial law is declared.

tras were replaced by communist slogans. The Buddha himself was accused of being a 'reactionary'.

Tibetan farmers were forced to collectivise into communes and were told what to grow and when to grow it. Anyone who objected was arrested and subjected to violent political struggle sessions, during which Tibetans were forced to denounce the Dalai Lama as a parasite and traitor. In an atmosphere of escalating madness, individual tragedies occurred on a national scale.

In 1972 restrictions on Tibetans' freedom of worship were lifted with much fanfare but little in the way of results. In 1975 a group of foreign journalists sympathetic to the Chinese cause were invited to Tibet. The reports they filed gave a sad picture of a land whose people had been battered by Chinese-imposed policies and atrocities that amounted to nothing less than cultural genocide.

The Dust Settles

By the time of Mao's death in 1976 even the Chinese had begun to realise that their rule in Tibet had taken a wrong turn. Mao's chosen successor, Hua Guofeng, decided to soften the government's line on Tibet and called for a revival of Tibetan customs. In mid-1977 China announced that it would welcome the return of the Dalai Lama and other Tibetan refugees, and shortly afterwards the Panchen Lama was released from more than 10 years of imprisonment.

The Tibetan government-in-exile received cautiously the invitation to return to Tibet, and the Dalai Lama suggested that he be allowed to send a fact-finding mission to Tibet first. To the surprise of all involved, the Chinese agreed. As the Dalai Lama remarked in his autobiography, *Freedom in Exile,* it seemed that the Chinese were of the opinion that the mission members would find such happiness in their homeland that 'they would see no point in remaining in exile'. In fact, the results of the mission were so damning that the Dalai Lama decided not to publish them.

Nevertheless, two more missions followed. Their conclusions were despairing. The missions claimed up to 1.2 million deaths (one in six Tibetans, according to the disputed report), the destruction of 6254 monasteries and nunneries, the absorption of two-thirds of Tibet into China, 100,000 Tibetans in labour camps and extensive deforestation. In a mere 30 years, the Chinese had turned Tibet into a land of nearly unrecognisable desolation.

In China, Hua Guofeng's short-lived political ascendancy had been eclipsed by Deng Xiaoping's rise to power. In 1980 Deng sent Hu Yaobang on a Chinese fact-finding mission that coincided with the visits of those sent by the Tibetan government-in-exile.

Cultural Revolution–Era Ruins

» Jampaling Chorten, Tsangpo Valley

» Thöling Monastery, Zanda

» Dradun Gompa, Zhongba

Sorrow Mountain: The Journey of a Tibetan Warrior Nun by Ani Pachen and Adelaide Donnelly is the story of a nun who became a resistance leader and was imprisoned by the Chinese for 21 years before escaping to India.

1988

The 14th Dalai Lama shifts his government's stand away from Tibetan independence, opting instead for the 'middle path' of autonomy.

1989

The Dalai Lama's efforts to achieve peace and freedom for his people are recognised when he is awarded the Nobel Peace Prize.

MERTEN SNIJDERS

» Video clips of the Qīnghǎi–Tibet railway, opened in 2006

Hu's conclusions, while not as damning as those of the Tibetans, painted a grim picture of life on the roof of the world. A six-point plan to improve the living conditions and freedoms of the Tibetans was drawn up, taxes were dropped for two years and limited private enterprise was allowed. The Jokhang was reopened for two days a month in 1978; the Potala opened in 1980. As in the rest of China, the government embarked on a program of extended personal and economic freedoms in concert with authoritarian one-party rule.

Reforms & Riots

The early 1980s saw the return of limited religious freedoms. Monasteries that had not been reduced to piles of rubble began to reopen and some religious artefacts were returned to Tibet from China.

Importantly, there was also a relaxation of the Chinese proscription on pilgrimage. Pictures of the Dalai Lama began to reappear on the streets of Lhasa. Talks aimed at bringing the Dalai Lama back into the ambit of Chinese influence continued, but with little result. Tibet, according to the Chinese government, became the 'front line of the struggle against splittism', a line that continues to be the official government position to this day.

In 1986 a new influx of foreigners arrived in Tibet, with the Chinese beginning to loosen restrictions on tourism. The trickle of tour groups and individual travellers soon became a flood. For the first time since the Chinese takeover, visitors from the West were given the opportunity to see the results of Chinese rule in Tibet.

When in September 1987 a group of 30 monks from Sera Monastery began circumambulating the Jokhang and crying out 'Independence for Tibet' and 'Long live his Holiness the Dalai Lama', their ranks were swollen by bystanders and arrests followed. Four days later, another group of monks repeated their actions, this time brandishing Tibetan flags. The monks were beaten and arrested. With Western tourists looking on, a crowd of 2000 to 3000 angry Tibetans gathered. Police vehicles were overturned and Chinese police began firing on the crowd.

The Chinese response was swift. Communications with the outside world were broken but this failed to prevent further protests in the following months. The Mönlam festival of March 1988 saw shooting in the streets of Lhasa, and that December a Dutch traveller was shot in the shoulder; 18 Tibetans died and 150 were wounded in the disturbances.

The Dalai Lama & the Search for Settlement

By the mid-1970s the Dalai Lama had become a prominent international figure, working tirelessly from his government-in-exile in Dharamsala to

The journalist Harrison Salisbury referred to Tibet in the mid-1980s as a 'dark and sorrowing land'.

Neither Mao Zedong nor Deng Xiaoping ever visited Tibet.

September 2006	2006	2007	10–14 March 2008
Western climbers on Mt Cho Oyu film Chinese border guards shooting unarmed nuns as they flee China over the Nangpa-la to Nepal.	The 4545m Nathu-la pass with Sikkim opens to local traders for the first time in 44 years, hinting at warmer ties between India and China.	The Chinese government passes a new law requiring all incarnate lamas to be approved by the government, part of an attempt to increase political control over Tibet's religious hierarchy.	In the run-up to the Olympic games in Běijīng, major riots hit Lhasa, spreading to southern Gānsù and western Sichuān. Nineteen people are killed and thousands are subsequently arrested.

make the world more aware of his people's plight. In 1987 he addressed the US Congress and outlined a five-point peace plan.

The plan called for Tibet to be established as a 'zone of peace'; for the policy of Han immigration to Tibet to be abandoned; for a return to basic human rights and democratic freedoms; for the protection of Tibet's natural heritage and an end to the dumping of nuclear waste on the high plateau; and for joint discussions between the Chinese and the Tibetans on the future of Tibet. The Chinese denounced the plan as an example of 'splittism'. They gave the same response when, a year later, the Dalai Lama elaborated on the speech before the European parliament at Strasbourg in France, dropping demands for full independence in favour of a form of autonomy and offering the Chinese the right to govern Tibet's foreign and military affairs.

On 5 March 1989 Lhasa erupted in the largest anti-Chinese demonstration since 1959. Běijīng reacted strongly, declaring martial law in Tibet, which lasted for more than a year. Despairing elements in the exiled Tibetan community began to talk of the need to take up arms. It was an option that for the Dalai Lama had consistently opposed. His efforts to achieve peace and freedom for his people were recognised on 4 October 1989, when he was awarded the Nobel Peace Prize.

In January 1989, after denouncing the Communist Party's policies in Tibet and while visiting Tashilhunpo, the traditional seat of all the Panchen Lamas, the 10th Panchen Lama died, triggering a succession crisis that remains unresolved (see p144). The Dalai Lama identified the 11th Panchen Lama in 1995, whereupon the Chinese authorities detained the boy and his family (who have not been seen since) and orchestrated the choice of their own preferred candidate. The Chinese began to toughen their policy towards the Dalai Lama and launched the anti-Dalai Lama campaign inside Tibet, compelling all government officials and monks to denounce the Dalai Lama.

The Chinese authorities believe that one of the reasons for continuing separatist sentiments and opposition is Tibet's lack of integration with China. The solution since the mid-1980s has been to encourage Han immigration to the high plateau, a policy already successfully carried out in Xīnjiáng, Inner Mongolia and Qīnghǎi. As Běijīng attempts to shift the economic gains of the east coast to its underdeveloped hinterland, hundreds of thousands of Han Chinese have taken advantage of attractive salaries and interest-free loans to 'modernise' the backward province of Tibet. By the end of the millennium Tibetans were facing the fastest and deepest-reaching changes in their history.

Education was once under the exclusive control of the monasteries, and the introduction of a secular education system has been a major goal of the communist government. These days most education is in the Chinese language.

The Panchen Lamas have their reincarnation confirmed by lots drawn from a golden urn. You can see the urn in the Tibet Museum in Lhasa.

2008	1 Oct 2009	2010	14 April 2010
Pro-Tibetan protests disrupt the procession of the Olympic flag in Paris, London and San Francisco, though not in Tibet where the flag is carried to the top of Mt Everest.	The 60th anniversary of communist rule in China is celebrated with tightly guarded parades in Běijīng.	The Dalai Lama celebrates his 75th birthday.	A huge 6.9 scale earthquake devastates Jyekundo (Yùshù) in Amdo (southeast Qīnghǎi), killing over 2000 people and leaving tens of thousands homeless.

Landscapes in the Land of the Snows

It's hard to overstate the global significance of the Tibetan plateau. Not only is it the earth's highest ecosystem and one of its last remaining great wildernesses, but it also contains the world's highest number of glaciers outside the poles, which is a major factor behind Tibet being the source of Asia's greatest rivers. In fact, rivers that start life on the Tibetan plateau deliver water to 85% of people in Asia – that's half the world's population!

Furthermore, it is thought that the high plateau affects global jet streams and even influences the Indian monsoon. It's perhaps understandable, then, that the Dalai Lama would like to see Tibet turned into a 'zone of peace' and maybe even the world's largest national park.

The Tibetan Buddhist view of the environment has long stressed the intricate and interconnected relationship between the natural world and human beings, a viewpoint closely linked to the concept of death and rebirth. Buddhist practice in general stands for moderation and against overconsumption, and tries to avoid wherever possible hunting, fishing and the taking of animal life. Tibetan nomads, in particular, live in a fine balance with their harsh environment.

These days it's the Chinese government rather than Tibetan nomads that holds the fate of this fragile ecosystem in its hands, and the way in which it deals with such a massive responsibility will undoubtedly shape the future of billions of people.

The dry, high altitudes of the Tibetan plateau make for climatic extremes – temperatures on the Changtang have been known to drop 27°C in a single day!

The Roof of the World

The Tibetan plateau is one of the most isolated regions in the world, bound to the south by the 2500km-long Himalaya, to the west by the Karakoram and to the north by the Kunlun and Altyn Tagh ranges, some of the least explored ranges on earth. Four of the world's 10 highest mountains straddle Tibet's southern border with Nepal. The northwest in particular is bound by the most remote and least explored wilderness left on earth, outside the polar regions. With an average altitude of 4000m and large swathes of the country well above 5000m, the Tibetan plateau (nearly the size of Western Europe) deserves the title 'the roof of the world'.

Much of Tibet is a harsh and uncompromising landscape, best described as a high-altitude desert. Little of the Indian monsoon makes it over the Himalayan watershed. Shifting sand dunes are a common sight along the Samye Valley and the road to Mt Kailash.

As early as 1642, the fifth Dalai Lama issued an edict protecting animals and the environment.

But the plateau's regions are diverse. Traditionally Tibet comprised three large regions: Kham, Amdo and Ütsang. But these were disbanded with the creation of the Chinese province, the Tibetan Autonomous Region (TAR). TAR only contains the central, southern and western regions of the Tibetan plateau. Amdo, for example, lies entirely outside the TAR in Qīnghǎi, Gānsù and northern Sìchuān provinces, while much of Kham is parcelled off into west Sìchuān and northwest Yúnnán. Even within TAR's borders, though, landscapes are vast and varied. These areas can be loosely divided into four major regions.

> The Chinese province commonly referred to as Tibet is officially called the Tibetan Autonomous Region (TAR) and has an area of 1.23 million sq km; bigger than the combined area of France, Spain and Portugal.

Ütsang

Made up of the combined regions of Ü and Tsang, which constitute central Tibet, Ütsang is the political, historical and agricultural heartland of Tibet. Its relatively fertile valleys enjoy a mild climate and are irrigated by wide rivers such as the Yarlung Tsangpo and the Kyi-chu.

Changtang

Towards the north of Ütsang are the harsh, high-altitude plains of the Changtang (northern plateau), the highest and largest plateau in the world, occupying an area of more than one million sq km (think France, the UK and Germany). This area has no river systems and supports very little in the way of life. The dead lakes of the Changtang are the brackish remnants of the Tethys Sea that found no run-off when the plateau started its skyward ascent.

> If you want to identify Tibetan medicinal plants, check out *Tibetan Medical Thangkas of the Four Medical Tantras*, a lavish coffee-table book available in most Lhasa bookshops.

Ngari

Ngari, or western Tibet, is similarly barren, although here river valleys provide grassy tracts that support nomads and their grazing animals. Indeed, the Kailash range in the far west of Tibet is the source of the subcontinent's four greatest rivers: the Ganges, Indus, Sutlej and Brahmaputra. The Ganges, Indus and Sutlej Rivers all cascade out of Tibet in its far west, not far from Mt Kailash itself. The Brahmaputra (known in Tibet as Yarlung Tsangpo) meanders along the northern spine of the Himalaya for 2000km, searching for a way south, before coiling back on itself in a dramatic U-turn and draining into India not far from the Myanmar border.

Kham

Eastern Tibet marks a tempestuous drop in elevation down to the Sìchuān plain. The concertina landscape produces some of the most

FLORA OR FAUNA?

In early summer (May and June) you will see nomads and entrepreneurs camped in the high passes of eastern Tibet, digging for a strange root known as *yartsa gunbu* (*Cordiceps sinensis*) that locals say is half vegetable, half caterpillar. It is actually a fusion of a caterpillar and the parasitic fungus that mummifies it. The Chinese name for the root is *dōngchóng xiàcǎo* (冬虫夏草; 'winter-worm, summer-grass'), a direct translation of the Tibetan name. Used by long-distance Chinese runners, it's also nicknamed Himalayan Viagra, and is used in Tibetan and Chinese medicine as an aphrodisiac and tonic similar to ginseng.

Fetching anywhere from Y3000 to Y40,000 per kilo, it's one of the most expensive commodities in Tibet. The business is most lucrative in Tengchen county, where amazingly it accounts for more than 60% of the local GDP. Entire tent villages spring up on the grasslands during harvest time, equipped with restaurants and shops, and it's not unusual for fights to erupt between the local communities and outside speculators. With the economic boom in Tibet and China, it's now being imported from Dolpo, Ladakh and Kashmir.

spectacular roller-coaster roads in Asia, as Himalayan extensions such as the Hengduan Mountains are sliced by the deep gorges of the Yangzi (Dri-chu in Tibetan; Jīnshā Jiāng in Chinese), Salween (Gyalmo Ngul-chu in Tibetan; Nù Jiāng in Chinese) and Mekong (Dza-chu in Tibetan; Láncáng Jiāng in Chinese) headwaters.

The Yarlung Tsangpo crashes through a 5km-deep gorge here (the world's deepest) as it swings around 7756m Namche Barwa. Many parts of this alpine region are lushly forested and support abundant wildlife, largely thanks to the lower altitudes and effects of the Indian monsoon.

In the arid climate of much of Tibet, water takes on a special significance. The *lu* (water spirits) guard the wellbeing of the community and are thought to be very dangerous if angered.

The Struggle for Life

The vast differences in altitude in Tibet give rise to a spread of eco-systems from alpine to subtropical, but generally speaking life on the Ti-betan Plateau is a harsh one and travellers are unlikely to encounter too much in the way of wildlife. Nevertheless, for those that have the time to get off the beaten track – particularly off the Friendship Hwy – or to go trekking in more remote areas, there are some unusual and understand-ably hardened species out there.

What Will I See?

On the road out to Mt Kailash, it is not unusual to see herds of fleet-footed Tibetan gazelles *(gowa)*, antelope *(tso)* and wild asses *(kyang)*, particularly along the northern route. During the breeding season antelope converge in groups numbering several hundred.

Trekkers might conceivably see the Himalayan black bear or, if they're exceeding lucky, the giant Tibetan blue bear searching for food in the alpine meadows. Herds of blue sheep, also known as bharal *(nawa na)*, are frequently spied on rocky slopes and outcrops (although the dwarf bharal is much rarer), but the argali, the largest species of wild sheep in the world, now only survives in the most remote mountain fastnesses of western Tibet.

Wolves of various colours can be seen all over the Tibetan plateau. Much rarer than the all-black wolf is the white wolf, one of the sacred animals of Tibet. Smaller carnivores include the lynx, marten and fox.

Marmots *(chiwa* or *piya)* are very common and can often be seen perched up on their hind legs sniffing the air curiously outside their bur-rows – they make a strange birdlike sound when distressed. The pika *(chipi)*, or Himalayan mouse-hare, a relative of the rabbit, is also com-mon. Pikas have been observed at 5250m on Mt Everest, thus earning the distinction of having the highest habitat of any mammal.

Geographically speaking, the Tibetan plateau makes up almost 25% of China's total landmass, spread over five provinces.

A surprising number of migratory birds make their way up to the lakes of the Tibetan plateau through spring and summer. Tibet has over 30 endemic birds, and 480 species have been recorded on the plateau. Birds include the black-necked crane (whose numbers in Tibet have

FROM SEABED TO SNOW CAPS: THE RISE OF TIBET

The high plateau of Tibet is the result of prodigious geological upheaval. The time scale is subject to much debate, but at some point in the last 100 million years the en-tire region lay beneath the Tethys Sea. And that is where it would have stayed had the mass of land now known as India not broken free from the protocontinent Gondwana and drifted off in a collision course with another protocontinent known as Laurasia. The impact of the two land masses sent the Indian plate burrowing under the Laur-asian landmass, and two vast parallel ridges, over 3000km in length and in places almost 9km high, piled up. These ridges, the Himalaya and associated ranges, are still rising at around 10cm a year. You may well find locals near Shegar selling fossils of marine animals – at an altitude of more than 4000m above sea level!

Two of the best places to go bird-watching are Yamdrok-tso and Nam-tso; a section of the latter has been designated a bird preserve, at least on paper. April and November are the best times.

doubled over the last decade), bar-headed goose and lammergeier, as well as grebes, pheasants, snow cocks and partridges. Watching a pair of black-necked cranes, loyal mates for life, is one of the joys of traipsing near the wetlands of northern and western Tibet. Flocks of huge vultures can often be seen circling monasteries looking for a sky burial.

Of course, you'll see lots and lots of yaks, but almost all them will be the domesticated variety rather than wild yaks (or *drong*), and many won't even be yaks at all, but will be *dzo,* a cross between a yak and a cow.

On the Brink

About 80 species of animal that are threatened with extinction have been listed as protected by the Chinese government. These include the almost-mythical snow leopard *(gang-zig)* as well as the wild yak *(drong).*

The Tibetan red deer was recently 'discovered' only 75km from Lhasa after a 50-year hiatus, as was a hitherto unknown breed of ancient wild horse in the Riwoche region of eastern Tibet. The horses, discovered in a remote valley in 1995 by French ethnologist Michel Peissel, bear a striking resemblance to those shown in Stone Age paintings. It is still unknown how many remain.

Wild yaks are mostly encountered in the far northern region of Changtang. The biggest bull yaks are reputed to be as large as a 4WD. Even rarer is the divine giant white yak, thought by Tibetans to inhabit the higher reaches of sacred mountains.

The *chiru,* a rare breed of antelope, was recently placed on the Red List (www.redlist.org), a list of threatened species maintained by the World Conservation Union. Numbers in Tibet dropped from over a million *chiru* 50 years ago to as few as 70,000, although they are believed to have picked up again in the past five years and may now number more 100,000. Poachers kill the animal for its *shatoosh* wool (wool from the animal's undercoat).

The illegal trade in antelope cashmere, musk, bear paws and gall bladders, deer antlers, and other body parts and bones remains a problem. You can often see Tibetan traders huddled on street corners in major Chinese cities selling these and other medicinal cures.

Tibet in Bloom

Juniper trees and willows are common in the valleys of central Tibet and it is possible to come across wildflowers such as the pansy and the oleander, as well as unique indigenous flowers such as the *tsi-tog* (a light-pink, high-altitude bloom).

PROTECTING THE PLATEAU

Nature reserves officially protect over 20% of the TAR, although many exist on paper only. The reserve with the highest profile is the Qomolangma Nature Reserve, a 34,000-sq-km protected area straddling the 'third pole' of the Everest region. The park promotes the involvement of the local population, which is essential as around 67,000 people live within the park.

Tibet's newest reserve is the Changtang Nature Reserve, set up in 1993 with the assistance of famous animal behaviourist George Schaller. At 247,120 sq km (larger than Arizona), this is the largest nature reserve in the world after Greenland National Park. Endangered species in the park include bharal, argali sheep, wolves, lynxes, gazelles, snow leopards, wild yaks, antelopes, brown bears and wild asses.

Other reserves include the Great Canyon of the Yarlung Tsangpo Nature Reserve (formerly the Metok reserve) to the south of Namche Barwa, the Dzayul (Zayu) Reserve along the far southeast border with Assam, and the Kyirong and Nyalam Reserves near the Nepali border. Unfortunately, these reserves enjoy little protection or policing.

Fifty years ago an estimated one million wild yaks roamed the Tibetan plateau. Now it is a rare treat to catch a glimpse of one of these huge creatures. They weigh up to a tonne and can reach 1.8m at the shoulder, while their sharp, slender horns often span 1m. Wild yaks have diminished in number to 15,000 as a result of the increased demand for yak meat and a rise in hunting, which is illegal.

Few, if any, of the yaks that travellers see are *drong* (wild yaks). In fact, most are not even yaks at all but rather *dzo*, a cross between a yak and a cow. A domestic yak rarely exceeds 1.5m in height. Unlike its wild relative, which is almost always black, the *dzo* varies in shade from black to grey and, primarily around Kokonor in Qīnghǎi, white.

With three times more red blood cells than the average cow, the yak thrives in the oxygen-depleted high altitudes. Its curious lung formation, surrounded by 14 or 15 pairs of ribs rather than the 13 typical of cattle, allows a large capacity for inhaling and expelling air. In fact, a descent below 3000m may impair the reproductive cycle and expose the yak to parasites and disease.

Tibetans rely on yak milk for cheese, as well as for butter for the ubiquitous butter tea and offerings to butter lamps in monasteries. The outer hair of the yak is woven into tent fabric and rope, and the soft inner wool is spun into *chara* (a type of felt) and used to make bags, blankets and tents. Tails are used in both Buddhist and Hindu religious practices. Yak hide is used for the soles of boots and the yak's heart is used in Tibetan medicine. In the nomadic tradition, no part of the animal is wasted and even yak dung is required as a fundamental fuel, left to dry in little cakes on the walls of most Tibetan houses. In fact, so important are yaks to the Tibetans that the animals are individually named, like children.

Eastern Tibet, which sees higher rainfall, has an amazing range of flora, from oak, elm and birch forests to bamboo, subtropical plants and flowers, including rhododendrons, azaleas and magnolias. It was from here that intrepid 19th-century plant hunters FM Bailey, Frank Kingdon Ward and Frank Ludlow took the seeds and cuttings of species that would eventually become staples in English gardening.

A Fragile Ecosystem

Tibet has an abundance of natural resources: many types of minerals, strong sunlight, fierce winds and raging rivers that supply water to an estimated 49% of the world's population.

How the Chinese government harnesses these resources, particularly Tibet's water, without harming their long-term sustainability could be vital for the future of half the planet.

Modern communist experiments, such as collectivisation and the changing of century-old farming patterns (for example, from barley to wheat and rice), upset the fragile balance in Tibet and resulted in a series of great disasters and famines in the 1960s (as, indeed, they did in the rest of China). By the mid-1970s, the failure of collectivisation was widely recognised and Tibetans have since been allowed to return to traditional methods of working the land.

The Tibetan plateau has rich deposits of gold, zinc, chromium, silver, boron, uranium and other metals. The plateau is home to most of China's huge copper reserves. A single mine in northern Tibet is said to hold over half the world's total deposits of lithium, while the Changtang holds five billion tonnes of oil and gas. Reports indicate mining now accounts for one-third of Tibet's industrial output. Mining has long been traditionally inimical to Tibetans, who believe it disturbs the sacred essence of the soil. The Chinese name for Tibet, Xīzàng – the Western Treasure House – now has a ring of prophetic irony.

The *sengye*, or snow lion, is one of Tibet's four sacred animals and acts as a mount for many Tibetan protector deities. The other three animals are the garuda (*khyung*), dragon (*druk*) and tiger (*dak*).

Yak-tail hair was the main material used to produce Father Christmas (Santa Claus) beards in 1950s America!

TIBET'S ENDANGERED SPECIES

SPECIES	ESTIMATED WORLD POPULATION	ESTIMATED TIBETAN POPULATION	CURRENT STATUS
snow leopard (gang-zig)	6500	2000	endangered
Tibetan antelope (chiru)	75,000–150,000	75,000–150,000	endangered
white-lipped deer (shawa chukar)	7000	5000	endangered
dwarf blue sheep, or dwarf bharal (nawa na)	7000	7000	endangered
Tibetan blue bear (dom gyamuk)	a few hundred	a few hundred	endangered
wild yak (drong)	15,000	8500	vulnerable
black-necked crane	11,000	7000	vulnerable
Tibetan gazelle (gowa)	100,000	100,000	near threatened
argali, or wild sheep	150,000	7000	near threatened
Tibetan wild ass (kyang)	60,000-70,000	37,000–48,000	least concern

Rapid modernisation threatens to bring industrial pollution, a hitherto almost unknown problem, onto the high plateau. Several cement factories at Lhasa's edge created clouds of noxious smoke, which blanketed parts of western Lhasa until the factories were shut down in the 1990s. Mass domestic tourism is also beginning to take its toll, with litter and unsustainable waste management a major problem in areas like Nam-tso and the Everest region.

Tibet has abundant supplies of geothermal energy thanks to its turbulent geological history. The Yangpachen Geothermal Plant already supplies Lhasa with much of its electricity. Portable solar panelling has also enjoyed some success; the plateau enjoys some of the longest and strongest sunlight outside the Saharan region. And experimental wind-power stations have been set up in northern Tibet.

But, much to the dismay of worried environmental groups worldwide, it's Tibet's enormous potential for hydroelectricity that has been the focus of the Chinese government in recent years. The undisputed king of dam building, China had 24 dams up and running on the Tibetan plateau at the time of research, and a further 76 in the pipeline. Plans to construct a so-called 'super-dam' (which could generate twice as much electricity as the Three Gorges Dam) on the Yarlung Tsangpo (Brahmaputra) in the remote southeast of Tibet still seem to be on the table and have the Indian government downstream deeply concerned.

In the long term, climate change is expected to affect Tibet as much as the earth's low-lying regions. Chinese scientists have admitted that Tibet's glaciers are retreating at a rate of 9% in the Everest region and up to 17% at Mt Amnye Machen near the source of the Yellow River in Qīnghǎi. The UN has warned that Tibet's glaciers could disappear within a century, with 80% predicted to disappear by 2035.

The results of glacial melting are likely to include initial flooding and erosion, followed by a long-term drought that may turn Tibet into a desert wasteland and the rest of Asia into a region desperately searching for new supplies of water.

Tibet has several thousand lakes (tso in Tibetan), of which the largest are Nam-tso, Yamdrok-tso, Manasarovar (Mapham yum-tso), Siling-tso and Pangong-tso, the last crossing the Indian border into Ladakh.

For more on environmental issues in Tibet, visit Tibet Environmental Watch at www.tew.org.

The People of Tibet

Tibetan Identity

Tibetans have a unique identity that mixes influences from their Himalayan neighbours, extreme mountain environment and war-like past. In terms of language, script, food, temperament and above all religion, they are poles apart from their Han Chinese neighbours. Where the Chinese drink their tea green, Tibetans take theirs with yak butter; when the rest of China eats rice, Tibetans eat tsampa (roasted barley); even when getting drunk Tibetans drink barley beer instead of shots of Chinese rice wine.

Tibetans are such a deeply religious people that a basic knowledge of Buddhism is essential in understanding their world view. Buddhism permeates most facets of Tibetan daily life and shapes aspirations in ways that are often quite alien to the Western frame of mind. The ideas of accumulating merit, of sending sons to be monks, of undertaking pilgrimages, and of devotion to the sanctity and power of natural places are all elements of the unique fusion between Buddhism and the older shamanistic Bön faith.

For travellers, the easy smile of most Tibetans is infectious and it is rare for major cultural differences to get in the way of communication. Tibetans are among the loveliest people in Asia and very easy to get along with: open, joyful, sincere, tolerant and good-humoured. This combination is all the more remarkable in view of the anger and long-harboured resentment that must lie just under the surface in Tibet.

In case you're wondering why your Tibetan guide can run up the side of a 4500m hill with ease, while you collapse gasping in the thin air after less than one minute, recent DNA research has shown that the Tibetan people are genetically adapted to living at high altitudes. In fact the 3000 years it took Tibetans to change their genes is considered the fastest genetic change ever observed in humans. You never stood a chance.

Traditional Lifestyle

Traditionally there have been at least three distinct segments of Tibetan society: the *drokpa* (nomads); *rongpa* (farmers of the Tibetan valleys); and *sangha* (communities of monks and nuns). All lead very different lives but share a deep faith in Buddhism.

These communities have also shared a remarkable resistance to change. Until the early 20th century Tibet was a land in which virtually the only use for the wheel was as a device for activating mantras. Tibet has changed more in the past 50 years than in the previous 500,

> Tibetans are often named after the day of week they were born on; thus you'll meet Nyima (Sunday), Dawa (Monday), Mingmar (Tuesday), Lhakpa (Wednesday), Phurba (Thursday), Pasang (Friday) and Pemba (Saturday). Popular names such as Sonam (merit) and Tashi (good fortune) carry religious connotations.

RESPONSIBLE TOURISM

Tourism has already affected many areas in Tibet. Most children will automatically stick their hand out for a sweet, a pen or anything. In some regions, locals have become frustrated at seeing a stream of rich tourist groups but few tangible economic results. Please try to bear the following in mind as you travel through Tibet:

» Try to patronise as many small local Tibetan businesses, restaurants and guesthouses as possible. Revenues created by organised group tourism go largely into the pockets of the Chinese authorities.

» Doling out medicines can encourage people not to seek proper medical advice, while handing out sweets or pens to children encourages begging. If you wish to contribute something constructive, it's better to give pens directly to schools and medicines to rural clinics, or make a donation to an established charity. See the box, p347.

» Monastery admission fees go largely to local authorities, so if you want to donate to the monastery, leave your offering on the altar.

» Don't buy skins or hats made from endangered animals such as snow leopards.

» Don't pay to take a photograph of someone, and don't photograph someone if they don't want you to. If you agree to send a photograph of someone, ensure you follow through on this.

» If you have any pro-Tibetan sympathies, be very careful with whom you discuss them. Don't put Tibetans in a politically difficult or even potentially dangerous situation. This includes handing out photos of the Dalai Lama (these are illegal in Tibet) and politically sensitive materials.

» Try to buy locally made souvenirs and handicrafts, especially authentic and traditionally made products whose profits go directly to artisans, such as Lhasa Village Handicrafts.

» If you have a guide, try to ensure that he or she is a Tibetan, as Chinese guides invariably know little about Tibetan Buddhism or monastery history.

For more on the ethical issues involved in visiting Tibet, visit www.tibetanvillage project.org and www.savetibet.org. For more on the etiquette of visiting monasteries, see the box, p92. For information on responsible trekking, see p235.

although many traditional social structures have endured Chinese attempts at iconoclasm.

As in most societies, there is some generational divide among Tibetans. The younger generation (in Lhasa and the main towns at least) is as enamoured with pop music, karaoke, mobile phones and the internet as most young people around the world and most know little about 'old' Tibet, having often grown up in a Chinese-language environment. That said, young Tibetans still have a remarkably strong sense of Tibetan identity and you'll still see many young Tibetans visiting monasteries, wearing traditional dress and making pilgrimages to holy sites.

The Conservancy for Tibetan Art & Culture (www.tibetanculture.org) offers bite-sized overviews of many aspects of Tibetan culture.

Farming & Trading

Farming communities in Tibet usually comprise a cluster of homes surrounded by agricultural lands that were once owned by the nearest large monastery and protected by a *dzong* (fort). The farming itself is carried out with the assistance of a *dzo,* a breed of cattle where bulls have been crossbred with yaks. Some wealthier farmers own a small 'walking tractor' (a very simple tractor engine that can pull a plough or a trailer). Harvested grain is carried by donkeys to a threshing ground where it is trampled by cattle or threshed with poles. The grain is then cast into the air from a basket and the task of winnowing carried out by the breeze. Animal husbandry is still extremely important in Tibet, and there are around 21 million head of livestock in the country.

Until recently such communities were effectively self-sufficient in their needs and, although theirs was a hard life, it could not be described as abject poverty. Village families pulled together in times of need. Plots of land were usually graded in terms of quality and then distributed so that the land of any one family included both better- and poorer-quality land. This is changing rapidly as many regions become more economically developed.

Imports such as tea, porcelain, copper and iron from China were traditionally exchanged for exports of wool and skins. Trading was usually carried out by nomads or in combination with pilgrimage. Most villages now have at least one entrepreneur who has set up a shop and begun to ship in Chinese goods from the nearest urban centre.

One significant change to rural life has been the government-sponsored construction of over 230,000 new houses across Tibet, providing new housing for some 1.3 million Tibetan farmers and herders. Families are given around Y10,000 to Y15,000 as a base subsidy to construct a home. A typical house might cost around Y33,000 to Y44,000 so farmers usually take out a loan (interest-free for three years) to cover the remaining costs. Critics of the scheme claim that many of the new homeowners then have to rent out their farmland to Chinese immigrants in order to pay off the loans. The new houses are recognisable by the addition of red Chinese flags fluttering 'harmoniously' with Tibetan prayer flags.

Individual households normally have a shrine in the home and some religious texts, held in a place of honour, which are reserved for occasions when a monk or holy man visits the village. Ceremonies for blessing yaks and other livestock to ensure a productive year are still held. One of the highlights of the year for rural Tibetans is visiting nearby monasteries at festival times or making a pilgrimage to a holy site.

Tibetans often gesture with their lips to indicate a particular direction, so if a member of the opposite sex pouts at you, they are just showing you where to go. Also, if a road worker looks like he's blowing you kisses, he probably just wants a cigarette. Then again, maybe he's just blowing you kisses...

THE PEOPLE OF TIBET TRADITIONAL LIFESTYLE

TIBET IN EXILE

About 120,000 Tibetans live in exile, mostly in India and Nepal but also in the United States, Canada and Switzerland. Hundreds of refugees a year continue to brave high passes and border guards to get to Kathmandu, paying as much as Y800 for a guide to help them across. The trek can take up to 25 days, with no supplies other than all the dried yak meat and tsampa (roasted-barley flour) they can carry, and no equipment except canvas shoes to help them get over the 6000m passes. Most make the crossing these days as educational refugees, travelling to Dharamsala to get a traditional education, learn Tibetan and English language and study Tibetan arts and history.

The dangers of the crossing were dramatically highlighted in September 2006 when climbers on Cho Oyu witnessed and videotaped the shooting of a 17-year-old Tibetan nun by Chinese border guards, as her group tried to cross the glaciers over the Nangpa-la into Nepal. The shocking incident is detailed in Jonathan Green's 2010 book *Murder in the High Himalaya*.

Dharamsala in India's Himachal Pradesh has become a de facto Tibetan town, although the Dalai Lama, after personally meeting each refugee, actively encourages many of them to return to Tibet. The great monasteries of Tibet have also relocated, many to the sweltering heat of South India, where you can find replicas of Sera, Ganden and Drepung Monasteries.

With exile has come an unexpected flowering of Tibetan Buddhism abroad; you can now find prayer flags gracing the Scottish glens of Samye Ling Monastery in Dumfrieshire and huge chörtens decorating the countryside of California.

As traditional life reasserts itself after 50 years of communist dogma and the disastrous Cultural Revolution, many of these traditions are slowly making a comeback.

Pilgrimage

When going over a pass, Tibetans say, '*La la so, lha gyelo!*' ('May the gods be victorious!').

Pilgrimage is practised throughout the world, although as a devotional exercise it has been raised to a level of particular importance in Tibet. This may be because of the nomadic element in Tibetan society; it may also be that in a mountainous country with no roads and no wheeled vehicles, walking long distances became a fact of life, and by visiting sacred places en route pilgrims could combine walking with accumulating merit. To most Tibetans their natural landscape is imbued with a series of sacred visions and holy 'power places': mountains can be perceived as mandala images, rocks assume spiritual dimensions and the earth is imbued with healing powers.

The motivations for pilgrimage are many, but for the ordinary Tibetan it amounts to a means of accumulating *sonam* (merit) or *tashi* (good fortune). The lay practitioner might go on pilgrimage in the hope of winning a better rebirth, to cure an illness, end a spate of bad luck or as thanks for an answered prayer.

Death

Although the early kings of Tibet were buried with complex funerary rites, ordinary Tibetans have not traditionally been buried. The bodies of the very poor were usually dumped in a river when they died and the bodies of the very holy were cremated and their ashes enshrined in a chörten (or their bodies dried in salt). But in a land where soil is at a premium and wood for cremation is scarcer still, most bodies were, and still are, disposed of by sky burial.

Tibetan babies are considered to be one year old at the time of birth, since reincarnation took place nine months previously upon conception.

After death, the body is kept for 24 hours in a sitting position while a lama recites prayers from *The Tibetan Book of the Dead* to help the soul on its journey through the 49 levels of Bardo, the state between death and rebirth. Three days after death, the body is blessed and early-morning prayers and offerings are made to the monastery. The body is folded up (the spine is broken and the body itself is folded into a surprisingly small package) and carried on the back of a close friend to the *dürtro* (burial site). Here, special body-breakers known as *rogyapas* cut off the deceased's hair, chop up the body and pound the bones together with tsampa (roasted-barley flour) for vultures to eat.

There is little overt sadness at a sky burial: the soul is considered to have already departed and the burial itself is considered to be mere disposal, or rather a final act of compassion to the birds. Sky burial is, however, very much a time to reflect on the impermanence of life. Death is seen as a powerful agent of transformation and spiritual progress. Tibetans are encouraged to witness the disposal of the body and to confront death openly and without fear. This is one reason that Tantric ritual objects such as trumpets and bowls are often made from human bone.

BOOKJACKING

Tibetans are a curious and devout people and so the slightest glimpse of a photo of a monastery or even a mention of a Dalai Lama picture will result in the temporary confiscation of your Lonely Planet guide. For many Tibetans this is their only chance to see other parts of their country, so try to be patient, even after the 10th request in five minutes. A good deed like this can often open hitherto locked doors (literally) in the monastery you are visiting.

In Tibet there are countless sacred destinations, ranging from lakes and mountains to monasteries and caves that once served as meditation retreats for important yogis. Specific pilgrimages are often prescribed for specific ills; certain mountains, for example, expiate certain sins. A circumambulation of Mt Kailash offers the possibility of liberation within three lifetimes, while a circuit of Lake Manasarovar can result in spontaneous buddhahood.

Pilgrimage is also more powerful in certain auspicious months: at certain times, circumambulations of Bönri are reckoned to be 700 million times more auspicious than those of other mountains.

Pilgrims often organise themselves into large groups, hire a truck and travel around the country visiting all the major sacred places in one go. Pilgrim guidebooks have existed for centuries to help travellers interpret the 24 'power places' of Tibet. Such guides even specify locations where you can urinate or fart without offending local spirits (and probably your fellow pilgrims).

Making a pilgrimage is not just a matter of walking to a sacred place and then going home. There are a number of activities that help focus the concentration of the pilgrim. The act of kora (circumambulating the object of devotion) is chief among these. Circuits of three, 13 or 108 koras are especially auspicious, with sunrise and sunset the most auspicious hours. The particularly devout prostrate their way along entire pilgrimages, stepping forward the length of their body after each prostration and starting all over again. The hardcore even do their koras sideways, advancing one side step at a time!

Most pilgrims make offerings during the course of a pilgrimage. *Kathaks* (white ceremonial scarves) are offered to lamas or holy statues as a token of respect (and then often returned by the lama as a blessing). Offerings of yak butter or oil, fruit, tsampa (dough made with roasted-barley flour), seeds and money are all left at altars, and bowls of water and *chang* (barley beer) are replenished.

Outside chapels, at holy mountain peaks, passes and bridges, you will see pilgrims throwing offerings of tsampa or printed prayers into the air. Pilgrims also collect sacred rocks, herbs, earth and water from a holy site to take back home to those who couldn't make the pilgrimage, and leave behind personal items as a break from the past, often leaving them hanging in a tree. Other activities in this spiritual assault course include adding stones to cairns, rubbing special healing rocks, and squeezing through narrow gaps in rocks as a method of sin detection.

Koras usually include stops that are of particular spiritual significance, such as rock-carved syllables or painted buddha images. Many of these carvings are said to be 'self-arising', meaning that they haven't been carved by a human hand. The Mt Kailash kora is a treasure trove of these, encompassing sky-burial sites, stones that have 'flown' from India, monasteries, bodhisattva footprints and even a lingam (phallic image).

Other pilgrimages are carried out to visit a renowned holy man or teacher. Blessings or *tsering rilbu* (long-life pills) from holy men, *trulkus* (reincarnated lamas) or *rinpoches* (highly esteemed lamas) are particularly valued, as are the possessions of famous holy men.

Pilgrimage Sites

MOUNTAINS	LAKES	CAVES
Mt Kailash, western Tibet	Manasarovar, western Tibet	Drak Yerpa, outside Lhasa
Bönri, eastern Tibet	Nam-tso, northern Ü	Chim-puk, near Samye
Tsari, southern Tibet	Yamdrok-tso, Tsang	Sheldrak, Yarlung Valley
Mt Labchi, east of Nyalam	Lhamo La-tso, eastern Ü	Drakyul, Yarlung Tsangpo Valley

Dress

Many Tibetans in Lhasa now wear modern clothes imported from China, but traditional dress is still the norm in the countryside. The Tibetan national dress is a *chuba* (long-sleeved sheepskin cloak), tied around the waist with a sash and worn off the shoulder with great bravado by nomads and Khampas (people from Kham). *Chubas* from eastern Tibet in particular have super-long sleeves, which are tied around the waist. An inner pouch is often used to store money belts, amulets, lunch and even small livestock. Most women wear a long dress, topped with a colourful striped apron known as a *pangden*. Traditional Tibetan boots have turned-up toes, so as to kill fewer bugs when walking (or so it is said).

Women generally set great store in jewellery, and their personal wealth and dowry are often invested in it. Coral is particularly valued (as Tibet is so far from the sea), as are amber, turquoise and silver. The Tibetan *zee*, a unique elongated agate stone with black and white markings, is highly prized for its protective qualities and can fetch tens of thousands of US dollars. Earrings are common in both men and women and they are normally tied on with a piece of cord. You can see all these goodies for sale around the Barkhor in Lhasa.

Tibetan women, especially those from Amdo (northeastern Tibet and Qīnghǎi), wear their hair in 108 braids, an auspicious number in Buddhism. Khampa men plait their hair with red or black tassels and wind the lot around their head. Cowboy hats are popular in summer and fur hats are common in winter. Most pilgrims carry a *gau* (amulet), with perhaps a picture of the owner's personal deity or the Dalai Lama inside.

Older country folk may stick out their tongue when they meet you, a very traditional form of respect that greeted the very first travellers to Tibet centuries ago. Some sources say that this is done to prove that the person is not a devil, since devils have green tongues, even when they take human form.

The Politics of People

Modern political boundaries and history have led to the fracture of the Tibetan nation. Large areas of historical and ethnic Tibet are now incorporated into the Chinese provinces of Qīnghǎi and Gānsù (traditionally known as Amdo), and Sìchuān and Yúnnán (traditionally known as Kham). More Tibetans now live outside the Tibetan Autonomous Region (TAR) than inside it.

Population Control

Population control is a cornerstone of Chinese government policy, but the regulations are generally less strictly enforced in Tibet. 'Minority nationalities' such as the Tibetans are allowed two children before they lose certain stipends and housing allowances. Ironically, the most effective form of birth control in modern Tibet still seems to be to join a monastery.

Ethnic Groups

Although local mythology has the Tibetan people descended from the union of a monkey and ogress, the Tibetan people probably descended

TOURISTS & SKY BURIAL

Sky burials are funeral services and, naturally, Tibetans are often very unhappy about camera-toting foreigners heading up to sky-burial sites. The Chinese authorities do not like it either and may fine foreigners who attend a burial. You should never pay to see a sky burial and you should *never* take photos. Even if Tibetans offer to take you up to a sky-burial site, it is unlikely that other Tibetans present will be very happy about it. If nobody has invited you, don't go.

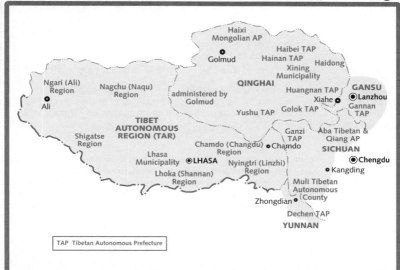

TAP Tibetan Autonomous Prefecture

from nomadic tribes who migrated from the north and settled to sedentary cultivation of Tibet's river valleys. About a quarter of Tibetans are still nomadic. There are considerable variations between regional groups of Tibetans. The most recognisable are the Khampas of eastern Tibet, who are generally larger and a bit more rough-and-ready than other Tibetans and who wear red or black tassels in their long hair. Women from Amdo are especially conspicuous because of their elaborate braided hairstyles and jewellery.

The people of Kongpo in eastern Tibet have a distinctive traditional dress that features a round hat with an upturned rim of golden brocade for men (known as a *gyasha*) and a pretty pillbox hat with winged edges (known as a *dieu*) for women. Men and women wear brown woollen tunics, belted around the waist. The former kingdom of Kongpo has for centuries been vilified by central Tibetan rulers as a land of incest and poison, whose inhabitants would routinely drug unsuspecting strangers to steal their souls.

There are pockets of other minority groups, such as the Lhopa (Lhoba) and Monpa in the southeast of Tibet, but these make up less than 1% of the total population and only very remote pockets remain. A more visible ethnic group are the Hui Muslims. Tibet's original Muslim inhabitants were largely traders or butchers (a profession that most Buddhists abhor), although the majority of recent migrants are traders and restaurant owners from southern Gansu province. Tibetans are also closely related to the Qiang people of northern Sìchuān, the Sherpas of Nepal and the Ladakhis of India.

Tibetans show respect to an honoured guest or a lama by placing a *kathak* (prayer scarf) around their neck. When reciprocating, hold the scarf out in both hands with palms turned upwards.

Han Migration

Official statistics claim 93% of the TAR's population is Tibetan, a figure that is hotly contested by almost everyone except the government. Chinese figures for the population of Lhasa, for example, suggest it is just over 87% Tibetan and just under 12% Han Chinese, a ratio that stretches

GUCCI GUCHI

Being a devout Buddhist region, Tibet has a long tradition of begging for alms. Generally, beggars will approach you with thumbs up and mumble 'guchi, guchi' – 'please, please' (not a request for Italian designer clothes).

Tibetans tend to be generous with beggars and usually hand out a couple of mao to anyone deserving. Banks and monasteries will swap a Y10 note for a wad of one-mao notes, which go a long way.

If you do give (and the choice is entirely yours), give the same amount Tibetans do; don't encourage the beggars to make foreigners a special target by handing out large denominations. It's worth keeping all your small change in one pocket – there's nothing worse than pulling out a Y100!

TORMA

Torma are small offerings made of yak butter and tsampa (roasted-barley flour) adorned with coloured medallions of butter. They probably developed as a substitute for animal sacrifice. Most are made during the Shö-tun festival and remain on display throughout the year.

the credulity of anyone who has visited the city in recent years. It is more likely that well over 50% of Lhasa's population is Han Chinese.

The current flood of Chinese immigrants into Tibet has been termed China's 'second invasion'. The Chinese government is very coy about releasing figures that would make it clear just how many Chinese there are in Tibet, but for visitors who have made repeated trips to Tibet the increased numbers of Han Chinese are undeniable.

Perhaps unsurprisingly, there's an endemic mistrust between the Tibetans and Chinese and ethnic tensions bubble just under the surface. Many Tibetans see the Han Chinese as land-hungry outsiders, while the Chinese often complain that the Tibetans are ungrateful and slow to adjust to economic opportunities. The Han Chinese word for Tibetan, zàng (藏), is a homonym for 'dirty' (zāng; 脏), which easily lends itself to racist slurs. Actual violence between the two communities is rare, but it's quickly apparent to visitors that most towns have quite separate Chinese and Tibetan (and in some cases also Hui Muslim) quarters.

Women in Tibet

Women have traditionally occupied a strong position in Tibetan society, often holding the family purse strings and running businesses like shops and guesthouses. Several of Tibet's most famous Buddhist practitioners, such as Yeshe Tsogyel and Machik Labdronma, were women, and Tibet's nuns remain at the vanguard of political dissent. Most of the road workers you see across the plateau are women!

Up until the Chinese invasion many Tibetan farming villages practised polyandry. When a woman married the eldest son of a family she also married his younger brothers (providing they did not become monks). The children of such marriages referred to all the brothers as their father. The practice was aimed at easing the inheritance of family property (mainly the farming land) and avoiding the break-up of small plots.

Tibetan Buddhism

A basic understanding of Buddhism is essential to getting beneath the skin of things in Tibet. Buddhism's values and goals permeate almost everything Tibetan. Exploring the monasteries and temples of Tibet and mixing with its people, yet knowing nothing of Buddhism, is like visiting the Vatican and knowing nothing of Roman Catholicism. To be sure, it might still seem an awe-inspiring experience, but much will remain hidden and indecipherable.

For those who already do know something of Buddhism – who have read something of Zen, for example – Tibet can be baffling on another level. The grandeur of the temples, the worship of images and the fierce protective deities that stand in doorways all seem to belie the basic tenets of an ascetic faith that is basically about renouncing the self and following a path of moderation.

On a purely superficial level, Buddhism has historically combined the moral precepts and devotional practices of lay followers, the scholastic tradition of the Indian Buddhist universities and a body of mystic Tantric teachings that had a particular appeal to followers of the shamanistic Bön faith.

Tibetan Buddhism's reaction with both existing Bön spirit worship and the Hindu pantheon created a huge range of deities, both wrathful and benign (although these are technically all merely aspects of the human ego). Apart from a whole range of different buddha aspects there are also general protector gods called *dharmapalas* and personal meditational deities called *yidams*, which Tantric students adopt early in their spiritual training. Yet for all its confusing iconography the basic tenets of Buddhism are very much rooted in daily experience. Even high lamas and monks come across as surprisingly down-to-earth.

Buddhism is perhaps the most tolerant of the world's religions. Wherever it has gone it has adapted to local conditions, like a dividing cell, creating countless new schools of thought. Its basic tenets have remained very much the same and all schools are bound together in their faith in the original teachings of Sakyamuni (Sakya Thukpa), the Historical Buddha. The Chinese invasion has ironically caused a flowering of Tibetan Buddhism abroad and you can now find Tibetan monasteries round the world.

Closely linked to both Bön and Buddhism is the folk religion of Tibet, known as *mi chös* (the dharma of man), which is primarily concerned with the appeasement of spirits. These spirits include *nyen*, which reside in rocks and trees; *lu* or *naga*, snake-bodied spirits, which live at the bottom of lakes, rivers and wells; *sadok,* lords of the earth, which are connected with agriculture; *tsen,* air or mountain spirits, which shoot arrows of illness and death at humans; and *dud,* demons linked

One result of the 1959 departure of the Dalai Lama is that Tibet has been largely cut off from its Buddhist teachers and lineage masters, most of who remain in exile.

What Makes You Not a Buddhist, by Dzongsar Jamyang Khyentse, is an illuminating introduction to Buddhism from the Bhutanese reincarnate lama and film director.

LOTUS

The lotus (*padma* in Sanskrit, *metok* in Tibetan) is an important Buddhist symbol and the thrones of many deities are made from a lotus leaf. The leaf symbolises purity and transcendence, in the world but not of it, rising as it does from muddy waters to become a flower of great beauty.

to the Buddhist demon Mara. Spirits of the hearth, roof and kitchen inhabit every Tibetan house. Like most Himalayan people, the religious beliefs of the average Tibetan are a fascinating melange of Buddhism, Bön and folk religion.

Buddha

Buddhism originated in the northeast of India around the 5th century BC, at a time when the local religion was Brahmanism. Some brahman, in preparation for presiding over offerings to their gods, partook of an asceticism that transported them to remote places where they fasted, meditated and practised yogic techniques.

Many of the fundamental concepts of Buddhism find their origin in the brahman society of this time. The Buddha (c 480–400 BC), born Siddhartha Gautama, was one of many wandering ascetics whose teachings led to the establishment of rival religious schools. Jainism was one of these schools; Buddhism was another.

Little is known about the life of Siddhartha. It was probably not until some 200 years after his death that biographies were compiled, and by that time many of the circumstances of his life had merged with legend. It is known that he was born in Lumbini (modern-day Nepal) of a noble family and that he married and had a son before renouncing a life of privilege and embarking on a quest to make sense of the suffering in the world.

After studying with many of the masters of his day he embarked on a course of intense asceticism, before concluding that such a path was too extreme. Finally, in the place that is now known as Bodhgaya in India, Siddhartha meditated beneath a *bo* (pipal) tree. At the break of dawn at the end of his third night of meditation he became a *buddha* (awakened one).

You'll see many famous stories from Buddha's life painted on monastery murals, from his birth (his mother Maya is depicted holding on to a tree) and his first seven steps (lotus flowers sprouted from the ground) to his skeletal ascetic phase and temptation by the demon Mara.

Buddhist Concepts

Buddhism's early teachings are based on the insights of the Buddha, known in Mahayana tradition as Sakyamuni (Sakya Thukpa in Tibetan), and form the basis of all further Buddhist thought. Buddhism is not based on a revealed prophecy or divine revelation but rather is rooted in human experience. The later Mahayana school (to which Tibetan Buddhism belongs) diverged from these early teachings in some respects, but not in its fundamentals.

The Buddha commenced his teachings by explaining that there was a Middle Way that steered a course between sensual indulgence and ascetic self-torment – a way of moderation rather than renunciation. This Middle Way could be pursued by following the Noble Eightfold Path. The philosophical underpinnings of this path were the Four Noble Truths, which addressed the problems of karma and rebirth. These basic concepts are the kernel of early Buddhist thought.

In a modern sense, Buddhist thought stresses nonviolence, compassion, equanimity (evenness of mind) and mindfulness (awareness of the present moment).

The dharma wheel symbolises the Buddha's first sermon at Sarnath. The eight spokes recall the Eightfold Path. The wheel was the earliest symbol of Buddhism, used long before images of the Buddha became popular.

Rebirth

Life is a cycle of endless rebirths. The Sanskrit word 'samsara' (Tibetan: *khorwa*), literally 'wandering on', is used to describe this cycle, and life is seen as wandering on limitlessly through time, and through the birth, extinction and rebirth of galaxies and worlds. There are six levels of rebirth or realms of existence, as depicted in the Wheel of Life. It is important to accumulate enough merit to avoid the three lower realms, although in the long cycle of rebirth, all beings pass through them at some point. All beings are fated to tread this wheel continuously until they make a commitment to enlightenment.

Karma

All beings pass through the same cycle of rebirths. Their enemy may once have been their mother, and like all beings they have lived as an insect and as a god, and suffered in one of the hell realms. Movement within this cycle, though, is not haphazard. It is governed by karma.

Karma (*las* in Tibetan) is a slippery concept. It is sometimes translated simply as 'action', but it also implies the consequences of action. Karma might be thought of as an overarching condition of life. Every action in life leaves a psychic trace that carries over into the next rebirth. It should not be thought of as a reward or punishment, but simply as a result. In Buddhist thought karma is frequently likened to a seed that ripens into a fruit: thus a human reborn as an insect is harvesting the fruits of a previous immoral existence.

Merit

Given that karma is a kind of accumulated psychic baggage that we must lug through countless rebirths, it is the aim of all practising Buddhists to try to accumulate as much 'good karma' – merit – as possible. Merit is best achieved through the act of rejoicing in giving. The giving

Butter lamps, or *chömay,* are kept lit continuously in all monasteries and many private homes, and are topped up continuously by visiting pilgrims equipped with a tub of butter and a spoon.

TIBETAN BUDDHISM BUDDHIST CONCEPTS

WHEEL OF LIFE

The Wheel of Life (Sipa Khorlo in Tibetan), depicted in the entryway to most monasteries, is an aid to realising the delusion of the mind. It's a complex pictorial representation of how desire chains us to samsara, the endless cycle of birth, death and rebirth.

The wheel is held in the mouth of Yama, the Lord of Death. The inner circle of interdependent desire shows a cockerel (representing desire or attachment) biting a pig (ignorance or delusion) biting a snake (hatred or anger). A second ring is divided into figures ascending through the realms on the left and descending on the right.

The six inner sectors of the wheel symbolise the six realms of rebirth: gods, battling demigods and humans (the upper realms); and hungry ghosts, hell and animals (the lower realms). All beings are reborn through this cycle dependent upon their karma. The Buddha is depicted outside the wheel, symbolising his release into a state of nirvana.

At the bottom of the wheel are hot and cold hells, where Yama holds a mirror that reflects one's lifetime. A demon to the side holds a scale with black and white pebbles, weighing up the good and bad deeds of one's lifetime.

The *pretas,* or hungry spirits, are recognisable by their huge stomachs, thin needle-like necks and tiny mouths, which cause them insatiable hunger and thirst. In each realm the Buddha attempts to convey his teachings (the dharma), offering hope to each realm.

The 12 outer segments depict the so-called '12 links of dependent origination', and the 12 interlinked, codependent and causal experiences of life that perpetuate the cycle of samsara. The 12 images (whose order may vary) are of a blind woman (representing ignorance), a potter (unconscious will), a monkey (consciousness), men in a boat (self-consciousness), a house (the five senses), lovers (contact), a man with an arrow in his eye (feeling), a drinking scene (desire), a figure grasping fruit from a tree (attachment), pregnancy, birth and death (a man carrying a corpse to a sky burial).

of alms to the needy and to monks, the relinquishing of a son to monkhood, and acts of compassion and understanding are all meritorious and have a positive karmic outcome.

The Four Noble Truths

If belief in rebirth, karma and merit are the basis of lay-followers' faith in Buddhism, the Four Noble Truths (Tibetan: *phakpay denpa shi*) might be thought of as its philosophical underpinning.

DUKKHA (SUFFERING)

The first of the Four Noble Truths is that life is suffering. This suffering extends through all the countless rebirths of beings, and finds its origin in the imperfection of life. Every rebirth brings with it the pain of birth, the pain of ageing, the pain of death, the pain of association with unpleasant things, the loss of things we are attached to and the failure to achieve the things we desire.

TANHA (DESIRE)

The reason for this suffering is the second Noble Truth, and lies in our dissatisfaction with imperfection, in our desire for things to be other than they are. What is more, this dissatisfaction leads to actions and karmic consequences that prolong the cycle of rebirths and may lead to even more suffering, much like a mouse running endlessly in a wheel.

NIBBANA (CESSATION OF DESIRE)

Known in English as nirvana, *nibbana* (Tibetan: *namtrol*) is the cessation of all desire; an end to attachment. With the cessation of desire comes an end to suffering, the achievement of complete nonattachment and an end to the cycle of rebirth. Nirvana is the ultimate goal of Buddhism. Nitpickers might point out that the will to achieve nirvana is a desire in itself. Buddhists answer that this desire is tolerated as a useful means to an end, but it is only when this desire, too, is extinguished that nirvana is truly achieved.

NOBLE EIGHTFOLD PATH

The fourth of the Noble Truths prescribes a course that for the lay practitioner will lead to the accumulation of merit, and for the serious devotee may lead to nirvana. The components of this path are (1) right understanding, (2) right thought, (3) right speech, (4) right action, (5) right livelihood, (6) right effort, (7) right mindfulness and (8) right concentration. Needless to say, each of these has a 'wrong' corollary.

Schools of Buddhism

Not long after the death of Sakyamuni, disagreements began to arise among his followers – as they tend to do in all religious movements – over whose interpretations best captured the true spirit of his teachings. The result was the development of numerous schools of thought and, eventually, a schism that saw the emergence of two principal schools: Hinayana and Mahayana.

Hinayana, also known as Theravada, encouraged scholasticism and close attention to what were considered the original teachings of Sakyamuni. Mahayana, on the other hand, with its elevation of compassion *(nyingje)* as an all-important idea, took Buddhism in a new direction. It was the Mahayana school that made its way up to the high plateau and took root there, at the same time travelling to China, Korea and Japan. Hinayana retreated into southern India and took root in Sri Lanka and Thailand.

The Ten Meritorious Deeds in Buddhism are to refrain from killing, stealing, inappropriate sexual activity, lying, gossiping, cursing, sowing discord, envy, malice and opinionatedness.

The Buddhist parable of the Four Harmonious Brothers is painted on walls at the entrance to many monasteries. The image is of a bird picking a tree-top fruit, while standing atop a hare, who is atop a monkey, who is atop an elephant. On its most basic level the image symbolises cooperation and harmony with the environment.

TIBETAN BUDDHISM SCHOOLS OF BUDDHISM

Mahayana

The claims that Mahayanists made for their faith were many, but the central issue was a change in orientation from individual pursuit of enlightenment to bodhisattvahood. Rather than striving for complete nonattachment, the bodhisattva aims, through compassion and self-sacrifice, to achieve enlightenment for the sake of all beings.

In the meantime, Sakyamuni slowly began to change shape. Mahayanists maintained that Sakyamuni had already attained buddhahood many aeons ago and that there were now many such transcendent beings living in heavens or 'pure lands'. The revolutionary concept had the effect of producing a pantheon of bodhisattvas, a feature that made Mahayana more palatable to cultures that already had gods of their own. In Tibet, China, Korea and Japan, the Mahayana pantheon came to be identified with local gods as their Mahayana equivalents replaced them.

The *dorje* (thunderbolt) and *drilbu* (bell) are ritual objects symbolising male and female aspects used in Tantric rites. They are held in the right and left hands respectively. The indestructible thunderbolt cuts through ignorance.

Tantrism (Vajrayana)

A further Mahayana development that is particularly relevant to Tibet is Tantrism. The words of Sakyamuni were recorded in sutras and studied by students of both Hinayana and Mahayana, but according to the followers of Tantrism, a school that emerged from around AD 600, Sakyamuni left a corpus of esoteric instructions to a select few of his disciples. These were known as Tantra (Gyü).

Tantric adepts claimed that through the use of unconventional techniques they could jolt themselves towards enlightenment, and shorten the long road to bodhisattvahood. The process involved identification with a tutelary deity invoked through deep meditation and recitation of the deity's mantra. The most famous of these mantras is the 'om mani padme hum' ('hail to the jewel in the lotus') mantra of Chenresig (Avalokiteshvara). Tantric practice employs Indian yogic techniques to channel energy towards the transformation to enlightenment. Such yogic techniques might even include sexual practices. Tantric techniques

RELIGIOUS FREEDOM IN TIBET

Religious freedoms in Tibet have certainly increased since the 1980s, though any form of nationalist or political protest is still quickly crushed. Monks and nuns, who have traditionally been at the vanguard of protests and Tibetan aspirations for independence, are regarded with particular suspicion by the authorities. The demonstrations of 2008 were initially led by monks from Sera, Drepung and Ramoche Monasteries and turned to riots after police beat a line of monks from Ramoche. Nuns, in particular, considering their small numbers, have been very politically active, accounting for 55 of the 126 independence protests in the mid-1990s. Regulations make it impossible for nuns, once arrested and imprisoned, to return to their nunneries.

Political indoctrination or education teams are frequent visitors to most monasteries, as are the recurring campaigns to denounce the Dalai Lama. Images of the current Dalai Lama are illegal, which is why you'll see pictures of the 13th Dalai Lama on most monastery thrones, as a symbolic stand-in. Since 2008 most monasteries now have a police station or army post on site and the numbers of resident monks are strictly controlled. The friendly orange-clad Chinese fire prevention teams you may see in larger monasteries are actually there to keep an eye on the monks, not potential arsonists.

While many monasteries now gleam after million-dollar renovations and are bustling with monks and tourists, the authorities are also there in the background, keeping a close eye open for the first sign of dissent.

TIBETAN BUDDHISM BUDDHISM IN TIBET

THE WORLD OF A MONK

The Western term 'monk' is slightly misleading when used in the context of Tibetan Buddhism. The Tibetan equivalent would probably be *trapa*, which means literally 'scholar' or 'student', and is an inclusive term that covers the three main categories of monastic inmates. Monks in these categories should also be distinguished from lamas who, as spiritual luminaries, have a privileged position in the monastic hierarchy, may have considerable wealth and, outside the Gelugpa order, are not necessarily celibate.

The first step for a monk, usually after completing some prior study, is to take one of two lesser vows, the *genyen* or *getsul* ordination – a renunciation of secular life that includes a vow of celibacy. This marks the beginning of a long course of study that is expected to lead to the full *gelong* vows of ordination. While most major monasteries have a number of *gelong* monks, not all monks achieve *gelong* status.

These three categories do not encompass all the monks in a monastery. There are usually specific monastic posts associated with administrative duties, with ritual and with teaching. *Gelong* vows are also supplemented by higher courses of study, which are rewarded in the Gelugpa order by the title *geshe*. In premodern Tibet the larger monasteries also had divisions of so-called 'fighting monks', or monastic militias. To a large extent they served as a kind of police force within a particular monastery, but there were also times when their services were used to hammer home a doctrinal dispute with a rival monastery.

In 1950, on the eve of the Chinese invasion, it was estimated that 30% of Tibet's male population were monks. Today there are around 47,000 monks in the Tibetan Autonomous Region.

are rarely written down, but rather are passed down verbally from tutor to student, increasing their secret allure.

Most of the ritual objects and images of deities in Tibetan monasteries and temples are Tantric in nature. Together they show the many facets of enlightenment – at times kindly, at times wrathful.

Despite its connotations abroad, the swastika is an ancient Indian religious symbol that was later adopted by Buddhism and is often found painted on Tibetan houses to bring good luck. Swastikas that point clockwise are Buddhist; those that point anticlockwise are Bön.

Buddhism in Tibet

The story of the introduction of Buddhism to Tibet is attended by legends of the taming of local gods and spirits and their conversion to Buddhism as protective deities. This magnificent array of buddhas, bodhisattvas and sages occupies a mythical world in the Tibetan imagination. Chenresig is perhaps chief among them, manifesting himself in the early Tibetan kings and later the Dalai Lamas. Guru Rinpoche, the Indian sage and Tantric magician who bound the native spirits and gods of Tibet into the service of Buddhism, is another, and there are countless others, including saints and protector gods. While the clerical side of Buddhism concerns itself largely with textual study and analysis, the Tantric shamanistic-based side seeks revelation through identification with these deified beings and through their *terma* ('revealed' words or writings).

It is useful to consider the various schools of Tibetan Buddhism as revealing something of a struggle between these two orientations: shamanism and clericalism. Each school finds its own resolution to the problem. In the case of the last major school to arise, the Gelugpa order, there was a search for a return to the doctrinal purity of clerical Buddhism. But even here, the Tantric forms were not completely discarded; it was merely felt that many years of scholarly work and preparation should precede the more esoteric Tantric practices.

The clerical and shamanistic orientations can also be explained as the difference between state-sponsored and popular Buddhism, respectively. There was always a tendency for the state to emphasise monastic Buddhism, with its communities of rule-abiding monks. Popular Buddhism, on the other hand, with its long-haired, wild-eyed ascetic recluses capable of performing great feats of magic, had a great appeal to the ordinary people of Tibet, for whom ghosts and demons and sorcerers were a daily reality.

Nyingmapa Order

Main Monasteries Mindroling (p113), Dorje Drak (p111)
Also known as Red Hats

The Nyingmapa order is the Old School, and traces its origins back to the teachings and practices of the 8th- or 9th-century Indian master Guru Rinpoche. Over the centuries the Nyingmapa failed to develop as a powerful, centralised school, and for the most part prospered in villages throughout rural Tibet, where it was administered by local shamanlike figures.

The Nyingma school was revitalised through the 'discovery' of hidden texts in the 'power places' of Tibet visited by Guru Rinpoche. In many cases these *terma* (revealed texts) were discovered through yogic-inspired visions by spiritually advanced Nyingmapa practitioners, rather than found under a pile of rocks or in a cave. Out of these *terma* arose the Dzogchen (Great Perfection) teachings, an appealing Tantric short cut to nirvana that teaches that enlightenment can come in a single lifetime. Today the Nyingmapa have a particularly strong presence in western Sìchuān.

Found on all altars and replenished twice a day, the seven bowls of water refer to the 'Seven Examined Men' – the first seven monks in Tibet, or the seven first steps of Buddha.

BÖN MONASTERIES

As a result of the historical predominance of Buddhism in Tibet, the Bön religion has been suppressed for centuries and has only recently started to attract the attention of scholars. Many Tibetans remain quite ignorant of Bön beliefs and your guide might refuse to even set foot in a Bön monastery. Yet Bön and Buddhism have influenced and interacted with each other for centuries, exchanging texts, traditions and rituals. In the words of Tibet scholar David Snellgrove, 'every Tibetan is a Bönpo at heart'.

To the casual observer it's often hard to differentiate between Bönpo and Buddhist practice. It can be said that in many ways Bön shares the same goals as Buddhism but takes a different path. The word 'Bön' has come to carry the same connotation as the Buddhist term 'dharma' *(chö)*. Shared concepts include those of samsara, karma and rebirth in the six states of existence. Even Bön monasteries, rituals and meditation practice are almost identical to Buddhist versions.

Still, there are obvious differences. Bön has its own Kangyur, a canon made up of texts translated from the Shang-Shung language, and Bönpos turn prayer wheels and circumambulate monasteries anticlockwise. The main difference comes down to the source of religious authority: Bönpos see the arrival of Buddhism as a catastrophe – the supplanting of the truth by a false religion.

Bönpo iconography is unique. Tonpa Shenrab is the most common central image, and is depicted as either a monk or a deity. He shares Sakyamuni's *mudra* (hand gesture) of 'enlightenment' but holds the Bön sceptre, which consists of two swastikas joined together by a column. Other gods of Bönpo include Satrid Ergang, who holds a swastika and mirror; Shenrab Wokar and his main emanation, Kuntu Zangpo, with a hooklike wand; and Sangpo Bumptri.

Complementing these gods is a large number of local deities – these are potentially harmful male spirits known as *gekho* (the protectors of Bön) and their female counterparts, *drapla*. Welchen Gekho is the king of the harmful *gekho,* and his consort Logbar Tsame is the queen of the *dralpa.*

EIGHT AUSPICIOUS SYMBOLS

The Eight Auspicious Symbols *(tashi targyel)* are associated with gifts made to Sakyamuni (Sakya Thukpa) upon his enlightenment and appear as protective motifs across Tibet.

Knot of eternity Representing the entwined, never-ending passage of time, harmony and love and the unity of all things, the knot of eternity is commonly seen on embroidery and tents.

Lotus flower The lotus flower, or *padma,* stands for the purity and compassion of Sakyamuni. The pure lotus rises from the muddy waters of earthly existence.

Pair of golden fishes Shown leaping from the waters of captivity, they represent liberation from the Wheel of Life.

Precious umbrella Usually placed over buddha images to protect them from evil influences, the precious umbrella is a common Buddhist motif also seen in Thailand and Japan.

Vase of treasure The vase is a sacred repository of the jewels of enlightenment or the water of eternity.

Victory banner Heralding the triumph of Buddhist wisdom over ignorance.

Wheel of Law Representing the Noble Eightfold Path to salvation, the wheel is also referred to as the Wheel of Dharma. The wheel turns 12 times, three times for each of the Four Noble Truths.

White conch shell Blown in celebration of the enlightenment of Sakyamuni and the potential of all beings to be awakened by the sound of dharma, the shell is often used to signal prayer time.

Knot of eternity

Lotus flower

Pair of golden fishes

Kagyupa Order

Main Monastery Tsurphu (p98)
Sub-schools Drigungpa (Drigung Til; p108); Taglungpa (Talung; p104)
Founder Milarepa
Also known as Black Hats

This resurgence of Buddhist influence in the 11th century led to many Tibetans travelling to India to study. The new ideas they brought back with them had a revitalising effect on Tibetan thought and produced other new schools of Tibetan Buddhism. Among them was the Kagyupa order, established by Milarepa (1040–1123), who was the disciple of Marpa the translator (1012–93).

The establishment of monasteries eventually overshadowed the ascetic-yogi origins of the Kagyupa. The yogi tradition did not die out completely, however, and Kagyupa monasteries also became important centres for synthesising the clerical and shamanistic orientations of Tibetan Buddhism.

In time, several suborders of the Kagyupa sprang up, the most prominent of which was the Karma Kagyupa, also known as the Karmapa. The practice of reincarnation originated with this suborder, when the abbot of Tsurphu Monastery, Dusum Khyenpa (1110–93), announced that he would be reincarnated as his own successor. The 16th Karmapa died in 1981, and his disputed successor fled to India in 1999 (see the box, p100).

Sakyapa Order

Main Monasteries Sakya (p147)
Sub-schools Tsarpa, Ngorpa
Founder Kongchog Gyelpo

From the 11th century many Tibetan monasteries became centres for the textual study and translation of Indian Buddhist texts. One of the earliest major figures in this movement was Kunga Gyaltsen (1182–1251), known as Sakya Pandita (literally 'scholar from Sakya').

Sakya Pandita's renown as a scholar led to him, and subsequent abbots of Sakya, being recognised as a manifestation of Jampelyang

(Manjushri), the Bodhisattva of Insight. Sakya Pandita travelled to the Mongolian court in China, with the result that his heir became the spiritual tutor of Kublai Khan. In the 13th and 14th centuries, the Sakyapa order became embroiled in politics and implicated in the Mongol overlordship of Tibet (see the box, p151).

Precious umbrella

Many Sakyapa monasteries contain images of the Sakyapa protector deity Gompo Gur and photographs of the school's four head lamas: the Sakya Trizin (in exile in the US), Ngawang Kunga (head of the Sakyapa order), Chogye Trichen Rinpoche (head of the Tsarpa subschool) and Ludhing Khenpo Rinpoche (head of the Ngorpa subschool). You can easily recognise Sakyapa monasteries from the three stripes painted on the generally grey walls.

Gelugpa Order

Main Monasteries Ganden (p89), Sera (p83), Drepung (p78), Tashilhunpo (p137)
Founder Tsongkhapa
Also known as Yellow Hats

Vase of treasure

It may not have been his intention, but Tsongkhapa (1357–1419), a monk who left his home in Amdo (Qīnghǎi) at the age of 17 to study in central Tibet, is regarded as the founder of the Gelugpa (Virtuous School) order, which came to dominate political and religious affairs in Tibet.

Tsongkhapa studied with all the major schools of his day, but was particularly influenced by the Sakyapa and the Kadampa orders, the latter based on the teachings of 11th-century Bengali sage Atisha. After experiencing a vision of Atisha, Tsongkhapa elaborated on the Bengali sage's clerical-Tantric synthesis in a doctrine that is known as *lamrim* (the graduated path). The Gelugpa school eventually subsumed the Kadampa school.

Victory banner

Tsongkhapa basically advocated a return to doctrinal purity and stressed the structure of the monastic body and monastic discipline as prerequisites to advanced Tantric studies. Tsongkhapa established Ganden Monastery, which became the head of the Gelugpa order. The abbot of Drepung is actually the titular head of the order, but it was the Dalai Lamas who came to be increasingly identified with the order's growing political and spiritual prestige.

Bön

Main Monasteries: Yungdrungling (p137), Tsedru (p211), Tengchen (p210)
Founder Shenrab Miwoche

Wheel of Law

In Tibet the establishment of Buddhism was marked by its interaction with the native religion Bön. This animist or shamanistic faith – which encompassed gods and spirits, exorcism, spells, talismans, ritual drumming, sacrifices and the cult of dead kings, among other things – had a major influence on the direction Buddhism took in Tibet, adding elements of magic, ritual and symbolic sacrifice.

Many popular Buddhist symbols and practices, such as prayer flags, sky burial, the rubbing of holy rocks, the tying of bits of cloth to trees and the construction of spirit traps, all have their roots deep in Bön tradition. The traditional blessing of dipping a finger in water or milk and flicking it to the sky derives from Bön and can still be seen today in the shamanistic folk practices of Mongolia.

White conch shell

But it was Bön that was transformed and tamed to the ends of Buddhism and not vice versa. The Bön order, as it survives today, is to all intents and purposes the fifth school of Tibetan Buddhism. Pockets of Bön exist in the Changtang region of northern Tibet and the Aba region of northern Sichuan (Kham).

Prayer flags are strung up to purify the air and pacify the gods. All feature the *longta*, or windhorse, which carries the prayers up into the heavens. The colours are highly symbolic – red, green, yellow, blue and white represent fire, wood, earth, water and iron.

PRAYER FLAGS

History of Bön

The word 'Bön' today has three main connotations. The first relates to the pre-Buddhist religion of Tibet, suppressed and supplanted by Buddhism in the 8th and 9th centuries. The second is the form of 'organised' Bön (Gyur Bön) systematised along Buddhist lines, which arose in the 11th century. Third, and linked to this, is a body of popular beliefs that involves the worship of local deities and spirit protectors.

The earliest form of Bön, sometimes referred to as Black Bön, also Dud Bön (the Bön of Devils) or Tsan Bön (the Bön of Spirits), was concerned with counteracting the effects of evil spirits through magical practices. Bönpo priests were entrusted with the wellbeing and fertility of the living, as well as curing sicknesses, affecting the weather and mediating between humans and the spirit world. A core component was control of the spirits, to ensure the safe passage of the soul into the next world. For centuries Bönpo priests controlled the complex burial rites of the Yarlung kings. Bön was the state religion of Tibet until the reign of Songtsen Gampo (r 630–49).

Bön is thought to have its geographical roots in the kingdom of Shang-Shung, which is located in western Tibet, and its capital at Kyunglung (Valley of the Garuda). Bön's founding father was Shenrab Miwoche, also known as Tonpa Shenrab, the Teacher of Knowledge, who was born in the second millennium BC in the mystical land of Olma Lungring in Tajik (thought to be possibly the Mt Kailash area or even Persia). Buddhists often claim that Shenrab is merely a carbon copy of Sakyamuni (Sakya Thukpa), and certainly there are similarities to be found. Biographies state that he was born a royal prince and ruled for 30 years before becoming an ascetic. His 10 wives bore him 10 children who formed the core of his religious disciples. Many of the tales of Shenrab Miwoche deal with his protracted struggles with the demon king Khyabpa Lagring.

Bön was first suppressed by the eighth Yarlung king, Drigum Tsenpo, and subsequently by King Trisong Detsen. The Bön master Gyerpung Drenpa Namkha (a *gyerpung* is the Bön equivalent of a lama or guru) struggled with Trisong Detsen to protect the Bön faith until the king finally broke Shang-Shung's political power. Following the founding of the Samye Monastery, many Bön priests went into exile or converted to Buddhism, and many of the Bön texts were hidden.

The modern Bön religion is known as Yungdrung (Eternal Bön). A *yungdrung* is a swastika, Bön's most important symbol. (Yungdrungling means 'swastika park' and is a common name for Bön monasteries.) *The Nine Ways of Bön* is the religion's major text. Bönpos still refer to Mt Kailash as Yungdrung Gutseg (Nine-Stacked-Swastika Mountain).

Prayer wheels are filled with up to a mile of prayers; the prayers are 'recited' with each revolution of the wheel. Pilgrims spin the wheels to gain merit and to concentrate the mind on the mantras and prayers they are reciting.

Important Figures of Tibetan Buddhism

This is a brief iconographical guide to some of the gods and goddesses of the vast Tibetan Buddhist pantheon, as well as to important historical figures. It is neither exhaustive nor scholarly, but it may help you to recognise a few of the statues you encounter during your trip. Tibetan names are given first, with Sanskrit names provided in parentheses. (The exception is Sakya Thukpa, who is generally known by his Sanskrit name, Sakyamuni.)

Buddhas
Sakyamuni (Sakya Thukpa)

Sakyamuni is the Historical Buddha (the Buddha of the Present Age), whose teachings set in motion the Buddhist faith. In Tibetan-style representations he is always pictured sitting cross-legged on a lotus-flower throne. His tight curled hair is dark blue and there is a halo of enlightenment around his head. The Buddha is recognised by 32 marks on his body, including a dot between his eyes, a bump on the top of his head, three folds of skin on his neck and the Wheel of Law on the soles of his feet. In his left hand he holds a begging bowl, and his right hand touches the earth in the 'witness' *mudra* (hand gesture). He is often flanked by his two principal disciples Sariputra and Maudgalyana.

Marmedze (Dipamkara)

The Past Buddha, Marmedze, came immediately before Sakyamuni and spent 100,000 years on earth. His hands are shown in the 'protection' *mudra* and he is often depicted in a trinity with the Present and Future Buddhas, known as the *dusum sangay*.

Sakyamuni
(Sakya Thukpa)

Öpagme (Amitabha)

The Buddha of Infinite Light resides in the 'pure land of the west'. The Panchen Lama is considered a reincarnation of this buddha. He is red, his hands are held together in his lap in a 'meditation' *mudra* and he holds a begging bowl.

Tsepame (Amitayus)

The Buddha of Longevity, like Öpagme, is red and holds his hands in a meditation gesture, but he holds a vase containing the nectar of immortality. He is often seen in groups of nine.

Tsepame
(Amitayus)

Medicine Buddhas (Menlha)

A medicine buddha holds a medicine bowl in his left hand and herbs in his right, while rays of healing light emanate from his body. He is often depicted in a group of eight.

Dhyani Buddhas (Gyalwa Ri Nga)

Each of the five Dhyani buddhas is a different colour, and each of them has different *mudras,* symbols and attributes. They are Öpagme, Nampar Namse (Vairocana), Mikyöba (or Mitrukpa; Akhshobya), Rinchen Jungne (Ratnasambhava) and Donyo Drupa (Amoghasiddhi).

Jampa (Maitreya)

Jampa, the Future Buddha, is passing the life of a bodhisattva until it is time to return to earth in human form 4000 years after the disappearance of Sakyamuni. He is normally seated in European fashion, with a scarf around his waist, often with a white stupa in his hair and his hands by his chest in the *mudra* of turning the Wheel of Law. Jampa is much larger than the average human and so statues of Jampa are often several storeys high.

Jampa (Maitreya)

Bodhisattvas

These are beings who have reached the state of enlightenment but vow to save everyone else in the world before they themselves enter nirvana. Unlike buddhas, they are often shown decorated with crowns and princely jewels.

Chenresig (Avalokiteshvara)

The 'glorious gentle one', Chenresig (Guanyin to the Chinese) is the Bodhisattva of Compassion. His name means 'he who gazes upon the world with suffering in his eyes'. The Dalai Lamas are considered to be reincarnations of Chenresig (as is King Songtsen Gampo), and pictures of the Dalai Lama and Chenresig are interchangeable, depending on the political climate. The current Dalai Lama is the 14th manifestation of Chenresig.

In the four-armed version (known more specifically in Tibetan as Tonje Chenpo), his body is white and he sits on a lotus blossom. He holds crystal rosary beads and a lotus, and clutches to his heart a jewel that fulfils all wishes. A deer skin is draped over his left shoulder.

Chenresig
(Avalokiteshvara)

There is also a powerful 11-headed, 1000-armed version, known as Chaktong Jentong. The head of this version is said to have exploded when confronted with myriad problems to solve. One of his heads is that of wrathful Chana Dorje (Vajrapani), and another (the top one) is that of Öpagme (Amitabha), who is said to have reassembled Chenresig's body after it exploded. Each of the 1000 arms has an eye in the palm. His eight main arms hold a bow and arrow, lotus, rosary, vase, wheel, staff and a wish-fulfilling jewel.

Jampelyang (Manjushri)

The Bodhisattva of Wisdom, Jampelyang is regarded as the first divine teacher of Buddhist doctrine. He is connected to science and agriculture and school children; architects and astrologers often offer prayers to him. His right hand holds the flaming sword of awareness, which cuts through delusion. His left arm cradles a scripture on a half-opened lotus blossom and his left hand is in the 'teaching' *mudra*. He is often yellow and may have blue hair or an elaborate crown. He is sometimes called Manjughosa.

Jampelyang
(Manjushri)

Drölma (Tara)

A female bodhisattva with 21 different manifestations or aspects, Drölma is also known as the saviouress. She was born from a tear of compassion that fell from the eyes of Chenresig and is thus considered the female version of Chenresig and a protector of the Tibetan people. She also symbolises purity and fertility and is believed to be able to fulfil wishes. Images usually represent Green Tara, who is associated with night, or Drölkar (White Tara), who is associated with day (and also Songtsen Gampo's Chinese wife). The green version sits in a half-lotus position with her right leg down, resting on a lotus flower. The white version sits in the full lotus position and has seven eyes, including ones in her forehead, both palms and both soles of her feet. She is often seen as part of a longevity triad, along with red Tsepame (Amitayus) and three-faced, eight-armed female Namgyelma (Vijaya).

Drölma (Tara)

Protector Deities

Protectors are easily recognised by their fierce expressions, bulging eyes, warrior stance (with one leg outstretched in a fencer's pose), halo of flames and Tantric implements. They either stand trampling on the human ego or sit astride an animal mount, dressed in military regalia and flayed animal or human skins. They represent on various levels the transformed original demons of Tibet, the wrathful aspects of other deities and, on one level at least, humankind's inner psychological demons.

Chökyong (Lokapalas)

The Chökyong (or Four Guardian Kings) are normally seen at the entrance hallway of monasteries and are possibly of Mongol origin. They are the protectors of the four cardinal directions: the eastern chief is white with a lute; the southern is green with a red beard and holds a sword; and the western is red and holds a green *naga*. Namtöse (Vaishravana), the protector of the north, doubles as the god of wealth (Zhambhala or Jambhala) and can be seen with an orange body (the colour of 100,000 suns) and clumpy beard, riding a snow lion, and holding a banner of victory, a jewel-spitting mongoose and a lemon. The Chinese connect the Chökyong to the four seasons.

Dorje Jigje (Yamantaka)

Dorje Jigje is a favourite protector of the Gelugpa order. A wrathful form of Jampelyang, he is also known as the destroyer of Yama (the Lord of Death). He is blue with eight heads, the main one of which is the head of a bull. He wears a garland of skulls around his neck and a belt of skulls around his waist, and holds a skull cup, butchers' chopper and a flaying knife in his 34 arms. He tramples on eight Hindu gods, eight mammals and eight birds with his 16 feet.

Nagpo Chenpo
(Mahakala)

Nagpo Chenpo (Mahakala)

A wrathful Tantric deity and manifestation of Chenresig, Nagpo Chenpo (Great Black One) has connections to the Hindu god Shiva. He can be seen in many varieties with anything from two to six arms. He is black ('as a water-laden cloud') with fanged teeth, wears a cloak of elephant skin and a tiara of skulls, carries a trident and skull cup, and has flaming hair. In a form known as Gompo (or Yeshe Gompo), he is believed by nomads to be the guardian of the tent.

Tamdrin (Hayagriva)

Another wrathful manifestation of Chenresig, Tamdrin (the 'horse necked') has a red body. His right face is white, his left face is green and he has a horse's head in his hair. He wears a tiara of skulls, a garland of 52 severed heads and a tiger skin around his waist. His six hands hold a skull cup, a lotus, a sword, a snare, an axe and a club, and his four legs stand on a sun disc, trampling corpses. On his back are the outspread wings of Garuda and the skins of a human and an elephant. He is sometimes shown embracing a blue consort. He has close connections to the Hindu god Vishnu and is popular among herders and nomads.

Tamdrin
(Hayagriva)

Chana Dorje (Vajrapani)

The name of the wrathful Bodhisattva of Energy means 'thunderbolt in hand'. In his right hand Chana Dorje holds a thunderbolt *(dorje or vajra),* which represents power and is a fundamental symbol of Tantric faith. He is blue with a tiger skin around his waist and a snake around his neck. He also has a peaceful, standing aspect. Together with Chenresig and Jampelyang, he forms part of the trinity known as the Rigsum Gonpo.

Chana Dorje
(Vajrapani)

Palden Lhamo (Shri Devi)

The special protector of Lhasa, the Dalai Lama and the Gelugpa order, Palden Lhamo is a female counterpart of Nagpo Chenpo. Her origins probably lie in the Hindu goddess Kali. She is blue, wears clothes of tiger skin, rides on a saddle of human skin, and has earrings made of a snake and a lion. She carries a club in her right hand and a skull cup full of blood in the left. She uses the black and white dice around her waist (tied to a bag of diseases) to determine people's fates. She holds the moon in her hair, the sun in her belly and a corpse in her mouth, and rides a mule with an eye in its rump.

Palden Lhamo
(Shri Devi)

Demchok (Chakrasamvara)

This meditational deity has a blue body with 12 arms, four faces and a crescent moon in his top knot. His main hands hold a thunderbolt and bell, and others hold an elephant skin, an axe, a hooked knife, a trident, a skull, a hand drum, a skull cup, a lasso and the head of Brahma. He also wears a garland of 52 heads, an apron of bone and clothes made from tiger skin.

Historical Figures

Guru Rinpoche (Padmasambhava)

Guru Rinpoche
(Padmasambhava)

The 'lotus-born' 8th-century Tantric master and magician from modern-day Swat in Pakistan, Guru Rinpoche subdued Tibet's evil spirits and helped to establish Buddhism in Tibet. Known in Sanskrit as Padmasambhava, he is regarded by followers of Nyingmapa Buddhism as the second Buddha and wears a red five-pointed Nyingmapa-style hat. His domain is the copper-coloured mountain called Zangdok Pelri. He has bug eyes and a curly moustache and holds a thunderbolt in his right hand, a skull cup in his left hand and a *katvanga* (staff) topped with three heads – one shrunken, one severed and one skull – in the crook of his left arm. He has a *phurbu* (ritual dagger) in his belt. Guru Rinpoche has eight manifestations, known collectively as the Guru Tsengye, which correspond to different stages of his life. He is often flanked by his consorts Mandarava and Yeshe Tsogyel.

Tsongkhapa

Tsongkhapa

Founder of the Gelugpa order and a manifestation of Jampelyang, Tsongkhapa (1357–1419) wears the yellow hat of the Gelugpas. Also known as Je Rinpoche, he is normally portrayed in the *yab-se sum* trinity with his two main disciples, Kedrub Je (later recognised as the first Panchen Lama) and Gyaltsab Je. His hands are in the 'teaching' *mudra* and he holds two lotuses. He was the founder and first abbot of Ganden Monastery and many images of him are found there.

Fifth Dalai Lama

Fifth Dalai Lama

The greatest of all the Dalai Lamas, the fifth (Ngawang Lobsang Gyatso; 1617–82) unified Tibet and built the bulk of the Potala. He was born at Chongye (in the Yarlung Valley) and was the first Dalai Lama to exercise temporal power. He wears the Gelugpa yellow hat and holds a flower or thunderbolt in his right hand and a bell *(drilbu)* in his left. He may also be depicted holding the Wheel of Law (symbolising the beginning of political control of the Dalai Lamas) and a lotus flower or other sacred objects.

King Songtsen Gampo

Tibet was unified under Songtsen Gampo (r 630–49). Together with his two wives, he is credited with introducing Buddhism to the country early in the 7th century. He has a moustache and wears a white turban with a tiny red Öpagme poking out of the top. He is flanked by Princess Wencheng Konjo, his Chinese wife, on the left, and Princess Bhrikuti, his Nepali wife, on his right.

King Trisong Detsen

King Songtsen
Gampo

The founder of Samye Monastery (r 755–97) is normally seen in a trio of kings with Songtsen Gampo and King Ralpachen (r 817–36). He is regarded as a manifestation of Jampelyang and so holds a scripture on a lotus in the crook of his left arm and a sword of wisdom in his right. Images show him with features similar to Songtsen Gampo's but without the buddha in his turban.

Milarepa

A great 11th-century Tibetan magician and poet, Milarepa (c 1040–1123) is believed to have attained enlightenment in the course of one lifetime. He became an alchemist in order to poison an uncle who had stolen his family's lands and then spent six years meditating in a cave in repentance. During this time he wore nothing but a cotton robe and so became known as Milarepa (Cotton-Clad Mila). Most images of Milarepa depict him smiling, sitting on an antelope skin, wearing a red meditation belt and holding his hand to his ear as he sings. He may also be depicted as green because he lived for many years on a diet of nettles. Milarepa's guru was the translator Marpa.

Milarepa

Tibetan Art

It is Buddhism that inspires almost all Tibetan art. Paintings, architecture, literature, even dance, all in some way or another attest to the influence of the Indian religion that found its most secure resting place in Tibet. Perhaps more unexpected is that, despite the harshness of their surroundings, Tibetans have great aesthetic taste, from traditional carpets and furniture of domestic architecture to jewellery and traditional dress.

The arts of Tibet represent the synthesis of many influences. The Buddhist art and architecture of the Pala and Newari kingdoms of India and Nepal were an important early influence in central Tibet, and the Buddhist cultures of Khotan and Kashmir were dominant in western Tibet. Newari influence is clearly visible in the early woodcarvings of the Jokhang, and Kashmiri influence is particularly strong in the murals of Tsaparang in western Tibet. As China came to play an increasingly major role in Tibetan affairs, Chinese influences, too, were assimilated, as is clear at Shalu Monastery near Shigatse and in the Karma Gadri style prevalent in eastern Kham. A later, clearly Tibetan style known as Menri was perfected in the monasteries of Drepung, Ganden and Sera.

Tibetan art is deeply conservative and conventional. Personal expression and innovation are not greatly valued, indeed individual interpretation is actually seen as an obstacle to Tibetan art's main purpose, which is to represent the path to enlightenment. The creation of religious art in particular is an act of merit and the creator generally remains anonymous.

Much of Tibet's artistic heritage fell victim to the Cultural Revolution. What was not destroyed was, in many cases, ferreted away to China or onto the Hong Kong art market. In recent years over 13,500 images have been returned to Tibet, still just a fraction of the number stolen. Many of Tibet's traditional artisans were persecuted or fled Tibet. It is only in recent years that remaining artists have again been able to return to their work and start to train young Tibetans in skills that faced the threat of extinction. New but traditional handicraft workshops are popping up all the time in Lhasa's old town.

Dance & Drama

Anyone who is lucky enough to attend a Tibetan festival should have the opportunity to see performances of *cham,* a ritual masked dance performed over several days by monks and lamas. Although every movement and gesture of *cham* has significance, it is no doubt the spectacle of the colourful masked dancers that awes the average pilgrim.

Cham is all about the suppression of malevolent spirits and is a clear throwback to the pre-Buddhist Bön faith. The chief officiant is an unmasked Black Hat lama who is surrounded by a mandalic grouping of masked monks representing manifestations of various protective deities.

If you live in London, check out the annual summer Tibetan Film Festival.

Tibetan Art Websites

» www.asianart.com – general

» www.mechakgallery.com – contemporary art

» www.himalayanart.org – online collections

The act of exorcism – it might be considered as such – is focused on a human effigy made of dough or perhaps wax or paper, through which the evil spirits are channelled.

The proceedings of *cham* can be interpreted on a number of levels. The Black Hat lama is sometimes identified with the monk who slew Langdharma, the anti-Buddhist king of the Yarlung era, and the dance is seen as echoing the suppression of malevolent forces inimical to the establishment of Buddhism in Tibet. Some anthropologists, on the other hand, have also seen in *cham* a metaphor for the gradual conquering of the ego, which is the ultimate aim of Buddhism. The ultimate destruction of the effigy that ends the dance might represent the destruction of the ego itself. Whatever the case, *cham* is a splendid, dramatic performance that marks the cultural highlight of the year for most Tibetans and it is well worth going out of your way to see.

Other festival dances might depict the slaying of Langdharma or the arrival of the Indian teachers in Tibet at the time of the second diffusion of Buddhism. Masked clowns provide light relief.

Lhasa's old town is stuffed with traditional workshops. Lhasa Village Handicrafts runs a two-hour walking tour of several old town artisans.

Lhamo Opera

Lighter forms of entertainment usually accompany performances of cham. *Lhamo,* not to be confused with *cham,* is Tibetan opera. A largely secular art form, it portrays the heroics of kings and the villainy of demons, and recounts events in the lives of historical figures. *Lhamo* was developed in the 14th century by Tangtong Gyelpo, known as Tibet's Leonardo da Vinci because he was also an engineer, a major bridge builder and a physician. Authentic performances still include a statue of Tangtong on the otherwise bare stage. After the stage has been purified, the narrator gives a plot summary in verse and the performers enter, each with his or her distinct step and dressed in the bright and colourful silks of the aristocracy.

The Art of Tibet by Robert Fisher is a portable colour guide to all the arts of Tibet, from the iconography of thangkas to statuary.

Music

Music is one aspect of Tibetan cultural life in which there is a strong secular heritage. In the urban centres, songs were an important vent for social criticism, news and political lampooning. In Tibetan social life, both work and play are seen as occasions for singing. Even today it is not uncommon to see the monastery reconstruction squads pounding on the roofs of buildings and singing in unison. Where there are groups of men and women, the singing alternates between the two groups in the form of rhythmic refrains. The ultimate night out in Lhasa is to a *nangma* venue, where house dancers and singers perform traditional songs and dances as part of a stage show, with members of the audience often joining in at smaller venues.

Tibet also has a secular tradition of wandering minstrels. It's still possible to see minstrels performing in Lhasa and Shigatse, where they play on the streets and occasionally (when they are not chased out by the owners) in restaurants. Generally, groups of two or three singers perform heroic epics and short songs to the accompaniment of a four-stringed guitar and a nifty little shuffle, before moving around tables soliciting donations with a grin. In times past, groups of such performers travelled around Tibet, providing entertainment for villagers who had few distractions from the constant round of daily chores.

The best places to see *lhamo* (Tibetan opera) are the Norbulinka Palace during a festival or the nightly shows at the Shöl Opera Troupe.

While the secular music of Tibet has an instant appeal for foreign listeners, the liturgical chants of Buddhist monks and the music that accompanies *cham* dances is a lot less accessible. Buddhist chanting creates an eerie haunting effect, but soon becomes very monotonous.

The music of *cham* is a discordant cacophony of trumpet blasts and boom-crash drums – atmospheric as an accompaniment to the dancing but not exactly the kind of thing you would want to slip into the MP3.

Tibetan religious rituals use *rolmo* and *silnyen* (cymbals), *nga* (suspended drums), *damaru* (hand drums), *drilbu* (bells), *dungchen* (long trumpets), *kangling* (conical oboes; formerly made from human thighbones) and *dungkar* (conch shells). Secular instruments include the *dramnyen* (a six-stringed lute), *piwang* (two-stringed fiddle), *lingbu* (flute) and *gyumang* (Chinese-style zither).

Recordings

Most recordings of traditional Tibetan music have been made in Dharamsala or Dalhousie in India. The country's biggest musical export (or rather exile) is Yungchen Lhamo, who fled Tibet in 1989 and has since released several excellent world-music recordings. She also appeared on Natalie Merchant's *Ophelia* album. Other Tibetan singers based abroad include Dadon Dawa Dolma and Kelsang Chukie Tethong (whose release *Voice from Tara* is worth checking out).

To see traditional Tibetan dancing and singing, check out our MC Tenzin's list of Lhasa's best *nangma* venues in the Entertainment section of the Lhasa chapter.

» *Chö* by Choying Drolma and Steve Tibbets (Hannibal, 1997). A deeply beautiful and highly recommended recording of chants and songs by a Tibetan nun. The follow-up, *Selwa* (Six Degrees Records), is also wonderful.

» *Coming Home* by Yungchen Lhamo (Real World, 1998). Tibetan world music with modern production. Try also *Ama* (2006), which features a duet with Annie Lennox.

» *Sacred Tibetan Chant* Even the monks of Sherab Ling Monastery in northern India were surprised when they won the 2003 Grammy for Best Traditional World Music Recording for this album of unadorned recording of traditional monk chanting. It's deep, guttural, and similar to what you'll hear in prayer halls across Tibet (Naxos, 2003).

Literature

The development of a Tibetan written script is credited to a monk by the name of Tonmi Sambhota and corresponded with the early introduction of Buddhism during the reign of King Songtsen Gampo. Before this, pre-Buddhist traditions were passed down as oral histories that told of the exploits of early kings, the spirits and the origins of the Tibetan people. Some of these oral traditions were later recorded using the Tibetan script.

But for the most part, literature in Tibet was dominated by Buddhism, first as a means of translating Buddhist scriptures from Sanskrit into Tibetan and second, as time went by, in association with the development of Tibetan Buddhist thought. There is nothing in the nature of a secular literary tradition – least of all novels – such as can be found in China or Japan.

The Tibetan epic *Gesar of Ling* is the world's longest epic poem, 25 times as long as *The Iliad*, and takes years to recite in full!

One of the great achievements of Tibetan culture was the development of a literary language that could, with remarkable faithfulness, reproduce the concepts of Sanskrit Buddhist texts. The compilation of Tibetan-Sanskrit dictionaries in the early 9th century ensured consistency in all subsequent translations.

Through the 12th and 13th centuries, Tibetan literary endeavour was almost entirely consumed by the monumental task of translating the complete Buddhist canon into Tibetan. The result was the 108 volumes of canonical texts (Kangyur), which record the words of the Historical Buddha, Sakyamuni, and 208 volumes of commentary (Tengyur) on the Kangyur by Indian masters that make up the basic Buddhist scriptures shared by all Tibetan religious orders. What time remained was used in the compilation of biographies and the collection of songs of revered lamas. Perhaps most famous among these is the *Hundred Thousand Songs of Milarepa*. Milarepa was an ascetic to whom many songs and poems concerning the quest for buddhahood are attributed.

Alongside Buddhist scriptures exists an ancient tradition of storytelling, usually concerning the taming of Tibet's malevolent spirits to allow the introduction of Buddhism. Many of these stories were passed from generation to generation orally, but some were recorded. Examples include the epic *Gesar of Ling* and the story of Guru Rinpoche, whose countless stories of miracles and battles with demons are known to peoples across the entire Himalayan region. The oral poetry of the Gesar epic is particularly popular in eastern Tibet, where a tiny number of ageing bards just keep alive a tradition that dates back to the 10th century.

Wood-block printing has been in use for centuries and is still the most common form of printing in monasteries. Blocks are carved in mirror image; printers then work in pairs putting strips of paper over the inky block and shuttling an ink roll over it. The pages of the text are kept loose, wrapped in cloth and stored along the walls of monasteries. Tibet's most famous printing presses were in Derge in modern-day Sichuan, at Nartang Monastery and at the Potala. You can see traditional block printing at Drepung, Ganden and Sera monasteries outside Lhasa.

Very little of the Tibetan literary tradition has been translated into English. Translations that may be of interest include the *Bardo Thödol,* or *Tibetan Book of the Dead,* a mysterious but fascinating account of the stages and visions that occur between death and rebirth.

Tales of Tibet – Sky Burials, Prayer Wheels & Wind Horses, edited by Herbert J Batt, gathers contemporary fiction by Tibetan and Chinese writers. The scholarly introduction explains how the nationality of the authors influences this sometimes elegiac, sometimes confronting collection.

TIBETAN ART ARCHITECTURE

Architecture

Most early religious architecture – the Jokhang in Lhasa for example – owed much to Pala (Indian) and especially Newari (Nepali) influences. A distinctively Tibetan style of architectural design gradually emerged, and found its expression in huge chörtens (stupas), hilltop *dzong*s (forts) and the great Gelugpa monastic complexes, as well as the lesser-known stone towers of Kongpo and the Qiang regions of western Sìchuān. The great American architect Frank Lloyd Wright is said to have had a picture of the Potala on the wall of his office.

Chörtens

Probably the most prominent Tibetan architectural motif is the chörten. Chörtens were originally built to house the cremated relics of the Historical Buddha and as such have become a powerful symbol of the Buddha and his teachings. Later, chörtens also served as reliquaries for lamas and holy men and monumental versions would often encase whole mummified bodies, as is the case with the tombs of the Dalai Lamas in the Potala. The tradition is very much alive: a stunning gold reliquary chörten was constructed in 1989 at Tashilhunpo Monastery to hold the body of the 10th Panchen Lama.

In the early stages of Buddhism, images of the Buddha did not exist and chörtens served as the major symbol of the new faith. Over the next two millennia, chörtens took many different forms across the Buddhist world, from the sensuous stupas of Burma to the pagodas of China and Japan. Most elaborate of all are the *kumbums* (100,000 Buddha images), of which the best remaining example in Tibet is at Gyantse. Many chörtens were built to hold ancient relics and sacred texts and have been plundered over the years by treasure seekers and vandals.

Chörtens are highly symbolic. The five levels represent the four elements, plus eternal space: the square base symbolises earth, the dome

Two years after killing off his main character, Arthur Conan Doyle explained the resurrection of Sherlock Holmes by saying that he had spent two years wandering in Tibet. Tibetan writer Jamyang Norbu cleverly conjectures on what Holmes may have been up to in his 2003 novel *The Mandala of Sherlock Holmes.*

is water, the spire is fire, and the top moon and sun are air and space. The 13 discs of the ceremonial umbrella can represent the branches of the tree of life or the 10 powers and three mindfulnesses of the Buddha. The top seed-shaped pinnacle symbolises enlightenment. The chörten as a whole can therefore be seen as a representation of the path to enlightenment. The construction can also physically represent the Buddha, with the base as his seat and the dome as his body.

Houses & Homes

Typical features of Tibetan secular architecture, which are also used to a certain extent in religious architecture, are buildings with inward-sloping walls made of large, tightly fitting stones or sun-baked bricks. Below the roof is a layer of twigs, squashed tight by the roof and painted to give Tibetan houses their characteristic brown band. Roofs are flat, as there is little rain or snow, made from pounded earth and edged with walls. You may well see singing bands of men and women pounding a new roof with sticks weighted with large stones. In the larger struc-

Tibet's Architectural Highlights

» Kumbum, Gyantse

» Potala Palace, Lhasa

» Tashilhunpo Monastery, Shigatse

» Samye Monastery, Yarlung Tsangpo Valley

MONASTERY LAYOUT

Tibetan monasteries are based on a conservative design and share a remarkable continuity of layout. Many are built in spectacular high locations above villages. Most were originally surrounded by an outer wall, built to defend the treasures of the monastery from bands of brigands, Mongolian hordes or even attacks from rival monasteries. Most monasteries have a kora (pilgrimage path) around the complex, replete with holy rocks and meditation retreats high on the hillside behind. A few monasteries have a sky-burial site and most are still surrounded by ruins dating from the Cultural Revolution.

Inside the gates there is usually a central courtyard used for special ceremonies and festivals and a darchen (flag pole). Surrounding buildings usually include a dukhang (main assembly or prayer hall) with gönkhang (protector chapels) and lhakhang (subsidiary chapels), as well as monks' quarters, a kangyur lhakhang (library) and, in the case of larger monasteries, tratsang (colleges), kangtsang (halls of residence), kitchens and a barkhang (printing press).

The main prayer hall consists of rows of low seats and tables, often strewn with cloaks, hats, ritual instruments, drums and huge telescopic horns. There is a small altar with seven bowls of water, butter lamps and offerings of mandalas made from seeds. The main altar houses the most significant statues, often Sakyamuni, Jampa (Maitreya) or a trinity of the Past, Present and Future Buddhas and perhaps the founder of the monastery or past lamas. Larger monasteries contain funeral chörtens of important lamas. There may be an tsangkhang (inner sanctum) behind the main hall, the entrance of which is flanked by protector gods, often one blue, Chana Dorje (Vajrapani) and the other red, Tamdrin (Hayagriva). There may well be an inner kora (korlam) of prayer wheels. At the entrance to most buildings are murals of the Four Guardian Kings and perhaps a Wheel of Life or a mandala mural. Side stairs lead up from here to higher floors.

Gönkhang are dark and spooky halls that hold wrathful manifestations of deities, frequently covered with a cloth because of their terrible appearance. Murals here are often traced against a black background and walls are decorated with Tantric deities, grinning skeletons or even dismembered bodies. The altars often have grain dice or mirrors, used for divination, and the pillars are decorated with festival masks, weapons and sometimes stuffed snakes and wolves. Women are often not allowed into protector chapels.

The monastery roof usually has excellent views as well as vases of immortality, victory banners, dragons and copper symbols of the Wheel of Law flanked by two deer, recalling the Buddha's first sermon at the deer park of Sarnath.

tures wooden pillars support the roof inside. The exteriors are generally whitewashed brick, although in some areas, such as Sakya in Tsang, other colours may be used. In rural Tibet, homes are often surrounded by walled compounds, and in some areas entrances are protected by painted scorpions and swastikas. Increasing numbers of new homes in Lhasa's old town are being made with concrete.

Over the last few years Tibet has seen a remarkable spate of new housing construction (over 300,000 new homes), driven and partly financed by the central government. See p299 for details.

Nomads, who take their homes with them, live in *bar* (yak-hair tents), which are normally roomy and can accommodate a whole family. An opening at the top of the tent lets out smoke from the fire.

Painting

As with other types of Tibetan art, painting is very symbolic and can be interpreted on many different levels. It is almost exclusively devotional in nature.

Tibetan mural painting was strongly influenced by Indian, Newari and, in the far West, Kashmiri painting styles, with later influence coming from China. Paintings usually followed stereotypical forms with a central Buddhist deity surrounded by smaller, lesser deities and emanations. The use of colour and proportion is decided purely by convention and rigid symbolism. Later came depictions of revered Tibetan lamas or Indian spiritual teachers, often surrounded by lineage lines or incidents from the lama's life.

Chinese influence began to manifest itself more frequently in Tibetan painting from around the 15th century. The freer approach of Chinese landscape painting allowed some Tibetan artists to break free from some of the more formalised aspects of Tibetan religious art and employ landscape as a decorative motif. The new, Chinese-influenced forms coexisted with older forms, largely because painting in Tibet was passed on from artisan to apprentice in much the same way that monastic communities maintained lineages of teaching.

Thangkas

Religious paintings mounted on brocade and rolled up between two sticks are called thangkas. Their eminent portability was essential in a land of nomads, as mendicant preachers and doctors often used them as a visual learning aid. Not so portable are the huge thangkas known as *gheku* or *koku*, the size of large buildings, that are unfurled every year during festivals. Traditionally, thangkas were never bought or sold.

The production of a thangka is an act of devotion and the process is carefully formalised. Linen (or now more commonly cotton) is stretched on a wooden frame, stiffened with glue and coated with a mix of chalk and lime called *gesso*. Iconography is bound by strict mathematical measurements. A grid is drawn onto the thangka before outlines are sketched in charcoal, starting with the main central deity and moving outwards.

Colours are added one at a time, starting with the background and ending with shading. Pigments were traditionally natural: blue from lapis, red from cinnabar and yellow from sulphur. Most thangkas are burnished with at least a little gold. The last part of the thangka to be painted is the eyes, which are filled in during a special 'opening the eyes' celebration. Finally a brocade backing of three colours and a protective 'curtain' are added, the latter to protect the thangka.

For an in-depth look at Lhasa's traditional Tibetan architecture and interactive maps of Lhasa, check out www.tibet heritagefund.org.

If you are interested in actually creating, not just understanding Tibetan art, look for the master work on the subject, *Tibetan Thangka Painting: Methods & Materials* by David P Jackson and Janice A Jackson.

See traditional craftsmen at the Ancient Art Restoration Centre (AARC) in Lhasa, next to Lhasa Village Handicrafts. The AARC managed the restoration of the Potala and Sera and Drepung Monasteries; craftsmen here include thangka painters, metal workers, woodcarvers and dye makers.

Statuary & Sculpture

Tibetan statuary, like Tibetan painting, is almost exclusively religious in nature. Ranging in height from several centimetres to several metres, statues usually depict deities and revered lamas. Most of the smaller statues are hollow and are stuffed with paper texts, prayers, amulets and juniper when consecrated. Very few clay or metal sculptures remaining in Tibet date from before 1959.

Metal statues are traditionally sculpted in wax and then covered in clay. When the clay is dry it is heated. The wax melts and is removed, leaving a mould that can be filled with molten metal. Statues are generally then gilded and painted.

Sculptures are most commonly made from bronze or stucco mixed with straw, but can even be made out of butter and tsampa, mounted on a wooden frame.

Handicrafts

A burgeoning economy in Lhasa has fuelled a real growth in traditional crafts in recent years, though these are partially for the Chinese tourist market.

To see a selection of Tibetan carpets visit the Gang Gyen Carpet Factory in Shigatse, the Tanva workshop in Nam village, or check out the Wangden style carpets at Lhasa Village Handicrafts.

Tibet has a 1000-year history of carpet making; the carpets are mostly used as seat covers, bed covers and saddle blankets. Knots are double tied (the best carpets have 100 knots per square inch), which results in a particularly thick pile. Tibet's secret carpet ingredient is its particularly high-quality sheep wool, which is hand spun and coloured with natural dyes such as indigo, walnut, madder and rhubarb. Tibetan cashmere goat's wool and *shahtoosh* antelope wool are also in great demand. Gyantse and Shigatse were the traditional centres of carpet production, although the modern industry is based almost exclusively in Tibetan exile communities in Nepal.

Inlaid handicrafts are common, particularly in the form of prayer wheels, daggers, butter lamps and bowls, although most of what you

---

MANDALAS

The mandala (*kyilkhor*, literally 'circle') is more than a beautiful artistic creation, it's also a three-dimensional meditational map. What on the surface appears to be a plain two-dimensional design emerges, with the right visual approach, as a three-dimensional picture. Mandalas can take the form of paintings, patterns of sand, three-dimensional models or even whole monastic structures, as at Samye. In the case of the two-dimensional mandala, the correct visual approach can be achieved only through meditation. The painstakingly created sand mandalas also perform the duty of illustrating the impermanence of life (they are generally swept away after a few days).

A typical mandala features a central deity surrounded by four or eight other deities who are aspects of the central figure. These surrounding deities are often accompanied by a consort. There may be several circles of these deities, totalling several hundred deities. These deities and all other elements of the mandala have to be visualised as the three-dimensional world of the central deity and even as a representation of the universe.

The mandala is associated with Tantric Buddhism and is chiefly used in a ritual known as *sadhana* (means for attainment). According to this ritual, the adept meditates on, invokes and identifies with a specific deity, before dissolving into emptiness and re-emerging as the deity itself. The process, in so far as it uses the mandala as an aid, involves a remarkable feat of imaginative concentration. One ritual calls for the adept to visualise 722 deities with enough clarity to be able to see the whites of their eyes and hold this visualisation for four hours.

see these days in Lhasa is made by Tibetan communities in Nepal. Nomads in particular wear stunning silver jewellery; you may also see silver flints, horse tack, amulets known as *gau,* and ornate chopstick and knife sets.

Tibetan singing bowls, made from a secret mix of seven different metals, are a meditation device that originated from pre-Buddhist Bön practices. The bowls produce a 'disassociated' mystic hum when a playing stick is rotated around the outer edge of the bowl.

Woodcarving is another valued handicraft, used in the production of brightly coloured Tibetan furniture and window panels, not to mention wood-print blocks.

Best Monastery Murals

» Shalu, near Shigatse

» Gongkar Chöde, Yarlung Valley

» Thöling, Zanda

TIBETAN ART HANDICRAFTS

The Future of Tibet

As Lhasa's economy booms and towns across the plateau are modernised and rebuilt, China's current policy in Tibet is clear: invest billions on a massive economic development to improve the lives of hundreds of thousands of Tibetans.

Unfortunately the modernisation is squarely on China's terms. Questions over the suitability and sustainability of hydroelectric projects and mass tourism remain unaddressed. Moreover, with a transient migrant Chinese population spearheading the economic boom, the bulk of the profits from mining, tourism and other industries in Tibet are flowing straight out of the plateau back into China. It's a bittersweet boom that looks set only to accelerate.

China believes that over time economic advancement will win Tibetan hearts and minds and compensate for the lack of religious and political freedoms; it's certainly a payoff that seems to be working in the rest of China. Many Tibetans reply that they are not so easily bought and that they must have more of a voice in the decision-making process. As Tibetans struggle to adjust to the perceived lack of control over their land, religion and resources, alienation and tensions look set to remain high.

> Encouragingly, Tibet is now seriously cool among Chinese backpackers from Běijīng to Guǎngzhōu, many of whom are as enamoured with Tibet as their Western counterparts.

The International Area

The more things change in Tibet, the more they stay the same outside. Talks between the Chinese and the Dharamsala-based Tibetan government in exile remain stalled, with the Chinese taking every opportunity to denounce the Nobel-peace prize winning Dalai Lama for being a 'wolf in sheep's clothing' or trying to 'split the motherland'. The Dalai Lama himself has abandoned any hope of nationhood, opting to push for genuine cultural, religious and linguistic autonomy within the Chinese state, yet even this 'middle path' of conciliation has yielded nothing. Fearful of upsetting their trade balance with China, foreign governments will continue to be careful not to receive the Dalai Lama in any way that recognises his political status as the head of an exiled government.

> One million people a year arrive in Tibet by train, one third of them visitors.

In an age of terrorism and rising religious extremism it is perhaps surprising how little attention the Dalai Lama's remarkable insistence on non-violence gets from the world community. As years pass with no discernable progress, tensions inside the Tibetan community are becoming apparent, with younger Tibetans increasingly pushing for direct, perhaps even violent, action.

For its part China seems incapable of seeing Tibetan dissent in any terms other than 'separatism' and 'splittism'. The fear in Běijīng is that continued unrest or concessions made to the Tibetans will cause a domino effect with other restive nationalities like the Uighurs of Xīnjiāng, a stand largely backed by an increasingly nationalist Chinese public. Until that changes, a political settlement will remain elusive. The political reality is that Tibet is firmly a part of China. No one expects that to change any time soon.

The Politics of Reincarnation

Only in Tibet could the 13th-century practice of reincarnation become a 21st-century political hot potato. Recent disputes between Dharamsala and Běijīng over the selection of various lamas, most notably the Panchen Lama, have spotlighted how religious decisions are becoming increasingly politicised, a trend that will doubtless only intensify as the Dalai Lama heads into his late 70s.

Both sides have their eyes firmly on the future here, for it is the Panchen Lama who traditionally assists in choosing the next Dalai Lama. The Chinese government knows that the struggle to control future reincarnations is fundamental to controlling Tibet; the rather bizarre result being that the avowedly atheist Chinese Communist Party is now in charge of choosing incarnate Buddhist lamas. For his part, the Dalai Lama has made it clear that he will only be reborn in Tibet if he is allowed to return there as part of a political settlement.

The spectre of the death of the Dalai Lama haunts the entire Tibetan world. More than just 'a simple monk' or even a god-king, the Dalai Lama has become a shining symbol of Tibetan identity. When he dies, Tibet will have lost something essential to its modern identity. Some commentators even believe that the death of Dalai Lama may herald the death of the Tibetan cause, one reason why both sides are laying the ground for future rebirth.

Cultural Survival

The greatest threat to Tibetan cultural life comes from indiscriminate economic change and Chinese migration, as government subsidies and huge infrastructure projects change the face and ethnic make-up of cities across the breadth of Tibet. As Tibetan culture becomes diluted, there is a fear that Tibetans will become a minority in their own country, a situation the Dalai Lama has described as 'cultural genocide'. Tibetans point to Amdo in Qīnghǎi, once a Tibetan-dominated area that now has three Han Chinese to every Tibetan.

Education is another sore point that has long-term cultural consequences. An education system that exclusively uses the (Mandarin) Chinese language reinforces the fact that only Sinicised Tibetans are able to actively participate in Tibet's economic advances. Parents face the unenviable balancing act of preserving Tibetan language and tradition, while preparing the coming generation for the realities of life in a Chinese-language dominated economy.

And yet for all the new roads, karaoke joints, brothels and mobile phones, Tibet's traditional and religious values remain at the core of most Tibetans' identities, and the quintessence of rural Tibet remains remarkably intact. Fifty years of political indoctrination and religious control has failed to dull the devotion of most Tibetans to either Buddhism or the Dalai Lama and there's little sign of this changing.

It's hard to separate myth from reality in Tibet. The half-truths and propaganda from all sides can be so enticing, so pervasive and so entrenched that it's hard to see the place through balanced eyes. The reality is that Tibet is no fragile Shangri-la but a resilient land underpinned by a unique culture and a deep faith, and it is perhaps this above all that offers Tibet's best hope for its future.

In 2010 the Dharamsala-backed 11th Panchen Lama turned 21 in his 15th year of house arrest.

PANCHEN LAMA

THE FUTURE OF TIBET THE POLITICS OF REINCARNATION

Survival Guide

DIRECTORY A–Z... 334

Accommodation.........334

Activities 335

Bathhouses............336

Business Hours 336

Children................336

Customs 336

Embassies &
Consulates 337

Food & Drink...........337

Gay & Lesbian
Travellers..............339

Insurance...............340

Internet Access 340

Language Courses......340

Legal Matters 340

Maps..................341

Money 342

Photography...........343

Post 343

Public Holidays.........343

Safe Travel 344

Telephone 345

Time 345

Toilets 345

Tourist Information......345

Travellers with
Disabilities.............345

Visas..................346

Volunteering...........347

Women Travellers 348

TRANSPORT...... 349

GETTING THERE & AWAY –
GATEWAY CITIES........349

Entering the Country.....349

Air.....................349

GETTING THERE
& AWAY – TIBET 352

Air.....................352

Land...................353

GETTING AROUND 357

Air.....................357

Bicycle 357

Bus 359

Car 359

Hitching...............359

Local Transport 359

HEALTH 361

LANGUAGE 368

Directory A–Z

Accommodation

Most towns in Tibet offer a decent range of hotels, many with hot showers and some three- or four-star options. In smaller towns you may be limited to rooms with a shared bathroom, while in the countryside electricity and running water are luxuries that cannot be relied on. Hotels are divided into *bīnguǎn* (宾馆), *fàndiàn* (饭店) or *dàjiǔdiàn* (大酒店; hotels), *zhāodàisuǒ* (招待所; guesthouses) and *lǚguǎn* (旅馆; simple hostels). The Tibetan terms are *drukhang* (hotel) and *dronkhang* (guesthouse).

Budget accommodation generally means a room without a bathroom, or at the top end of the scale a simple room with a hot-water bathroom. Lhasa in particular has many budget guesthouses and youth hostels. Midrange hotels generally have rooms with a private bathroom and hot-water showers, at least for part of the day. Top-end hotels are limited to the main cities and Lhasa now boasts several luxury and boutique hotels.

Hot water is provided everywhere in thermoses and even in the simplest places a basin and drum of cold water is usually provided for washing. Bedding is provided, but in the cheapest places it's often not that clean and a sleeping bag is a nice luxury.

In some towns (such as Tsetang, Ali and Purang) the local Public Security Bureau (PSB) keeps a frustratingly tight lid on which places can and cannot accept foreigners, and budget hotels are often not permitted to accept foreigners.

Groups are sometimes expected to share rooms at remote truck-stop places, since many only have four- or five-bed rooms. If you want your own room, you may be able to either pay for only the number of beds you require, or for all the beds in a room.

The price ranges listed in this book are for a standard double room before discounts and are defined as follows:

$	under Y130
$$	Y130 to Y400
$$$	over Y400

Midrange and top-end hotels in Lhasa are 30% more expensive than elsewhere, though standards are 40% higher. You can sometimes get good deals on midrange and top-end hotels in China at booking sites such as **China Hotel Reservation** (www.chinahotels reservation.com), **Sinohotel** (www.sinohotel.com), **Asiarooms** (www.asiarooms.com), **Ctrip** (www.english.ctrip.com) and **Elong** (www.elong.com), though many of the Lhasa hotels listed on these sites are dull Chinese places with poor locations.

Camping

Camping out is well understood by Tibetans, many of whom still spend their summers herding livestock in mountain valleys. Always ask permission if camping near a settlement or encampment, watch out for the dogs (see p344) and expect an audience.

Guesthouses & Hotels

Lhasa is full of clean, well-run Tibetan-style guesthouses and hostels, many of which are aimed at Chinese backpackers. Similar set-ups can be found in Shigatse, Sakya and Tingri.

Monasteries such as Samye, Ganden, Drigung Til, Dorje Drak, Mindroling, Tidrum and Reting have their own pilgrim guesthouses –

BOOK YOUR STAY ONLINE

For more accommodation reviews by Lonely Planet authors, check out hotels.lonelyplanet.com/Tibet. You'll find independent reviews, as well as recommendations on the best places to stay. Best of all, you can book online.

DISCOUNTS

In some areas of Tibet, notably in Lhasa, accommodation prices vary seasonally. Midrange and top-end hotels in particular almost always discount their rooms from the largely fictitious rack rates. Throughout this book, we list full high-season rates (May to September), followed by the range of discounts you could expect at the time of research. Prices will be lower still in winter.

normally a bank of carpeted seats that double as beds – and a night here can be a magical experience. Your guide may be reluctant for you to overnight at a monastery guesthouse, but this may change if travel regulations ease.

Most of the larger hotels are anonymous Chinese-style places that share several traits: the plumbing is often dodgy, the toilets stinky, the carpets dotted with a mosaic of cigarette burns and the light bulbs too dim to read by. The one thing that will always work is the TV.

Rooms are generally divided into *biāozhǔn* (标准; standard), which come with a bathroom, and *pǔtōng* (普通; ordinary). Standard rooms are often divided into *jīngjì* (经济; economy) and *háohuá* (豪华; deluxe) rooms.

Some hotels (generally the cheaper ones) price their accommodation per bed rather than per room, which can work out well for solo travellers. To guarantee that you have the room to yourself, you would theoretically have to pay for all beds (and a few hotel owners will try to force you to do so), but usually that's not necessary.

Strangely single rooms are normally the same price (or even more expensive!) as a double room. Where they are cheaper they are generally much smaller than a double.

Activities

Tibet offers the type of topography to delight horse riders, mountaineers, white-water rafters and others, though the problem, as always, is the confusing travel permit system, which many authorities manipulate to their own financial advantage.

Cycling

Tibet offers some of the most extreme and exhilarating mountain biking in the world. Unfortunately the current permit system (see p29) means that independent tours on bikes are effectively impossible, or at least much more expensive than a few years ago, since cyclists require a guide and vehicle support like everyone else.

If things change and if you are fit and well equipped, it's possible to visit most places in this book by bike, although the most popular route is the paved roller-coaster ride along the Friendship Hwy from Lhasa down to Kathmandu. Mountain bikes can be hired in Lhasa for short trips around the city and surrounding valley.

Thaizand Bicycle Tours (p78) Offers route information and can provide bikes and logistical support for all kinds of trips, including a 10-day ride to the Nepal border with jeep support.

Bike China (☎1-800-818 1778; www.bikechina.com) US-based company is another good resource and offers organised supported bike rides, including from Chéngdū to Lhasa.

For information on long-distance touring, see p357. For a double shot of inspiration, check out the home page of Martin Adserballe (www.adserballe.com).

Horse Riding

There's something romantic about travelling across Tibet on horseback. The easiest place to arrange this is in the Kham region of western Sìchuān, but even there it's just a matter of coming to an agreement with local herdsmen. A kora of Lake Manasarovar on horseback is a great idea and a few travellers have managed to arrange this.

Tibet Wind Horse Adventure (☎136 3890 0332; www.windhorsetibet.com) offers day trips on horseback in the Drigung and Tolung Valley regions (Y760) and can customise longer adventures.

Foreign travel companies, such as Hidden Trails (www.hiddentrails.com) and Boojum Expeditions (www.boojum.com), offer expensive horse-riding tours in Kham (western Sìchuān).

Mountaineering

There are some huge peaks in Tibet, including the 8000m-plus giants of Cho Oyu, Shishapangma and, of course, Everest, which are enough to send a quiver of excitement through vertically inclined explorers. Unfortunately, the Chinese government charges exorbitant fees for mountaineering permits, which puts mountaineering in Tibet out of the range of most individuals or groups devoid of commercial sponsorship.

Foreign travel companies, such as Alpine Ascents (www.alpineascents.com) and Jagged Globe (www.jagged-globe.co.uk) can arrange mountaineering trips to Cho Oyu and

Shishapangma in Tibet, but they don't come cheap.

Rafting

Tibet Wind Horse Adventure (☎136 3890 0332; www.windhorsetibet.com) offers rafting trips between June and October, either a half-day on the Tolung-chu (Y600), one/two days on the Drigung-chu (Y760/1520) or an ambitious five-day trip on the Reting Tsangpo. Both horse and rafting trips can be joined in Lhasa or added onto another company's itinerary without special permits.

Trekking

Tibet offers some of the most spectacular trekking on earth. For detailed information on the most popular trekking routes, see p230.

Bathhouses

Cheap hotels often don't have hot showers, but staff can normally direct you to a simple bathhouse (淋浴; *línyù; sugpo truya* in Tibetan), where you can get a hot shower for Y10 to Y20. These are purely functional places, and sometimes a bit grotty, but after a few days on the road you'll be glad for the chance to wash. Bring your own towel and flip-flops.

Business Hours

Standard opening hours for banks, government offices and PSB offices are 9.30am to 1pm and 3pm to 6.30pm Monday to Friday, and sometimes 10am to 1pm Saturday.

Hours for shops and restaurants vary considerably, but generally shops open from 10am to 9pm and restaurants 10am to 10pm. Bars may close at 8pm or 2am, depending on their location and clientele.

Opening hours listed in this guide are for summer; winter hours generally start half an hour later and finish half an hour earlier. Hours are only listed in reviews if they differ from these standards.

Many smaller monasteries have no set opening hours and will open up chapels once you've tracked down the right monk. Others, such as Samye, are notorious for only opening certain rooms at certain times. In general it's best to try to tag along with pilgrims or a tour group.

Children

Children can be a great ice-breaker in Tibet and generally generate a lot of interest. Many hotels have family rooms, which normally have three or four beds arranged in two connected rooms. On the down side, children don't get on with Tibetan food or toilets any better than grown-ups. They also tire more easily from an endless round of visiting monasteries. Bring along a copy of *Tintin in Tibet* for when morale flags. In Kathmandu several bookshops sell Tibetan thangka (religious paintings) and mandala colouring books. Children under 1.5m (5ft) or under eight years old (the definition depends on the site) get in free at most sights in Tibet.

Tibet is probably not a great place to bring a very small child. You should bring all supplies (including nappies and medicines) with you. Small spoons can be useful as most places have only chopsticks. There's plenty of boiling water to sterilise bottles etc. It's possible to make a cot from the copious numbers of duvets supplied with most hotel rooms.

Be especially careful with children, as they won't be on the lookout for signs of altitude sickness.

Customs

Chinese border crossings have gone from being severely traumatic to exceedingly easy for travellers. You are unlikely to be even checked when flying in or out of the country.

You can legally bring in or take out only Y6000 in Chinese currency and must declare any cash amount exceeding US$5000 or its equivalent. It's also officially forbidden to bring more than 20 pieces of underwear into the PRC (we kid you not!).

It is illegal to import any printed material, film, tapes etc 'detrimental to China's politics, economy, culture and ethics'. This is a particularly sensitive subject in Tibet, but even here it is highly unusual to have Chinese customs officials grilling travellers about their reading matter. Maps and political books printed in Dharamsala, India, could cause a problem.

Climate

Lhasa

It is currently illegal to bring into China pictures, books, videos or speeches of or by the Dalai Lama. Moreover, you may be placing the recipient of these in danger of a fine or jail sentence from the Chinese authorities. Images of the Tibetan national flag are even 'more' illegal.

If travelling from Nepal to Tibet by air or overland it's a good idea to bury this guide deep in your pack or sleeping bag, as overzealous customs officials have been known to confiscate Lonely Planet *Tibet* guides.

Be very circumspect if you are asked to take any packages, letters or photos out of Tibet for anyone else, including monks. If caught, you'll most likely be detained, interrogated and then probably expelled.

Anything made in China before 1949 is considered an antique and needs a certificate to take it out of the country. If it was made before 1795, it cannot legally be taken out of the country.

Embassies & Consulates

For Chinese embassies abroad, consult the Chinese Foreign Ministry website at www.fmprc.gov.cn/eng and click on 'Missions Overseas'.

Consulates in Tibet

The only diplomatic representation in Tibet is the **Nepali Consulate-General** (尼泊尔领事馆; Nípóěr Lǐngshìguǎn; Map p44; ☎ 0891-681 5744; www.nepalembassy.org.cn; 13 Luobulinka Beilu; ☺10am-noon Mon-Fri) in Lhasa. Visas are issued the next day at 4.30pm, though you can sometimes get your passport back the same day. It's located on a side street between the Lhasa Hotel and the Norbulingka.

Visa fees change frequently, but at the time of research a 15-/30-/90-day multiple entry visa cost

Y175/280/700. All visas are valid for six months from the date of issue. Bring one visa photo. Visits of less than 24 hours are currently visa-free.

It is also possible to obtain the same Nepali visas for US$25/40/100 (in US dollars cash) at Kodari, the Nepali border town, although it would be sensible to check first that this has not changed.

Consulates in Chéngdū

France (☎028-6666 6060; www.consulfrance-chengdu.org; 30th fl, Tianfu Time Sq, 2 Zongfu Lu)

US (☎028-8558 3992; http://chengdu.usembassy-china.org.cn; 4 Lingshiguan Lu)

Embassies in Běijīng

In case of emergency in Tibet, your nearest embassy is most likely in Běijīng:

Australia (☎010-5140 4111; www.austemb.org.cn)

Canada (☎010-6532 3536; www.canada.org.cn)

France (☎010-8532 8080; www.ambafrance-cn.org)

Germany (☎010-8532 9000; www.peking.diplo.de)

Ireland (☎010-6532 5486; www.embassyofireland.cn)

Netherlands (☎010-8532 0200; www.hollandinchina.org)

New Zealand (☎010-8532 0200; www.nzembassy.com/china)

UK (☎010-5192 4000; www.ukinchina.fco.gov.uk)

USA (☎010-6532 3831; www.beijing.usembassy-china.org.cn)

Food & Drink

Though you won't starve, food will probably not be a highlight of your trip to Tibet. A few restaurants in Lhasa have elevated a subsistence diet into the beginnings of a cuisine, but outside the urban centres Tibetan food is more about survival than pleasure. On the plus

side, fresh vegetables and packaged goods are now widely available and you are never far away from a good Chinese *fànguǎn* (饭馆) or *cāntīng* (餐厅) restaurant.

Price ranges for restaurants in this guide are defined as the following. Prices are defined as per dish in Chinese restaurants, or per main course in Western restaurants:

$ less than Y30 per dish
$$ Y30 to Y80
$$$ over Y80

Staples & Specialities
TIBETAN

The basic Tibetan meal is *tsampa*, a kind of dough made with roasted-barley flour and yak butter mixed with water, tea or beer – something wet. Tibetans skilfully knead and mix the paste by hand into dough-like balls, which is not as easy as it looks! Tsampa with milk powder and sugar makes a pretty good porridge and is a fine trekking staple, but only a Tibetan can eat it every day and still look forward to the next meal.

Outside of Lhasa, Tibetan food is limited to greasy *momos* and *thugpa*. Momos are small dumplings filled with meat or vegetables or both. They are normally steamed but can be fried and are pretty good. More common is *thugpa*, a noodle soup with meat or vegetables or both. Variations on the theme include *hipthuk* (squares of noodles and yak meat in a soup) and *thenthuk* (more noodles). Glass noodles known as *phing* are also sometimes used.

The other main option is *shemdre* (sometimes called curried beef), a stew of potatoes and yak meat on a bed of rice. In smarter restaurants in Lhasa or Shigatse you can try dishes like *damje* or *shomday* (butter fried rice with raisins and yoghurt), *droma desi* (wild ginseng

DHARMA FOOD

Need to cook dinner for a visiting rinpoche? Try *Tibetan Cooking: Recipes for Daily Living, Celebration, and Ceremony* by Elizabeth Kelly or *The Lhasa Moon Tibetan Cookbook* by Tsering Wangmo. Both books offer recipes for everything from *momos* to Milarepa-style nettle soup.

with raisins, sugar, butter and rice) and *shya vale* (fried pancake-style pasties with a yak-meat filling). Formal Tibetan restaurants (*sakhang* in Tibetan) in particular are very big on yak offal, with large sections of menus sumptuously detailing the various ways of serving up yak tongues, stomachs and lungs.

In rural areas and markets you might see strings of little white lumps drying in the sun that even the flies leave alone – this is dried yak cheese and it's eaten like a boiled sweet. For the first half-hour it is like having a small rock in your mouth, but eventually it starts to soften up and taste like old, dried yak cheese.

Also popular among nomads is *yak sha* (dried yak jerky). It is normally cut into strips and left to dry on tent lines and is pretty chewy stuff.

CHINESE

Han immigration into Tibet may be a threat to the very essence of Tibetan culture, but it's done wonders for the restaurant scene. Even most Tibetans admit that Chinese food is better than tsampa, *momos* and *thugpa*. Chinese restaurants can be found in every settlement in Tibet these days, but are around

50% more expensive than elsewhere in China.

Chinese food in Tibet is almost exclusively Sichuanese, the spiciest of China's regional cuisines. One popular Sichuanese sauce is *yúxiāng* (鱼香), a spicy, piquant sauce of garlic, vinegar and chilli that is supposed to resemble the taste of fish (probably the closest thing you'll get to fish in Tibet). You'll also taste *huājiāo* (花椒; wild Asian flower pepper), a curious mouth-numbing spice popular in Sichuanese food. See p381 for a list of the most common Chinese dishes.

Outside of Lhasa, few Chinese restaurants have menus in English and when they do the prices are often marked up by as much as 50%. We indicate restaurants with English menus by the icon 🔲. In most restaurants you can simply wander out into the kitchen and point to the vegetables and meats you want fried up, but you'll miss out on many of the most interesting sauces and styles this way.

Chinese snacks are excellent and make for a fine light meal. The most common are *shuǐjiǎo* (ravioli-style dumplings) ordered by the bowl or weight (half a *jin*, or 250g, is enough for one person), and *bāozi* (thicker steamed dumplings), which are similar to *momos* and are normally ordered by the steamer. Both are dipped in soy sauce, vinegar or chilli (or a mix of all). You can normally get a bowl of noodles anywhere for around Y5; *shāguō mǐxiàn* is a particularly tasty form of rice noodles cooked in a clay pot. *Chǎomiàn* (fried noodles) and *dan chao fan* (egg fried rice) are not as popular as in the West, but you can get them in many Chinese and backpacker restaurants.

You can get decent breakfasts of yoghurt, muesli and toast at backpacker hotels in Lhasa, Gyantse and Shi-

gatse, but elsewhere you are more likely to be confronted by Chinese-style dumplings, fried bread sticks (油条; *youtiao*) and tasteless rice porridge (稀饭; *xifan*). One good breakfast-type food that is widely available is scrambled eggs and tomato (*fānqié chǎodàn*).

MUSLIM

The Muslim restaurants found in almost all urban centres in Tibet are an interesting alternative to Chinese or Tibetan food. They are normally recognisable by a green flag hanging outside or Arabic script on the restaurant sign. Most chefs come from the Línxià area of Gānsù. The food is based on noodles, and, of course, there's no pork.

Dishes worth trying include *gānbànmiàn*, a kind of stir-fried spaghetti bolognaise made with beef (or yak) and sometimes green peppers; and *chǎomiànpiàn*, fried noodle squares with meat and vegetables. *Xīnjiāng bànmiàn* (Xīnjiāng noodles) are similar, but the sauce comes in a separate bowl, to be poured over the noodles. It's fun to go into the kitchen and see your noodles being handmade on the spot.

Muslim restaurants also offer good breads and excellent *babao chá* (eight treasure tea), which is made with dried raisins, plums and rock sugar, and only releases its true flavour after several cups.

SELF-CATERING

There will likely be a time somewhere on your trip when you'll need to be self-sufficient, whether you're staying overnight at a monastery or are caught between towns on an overland trip. Unless you have a stove, your main saviour will be instant noodles. Vegetables such as onions, carrots and bok choy (even seaweed and pickled vegetables) can save even the cheapest pack of noodles from culinary oblivion, as can a packet of mixed spices brought from home.

It's a good idea to stock up on instant coffee, hot chocolate and soups, as flasks of boiling water are offered in every hotel and restaurant.

Drinks

NONALCOHOLIC DRINKS

The local beverage that every traveller ends up trying at least once is yak-butter tea (see the box, p339). Modern Tibetans these days use an electric blender to mix their yak-butter tea.

The more palatable alternative to yak-butter tea is sweet, milky tea, or *cha ngamo*. It is similar to the tea drunk in neighbouring Nepal or Pakistan. Soft drinks and mineral water are available everywhere.

ALCOHOLIC DRINKS

The Tibetan brew is known as chang (青稞酒; *qingkèjiǔ* in Chinese), a fermented barley beer. It has a rich, fruity taste and ranges from disgusting to pretty good. True connoisseurs serve it out of a jerry can. Those trekking in the Everest region should try the local variety (similar to Nepali *tongba*), which is served in a big pot. Hot water is poured into the fermenting barley and the liquid is drunk through a wooden straw – it is very good. Sharing *chang* is a good way to get to know local people, if drunk in small quantities. On our research trips we have never suffered any adverse effects from drinking copious amounts of chang. However, you should be aware that it is often made with contaminated water, and there is always some risk in drinking it.

The main brands of local beer are Lhasa Beer, now brewed in Lhasa in a joint venture with Carlsberg, and the better (and pricier) Tibet Spring Green Barley

---

YAK-BUTTER TEA

Bö cha, literally 'Tibetan tea', is unlikely to be a highlight of your trip to Tibet. Made from yak butter mixed with salt, milk, soda, tea leaves and hot water all churned up in a wooden tube, the soupy mixture has more the consistency of bouillon than of tea (one traveller described it as 'a cross between brewed old socks and sump oil'). When mixed with tsampa (roasted barley flour) and yak butter it becomes the staple meal of most Tibetans, and you may well be offered it at monasteries, people's houses and even while waiting for a bus by the side of the road.

At most restaurants you mercifully have the option of drinking *cha ngamo* (sweet, milky tea), but there will be times when you just have to be polite and down a cupful of *bö cha* (without gagging). Most nomads think nothing of drinking up to 40 cups of the stuff a day. On the plus side it does replenish your body's lost salts and prevents your lips from cracking. As one reader told us, 'Personally we like yak-butter tea, not so much for the taste as the view'.

Most distressing for those not sold on the delights of yak-butter tea is the fact that your cup will be refilled every time you take even the smallest sip, as a mark of the host's respect. There's a pragmatic reason for this as well; there's only one thing worse than hot yak-butter tea – cold yak-butter tea.

Beer. Domestic beer costs around Y4 in a shop, Y8 in most restaurants and Y12 in swanky bars.

Supermarkets in Lhasa stock several types of Chinese red wine, including Shangri-La, produced in the Tibetan areas of northeast Yunnan using methods handed down by French missionaries at the beginning of the 19th century.

Gay & Lesbian Travellers

Homosexuality has historical precedents in Tibet, especially in Tibetan monasteries, where male lovers were known as *trap'i kedmen*, or 'monk's wife'. The Dalai Lama has sent mixed signals about homosexuality, describing gay sex as 'sexual misconduct', 'improper' and 'inappropriate', but also by saying, 'There are no acts of love between adults that one can or should condemn'.

The official attitude to gays and lesbians in China is also ambiguous, with responses ranging from draconian penalties to tacit acceptance. Travellers are advised to act with discretion. Chinese men routinely hold hands and drape their arms around each other without anyone inferring any sexual overtones.

Gay + Tibet (www.gaytibet. blogspot.com) An interesting blog.

Hanns Ebensten Travel (☏866-294 8174; www. hetravel.com) This US-based company has organised gay and lesbian group trips to Tibet in the past.

Out Adventures (☏1-888-360 1152; www.out-adventures. com) A Canada-based company that markets gay and lesbian tours to Tibet, including the train trip to Lhasa.

Utopia (www.utopia-asia. com/tipschin.htm) Has a good website and publishes a guide to gay travel in China, though with little specific to Tibet.

Insurance

Travel insurance is particularly recommended in a remote and wild region like Tibet. Check particularly that the policy covers ambulances or an emergency flight home, which is essential in the case of altitude sickness. Some policies specifically exclude 'dangerous activities' such as rafting and even trekking.

You may prefer a policy that pays doctors or hospitals directly rather than you having to pay on the spot and claim later. If you have to claim later, make sure you keep all documentation. Some policies ask you to call to a centre in your home country where an immediate assessment of your problem is made. Note that reverse charge (collect) calls are not possible in Tibet.

Worldwide travel insurance is available at www. lonelyplanet.com/travel_ services. You can buy, extend and claim online any time – even if you're already on the road.

See p361 for information on health insurance.

Internet Access

Internet cafes (网吧; *wǎngbā* in Chinese) are available in almost every town in Tibet, though locals use them more to play computer games and smoke cigarettes than to surf the web. Most charge around Y3 per hour, though places in Western Tibet cost up to Y8. A surprising number operate 24 hours. Speeds are pretty good considering you're in Tibet.

To get online you may need to show your passport. You'll most likely prepay for a fixed amount of time and you'll then be assigned a card number (证件号; *zhèngjiànhào*) and a password (密码; *mì mǎ*), which you enter into the onscreen box.

Some social networking sites (such as YouTube and Blogspot) and websites (eg those of the Dalai Lama) have been blacklisted by the Chinese government and are unavailable inside China.

Several hotels and restaurants in Lhasa offer free wi-fi access (无线网; *wúxiàn wǎng*).

In this guide 🛜 means that a hotel or cafe provides either wi-fi or a LAN cable in the room (normally free), and @ means that an internet-connected computer is available for guests (normally for a fee).

Language Courses

It is possible to enrol in a Tibetan-language course at Lhasa's Tibet University. Tuition costs US$1000 per semester; semesters run from March to July and September to January. There are two hours of classes a day and around 70 foreign students generally attend. For an application form contact the **Foreign Affairs Office** (☎0891-634 3254; www.utibet. edu.cn, in Chinese; fsd@utibet. edu.cn; Tibet University, Lhasa 850000, Tibetan Autonomous Region). Once you are accepted, the university will help arrange a student ('X') visa and, after three months, residency status in Lhasa. Students have to stay in campus accommodation. It should also be possible to hire a private tutor from the university for around Y20 per hour. Look for the Tibet University Foreign Student forum on Facebook.

Many travellers find it more convenient to study at

Dharamsala or Kathmandu, although students say that the mix of dialects and high levels of English make them less effective places to study. Courses offered there include Tibetan Buddhist philosophy, Tibetan language and Tibetan performing arts.

A good resource for finding Tibetan language courses is www.learntibetan.net.

Legal Matters

Most crimes are handled administratively by the Public Security Bureau (PSB; 公安局; *Gōng'ānjú*), which acts as police, judge and executioner.

China takes a particularly dim view of opium and all its derivatives. Foreigners have been executed for drug offences (trafficking in more than 50g of heroin can result in the death penalty). It's difficult to say what attitude the Chinese police will take towards foreigners caught using marijuana – they often don't care what foreigners do if it's not political, and if Chinese or Tibetans aren't involved. Then again the Chinese are fond of making examples of wrongdoings and you don't want to be the example. If arrested you should immediately contact your nearest embassy, probably in Běijīng.

New regulations forbid foreigners from visiting private Tibetan homes without special permission.

Public Security Bureau (PSB)

The PSB is the name given to China's police, both uniformed and plain clothed. The foreign affairs branch of the PSB deals with foreigners. This branch (also known as the 'entry-exit branch') is responsible for issuing visa extensions and Alien Travel Permits.

In Tibet it is fairly unusual for foreigners to have problems with the PSB, though making an obvious display of pro-Tibetan political sympathies is guaranteed to lead to problems. Photographing Tibetan protests or military sites will lead to the confiscation of your film and possibly a brief detention.

Attempting to travel into, through or out of Tibet without a travel permit is likely to end in an encounter somewhere en route, most likely when checking into a hotel in a closed area, or trying to board public transport at the bus station. If you are caught in a closed area without a permit, you face a fine of between Y200 and Y600, which can often be bargained down (some officers have been known to offer a 'student discount'!). Make sure you are friendly and repentant: the only times things get nasty is if you (or the police) lose your cool. Get a receipt to make sure you don't get fined a second time during your return to where you came from.

If you do have a serious run-in with the PSB, you may have to write a confession of guilt. In the most serious cases, you can be expelled from China (at your own expense).

Maps

Good mapping for Tibet is not easy to come by, especially inside China, so stock up on maps before you leave. Good online map shops include Stanfords (www.stanfords.co.uk), Map Shop (www.themapshop.co.uk), Mapland (www.mapland.com.au) and Map Link (www.maplink.com). For information on trekking-specific maps, see p232.

MAPS OF TIBET

Chinese provincial atlases to Tibet are available in bookshops throughout China. They show the most detail, but are of little use if you or the person you are asking

PRACTICALITIES

» **Currency** Renminbi, referred to as yuan or colloquially as kuai; Y1 = 10 mao.

» **Electricity** 220V, 50 cycles AC. Note that electronics such as laptops and iPods (anything with a hard drive) are often affected by altitudes above 4500m and may stop working.

» **Plugs** At least five designs: three-pronged angled pins (like in Australia); three-pronged round pins (like in Hong Kong); two flat pins (US style but without the ground wire), two narrow round pins (European style) and three rectangular pins (British style).

» **Weights & Measures** Metric, though traders measure fruit and vegetables by the *jin* (500g).

doesn't read Chinese characters. Most locals know place names in Tibetan only, not Chinese.

The English-language map *China Tibet Tour Map*, by the Mapping Bureau of the Tibet Autonomous Region, is the best locally produced English-language map and is OK if you are just travelling around Tibet by road.

Road maps available in Kathmandu include *Tibet – South-Central* by Nepa Maps, *Latest Map of Kathmandu to Tibet* by Mandala Maps, the *Namaste Trekking Map* and *Lhasa to Kathmandu*, which is a mountain-biking map by Himalayan Map House. They are marginally better than Chinese-produced maps, but still aren't up to scratch.

Amnye Machen Institute in Dharamsala (www.amnyemachen.org) The *Tibet and Adjacent Areas under Chinese Communist Occupation* is an unusual map that covers the entire Tibetan world. It uses traditional Tibetan place names, which not everyone in Tibet (certainly not the many Chinese immigrants) will know.

Gecko Maps (www.geckomaps.com; formerly Karto Atelier) Produces an excellent general *Himalaya-Tibet* map, as well as trekking

and panoramic maps of Mt Kailash.

Google Earth (http://earth.google.com) Offers fascinating detail on Tibet, including many monasteries and several treks. Be warned: it's utterly addictive.

ITMB (www.itmb.com) Publishes a good and (usefully) waterproof *Tibet* map (1:1,850,000; 2006).

Nelles Verlag (www.nelles-verlag.de) Their *Himalaya* map covers the entire range and has good detail of central Tibet.

Reise Know-How (www.reise-know-how.de) Perhaps the best overview is this 1:1,500,000 scale *Tibet* map.

Tibet Map Institute (www.tibetmap.com) Try this website for detailed and downloadable online maps of Tibet.

MAPS OF LHASA

Gecko Maps produce *The Lhasa Map*, with awesome architectural detail of the old town. More offbeat, and quite dated these days (published in 1995), is the Amnye Machen Institute *Lhasa City* (1:12,500).

On This Spot – Lhasa, published by the **International Campaign for Tibet** (ICT; www.savetibet.org) in 2001, is a unique political map of the Lhasa region, pinpointing the location of prisons, demonstrations, human-rights abuses and more. It's a really fascinating read, but it's too politically subversive to take into Tibet. It can be ordered from ICT.

Money

The Chinese currency is known as Renminbi (RMB) or 'people's money'. The basic unit of this currency is the yuan, and is designated in this book by a 'Y'. In spoken Chinese, the word kuai is almost always substituted for the yuan. Ten jiao (commonly known as mao) make up one yuan.

For your trip to Tibet bring a mix of travellers cheques (say 60%), cash in US dollars (40%) and a credit card or two. See p16 for a table of exchange rates and basic information on costs.

ATMs

Several ATMs (自动取款机; *zìdòng qǔkuǎnjī*) in Lhasa and Shigatse and even as far afield as Ali accept foreign cards. The Bank of China accepts Visa, MasterCard, Diners Club, American Express, Maestro, Cirrus and Plus. The Agricultural Bank accepts Visa, Plus and Electron. Check before trying your card as many ATMs can only be used by domestic account holders.

The maximum amount you can withdraw per transaction is around Y2000 with the Bank of China and Y1000 with the Agricultural Bank. Cards are occasionally eaten, so try to make your transaction during bank hours.

For those without an ATM card or credit card, a PIN-activated **Visa Travel-Money card** (www.usa.visa.com/personal/cards/prepaid; www.visa.co.uk/visacards/travel.html) gives access to predeposited cash through the Visa/Plus ATM network.

Credit Cards

You'll get very few opportunities to splurge on the plastic in Tibet, unless you spend a few nights in a top-end hotel. Most local tours, train tickets and even flights out of Lhasa still can't be paid for using a credit card. The few shops that do accept credit cards often charge a 4% surcharge.

The Lhasa central branch of the Bank of China is the only place in Tibet that provides cash advances on a credit card. A 3% commission is deducted.

Exchanging Money

In Tibet, the main place to change foreign currency is the Bank of China. Top-end hotels in Lhasa have exchange services, but only for guests. Outside of Lhasa the only other locations to change money are in Shigatse, Zhangmu, Purang (cash only), Ali, and at the airport. If you are travelling upcountry, try to get your cash in small denominations: Y100 and Y50 bills are sometimes difficult to get rid of in rural Tibet.

The currencies of Australia, Canada, the US, the UK, Hong Kong, Japan, the euro zone and most of the rest of Western Europe are acceptable at the Lhasa Bank of China. The official rate is given at all banks and most hotels, so there is little need to shop around for the best deal. There's generally no commission to change cash.

The only place in Tibet to officially change yuan back into foreign currency is the central Lhasa branch of the Bank of China. You will need your original exchange receipts.

Moneychangers at Zhangmu (by the Nepal border) will change yuan into Nepali rupees and vice versa. Yuan can also easily be reconverted in Hong Kong and, increasingly, in many Southeast Asian countries.

China has a problem with counterfeit notes. Very few Tibetans or Chinese will accept a Y100 or Y50 note without first subjecting it to intense scrutiny, and many will not accept old, tattered notes or coins. Check the watermark when receiving any Y100 note.

International Transfers

Getting money sent to you in Lhasa is possible, but it can be a drag. One option is by using the Bank of China's central office in Lhasa. Money should be wired to the Bank of China, Tibet/Lhasa branch, 28 Linkuo Xilu, bank account No 90600668341, SWIFT code BKCHCNBJ900. Double-check wiring instructions with the bank beforehand.

The second option is via **Western Union** (www.westernunion.com), which can wire money via the Express Mail Service (EMS; see p343) at Lhasa's main post office.

Taxes

Although big hotels may add a tax or 'service charge' of 10% to 15%, all other taxes are included in the price tag, including airline departure tax.

Tipping & Bargaining

Tibet is one of those wonderful places where tipping is not done and almost no one asks for a tip. If you go on a long organised trip out to Eastern or Western Tibet, your guide and driver will probably expect a tip at the end of the trip, assuming all went well.

Basic bargaining skills are essential for travel in Tibet. You can bargain in shops, hotels, street stalls and travel agencies, and with pedicab drivers and most people – but not everywhere. In small shops and street stalls, bargaining is expected, but there is one important rule to follow: be polite.

Tibetans are no less adept at driving a hard deal than the Chinese and, like when dealing with the Chinese, aggressive bargaining will usually only serve to firm their conviction that the original asking price is the one they want. Try to keep smiling and firmly whittle away at the price. If this does not work, try walking away. They might call you back, and if they don't there is always somewhere else.

Travellers Cheques

Besides the advantage of safety, travellers cheques are useful to carry in Tibet because the exchange rate is higher (by about 3%) than it is for cash. The Bank of China charges a 0.75% commission to cash travellers cheques. Cheques from the major companies such as Thomas Cook, Citibank, American Express and Bank of America are accepted.

Photography

Film & Equipment

Shops in Lhasa stock a decent range of memory cards and rechargeable batteries. Internet cafes or photo shops in Lhasa, Shigatse, Chamdo and Ali can burn your photos onto a CD for around Y20. Opt for brand-name CDs rather than the cheaper Chinese-made versions. It is possible to make digital prints in Lhasa.

Battery life plummets at Tibet's higher elevations and lower temperatures. Keep your batteries warm and separate from your camera overnight and during cold weather. Just heating up batteries in your pocket or the sun can draw some extra juice from them. Chinese batteries are invariably useless.

Restrictions

Photographs of airports and military installations are prohibited, and bridges are also a touchy subject. Don't take any photos or especially video footage of civil unrest or public demonstrations. Chinese authorities are paranoid about foreign TV crews filming unauthorised documentaries on Tibet.

Restrictions on photography are also imposed at most monasteries and museums. This is partly an attempt to stop the trade of antiquities out of Tibet (statues are often stolen to order from photos taken by seemingly innocuous 'tourists'). In the case of flash photography, such restrictions protect wall murals from damage. Inside the larger monasteries, a fee of Y20 to Y50 is often imposed in each chapel for taking a photograph. Video fees can be up to Y800 (US$100!) in some monasteries. You are free, however, to take any photos of the exteriors of monasteries.

Technical Tips

» Dust gets into everything in Tibet, so make a point of carefully cleaning your lenses as often as possible.

» Take photographs early in the morning and late in the afternoon, to cope with the harsh light conditions.

» Use a polarising filter to deepen contrast and blue skies.

Lonely Planet's full-colour *Travel Photography: A Guide to Taking Better Pictures*, written by internationally renowned travel photographer Richard I'Anson, is full of handy hints and is designed to be taken on the road.

Post

China's post service is pretty efficient and airmail letters take around a week to reach most destinations. Writing the country of destination in Chinese can speed up the delivery. Postal rates are as follows:

Y6 to any country, plus Y1.8 per additional 10g
Postcard Y4.50
Aerogram Y5.20

Rates for parcels vary depending on the country of destination and seem quite random. As a rough guide, a 1kg airmail package costs around Y160 to Australia, the UK or USA. Cheaper options include surface mail (which takes around one month) or sea mail (which takes from two to three months); a good compromise is Sea, Air and Land (SAL), which takes about six weeks to the USA. The maximum weight you can send or receive is 30kg. Lhasa is the only place in Tibet from which it's possible to send international parcels. Domestic parcels are cheap: around Y27 for a 4kg parcel by train to Shànghǎi.

Post offices are very picky about how you pack things; do not finalise your packing until the parcel has its last customs clearance. If you have a receipt for the goods, then put it in the box when you are mailing it, since it may be opened again by customs further down the line.

Express Mail Service (EMS), a worldwide priority mail service, can courier documents to most foreign countries in around five days. Documents up to 500g cost Y160/220/190 to Australia/Europe/US. Documents to Hong Kong cost Y110, plus Y30 each additional 500g. There are charges of Y2.30 for recorded delivery and Y6.50 for registered mail.

DHL has an office in Lhasa (see p76). A 500g document couriered to the USA costs Y228 (depending on the fuel surcharge) and a 10kg jumbo box costs Y1126.

Public Holidays

The PRC has several traditional and modern national holidays. These are mainly

Chinese holidays and mean little to many Tibetans, but government offices and banks will be closed on many of these dates.

New Year's Day 1 January
Chinese New Year 23 January 2012, 10 February 2013, 31 January 2014
Serf Emancipation Day 28 March
Qing Ming Jie (Tomb Sweeping Day) 4/5 April, not really observed in Tibet
Labour Day 1 May, a three-day holiday
Youth Day 4 May
National Day 1 October, a three-day holiday

Chinese New Year, otherwise known as the Spring Festival, officially lasts only three days but many people take a week off from work. Be warned: this is definitely not the time to travel around China, cross borders (especially the Hong Kong one) or to be caught short of money.

Serf Emancipation Day was introduced as a public holiday in Tibet in 2009 to commemorate 50 years of Communist Chinese control in Tibet and what China's says was the freeing of one million Tibetan 'serfs'. Don't expect much in the way of celebration among the ex-serfs.

Many Tibetan businesses, restaurants, shops and travel agencies are closed on the days of Losar and Saga Dawa (for more on these and other festivals, see p21). Tibetan festivals like these are held according to the Tibetan lunar calendar, which usually lags at least a month behind our Gregorian calendar. Ask around for the exact dates of religious festivals because monasteries often only fix these a few months in advance. Check Tibetan lunar dates against Gregorian dates at www.kalachakranet. org/ta_tibetan_calendar. html.

The following are politically sensitive dates, as are 5 March, 27 September, 10 December and 1 October, which mark past political protests. It may be difficult for travellers to fly into Tibet for a few days before these dates.

10 March Anniversary of the 1959 Tibetan uprising and flight of the Dalai Lama
23 May Anniversary of the signing of the *Agreement on Measures for the Peaceful Liberation of Tibet*
1 September Anniversary of the founding of the Tibetan Autonomous Region (TAR)

Safe Travel
Dogs

If you are exploring remote monasteries or village on foot, you should keep an eye open for dogs, especially at remote homesteads or nomad encampments, where the powerful and aggressive mastiffs should be given a very wide berth. Travelling with a walking pole or stick is recommended. Some cyclists and trekkers even carry pepper spray or Chinese fireworks to scare off the brutes. See p363 for information on what to do if you are bitten.

Political Disturbances

Tourists can be caught up in Tibet's political violence and backpackers have even been injured in crossfire in the past. If a demonstration or full-blown riot breaks out (as it did in 2008) it's safest to stay in your hotel. If things get really bad local authorities or you embassy may organise emergency flights out of Lhasa.

Staring Squads

It is very unusual to be surrounded by staring Tibetans and Chinese in Lhasa, but visiting upcountry is another matter. Trekkers will soon discover that it is not a good idea to set up camp beside Tibetan villages. The spectacle of a few foreigners putting up tents is probably the closest some villagers will ever come to TV.

Theft

Theft is rare in Tibet, which is generally safer than other provinces of China. Trekkers in the Everest region have reported problems with petty theft, and pickpockets work parts of Lhasa.

Small padlocks are useful for backpacks and some dodgy hotel rooms. Bicycle chain locks come in handy not only for hired bikes but

---

GOVERNMENT TRAVEL ADVICE

The following government websites offer travel advisories and information on current hot spots.

Australian Department of Foreign Affairs & Trade (☎1300 139 281; www.smarttraveller.gov.au) Register online at www.orao.dfat.gov.au.

British Foreign Office (☎0845-850-2829; www.fco.gov.uk/travel)

Canadian Department of Foreign Affairs (☎800-267 6788; www.voyage.gc.ca)

New Zealand Ministry of Foreign Affairs & Trade (☎439 8000; www.safetravel.govt.nz) Register online at https://register.safetravel.govt.nz.

US State Department (☎888-407 4747; http://travel.state.gov) Register online at https://travelregistration.state.gov.

also for attaching backpacks to railings or luggage racks.

If something of yours is stolen, you should report it immediately to the nearest foreign affairs branch of the PSB. They will ask you to fill in a loss report, which you will also need to claim the loss on your travel insurance.

Telephone

The cheapest way to make an international call is through one of the private telephone booths known as 'Telecom Supermarkets'. Rates are Y2.40 per minute to the US, Y2.90 to India and Nepal, Y3.60 to Australia, Europe and Southeast Asia, and Y4.60 to most other countries. 'Domestic' long-distance calls cost Y1.50 per minute to Hong Kong, Macau and Taiwan and Y0.30 elsewhere in China. Local city calls cost Y0.20 per minute.

Most hotels in Lhasa have International Direct-Dial (IDD) telephones, but levy a hefty 30% surcharge on calls.

It is still impossible to make reverse-charge (collect) calls or to use foreign telephone debit cards. The best you can do is give someone your number and get them to call you back.

China country code is ✏️86. Local area codes are given at the start of each town's entry within this guidebook.

Mobile phone coverage is generally excellent, even in far Western Tibet and at Everest Base Camp! The easiest way to use your mobile phone in Tibet is to buy a local SIM card in Lhasa from someone like China Mobile (Y60 to Y100, including Y50 worth of credit). Top it up by buying a scratch card (充值卡; *chōngzhí ka*) for Y50 or Y100 of credits.

Most internet cafes come equipped with headphones and microphones, but few have Skype pre-loaded.

> ## SLEEPING BAGS
>
> The question of whether you need a sleeping bag or not depends entirely on where you plan to go and how you plan to travel. Those who aim to spend time in Lhasa and then head down to Nepal via the sights of Tsang could do without one, although they are always a nice comfort, especially in budget hotels. Anyone planning on trekking or heading out to more remote areas, such as Nam-tso, Everest or Western Tibet, should definitely bring one along. See also Equipment, p232.

Time

Time throughout China – including Tibet – is set to Běijīng time, which is eight hours ahead of GMT/UTC. When it is noon in Běijīng it is also noon in far-off Lhasa, even if the sun only indicates around 9am or 10am.

Toilets

Chinese toilets might be fairly dismal, but Tibetan toilets make them look like little bowers of heaven. The standard model is a deep hole in the ground, often without partitions, that bubbles and gives off noxious vapours. Many Tibetans (including women with long skirts) prefer to urinate in the street.

On the plus side there are some fabulous 'toilets with a view'. Honours go to the Samye Monastery Guesthouse, the Sakya Guesthouse, the public toilets in the Potala and the small village of Pasum on the way to Everest Base Camp.

With the exception of midrange and top-end hotels, hotel toilets in Tibet are of the squat variety – as the clichés go, good for the digestion and character building, too. *Always* carry an emergency stash of toilet paper or tissues with you.

Tourist Information

Tibet is officially a province of China and does not have tourist offices as such. Similarly, the Tibetan government-in-exile does not provide information specifically relating to travel in Tibet. Several of the pro-Tibetan organisations abroad offer travel advice (see the box, p347).

Tibet Tourism Bureau (TTB; Luobulinka Lu, Lhasa; ⏱️8.30am-1.30pm & 3-5.30pm) State-sponsored agency that issues the permits necessary to enter Tibet (see p29), although very few travellers deal with it directly. The TTB branches in Shànghǎi (www.cn-tibet. com) and Běijīng (www. tibettour.net.cn/en) operate like normal travel agencies.

Travellers with Disabilities

High altitudes, rough roads and lack of access make Tibet a hard place for people with mobility difficulties. Monasteries in particular often involve a hike up a hillside or steep, very narrow steps. Few of the hotels offer any facilities for the disabled.

Braille Without Borders (www.braillewithoutborders. org) Blind visitors can contact this excellent organisation based in Lhasa. It developed the first Tibetan Braille system and runs a school for blind Tibetan kids, as well as supporting a blind massage clinic in Lhasa (see p63). The co-founder, Sabriye Tenberken, is the author of the book *My Path Leads to Tibet: The Inspiring Story of How One Young Blind Woman Brought Hope to the Blind Children of Tibet* and stars alongside blind climber Erik Weihenmayer in the moving documentary film *Blindsight* (www.blindsightthemovie.com).

Navyo Nepal (☑01-691 6359; www.navyonepal.com; Kathmandu, Nepal) This Nepal-based company has some experience in running tours for the disabled to Tibet and Nepal.

Visas

Apart from citizens of Brunei, Japan and Singapore, all visitors to Tibet require a valid China visa. Visas for individual travel in China are easy to get from most Chinese embassies, though it's important not to mention Tibet on your application. The Chinese government has been known to stop issuing individual visas in summer or the run-up to sensitive political events, as a control of tourist numbers.

Most Chinese embassies and consulates will issue a standard 30- or 60-day, single-entry tourist (an 'L' category) visa in three to five working days. The 'L' means *lüxing* (travel). Fees vary according to how much your country charges Chinese citizens for a visa (US citizens pay a lot more than anyone else). Fees must be paid in cash at the time of application and you'll need two passport-sized photos. It's possible to download an application form at embassy or visa agency websites. Express services cost double the normal fee. Your application must be written in

English, and you must have one entire blank page in your passport for the visa.

Some Chinese embassies offer a postal service for a fee, but this takes around three weeks. Chinese embassies in the USA do not accept mail-in applications, so unless you live in a major city you'll have to use a visa agent such as China Visa Service Center (www.my chinavisa.com) or Oasis China Visa (www.oasischinavisa. com). In some countries (eg the UK; www.visaforchina. org.uk) the visa service has been outsourced to a visa-issuing servicing centre that levies an administration fee, which effectively doubles the cost of your visa.

The visa application form asks you a lot of questions (your entry and exit points, travel itinerary, means of transport etc), but once in China you can deviate from this as much as you like. When listing your itinerary, pick the obvious contenders: Běijīng, Shànghǎi and so on. Don't mention Tibet and don't list your occupation as journalist.

Visas valid for more than 30 days can be difficult to obtain anywhere other than Hong Kong, although some embassies abroad (in the US and UK, for example) often give you 60 or even 90 days if you ask nicely. This saves you the considerable difficulty of getting a visa extension in Tibet. Most agencies in Hong Kong can arrange a 90-day visa. Most Chinese embassies abroad will issue a double-entry visa.

A standard single-entry visa is activated on the date you enter China, and must be used within three months from the date of issue. There is some confusion over the validity of Chinese visas. Most Chinese officials look at the 'valid until' date, but on most 30-day visas this is actually the date by which you must have *entered* the country, not the visa's expiry

date. Longer-stay visas are often activated on the day of issue, not the day you enter the country, so there's no point in getting one too far in advance of your planned entry date. Check with the embassy if you are unsure.

It's possible to travel in Tibet with a student ('X' visa), resident ('D') or business ('F' or 'Z') visa, but not on a journalist ('J') visa.

Hong Kong

Double, multiple-entry, six-month and business visas are easily available at the following places in Hong Kong:

China Travel Service (CTS; ☑2315 7171; www.ctshk.com; 1st fl, Alpha House, 27-33 Nathan Rd, Tsim Sha Tsui, enter from Peking Rd)

Forever Bright Trading Limited (☑852-2369 3188; www.fbt-chinavisa.com.hk; Room 916-917, Tower B, New Mandarin Plaza, 14 Science Museum Rd, Tsim Sha Tsui East, Kowloon)

Visa Office of the People's Republic of China (☑3413 2300; 7th fl, Lower Block, China Resources Centre, 26 Harbour Rd, Wan Chai; ⊙9am-noon & 2-5pm Mon-Fri)

Kathmandu

For the last few years the Chinese embassy in Kathmandu has not been issuing visas to individual travellers, only to those booked on a tour and then only group visas. If you turn up with a Chinese visa in your passport, it will be cancelled.

A group visa is a separate sheet of paper with all the names and passport numbers of the group members. It's important to get your own individual 'group' visa (a 'group' can be as small as one person!), as otherwise, come the end of your tour in Lhasa, you will either have to exit China with your fellow group members or split from this group visa, at considerable cost and hassle. Splitting from a group visa can only be done by the Chinese partner of the Nepali travel agency that arranged your travel into Tibet. It is a *real* pain to be avoided at all costs.

Group visas are generally issued for 15 days, though 21 days or more is possible, especially for trips to Kailash. Note that it is very difficult, if not impossible, to extend the duration of a group visa, regardless of what agents in Kathmandu may tell you. It's easier to split from a group visa (ie convert this into a normal tourist visa) and then extend that, but this is still difficult and best avoided.

Nepali agencies currently charge US$58/80/114 to process a group visa in 10/three/one days, plus a possible US$20 agency service charge. US citizens pay US$142/164/198.

The visa office at Nepal's **Chinese Embassy** (☏01-4440286; www.chinaembassy.org.np; Hattisar, Kathmandu) accepts applications 9.30am to 11.30am on Monday, Wednesday and Friday only. Note that the main embassy is in Baluwatar but the separate visa office is in Hattisar.

If you are flying from Kathmandu directly to Chinese cities outside Tibet (ie Chéngdū or Shànghǎi), you can enter China on an individual tourist visa issued from abroad. Thus if you want to continue travelling in China after your Tibet trip the easiest thing is to fly from Kathmandu to Chéngdū (the plane stops in Lhasa but TTB permits are not required for transfer) and then fly back to Lhasa with your TTB permit and on your normal China visa.

Visa Extensions

The *waishike* (foreign affairs) section of the local PSB handles visa extensions. Extensions of one week are generally obtainable in Lhasa (and theoretically in Ali or Chamdo), but only a

few days before your visa expires and only through the travel company that arranged your TTB permit. It is far easier to extend your visa in other areas of China such as Chéngdū, Lèshān, Zhōngdiàn, Xīníng or Xī'ān, where a 30-day extension is commonplace.

Fees vary according to your nationality, but generally cost around Y160 (except for American citizens who pay around Y400).

FINDING OUT MORE

The following organisations do excellent work to help the people of the Tibetan plateau and several have been instrumental in assisting in the wake of the huge 2010 earthquake in Jyekundo (Yùshù).

Braille Without Borders www.braillewithoutborders.org

Jinpa www.jinpa.org

Kham Aid Foundation www.khamaid.org

Machik www.machik.org

Plateau Perspectives www.plateauperspectives.com, www.yushuearthquakerelief.com

Seva www.seva.ca/sevaintibet.htm

Tendol Gyalzur Orphanage www.tendol-gyalzur-tibet.ch

Tibet Foundation www.tibet-foundation.org

Tibet Fund www.tibetfund.org

Tibet Poverty Alleviation Fund www.tpaf.org

Tibetan Village Project www.tibetanvillageproject.org

Pro-Tibetan organisations abroad have good news services and some cultural coverage. The ICT website includes an interesting guide for tourists visiting Tibet. The Tibet Support Group (www.tibet.org) offers online links to most pro-Tibet organisations.

Australia Tibet Council www.atc.org.au

Canada Tibet Committee www.tibet.ca

Free Tibet Campaign (UK) www.freetibet.org

International Campaign for Tibet (ICT) www.savetibet.org

Students for a Free Tibet www.studentsforafreetibet.org

Tibet Foundation (UK) www.tibet-foundation.org

Tibet House www.tibethouse.org

Tibet Information Network www.tibetinfonet.net

Tibet Society www.tibetsociety.com

Tibetan Centre for Human Rights and Democracy www.tchrd.org

Volunteering

There are limited opportunities for volunteer work in the TAR. There are considerable more opportunities outside the TAR, in Tibetan areas of Sìchuān and Qīnghǎi, and especially in Dharamsala (see www.volunteertibet.org.in), and you can always volunteer at any of pro-Tibet organisations (see the box, p347).

Conscious Journeys (www.conciousjourneys.org) Runs

medical 'voluntourism' trips to Tibetan areas of Sìchuān, as well as responsibly run tours in Tibet.

Rokpa (www.rokpauk.org/volunteering.html) Volunteer teaching positions in the Jyekundo (Yùshù) region of Qīnghǎi.

United Planet (www.unitedplanet.org) Also in the Jyekundo (Yùshù) region of Qīnghǎi.

Women Travellers

Sexual harassment is extremely rare in Tibet and foreign women seem to be able to travel here with few problems. Naturally, it's worth noticing what local women are wearing and how they are behaving, and making a bit of an effort to fit in, as you would in any other foreign country. Probably because of the harsh climate, Tibetan women dress in bulky layers of clothing that mask their femininity. It would be wise to follow their example and dress modestly, especially when visiting a monastery. Several women have written of the favourable reactions they have received from Tibetan women when wearing Tibetan dress; you can get one made in Lhasa.

Women are generally not permitted to enter the *gönkhang* (protector chapel) in a monastery, ostensibly for fear of upsetting the powerful protector deities inside.

Transport

For most international travellers, getting to Tibet will involve at least two legs: the first to the gateways of Kathmandu (Nepal) or Chéngdū (China) and the second from these cities into Tibet. The first section of this chapter details long-haul options to/from China and Nepal, while the second section details the practicalities of actually getting into and around Tibet. The Gateway Cities chapter (p261) offers basic information for travellers transiting through Kathmandu or Chéngdū.

Once you are within the region, the most popular options into Tibet are flights from Kathmandu, Chéngdū, Zhōngdiàn or Xī'ān; the train link from Qīnghǎi to Lhasa;

or the overland drive from Kathmandu to Lhasa along the Friendship Hwy.

At the time of writing, bureaucratic obstacles to entering Tibet from China were tight and involved either signing up for a pre-planned and pre-paid tour. The situation from Nepal is trickier because of ever-changing visa requirements. We still get the occasional report of travellers sneaking into Tibet illegally, but this is becoming more difficult and the consequences more severe.

Political events, both domestic and international, can change overnight the regulations for entry into Tibet. It would be wise to check on the latest developments in Tibet before setting out. It

can be very hard to get hold of air and train tickets to Lhasa around the Chinese New Year and the week-long holidays around 1 May and 1 October.

Flights, hotels and tours can be booked online at www.lonelyplanet.com/travel_services.

GETTING THERE & AWAY – GATEWAY CITIES

Entering the Country

Arriving in China is pretty painless these days. All travellers fill in a health declaration form on arrival in China. Expect closer scrutiny of your group documents and luggage when crossing into Tibet from Nepal at Zhāngmù, where some travellers have on occasion had Tibetan-related books and images confiscated.

Passport

Chinese embassies will not issue a visa if your passport has less than six months of validity remaining. See also Visas (p346) and Tours & Permits (p29).

Air

There are no direct long-haul flights to Tibet. You will probably have to stop over in Kathmandu, Chéngdū or

---

CLIMATE CHANGE & TRAVEL

Every form of transport that relies on carbon-based fuel generates CO_2, the main cause of human-induced climate change. Modern travel is dependent on aeroplanes, which might use less fuel per kilometre per person than most cars but travel much greater distances. The altitude at which aircraft emit gases (including CO_2) and particles also contributes to their climate change impact. Many websites offer 'carbon calculators' that allow people to estimate the carbon emissions generated by their journey and, for those who wish to do so, to offset the impact of the greenhouse gases emitted with contributions to portfolios of climate-friendly initiatives throughout the world. Lonely Planet offsets the carbon footprint of all staff and author travel.

FLIGHTS TO/FROM KATHMANDU

TO/FROM	AIRLINE	FREQUENCY	RETURN FARE (US$)
Auckland (via Bangkok)	Cathay Pacific	4 weekly	2250
Bangkok	Thai Airways	daily	1350
Bangkok (via Delhi)	Jet Airways	daily	730
Frankfurt (via Bahrain)	Gulf Air	daily	1260
Hong Kong	Dragonair	3 weekly	440
Kūnmíng (possible stop in Guǎngzhōu)	China Eastern	3 weekly	425
London (via Bahrain)	Gulf Air	daily	890
Los Angeles (via Hong Kong)	Cathay Pacific	6 weekly	1300
New Delhi	Air India	2-3 daily	325
New Delhi	Jet Airways	2 daily	320
Paris (via Bahrain)	Gulf Air	daily	1200
Seoul	Korean	2 weekly	1200
Singapore	Silk Air	6 weekly	1300
Sydney (via Bangkok)	Thai Airways	daily	900-1400

Xī'ān, even if you are making a beeline for Lhasa.

Airports & Airlines

To China, you generally have the choice of flying first to Běijīng, Shànghǎi or Hong Kong, although there are a small but growing number of flights direct to Chéngdū or Kūnmíng. The new terminal at Běijīng Capital Airport (www.bcia.com.cn) is the world's largest. Hong Kong's Chek Lap Kok Airport (www.hkairport.com) is also new. There's little difference in fares to these airports.

The tables in this section indicate sample high season prices and mid-week travel. Fares can fluctuate by the day (Monday and Tuesday flights are generally cheaper than Friday and Saturday flights). While most major international airlines fly to China's east coast cities, you'll probably need to connect with a domestic carrier to reach Chéngdū or Xī'ān.

TO/FROM KATHMANDU

Generally speaking, fares to/from Kathmandu are not all that cheap as there is a limited number of carriers operating out of the Nepali capital. The national carrier, Nepal Airlines, is to be avoided if possible. Depending on where you are coming from, it may be cheaper to fly to Delhi and make your way overland from there. International airlines that operate out of Kathmandu include the following:

Air India (☎4415367; www.airindia.com; Hattisar)

China Eastern (☎4411666; ceaktm@gmail.com; House 601 Hattisar, next to Gulf Air)

China Southern (☎4440761; www.flychinasouthern.com; Marcopolo Business Hotel, Kamalpokhari)

Dragonair (☎4248944; www.dragonair.com; Kamaladi)

DEPARTURE TAX

Departure tax in China is worked into the price of both domestic and international tickets, so there's nothing additional to pay at the airport.

Gulf Air (☎4435322; www.gulfair.com; Hattisar)

Jet Airways (☎4446375; www.jetairways.com; Sundar Bhawan, Hattisar)

Kingfisher Airlines (www.flykingfisher.com)

Korean Airlines (☎4252048; www.koreanair.com; Heritage Plaza, Kamaladi)

Nepal Airlines Corporation (☎4220757; Kantipath)

Silk Air (☎4226582; www.silkair.com; Kamaladi)

Thai Airways (☎4223565; www.thaiair.com; Durbar Marg)

TO/FROM CHÉNGDŪ

Chéngdū is well connected to other cities in China, with daily flights arriving from Běijīng, Shànghǎi, Guǎngzhōu, Kūnmíng and Hong Kong, among others. There is also a handful of international carriers making nonstop flights into Chéngdū, mainly from Southeast Asian hubs like Bangkok and Singapore. From Europe, it's possible to reach Chéngdū nonstop from Amsterdam on KLM. Arriving from other international destinations will likely require a layover in a mainland Chinese hub.

Chéngdū is also well connected by rail, so if you want to see a bit of China, fly into a major city and spend a few days travelling by train to Chéngdū. Lonely Planet's *China* guide has more on getting around China by train.

International airlines that operate out of Chéngdū:

Air China (国航世界中心; Guóháng Shìjiè Zhōngxīn; ☑24hr hotline 4008 100 999; 1 Hangkong Lu, off Renmin Nanlu; ◷8.30am-5pm)

Asiana (☑8451 0101; Room 1-2-1904, Sun Dynasty Plaza, No 27, Section 4, Renmin Nanlu)

China Airlines (☑8602 7508; Room 1-2-504, Sun Dynasty Plaza, No. 27, Section 4, Renmin Nanlu)

China Southern Airlines (中国南方航空; Zhōngguó Nánfāng Hángkōng; ☑8666 3618; 278 Shangdong Dajie; ◷8.30am-5.30pm)

Dragonair (港龙航空; Gǎnglóng Hángkōng; ☑8676 8828; Sheraton Chéngdū Lido Hotel, Section 1, 15 Renmin Zhonglu)

Hainan Airlines (☑8526 8268; Renmin Nanlu, 4th district, Weisidun Bldg, 9th fl)

KLM (☑4008 808 222; 1603B, Bldg A, Times Plaza, 2 Zongfu Lu)

Thai Airways (☑8666 7171; Room 02-03, 12th fl, Tower 1, Central Plaza, 8 Shuncheng Lu)

Tickets

If you want to get to Tibet as quickly as possible (perhaps to get the maximum use from your visa), consider buying a domestic Air China ticket to Chéngdū as part of your international ticket. Some Air China offices will give you a discount on the domestic leg if you buy the long-haul leg through them. Airfares to China peak between June and September. Airline offices will generally not sell you a ticket to Lhasa without a Tibet Tourism Bureau (TTB) permit.

Another ticket worth looking into is an open-jaw ticket. This option might involve, for example, flying into Hong Kong and then flying out of Kathmandu, allowing you to travel overland across Tibet.

Buying domestic Chinese tickets abroad is possible but at relatively high fares. Better value online Chinese ticket agencies such as Elong (www.elong.net), Ctrip

(www.ctrip.net) and China Tour (www.chinatour.net) sell heavily discounted domestic flights in the form of e-tickets.

The following online ticket agencies book flights originating in the USA but have links to specific country websites across the world:

Cheapflights.com (www.cheapflights.com)

China Travel Service (CTS; www.ctshk.com)

Expedia (www.expedia.com) Good for buying tickets in China as it's paired with a Chinese affiliate.

Flight Centre (www.flight centre.com)

Last Minute.com (www.lastminute.com)

Lonely Planet (www.lonely planet.com) Click on 'Travel services' to book flight tickets.

Nouvelles Frontières (www.nouvelles-frontieres.fr)

Orbitz (www.orbitz.com)

Priceline (www.priceline.com) Aims to match the ticket price to your budget.

STA Travel (www.statravel.com)

Travelocity (www.travelocity.com)

FLIGHTS TO/FROM CHÉNGDŪ

TO/FROM	AIRLINE	FREQUENCY	RETURN FARE (US$)
Amsterdam	KLM	4 weekly	1120
Bangkok	Thai Airways	daily	400
Běijīng	Air China	daily	230
Guǎngzhōu	China Southern Airlines	daily	220
Hong Kong	Dragonair	daily	410
Kathmandu (via Lhasa)	Air China	2 weekly	370
Kuala Lumpur	Air Asia	4 weekly	275
Kūnmíng	Air China	daily	140
Seoul	Asiana	daily	450
Shēnzhèn	Hainan Airlines	daily	380
Singapore	Air China	daily	490
Taipei	China Airlines	4 weekly	520
Tokyo (via Běijīng)	Air China	daily	955

GETTING THERE & AWAY – TIBET

This section has detailed information about getting directly into Tibet from Nepal or China.

Air

Flights into Lhasa are shared by Air China (CA; www.airchina.com.cn), China Southern (CZ; www.csair.com), Sichuan Airlines (3U; www.scal.com.cn), Hainan Airlines (HU; www.hnair.com) and China Eastern (MU; www.ce-air.com).

There are flight connections to Lhasa from half a dozen Chinese cities but most travellers fly from Chéngdū. Airport tax (Y50) and a fuel surcharge (around Y80) are figured into the cost of domestic airfares.

Besides Lhasa, there are domestic airports at Nyingtri and Chamdo, though these are of very limited use to tourists. Ngari Kunsha Airport in Ali and Peace Airport in Shigatse both opened in 2010.

Permits are very rarely checked on arrival at or departure from Lhasa's Gongkar airport, though they are checked when checking in for your flight to Lhasa.

While it can be difficult to get a ticket into Tibet, once there you face no restrictions on buying air tickets out of the province. You can buy the ticket online. Some agents or sites may ask about the TTB permit, but this is uncommon.

Air China cancellation policies usually depend on the type of ticket you have purchased. Some ticket classes allow refunds (but these tickets are more expensive). If you do need to change or cancel a ticket do so as soon as possible. The process can be dearer and more difficult if you wait until the last minute. A date change is usually valid for 12 months of the originally scheduled flight.

Note that flights to and from Lhasa are sometimes cancelled or delayed in the winter months, so if you are flying at this time give yourself a couple of days' leeway if you have a connecting flight.

Baggage allowance on domestic flights to Lhasa is 20kg in economy class and 40kg in 1st class, so you'll have to limit your gear to that to avoid penalties, regardless of what you are allowed to bring on your international flight into China.

Nepal

Flights between Kathmandu and Lhasa run four times a week in the high summer season. From April to October flights are organised by demand only, usually operating once or twice a week.

Individual travellers can't buy air tickets from the Air China office in Kathmandu without a TTB permit. To get a ticket you'll have to purchase a three- to eight-day package tour through a travel agency.

At the time of research, the cheapest air package was a three-day tour for around US$550. This includes the flight ticket (around US$380), airport transfers, TTB permit and accommodation for three nights in Lhasa. With this package you'll probably only get a 15-day group visa. For a list of travel companies in Kathmandu, see p263.

The Chinese embassy in Kathmandu does not give Chinese visas to individual travellers and will even cancel any existing Chinese visa you have. See p346 for more on visa headaches in Kathmandu.

It is possible to buy air tickets from Kathmandu to other destinations in China; you don't need a TTB permit to take these flights.

FLIGHTS TO/FROM OTHER CHINESE CITIES

FROM	TO	AIRLINE	FREQUENCY	RETURN FARE (US$)
Auckland	Hong Kong	Air New Zealand	daily	1340
Chicago	Běijīng	American	daily	1130
Frankfurt	Běijīng	Emirates	daily	800
London	Běijīng	British Airways	daily	870
London	Hong Kong	Virgin Atlantic	daily	930
Madrid	Běijīng	Air China	daily	850
San Francisco	Běijīng	United	daily	1020
Sydney	Hong Kong	Virgin Atlantic	daily	1180
Toronto	Běijīng	Air Canada	daily	1430
Vancouver	Shànghǎi	Air Canada	daily	1140

All of the following flights operate in both directions. Fares given are one way.

FROM	TO	FREQUENCY	FARE (Y)
Lhasa	Běijīng (via Chéngdū)	7 weekly	2520
Lhasa	Chamdo (Bamda/Bangda)	2 weekly	900
Lhasa	Chéngdū	60-70 weekly	1590
Lhasa	Chóngqìng	7 weekly	1720
Lhasa	Guǎngzhōu (via Chóngqìng)	2 weekly	2590
Lhasa	Kathmandu	3-4 weekly	2540
Lhasa	Kūnmíng (via Zhōngdiàn)	7 weekly	2050
Lhasa	Shànghǎi Pudong (via Xī'ān)	2 weekly	2850
Lhasa	Xī'ān	4 weekly	1740
Lhasa	Xīníng (via Chéngdū)	4 weekly	1750
Lhasa	Zhōngdiàn (summer only)	7 weekly	1470
Chamdo (Bamda/Bangda)	Chéngdū	6 weekly	990
Nyingtri	Chéngdū	21 weekly	1470
Lhasa	Ali	2 weekly	250

Chéngdū

Flights between Chéngdū and Lhasa cost around Y1600 (through Air China; www.airchina.com). You can buy them online or though an agent, but you won't be able to board the plane unless you also have a TTB permit, which you show at customs and check-in in Chéngdū. Chéngdū has long been the main gateway to Lhasa for travellers coming by air and up to seven flights a day go to Lhasa in the height of summer. Try to book the first flight of the day as weather conditions and visibility will be optimal in the morning. Getting into Lhasa early also gives you a little more time to acclimatise if you are on a short tour.

If you are coming to Tibet from somewhere outside China, have your agency mail your permit to a hotel in Chéngdū where you can pick it up and fly out the next day. See p29 for more information on organising your permit.

On a clear day the views from the plane are stupendous, so try to get a window seat. In general the best views are from the left side of the plane from Chéngdū to Lhasa and the right side from Lhasa to Chéngdū.

Zhōngdiàn & Kūnmíng

China Eastern (www.flychinaeastern.com) operates a useful daily flight from Kūnmíng to Lhasa via Zhōngdiàn in northwest Yúnnán (also rather ridiculously called Shangri-La by the Chinese). China Southern also flies from Lhasa to Zhōngdiàn en route to Guǎngzhōu. As with other flights to Lhasa, foreigners won't be allowed on board without a TTB permit.

Land

Many individual travellers make their way to Tibet as part of a grand overland trip through China, Nepal, India and onwards. In many ways, land travel to Tibet is the best way to go, not only for the scenery en route but also because it can help spread the altitude gain over a few days.

Road

In theory there are several land routes into Tibet. The bulk of overland travellers take the Friendship Hwy between Kathmandu to Lhasa. Other possible routes (officially closed to permitless travellers) are the Sìchuān–Tibet Hwy, the Yúnnán–Tibet Hwy and the Xīnjiāng–Tibet Hwy.

However, in the current climate it's most unwise to try these latter routes on your own (ie not in a 4WD tour) – you have a very good chance of being caught, fined and sent back in the direction you came. If you do get stopped by the Public Security Bureau (PSB), always claim to be heading in the opposite direction. Then you'll be sent 'back' in the direction in which you actually want to travel!

See p359 for advice on hitching through Tibet.

FRIENDSHIP HIGHWAY (NEPAL TO TIBET)

The 865km stretch of road between Kathmandu and Lhasa is known as the Friendship Hwy. The journey is without a doubt one of the most spectacular in the world.

From Kathmandu (elevation 1300m) the road travels gently up to Kodari (1873m), before leaving Nepal to make a steep switchback ascent to Zhāngmù (2250m), the Tibetan border town, and then Nyalam (3750m), where most people spend their first night. The road then climbs to the top of the Tong-la (4950m), continuing to Tingri (4250m) for the second night. The road is paved the whole way.

It is essential to watch out for the effects of altitude sickness during the early stages of this trip (see p364). If you intend to head up to Everest Base Camp (5150m) you really need to slip in a rest day at Tingri or Nyalam.

Your guide and driver must meet you at the border and at customs you'll be asked to present your TTB permit. Travel agents in Kathmandu offer 'budget' tours of Tibet to get you into Lhasa. At the time of research the cheapest of these tours cost from around US$350 per person for a basic seven-day trip to Lhasa, stopping in Zhāngmù/Nyalam, Lhatse, Shigatse, Gyantse and then Lhasa for two days. These trips generally run every Tuesday and Saturday. A nine-day trip that adds on a visit to Everest Base Camp costs US$650 per person but these are harder to find. Prices include transport, permits, a Chinese group visa, dormitory accommodation for the first two nights and then shared twins, a fairly useless guide and admission fees.

Bear in mind that most agencies are just subcontractors and normally pool clients, so you could find yourself travelling in a larger group than expected and probably on a bus instead of the promised 4WD. Other potential inconsistencies may include having to share a room when you were told you would be given a single, or paying a double room supplement and ending up in a dorm. We do get a fair number of complaints about the service of some of these tours; it's best just to view it as the cheapest way to get to Tibet.

For more information about the visa snags involved in a trip from Kathmandu, see p346.

Headed in the other direction, a private 4WD tour from Lhasa to the Nepali border costs around Y7000 for a four- or five-day trip, which works out around US$250 per person. This includes a guide, permits and transport only.

A direct bus runs twice a week from Lhasa's Northern Bus Station to Zhāngmù and back, but foreigners are currently not allowed on this.

Under current regulations tourists are required to pre-book their trip and itinerary. Should this change, and you need a lift to Nepal, ask around the agencies as they often send empty 4WDs to the border to pick up groups. These 4WDs generally drive nonstop through the night.

See p162 for details of the border crossing to Nepal. China is 2¼ hours ahead of Nepali time.

QĪNGHǍI–TIBET HIGHWAY

It takes about 20 hours to travel along the 1115km road between Golmud and Lhasa. In the past it was possible to buy tickets at the **CITS** (☎0979-413 003; 2nd fl, Golmud Hotel) in Golmud at a massive mark-up. However, as of our last research trip, foreigners were not allowed to buy a ticket for the bus.

A few hardy souls make the trip by bike, crossing into Tibet over the 5180m Tangula pass. A checkpoint 30km south of Golmud checks for permits. Under current regulations, a guide would need to accompany you in a support vehicle.

An unusual route into Tibet is the back-door route from Yùshù (Jyekundo) in southeastern Qīnghǎi to Chamdo in eastern Tibet, via the towns of Nangchen and Riwoche. At the time of research part of this route was off-limits to foreigners (both individuals and groups).

SÌCHUĀN–TIBET HIGHWAY

The road between Chéngdū and Lhasa is an epic 2400km or 2100km, depending on whether you take the northern or southern route. Either way, it would take between 10 to 14 days to make the entire journey.

The Sìchuān section of the Sìchuān–Tibet Hwy is open to foreigners as far as the Tibetan border. In good times, foreign tour groups have been allowed to continue past the checkpoints and onto Lhasa. But permits have been increasing hard to come by; in 2010 no foreign tour groups were allowed along this route because Chamdo prefecture was closed.

For coverage of the sights along the route, see the Overland Routes from Sìchuān (p216) and Eastern Tibet (Kham) (p189) chapters. For an overview of routes, see p28.

Foreigners attempting to smuggle themselves into Tibet should be aware that the 780km stretch of road between Markham and Bayi is likely to be the biggest hurdle on the journey to Lhasa. Markham is where the Yúnnán–Tibet Hwy joins the Sìchuān–Tibet Hwy and so the local PSB is pretty vigilant about making sure that no travellers continue on to Lhasa. Nyingtri, Bayi and Chamdo also have pretty strict PSB offices.

A 4WD tour from Lhasa to Chéngdū costs from Y16,000 to Y20,000.

YÚNNÁN–TIBET HIGHWAY

The Yúnnán–Tibet Hwy is a wonderful way to approach Tibet, though once again the route is officially limited to organised groups. Even group permits can be denied, as they were in 2010 when Chamdo prefecture was closed.

From Lijiang a road heads up to the Tibetan towns and monasteries of Zhōngdiàn (Gyeltang), Benzalin and Déqīn (Jol), from where there are public buses north across the Tibetan border (and checkpost) 112km to Yanjing. From here it's 111km to Markham, where the road joins the Sìchuān southern route.

Travellers trying to get in without a permit are often caught at Markham and sent back. When the roads are open to foreigners, some travel companies can organise nine- or 10-day overland tours on this route, including the excellent Khampa Caravan in Zhōngdiàn (see the box, p33). TTB permits take around five days to arrange so contact these agencies in advance.

XĪNJIĀNG–TIBET HIGHWAY

The Xīnjiāng–Tibet Hwy is off limits without travel permits. In the past many travellers, even cyclists, had gotten through this road with few difficulties, but the situation has changed since 2008 and permit-less travellers are being sent back. If the situation loosens up, the approximately 1350km route from Kashgar to Ali is an epic journey that can form a wild extension to a trip along the Karakoram Hwy.

With at least two passes more than 5400m, the Xīnjiāng–Tibet Hwy is the highest road in the world. It can be bitterly cold and closes down for the winter months from December to February. The whole trip takes at least four days of travel. There are truck stops along the way, about a day's

travel apart, but it's wise to bring food and a sleeping bag. A tent can be useful in emergencies. Coming from Kashgar, you have to be particularly careful about altitude sickness as the initial rate of altitude gain is dramatic.

It is possible to travel this route as part of a 4WD tour. FIT Snowlands in Lhasa (see p76) offers a three-week Mt Everest–Kailash–Guge Kingdom–Yecheng–Kashgar 4WD trip for about Y20,000 to Y25,000, which works out at around US$830 per person for four sharing.

Kashgar Guide (☎295 1029; www.kashgarguide.com; 337 Seman Lu) in Kashgar and **John's Café** (www.johncafe.net), with branches in Lhasa and Kashgar, can arrange 15- to 18-day vehicle hire along this route from Y45,000.

The Route

Leaving Karghilik, the road climbs past Akmeqit village to Kudi Pass (kilometre marker 113; 3240m) then follows a narrow gorge to the truck stop and checkpost at Kudi (kilometre marker 161, 2960m). From Kudi it's 80km over the Chiragsaldi Pass (kilometre marker 217; 4960m) to the village of Mazar (kilometre marker 241; 3700m). The road turns east and climbs over the Kirgizjangal Pass (kilometre marker 09; 4930m) to the large village of Xaidulla (Sài Túlá; kilometre marker 363; 3700m), the largest town en route. The road climbs again over the 4250m Koshbel Pass to the truck stop of Dahongliutan (kilometre marker 488; 4200m), which offers basic food and lodging.

From here the road turns south, and climbs to the Khitai Pass (kilometre marker 535; 5150m), past the military base of Tianshuihai. About 100km from the pass you cross another 5180m pass (kilometre marker 670) to enter the remote region of Aksai Chin. For the next

170km road conditions are bad and progress is slow. The construction of the road here, through a triangle of territory that India claimed as part of Ladakh, was a principal cause of the border war between India and China in 1962. The fact that the Chinese managed to build this road without India even realising that it was under construction is an indication of the utter isolation of the region!

The road passes Lungma-tso, shortly afterwards entering the Changtang Nature Reserve, and 15km later reaches the small village of Sumzhi (Sōngxī) (kilometre marker 720; 5200m). Finally at kilometre marker 740 you come to the edge of the Aksai Chin region and climb up to the Jieshan Daban pass (5200m). From here, Ali is around 420km away via the village of Domar (kilometre marker 828; 4440m), the eastern end of Pangong-tso (Palgon-tso; 4270m) and Rutok Xian (kilometre marker 930). From here it is 130km south to Ali.

OTHER ROUTES INTO TIBET

Another route into Tibet, for trekking groups only, passes through Purang (Nepali: Taklakot). Special visas are required for this trip. Trekkers start by travelling by road or flying from Kathmandu to Nepalganj, then flying from there to Simikot in the far west of Nepal. From Simikot it's a five- or six-day walk to the Tibetan border, crossing the Humla Karnali. You can then drive the 28km to Purang and 107km on to the Mt Kailash area via Lake Manasarovar. See Lonely Planet's *Trekking in the Nepal Himalaya* for details of the trek. For details on the route from the Nepali border to Mt Kailash, see p187.

Tibetan, Chinese and Hong Kong travellers can cross into Tibet's Yadong region from Gangtok in Sikkim via the 4310m Nathu-la, tracing the former trading routes between Lhasa, Kalimpong and Calcutta, and the path taken by Younghusband's invasion of Tibet in 1903. The route opened to locals in 2006, but is not scheduled to open to third-party nationals until 2011.

There is talk of opening the Kyirong-la (Kerong-la) to organised tour groups headed to/from the Langtang region of Nepal, but there are no definite plans as yet. Roads are in place on both sides of the border.

Indian pilgrims on a quota system travel to Purang via the Lipu Lekh pass from Pithoragarh.

Train

The trains to Lhasa originate from Běijīng, Chéngdū and Xīníng daily, and every other day from Guǎngzhōu and Shànghǎi. Trains also run every other day from Chóngqìng (via Xī'ān) and Lánzhōu, which link up with the Chéngdū and Xīníng trains respectively. See the box, p358 for schedules and fares. A 250km extension

line to Shigatse is due to open by 2014.

All trains cross the Tibetan plateau during daylight, guaranteeing you great views (the scenery is impressive in scale rather than beautiful). From Golmud the train climbs through desert into the jagged caramel-coloured mountains of Nanshankou (Southern Pass), passing what feels like a stone's throw from the impressive glaciers beside Yuzhu Feng (Jade Pearl Peak; 6178m). Other highlights include the nearby tunnel through the 4776m Kunlun Pass, where you can see the prayer flags at the top of the pass, and Tsonak Lake, 9½ hours from Golmud near Amdo, claimed to be the highest freshwater lake in the world at 4608m. Keep your eyes peeled throughout the journey for antelope, fox and wild asses, plus the occasional nomad. The train crosses into Tibet over the 5072m Tangu-la (Tanggula Shankou) Pass, the line's high point.

For more details on services and schedules see the following:

China Highlights (www.chinahighlights.com/china-trains/index.htm) Searchable timetables.

China Tibet Train (www.chinatibettrain.com) Good background info.

Lulutong (www.railway.com.cn) Chinese-language website.

Seat 61 (www.seat61.com) General info on trains in China.

Tibet Train Travel (www.tibettraintravel.com) Background info and mini-tours.

Travel China Guide (www.travelchinaguide.com/china-trains/) Searchable timetables.

The luxurious *Tangula Express* – a sort of 21st century *Orient Express* – is expected to run between Běijīng and Lhasa. Each carriage contains just four private rooms, each one like a small five-star hotel room complete with bathroom, shower, TV, wi-fi

---

THE WORLD'S HIGHEST TRAIN RIDE

There's no doubt the Qīnghǎi–Tibet train line is an engineering marvel. Topping out at 5072m, it is the world's highest railway, snatching the title from a Peruvian line. The statistics speak for themselves: 86% of the line is above 4000m, and half the track lies on permafrost, requiring a cooling system of pipes driven into the ground to keep it frozen year-round and avoid a rail-buckling summer thaw. Construction of the line involved building 160km of bridges and elevated track, seven tunnels (including the world's highest) and 24 hyperbaric chambers, the latter to treat altitude-sick workers.

Aside from the environmental concerns, Tibetans are most deeply concerned about the cultural impact of the train. While the highly subsidised line will doubtless boost the Tibetan economy, decreasing transport costs for imports by up to 75%, the trains also unload 2500 Chinese tourists and immigrants into Lhasa every day.

The authorities like to stress the economic benefits of the line, but Tibetans remain economically marginalised. More than 90% of the 100,000 workers employed to build the line came from other provinces and few, if any, Tibetan staff actually work on the trains. The US$4.1 billion cost of building the line is greater than the amount Běijīng has spent on hospitals and schools in Tibet over the last 50 years.

As with most of Běijīng's epic engineering projects, the results are as much symbolic as real, connecting China's rail network to the only province in China lacking a rail link and forging Tibet and China together in an iron grip. It did a similar thing with the 1999 railway line to Kashgar in Xīnjiāng; now it's the turn of its other troublesome border province.

and over-sized viewing windows. The train is managed by Kempinski (www.kempinski.com) and includes a bar and gourmet restaurant. The service had not yet started at the time of writing.

PRACTICALITIES
At the time of writing, foreigners needed a TTB permit (see p29) to buy a ticket and board the train, though some travellers have managed to take the train without one. Golmud and Xī'ān seem to be the most difficult places to buy tickets without a TTB permit. Several agencies such as Leo's Hostel in Běijīng and Sim's Cozy Guesthouse in Chéngdū sell tickets and TTB permits, though sleeper berths can be hard to secure from Běijīng, Chéngdū and Xī'ān. You can buy tickets up to 10 days in advance.

The online agency www.china-train-ticket.com sells train tickets and will deliver them to your hotel in China, for a fairly hefty 40% mark-up on the ticket price. Chinese sites such as www.piao.com/train are cheaper, if you read Chinese. Either way you face complications getting a TTB permit this way.

The carriages are much better than your average Chinese train and are more like the express trains that link Běijīng with Shànghǎi. All passengers have access to piped-in oxygen through a special socket beside each seat or berth and all carriages are nonsmoking after Golmud. There are power sockets by the window seats, though be aware that laptops and MP3 players often stop working at points during the trip, due to the altitude. Each train has a small but decent dining car (mains Y15 to Y25).

Hard-sleeper (硬卧; yìng wò) carriages are made up of doorless six-berth compartments with bunks in three tiers, with sheets, pillows and blankets provided.

There is a small price difference between berths, with the lowest bunk the most expensive and the top-most bunk the cheapest. Four-bed soft-sleeper (软卧; ruǎn wò) berths come with individual TVs and doors that close and lock. Hard seats (硬座; yìng zuò) are just that.

Sleeper tickets to Lhasa sell out quickly in summer and during holidays, so it's essential that you book your tickets as early as possible. Tickets can be purchased up to 10 days in advance, but scalpers are known to buy them as soon as they go on sale. As you might expect, scalpers hang around the ticket window at the railway station in Běijīng, ever on the look out for foreigners trying to score a ticket. They will find you. If you have to deal with a scalper, at least try to bargain. Getting tickets for trains out of Lhasa is easier than getting a ticket into Lhasa.

GETTING AROUND

Tibet's transport infrastructure has developed rapidly in recent years. While some areas are still a patchwork of rough roads most of the main highways are now paved. Airports are springing up on the plateau and the railway line is extending beyond Lhasa. Tibet's Metok country was the very last of China's 2100 counties to be connected by road, completed in 2011 via a 3km tunnel.

Air

Tibet is one of China's biggest provinces, but flights within the TAR are few and far between. At the time of writing the only option is the new twice-weekly route between Lhasa and Ali (Y900).

Construction on a new airport in Nagchu is slated to commence in 2011, to be finished by 2014. If it gets

built it would be the highest civilian airport in the world.

Shigatse's Peace Airport was completed in 2010. At the time of research no flights were scheduled. However, if flights connect Shigatse with mainland China (or international destinations), this could be a handy way of flying out of Tibet without having to retreat all the way back to Gongkar.

Bicycle

Long-distance cyclists are an increasingly frequent sight on the roads of Tibet, especially along the Friendship Hwy, though also through eastern Tibet. Cycling is no longer a free and easy adventure in Tibet; you still need a guide, who will likely follow you in a support vehicle.

You can rent Taiwanese-made mountain bikes in Lhasa for around Y30 per day, which are fine for getting around town. Test the brakes and tyres before taking the bike out onto the streets. An extra padlock is a good idea, as there is a problem with bicycle theft in the capital.

Most long distance cyclists bring their own bikes to Tibet, though a few buy mountain bikes in China or Lhasa. Nowadays it is possible to buy a Chinese-made or (better) Taiwanese-made mountain bike in Lhasa for about Y500 or, if you are lucky, a good-quality Thai bike for around Y2000. Standards aren't all that bad, although you should check the gears in particular. Do not expect the quality of such bikes to be equal to those you might buy at home – bring plenty of spare parts. Bikes have a relatively high resale value in Kathmandu and you might even make a profit if the bike is in good shape (which is unlikely after a trip across Tibet!).

Touring

Tibet poses unique challenges to individual cyclists. The good news is that the main roads are in surprisingly good condition (the Friendship Hwy was recently upgraded and roads everywhere are under improvement) and the traffic is fairly light. The main physical challenges come from the climate, terrain and altitude: wind squalls and dust storms can make your work particularly arduous; the warm summer months can bring flash flooding; and then there is the question of your fitness in the face of Tibet's high-altitude mountainous terrain.

A full bicycle-repair kit, several spare inner tubes, and a spare tyre and chain are essential. Preferably bring an extra rim and some spare spokes. Extra brake wire and brake pads are useful (you'll be descending 3000m from Lhasa to Kathmandu!). Other useful equipment includes reflective clothing, a helmet, a dust mask, goggles, gloves and padded trousers.

You will also need to be prepared with supplies such as food, water-purifying tablets and camping equipment, just as if you were trekking. Most long-distance cyclists will probably find formal accommodation and restaurants only available at two- or three-day intervals. It may be possible to stay with road repair camps (known as daoban in Chinese) in remote places.

The Trailblazer guidebook *Tibet Overland: A Route and Planning Guide for Mountain Bikers and Other Overlanders*, by Kym McConnell, has useful route plans and gradient charts aimed at mountain bikers, with a notice board at www.tibetoverland.com. The website www.bikechina.com is another good resource.

Obviously, you need to be physically fit to undertake road touring in Tibet. Spend some time acclimatising to the altitude and taking leisurely rides around Lhasa (for example) before setting off on a long trip.

On the plus side, Tibet has some of the highest-altitude roads in the world, but gradients are usually quite manageable. The Tibetan roads are designed for low-powered Chinese trucks, and tackle the many high passes of the region with its low-gradient switchback roads. And apart from the military convoys, which can include a hundred or more trucks, you rarely have to put up with much traffic.

Touring Routes

The most popular touring route at present is Lhasa to Kathmandu, along the Friendship Hwy. It is an ideal route in that it takes in most of Tibet's main sights, offers superb scenery and (for those leaving from Lhasa) features a spectacular roller-coaster ride down from the heights of the La Lung-la into the Kathmandu Valley. The trip will take a minimum of two weeks, although to do it justice and include stopovers at Gyantse, Shigatse and Sakya, budget for 20 days. The entire trip is just over 940km, though most people start from Shigatse. The roadside kilometre markers

TRAIN SCHEDULES TO LHASA

TRAIN NO	TO/FROM	DEPARTURE	DISTANCE (KM)	DURATION (HR)	HARD SEAT/HARD SLEEPER/SOFT SLEEPER
T27/8	Běijīng	daily 9.30pm	4064	48hr	Y389/813/1262
T22/3	Chéngdū	daily 6.18pm	3360	48hr	Y331/712/1104
T223/4	Chóngqìng	7.20pm	3654	48	Y355/754/1168
T264/5	Guǎngzhōu	1.07pm	4980	58	Y451/923/1530
T164/5	Shànghǎi	4.11pm	4373	52	Y406/845/1314
K917/8	Xīníng	daily 4.45pm	1972	27	Y226/523/810
K917/8	Lánzhōu	4.45pm	2188	30	Y242/552/854
**	Xī'ān	-	2864	27	Y296/650/1008*
**	Golmud	-	1135k	14	Y143/377/583

NB Sleeper fares are for lower berth. Unless noted, services run every other day.
* Fares slightly more expensive on the Chóngqìng train
** Multiple train options

are a useful way of knowing exactly how far you have gone and how far you still have to go. For a rundown of the route and its markers, see the box, p149.

If you are travelling via Kathmandu, Nepali mountain-bike agencies such as Massif Mountain Bikes (www.massifmountainbike. com), Himalayan Mountain Bikes (www.bikeasia.info) and Dawn Til Dusk (www. nepalbiking.com) can offer tips, equipment and organised biking tours in Tibet.

Keen cyclists with good mountain bikes might want to consider the detour to Everest Base Camp as a side trip on the Lhasa–Kathmandu route. The 108km one-way trip starts from the Shegar turn-off, and it takes around two days to Rongphu Monastery.

Other possibilities are endless. Tsurphu, Ganden and Drigung Til Monasteries are relatively easy trips and good for acclimatisation (though the road to Tsurphu is rough and Ganden has a fierce final 10km uphill section). The Gyama Valley is an easy detour on a bike if you are headed to Ganden. Cycling in the Yarlung Valley region is another fine option. Some cyclists even tackle the paved road to Nam-tso, although the nomads' dogs can be a problem here.

Permits

It's currently not possible to cycle anywhere in Tibet independently. You must sign up for a 'tour', which essentially means being followed by a support vehicle and guide. There are no specific permits for cycling but you will need all the usual permits as if you were travelling by 4WD.

Hazards

Cycling in Tibet is not to be taken lightly. Dogs are a major problem, especially in more remote areas. You may have to pedal like mad to outpace them. Children have

been known to throw stones at cyclists. Erratic driving is another serious concern.

Wear a cycling helmet and lightweight leather gloves and, weather permitting, try to keep as much of your body covered with protective clothing as possible. It goes without saying that cyclists should also be prepared with a comprehensive medical kit (see p362).

Bus

Bus travel in Tibet is limited but most places in this book are connected to some sort of public transport. Most services originate in Lhasa or Shigatse and run to any town that has a sizeable Chinese presence. See individual towns for details.

Many bus stations in Tibet will not sell bus tickets to foreigners, which leaves you in the hands of private or pilgrim bus services. Even the larger private buses may be reluctant to take foreigners (notably between Lhasa and Shigatse) because they don't have government permission and/or insurance to take foreigners. Given the current climate of tourism in Tibet, very few people will even need to consider public transport as almost everyone is on a guided 4WD tour.

Car

For information on travelling by hired vehicle in Tibet, see Tours & Permits (p29).

PUBLIC TRANSPORT

At the time of research, foreigners were not allowed to travel on public transport in Tibet. Basic information is included here in case the situation changes.

Hitching

Hitching is never entirely safe in any country in the world, and we don't necessarily recommend it. Travellers who decide to hitch should understand that they are taking a small but potentially serious risk.

It goes without saying that if you are hitching in Tibet you are doing so because you decided to forgo the permit-and-tour route (tsk! tsk!) and risk fines or expulsion by the PSB. At the moment, one of the biggest hurdles to hitching is simply getting a ride. Drivers will be reluctant to give you a ride because the authorities impose heavy fines on anyone transporting foreign travellers and may even confiscate their licence.

If things do change, sometimes you can get a lift on a pilgrim truck or an organised passenger truck. If you are headed out to fairly remote destinations you should be equipped to camp out for the night if you don't get a ride. There are also plenty of half-empty 4WDs heading down the Friendship Hwy to pick up a group, or returning after having dropped one off.

Normally you will be expected to pay for your lift. The amount is entirely negotiable, but in areas where traffic is minimal, drivers will often demand quite large sums.

It's a good idea to start hitching a few kilometres out of town because then you know that traffic is going in your direction and is not about to turn off after 400m.

The most common hitching gesture is to stick out one or two fingers towards the ground and wave them up or down.

Local Transport

Local city transport only really operates in Lhasa and Shigatse. Minibuses run on set routes around Lhasa and Shigatse and they charge a fixed fare of Y2.

Pedicabs (pedal-operated tricycles transporting passengers) are available in Lhasa, Gyantse, Shigatse and Bayi, but require some extensive haggling.

A couple of towns in eastern Tibet have motorised three-wheeler rickshaws that take passengers around town or to destinations (eg monasteries) just outside of town. Negotiate the fare before you set off.

One result of China's economic infusion into Tibet is the large number of taxis now available in most towns, even Ali in western Tibet (you have to wonder how they got there!). Taxis in Lhasa, Shigatse and Ali charge a standard Y10 to anywhere in the city; for longer trips negotiate a fare. Fixed-route passenger taxis (which you can pay for by the seat) run between several cities, including Lhasa and Tsetang.

Tractors can be an option for short trips in rural areas, especially in the Yarlung Valley. For a few yuan, drivers are normally quite happy to have some passengers in the back. Rides of anything over 10 minutes quickly become seriously uncomfortable unless on a tarmac road.

Health

Tibet poses some unique and particular risks to your health, although for the large part these are associated with the high average altitude of the plateau.

There is no need to be overly worried: very few travellers are adversely affected by the altitude for very long, and greater risks are present in the form of road accidents and dog bites. Insect-borne and infectious diseases are quite rare because of the high altitude.

Sensible travellers will rely on their own medical knowledge and supplies when travelling throughout Tibet. It is a very isolated place, and outside the city of Lhasa there is very little in the way of expert medical care available. Make sure you travel with a well-stocked medical kit and the knowledge of how to use it.

BEFORE YOU GO

Make sure you're healthy before you start travelling. If you are going on a long trip, make sure your teeth are OK. If you wear glasses, take a spare pair and your prescription.

If you require a particular medication take a good supply, as it may not be available in Tibet. Take along part of the packaging showing the generic name rather than the brand to make getting replacements easier. To avoid problems, it's a good idea to have a legible prescription or letter from your doctor to show that you legally use the medication.

Insurance

Keep in mind that Tibet is a remote location, and if you become seriously injured or very sick, you may need to be evacuated by air. Under these circumstances, you don't want to be without adequate health insurance. Be sure your policy covers evacuation. See p340 for details.

Recommended Vaccinations

China doesn't officially require any immunisations for entry into the country; however, the further off the beaten track you go, the more necessary it is to take all precautions.

Plan well ahead (at least eight weeks before travel) and schedule your vaccinations – some require more than one injection, while others should not be given together. Note that some vaccinations should not be given during pregnancy or to people with allergies.

Discuss your requirements with your doctor, but vaccinations you should consider for this trip include the following:

Chickenpox (Varicella) Discuss this vaccine with your doctor if you have not had chickenpox.

Diphtheria & Tetanus Vaccinations for these two diseases are usually combined and are recommended for everyone. After an initial course of three injections (usually given in childhood), boosters are necessary every 10 years.

Hepatitis A The vaccine for Hepatitis A (eg Avaxim, Havrix 1440 or VAQTA) provides long-term immunity (at least 20 years) after an initial injection and a booster at six to 12 months. Hepatitis A vaccine is also available in a combined form, Twinrix, with hepatitis B vaccine. Three injections over a six-month period are required, the first two providing substantial protection against hepatitis A.

Hepatitis B China (although not so much Tibet) is one of the world's great reservoirs of hepatitis B infection, a disease spread by contact with blood or by sexual activity. Vaccination involves three injections, the quickest course being over three weeks with a booster at 12 months.

Influenza The flu vaccine is recommended for anyone with chronic diseases, such as diabetes, lung or heart disease. Tibet has a high rate of respiratory illness, so all travellers should consider vaccination.

Measles-mumps-rubella (MMR) All travellers should ensure they are immune to these diseases, either through infection or vaccination. Most people born before 1966 will be immune; those born after this date should have received two MMR vaccines in their lifetime.

Pneumonia A vaccine is recommended for anyone over 65 or those over 55 with certain medical conditions.

Polio Everyone should keep up-to-date with this vaccination, which is normally given in childhood. One adult booster is then needed (as long as the full childhood course was completed), particularly if travelling to a country with recent polio activity such as Nepal. This should be discussed with your doctor.

Rabies Rabies is the most common infectious disease cause of death in China. Vaccination is strongly recommended for those spending more than a month in Tibet (especially if you are cycling, handling animals, caving or travelling in remote areas) and for children. Pretravel vaccination means you do not need to receive Rabies Immuno Globulin (RIG) after a bite. RIG is very unlikely to be available in Tibet. If you are prevaccinated and then bitten, you need only get two further shots of vaccine, as soon as possible, three days apart. If not prevaccinated, you require RIG plus five shots of vaccine over the course of 28 days. The full series of vaccination does not require any boosters *unless* a bite occurs.

Tuberculosis The risk of tuberculosis (TB) to travellers is usually very low, unless you'll be living with or closely associated with local people in high-risk areas. Recommendations for BCG vaccination vary consider-

ably around the world. Discuss with your doctor if you feel you may be at risk. It is strongly recommended for children under five who are spending more than three months in a high-risk area.

Typhoid This is an important vaccination to have for Tibet, where hygiene standards are low. It is available either as an injection or oral capsules. A combined hepatitis A-typhoid vaccine was launched recently; check with your doctor to find out its availability in your country.

Yellow Fever This disease is not endemic in China or Tibet and a vaccine (proven by an International Health Certificate) is only required if you are coming from an infected area (parts of South America and Africa).

Medical Checklist

Following is a list of items you should consider including in your medical kit for travelling – consult your pharmacist for brands available in your country.

» Antibiotics – useful for everyone travelling to Tibet to avoid risks of receiving poorly stored local medications; see your doctor (antibiotics must be prescribed) and carry the prescription with you

» Antifungal cream or powder – for fungal skin infections and thrush

» Antihistamine – for allergies (eg hay fever), to ease the itch from insect bites or stings, and to prevent motion sickness

» Antiseptic (such as povidone-iodine) – for cuts and grazes

» Bandages, Band-Aids (plasters) and other wound dressings

» Calamine lotion, sting-relief spray or aloe vera – to ease irritation from sunburn and insect bites or stings

» Cold and flu tablets, throat lozenges and nasal decongestant

» Homeopathic medicines – useful homeopathic medicines include gentiana for altitude sickness, echinacea for warding off infections, and tea-tree oil for cuts and scrapes

» Insect repellent, sunscreen, lip balm and eye drops

» Loperamide or diphenoxylate – 'blockers' for diarrhoea

» Multivitamins – for long trips, when dietary vitamin intake may be inadequate

» Paracetamol (acetaminophen in the USA) – for pain or fever

» Prochlorperazine or metaclopramide – for nausea and vomiting

» Rehydration mixture – to prevent dehydration (eg during bouts of diarrhoea); particularly important when travelling with children

» Scissors, tweezers and a thermometer – note that mercury thermometers are prohibited by airlines

» Sterile kit – in case you need injections in a country with medical hygiene problems; discuss with your doctor

» Water purification tablets or iodine

Websites

There are a number of excellent travel-health sites on the internet. From the Lonely Planet website (lonelyplanet. com) there are links to the WHO and the US Centers for Disease Control & Prevention.

Further Reading

Lonely Planet's *Healthy Travel – Asia & India* is a handy pocket size and packed with useful information, including pretrip planning, emergency first aid, immunisation and disease information, and what to do if you get sick on the road. *Travel with Children* from Lonely Planet also includes advice on travel health for younger children.

Other detailed health guides you may find useful:

Complete Guide to Healthy Travel provides recommendations for international travel from the US Centers for Disease Control & Prevention.

Medicine for Mountaineering by James Wilkerson is still the classic text for trekking first aid and medical advice.

Pocket First Aid and Wilderness Medicine by Jim Duff and Peter Gormly is a great pocket-sized guide that's easily carried on a trek or climb.

The High Altitude Medicine Handbook by Andrew J Pollard and David R Murdoch is a small-format guide full of valuable information on prevention and emergency care.

Travellers' Health by Dr Richard Dawood is comprehensive, easy to read, authoritative and highly recommended, although it's rather large to lug around.

IN TIBET

Availability & Cost of Health Care

Self-diagnosis and treatment can be risky, so you should always seek medical help where possible. Although we do give drug dosages in this section, they are for emergency use only. Correct diagnosis is vital.

Top-end hotels can usually recommend a good place to go for advice. Standards of medical attention are so low in most places in Tibet that for some ailments the best advice is to go straight to Lhasa, and in extreme cases get on a plane to Kathmandu and Chéngdū:

CIWEC Clinic Travel Medicine Center (☑442 4111; www.ciwec-clinic.com; Lazimpath, Kathmandu, near British Embassy) Has lots of experience with altitude-related illnesses and is a good resource if on the way to or coming from Tibet. The website also offers useful medical advice.

Global Doctor Chengdu Clinic (☑8528 3638, 24hr emergency 139-8225 6966; www.globaldoctor.com.au; 62 Kehua Beilu, Lippo Tower, Section S, 2nd fl, No 9-11) Offers pre-Tibet medical examinations and a Tibet Travellers Assist Package that can be useful if you are worried about an existing medical condition.

Infectious Diseases

AVIAN INFLUENZA (BIRD FLU)
Influenza A (H5N1) or 'bird flu' is a subtype of the type A influenza virus. This virus typically infects birds and not humans. There have been some cases of bird-to-human transmission, though this does not easily occur. Very close contact with dead or sick birds is the currently principal source of infection. There is currently no vaccine available to prevent bird flu.

Symptoms include high fever and typical influenza-like indicators, with rapid deterioration leading to respiratory failure and, in many cases, death. The early administration of antiviral drugs such as Tamiflu is recommended to improve the chances of survival. Immediate medical care should be sought if bird flu is suspected.

RABIES
This fatal viral infection is found in Tibet. Many animals (such as dogs, cats, bats and monkeys) can be infected and it is their saliva that is infectious. Any bite, scratch or even lick from an animal should be cleaned immediately and thoroughly. Scrub gently with soap and running water, and then apply alcohol or iodine solution. Prompt medical help should be sought to receive a course of injections to prevent the onset of symptoms and save the patient from death.

Several travellers have written to say that they received treatment for rabies In Lhasa, though you'll likely have to visit several hospitals before finding the vaccine. If you have any potential exposure to rabies, seek medical advice in Lhasa (or ideally Kathmandu, Chéngdū or Běijīng) as soon as possible in order to receive post-exposure treatment. Even in these centres full treatment may not be available and you may need to travel to Bangkok or Hong Kong.

RESPIRATORY INFECTIONS
Upper respiratory tract infections (like the common cold) are frequent ailments all over China, including Tibet, where the high altitude aggravates symptoms.

Some of the symptoms of influenza include a sore throat, fever and weakness. Any upper-respiratory-tract infection, including influenza, can lead to complications such as bronchitis and pneumonia, which may need to be treated with antibiotics. Seek medical help in this situation.

No vaccine offers complete protection, but there are vaccines against influenza and pneumococcal pneumonia that might help. The influenza vaccine is highly recommended for travellers to China and Tibet, and is good for up to one year.

AMOEBIC DYSENTERY
Caused by the protozoan *Entamoeba histolytica*, amoebic dysentery is characterised by a gradual onset

of low-grade diarrhoea, often with blood and mucus. Cramping abdominal pain and vomiting are less likely than in other types of diarrhoea, and fever may not be present. It will persist until treated and can recur and cause other health problems.

You should seek medical advice if you think you have giardiasis or amoebic dysentery, but where this is not possible, tinidazole or metronidazole are the recommended drugs. The better option of the two is tinidazole, which is not easily obtained in Tibet. If you are going to be travelling in high mountain areas, it's a good idea to keep your own stock with you.

CHOLERA

This is the worst of the watery diarrhoeas. Outbreaks are generally widely reported, so you can avoid problem areas. Fluid replacement is the most vital treatment: the risk of dehydration is severe, as you may lose up to 20L a day. If there is a delay in getting to hospital, begin taking Doxycycline. This may help shorten the illness, but adequate fluids are required to save lives. Seek medical advice if you think you may have this disease.

GIARDIASIS

Known as giardia, giardiasis is a type of diarrhoea that is relatively common in Tibet and is caused by a parasite, *Giardia lamblia*. Mountaineers often suffer from this problem. The parasite causing this intestinal disorder is present in contaminated water. Many kinds of mammals harbour the parasite, so you can easily get it from drinking 'pure mountain water' unless the area is devoid of animals. Brushing your teeth using contaminated water is sufficient to get giardiasis, or any other gut bug. Symptoms include stomach cramps, nausea, a bloated stomach, watery,

foul-smelling diarrhoea and frequent gas. Giardiasis can appear several weeks after you have been exposed to the parasite. The symptoms may disappear for a few days and then return; this can go on for several weeks. Treatment is with tinidazole, 2g in a single dose for one to two days.

Environmental Hazards

ACUTE MOUNTAIN SICKNESS

Acute mountain sickness (AMS, also known as altitude sickness) is common at high elevations; relevant factors are the rate of ascent and individual susceptibility. The former is the major risk factor. On average, one tourist a year dies in Tibet from AMS. Any traveller who flies or buses into Lhasa, where the elevation is around 3600m, is likely to experience some symptoms of AMS.

AMS is a notoriously fickle affliction and can also affect trekkers and walkers accustomed to walking at high altitudes. It has been fatal at 3000m, although 3500m to 4500m is the usual range.

Acclimatisation

AMS is linked to low atmospheric pressure. Those who travel up to Everest Base Camp, for instance, reach an altitude where atmospheric pressure is about half of that at sea level.

With an increase in altitude, the human body needs time to develop physiological mechanisms to cope with the decreased oxygen. This process of acclimatisation is still not fully understood, but is known to involve modifications in breathing patterns and heart rate induced by the autonomic nervous system, and an increase in the blood's oxygen-carrying capabilities. These compen-

satory mechanisms usually take about one to three days to develop at a particular altitude. You are unlikely to get AMS once you are acclimatised to a given height, but you can still get ill when you travel higher. If the ascent is too high and too fast, these compensatory reactions may not kick into gear fast enough.

Symptoms

Mild symptoms of AMS usually develop during the first 24 hours at altitude. Most visitors to Tibet will suffer from some symptoms; these will generally disappear through acclimatisation in several hours to several days.

Symptoms tend to be worse at night and include headache, dizziness, lethargy, loss of appetite, nausea, breathlessness and irritability. Difficulty sleeping is another common symptom, and many travellers have trouble for the first few days after arriving in Lhasa.

AMS may become more serious without warning and can be fatal. Symptoms are caused by the accumulation of fluid in the lungs and brain, and include breathlessness at rest, a dry irritative cough (which may progress to the production of pink, frothy sputum), severe headache, lack of coordination (typically leading to a 'drunken walk'), confusion, irrational behaviour, vomiting and eventually unconsciousness.

The symptoms of AMS, however mild, are a warning: be sure to take them seriously! Trekkers should keep an eye on each other as those experiencing symptoms, especially severe symptoms, may not be in a position to recognise them. One thing to note is that while the symptoms of mild AMS often precede those of severe AMS, this is not always the case. Severe AMS can strike with little or no warning.

Prevention

If you are driving up from Kathmandu, you will experience rapid altitude gain. An itinerary that takes you straight up to Everest Base Camp is unwise; plan to see it on your way back if possible. The best way to prevent AMS is to avoid rapid ascents to high altitudes. If you fly or bus into Lhasa, take it easy for at least three days; this is enough for most travellers to get over any initial ill-effects.

To prevent acute mountain sickness:

» Ascend slowly. Have frequent rest days, spending two to three nights at each rise of 1000m. If you reach a high altitude by trekking, acclimatisation takes place gradually and you are less likely to be affected than if you fly or drive directly to high altitude.

» Trekkers should bear in mind the climber's adage of 'climb high, sleep low'. It is always wise to sleep at a lower altitude than the greatest height that's reached during the day.

» Once above 3000m, care should be taken not to increase the sleeping altitude by more than 400m per day.

» Drink extra fluids. Tibet's mountain air is cold and dry, and moisture is lost as you breathe. Evaporation of sweat may occur unnoticed and result in dehydration.

» Avoid alcohol as it may increase the risk of dehydration, and don't smoke.

» Avoid sedatives.

» When trekking, take a day off to rest and acclimatise if feeling overtired. If you or anyone else in your party is having a tough time, make allowances for unscheduled stops.

» Don't push yourself when climbing up to passes; rather, take plenty of breaks. You can usually get over the pass as easily tomorrow as you can today. Try to plan your itinerary so that long ascents can be divided into two or more days. Given the complexity and unknown variables involved with AMS and acclimatisation, trekkers should always err on the side of caution and ascend mountains slowly.

Treatment

Treat mild symptoms by resting at the same altitude until recovery, usually a day or two. Take paracetamol or acetaminophen for headaches. If symptoms persist or become worse, however, *immediate* descent is necessary. Even 500m can help.

The most effective treatment for severe AMS is to get down to a lower altitude as quickly as possible. In less severe cases the victim will be able to stagger down with some support; in other cases they may need to be carried down. Whatever the case, any delay could be fatal.

AMS victims may need to be flown out of Tibet as quickly as possible, so make sure you have adequate travel insurance.

The drug acetazolamide (Diamox) is recommended for the prevention of AMS – take 125mg twice a day as a preventive dose. Be aware that even when you are on Diamox, you should not ignore any symptoms of AMS. Diamox should be avoided in those with a sulphur allergy.

Drug treatments should never be used to avoid descent or to enable further ascent (although they can help get people well enough to descend).

Several hotels in Lhasa sell a Tibetan herbal medicine recommended by locals for easing the symptoms of mild altitude sickness. The medicine is known as *solomano* in Tibetan and *hongjingtian* (红景天) in Chinese, though locals also recommend *gaoyuanning* (高原宁) and *gaoyuankang* (高原康). A box of vials costs around Y20 to Y35; take three vials a day.

FOOD

There is an old colonial adage: 'If you can cook it, boil it or peel it, you can eat it... otherwise forget it.' Vegetables and fruit should be washed with purified or bottled water or peeled where possible. Beware of ice cream that is sold in the street or anywhere it might have been melted and refrozen; if there's any doubt (eg a power cut in the last day or two) steer clear. Avoid undercooked meat.

In general, places that are packed with travellers or locals will be fine, while empty restaurants are questionable. Chinese food in particular is cooked over a high heat, which kills most germs.

FROSTBITE

This is the freezing of extremities, including fingers, toes and nose. Signs and symptoms of frostbite include a whitish or waxy cast to the skin, or even crystals on the surface, plus itching, numbness and pain. Warm the affected areas by immersing them in warm (not hot) water or with blankets or clothes, only until the skin becomes flushed. Note: frostbitten areas should only be rewarmed if there is not a likelihood they can be frostbitten again prior to reaching medical care. Frostbitten parts should not be rubbed. Pain and swelling are inevitable. Blisters should not be broken. Get medical attention right away.

HEAT EXHAUSTION

Dehydration and salt deficiency can cause heat exhaustion. Take time to acclimatise to high temperatures, be sure to drink sufficient liquids and do not do anything too physically demanding.

Salt deficiency is characterised by fatigue, lethargy,

headaches, giddiness and muscle cramps; salt tablets may help, but adding extra salt to your food is better.

HYPOTHERMIA

Tibet's cold climate must be treated with respect. Subfreezing temperatures mean there is a risk of hypothermia, even during the summer season. Even in midsummer, passes and high areas around western Tibet and the northern Changtang can be hit without warning by sudden snow storms. Exposed plains and ridges are prone to extremely high winds and this significantly adds to the cold. For example, on a 5000m pass in central Tibet in July, the absolute minimum temperature is roughly -4°C, but regularly occurring 70km/h winds plunge the wind-chill factor or apparent temperature to -20°C.

The message is that you should always be prepared for cold, wet or windy conditions, especially if you're out walking at high altitudes or even taking a long bus trip over mountains (particularly at night).

Hypothermia occurs when the body loses heat faster than it can produce it and the core temperature of the body falls. It is surprisingly easy to progress from very cold to dangerously cold through a combination of wind, wet clothing, fatigue and hunger, even if the air temperature is above freezing.

Symptoms of hypothermia are exhaustion, numb skin (particularly toes and fingers), shivering, slurred speech, irrational or violent behaviour, lethargy, stumbling, dizzy spells, muscle cramps and violent bursts of energy. Irrationality may take the form of sufferers claiming they are warm and trying to take off their clothes.

To treat mild hypothermia, first get the person out of the wind and rain, remove their clothing if it's wet and replace it with dry, warm clothing. Give them hot liquids (not alcohol) and some high-energy, easily digestible food. Do not rub victims; instead, allow them to slowly warm themselves. This should be enough to treat the early stages of hypothermia. The early recognition and treatment of mild hypothermia is the only way to prevent severe hypothermia, which is a critical condition.

SUNBURN

It's very easy to get sunburnt in Tibet's high altitudes, especially if you're trekking. Sunburn is more than just being uncomfortable. Among the undesirable effects (apart from the immediate pain) are premature skin ageing and possible skin cancer in later years. Wear sunglasses, loose-fitting clothes that cover your arms, legs and neck, and a wide-brimmed hat like the ones Tibetans wear (not a baseball cap).

Choose sunscreen with a high sun protection factor (SPF). Those with fair complexions should bring reflective sunscreen (containing zinc oxide or titanium oxide) with them. Apply the sunscreen to your nose and lips (and especially the tops of your ears if you are not wearing a hat).

WATER

The number-one rule is don't drink the tap water, including ice. In urban centres Tibetans, like the Chinese, boil their drinking water making it safe to drink hot or cooled. In the country and while trekking you should boil your own water or treat it with water-purification tablets, as livestock contaminate many of the water sources. Tea is always safe to drink. Locally brewed beer (*chang*) is another matter. It is often made with contaminated well water and there is always some risk in drinking it.

Water Purification

The simplest way to purify water is to boil it thoroughly. At Tibet's high altitude water boils at a lower temperature and germs are less likely to be killed, so make sure you boil water for at least 10 minutes.

Consider purchasing a water filter for a long trip. Total filters take out all parasites, bacteria and viruses, and make water safe to drink. They are often expensive, but can be more cost-effective than buying bottled water.

Chlorine tablets (eg Puritabs or Steritabs) will kill many pathogens, but not giardia and amoebic cysts. Iodine is more effective for purifying water and is available in liquid (Lugol's solution) or tablet form (eg Potable Aqua). Follow the directions carefully and remember that too much iodine can be harmful.

Tibetan Medicine

The basic teachings of Tibetan medicine share much with those of other Asian medical traditions, which, according to some scholars, made their way to the East via India from ancient Greece. While the Western medical tradition treats symptoms that indicate a known medical condition (measles or mumps, for example), the Eastern medical tradition looks at symptoms as indications of an imbalance in the body and seeks to restore that balance.

The Tibetan medical tradition is largely textual. It derives from Indian sources and was studied in some monasteries in much the same way that Buddhist scriptures were studied. When Tibetans needed medical help they usually went to a local 'apothecary' who sold concoctions of herbs and blessed pills; equally, help was sought in prayers and good-luck charms.

The theory of Tibetan medicine is based on an extremely complex system of checks and balances between what can be broadly described as three 'humours' (related to state of mind), seven 'bodily sustainers' (related to the digestive tract) and three 'eliminators' (related to the elimination of bodily wastes). And if the relationship between bodily functions and the three humours of desire, egoism and ignorance were not complex enough, there is the influence of harmful spirits to consider. There are 360 harmful female influences, 360 harmful male influences, 360 *naga* (water spirits) influences and, finally, 360 influences stemming from past karma. All these combine to produce 404 basic disorders and 84,000 illnesses!

How does a Tibetan doctor assess the condition of a patient? The most important skill is pulse diagnosis. A Tibetan doctor is attuned to 360 'subtle channels' of energy that run through the body's skin and muscle, internal organs and bone and marrow. The condition of these channels can be ascertained through six of the doctor's fingers (the first three fingers of each hand). Tibetan medicine also relies on urine analysis as an important diagnostic tool.

If Tibetan diagnostic theory is mainly Indian in influence, the treatment owes as much to Chinese medicine as to Indian practices. Herbal concoctions, moxibustion and acupuncture are all used to restore balance to the body. Surgery was practised in the early days of Tibetan medicine, but was outlawed in the 9th century when a king's mother died during an operation.

Yuthok Yongten Gonpo (1182–1251), the physician of King Trisong Detsen, who was born near Ralung Monastery, is credited as the founder of the Tibetan medical system. For more on Tibetan medicine see the website www.tibetan -medicine.org.

If you get sick, you can get a diagnosis from Lhasa's **Mentsikhang** (Traditional Tibetan Hospital; Map p48; ◎9.30am-12.30pm & 3.30-6pm) opposite the Barkhor. Two English-speaking doctors attend to foreigners on the 3rd floor.

Language

WANT MORE?
For in-depth language information and handy phrases, check out Lonely Planet's *Tibet Phrasebook* and *China Phrasebook*. You'll find them at **shop. lonelyplanet.com**, or you can buy Lonely Planet's iPhone phrasebooks at the Apple App Store.

The two principal languages of Tibet are Tibetan and Mandarin Chinese. In urban Tibet (the countryside is another matter) almost all Tibetans speak Tibetan and Mandarin, and all Tibetans undertaking higher studies do so in Chinese. Linguistically, Chinese and Tibetan have little in common. They use different sentence structures, and the tones are far less crucial in Tibetan than in Chinese. Also, unlike the dialects of China, Tibetan has never used Chinese characters for its written language.

TIBETAN

Tibetan belongs to the Tibeto-Burman group of languages, and is spoken by around six million people, mainly in Tibet but also within Tibetan communities in Nepal, India, Bhutan and Pakistan. The Lhasa dialect is the standard form of Tibetan.

Most sounds in Tibetan are similar to those in English, so if you read our coloured pronunciation guides as if they were English, you'll be understood. Note that the symbol â is pronounced as the 'a' in 'ago', ö as the 'er' in 'her', and ü as the 'u' in 'flute' but with a raised tongue.

When a vowel is followed by n, m or ng, this indicates a nasalised sound (pronounced with air escaping through the nose). When a consonant is followed by h, the consonant is aspirated (ie accompanied by a puff of air).

Basics

There are no words in Tibetan that are the direct equivalents of the English 'yes' and 'no'. You'll be understood if you use *la ong* for 'yes' and *la men* for 'no'.

Hello.	བཀྲ་ཤིས་བདེ་ལེགས།	ta·shi de·lek
Goodbye.	ག་ལེར་ཕེབས།	ka·lee pay
	(said when staying)	
	ག་ལེར་བཞུགས།	ka·lee shu
	(said when leaving)	
Sorry.	དགོངས་དག	gong·da
Excuse me.	དགོངས་དག	gong·da
Please.	ཐུགས་རྗེ་གཟིགས།	tu·jay·sig
Thank you.	ཐུགས་རྗེ་ཆེ།	tu·jay·chay

How are you?
ཁྱེད་རང་སྐུ་གཟུགས་ kay·râng ku·su
བདེ་པོ་ཡིན་པས། de·po yin·bay

Fine, and you?
བདེ་པོ་ཡིན། ཁྱེད་རང་ཡང་ de·bo·yin kay·râng·yâng
སྐུ་གཟུགས་བདེ་པོ་ཡིན་པས། ku·su de·po yin·bay

What's your name?
ཁྱེད་རང་གི་མཚན་ལ་ kay·râng·gi tsen·lâ
ག་རེ་རེད། kâ·ray·ray

My name is ...
ངའི་མིང་ལ་ ... རེད། ngay·ming·la ... ray

Do you speak English?
ཁྱེད་རང་དབྱིན་ཇི་སྐད་ kay·râng in·ji·kay
ཤེས་ཀྱི་ཡོད་པས། shing·gi yö·bay

I don't understand.
ཧ་གོ་མ་སོང་། ha ko ma·song

Tibetan Trekking Essentials

How many hours to ...?
... བར་དུ་ཆུ་ཚོད་ཚོད་འགོར་གི་རེད།
... bah·tu chu·tsö kâ·tsay go·gi·ray

I want to rent a yak/horse.
ངས་ཡཱག/ཪྟ་གཅིག་གླ་དགོས་ཡོད།
nga yâk/ta·chig la·gö·yö

I need a porter.
ངར་དོ་པོ་ཁུར་མཁན་གཅིག་དགོས།
nga doh·bo khu·khen·chig gö

I need a guide.
ང་ལམ་རྒྱུས་ཆེ་མཁན་གཅིག་དགོས།
nga lâm·gyü chay·khen·chig gö

How much does it cost per day?
ཉིན་མ་རེ་རེ་ལ་གླ་ཆག་ཚོད་རེད།
nyi·ma ray·ray·la la·ja kâ·tsay ray

Which way to ...?
... འགྲོ་ཡག་གི་ལམ་ག་ག་གི་རེད།
... doh·ya·gi lâm·ga ka·gi·ray

Is this the trail to ...?
འདི་ ... འགྲོ་ཡག་གི་ལམ་ག་རེད་པས།
di ... doh·ya·gi lâm·ga re·bay

What is the next village on the trail?
ལམ་ག་དེ་ནས་ཕྱིན་ན་དང་པོ་ལུང་པ་ག་རེ་སླེབས་ཀྱི་རེད།
lâm·ga te·nay chin·na dâng·po loong·pa ka·ray leb·ki·ray

I have altitude sickness.
ངར་ལ་དུག་ན་གིས།
nga lâ·du na·gi

I must get to low ground as quickly as possible.
ངས་ས་མའ་ས་གང་མགྱོགས་མགྱོགས་འཚོར་དགོས་ཀྱི་འདུག
nga sa mah·sa gâng gyok·gyok joh go·ki·du

Slowly, slowly!	ག་ལེ་ག་ལེ།	ka·lee ka·lee
Let's go!	ད་འགྲོ།	ta doh
north	བྱང་	châng
south	ལྷོ་	lho
east	ཤར་	shâr
west	ནུབ་	noob
cave	བྲག་ཕུག་	dâg·phuk
hot spring	ཆུ་ཚན་	chu·tsen
lake	མཚོ་	tso
mountain	རི་	ri
pass	ལ་	la
river	གཙང་པོ་	tsâng·po
road/trail	ལམ་	lam
sleeping bag	ཉལ་ཁུག་	nye·koog
tent	གུར་	gur
valley	ལུང་གཤོང་	loong shong

I need some hot water.
ང་ལ་ཆུ་ཚ་པོ་དགོས།
nga·la chu tsa·po gö

Accommodation

I'm looking	... གཅིག་མིག་	...·chig mig
for a ...	བལྟ་གི་ཡོད།	ta·gi·yö
campsite	གུར་བརྒྱབ་ནས་	gur gyâb·nay
	སྡོད་སའི་ས་ཆ་	dö·say sa·cha
guesthouse	མགྲོན་ཁང་	drön·khâng
hotel	འགྲུལ་ཁང་	drü·khâng

I'd like to book a room.
ཁང་མིག་ཅིག་གླ་དགོས་ཡོད།
khâng·mi·chig la gö·yö

How much for one night?
མཚན་གཅིག་ལ་གོང་
tsen chig·la gong
ག་ཚོད་རེད།
kâ·tsay ray

I'd like to stay with a Tibetan family.
ངར་བོད་པའི་མི་ཚང་
nga bö·pay mi·tsâng
མཉམ་དུ་བསྡད་འདོད་ཡོད།
nyâm·do den·dö yö

Directions

Where is ...?
... ག་བར་ཡོད་རེད།
... ka·bah yö·ray

Can you show me (on the map)?
(ས་བཀྲ་འདི་ནང་) (sâp·ta di·nâng)
སྟོན་གནང་དང་། tön nâng·da

Turn left/right.
གཡོན་ལ་/གཡས་ལ་ yön·la/yeh·la
སྐྱོགས་གནང་། kyog·nâng

straight ahead	ཁ་ཐུག་འགྲོ།	ka·toog·do
behind ...	... རྒྱབ་ལ་	... gyâb·lâ
in front of ...	... མདུན་ལ་	... dün·lâ

Signs – Tibetan	
འཛུལ་ས་	Entrance
དོན་ས་	Exit
སྒོ་ཕྱེ	Open
སྒོ་བརྒྱབ་	Closed
པར་བརྒྱབ་མི་ཆོག	No Photographs
གསང་སྤྱོད་	Toilets

near (to) ...	... འཁྲིས་ལ་	... tee·lâ
opposite ...	... པར་ཕྱོགས་ལ་	... pha·chog·lâ

Eating & Drinking

What do you recommend?
ཁྱེད་རང་བྱེད་ན་ག་རེ་ / ཡག་གི་རེད།   kay·râng chay·na kâ·ray yâ·gi·ray

What's in that dish?
ཁ་ལག་ཕ་གིའི་ནང་ག་རེ་ / ཡོད་རེད།   kha·la pha·gi·nâng kâ·ray yö·ray

I'm vegetarian.
ང་ཤ་མི་ཟ་མཁན་ཡིན།   nga sha mi·sa·ken yin

That meal was delicious.
ཁ་ལག་ཞིམ་པོ་ཞི་དྲགས་ / བྱུང་།   kha·la shim·bu shay·ta choong

breakfast	ཞོག་སྐད་ཁ་ལག	shog·kay kha·la
coffee	ཇ་ཀོ་པི་	cha ka·bi
dinner	དགོང་དག་ཁ་ལག	gong·da kha·la
fish	ཉ་ཤ	nya·sha
food	ཁ་ལག	kha·la
fruit	ཤིང་ཏོག	shing·tog
juice	ཁུ་བ་	khu·wa
lunch	ཉིན་གུང་	nyin·goong
	ཁ་ལག	kha·la
meat	ཤ	sha
milk	འོ་མ	oh·ma
restaurant	ཟ་ཁང་	sa·khâng
tea	ཇ་	cha
vegetable	སྔོ་ཚལ་	ngo·tsay
(boiled) water	ཆུ (འཁོལ་མ་)	chu (khö·ma)

For more food terms, see the Glossary.

Emergencies

Help!	རོགས་གནང་དང་།	rog nâng·da
Go away!	པར་རྒྱུགས།	phâh gyook
Call ...	... སྐད་	... kay
	གཏོང་དང་།	tong·da
a doctor	ཨེམ་ཆི	ahm·chi
the police	སྐོར་སྲུང་བ་	kor·soong·wa

I'm lost.
ང་ལམ་ཀ་བརྒྱགས་ཤག   nga lâm·ga la·sha

I'm allergic to ...
ངར་ ... ཕོགས་ཀྱི་ཡོད།   ngah ... pho·gi·yö

Shopping & Services

Do you have any ... ?
ཁྱེད་རང་ལ་ ... / བཙོང་ཡག་ཡོད་པས།   kay·râng·la ... tsong·ya yö·bay

How much is it?
གོང་ག་ཚད་རེད།   gong kâ·tsay ray

It's too expensive.
གོང་ཆེ་དྲགས་ཤག   gong chay·ta·sha

I'll give you ...
ངས་ ... སྤྲད་དགོས།   ngay ... tay go

bank	དངུལ་ཁང་	ngü·khâng
post office	སྦྲག་ཁང་	da·khâng
tourist office	ཡུལ་སྐོར་	yu·kor
	སྒོ་འཆམ་པའི་	to·châm·pay
	ལས་ཁུངས་	lay·khoong

Time & Dates

What time it is?
དལྟ་ཆུ་ཚོད་ག་ཚོད་རེད།   tân·da chu·tsö kâ·tsay·ray

It's half past (two).
ཆུ་ཚོད་ (གཉིས་) དང་ / ཕྱེད་ཀ་རེད།   chu·tsö (nyi)·dâng chay·ka ray

It's (two) o'clock.
ཆུ་ཚོད་ (གཉིས་) པ་རེད།   chu·tsö (nyi)·pa ray

Numbers – Tibetan

1	༡	chig
2	༢	nyi
3	༣	soom
4	༤	shi
5	༥	nga
6	༦	doog
7	༧	dün
8	༨	gye
9	༩	gu
10	༡༠	chu
20	༢༠	nyi·shu
30	༣༠	soom·chu
40	༤༠	shib·chu
50	༥༠	ngâb·chu
60	༦༠	doog·chu
70	༧༠	dün·chu
80	༨༠	gyay·chu
90	༩༠	goob·chu
100	༡༠༠	gya
1000	༡༠༠༠	chig·tong

yesterday	ཁ་ས་	kay·sa
today	དེ་རིང་	te·ring
tomorrow	སང་ཉིན་	sa·nyin
Monday	གཟའ་ཟླ་བ་	sa da·wa
Tuesday	གཟའ་མིག་དམར་	sa mig·ma
Wednesday	གཟའ་ལྷག་པ་	sa lhâg·bâ
Thursday	གཟའ་ཕུར་བུ་	sa phu·bu
Friday	གཟའ་པ་སངས་	sa pa·sâng
Saturday	གཟའ་སྤེན་པ་	sa pem·pa
Sunday	གཟའ་ཉི་མ་	sa nyi·mâ

Transport

Where is this	... འདི་ག་པར་	... ka·bah
... going?	འགྲོ་གི་རེད།	doh·gi ray
boat	གྲུ་གཟིངས་	dru·zing
bus	སྤྱི་སྤྱོད་	chi·chö
	རླངས་འཁོར་	lâng·kho
plane	གནམ་གྲུ་	nâm·du

I'd like to	ང་ ... གཅིག	nga ...·chig
hire a ...	གཡར་འདོད་ཡོད།	yar dhö·yö
car	མོ་ཊ་	mo·ta
donkey	བོང་གུ་	boong·gu
landcruiser	ལེན་ཀུ་རུ་ས་	len ku·ru·sa
pack animals	ཁལ་སེམས་ཅན་/	kel sem·chen/
	ཁལ་མ་	kel·ma
porter	དོ་པོ་ཁུར་མཁན་	doh·po khu·khen
yak	གཡག་	yak

How much is it daily/weekly?

ཉིན་/བདུན་ཕྲག་རེ་རེར་	nyin/dun·tâg ray·ray
གོང་ག་ཚད་རེད།	gong kâ·tsay ray

Does this road lead to ...?

ལམ་ག་འདི་ ...	lâm·ga·di ...
འགྲོ་ཡག་རེད་པས།	doh·ya re·bay

Can I get there on foot?

ཕ་གིར་གོམ་པ་བརྒྱབ་ནས་	pha·gay gom·pa gyâb·nay
སླེབས་ཐུབ་ཀྱི་རེད་པས།	leb thoob·ki re·bay

MANDARIN

Pronunciation

In this section we've provided Pinyin (a system of writing Chinese using the Roman alphabet) alongside the Mandarin script.

Vowels

a	as in 'father'
ai	as in 'aisle'
ao	as the 'ow' in 'cow'
e	as in 'her', with no 'r' sound
ei	as in 'weigh'
i	as the 'ee' in 'meet' (or like a light 'r' as in 'Grrr!' after c, ch, r, s, sh, z or zh)
ian	as the word 'yen'
ie	as the English word 'yeah'
o	as in 'or', with no 'r' sound
ou	as the 'oa' in 'boat'
u	as in 'flute'
ui	as the word 'way'
uo	like a 'w' followed by 'o'
yu/ü	like 'ee' with lips pursed

Consonants

Note that in Pinyin apostrophes are sometimes used to separate syllables in order to avoid mispronunciation, eg píng'ān.

c	as the 'ts' in 'bits'
ch	as in 'chop', but with the tongue curled up and back
h	as in 'hay', but articulated from farther back in the throat
q	as the 'ch' in 'cheese'
r	as the 's' in 'pleasure'
sh	as in 'ship', but with the tongue curled up and back
x	as in 'ship'
z	as the 'dz' in 'suds'
zh	as the 'j' in 'judge' but with the tongue curled up and back

Tones

Mandarin has many words with the same pronunciation but a different meaning. What distinguishes these words is their 'tonal' quality – the raising and the lowering of pitch on certain syllables. For example, the word ma has four different meanings according to tone, as shown below. Tones are indicated in Pinyin by the following accent marks on vowels:

high tone	mā (mother)
rising tone	má (hemp, numb)
falling-rising tone	mǎ (horse)
falling tone	mà (scold, swear)

Basics

Hello.	你好。	Nǐhǎo.
Goodbye.	再见。	Zàijiàn.
How are you?	你好吗？	Nǐhǎo ma?
Fine. And you?	好。你呢？	Hǎo. Nǐ ne?
Yes./No.	是。/不是。	Shì./Bùshì.
Please ...	请……	Qǐng ...
Thank you.	谢谢你。	Xièxie nǐ.
You're welcome.	不客气。	Bù kèqi.
Excuse me.	劳驾。	Láojià.
Sorry.	对不起。	Duìbùqǐ.

What's your name?
你叫什么名字？ Nǐ jiào shénme míngzi?

My name is ...
我叫…… Wǒ jiào ...

Do you speak English?
你会说英文吗？ Nǐ huìshuō Yīngwén ma?

I don't understand.
我不明白。 Wǒ bù míngbai.

Accommodation

Do you have a single/double room?
有没有（单人/
套）房？ Yǒuméiyǒu (dānrén/tào) fáng?

How much is it per night/person?
每天/人多少钱？ Měi tiān/rén duōshǎo qián?

campsite	露营地	lùyíngdì
guesthouse	宾馆	bīnguǎn
hostel	招待所	zhāodàisuǒ
hotel	酒店	jiǔdiàn

air-con	空调	kōngtiáo
bathroom	浴室	yùshì
bed	床	chuáng
window	窗	chuāng

Directions

Where's (a bank)?
（银行）在哪儿？ (Yínháng) zài nǎr?

What is the address?
地址在哪儿？ Dìzhǐ zài nǎr?

Could you write the address, please?
能不能请你
把地址写下来？ Néngbunéng qǐng nǐ bǎ dìzhǐ xiě xiàlái?

Can you show me where it is on the map?
请帮我找它在
地图上的位置。 Qǐng bāngwǒ zhǎo tā zài dìtú shàng de wèizhi.

Go straight ahead.
一直走。 Yīzhí zǒu.

at the next corner
在下一个拐角 zài xià yīge guǎijiǎo

at the traffic lights
在红绿灯 zài hónglǜdēng

behind	背面	bèimiàn
far	远	yuǎn
in front of ...	……的前面	... de qiánmian
near	近	jìn
next to	旁边	pángbiān
on the corner	拐角	guǎijiǎo
opposite	对面	duìmiàn
Turn left/right.	左/右转。	Zuǒ/Yòu zhuǎn.

Signs – Mandarin		
入口	Rùkǒu	**Entrance**
出口	Chūkǒu	**Exit**
问讯处	Wènxùnchù	**Information**
开	Kāi	**Open**
关	Guān	**Closed**
禁止	Jìnzhǐ	**Prohibited**
厕所	Cèsuǒ	**Toilets**
男	Nán	**Men**
女	Nǚ	**Women**

Eating & Drinking

What would you recommend?
有什么菜可以 | Yǒu shénme cài kěyǐ
推荐的? | tuījiàn de?

What's in that dish?
这道菜用什么 | Zhèdào cài yòng shénme
东西做的? | dōngxi zuòde?

That was delicious!
真好吃! | Zhēn hǎochī!

The bill, please! 买单! | Mǎidān!
Cheers! 干杯! | Gānbēi!

I don't eat ... 我不吃…… | Wǒ bùchī ...
  fish 鱼 | yú
  nuts 果仁 | guǒrén
  poultry 家禽 | jiāqín
  red meat 牛羊肉 | niúyángròu

Emergencies

Help! 救命! | Jiùmìng!
I'm lost. 我迷路了。 | Wǒ mílù le.
Go away! 走开! | Zǒukāi!

There's been an accident!
出事了! | Chūshì le!

Call a doctor!
请叫医生来! | Qǐng jiào yīshēng lái!

Call the police!
请叫警察! | Qǐng jiào jǐngchá!

I'm ill.
我生病了。 | Wǒ shēngbìng le.

I'm allergic to (antibiotics).
我对(抗菌素) | Wǒ duì (kàngjūnsù)
过敏。 | guòmǐn.

Shopping & Services

I'd like to buy ...
我想买…… | Wǒ xiǎng mǎi ...

Can I look at it?
我能看看吗? | Wǒ néng kànkan ma?

How much is it?
多少钱? | Duōshǎo qián?

That's too expensive!
太贵了! | Tàiguì le!

Can you lower the price?
能便宜一点吗? | Néng piányi yìdiǎn ma?

There's a mistake in the bill.
帐单上 | Zhàngdān shàng
有问题。 | yǒu wèntí.

Numbers – Mandarin

1	一	yī
2	二/两	èr/liǎng
3	三	sān
4	四	sì
5	五	wǔ
6	六	liù
7	七	qī
8	八	bā
9	九	jiǔ
10	十	shí
20	二十	èrshí
30	三十	sānshí
40	四十	sìshí
50	五十	wǔshí
60	六十	liùshí
70	七十	qīshí
80	八十	bāshí
90	九十	jiǔshí
100	一百	yībǎi
1000	一千	yīqiān

internet cafe	网吧	wǎngbā
post office	邮局	yóujú
tourist office	旅行店	lǚxíng diàn

Time & Dates

What time is it?
现在几点钟? | Xiànzài jǐdiǎn zhōng?

It's (10) o'clock.
(十)点钟。 | (Shí)diǎn zhōng.

Half past (10).
(十)点三十分。 | (Shí)diǎn sānshífēn.

morning	早上	zǎoshang
afternoon	下午	xiàwǔ
evening	晚上	wǎnshàng
yesterday	昨天	zuótiān
today	今天	jīntiān
tomorrow	明天	míngtiān
Monday	星期一	xīngqī yī
Tuesday	星期二	xīngqī èr
Wednesday	星期三	xīngqī sān
Thursday	星期四	xīngqī sì
Friday	星期五	xīngqī wǔ
Saturday	星期六	xīngqī liù
Sunday	星期天	xīngqī tiān

Transport

boat	船	chuán
bus	长途车	chángtú chē
plane	飞机	fēijī
taxi	出租车	chūzū chē
train	火车	huǒchē

I want to go to ...
我要去…… Wǒ yào qù ...

What time does it leave?
几点钟出发? Jǐdiǎnzhōng chūfā?

What time does it get to ...?
几点钟到……? Jǐdiǎnzhōng dào ...?

I want to get off here.
我想这儿下车。 Wǒ xiǎng zhèr xiàchē.

When's the ... (bus)? 几点走?	……(车) 	... (chē) jǐdiǎn zǒu?
first	首趟	Shǒutàng
last	末趟	Mòtàng
next	下一趟	Xià yītàng

A ... ticket to (Dalian). 	一张到 (大连)的 ……票。	Yīzhāng dào (Dàlián) de ... piào.
1st-class	头等	tóuděng
2nd-class	二等	èrděng
one-way	单程	dānchéng
return	双程	shuāngchéng

cancelled	取消	qǔxiāo
delayed	晚点	wǎndiǎn
ticket office	售票处	shòupiàochù
timetable	时刻表	shíkè biǎo

I'd like to hire a ... 	我要租 一辆…… 	Wǒ yào zū yīliàng ...
4WD	四轮驱动	silún qūdòng
bicycle	自行车	zìxíngchē
car	汽车	qìchē
motorcycle	摩托车	mótuochē

Does this road lead to ...?
这条路到……吗? Zhè tiáo lù dào ... ma?

How long can I park here?
这儿可以停多久? Zhèr kěyi tíng duōjiǔ?

The car has broken down (at ...).
汽车是(在……)坏的。 Qìchē shì (zài ...) huài de.

I have a flat tyre.
轮胎瘪了。 Lúntāi biě le.

I've run out of petrol.
没有汽油了。 Méiyou qìyóu le.

bicycle pump	打气筒	dǎqìtóng
child seat	婴儿座	yīng'érzuò
diesel	柴油	cháiyóu
helmet	头盔	tóukuī
gas/petrol	汽油	qìyóu
mechanic	机修工	jīxiūgōng
service station	加油站	jiāyóu zhàn

GLOSSARY

The main entries in this chapter are the Tibetan terms, unless otherwise indicated. (S) denotes Sanskrit and (M) stands for Mandarin.

Who's Who

This section presents some of the deities, historical figures and other people mentioned in this book. Many terms are of Sanskrit origin.

Akshobhya – see *Mikyöba*
Amitabha – see *Öpagme*
Amitayus – see *Tsepame*
Atisha – see *Jowo-je*
Avalokiteshvara – see *Chenresig*

Bhrikuti – the Nepali consort of King Songtsen Gampo
Büton Rinchen Drup – compiler of the Tibetan Buddhist canon; established

a sub-school of Tibetan Buddhism, based in Shalu Monastery

Chana Dorje (S: Vajrapani) – the wrathful Bodhisattva of Energy whose name means 'thunderbolt in hand'
Chenresig (S: Avalokiteshvara) – an embodiment of compassionate bodhisattvahood and the patron saint of Tibet; the Dalai Lamas are

considered to be manifestations of this deity

Chögyel (S: Dharmaraja) – Gelugpa protector deity; blue, with the head of a bull

Chökyong (S: Lokapalas) – the Four Guardian Kings

Citipati – dancing skeletons, often seen in protector chapels

Dalai Lama – spiritual head of the Gelugpa order, which ruled over Tibet from 1642 until 1959; the term is an honorific that means 'ocean of wisdom' and was bestowed by the Mongolian Altyn Khan; also believed to be the manifestation of Chenresig (Avalokiteshvara)

Dharmaraja – see *Chögyel*

Dorje Chang (S: Vajradhara) – one of the five Dhyani buddhas, recognisable by his crossed arms holding a bell and thunderbolt

Dorje Drolo – wrathful form of Guru Rinpoche, seated on a tiger

Dorje Jigje (S: Yamantaka) – a meditational deity who comes in various aspects; the Red and Black aspects are probably the most common

Dorje Lekpa – Dzogchen deity, recognisable by his round green hat and goat mount

Dorje Semba (S: Vajrasattva) – Buddha of purification

Dorje Shugden – controversial protector deity outlawed by the Dalai Lama

Drölma (S: Tara) – a female meditational deity who is a manifestation of the enlightened mind of all buddhas; she is sometimes referred to as the mother of all buddhas, and has many aspects, but is most often seen as Green Tara or as Drölkar (White Tara)

Dromtönpa – 11th-century disciple of Jowo-je *(Atisha)* who founded the Kadampa order and Reting Monastery

Dusum Sangye – trinity of the Past, Present and Future Buddhas

Ekajati – see *Tsechigma*

Gesar – a legendary king and also the name of an epic concerning his fabulous exploits; the king's empire is known as Ling, and thus the stories, which are usually sung and told by professional bards, are known as the *Stories of Ling*

Gompo Gur – a form of Nagpo Chenpo (Mahakala) and protector of the Sakyapa school

Guru Rinpoche – credited with having suppressed demons and other malevolent forces in order to introduce Buddhism into Tibet during the 8th century; in the Nyingmapa order he is revered as the Second Buddha

Hayagriva – see *Tamdrin*

Jamchen Chöde – disciple of Tsongkhapa and founder of Sera Monastery; also known as Sakya Yeshe

Jampa (S: Maitreya) – the Buddha of Loving Kindness; also the Future Buddha, the fifth of the 1000 buddhas who will descend to earth (Sakyamuni or Sakya Thukpa was the fourth)

Jampelyang (S: Manjushri) – the Bodhisattva of Insight; usually depicted holding a sword (which symbolises discriminative awareness) in one hand and a book (which symbolises his mastery of all knowledge) in the other

Jamyang Chöje – founder of Drepung Monastery

Je Rinpoche – see *Tsongkhapa*

Jowo-je (S: Atisha) – 11th-century Buddhist scholar from contemporary Bengal whose arrival in Tibet at the invitation of the king of Guge was a catalyst for the revival of Buddhism on the high plateau

Jowo Sakyamuni – the most revered image of Sakyamuni (Sakya Thukpa) in Tibet, it depicts the

Historical Buddha at the age of 12 and is kept in the Jokhang in Lhasa

Karmapa – a lineage (17 so far) of spiritual leaders of the Karma Kagyupa; also known as the Black Hats

Khenlop Chösum – Trinity of Guru Rinpoche, Trisong Detsen and Shantarakshita, found at Samye Monastery

Kunga Gyaltsen – see *Sakya Pandita*

Langdharma – the 9th-century Tibetan king accused of having persecuted Buddhists

Lokapalas – see *Chökyong*

Longchen Rabjampa – (1308–63) *Nyingmapa* and *Dzogchen* teacher and writer, revered as a manifestation of Jampelyang; also known as Longchenpa

Machik Labdronma – (1031–1129) female yogini connected to Shugsheb Nunnery

Maitreya – see *Jampa*

Mahakala – Sanskrit name for Nagpo Chenpo

Manjushri – see *Jampelyang*

Marpa – 11th-century ascetic whose disciple, Milarepa, founded the Kagyupa order

Mikyöba (S: Akshobhya) – the Buddha of the State of Perfected Consciousness, or Perfect Cognition; literally 'unchanging', 'the immutable one'

Milarepa – (1040–1123) disciple of Marpa and founder of the Kagyupa order; renowned for his songs

Nagpo Chenpo – The Great Black One, wrathful manifestation of Chenresig that carries echoes of the Indian god Shiva; see *Mahakala*.

Namgyelma – three-faced, eight-armed female deity and one of the three deities of longevity

Namse (S: Vairocana) – Buddha of Enlightened Consciousness, generally white;

also a renowned Tibetan translator

Namtöse (S: Vaishravana) – the Guardian of the North, one of the Lokapalas or Four Guardian Kings

Nechung – protector deity of Tibet and the Dalai Lamas; manifested in the State Oracle, who is traditionally installed at Nechung Monastery

Nyenchen Tanglha – mountain spirit and protector deity that has its roots in Bön

Nyentri Tsenpo – legendary first king of Tibet

Öpagme (S: Amitabha) – the Buddha of Perfected Perception; literally 'infinite light'

Palden Lhamo (S: Shri Devi) – special protector of Lhasa, the Dalai Lama and the Gelugpa order; the female counterpart of Nagpo Chenpo (Mahakala)

Panchen Lama – literally 'guru and great teacher'; the lineage is associated with Tashilhunpo Monastery, Shigatse, and goes back to the 17th century; the Panchen Lama is a manifestation of Öpagme (Amitabha)

Pehar – oracle and protector of the Buddhist state, depicted with six arms, wearing a round hat and riding a snow lion

Rahulla – Dzogchen deity with nine heads, eyes all over his body, a mouth in his belly and the lower half of a serpent (coiled on the dead body of ego)

Ralpachen – 9th-century king whose assassination marked the end of the Yarlung Valley dynasty

Rigsum Gonpo – trinity of bodhisattvas consisting of Chenresig (Avalokiteshvara), Jampelyang (Manjushri) and Chana Dorje (Vajrapani)

Rinchen Zangpo – (958–1055), the Great Translator, who travelled to India for 17 years and established

monasteries across Ladakh, Spiti and Western Tibet

Sakyamuni (S) – literally the 'sage of Sakya'; the founder of Buddhism, the Historical Buddha; known in Tibetan as Sakya Thukpa; see also *Siddhartha Gautama* and *buddha*

Sakya Pandita (S) – literally 'scholar from Sakya'; former abbot of Sakya Monastery who established the priest-patron system with the Mongols; also known as Kunga Gyaltsen

Sakya Thukpa – see *Sakyamuni*

Samvara – a wrathful multi-armed deity and manifestation of Sakyamuni (Demchok in Tibetan)

Shantarakshita – Indian scholar of the 8th century and first abbot of Samye Monastery; Kende Shewa in Tibetan

Shenrab – founder of the Bön faith

Shiromo – Bönpo deity, the equivalent of Sakyamuni

Shri Devi – see *Palden Lhamo*

Siddhartha Gautama (S) – the personal name of the Historical Buddha; see also *Sakyamuni* (Sakya Thukpa)

Songtsen Gampo – the 7th-century king associated with the introduction of Buddhism to Tibet

Tamdrin (S: Hayagriva) – literally 'horse necked'; a wrathful meditational deity and manifestation of Chenresig, usually associated with the Nyingmapa order

Tangtong Gyelpo – (1385–1464) Tibetan yogi, treasure finder *(terton)*, bridge builder, medic and developer of Tibetan opera; often depicted holding a chain link in his hands

Tara – see *Drölma*

Tenzin Gyatso – the 14th and current Dalai Lama

Terdak Lingpa – founder of Mindroling Monastery

Trisong Detsen – 8th-century Tibetan king; founder of Samye Monastery

Tsechigma (S: Ekajati) – protectress with one eye, one tooth and one breast, associated with the Dzogchen movement

Tsepame (S: Amitayus) – a meditational deity associated with longevity; literally 'limitless life'; often featured in a trinity with Drölma (Tara) and Namgyelma (Vijaya)

Tseringma – protector goddess of Mt Everest, depicted riding a snow lion

Tsongkhapa – 14th-century founder of the Gelugpa order and Ganden Monastery, also known as 'Je Rinpoche'

Vairocana – see *Namse*

Vaishravana – see *Namtöse*

Vajradhara – see *Dorje Chang*

Vajrapani – see *Chana Dorje*

Vajrasattva – see *Dorje Semba*

Vijaya – Sanskrit name for Namgyelma

Wencheng – Chinese wife of King Songtsen Gampo; called Wencheng Konjo in Tibetan

Yama (S) – Lord of Death, who resides in sky burial sites

Yamantaka – see *Dorje Jigje*

Yeshe Tsogyel – female consort of Guru Rinpoche and one-time wife of King Trisong Detsen

General Terms

Amdo – a traditional province of Tibet, now Qīnghǎi province

AMS – acute mountain sickness; often referred to as altitude sickness

ani – Tibetan for 'nun', as in ani gompa (nunnery)

arhat (S) – literally 'worthy one'; a person who has

achieved nirvana; the Tibetan term is 'neten'

Bardo – as detailed in the *Tibetan Book of the Dead*, this term refers to the intermediate stages between death and rebirth

Barkhor – an intermediate circumambulation circuit, or kora, but most often specifically the intermediate circuit around the Jokhang temple of Lhasa

binguan (M) – guesthouse or hotel

Black Hat – strictly speaking, this refers to the black hat embellished with gold that was presented to the second Karmapa of the Karma Kagyupa order of Tsurphu Monastery by a Mongol prince, and worn ceremoniously by all subsequent incarnations of the Karmapa; by extension the black hat represents the Karma Kagyupa order

Bö – Tibetans' name for their own land, sometimes written 'Bod' or 'Po'

Bodhgaya – the place in contemporary Bihar, India, where Sakyamuni, the Historical Buddha, attained enlightenment

bodhisattva (S) – literally 'enlightenment hero'; the bodhisattva chooses not to take the step to nirvana, being motivated to stay within the Wheel of Life by compassion for all sentient beings

Bön – the indigenous religion of Tibet and the Himalayan borderlands; in its ancient form its main components were royal burial rites, the cult of indigenous deities and magical practices; in the 11th century, Bön was systematised along Buddhist lines and it is this form that survives today

Bönpo – a practitioner of Bön

buddha (S) – literally 'awakened one'; a being who through spiritual training has broken free of all illusion and karmic consequences and is 'enlightened'; most often specifically the Historical Buddha, Sakyamuni

Büton – suborder of Tibetan Buddhism based on the teachings of Büton Rinchen Drup, the 14th-century compiler of the major Buddhist texts; associated with Shalu Monastery, near Shigatse

CAAC – Civil Aviation Authority of China

chakje – handprint of a deity or a religious figure made in rock

chaktsal – ritual prostration

chaktsal gang – prostration point

cham – a ritual dance carried out by monks and lamas, usually at festivals; all participants except the central lama are masked

chang – Tibetan barley beer

Changtang – vast plains of north Tibet extending into Xīnjiāng and Qīnghǎi; the world's largest and highest plateau

chö – see *dharma*

chömay – butter lamp

chörten – Tibetan for stupa; usually used as reliquary for the cremated remains of important lamas

chu – river, stream, brook etc

chuba – long-sleeved sheepskin cloak

CITS – China International Travel Service

CTS – China Travel Service

cun (M) – village; 'tson' in Tibetan

dakini – see *khandroma*

dharma (S) – 'chö' in Tibetan, and sometimes translated as 'law', this very broad term covers the truths expounded by Sakyamuni, the Buddhist teachings, the path and goal of nirvana; in effect it is the 'law' that must be understood, followed and achieved in order for one to be a Buddhist

doring – stele; carved obelisk commemorating a historic event or edict

dorje – literally 'diamond' or 'thunderbolt'; a metaphor for the indestructible, indivisible nature of buddhahood; also a Tantric hand-held sceptre symbolising 'skilful means'

drokpa – nomad

drubkhang – meditation chamber

dukhang – assembly hall

dukkha (S) – suffering, the essential condition of all life

dungkhar – conch shell

dürtro – sky-burial site

dzo – domesticated cross between a bull and a female yak

Dzogchen – the Great Perfection teachings associated with the Nyingmapa order

dzong – fort

Eightfold Path – one of the Four Noble Truths taught by Sakyamuni; the path that must be taken to achieve enlightenment and liberation from the Wheel of Life

FIT office – Family (or Foreign) and Independent Traveller office

Four Noble Truths – as stated in the first speech given by Sakyamuni after he achieved enlightenment, the Four Noble Truths are: the truth that all life is suffering; the truth that suffering originates in desire; the truth that desire may be extinguished; and the truth that there is a path to this end

Ganden (S) – the pure land of Jampa (Maitreya) and the seat of the Gelugpa order; 'Tushita' in Tibetan

garuda – mythological bird associated with Hinduism; in Tibetan Tantric Buddhism it is seen as a wrathful force that transforms malevolent influences; 'khyung' in Sanskrit

gau – an amulet or 'portable shrine' worn around the

neck, containing the image of an important spiritual figure, usually the Dalai Lama

Gelugpa – major order of Tibetan Buddhism, associated with the Dalai Lamas, the Panchen Lamas, and the Drepung, Sera, Ganden and Tashilhunpo Monasteries; founded by Tsongkhapa in the 14th century and sometimes known as the Yellow Hats

geshe – title awarded on completion of the highest level of study (something like a doctorate) that monks may undertake after completing their full indoctrinal vows; usually associated with the Gelugpa order

gompa – monastery

gönkhang – protector chapel

Guge – a 9th-century kingdom of western Tibet

guru (S) – spiritual teacher; literally 'heavy'; the Tibetan equivalent is lama

Hinayana (S) – also called Theravada, this is a major school of Buddhism that follows the original teachings of the Historical Buddha, Sakyamuni, and places less importance on the compassionate bodhisattva ideal and more on individual enlightenment; see also *Mahayana*

Jokhang – situated in Lhasa, this is the most sacred and one of the most ancient of Tibet's temples; also known as the Tsuglhakhang

Kadampa – order of Tibetan Buddhism based on the teachings of the Indian scholar Atisha (Jowo-je); the school was a major influence on the Gelugpa order

Kagyupa – order of Tibetan Buddhism that traces its lineage back through Milarepa and Marpa and eventually to the Indian mahasiddhas; divided into numerous suborders, the most famous of which is the Karma Kagyupa, or the Karmapa; also known as Kagyud

kangtsang – monastic residential quarters

Kangyur – the Tibetan Buddhist canon; its complement is the *Tengyur*

karma (S) – action and its consequences, the psychic 'imprint' that action leaves on the mind and that continues into further rebirths; the term is found in both Hinduism and Buddhism, and may be likened to the law of cause and effect

Karma Kagyupa – suborder of the Kagyupa order, established by Gampopa and Dusum Khyenpa in the 12th century; represented by the Black Hat

Kashag – the cabinet of the Gelugpa lamaist government

kathak – prayer scarf; used as a ritual offering or as a gift

Kham – traditional eastern Tibetan province; much of it is now part of western Sìchuān and northwestern Yúnnán

Khampa – a person from Kham

khandroma (S: dakini) – literally 'sky dancer' or 'sky walker'; a flying angel-like astral being that communicates between the worlds of Buddhas, man and demons

Khangjung – Land of Snows

khenpo – abbot

kora – ritual circumambulation circuit; pilgrimage circuit

kumbum – literally '100,000 images', this is a chörten that contains statuary and paintings; the most famous in Tibet is the Gyantse Kumbum in Tsang

la – mountain pass

lama – literally 'unsurpassed'; Tibetan equivalent of guru; a title bestowed on monks of particularly high spiritual attainment

lamaism – term used by early Western writers on the subject of Tibet to describe Tibetan Buddhism; also used by the Chinese in the term 'lamajiao', literally 'lama religion'

lamrim – the stages on the path to enlightenment; a graduated approach to enlightenment as expounded by Tsongkhapa; associated with the Gelugpa order

lapse – a cairn

lha – life spirit; it may also be present in inanimate objects such as lakes, mountains and trees

lhakhang – chapel

ling – Tibetan term meaning 'royal', usually associated with lesser, outlying temples

lingkhor – an outer pilgrimage circuit; famously, the outer pilgrimage of Lhasa

Losar – Tibetan New Year

lu (M) – road; see also *naga*

mahasiddha – literally 'of great spiritual accomplishment'; a Tantric practitioner who has reached a high level of awareness; there are 84 famous mahasiddhas; the Tibetan term is 'drubchen'

Mahayana (S) – the other major school of Buddhism along with Hinayana; this school emphasises compassion and the altruism of the bodhisattva who remains on the Wheel of Life for the sake of all sentient beings

mandala – a circular representation of the three-dimensional world of a meditational deity; used as a meditation device; the Tibetan term is 'kyilkhor'

mani – prayer

mani lhakhang – small chapel housing a single large prayer wheel

mani stone – a stone with the mantra 'om mani padme hum' ('hail to the jewel in the lotus') carved on it

mani wall – a wall made with mani stones

mantra (S) – literally 'protection of the mind'; one of the Tantric devices used to achieve identity with a meditational deity and break through the world of illusion; a series of syllables recited as the pure sound made by an enlightened being

meditational deity – a deified manifestation of the enlightened mind with which, according to Tantric ritual, the adept seeks union and thus experience of enlightenment

momo – Tibetan dumpling

Mönlam – a major Lhasa festival established by Tsongkhapa

Mt Meru – the sacred mountain at the centre of the universe; also known as Sumeru

naga (S) – water spirits that may take the form of serpents or semi-humans; the latter can be seen in images of the *naga* kings; the Tibetan term is 'lu'

nangkhor – inner circumambulation circuit, usually within the interior of a temple or monastic assembly hall, and taking in various chapels en route

neten – see *arhat*

Newari – the people of the Nepali Buddhist kingdoms in the Kathmandu Valley

Ngorpa – sub-school of the Sakya school of Tibetan Buddhism founded by Ngorchen Kunga Sangpo and based at Ngor Monastery in Tsang

Ngari – ancient name for the province of western Tibet; later incorporated into Ütsang.

nirvana (S) – literally 'beyond sorrow'; an end to desire and suffering, and an end to the cycle of rebirth

Norbulingka – the summer palace of the Dalai Lamas in Lhasa

Nyingmapa – the earliest order of Tibetan Buddhism, based largely on the Buddhism brought to Tibet by Guru Rinpoche

om mani padme hum – this mantra means 'hail to the jewel in the lotus' and is associated with Chenresig, patron deity of Tibet

oracle – in Tibetan Buddhism an oracle serves as a medium for protective deities, as in the State Oracle of Nechung Monastery near Drepung, Lhasa; the State Oracle was consulted on all important matters of state

Pandita – a title conferred on great scholars of Buddhism, as in Sakya Pandita

parikrama – the Hindu equivalent of a kora

PLA – People's Liberation Army (Chinese army)

PRC – People's Republic of China

protector deities – deities who can manifest themselves in either male or female forms and serve to protect Buddhist teachings and followers; they may be either wrathful aspects of enlightened beings or worldly powers who have been tamed by *Tantric* masters; the Tibetan term is 'chojung'

PSB – Public Security Bureau

puk – cave

pure lands – otherworldly realms that are the domains of buddhas; realms completely free of suffering, and in the popular Buddhist imagination are probably something like the Christian heaven

Qiang – proto-Tibetan tribes that troubled the borders of the Chinese empire

Qomolangma – Tibetan name for Mt Everest as transliterated by the Chinese; also spelt 'Chomolangma'

Qu (M) – administrative district

rangjung – self-manifesting or self-arising; for example, a rock spire could be a rangjung chörten

rebirth – a condition of the Wheel of Life; all beings experience limitless rebirths until they achieve enlightenment

regent – a representative of an incarnate lama who presides over a monastic community during the lama's minority; regents came to play an important political role in the Gelugpa lamaist government

ri – mountain

Rinpoche – literally 'high in esteem', a title bestowed on highly revered lamas; such lamas are usually incarnate but this is not a requirement

ritrö – hermitage

RMB – acronym for Renminbi or 'people's money', the currency of China

rogyapas – the 'body breakers' who prepare bodies for sky burial

sadhu – an Indian ascetic who has renounced all attachments

Saga Dawa – festival held at the full moon of the fourth lunar month to celebrate the enlightenment of Sakyamuni

Sakyapa – Tibetan Buddhist order associated with Sakya Monastery and founded in the 11th century; also known as the Red Hats

samsara (S) – 'kyor dumi' in Tibetan; the cycle of birth, death and rebirth

Samye – the first Buddhist monastery in Tibet, founded by King Trisong Detsen in the 8th century

sang – incense

sangha (S) – community of Buddhist monks or nuns

sangkang – pot-bellied incense burners

Sanskrit – ancient language of India; a classical mode of expression with the status that Latin had in earlier Western society

self-arising – thought to have been created naturally (ie not by humans); often applied to rock carvings; see also *rangjung*

serdung – golden funeral stupa

shabje – footprint of a deity or a religious figure made in rock that has become a sacred icon

Shambhala – the mythical great northern paradise, believed to be near the Kunlun mountains

Shangshung – ancient kingdom of western Tibet and place of origin of the Bön faith

shedra – Buddhist college

sky burial – funerary practice of chopping up the corpses of the dead in designated high places (dürtro) and leaving them for the birds

spirit trap – collection of coloured threads wrapped around a wooden frame, used to trap evil spirits

stupa – see *chörten*

sutra (S) – Buddhist scriptures that record the teachings of the Historical Buddha, Sakyamuni

suzerainty – system whereby a dominant power controls a region or country's foreign relations but allows it sovereignty in its internal affairs

Tantra – scriptures and oral lineages associated with Tantric Buddhism

Tantric – of Tantric Buddhism, a movement combining mysticism with Buddhist scripture

TAR – Tibetan Autonomous Region

tarchok – string of prayer flags

Tengyur – a Tibetan Buddhist canonical text of collected commentaries on the teachings of Sakyamuni

terma – 'discovered' or 'revealed' teachings; teachings that have been hidden until the world is ready to receive them; one of the

most famous *termas* is the *Tibetan Book of the Dead*

terton – discoverer of *terma*, sometimes referred to as a 'treasure finder'

thamzing (M) – 'struggle sessions', a misconceived Chinese tool for changing the ideological orientation of individuals; ultimately a coercive tool that encouraged deceit under the threat of torture

thangka – a Tibetan religious painting usually framed by a silk brocade

Theravada – see *Hinayana*

thugpa – traditional Tibetan noodle dish

torana – halo-like garland that surrounds Buddhist statues

torma – offerings of sculptured *tsampa*

trapa – Tibetan for 'monk'

tratsang – monastic college

Tripa – the post of abbot at Ganden Monastery; head of the Gelugpa order

trulku – incarnate lama, sometimes inaccurately called a 'Living Buddha' by the Chinese

tsampa – roasted-barley flour, traditional staple of the Tibetan people

tsangkhang – inner chapel

tsangpo – large river

tsatsa – stamped clay religious icons

tsenyi lhakhang – debating hall

tso – 'lake'

tsogchen – cathedral or great chapel, also an assembly hall

tsuglhakhang – literally 'grand temple', but often specifically the Jokhang of Lhasa

TTB – Tibetan Tourism Bureau

Ütsang – the area comprising the provinces of Ü and Tsang, also incorporating Ngari, or western Tibet; effectively central Tibet, the political, historical and

agricultural heartland of Tibet

Vajrayana (S) – literally the 'diamond vehicle', a branch of Mahayana Buddhism that finds a more direct route to bodhisattvahood through identification with meditational deities; vajrayana is the Sanskrit term for the form of Buddhism found in Tibet, known in the West as tantrism

Wheel of Life – this term refers to the cyclical nature of existence and the six realms where rebirth take place; often depicted in monasteries

xian (M) – country town

xiang (M) – village

yabyum – Tantric sexual union, symbolising the mental union of female insight and male compassion; fierce deities are often depicted in yabyum with their consorts

yidam – see *meditational deity;* may also have the function of being a personal protector deity that looks over an individual or family

yogin – an adept of Tibetan Buddhist techniques for achieving a union with the fundamental nature of reality ('yoga' in Sanskrit); the techniques include meditation and identification with a meditational deity

yuan (M) – unit of Chinese currency

zhaodaisuo (M) – guesthouse, usually a basic hostel

Food & Drink Terms

bābǎo wǎnzi (M) – meatballs with eight delicacies

bāozi (M) – steamed meat buns

beeyar – beer (bottled)

bīngde (M) – ice-cold
bōcài (M) – spinach
böja – butter tea
butogchu – mineral water

chá (M) – tea
cha süma – butter tea
châng – beer (home-brew)
chǎomiànpiàn (M) – fried noodle squares
chayma kara/chini – sugar
chu khöma – boiled water

dànhuā tāng (M) – egg soup

fānqié chǎodàn (M) – fried egg and tomato

gānbàn miàn (M) – fried Muslim noodles and beef
gānbiān sìjìdòu (M) – dry-fried runner beans
gōngbào jīdīng (M) – spicy chicken with peanuts
gongdre ngöpâ – omelette
guōbā ròupiàn (M) – pork and sizzling rice crust
gyâthuk – fried noodles

hóngshāo qiézi (M) – red-cooked eggplant
huíguō ròu (M) – double-cooked fatty pork
húntun (tāng) (M) – won-ton (soup)

jiācháng dòufu (M) – home-style tofu
jīdàn chǎofàn (M) – fried rice with egg

jīngjiàng ròusī (M) – pork in soy sauce
kāi shuǐ (M) – boiled water
kuàng quán shuǐ (M) – mineral water

lāmiàn (M) – handmade string noodles

málà dòufu (M) – spicy tofu
mápó dòufu (M) – pock-marked Mother Chen's bean curd
mǐfàn (M) – steamed white rice
momo – dumplings
mùěr ròu (M) – 'wooden ear' mushrooms and pork

niúròu miàn (M) – beef noodles in a soup
niúròusī chǎofàn (M) – fried rice with beef

píjiǔ (M) – beer

qīngcài (M) – bok choy; also called *yóucài*
qīngjiāo ròupiàn (M) – pork and green peppers

rède (M) – hot

shāguō mǐxiàn (M) – vermicelli noodles in casserole pot
sha-momo – yak-meat dumplings
shemdre – rice, potato and yak-meat stew
sho – yoghurt

shūcài chǎofàn (M) – fried rice with vegetables
shūcài chǎomiàn (M) – fried noodles and vegetables
shuǐjiǎo (M) – boiled dumplings
shuǐzhǔ yú (M) – boiled fish in a fiery sauce
sùchǎo biǎndòu (M) – fried green beans
sùchǎo sùcài (M) – fried vegetables

tángcù lǐjī (M) – sweet and sour pork fillets
thugpa – thick noodle soup
tsampa – roasted-barley flour
tsay ngöpâ – stir-fried vegetable dishes
tse-momo – vegetable dumplings
tsha – salt

xiāngzhá jīkuài (M) – crispy chicken
xiǎo báicài (M) – baby bok choy
xīlánhuā (M) – broccoli
xīnjiāng bànmiàn (M) – xinjiang noodles

yâksha – yak meat
yóucài (M) – bok choy; also called *qīngcài*
yúxiāng qiézi (M) – 'fish-scented' eggplant
yúxiāng ròusī (M) – 'fish-scented' pork

behind the scenes

SEND US YOUR FEEDBACK

We love to hear from travellers – your comments keep us on our toes and help make our books better. Our well-travelled team reads every word on what you loved or loathed about this book. Although we cannot reply individually to postal submissions, we always guarantee that your feedback goes straight to the appropriate authors, in time for the next edition. Each person who sends us information is thanked in the next edition – and the most useful submissions are rewarded with a free book.

Visit **lonelyplanet.com/contact** to submit your updates and suggestions or to ask for help. Our award-winning website also features inspirational travel stories, news and discussions.

Note: We may edit, reproduce and incorporate your comments in Lonely Planet products such as guidebooks, websites and digital products, so let us know if you don't want your comments reproduced or your name acknowledged. For a copy of our privacy policy visit lonelyplanet.com/privacy.

OUR READERS

Many thanks to the travellers who used the last edition and wrote to us with helpful hints, useful advice and interesting anecdotes:

Myriam Altmeyer, Arratee Ayuttacorn, Patrick Bruyere, Martin Checinski, Claus Drunkenmölle, Rainer Engels, Pescia Gerald, Amy Iacopi, Martin Irle, Ralpha Jacobson, Michelle Johnson, Markus Kalén, David Kerkhoff, Cor Keuning, Frederick Kilner, Judy Magnussen, Cristina N, Lidia Pieri, Thomas Plesser, Ine Reijnen, David Simpson, Eline, Michelle & John Small, Janet Spence, Brian Stepanic, Jackie Tang, Emanuela Tasinato, Steve & Joanne Tibbetts, Christiaan van der Blij, Frank van der Heyden, Remmelt van der Wal, Julie Washer, Mervyn Williams, Julianne Ye, David Zucker

AUTHOR THANKS

Bradley Mayhew

To Bill of Tibetan Connections and Tenzin and Xiaojin for help arranging my trip. Lumbum was a great guide. Cheers to Andre and Alyson for another fine trip and to university chum Garth Edwards for his info from his out-there Ngari–Xinjiang trip. To Tashi at Yabshi Phunkang, Nyima and Tashi at Dropenling, and Lobsang and Chris Jones, who always offers helpful tips. Also to fine co-authors John, Daniel and Mike, and to Liz Heynes for helping with style issues.

Michael Kohn

A warm thanks to the kind Tibetan people who made the experience worthwhile. Special thanks to Tenzin at FIT for keeping things on track during research, and to my host at Everest Base Camp for finding me extra blankets! Thanks to coordinating author Bradley for encouragement and camaraderie, and to fellow author Daniel. Behind the scenes, thanks to Emily Wolman and Liz Heynes. And thanks to Baigal and Molly, who make coming home the best part of the trip.

Daniel McCrohan

Massive thanks to Xiao Bianr for coming to the rescue when my first Tibet permit was denied. Equally massive thanks, for all the fact-checking, translating and general suggestions, to Pazu Kong of the Spinn Cafe. For other great tips, thanks to Wangden Tsering of Snow Lion Tours and Jamin Losang. In LP land, big thanks to Megan Fraser, Emily and Bradley. And finally, back home: Taotao, you're amazing; Dudu and Yoyo, you light up our lives.

John Vincent Bellezza

Travelling in Tibet for Lonely Planet is as much a social enterprise as it is a physical journey. For all those who pointed the way, offered moral support or cups of tea, I doff my cap in thanks. I especially want to express gratitude to my vermillion-clad teachers of Tibetan history and culture, individuals of the highest order.

ACKNOWLEDGMENTS

Climate map data adapted from Peel MC, Finlayson BL & McMahon TA (2007) 'Updated World Map of the Köppen-Geiger Climate Classification', *Hydrology and Earth System Sciences*, 11, 163344.

Cover photograph: Tibetan woman herding yaks, between Lhasa and Shigatse/Keren Su/Lonely Planet Images. Many of the images in this guide are available for licensing from Lonely Planet Images: www.lonely planetimages.com.

THIS BOOK

This 8th edition of Lonely Planet's *Tibet* guidebook was researched and written by Bradley Mayhew, Michael Kohn, Daniel McCrohan and John Vincent Bellezza. Xiao Bianr assisted with research. The previous edition was written by Bradley Mayhew, John Vincent Bellezza and Robert Kelly. This guidebook was commissioned in Lonely Planet's Oakland office and produced by the following:

Commissioning Editor Emily K Wolman

Coordinating Editors Pete Cruttenden, Branislava Vladisavljevic

Coordinating Cartographer Andrew Smith

Coordinating Layout Designer Carol Jackson

Managing Editors Liz Heynes, Annelies Mertens

Managing Cartographers Shahara Ahmed, Alison Lyall, Adrian Persoglia

Managing Layout Designer Celia Wood

Assisting Editors Holly Alexander, Carolyn Boicos, Jocelyn Harewood, Helen Yeates

Assisting Cartographers Ildiko Bogdanovits, Julie Dodkins

Cover Research Naomi Parker, lonelyplanetimages. com

Internal Image Research Rebecca Skinner

Expert Language Advice Michael Essex (Tibetan), Tim Lu (Mandarin)

Thanks to Mark Adams, Imogen Bannister, Xiao Bianr, David Connolly, Melanie Dankel, Stefanie Di Trocchio, Heather Dickson, Janine Eberle, Joshua Geoghegan, Mark Germanchis, Michelle Glynn, Lauren Hunt, Laura Jane, David Kemp, Lisa Knights, Rebecca Lalor, Nic Lehman, Katie Lynch, John Mazzocchi, Wayne Murphy, Piers Pickard, Lachlan Ross, Michael Ruff, Julie Sheridan, Laura Stansfeld, John Taufa, Sam Trafford, Juan Winata, Nick Wood

index

1959 uprising 287

A

accommodation 334-5, *see also individual locations*
activities 20, 335-6, *see also individual activities*
acute mountain sickness 43, 154, 168, 364-5
agriculture 300-2
air travel
regional air routes 353
to/from major Chinese cities 268-9, 350-2, 353
to/from Nepal 265, 350, 352-3
to/from Tibet 352-3
within Tibet 357
Ali 173-5, **174**
Alien Travel Permit 31
altitude sickness, *see* acute mountain sickness
Amitabha 317
Amitayus 317
amoebic dysentery 363-4
AMS, *see* acute mountain sickness
animals 295-8, *see also individual animals*
architecture 325-7
area codes 17, 345
arts 322-9
books 323, 327
Atisha 93, 94, 277, 278, 315
ATMs 342
Avalokiteshvara 317-18
avian influenza (bird flu) 363

B

Baber 152-4
Baha Gompa 197-8
Bakong Scripture Printing Press & Monastery 226
bargaining 342-3

Map Pages **p000**
Image Pages **p000**

Barkhor area 42-5, **48-50**
Barkhor circuit 45, **11**
Barkhor Square 43-5
Bathang 229
bathhouses 336
bathrooms 345
Bāyī 199-200, **199**
begging 306
bicycle travel, *see* cycling
bird flu 363
birds 295-6
bird-watching 296
Biru 214
bodhisattvas 317-18
body language 301, 304
Bön 313, 315-16
Bönri 200
bookjacking 302
books, *see also* literature
arts 323, 327
biographies 272-3, 290
Buddhism 307
cooking 338
Dalai Lama (present) 289
Dalai Lamas 272
health 294, 362-3
history 275, 281, 285, 286, 287, 289
Lake Manasarovar 178
Mt Kailash 178
travelogues 282, 284
border crossings 162, 217, 336
British-Tibetan relations 136, 282-5
Buchu Monastery 201
Buddha, the 308
buddhas 316-17
Buddhism 307-21, *see also* Dalai Lamas, Panchen Lamas
books 307
concepts 280, 282, 302, 308-10
historical figures 320-1
history 276-8
important figures 316-20
in Tibet 312-16
protector deities 318-20
schools of Buddhism 310-12
symbols 308, 313
budget 16
Bumpa Ri 82
bus travel 359
business hours 336
butter lamps 309

C

camping 334
car travel 17, 32, 359, **12**
carpets 328
cave paintings (Dungkar) 185
caves 93, 109, 112, 120, 157-8

cell phones 17, 345
Chakrasamvara 319-20
cham 322-3
Chamdo 205-9, 288, **206-7**
Chana Dorje 319
Changtang Nature Reserve 296
Chayab Monastery 211
Chéngdū 261, 265-9, **266-7**
travel to/from 350-2, 353
Chenresig 317-18
children, travel with 336
Chim-puk Hermitage 118-19
Chinese language 371-4
Chinese occupation of Tibet 286-92
Chinese-Tibetan relations 272-3, 274-5, 305-6, 330-1
Chingwa Tagtse Dzong 124-5
Chiu Monastery 179, 260
Chökyong 318-19
cholera 364
Chongye 124
Chongye burial mounds 124
Chongye Valley 124-5, **123**
Chörten Kangnyi 252
chörtens 325-6
cinema 273
circumambulation 201
climate 16, 230, 336, *see also individual regions*
climate change 298, 349
clothing
for travellers 92
for trekkers 231
souvenirs 74
traditional Tibetan 304
consulates 337
courses (language) 340
crafts 75, 323, 328-9
credit cards 342
cultural considerations 92, 272, 301, 304, 305
Cultural Revolution 289-90
culture 19, 272-3, 299-306, 331
currency 16, 17, 221, 341
customs regulations 336-7
cycling 335, 357-9

D

Dala Gong 225
Dalai Lama (present) 13, 285, 286-92, 330-1
Dalai Lamas 62-3, 272, 279-85
fifth Dalai Lama 280, 293, 320
dance 322-3
dangers, *see* safe travel
Darchen 176-7
Dardo 217-21, **220**
Dawa-tso 172

death 302, *see also* sky burials
Demchok 319-20
demoness-subduing temples 56
departure tax 350
Derge 226-7
Deyang College 82
dharma wheel 308
Dhyani buddhas 317
digital photography 343
Dipamkara 317
disabilities, travellers with 345-6
discounts 335
documents, *see* passports, travel
    permits, visas
Dode Valley 86
Dodoka Gompa skull wall 214
dogs 344
Dorje Drak Monastery 111-12
Dorje Jigje 319
Drak Yangdzong 112-13
    caves 112
Drak Yerpa 92-3
    caves 93
Draksum-tso 201-3
Dram 160-2, **160**
drama 322-3
Drampa Gyang Temple 146
Dratang Monastery 113
Drepung Monastery 78-83, **80-1**, 8
Drigung Qu 107-8
Drigung Til Monastery 108-9
drinks 339
    water 295, 366
    when trekking 236
    yak-butter tea **7**
driving, *see* car travel
drokpas 102
Drölma 318
Drölma Lhakhang 93-4
Drölma Valley 215
Dromochen Lhakhang 112
Dungkar 185-6
Dung-tso 172
Dzong Kumbum 112
dzongs 18

E
eastern Tibet, *see* Kham
ecology, *see* environment
economy 272-3
education 292, 331
Eight Auspicious Symbols 314, **314-5**
electricity 341

Map Pages **p000**
Image Pages **p000**

elevations 236
embassies 337
emergencies 17
endangered species 298
environment 293-8
environmental hazards 364-6
environmental issues 297-8
ethnic groups 304-5, **305**
etiquette tips 92, 272, 301, 304, 305
events, *see* festivals
Everest Base Camp 155, *see also*
    Mt Everest
    trekking to Tingri 247-50, **249**
exchange rates 17
exiled communities 301
    Tibetan government in exile 290-2,
    330-1
explorers 158-9, 166, 178, 277

F
farming 300-2
fauna, *see* animals, birds
festivals 21-3, **8**, **19**, *see also*
    individual festivals
fifth Dalai Lama 280, 293, 320
films 273
flora, *see* plants
food 337-9
    books 338
    vocabulary 370, 373, 380
    when trekking 235-6
forts 18
Four Harmonious Brothers 310
Four Noble Truths 310
Friendship Highway 353
    kilometre markers 148-9
frostbite 365

G
Ganden Monastery 89-92, **90-1**, 9
    trekking to Samye Monastery
    237-40, **238**, 9
Gangpo Ri 120
Gângzî 223-4
Garuda Valley 181
Garzê 223-4
gay travellers 339-40
Gegye 173
Gelugpa order 279-80, 315-16
Genghis Khan 278
geography 293-5
geology 293-5
Gertse 172
giardiasis 364
gods 316-20, **317-19**
Gomang College 82
Gongkar 109-11
Gongkar Chöde Monastery 109-10

Gongkar Xian 110
Gossul Monastery 179
government in exile 290-2, 330-1
Guge Kingdom 166, 180-5, **9**
Guru Rinpoche 179, 320
Gyalwa Ri Nga 317
Gyama Valley 106
Gyantse 131-5, **132**
Gyantse Dzong 133
Gyantse Horse-Racing Festival 22, **19**
Gyantse Kumbum 132-3, **10**
Gyelpo Gongkar 106

H
Han immigration 292, 305-6
handicrafts 75, 323, 328-9
Hayagriva 319
health 361-7
    books 294, 362-3
    insurance 361
    internet resources 362
    Tibetan medicine 366-7
    vaccinations 361-2
    when trekking 233
heat exhaustion 365-6
Hepo Ri 117-18
hiking, *see* trekking
history 274-92
    1959 uprising 287
    books 275, 281, 285, 286, 287, 289
    British-Tibetan relations 136, 282-5
    Buddhism 276-8, 313-16, 320-1
    Chinese occupation 286-92
    Chinese-Tibetan relations 272-3,
    274-5, 305-6, 330-1
    Cultural Revolution 289-90
    Dalai Lamas 279-85
    Gelugpa order 279-80
    government in exile 290-2
    independence of Tibet 278-9, 284
    Manchus 280-2
    Mongols 151, 278, 279, 280-2
    post–Cultural Revolution 290-2
    Sakyapa rule 151, 278
    Yarlung Valley kings 276
hitching 359-60
holidays 343-4
Holmes, Sherlock 325
Hor Qu 170
horse riding 335
horse-racing festivals 22, 23, 213,
    223, 228, **19**
hot springs
    Kângding 220
    King Tiger Hot Springs 170-1
    Kongpo region 204
    Lake Manasarovar 179
    Tidrum Nunnery 109

Tirthapuri Hot Springs 179-80, **180**
Tsamda Hot Springs 157
Xiqian Hot Springs 152
hydroelectric power 111, 298
hypothermia 366

I
immigration 272, 349
    Han immigration 292, 305-6
independence of Tibet 278-9, 284
insurance
    health 361
    travel 222, 340
internet access 340
internet resources 17
    architecture 327
    arts 322
    culture 300
    environment 298
    health 362
    organisations 347
    safe travel 344
itineraries 24-8
    eastern Tibet 27, **27**
    Lhasa 24, 43, **24**
    Lhasa to Kathmandu 25, **25**, **12**
    Mt Kailash 26, **26**
    overland trips 28, **28**

J
Jampa 317
Jampaling Kumbum 113
Jampelyang 318
jewellery 74
Jinkar Monastery 211
Jokhang, the 45-52, **52-3**, **6**
Jomda 204-5
Jonang Kumbum 146

K
Kagyupa order 314
Kāngding 217-21, **220**
karma 309
Karmapa 100
Kathmandu 261, 262-5, **262-3**
    Lhasa to 25, **25**, **12**
    travel to/from 350, 352-3
Keutsang Ritrö 86
Kham 36, 189-215, **190-1**
    accommodation 189, 195
    climate 189
    food 189
    highlights 190-1
    history 192
    itineraries 27, 192-3, **27**
    permits 192

    planning information 189-93
    travel seasons 189
Khampa Resistance 193
Khojarnath 187
King Tiger Hot Springs 170-1
Kiri Yangdzong caves 109
Kongpo Gyamda 203-4
Kongpo region **202-3**
koras 19, 201, 303, **12**
    Barkhor circuit 45, **11**
    Bönri 200
    Dorje Drak Monastery 111
    Drepung Monastery 82
    Drigung Til Monastery 108
    Ganden Monastery 91
    Lake Manasarovar 259-60, **260**
    Lhasa 51
    Lingkhor 68, **68**
    Mt Kailash 26, 250-6, **26**, **252**, **4**
    Pabonka Monastery 88
    Potala, the 59
    Reting Monastery 105
    Sera Monastery 87
    Tashi Dor Monastery 101-2
    Tashilhunpo Monastery 141
    Tirthapuri Hot Springs 179-80, **180**
    Tsedru Monastery 211
    Tsetang 119-20
    Tsurphu Monastery 99-100
    Ü 104
Kyi-chu kilometre markers 107

L
Lake Manasarovar 178-9, 259-60,
    260
lakes 20, 298, see also individual
    lakes
Lamaling Temple 200
Lang-tso 167-8
language 16, 368-81
    courses 340
    food vocabulary 370, 373, 380
    Mandarin Chinese 371-4
    street names 46
    Tibetan 368-71
    trekking vocabulary 369
legal matters 340-1
legends 55, 56, 256, 295
lesbian travellers 339-40
Lhagong 222-3
lhamo 323
Lhamo La-tso 125
Lhasa 35, 40-94, **41**, **44-5**, **79**, **5**,
    6, **11**
    accommodation 40, 64-71
    activities 63
    climate 40, 336
    drinking 73

    entertainment 73
    festivals 63
    food 40, 71-3
    highlights 41
    history 42
    information 76-7
    internet access 76
    itineraries 24, 43, **24**
    koras 45, 51, 59-60
    medical services 76
    nightlife 74
    permits 42
    planning information 40
    postal services 76
    safe travel 43
    shopping 73-6
    sights 42-63
    telephone services 76
    travel agencies 76
    travel seasons 40
    travel to/from 77
    travel within 77
    walking tours 66-8, **66**, **68**
Lhatse 151-2
Lhatse Chöde 146
Lhegu Glacier 197
Lhundrub 103-4
Lhundrub County 103-4
Lingkhor 68, **68**
literature 324-5, see also books
Lithang 227-9
Lokapalas 318-19
Losar (New Year Festival) 21
Loseling College 81-2
lotus 308
Lukhang 60
Lurulangkar 186

M
Mahakala 319
Mahayana 311
Maitreya 317
Manasarovar, Lake 178-9, 259-60,
    260
Manchus 280-2
mandalas 116, 328
Mandarin Chinese language 371-4
Manigango 224-5
Manjushri 318
maps 232, 341-2
Marco Polo 277, 279
Markham 194
Marmedze 317
MC Tenzin 74
measures 341
medical services 363
medicine buddhas 317
Medro Gongkar 106-7

Menlha 317
merit 309-10
Midui Glacier 197
Milarepa 256, 321
Milarepa's Cave 157-8
military permits 31
Mindroling Monastery 113-14
mineral resources 297
minibus travel 360
Miru 200
mobile phones 17, 345
Moincer 180
momos 337
monasteries & nunneries 18, 88, 92, 326, *see also* monkhood
Baha Gompa 197-8
Bakong Monastery 226
Beri Gompa 224
Buchu Monastery 201
Changmoche Monastery 152
Chayab Monastery 211
Chiu Monastery 179, 260
Chöde Gaden Pendeling Gompa 229
Chöde Gompa 227-8
Chökorgye Monastery 125
Chugu Gompa 205
Chuku Monastery 252-3
Chusi Nunnery 112
Dargyeling Monastery 169
Darjay Gompa 224
Dechen Chokhor Monastery 110
Dira-puk (Lhalung Dira) Monastery 254
Dodoka Gompa 214
Dodung Monastery 196-7
Dola Gompa Monastery 195
Dorje Drak Monastery 111-12
Dragu Monastery 209
Dramaje Monastery 136-7
Drapchi Monastery 86
Drapsang Monastery 168
Dratang Monastery 113
Drepung Monastery 78-83, **80-1**, 8
Drigung Til Monastery 108-9
Drölma Lhakhang 93-4
Drongtse Monastery 135-6
Drubthub Nunnery 60
Dzongsar Monastery 107
Galden Jampaling Monastery 205-7
Ganden Chökhorling Monastery 103, 119
Ganden Monastery 89-92, **90-1**, 9
Garzê Gompa 223-4

Gokung (Tsegu) Monastery 188
Gongkar Chöde Monastery 109-10
Gossul Monastery 179
Gurugyam Monastery 181
Gyangdrak Monastery 176
Héping Fǎhui 222-3
Jinkar Monastery 211
Kangchen Monastery 144
Kathok Nunnery 203-4
Katsel Monastery 106
Korjak Monastery 187
Kyang-rag Monastery 257
Langbona Monastery 260
Mendong Monastery 171
Mindroling Monastery 113-14
Nalendra Monastery 104
Nartang Monastery 144
Neche Goshog Monastery 201
Nechung Monastery 83
Neru Monastery 195
Ngadrak Monastery 112
Ngamchö Monastery 119
Ngor Monastery 247
Oserling Nunnery 168
Pabonka Monastery 87-8
Pelkor Chöde Monastery 131-2
Phuntsoling Monastery 146
Phurbu Chok Monastery 86
Pomda Monastery 194
Rabse Nunnery 134
Rajye Ling Monastery 106
Ralung Monastery 130
Rechung-puk Monastery 123-4
Reting Monastery 105-6
Retok Ganden Retreat 135
Riwo Dechen Monastery 125
Riwoche Tsuglhakhang 209-10, **11**
Rongphu Monastery 155, **6**
Rotung Monastery 211
Rugo Monastery 260
Rutok Monastery 186
Sakya Monastery 147-9
Samding Monastery 130-1
Samtenling Nunnery 106
Samye Monastery 114-18, **115**, **7**, **276**
Sang-ngag Zimche Nunnery 119-20
Selung Monastery 176
Sera Monastery 83-7, **84-5**, 8
Seralung Monastery 260
Sha Monastery 107-8
Shabten Monastery 213
Shalu Monastery 144-6
Shegar Chöde Monastery 153
Shepeling (Simbaling) Monastery 188
Shugsheb Nunnery 94
Söda Gompa 205

Sok Tsanden Monastery 212
Tāgōng Monastery 222
Takdrugtse Monastery 199
Taktse Yungdrungling Monastery 200
Talung Monastery 104-5
Tangboche Monastery 124
Tashi Dor Monastery 101-2
Tashilhunpo Monastery 137-40, **140**, **280**
Tengchen Monastery 210
Thöling Monastery 182-3
Tidrum Nunnery 109
Trandruk Monastery 122-3
Tsechen Monastery 135
Tsedru Monastery 211
Tsi Nesar Monastery 136
Tsodzong Monastery 202-3
Tsurphu Monastery 98-101
Wara Monastery 205
Yangpachen Monastery 244
Yungdrungling Monastery 137
Yushig Monastery 208
Zutul-puk Monastery 256
money 16-17, 221, 342-3
Mongols 151, 278, 279, 280-2
Monkey Cave 120
monkhood 88, 277, 285, 289, 312, *see also* monasteries & nunneries
motorcycle travel 359
movies 273
Mt Everest 154-6, **6**
Everest East Face trekking route 260
expeditions 158-9
Mt Kailash 175-8, 250-6, **252**, **4**
itineraries 26, **26**
mountaineering 335-6
murals 327
museums 63
music 323-4
myths 55, 56, 256, 295

N
Nagchu 213-15
Nagchu Horse Festival 23
Nagpo Chenpo 319
Nalendra Monastery 104
Namseling Manor 119
Nam-tso 101-3, **10**
Nangartse 130-1
Naro Bönchung 256
Nartang Monastery 144
trekking from Shalu Monastery 244-7, **245**
nature reserves 153, 154, 156, 296
Neche Goshog Monastery 201
Nechung Monastery 83

Map Pages **p000**
Image Pages **p000**

Nechung oracle 83
Nepal, Tibet to 25, **25**, 12
Ngagpa College 81
Ngamring-tso 168
Ngan-tso 196, 12
Ngari 36, 163-88, **164-5**
  climate 163
  highlights 163, 164-5
  history 166
  itineraries 166-7
  permits 166
  planning information 163-7
  travel seasons 163
Noble Eightfold Path 310
nomads 102
Nor Gwa-la 172
Norbulingka, the 62-3, **287**
nunneries, see monasteries &
  nunneries
Nyalam 157-60
Nyenchen Tanglha Traverse 256-9, **259**
Nyima Jiangre 107-8
Nyingmapa order 313

O
Oma-chu 172
Öpagme 317
opening hours 336
opera 323
overland trips 20, 353-6
  cycling routes 358-9
  Friendship Highway 353
  from Sìchuān 216-29, **218-19**
  itineraries 28, **28**
  Lhasa to Kathmandu 25, **25**, 12
  Qīnghǎi–Tibet Highway 354
  Qīnghǎi–Tibet railway line 273,
    356, **7**, **290**
  Sìchuān–Tibet Highway 354-5
  Xīnjiāng–Tibet Highway 167, 355
  Yúnnán–Tibet Highway 355

P
Pabonka Monastery 87-8
Padmasambhava 320
painting 327
palaces 18
Palden Lhamo 257, 319
Palha Lu-puk 60
Panchen Lamas 144-5, 257, 282, 283,
  285, 289, 292, 331
Pangong-tso 186
Parma Ri 60
Paryang 170
Pasho 194-5
passports 349, see also visas
pedicabs 360
Peiku-tso 169

Pelkor Chöde Monastery 131-2
permits, see travel permits
petroglyphs 186, 274
Phongdo 105
photography 43, 188, 343
Phuntsoling Monastery 146
pilgrimage 201, 302, 303, 12
pilgrimage circuits, see koras
Piyang 185-6
planning, see also individual regions
  basics 16-17
  budgeting 16
  calendar of events 21-3
  internet resources 17
  itineraries 24-8
  regions 35-7
  tours & permits 29-34
  travel seasons 16
plants 294, 296-7
Pode Kangtsang 62
police, see Public Security Bureau
  (PSB)
politics 272-3, 330-1
Pomda 194
Pomi 196-7
population 272-3, 304-6, **305**
postal services 343
Potala, the 52-9, **54-5**, **58-9**, 5
prayer flags 316, 11
prayer wheels 316
Princess Bhrikuti 276
Princess Wencheng 55, 56, 276
protector deities 318-20
public holidays 343-4
Public Security Bureau (PSB) 340-1
public transport 359
Purang 187-8, **187**

Q
Qīnghǎi–Tibet Highway 354
Qīnghǎi–Tibet railway line 273, 356,
  7, **290**
Qomolangma Nature Reserve 153,
  154, 156, 296

R
rabies 363
rafting 336
Raka 168
Rakadrak 86
Ralung Monastery 130
Ramoche Lam 61
Ramoche Temple 61
Rawok 196
Rawok-tso 12, 196
rebirth 308-9, see also reincarnation
Rechung-puk Monastery 123-4
Red Palace (Potala) 56-9, **58-9**

reincarnation 280, 282, 302, 331
  lineages 280-1, 283
religion 307-21, see also Buddhism
religious freedom 311
respiratory infections 363
responsible travel 234-5, 300
Reting Monastery 105-6
Retok Ganden Retreat 135
Rìbā Sì 211
rickshaws 360
Rigsum Lhakhang 62
Riwo Dechen Monastery 125
Riwoche 209
Riwoche Tsuglhakhang 209-10, **11**
rock carvings 60-1, 186
Rongphu Monastery 155, **6**
Rotung Monastery 211
Rumudong 186
Rutok 186, 204
Rutok Dzong 186

S
sacred animals 297
safe travel 344
  cycling 359
  hitching 359-60
  internet resources 344
  Lhasa 43
  Nepal 262
  trekking 233, 243
Saga 169
Saga Dawa Festival 22, 63, 177, **8**
Sakya 147-51
Sakya Monastery 147-9
Sakya Thukpa 316-17
Sakyamuni 316-17
Sakyapa order 314
Sakyapa reign 151, 278
Samding Monastery 130-1
Samye Monastery 114-18, **115**, **7**, **276**
  trekking from Ganden Monastery
    237-40, **238**, **9**
Sangsang 168
scenery 19
sculpture 328
Sera Je College 85
Sera Me College 84-5
Sera Monastery 83-7, **84-5**, **8**
Sera Ngagpa College 85
Sera Ütse 86
Serkhang chörten 182
Shalu Monastery 144-6
  trekking to Nartang 244-7, **245**
Shangri-la 275
Shangshung 181
Shegar 152-4
Shegar Dzong 153
Shide Tratsang 61-2

Shigatse 137-43, **138-9**
Shigatse Dzong 140
Shishapangma 169
Shöl 55
Shötun (Yogurt Festival) 22-3
Shri Devi 319
Shuba Ancient Fort 203-4
Shugsheb Nunnery 94
Sìchuān, overland trips from 216-29, **218-19**
    accommodation 216
    climate 216
    food 216
    highlights 218
    planning information 216, 221
    travel seasons 216
Sìchuān–Tibet Highway 354-5
    northern route 204-15, 222-7
    southern route 193-204, 227-9
Sili Götsang 105
Siling 169
skull wall (Dodoka Gompa) 214
sky burials 108, 214, 228, 304
sleeping bags 345
snow lion 297
Sok 212-13
Songdo 204
Songtsen Gampo 42, 106, 124, 276, 320
souvenirs 73-4
statuary 328
street names 46
stupas, see chörtens
Summer Palace of the Panchen Lamas 140-1
sunburn 366
swastikas 312

T
Tăgōng 222-3
Tăgōng Monastery 222
Tagyel-tso 171
Talung Monastery 104-5
Tamdrin 319
Tangboche Monastery 124
Tangmi 198
Tangtong Gyelpo 279
Tantrism 311-12
Tara 318
Tashi Dor Monastery 101-2
Tashigang 198
Tashilhunpo Festival 22
Tashilhunpo Monastery 137-40, **140**, **280**

taxes 342
taxi travel 360
telephone services 17, 345-6
temples 18, 56, see also individual temples
    etiquette 92
Ten Meritorious Deeds 310
Tengchen 210-12
Tengye Ling 61
Tent Camp 155, see also Mt Everest
thangkas 327
theft 344
Thöling Monastery 182-3
thugpa 337
Tibet Museum 63
Tibet Tourism Bureau (TTB) Permit 29-31
Tibetan government in exile 290-2, 330-1
Tibetan language 302, 368-71
Tibetan medicine 366-7
Tibetan names 299
Tidrum Nunnery 109
time 345
Tingri 156-7
    trekking from Everest Base Camp 247-50, **249**
tipping 342
Tirthapuri Hot Springs & Kora 179-80, **180**
toilets 345
Topa 205
torma 306
tourist information 345
tours 17, 29-34, see also travel agencies
tractor travel 360
traditional lifestyle 299-304, 331
train travel 356-7
    Qīnghǎi–Tibet railway line 273, 356, **7**, **290**
    train schedules to Lhasa 358
Trandruk Monastery 122-3
travel agencies 33-4
    for trekking 232-4
    in China 33-4
    in Nepal 263
travel permits 17, 29-34, 234, 359
    Kham 192
    Lhasa 42
    Mt Everest 154
    Ngari 166
    Tsang 127
    Ü 98
travel to/from China 268-9, 350-2, 353
travel to/from Nepal 265, 350, 352-3
travellers cheques 343

trekking 18, 230-60, 336
    agencies 232-4
    climate 230
    clothing & footwear 231
    drinks 236
    equipment 232
    food 235-6
    guides 234-5
    health 233
    highlights 230
    language 369
    maps 232
    pack animals 234-5
    permits 234
    planning information 230-5
    responsible travel 234-5
    safe travel 233, 243
    travel seasons 230
trekking routes 236-60
    Bumpa Ri 82
    Dode Valley 86
    Draksum-tso 203-4
    Everest Base Camp to Tingri 247-50, **249**
    Everest East Face 260
    Ganden to Samye 237-40, **238**, **9**
    Lake Manasarovar 179, 259-60, **260**
    Mt Kailash 176, 250-6, **252**, **4**
    Nyenchen Tanglha Traverse 256-9, **259**
    Shalu to Nartang 244-7, **245**
    Tsurphu to Yangpachen 240-4, **241**
    Ü 104
    Yarlung Valley 122
Trisong Detsen 320
Tsaka 172
Tsamda Hot Springs 157
tsampa 337
Tsang 36, 126-62, **128-9**
    accommodation 126
    climate 126
    food 126
    highlights 128-9
    history 127
    itineraries 127
    permits 127
    planning information 126-7
    travel seasons 126
Tsangyang Gyatso 281
Tsaparang 183-5, **183**
Tsechen Fort 135
Tsechen Monastery 135
Tsedru Monastery 211
Tsepame 317
Tsetang 119-21, **120**
Tsochen 171
Tsogyel La-tso 112
Tsome Ling 61

Tsongkhapa 89, 320
Tsurphu Monastery 98-101
   trekking to Yangpachen Monastery 240-4, **241**

U
Ü 35, 95-125, **96-7**
   accommodation 95
   climate 95
   food 95
   highlights 96-7
   itineraries 98
   permits 98
   planning information 95-8
   travel seasons 95

V
vacations 343-4
vaccinations 361-2
Vajrapani 319
Vajrayana 311-12
visas 17, 346-7, see also passports
volunteering 347-8

W
walking, see trekking
walking tours (Lhasa) 66-8, **66**, **68**
water (drinkable) 236, 295, 366
weather 16, 336, see also individual regions
weights 341
western Tibet, see Ngari
Wheel of Life 309
wildlife, see animals, birds
wildlife-watching 20
women in Tibet 306
women travellers 348

X
Xīnjiāng–Tibet Highway 167, 355
Xiqian Hot Springs 152

Y
yak-butter tea 236, 339, **7**
yaks 296, 297, **19**
Yamalung Hermitage 119, 240
Yamantaka 319
Yamdrok-tso 127-30
Yangpachen Monastery 244
   trekking from Tsurphu Monastery 240-4, **241**
Yarlung Tsangpo Valley 109-25
   kilometre markers 110
Yarlung Valley 121-4, **123**
Yarlung Valley kings 276
Yigong-tso 198
Yilhun Lha-tso 225-6
Younghusband expedition 136, 283-4, 285
Yumbulagang 123
Yungdrungling Monastery 137
Yúnnán–Tibet Highway 355
Yushig Monastery 208

Z
Zanda 181-2
Zhāngmù 160-2, **160**
Zhari (Tsari) Nam-tso 171
Zhongba 169-70
Zhungba 173
Zutul-puk Monastery 256

how to use this book

These symbols will help you find the listings you want:

👁 Sights	🎊 Festivals & Events	☆ Entertainment
🏃 Activities	🛌 Sleeping	🛍 Shopping
🥢 Courses	🍴 Eating	ℹ Information/Transport
👉 Tours	🍷 Drinking	

These symbols give you the vital information for each listing:

📞 Telephone Numbers	🔊 Wi-Fi Access	🚍 Bus
🕐 Opening Hours	🏊 Swimming Pool	🚢 Ferry
🅿 Parking	🥗 Vegetarian Selection	Ⓜ Metro
🚭 Nonsmoking	🍴 English-Language Menu	Ⓢ Subway
❄ Air-Conditioning	👪 Family-Friendly	⊖ London Tube
@ Internet Access	🐾 Pet-Friendly	🚋 Tram
		🚆 Train

Look out for these icons:

TOP CHOICE	Our author's recommendation
FREE	No payment required
🍃	A green or sustainable option

Our authors have nominated these places as demonstrating a strong commitment to sustainability – for example by supporting local communities and producers, operating in an environmentally friendly way, or supporting conservation projects.

Reviews are organised by author preference.

Map Legend

Sights
- 🟢 Beach
- 🔺 Buddhist
- 🟠 Castle
- 🟢 Christian
- 🟣 Hindu
- 🔵 Islamic
- 🟢 Jewish
- 🔵 Monument
- 🟤 Museum/Gallery
- 🟠 Ruin
- 🟢 Winery/Vineyard
- 🟢 Zoo
- 🟢 Other Sight

Activities, Courses & Tours
- 🟢 Diving/Snorkelling
- 🟢 Canoeing/Kayaking
- 🟢 Skiing
- 🔵 Surfing
- 🟢 Swimming/Pool
- 🟢 Walking
- 🟢 Windsurfing
- • Other Activity/Course/Tour

Sleeping
- 🟢 Sleeping
- 🟢 Camping

Eating
- ⊗ Eating

Drinking
- 🟢 Drinking
- 🟢 Cafe

Entertainment
- ⊙ Entertainment

Shopping
- 🟢 Shopping

Information
- 🟢 Post Office
- ℹ Tourist Information

Transport
- 🟢 Airport
- ⊗ Border Crossing
- 🟢 Bus
- ⊕ Cable Car/Funicular
- 🟢 Cycling
- 🟢 Ferry
- Ⓜ Metro
- 🟢 Monorail
- 🅿 Parking
- 🟢 S-Bahn
- 🟢 Taxi
- 🟢 Train/Railway
- 🟢 Tram
- 🟢 Tube Station
- 🟢 U-Bahn
- • Other Transport

Routes
- Tollway
- Freeway
- Primary
- Secondary
- Tertiary
- Lane
- Unsealed Road
- Plaza/Mall
- Steps
- Tunnel
- Pedestrian Overpass
- Walking Tour
- Walking Tour Detour
- Path

Boundaries
- International
- State/Province
- Disputed
- Regional/Suburb
- Marine Park
- Cliff
- Wall

Population
- 🟢 Capital (National)
- ◉ Capital (State/Province)
- 🟢 City/Large Town
- 🟢 Town/Village

Geographic
- 🟢 Hut/Shelter
- 🟢 Lighthouse
- 🟢 Lookout
- ▲ Mountain/Volcano
- 🟢 Oasis
- 🟢 Park
-)(Pass
- 🟢 Picnic Area
- 🟢 Waterfall

Hydrography
- River/Creek
- Intermittent River
- Swamp/Mangrove
- Reef
- Canal
- Water
- Dry/Salt/Intermittent Lake
- Glacier

Areas
- Beach/Desert
- + + + Cemetery (Christian)
- × × × Cemetery (Other)
- Park/Forest
- Sportsground
- Sight (Building)
- Top Sight (Building)

Contributing Author
John Vincent Bellezza John has been living and travelling in Tibet and the Himalaya since 1983. A leading authority in the pre-Buddhist civilization of Tibet, he is affiliated with the Tibet Center, University of Virginia, as a senior research fellow. He has been charting Zhang Zhung and Sumpa, fabled cultures of Upper Tibet that had attained a surprising level of sophistication more than 2000 years ago. His most recent work, *Antiquities of Zhang Zhung*, is freely available online at http://thlib.org. He researched the Tibetan Treks chapter for this book. More information about John's life and work are available on his website: http://tibetarchaeology.com.

OUR STORY

A beat-up old car, a few dollars in the pocket and a sense of adventure. In 1972 that's all Tony and Maureen Wheeler needed for the trip of a lifetime – across Europe and Asia overland to Australia. It took several months, and at the end – broke but inspired – they sat at their kitchen table writing and stapling together their first travel guide, *Across Asia on the Cheap*. Within a week they'd sold 1500 copies. Lonely Planet was born.

Today, Lonely Planet has offices in Melbourne, London and Oakland, with more than 600 staff and writers. We share Tony's belief that 'a great guidebook should do three things: inform, educate and amuse'.

OUR WRITERS

Bradley Mayhew
Coordinating Author, Lhasa, Western Tibet, Tibetan Treks (Mt Kailash), Gateway Cities A self-professed mountain junkie, Bradley has been visiting the Tibetan plateau for 20 years now, since studying Chinese for four long years at Oxford University. So far he's been horse trekking in Kham, travelled for four months in Bhutan, gompa-stomped in Ladakh, trekked in Dolpo, done the Kailash kora twice and was last seen heading to Sikkim for Lonely Planet's India guide. Bradley has coordinated the last four editions of this guide and is also the co-author of over 25 Lonely Planet titles, including *Bhutan, Nepal, Trekking in the Nepal Himalaya* and *Central Asia*. He has lectured on Central Asia to the Royal Geographical Society and was recently the subject of a five-part Arte/SWR documentary retracing the route of Marco Polo from Venice to Xanadu, via Iran, Afghanistan and Central Asia. See what he's currently up to at www.bradley mayhew.blogspot.com.

Michael Kohn
Ü, Tsang Michael studied journalism at UCSB and took time off in 1994 to make a round-the-world journey that included a trip to Tibet. After roaming the Yarlung Tsangpo Valley he went overland to Nepal on an eight-day epic ride across the plateau. The trip had him hooked on Tibet. Michael returned to Tibet in 2004 to update the 6th edition of this guide. That time he covered Ü and Kham provinces before a second overland journey to Nepal. Michael has researched Lonely Planet guides to China, Central Asia and Mongolia and has written two books of his own: *Dateline Mongolia: An American Journalist in Nomads Land;* and *Lama of the Gobi*, the first biography of Mongolia's famed monk Danzan Ravjaa. Michael is currently based in Ulaanbaatar with wife Baigal and daughter Molly.

Daniel McCrohan
Eastern Tibet, Overland Routes from Sìchuān Daniel worked as journalist in the UK for seven years before turning his hand to travel writing. An Asia fanatic, he has been travelling regularly to the Tibetan plateau ever since he moved to China six years ago. He lives with his wife and two children in Beijing, but makes forays into the more remote pockets of western China as often as he can. Daniel has co-written Lonely Planet guides to China, Tibet, India and Shanghai. He also worked as a presenter for Lonely Planet TV's *Best in China* series. His research trip for this book was detailed every step of the way on http://twitter.com/dani**R.C.L.** – the first time Lonely Planet has commissioned an author to tweet! To find out more about Daniel, visit his website: http://danielmccrohan.com.

JUIN 2011

OVER MORE
PAGE WRITERS

G

Published by Lonely Planet Publications Pty Ltd
ABN 36 005 607 983
8th edition – March 2011
ISBN 978 1 74179 218 8
© Lonely Planet 2011   Photographs © as indicated 2011
10 9 8 7 6 5 4 3 2 1
Printed in Singapore